THE DOW JONES-IRWIN
GUIDE TO
COMMODITIES TRADING

THE DOW JONES-IRWIN GUIDE TO
COMMODITIES TRADING

BRUCE G. GOULD

Revised Edition

 DOW JONES-IRWIN Homewood, Illinois 60430

© DOW JONES-IRWIN, INC., 1973 and 1981

ISBN 0-87094-193-3
Library of Congress Catalog Card No. 80–70272

Printed in the United States of America

1 2 3 4 5 6 7 8 9 0 K 8 7 6 5 4 3 2 1

PREFACE TO THE SECOND EDITION

Since the appearance of the first edition of the *Guide* in 1973, spectacular changes have transformed the scene of commodity futures trading. The number of futures contracts traded rose from 25.8 million to 76 million. The value of these contracts skyrocketed from $520 billion to well over $2 *trillion.* New volume and value records were set every year during the 1970s. Thousands of new players—traders, speculators, brokers, hedgers—have entered the game, and they have come from all walks of life to seek the extraordinary profits offered to the minority of skillful winners. Always an integral component of the American economy, futures trading has dramatically taken a leading role recently in international economic affairs. Headlines at home and abroad trumpet the ups and downs of wheat and soybeans, gold and silver, Treasury Bills and foreign currencies. Futures trading has arrived in a very big way.

The accelerating importance of the futures markets has revolutionized the institutions of trading itself. In the last eight years, a flurry of entirely new futures contracts has created a tremendous market in futures for precious metals and financial instruments. This innovation and success story itself made most earlier accounts of the futures business obsolete. The growth of lucrative opportunities in futures prompted the once-disinterested brokerage industry to alter its ways and jump aboard. Brokers now crowd together with trading advisors, analysts, pool and fund managers in a scramble for escalating profits. All offer the trader a bewildering assortment of opinions, methods, and programs. The adjustment has not always been an easy one, as in boom times con artists or the merely incompetent take their inevitable toll. As a direct result, government regulation has increased significantly with the creation (1974) of the Commodity Futures Trading Commission. Meanwhile the futures exchanges themselves have expanded the size and sophistication of their operations to meet the conditions of a new age.

This new edition of the *Guide* has been totally reworked to take account of these unprecedented developments. *Every* page has been revised or entirely rewritten to cover recent events and prepare for the decades ahead. Most of the illustrations have been replaced with newer figures.

v

However, the qualities that I think made for the popular success of the first edition—clear explanation, common sense, concern for the average speculator—have been retained. New sections and chapters have been added, covering such topics as the history of futures to the present, women in commodities, selecting a broker, pools and funds, the CFTC, commodity options, metals, financial futures, and individual account management.

The book's revisions and additions, as they respond to new events, also grow out of my continuing work as a speculator and author. In 1969 when I was fresh out of law school, I made $80,000 on a $5,000 investment in less than seven months. I have since never turned my back on commodities trading.

Whether you are a novice, a practiced trader, a student or a broker, the statistical odds are that you are losing money, or at best not making as much as is easily possible. Few have the excuse of great success that would allow skipping even the most introductory chapters here, for in these is much of the general consensus and common sense advice all too often forgotten in the dash for profits. The *Guide* will now take you from a simple definition of commodities and futures, through a complete overview of trading and its mechanics, into the complexities of pricing for the principal commodities, and lastly to instructions for designing your own trading program.

Without apology, the *Guide* reflects my own trading philosophy as it has been refined through years of research and actual trading. Readers already familiar with the markets and how to trade will thus find value here in the particular perspective with which old facts and new events are viewed and explained. The newcomer may

be assured, however, that the *Guide* has been written with constant consultation of other viewpoints, and has incorporated these whenever they contributed to a balanced, thorough presentation of topics notoriously subject to sharp disagreements.

The book is divided into three parts, beginning with a general overview of the futures market: why it exists, who uses it, how it is used. This gives a comprehensive but not overwhelming introduction, providing a framework with which the reader can understand the difficulties of pricing and then construct a trading program. Along with the facts, I have given whenever appropriate an interpretation of them that will aid the speculator in his attempt to beat the odds. The speculator plays price changes, and the second part of the book is limited solely to the whys and hows of price analysis. After a look at a general theory of price moves, chapters examine the determinants of cash price, and in turn of the futures price which is tied to but independent of the cash market price. A logical chain of relationships is established that will serve in the analysis of any commodity's cash and futures prices, which is after all the trader's main concern. A final chapter of the section details the nature and price factors of all the major commodities currently being traded on the futures exchanges.

In Part III, attention shifts to the actual program for futures trading and speculation. Although the book, as a matter of principle, takes a sceptical stance toward predicting the future, the speculator is going to come across prediction systems by the dozens, and will eventually develop one of his own. Thus every widely used forecasting method is included and discussed: supply and demand, chart reading, moving averages and oscillators, seasonal trends, etc. Inclusion does not necessarily mean recommendation. I have attempted to be objective, and work them all in, so that the newcomer may pick and choose on his own. My own preferences, I believe, are clear, but these matters and my own personal trading methods have been reserved for detailed discussion in other writings. Finally, the last chapter covers the general rules for designing a trading program, organizing the account, and managing the positions taken in the market. Price analysis and forecasting are the basis of any program. What to do when a position is actually chosen will determine a trader's success.

In constructing the book so that the entire market can be understood by someone with no prior knowledge of commodities, surprisingly little specific data had to be left out. More complex matters are dealt with as the argument proceeds from definition to detail. The book does admit to distinct limitations, however. Prices and dates, although almost all have been revised, will soon be once more out of date; but the principles they illustrate will remain unchanged. A balance of coverage among the many types of commodities has been sought. Yet in harmony with the market's own character, agricultural products still receive heavy attention. Specific markets and their special aspects are covered in other books on commodities (see Appendix I). The trader is encouraged to acquire much more information than can fit between the covers of this book, and to use that data to build an individual plan. It should also be noted that the *Guide* is written from the viewpoint of the speculator. I believe farmers, hedgers, and other industrial and commercial players will find it a valuable in-

troduction to futures trading, but they will have to go on to other more programmatic writings for in-depth coverage of hedging practices.

Trading commodities is one of the last fields of speculative investment in this country which is both rational and legal. Its economic stature and importance do not prevent it, happily, from also being fun. It does require hard work and time, though less than many think, and the person serious about profiting will drop most other after-hours diversions for a while. I have traded stocks and bonds, and continue to do so, but for entirely different reasons than I trade commodities. My investment portfolio is designed to complement my life insurance, real estate, and other holdings, and centers on blue-chip and high-rated issues. These are treated by me in very somber terms of "estate planning," wealth storage and value accumulation. To me, commodities is best thought of and played as a game, not an investment. I do not mix the two in my planning or in my cash accounts. Futures trading is too volatile and risky to act as the foundation for financial security.

Some people will never become successful commodity speculators. Either their open positions (contracts still held and thus subject to gains and losses) take over their entire waking consciousness and ruin their sleep, or they get a taste of success and dive in as though the country were going to give up bread. Commodities, whatever the appearances, is not a Roman Circus. The successful trader is the actuary who keeps his cool when large masses of money make their move, not the self-styled "hero" who believes soybeans must be worth $8.00 a bushel and that any other price is un-American. A good cliche is "sell down to the sleeping point." Keep positions you can live with sanely. If you are strung out in your account to the point where the least reversal will wipe you out, you'll miss the fun and never be around to play the winning odds. Nor will you be in control of your position, for your broker must by law close you out.

I am a professional speculator, yet I often have no position at all. Sometimes I see no risk *I wish to take, but more often* I get out for awhile to regain perspective and take a vacation. If you can't get out, you have no business trading commodities. I am biased in favor of commodities speculation. I enjoy it immensely. This book is going to reflect that bias. But at the same time I have no interest in talking anybody into trading, though I would like to prevent people who do trade from unnecessarily losing so much money.

For those who can make it, commodities can quickly become the only game in town.

ACKNOWLEDGMENTS

I wish to express my appreciation to the following individuals who have, either directly or indirectly, been responsible for whatever measure of success I have achieved in the world of the commodity markets—Richard G. Jeffers (who will always be Number One in my book), Stephen K. Husby, Donald J. Sankus, Palmer Peterson, Gary and Mary Ann Burrus, Fred, Doreen, and Peter Pomeroy.

I also wish to express my appreciation to Jack L. Hofer (a scholar in the field of computers and commodities), to Edward J. Mader (my longtime friend and now the Director of Commodity Research for E. F. Hutton & Company in New York—"When Ed Mader talks, E. F. Hutton listens"), and to Houston Cox, a credit to the professional world of commodity analysis.

My very special thanks go to Greg Jay who was deeply involved in the preparation of this book and who will one day use the knowledge gained in his research to make himself a wealthy man.

I wish to dedicate this book to Lawrence Douglass Gould—a more understanding father no son ever had—and to Magda F. Pomeroy (may God take good care of her . . . wherever she may be).

BRUCE GRANT GOULD

CONTENTS

LIST OF CHARTS

PART ONE

AN OVERVIEW

Chapter 1 —————————————————————

INTRODUCTION: A FORTUNE IN COMMODITIES

WHAT ARE COMMODITIES?

What are "commodities"? What are "commodity futures"? Who trades them? How? Why? Answering these questions is the fundamental purpose of this book. The air of mystery surrounding the commodities markets and traders can be blown away by a little thought and a lot of common sense.

Anything that people buy and sell is a commodity. The material life of all human societies is simply the production and exchange of commodities. When people ask me, "How can I get into commodities?" I first tell them, "You are already in the commodities business. Everybody is a buyer, seller, or trader of commodities." Take a look at the clothes you are wearing. Is there any cotton or wool in them? Are there leather hides in your shoes or belt or handbag? Look around your home. Is there plywood in its construction? Did you realize that the electricity you buy with your payments to the power company is also a commodity, itself transformed from purchases of water, coal, oil, or uranium? Remember the gold in your jewelry, the silver in your kitchen, the copper in your plumbing—all are commodities. What did you have for

breakfast? The bacon, bread, potatoes, orange juice, and coffee came courtesy of a series of commodity deals that included yourself, the restaurant or supermarket, the warehouse, the processor, the transporter, the producer, and all the other players in the game of creation and consumption. From an economic standpoint, you yourself are a commodity when you sell your labor, talents, or knowledge in the open job market. If you're a champion athlete or a superb attorney, the return on your investment in yourself may be handsome indeed. There is no mystery, then, about commodities themselves. The commodities most often traded number less than forty and are only massive quantities of real things each of us handles every day.

FUTURES

"Ok," the inquirer says, "I can understand what commodities are, but what in heaven's name are 'futures'? Isn't commodity trading a very complex economic operation that only experts in its science and technology can possibly comprehend?" In reality, the principles of futures, commodities, and trading are rather simple. Those who perpetuate the myth of mysterious secrets and unexplainable intricacies are either profiting by the ignorance of others or are ignorant themselves. Simple commodities transactions, like buying a newspaper or selling furniture at a garage sale, may take place immediately. Contract, delivery, and payment happen simultaneously. Complex commodity transactions, including the purchase or sale of homes, cars, soybeans, and pork bellies involve delays between contract, delivery, and payment. All such arrangements call for some kind of "futures contract." A futures contract is simply an agreement that a fixed commodity at a fixed price be delivered at a fixed date. Actual delivery and payment are postponed until some established future time. Most of us engage in making futures contracts throughout our lives. Car loans, mortgages, credit card purchases—all are kinds of futures contracts. What we rarely do in our daily lives, however, is to turn such contracts *themselves* into commodities. This is what happens in the trading exchanges and financial instrument markets. Contracts concerning thousands of bushels of wheat or government sponsored mortgages are bought and sold, traded back and forth, as the market players speculate about what changes prices will go through in the period between contract and delivery. Control of these contracts and their huge amounts can be had for comparatively little money, as the risks of speculation can be very high. Since a wheat contract, for example, contains 5,000 bushels, a price change of a few cents per bushel may make or break the trader.

Between the time it opens and the date it closes (usually from 8 to 18 months), traders will buy and sell the futures con-

tracts thousands and thousands of times, hoping to position themselves on the right side of price changes, taking profits and losses from their positions, until the contract close, when most positions have been liquidated. Few futures contracts are ever delivered on, though they are written so as to be useful for actual transactions. Most commodities are purchased on the cash or spot markets. Futures contracts are thus chiefly an economic management mechanism. They are also the lifeblood of the speculator.

SPECULATIVE POSITIONS

Everyone is familiar with how speculation works. One invests in a commodity in hopes that over time its rise in price, relative to the price originally paid, will yield a profit. Such buying is called taking a "long" position. It is the kind of speculation most people know well when it comes to real estate, antiques, and art work. But it takes two to make a contract. One can make a contract to deliver a commodity (even if one doesn't have it yet, as when a manufacturer takes orders for products that have yet to be made) at a fixed price sometime in the future, hoping that declining prices will bring a profitable price differential between the contracted price and the price paid to eventually acquire the commodity (or in the case of the manufacturer, the price paid to produce it), so that the delivery can actually be made when the contract closes. This is called selling "short," as one is "short" the commodity one contracts to deliver. Commodity futures trading, allowing for gross simplification, is just this process of making futures contracts, trading them long or short, and speculating that price movements will produce a profit before any ad-

FIGURE 1–1

AN ANALYSIS OF SPECULATIVE TRADING IN GRAIN FUTURES

SUMMARY

This study is concerned primarily with the trading behavior of small speculators in grain futures, and the results of their trading. Statistics were analyzed on the futures operations of nearly 9,000 traders, extending over a 9-year period (1924–32) and involving more than 400,000 individual futures transactions. This wealth of data, set up on punch cards and processed by machine-tabulation methods, provided comprehensive evidence for the first time on some of the most important questions in the field of futures trading. The study confirms a number of commonly held opinions as to the results of speculative trading; it tends to disprove others which have also been widely accepted.

The first obvious conclusion from the analysis is that the great majority of small speculators lost money in the grain futures market. There were 6,598 speculators in the sample with net losses, compared with 2,184 with net profits, or three times as many loss traders as profit traders. Net losses of speculators were approximately six times net profits, or nearly $12,000,000 of losses, compared with about $2,000,000 of profits. Speculative traders in the sample lost money in each of the four grains traded—wheat, corn, oats, and rye.

Primarily responsible for the high ratio of losses was the small speculator's characteristic hesitation in closing out loss positions. An often-quoted maxim for speculative trading is "Cut your losses and let your profits run." Contrary to this advice, speculators in the sample showed a clear tendency to cut their profits and let their losses run. Futures positions or cycles resulting in losses were held open for consistently longer durations than profit cycles—average losses were larger than average profits—and long cycles were kept open for a greater number of days than short cycles. In wheat futures, for example, the average duration of profit cycles was only 10.5 days, compared with 16.3 days for loss cycles. The average duration of the profit trader in wheat futures was 114.8 days, compared with 182.5 days for the loss trader.

Speculators who did make profits on individual trades were inclined to cut them short. The tendency on individual cycles was to settle for profits which were much smaller on the average than the average loss on trades closed out unprofitably. With this situation, plus the shorter time duration of profit cycles, it is not surprising that there were actually more individual profit cycles than loss cycles.

It has not been possible in this study to explore all the aspects of speculative trading on grain futures markets, nor to answer all the questions which have been raised. A final comment should be made involving a most important question. As already indicated, the losses of traders in the sample were much greater than their profits. If these results are representative of trading by small speculators generally, there must be other groups—large speculators, scalpers, spreaders, or hedgers—which make very large profits.

There is no known empirical study, however, which reveals other groups of traders with net profits sufficient to balance such large losses as those suffered by small speculators in the sample. Yet the nature of futures trading is such that all losses are balanced by profits. This raises the most important question left unanswered by this study. Was the sample in this respect not typical of small speculative traders? There is no apparent reason for pronounced bias in the direction of losses. If the sample is representative, is there another group of traders who consistently make profits large enough to balance the losses of small speculators? There is no convincing evidence that such large profits are made by any class of traders. These are questions which can be answered only by further studies of the results of futures trading.

Source: U.S. Department of Agriculture, *Technical Bulletin No. 1001.*

verse change wipes out the trader's capital.

Commodity futures trading came about as an answer to the immediate problem faced by all buyers and sellers of commodities: "How do I get out of a contract I can't perform on, or don't wish to perform on, because it will mean inconvenience or financial loss?" This problem, "liquidating" the trader's position, became acute as national commodity economies grew. The time delays naturally involved in agricultural and lifecycle commodities (such as grains and meats), coupled with the uncertainties of weather, disease, and insects, prompted producers and buyers to seek a mechanism for getting out of their positions if prices turned against them. Trading futures contracts is that mechanism. It allows the risks inherent in marketing to be assumed by a third party, the speculator, who relieves the farmer or grain company of a position in return for a chance to make substantial profits from advantageous price shifts.

Every action in the commodities market takes someone out of a position. The buyer of immediately delivered wheat liquidates someone else's short position. The rancher who increases the size of his cattle herd goes long, as he now has more to sell. The liquidity of the commodities futures market is made possible by all these players, but the key to the whole operation's existence is the speculator. He makes possible the position changes of those players with real cash positions in the industry by taking a position in the market opposite from theirs; in effect, he buys wheat from the farmer or sells gold to the jeweler. They, in turn, with these futures contracts can plan the prices they pay or receive for the materials their businesses depend upon. For this service the speculator receives the right to lose his capital (as most do) or to rack up huge profits in a very short space of time. The odds are heavily against him. Observers disagree as to the ratio of winners to losers, with most finding that almost two-thirds of all speculators end up with net losses. (See Figure 1–1.) In defiance of the odds, they keep on coming, and in ever growing numbers. To understand the workings of the futures markets one must know the advantages that this game, and no other, can offer.

THE ATTRACTION OF THE GAME

The interest and importance of commodity trading could easily be established with mere numbers. The statistics on the major role played by commodities in the national and world economies will, indeed, be cited often in the pages that follow. But commodity trading is a special speculative enterprise, and that means it is a business of human choices and personal motives. The uniqueness of the commodities game stems from the special demands it makes on the people who play it, and on the unique opportunities it allows them. Commodity trading is first and foremost a story of people, not of impersonal data. Behind the avalanche of graphs and the headlines of events are the traders, producers, brokers, and buyers— all engaged in a competition of wits. Anyone who tries to understand the world of commodities, much less make a fortune there, must have more than a grasp of the mechanics or a storehouse of facts. These are essentials, as we shall see, but the heart of the commodities game is located elsewhere, in the attractions and risks only it can provide.

What makes trading in commodity futures so rewarding, personally and financially? The producer, the processor, and the buyer of commodities each use the futures market primarily to regulate their cash selling and buying, to create some degree of predictability in prices. They rarely use it directly for profit taking. The broker, mortgage company, bank, or corporation likewise buys and sells futures contracts for purposes other than speculative gain. The place of all these participants will be considered in turn. Who, though, is the speculative trader? Why is he willing to make the system possible by assuming the risks hedged by these other players?

The answers, again, are more than financial, though the prospect of enormous profits acts as a substantial lure. In a world where personal initiative and freedom seem more and more constrained, commodity trading offers one of the last great opportunities for decisive individual action. Properly informed and intelligently managed, commodity trading can be the trader's own private enterprise. Once free of the myth that the "insiders" have the edge, the speculator proceeds to build a trading program of his own devising, dependent on his own skills, methods, and luck. The single most important lesson in commodity trading is that of independent thinking. The trader must be able to sift through all the conflicting data and advice, weigh the opinions and events, and decide for himself which positions promise profit and which will bring him ruin. Most of the horror stories I have heard about catastrophic losses in commodity trading have involved traders who blindly followed the suggestions of friends, shoeshine boys, and "expert" newsletters, "how-to" books, brokers, computers, or

gut feeling. The good trader is his own boss, ready to exercise his freedom and his knowledge for his own profit. The risks are great, but that is part of the excitement that the trader thrives on. Any sound guidebook to commodity trading includes this percept: Nothing truly valuable is gained without risk. The risks are the price the trader pays for the freedom to make his own decisions and destiny in the market place.

THE TRADER'S LIFE

The trader must quickly begin to learn about himself as well as about commodities, for it is on his shoulders that the success of the trade ultimately rests. One result of financial success and security (or of financial ruin) is a new sense of identity, a self-knowledge tried and tested in keen worldly competition, and the product of pitting one's expertise against 50,000 traders and coming out on top. Only a fool would insist, however, that the trader controls the market. He does not. He rides the market like a wild horse, trying to stay aboard during the ups and downs, or sitting patiently when the animal refuses to budge. The speculative trader makes his way against the other forces in the market, including farmers, producers, processors, giant corporations, brokerage houses, other traders, the weather, and politicians (the unpredictability of the last two can often be exasperating). The speculator isn't competing with the hedger or corporate investor, though he must keep apprised of their moves. The real competition is other speculators. The commodity futures market is an instrument with a variety of uses. The farmer's use of futures differs from the speculator's, as does the grain company's and the bank's. Each must, nevertheless, abide by the same laws of supply and demand, price and profit. The difference is that the trader has more flexibility and independence when it comes to establishing or liquidating his market positions. On the other hand, his relatively risky position as an isolated speculator means he may be completely wiped out by an unforeseen or poorly prepared for price move.

The individual liberty available to the trader has its physical and geographical aspects as well. The trader need not be on the floor of the exchange at Chicago, New York, or Winnipeg. In fact, for most kinds of trading, other than scalping, distance from the madness of the pits is a distinct advantage. For some years now I have done all my trading from Seattle, Washington. One trader and analyst set up shop in a log cabin on a remote river in Oregon. If you have a phone line, electricity, and a mail box, you can trade commodities with the best. Advances in communications technology may eventually eliminate the physical exchange and pit altogether, or transform them beyond recognition as electronic processing of orders, accounts, and facts becomes easier, cheaper, and more widespread. Global information networks now bring the Iowa farmer, New York gold dealer, Arab millionaire, and Indonesian oil driller into virtually instant contact, increasing the quality of data and economic options for each.

There is a similar liberty in the trader's choice of market positions. In this the speculator has a real advantage over the farmer or money institution. The farmer is always "long," always hoping for prices to advance, always looking for an expanding market. The farmer must stay with the crop he planted in the spring or with

the piglets that were recently weaned. But the futures trader can trade the markets from the "short" side as easily as from the long. If prices are declining, the commodity trader (unlike the farmer, unless he has hedged his position more than 100 percent using the futures market) can profit nicely on the ride down. If hog prices are stagnant, the speculator can switch to beef, or wheat, or plywood, or Treasury Bills. He can do this as quickly as he can pick up his telephone and call in his order. If prices are advancing, the trader can increase his holdings in a commodity in a matter of minutes with further orders. The farmer is not so lucky, because Mother Nature requires more time than does the futures market. Likewise, the bank or corporation using financial instruments (Commercial Paper, Ginnie Maes, etc.) becomes a hostage to interest rate fluctuations and money supply shifts, unable to form or liquidate positions with the speed and freedom of the individual trader.

PROFITS

The fast pace and flexibility of the commodities market means that fortunes can be made or lost in a very short time. The constant opportunity to rapidly accumulate wealth is one of commodity trading's great advantages. If you're a young person in a hurry, or middle-aged and running out of time, or retired and still ready for action, you'll find no other investment that will return the profits of commodities trading in the same short length of time. The profits for those who do succeed are often staggering. They can run from a comparatively modest 100 percent to as high as 5,000 percent *in less than a single year*. The history books give countless ex-

FIGURE 1–2

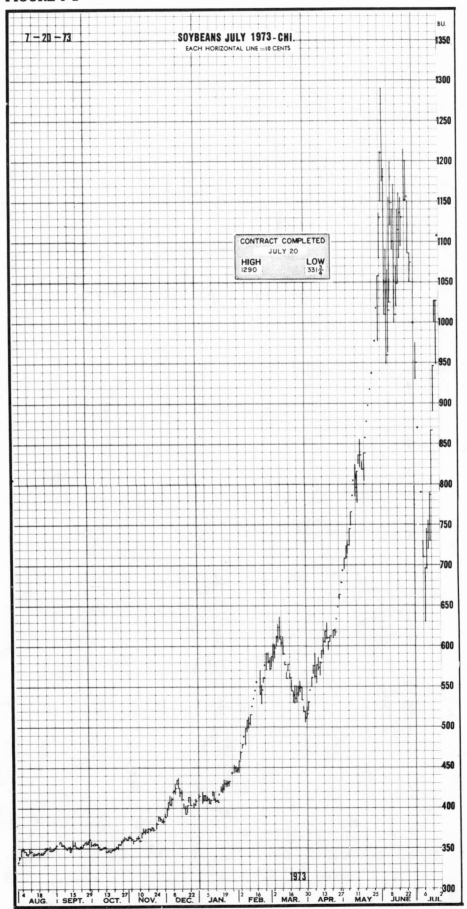

Source: Commodity Research Bureau, Inc.

amples, and the future promises even more. Since relatively small amounts of margin money are required to control a commodities contract, such profit opportunities occur every year in a number of price moves. (See Figures 1–2, 1–3, 1–4.)

FIGURE 1–3

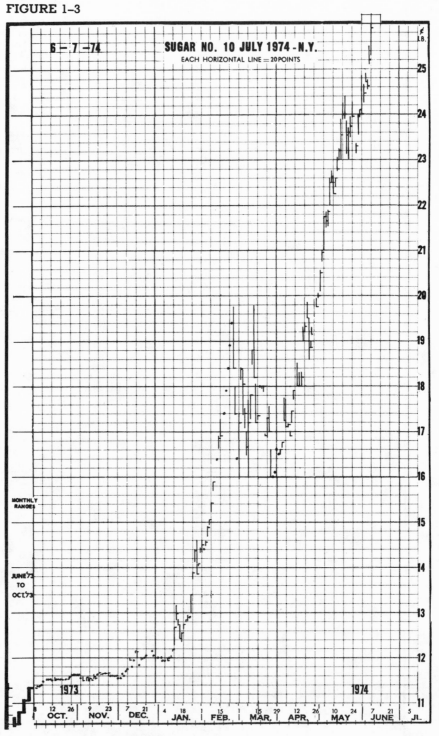

Source: Commodity Research Bureau, Inc.

FIGURE 1-4

Source: Commodity Research Bureau, Inc.

For the speculator who bought July 1973 soybeans when the line first moved up out of its "sideways channel," a profit of $45,000 could have been earned on each $1,000 invested—a profit of 4,500 percent in eight months time. The profit possible on each $1,000 invested in July 1974 sugar was $15,680, or 1,568 percent. The cocoa contract of May 1977 offered, in less than a single year, a return of 4,200 percent ($42,000 per contract) on each $1,000 invested. Fortunes can be made whether prices go up or down. September 1977 contracts for coffee were just such a dou-

ble opportunity for the trader who took first a long, and then a short, position. The profit on the way up was $75,000 per contract; on the way down, $52,500 per contract. The extraordinary surge in the price of gold from 1979 into 1980, spurred by international political fears and by doubts about the strength of the U.S. dollar, carried other precious metals upwards to create a number of fabulous profit potentials for those who got on board early and rode the trend. (See Figure 1–5.) No matter the type of commodity or the year it is traded, the speculator

FIGURE 1–5

Source: Commodity Research Bureau, Inc.

who can cut losses short, wait patiently for the big moves, and run profits with the trends stands to make more in a few months time than many earn in years or a lifetime.

As long as a commodity market exists profits will be available, whatever the state of the economy may be. There are few recession-proof or depression-proof occupations, but commodity trading is one. The speculator trades only the line of the price move—up, down, or sideways—and can profit in any case. Price fluctuation means profit opportunity. As economic uncertainty increases, more and more investors of every kind find in commodity trading a hedge against inflations and recessions and protection from interest rate changes and oil price hikes. The role of commodity trading in national and global economic life has increased tremendously in the last decades, as has participation in it, until no one concerned with money (and who isn't?) can afford to be ignorant of the workings of this basic enterprise.

The amount of money required to earn substantial profits from futures trading is not as great as many people believe. Most brokerage firms would prefer that their customers have from $10,000 to $50,000 in trading capital. This is principally because the larger a trader's account, the more commissions that can be generated for the firm. My own rule of thumb is: If you can't profit from a $5,000 account, you can't profit from a $50,000 account. There is no reason to have large sums of money invested in the markets. Many of the very successful traders, in my experience, trade with far less money than do the unsuccessful speculators. When a successful trader runs a $5,000 account to $50,000 or $100,000, he withdraws his profits and starts over again with the mini-

mum. If you have a few thousand dollars you can easily afford to lose, without hardship to your basic financial security, then you can begin to trade commodities.

SIMPLICITY

Despite its reputation, commodity trading is quite a simple business. Though there are endless sources of information, mountains of bulletins, journals, facts, and charts, the skillful trader needs surprisingly little data to trade profitably. Whatever the complexities of crop harvest forecasts, Federal Reserve Board monetary actions, or feed grain intercommodity relations, the trader is concerned with price patterns as they really occur. Prices can only go in three directions, and the trader need only follow the line and trade it profitably. Too much time spent becoming an "expert" in all aspects of one particular commodity wastes the trader's time. I once spent three years studying corn. I doubt that there were fifty people in the world who knew more about corn statistics than I did. At twenty-six I had become "feed grain analyst" for the Pillsbury Corporation, with a library of data on the price of corn going back to the 1860s. But no amount of numbers can infallibly predict future prices. Too many factors (rain, strikes, insects, new crops, government actions, etc.) upset the projections. (Historically, there are "odds" for price changes in seasonal commodities that do aid in selecting a position. These are dealt with in a later chapter.)

There is nothing very mysterious about the commodities themselves. They are (with the exception of financial instruments such as Ginnie Maes, a group of mortgages sold as a security) common household words: eggs, cotton, sugar, wheat, potatoes, soybeans, gold, plywood, et. al. There are actually only about thirty to thirty-five commodity substances that the average trader will ever deal in often, though the list of possible contracts grows with cross-listing on different exchanges and inclusion of rarely traded items. (See Figure 1–6.) Trading the stock market, one faces up to 40,000 choices. In commodities, the relatively small number and type of materials traded makes sufficient expertise in a few (and that is enough at any one time for most traders) a realistic, though challenging, task. The beginning trader starts with a familiar knowledge of most commodities just by reason of experience in normal life activities such as grocery shopping or banking. The same cannot be said for the investor in stocks who is trying to understand the nature and prospects of some giant conglomerate or new industrial firm.

FIGURE 1–6

1978's big volume gainers: Gold, currencies, cattle, interest rates

Commodity (Exchange in parentheses)	1977	1978	Change
Grains, oilseeds			
Wheat (CBT)	1,820,790	2,556,034	+ 40.4%
Wheat (KCBT)	617,122	755,949	+ 22.5%
Wheat (MidAm)	151,433	205,629	+ 35.8%
Wheat (MGE)	191,134	284,313	+ 48.6%
Corn (CBT)	5,021,827	6,127,099	+ 22.0%
Corn (MidAm)	280,268	256,022	− 8.6%
Oats (CBT)	109,970	215,774	+ 96.2%
Oats (MidAm)	1,172	1,423	+ 21.4%
Soybeans (CBT)	7,996,139	8,477,277	+ 6.0%
Soybeans (MidAm)	1,104,73	994,932	− 10.0%
Soy oil (CBT)	2,535,046	2,909,284	+ 14.8%
Soybean meal (CBT)	2,373,453	2,493,086	+ 5.1%
Livestock, products			
Live cattle (CME)	2,639,517	5,603,375	+112.2%
Live cattle (MidAm)	—	54,054	—
Feeder cattle (CME)	133,274	568,181	+326.3%
Live hogs (CME)	1,307,712	1,767,634	+ 35.2%
Live hogs (MidAm)	159,324	185,927	+ 6.2%
Pork bellies (CME)	1,358,730	1,442,362	+ 6.2%
Boneless beef (NYME)	2,690	5,870	+118.2%
Iced broilers (CBT)	64,938	74,684	+ 15.0%
Fresh eggs (CME)	130,042	73,210	− 43.9%
Food, fiber			
Coffee C (NYC&SE)	214,202	163,959	− 23.5%
Sugar #11 (NYC&SE)	1,055,984	1,016,773	− 3.7%
Sugar #12 (NYC&SE)	15,676	21,875	+ 39.5%
Cocoa (NYCoE)	307,628	222,732	− 27.6%
Rubber (NYCoE)	53	—	—
Idaho potatoes (CME)	4,727	90	—
Round white potatoes (NYME)	478,558	454,195	− 5.1%
Cotton (NYCE)	826,395	1,155,801	+ 39.9%
FC orange juice (NYCE)	377,921	285,405	− 24.5%
Woods			
Plywood (CBT)	368,770	261,483	− 29.1%
Lumber (CME)	486,691	560,368	+ 15.1%
Stud lumber (CME)	687	9,372	—

	1977	1978	Change
Metals			
Gold (CBT)	13,758	56,470	+310.5%
Gold (MidAm, 1 Kg)	2,650	3,214	+ 21.3%
Gold (MidAm, 33.2 oz.)	—	41,939	—
Gold (IMM)	908,180	2,814,572	+209.9%
Gold (NYME, 1 Kg)	1,017	624	− 38.6%
Gold (NYME, 400 oz.)	2,633	2,746	+ 4.3%
Gold (Comex)	981,551	3,742,091	+281.2%
Silver (CBT)	2,257,059	2,657,833	+ 17.8%
Silver (MidAm)	366,585	378,049	+ 3.1%
Silver (Comex)	3,573,301	3,822,085	+ 7.0%
U.S. silver coins (CME)	371	275	− 25.9%
U.S. silver coins (NYME)	15,514	9,823	− 36.8%
Palladium (NYME)	119,971	45,227	+126.5%
Platinum (NYME)	122,924	405,552	+229.9%
Copper (Comex)	1,070,210	1,408,688	+ 31.6%
Zinc (Comex)	—	677	—
Financial instruments			
GNMA CDR (CBT)	422,421	953,161	+120.0%
GNMA CD (CBT)	—	6,532	—
Commercial paper (CBT)	3,553	18,767	—
T-bonds (CBT)	32,101	555,350	—
T-bills (CME, 13-week)	321,703	766,352	+138.2%
T-bills (CME, 1-year)	—	5,512	—
Total financial instruments	779,778	2,305,674	+195.7%
Currencies (all IMM)			
British pound	78,701	243,337	+209.2%
Canadian dollar	161,139	209,303	+ 29.9%
Deutschemark	134,368	400,541	+198.1%
Dutch guilder	2,812	3,585	+ 27.5%
French franc	3,150	4,449	+ 41.2%
Japanese yen	82,261	362,600	+340.8%
Mexican peso	17,029	17,927	+ 5.3%
Swiss franc	106,968	321,339	+200.4%
Total IMM currencies	586,428	1,563,081	+166.5%

Source: Commodities Magazine.

While it is common for there to be "inside information" about businesses that can give a stock trader decided advantages, the fundamental and technical data about commodities are public knowledge and equally accessible to everyone. The departments of Agriculture, Commerce, and Treasury must make information about crops, inflation, and interest rates available to all at the same time. Long-term price determinants reduce further the importance of minute-by-minute news, and in any case the really significant fortunes to be made in commodities come over periods of time from a few weeks to a year. Anyone can obtain charts and graphs depicting past price patterns in a given commodity, and these are the trader's allies. They provide some of the most realistic figures for computing and forecasting prices. If soybean meal prices have been higher in December than they were in September for nineteen years out of twenty, the probability of higher prices this December is 95 percent, better odds that you can get in Las Vegas or on Wall Street. Though nonlifecycle commodities, such as silver and financials, have no real seasonal trends, they can be traded with the same basic methods applied to wheat, soybeans, or corn. Charts of the price fluctuations of pork bellies and of gold are constructed in the same way, and their significance can be read with the same trading rules, no matter the difference in the substance of the actual commodity.

COMMODITIES AND THE REAL WORLD

Prices found in commodity trading are true tangible values which relate to specific goods. The price of eggs depends on what the consumer will pay for eggs at the supermarket. The price of cotton depends on how sweaters are selling, or on how the price of oil affects cotton's competition, the synthetics. The price of silver depends on actual usage. The price of beef is determined by grain harvests, feed costs, herd supplies, and consumer preference. Classic supply and demand determinants, joined to intercommodity relations and diverse price influences, still govern commodity prices. The situation grows more complex with time, however; the increasing influence of government policies, foreign and domestic, on commodity prices upsets the old market mechanisms, as does the large-scale use of the commodities markets by worried investors and oil billionaires (witness the wild careers of gold and silver). Fortunately, whatever determines prices, profits can be had from price movements, and the commodities market can operate to absorb changes in policy or economic emotion, eventually readjusting prices according to tangible factors. The mechanisms that determine commodity price changes are, in most cases, rational. Stock values, on the other hand, are not real and tangible, but arbitrary and emotional. Though the boom in the volume of commodity trading can create some circuslike scenes, commodity prices remain firmly tied to real world conditions.

This relation between commodities and real life extends to history itself. The commodity trader quickly finds himself caught up in the drama of human affairs. Commodity production, distribution, and pricing are all affected by events at home and abroad. A freeze in Brazil sends coffee futures shooting upwards. Poor harvests in the Ukraine may mean more U.S. exports, hence higher prices for the American farmer. A Russian invasion of Afghanistan halts grain sales to the Soviet Union, sending prices down and up as traders guess how governments and supplies will respond. A president running for reelection manipulates price-support levels and farm loan programs to temporarily boost farm income, supermarket prices, and perhaps his own standing in the polls. The commodity trader becomes involved in history; better still, he profits by it, which is rare indeed. Trading means taking an exhilirating part in the fast-paced worlds of international diplomacy, high finance, and global economics. The education it can offer benefits the student of commodities in a variety of ways—practical, intellectual, and monetary—even if he never makes a real trade. The workings of the commodity market now are intertwined with almost every aspect of our daily lives. Whatever your vocation—trader, secretary, teacher, government worker, banker, housewife, laborer—you are already working with commodities. The chapters that follow provide an introduction on how those commodities are traded, how they are priced, and how people from all walks of life and from every economic bracket have learned to profit in the marketing process.

Chapter 2

HOW FORTUNES ARE MADE

Before going into detail about how fortunes are made in commodities, I feel obliged to give a few words of caution in the form of some old-fashioned and time-honored truths. The desire to make a great deal of money may be of help in your career in commodities. An excessive greed for profits will surely take you down, eventually, into ruin. In this case ethical and moral perspectives go hand-in-hand with financial wisdom and sound business practice. When the lust for grabbing every last dollar gets the better of you, your account is in real danger. Remind yourself that success is not counted in stacks of money. "Success" denotes the achievement of a goal, the realization of an aspiration to do something or be somebody of lasting value. Money is transient, valueless by itself. Money in itself is a means to other ends, and without worth except as it is used for purposes which are themselves of true value. The obsessive quest for riches has duped the ignorant and the brilliant, the great and the small. History is littered with the sad and sorry stories of those fools who thought that money would bring them happiness. Concentration solely upon the accumulation of wealth is not a pursuit I would recommend to anyone—friend or foe.

Greed inevitably destroys human relationships and degrades human activities. It is too high a price to pay for money. For many people, especially those who seek money as the sole object of trust within their environment, a cruel joke is taking place. The more money one accumulates, the less trusting one becomes of other people; the more one turns to money itself as security, the less and less secure one becomes. Greed and insecurity feed upon one another, so that additional sums do not add happiness and security but add fear and unhappiness. Once money becomes more important than living, loving, caring, sharing, giving—once suspicion and avarice replace kindness and laughter—money becomes the devil in disguise.

There are certain universal laws that govern life as we know it, laws which (when followed) allow one to squeeze more out of life than could be had were those laws ignored. Wronging other people for one's own ends will not bring real happiness. Violating mores or rules worked out through centuries of human development may bring some people a perverse form of "satisfaction," but none could be honestly described as "happy" when that satisfaction comes at the unjust expense of others, and at the cost of the

17

individual's own human integrity and dignity. The truisms and moral rules of human societies are far more likely to bring beneficial returns, and these riches will be of a wider variety and deeper nature than mere coins can bring. The golden rules of human conduct are the product of thousands of years of human experience both happy and unhappy. Few of us have not seen these rules at work firsthand, or failed to benefit when others abided by them.

With our sense of how to approach the game now refreshed, how *can* we make a fortune in commodities? In the accumulation of wealth, once again we find certain laws and time-tested rules that yield superior results. Fortunes are rarely made accidentally. Fortunes are made by those with a rational *plan,* by people who consider the broader context as well as the details, and who arrive at a simple-yet-efficient program for reaching their goal. A primary avenue to follow in your quest for wealth accumulation is that of *horizontal and vertical analysis.*

Along the horizontal plane, we encounter a series of discrete profit opportunities. These may be jobs, careers, or commodity futures contracts. Whenever one of these opportunities takes off, we move in a vertical direction as we exploit the success of

this winner. In the span of a lifetime, each of us will encounter many such horizontal opportunities (the number will depend upon the individual, his resources, his luck and abilities). Let's take a typical small businessperson. Assume a try at several enterprises during a life span, some failures and some successes. Our entrepreneur is at one time or another involved in the following:

1. Grocery store box boy
2. Grocery store assistant manager
3. Owner of own grocery store (goes broke)
4. Owner of small shoe store (goes broke)
5. Hires on to retail hardware outlet, assistant manager
6. Buys hardware store (marginally successful)
7. Buys franchised quick-stop market (moderate success)
8. Buys second market; 2 stores now earn him $40,000 annually
9. Buys third, fourth, fifth stores; income exceeds $100,000
10. Buys entire Kansas state franchise of 7–11 markets, 45 stores; annual personal income exceeds $500,000 annually
11. Retires at age 62; net after tax capital upon retirement exceeds $1 million
12. Judged a success by his peers. *Accumulation of wealth accomplished.*

The Horizontal Plane—the seven different business and employment opportunities experienced by this person during a working life. Across the plane the person went—no financial accumulation as a box boy, assistant manager, grocery store involvement, shoe store involvement, work-

ing in a hardware, or owning a hardware. Of the first 6 boxes in this person's plane of experience, it wasn't until he came to box 7 that wealth accumulation really began. In terms of making a fortune, the first 6 boxes can be judged a total failure (in and of themselves except as they pre-

1	2	3	4	5	6	7
Box Boy	Assistant Manager	Grocery Store	Shoes	Hardware	Hardware	7–11

pared this person for later work and ownership opportunities).

How did wealth accumulation come about? Simple. It came about from testing many of life's opportunities in a horizontal plane and when success started in one of the boxes on that horizontal plane, the person whose goal it was to achieve wealth shifted from a horizontal plane to a vertical plane. On paper it looked like this:

Wealth accumulation came when the person shifted from a horizontal plane to a vertical plane . . . when the person had the good sense to recognize that he was finally aboard a "winner" and maximized his efforts and capital staying aboard that winner.

"Grab it if it comes your way" is a line out of a song by Cat Stevens and it has more meaning than the 7 words convey at first listening. When (as you define it) you are on board a winner, grab it and stick with it and run with it as your time and effort will allow. For it is by sticking with winners that goals are achieved and by cutting losing positions (endeavors) short that defeat is minimized.

Success in business is not the rule. It is the exception. Success is highly unlikely. Failure is the norm. If you fail in your venture, that is to be expected. It

have failed at a given activity, but because they do not have the time, capital, or endurance to push on until the winner comes. They simply give up and assume they are failures. They are *not* failures. They are, in fact, simply proving that success is difficult and that when one looks at opportunities along a horizontal line, *failure is quite common.* But it is hard to convince someone who has worked 5 years in a grocery store, 5 years in a hardware store, 7 years in shoes, 3 years here and 4 years there and 5 years another place that success may come. Twenty-nine years of one's life is a lot of time, a lot of money, and a lot of effort. Success may, in fact, never come to that person. That person may never hit "his 7–11 bonanza" and may struggle on from one opportunity

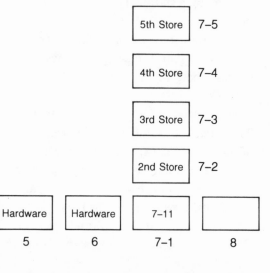

is success that should cause surprise. You should expect to fail in your various business activities, for more likely than not you will. Failure is the rule; success is the exception.

The reason so few business oriented people accumulate wealth is not because they

on the horizontal plane to another and another and another and finally simply quit. He may well judge his life a failure, *but it is not.* It is simply stated by saying that this person never hit (or didn't recognize) a winner within the boxes on that person's horizontal opportunity frame. He wasn't a failure; he simply just never hit a winner (or didn't recognize it when he did).

WHAT DOES THIS ALL HAVE TO DO WITH MAKING A FORTUNE AND THE COMMODITY FUTURES MARKETS? *A great deal!* Commodity trading is business shoved into a short time span—nothing else. It is 50 years shoved into 1 year. It is 25 years shoved into 6 months. It is 6 months shoved into 24 hours. It is opportunity on a horizontal plane shoved before us as traders day after day after day . . . *it is an entrepreneur's dream. It is life without having to wait 50 years to find out if you have the ability to accumulate capital when you have hold of a winner.*

What does the grocery business, a gas station, being an attorney, being involved in real estate, owning land where oil might exist, having a cattle ranch, owning a car dealership, a stationery store, a mail order business, a candy shop, or a wheat ranch have to do with the commodities of cattle, corn, yen, ginnie mae, gold, hogs, pork bellies, cotton, soybeans, sugar, and wheat?

Everything. The games are identical. The object of each (from a financial point of view only) is (a) living income and (b) wealth accumulation. The people involved in real estate or owning a cattle ranch are identical with the people having 5 contracts of cotton and 3 contracts of sugar. Both wish to earn a regular sum of money

and also to accumulate money beyond needs. We in the commodity futures trade are not doing anything which any other person who is seeking those goals is not doing. We are business people just like all the others are business people.

NOW, STOP AND THINK OF OUR ADVANTAGES IN TERMS OF WEALTH ACCUMULATION.

Question (1) Could any person be involved in all 11 occupations mentioned previously during a single lifetime. Probably not. It would be very unlikely that any single person would be involved in all 11 activities in a single life. SO, if those 11 are the choices you wish to involve yourself in—in the search for wealth accumulation—you will have to start off by eliminating several of them, for you won't have the time to engage in all 11.

Question (2) Could any person have financial interests in all 11 commodities listed in the second horizontal line? *Sure,* not just those 11, but 111 more. No problem at all in having a financial interest in live cattle, corn, yen, ginnie mae contracts, gold, hogs, pork bellies, cotton, soybeans, sugar, and wheat. We could even toss in the British Pound, Canadian Dollar, Canadian Barley, Rapeseed, and platinum if we liked. The point is that we, as commodity traders, have a *tremendous advantage from the start* in wealth accumulation because we can be involved in several financial activities at a single time.

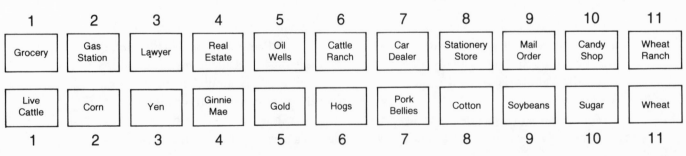

Now, assume the businessman is involved in the first line but he has to select a reasonable list from that 11—say, he picks a grocery store, gas station, cattle ranch, car dealer, and stationery store. That is 5 from the 11. The chances are that those 5 *will occupy him for his entire life.* He will have no more time or money left if he does not accumulate money from one of the five selected. He has five chances. It will require the major portion of his life to succeed, so he had better select his five well. Maybe a *candy shop,* which was *not* selected, is the business which can be taken from a horizontal to

STAY WITH EACH MARKET UNTIL YOU LOSE $1,000 CAPITAL. IF $1,000 IS LOST, CUT YOUR LOSSES SHORT AND GET OUT.

Here are the positions you have:

1. long 2 cattle
2. short 1 corn
3. long 1 yen
4. short 2 ginnie mae
5. long 2 gold
6. 'short 2 hogs
7. long 1 pork belly
8. short 1 cotton
9. long 2 soybeans
10. short 1 sugar
11. long 2 wheat

------------------------------------ $1000 Loss Line -------------------------------------

a vertical emphasis. Maybe the business-person selected 5, stopped before the candy store, and never got to 6. He never made his fortune because he ran out of time and money before the candy store idea ever came to him. He worked all his life on a *horizontal plane* and never got to see how skillful he was at making money from a vertical plane. Never had the chance.

BUT THE COMMODITY TRADER is not limited by time. He may be limited by money, but not by time. We have all the time in the world to work on vertical skills. Our excuse for failure will not be that we never got a market which gave us a vertical opportunity. If we fail to accumulate capital it will be because we did not learn how to squeeze capital out of vertical opportunities.

Take the list we started with . . . and start with this requirement:

You will stay with all your positions until they cross the $1,000 loss line. Whether it be 3 hours, 3 days, 3 weeks, or 3 months, you will stay with the position until the $1,000 loss line is crossed. All on a horizontal plane, all have an equal chance (if your ability of picking winners and losers was equal) of crossing that line. And what happens on this horizontal plane? Within one month, you have a loss in 7 of the 11 commodities. You have a $7,000 loss and are out of 63 percent of your positions. You are a loser already in nearly ⅔ of the positions you took.

What has really happened? What has really happened is not that you are a loser at all. You have merely experienced an economic fact of life that most business opportunities do not provide financial rewards. Failure is the rule; success is the exception. You have not failed. You have

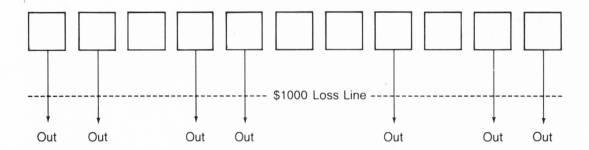

succeeded—succeeded in proving that failure is the rule—for you, 63% of the time you have lost $1,000 of your capital.

What else has happened? In one month you have been involved in 11 different financial opportunities. Eleven in one month. Remember our businessperson who had to limit his total list to 5 because there was not enough time in that person's life to experience more than 5. You, as a commodity investor, have already progressed through 11 different financial arenas in a month's time. Seven of the markets have provided losses. You have a 63 percent loss ratio. But this loss ratio should not disguise from you the fact that you have lived through more markets than a businessman can live through in a lifetime. The opportunities you have experienced exceed the average horizontal opportunities of an average businessman during an entire lifetime. Think about that for a while. *The opportunities you have experienced exceed the average horizontal opportunities of an average businessman during an entire lifetime.*

Now there is something else. . . .

You, unlike the 5 business businessman, have an opportunity to test your skills at accumulating capital through vertical application.

What happened to the 4 markets (the 37 percent of your positions) which did not result in a $1,000 loss? They are still

around. You have been kicked out of 7 of your 11, but 4 are still around and earning a profit. Let's take a look at them.

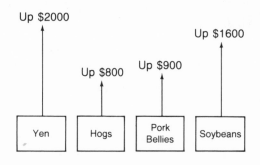

Unlike the businessman who would not experience 11 opportunities in a lifetime of business and who might never experience vertical success, in a month's time as an investor you have experienced 11 opportunities, have failed in 7, but have had success in 4. You have 4 opportunities to work with vertical application within a single month, while the businessman never had 1 chance during an entire life. It is sad, but it is very true. Very, very true. As a commodity investor, you will have more business opportunities in a single month than the average businessperson has in a lifetime, and your skills in working with winners will be tested, while the average businessman's skills may never be tested due to a lack of opportunity. It is sad from the businessman's point of view, but this is a true statement.

Wealth accumulation, then, is nothing

more than your ability to work with winners. You don't have to worry about accumulating wealth from losers, for few have that ability. Your wealth accumulation will come solely from your ability to work with winners . . . and in our example you have 4 chances to work with winners in a single month. If you don't accumulate wealth it will not be because you have not been given the opportunity (assuming you have sufficient capital to trade more than one market). It will be because you did not develop sufficient skills and patience to wring money from the winners you will be given. You won't have to worry about never having a chance to work with vertical procedures, for you will have plenty of chances. And the more you work with such, the greater your skills will become in making such markets give you the money you deserve for surviving and becoming skillful at your trade.

Forget about commodities for a minute and think of all the successful (financially successful) people you know. How many made their money from horizontal analysis trading and how many from vertical? How many truly wealthy people do you know or have read about who were successful on a horizontal plane? *Virtually none.* They were all successful vertically. Conrad Hilton didn't make his fortune by building only one hotel and then opening a car wash. He may have had a car wash before he had a hotel, but once he found hotels and they succeeded, it was hotels, hotels, and more hotels. He had gone from horizontal to vertical. J. D. Rockefeller didn't make his family wealthy by horizontal application. He discovered oil and then continued in the field where success lay. I know a man (know of him but do not know him personally) in Seattle who had a small store in a key

location. It wasn't his first venture. It was one of many along a horizontal line. The store started to earn some income. He started to get a name. He started to sell some of his products by catalog and mail order. He kept his name and put in more stores. He had no special skills beyond those of hundreds of thousands of businessmen in America, but he did recognize opportunity on a vertical scale and he maximized that opportunity. Within a period of years his ownership of that small store and what he had developed was sold for millions. He had accumulated wealth through vertical development of what had started as a horizontal opportunity experience. Did Ray Kroc, who owned MacDonalds, start one hamburger stand and then open a dry cleaners? No. He is almost a billionaire because the first MacDonalds became the first of many thousands. He had a winner, he stayed with it, and wealth was accumulated.

Well, our commodity trader of one month has some winners, too—winners in the Japanese yen, live hogs, pork bellies, and soybeans. Four winners (Ray Kroc only had one) and each can help our commodity trader accumulate wealth. Not one chance . . . but four. And not in a lifetime, but in a single month.

Cocoa is worth $300 per/penny. The advance from 50 cents a pound to $1.50 was worth $30,000 per/contract. Ten contracts were worth $300,000. A hundred contracts were worth $3 million. *Yet cocoa may well have started simply as a horizontal opportunity.* It may have been one of 11 trades for a person in 1976. Maybe that person lost $1,000 on 9 of those 11 trades, but the inventory also included cocoa as part of the portfolio. And maybe—just maybe—that person knew how to succeed in working with winners, and while that person may have started out with 2 contracts long the cocoa market, by the time the price reached 70 cents, that person may have had 50 contracts. And when the price reached $1.00 maybe that person sold. He or she didn't get $1.50 per/pound. They sold for only $1.00. Yet, 50 contracts at an average price of 60 cents sold for $1.00, yielding a profit of $600,000. What started with 2 contracts might have ended up with $600,000 in profits in the year 1976. (See Figure 2–1.

There are plenty of other examples to use: big markets in most commodities from plywood to soybeans to the drop in hogs this past year and perhaps to the rise in sugar now. Perhaps not, but certainly a horizontal opportunity worth testing.

Big money is made in commodity markets the same way it is made in any other business venture. It is made by testing many products, investments, and opportunities and cutting losses short on those which are unsuccessful and maximizing

FIGURE 2–1

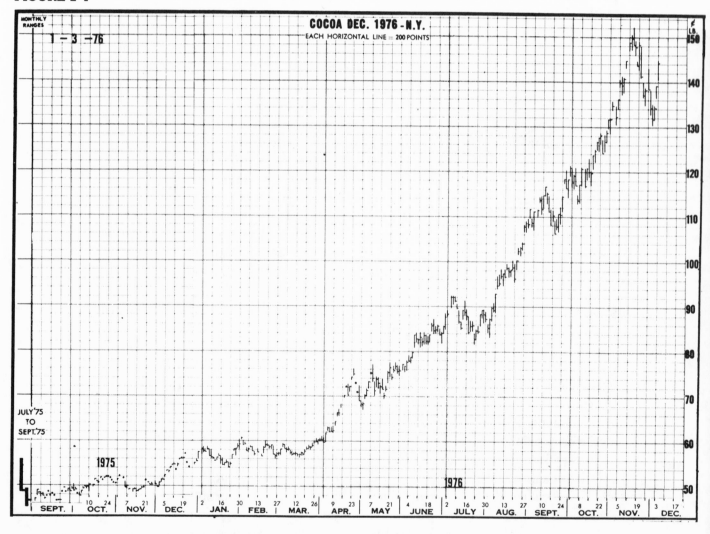

profits on those which are successful. It is taking horizontal opportunities and turning the winners into vertical successes. It is that simple. Just as there are maxims and rules for life, there are maxims and rules for successful commodity trading on a vertical scale which, when applied with some discipline, will yield success more often than not. Let's look at a few.

    a. Don't pour good money after bad. What does that mean? It means if you have a horizontal opportunity which results in a loss, get out and look for another opportunity. Don't continue to put money into a losing opportunity.

    b. Pour good money after good. When you get a winner, add to your investment if you consider the opportunity a sustained one. If you wish to switch from 2 contracts to 10, do it with the winners rather than starting with 2 contracts and averaging down, hoping to break even in a losing position.

    c. Scale in your orders. This means to add to winning positions when the profits continue to mount in your favor (if you think the position's move, again, will be sustained).

    d. Realize that big profits take considerable periods of time to be achieved (months generally) and be patient through the use of trailing stops or other trend following methods during this period of time. Don't be too eager to get out from a winner.

There are many others. The important consideration which one should reflect on is that, as commodity traders, we have many advantages which an ordinary businessman does not have—both in the opportunities for trading and also in the time span in which success can come. We will have more opportunities for failure (and we will fail many times which will keep us humble) but we will also have more opportunities for success (and many of us will succeed, time and time again).

We must learn to view opportunities horizontally and not be afraid if we lose now and then. But when we have a winner, we must learn to trade on a vertical scale, maximizing our efforts, time, and capital to earn the money which a winner delivers to those who accurately ride with her.

Not long ago I had a discussion with a friend who works for IBM and who has just gotten involved in commodity trading. He knew me from several years ago when he sold me a typewriter and so, after suffering a loss in the soybean market, he came by to discuss trading. He said that he and two of his friends had split an investment in soybeans, 3 or 4 contracts. This was the only position they had. They bought soybeans with the trend, rode it down against the trend, hated to take a loss, held on, rode it back up with the trend, were about even, it came back down again, and they suffered a loss—probably around $3,000 in total, I would guess, though I didn't ask the precise amount. My own response to this person was as follows: "*The first mistake* you made was to assume that your soybean position had any importance at all. It did not. It had no more importance than the first five cards you might have been dealt in a poker game. You no more had to win with that position in soybeans (to be successful long term) than you have to win with the first hand in poker you are given. That position was totally immaterial in your overall success and abilities to succeed. By watching that position the three of you were attaching more importance to it than it deserved. By forming any conclusions from your loss, you are giving it significance it does not deserve. It is nothing in your trading program. Absolutely nothing. It matters not. What you have to do is not succeed on the first contract you buy or sell; you have to succeed over a series. That is what is important. If you cannot succeed over a series, you will not accumulate money. If you cannot succeed over a single position, that means nothing. Absolutely nothing. You would be far, far better off rather than taking 4 contracts in soybeans to have 1 in cotton, 1 in sugar, and 1 in wheat and soybeans. Then you will not attach more importance to your soybean position than you will to any of the others. If you lose $700 in soybeans, so what; you may make $1,500 in sugar. You will not draw conclusions based on a single commodity which the 3 of you watch day in and day out. Would the 3 of you stand behind a single poker hand (the first one dealt that evening) and all bet on it and draw conclusions as to how good a poker player you are because you lost? It makes no more sense to see a commodity position as an entity any more than it makes sense to see a poker hand separate from the end results when the chips are finally counted."

TO WIN YOU SIMPLY MUST HAVE THIS ABILITY

a. The ability to make reasonable judgments on a horizontal plane so you can increase your likelihood of hitting winning positions (which you can work on a vertical plane) beyond the mere chance of 50/50.

b. Once you develop that ability, then you must develop the ability to work with winners, be patient, learn how to add to markets, decide how much capital to commit, and develop all the skills which any successful businessman must develop.

c. Once you develop that ability, then you must overcome the problems which excess money will cause. Handling money itself is a problem. You must learn to exist in a world where normal sums of capital are dwarfed by the figures with which you will be dealing. You must learn that money is simply a means to other ends. It is nothing in itself. It is something to work with, to develop with, to grow with, and to do good with. It is not good in and of itself. It is nothing in and of itself. It is simply money, just as a tree is a tree or a rock is a rock. It is what you can do with money that counts and whether you learn to master it or it learns to master you.

Chapter 3

SOME MYTHS AND TRUTHS ABOUT THE COMMODITY MARKET

For some time now, futures trading has been a featured part of our economic life. The ups and downs of gold, soybeans, and wheat find their way onto the nightly news shows and into the living rooms of millions. Most people have heard of commodity trading, listened to reports of great market moves, heard analyzed the effects of embargoes or droughts on futures prices, or known someone made fabulously rich or grimly poor by the game of speculation. The increase in the number of traders, in the kinds of commodities traded, and in the publicity surrounding the markets does not necessarily indicate a deeper understanding of the system itself. Most speculators still come to futures trading after studying or engaging in other kinds of financial enterprises, bringing with them the myths that can be expected to obscure any relatively new or unique activity. More talk about the commodity markets has not been universally accompanied by more knowledge of their real nature. By attacking some of these myths first, it is hoped the air will be cleared for the fuller, but inevitably slower, text to follow. Each subject discussed in this chapter is handled in the course of the text, although not in the same manner.

The novice will find here a debunking of follies often heard in the media, in brokers' offices, from other speculators, or on the floor of the exchanges themselves. Those already familiar with trading may discover that their education has only just begun.

Here, then, are some of the myths most commonly held about commodity trading.

MYTH NUMBER 1

Trading commodities requires a great deal of money. The fact is that a commodity account can be set up, and played, with surprisingly small sums. Many traders have less than $10,000 invested in commodity futures (this and other money figures throughout the book will, of course, vary in time with general economic and market conditions; the *relative* financial advantages of commodity trading remain unaffected). An average account might be $5,000 or $7,000. Compare this to the average stock market account of $50,000 to $100,000. Too much money invested in commodity futures is often a handicap to successful trading. If you can't profit from a small speculation, you'll lose your shirt on a

27

larger one. Success in the game depends on skill and research, not on the size of your capital. It would be unwise to sink many thousands of dollars in the markets until hundreds of trades and months or years of practice signal that you're ready. Even then, betting too many chips on a single hand may be fatal. One of commodity futures trading's prominent attractions is precisely the opportunity to get in-

FIGURE 3–1

MARKETS	LARGE HEDGERS				LARGE SPECULATORS				SMALL TRADERS			
	LONG	SHORT	NET	△	LONG	SHORT	NET	△	LONG	SHORT	NET	△
Broilers–C. B. T.	17	64	– 47	– 47	*	17	– 17	– 21	83	19	+ 64	+ 68
Cattle (Live)	12	30	– 18	Unch	10	12	– 2	Unch	72	52	+ 20	– 1
Cattle (Feeder)	20	29	– 9	– 5	16	15	+ 1	+ 10	60	52	+ 8	– 5
Cocoa (Old)	37	51	– 14	+ 8	15	10	+ 5	– 10	46	38	+ 8	+ 2
Coffee	8	37	– 29	– 13	15	6	+ 9	+ 10	73	54	+ 19	+ 1
Corn	60	51	+ 9	+ 1	4	5	– 1	– 2	29	38	– 9	Unch
Cotton	12	66	– 54	+ 4	18	1	+ 17	+ 2	62	24	+ 38	– 5
Eggs	0	0	0	Unch	0	0	0	Unch	100	100	0	Unch
Hogs	5	7	– 2	+ 2	15	26	– 11	– 10	69	56	+ 13	+ 7
Lumber	20	27	– 7	– 1	8	13	– 5	– 9	54	39	+ 15	+ 11
Oats	13	48	– 35	+ 7	5	11	– 6	+ 5	74	32	+ 42	– 12
Orange Juice	40	48	– 8	+ 19	12	8	+ 4	+ 3	42	38	+ 4	– 21
Platinum	3	31	– 28	– 3	22	3	+ 19	+ 10	67	58	+ 9	– 7
Pork Bellies	*	8	– 8	Unch	11	30	– 19	– 7	78	51	+ 27	+ 7
Potatoes (NY)	5	35	– 30	– 11	18	20	– 2	+ 9	74	43	+ 31	+ 1
Soybeans	45	39	+ 6	– 4	3	8	– 5	– 1	33	34	– 1	+ 7
Soybean Meal	65	68	– 3	+ 3	5	3	+ 2	+ 1	25	23	+ 2	– 2
Soybean Oil	51	67	– 16	– 9	5	3	+ 2	+ 1	31	17	+ 14	+ 7
Sugar "11"	28	50	– 22	+ 14	16	3	+ 13	– 1	46	38	+ 8	– 14
Wheat (Chi)	25	43	– 18	– 6	12	6	+ 6	– 1	49	37	+ 12	+ 7
Wheat (K.C.)	75	66	+ 9	+ 7	3	1	+ 2	+ 2	19	29	– 10	– 6
Wheat (Minn)	49	86	– 37	– 15	1	*	+ 1	+ 1	44	14	+ 30	+ 11
Ginnie Maes (Chi)	38	41	– 3	Unch	5	4	+ 1	+ 3	23	22	+ 1	– 3
T-Bills (90 Days)	13	26	– 13	+ 7	22	15	+ 7	+ 9	43	37	+ 6	+ 2
T-Bonds	17	25	– 8	– 5	11	5	+ 6	+ 3	38	35	+ 3	+ 4

Open Interest—Large Hedgers, Speculators and Small Traders
Positions Shown in Percent (Rounded) as of February 29, 1980

* Less Than .05%   △ CHANGE IN % NET FROM PREVIOUS MONTH

Source: Commodity Research Bureau, Inc.

volved, and realize handsome returns, with only a small initial investment.

MYTH NUMBER 2

Commodity markets exist to serve speculators and gamblers both inside and outside the industry. On the contrary, the majority of trading in any market is usually done by hedgers who use the markets to *avoid* gambling on coming cash commodity prices. These hedgers reduce or specialize the price risks inherent in any marketing operation by trading contracts in such a way as to offset cash positions, establish predictable levels of purchase cost, and to generally plan their expenses and receipts with more assurance than they could without futures markets. The flexibility afforded producers and processors by futures hedging enables economic planning, defuses momentary price crises, and is the futures market's most famous justification. During a typical month, large hedgers might comprise 56 percent of open interest in corn, 34 percent in Chicago wheat, 71 percent in Kansas City wheat, 42 percent in soybeans, 18 percent in Treasury Bills, etc. (See Figure 3–1.) There will be sharp fluctuations in hedger interest from day to day and in seasonal patterns, but their involvement remains substantial.

Hedgers include banks, grain companies, farmers, and anyone whose business depends on the sale or purchase of large amounts of a certain commodity. In its simplest, but by no means exclusive form, a hedge would be a position taken directly opposite one's cash or actual situation. Any change in one would be offset by the other (it rarely works so neatly in fact, but the theory remains basic to practical hedges). For instance, an orange farmer

is "long" by virtue of his role as producer. If prices between blossom and harvest dip to 75 cents a pound, rocket upwards towards $1.00 during a freeze in the Florida orange belt, and settle at 92 cents (at which price delivery is made in the cash market), such price shenanigans make the farmer's attempts at budgeting or planning totally meaningless. He cannot finance new land purchases or crop handling equipment if he does not know his income within fairly close limits. Nor can he borrow from the bank without a sure estimate of his collateral's value. The producer's projected income, and thus his entire financial position, rides precariously on the moods of the market place, on consumers, on the weather, and on the fortunes of other farmers. The inevitable risk of price changes may be passed on, however, if the farmer trades futures. He can sell a number of futures contracts roughly equal to the size of his projected crop if he fears an upcoming decline in prices. If prices fall, his loss on his crop's real market value will be mostly offset when he closes his short futures position for a profit, as cash and futures prices move together. Futures markets don't eliminate risks; they simply shift them from the hedgers to the person out of the industry who chooses to bear them. The speculator may or may not be able to afford the gamble, but at least he chooses to do so.

MYTH NUMBER 3

You have to be an expert to deal in commodities. Obviously, it helps if you know what you are doing, but a Ph.D. in pork bellies wouldn't guarantee a dime's worth of profits. Who is more of an "expert" when it comes to the price of potatoes, corn, beef, pork, cooking oil, cocoa, coffee, orange juice, or home mortgages than today's consumer? The commodity markets offer an opportunity for those battered by price fluctuations at the grocery store, gas pump, and bank to do a little hedging of their own, applying that knowledge of price changes every American has been forced to acquire in the last tumultuous decades. Most commodity names are much more familiar to us than such stock market terms as "convertible bonds," "price/earnings ratio," or "book value." Everyone knows what is meant when it is predicted that wheat prices will rise 50 cents in five months time, and it doesn't take an expert to know that prices can only go three ways—up, down, or sideways.

The commodity trader doesn't have to master the profile of Pillsbury Corporation or Hershey Foods or of the U.S. Department of Agriculture. The speculator is playing a mathematical game into a set of random events. You need know nothing about corn—who grows it, who buys it, or even what it looks like—to see that the corn market represented by the graph offered substantial profits on the May–July rise and equally rewarding positions if sold short on the July–August decline. (See Figure 3–2.) A reasonable amount of fundamental information on corn supply and demand and charts of past corn

FIGURE 3–2

Source: Commodity Research Bureau, Inc.

market trends might have aided the trader, but skill in profiting from price moves is the real expertise required. It makes no difference to the speculator what commodity is moving, or why. The movement alone, chosen even at random, produces the gain or loss. The increasing prominence of financial futures may scare off traders, as the jargon in such circles can become truly formidable. Yet the economic sophistication necessary to trade in these new futures markets is less than many believe. Certainly a little homework on the fundamentals of interest rates, money supplies, and financing systems would be of assistance, but again the "expert" is the one who accumulates profits, not a mountain of statistics or library of theories.

MYTH NUMBER 4

The novice ought to confine himself to one single commodity and learn all there is to know about it. Once more, this myth is a follow over from stock handling. There is no way of knowing in advance whether a particular commodity will make price moves of a profitable nature. A commodity could trade for months or years without presenting the opportunity for any significant speculative profit. One could die of old age waiting for such a market to move. If a single commodity could be mastered and its price scientifically forecast with perfect accuracy, then General Mills or Chase Manhattan would be doing it and there would be no need of futures markets. Nor would there be a possibility of making a profit in them. Large industrial players trade the futures markets precisely because they cannot know what prices may do. With all their staffs of investigative researchers they,

too, are at the mercy of the chart line's random walk.

The novice ought, then, to play a variety of markets simultaneously. The trading program seeks out markets where profits are to be had and cuts short deals in slow or adverse moves. The trader looks for opportunities and takes them where they are found, regardless of the individual commodity involved. Each position is only one move in an overall strategy, hoping to come out on the plus side when wins and losses are weighed against each other. No degree of patience or knowledge is capable of forcing an unprofitable market to yield winning positions. The trader's allegiance is to the game and to his trading program, not to plywood, cotton, gold, or Treasury Bonds. No commodity, however glamorous its past or future may appear, is a sure bet. No market should be treated like a special or favorite child. Chances are it will return a quick kick in the financial shins.

MYTH NUMBER 5

Good Lord, the driveway is full of corn and the trucks are still coming! Commodity players and commentators delight in this tall tale. Hundreds of hilarious versions continue to circulate, each involving some poor innocent who comes home to find himself delivered on—his house buried under coffee beans, his yard swarming with live hogs, or his swimming pool an ocean of soybean oil. It doesn't happen. Should the holder of a long position hang onto his contracts up to the delivery date, the most he will ever receive is a slip of paper that indicates he now owns so many bushels of wheat or so many pounds of cattle. This paper is his warehouse receipt or ownership statement, telling the location of the contracted goods. Ownership registries are supplied by short contract holders in fulfillment of their contracts and given to the oldest standing long in the market. The receiver of the slip can generally mark it "don't want" and it will be passed onto the next oldest long in line ("re-tendering"). You should be warned, though, that in the case of shell eggs, soybean meal, and a few other commodities the process can sometimes be quite complicated and often financially costly. This should be discussed with your broker prior to purchasing contracts that may be delivered upon.

Should you hold an open long position to the very last delivery day and be unable to pass the receipt along, your broker will sell the "actuals" for you, although there is a charge for this extra service. Carrying costs, the price of storing and handling the commodity, may also be a factor. As a rule it is wise for most speculators to stay out of the delivery month altogether, as contracts are matched against the actual goods in warehouses. The expiring days of a contract have special trading characteristics and pitfalls and may be very volatile and illiquid. This is a game to be left largely to the processors and warehousemen.

MYTH NUMBER 6

The insiders know it all. Literally all information of any importance whatsoever to the commodity business, both cash and future, originates with government agencies like the Department of Agriculture as a normal adjunct to their business with the nation's industries. Elaborate precautions are taken to prevent leaks. Reports are literally assembled behind locked doors—in rooms without windows

or telephones—and only released at preannounced times. All interested parties get the information on the same day.

In addition, wire services provide subscribing brokerage firms and traders with minute-by-minute reports on the markets, prices, political developments, crop reports, and other issues of concern to the trader, who thus has an effective equality of information with other traders. (See Figures 3–3 and 3–4.) There is no reliable inside information when it comes to the weather or international political events; these strike the beginner and the expert alike whenever nature or governments decide to act.

It should also be said that many insiders know it all, and that is exactly their problem. Too much specialization, too much data, and too little perspective on the game can cause tremendous mistakes. The insider may be like the person who can't see the forest for the trees. Finally, many so-called insiders are not in competition with the speculator. The broker and the pit trader make their money on commissions, whether the trade is a winner or a loser. Their concern is not how well you do, but how often you do it. Government officials are not the speculator's competition, but regulators and sources of information. If they knew all the answers they would be out trading commodities, not locked away in government service where conflict of interest laws essentially prohibit them from using inside information.

MYTH NUMBER 7

In commodities you can come face to face with General Mills. The insiders at the large industrial companies and the positions those companies take in the mar-

FIGURE 3–3

MEAT PRODUCTION DECLINES 2 PCT FROM WEEK AGO

   WASHINGTON--MAY 2--CNS--TOTAL MEAT PRODUCTION UNDER INSPECTION
FOR THE WEEK ENDED MAY 3 WAS ESTIMTED TODAY AT 729 MILLION POUNDS
BY THE U.S. DEPARTMENT OF AGRICULTURE. THE FIGURE IS 2 PCT BELOW
A WEEK AGO AND 8 PCT ABOVE A YEAR AGO.   MORE
1403 CDT#

CCC SELLS CONTRACT RIGHTS FOR 50,000 TONNES SOYBEANS

   WASHINGTON--MAY 2--CNS--THE U.S. DEPARTMENT OF AGRICULTURE SAID
TODAY THAT THE COMMODITY CREDIT CORP. SOLD CONTRACT RIGHTS FOR 50,000
TONNES OF SOYBEANS IN TODAY'S CONTRACT RETENDER.
   THE CONTRACTS WERE SOLD AT A WEIGHTED AVERAGE PRICE OF 6.305 DLRS
PER BUSHEL FOR JUNE SHIPMENT, FOB GULF PORTS.   MORE
1359 CDT#

   CME LUMBER: DEFERRED BUYING PULLS UP NEARBYS--5/2--CNS

   TECHNICAL BUYING OF THE DEFERRED LUMBER CONTRACTS HAS TRIGGERED
SOME BUYING OF THE NEARBYS, DESPITE BEARISH FUNDAMENTAL FACTORS,
SOURCES SAID. AT 1105 CDT, PRICES WERE UP 120 TO 60 POINTS WITH SPOT
MAY UP 80 POINTS AT 15800.
   SOURCES SAID BEAR SPREADING OR BUYING OF THE DEFERRED CONTRACTS
AND SELLING THE NEARBYS HAS BEEN THE MAJOR FEATURE THIS MORNING.
HOWEVER, THEY SAID THERE ALSO HAVE BEEN INDICATIONS THAT SOME OF THE
BUYING IN THE DEFERREDS HAS BEEN NEW BUYING BASED MOSTLY ON TECHNICAL
FACTORS BUT ALSO ON IDEAS THAT THE RECESSION WILL BE OVER BY THE
SECOND QUARTER OF 1981, RESULTING IN A NEW BUILDING BOOM.
   ALTHOUGH FUTURES HAD BEEN EXPECTED TO OPEN LOWER ON BEARISH
FUNDAMENTALS, THEY OPENED HIGHER, WITH THE GAINS IN THE NEARBY
CONTRACTS BEING PARED THROUGH THE MORNING. SOURCES SAID A LABOR
DEPARTMENT RELEASE THAT UNEMPLOYMENT HAD INCREASED TO 7 PCT AND
THURSDAY'S RELEASE OF NEW CONSTRUCTION FOR MARCH BEING DOWN A RECORD
5.8 PCT SHOULD HAVE EXERTED SOME PRESSURE ON FUTURES, BUT HAD LITTLE
EFFECT.
   A LOCAL HOUSE HAS BEEN A FAIRLY SUBSTANTIAL BUYER, WHILE
COMMISSION HOUSES HAVE BEEN LIGHT SELLERS, SOURCES SAID. THUS FAR, AN
ESTIMATED 1,355 CONTRACTS HAVE CHANGED HANDS.   END
1124 CDT#

Source: Commodity News Service.

FIGURE 3-4

NY MONEY MARKET: PRICES RALLY ON FED INTERVENTION--5/2--CNS

GOVERNMENT SECURITIES PRICES SETTLED WITH LARGE GAINS ON THE DAY AFTER THE MARKET RALLIED IN RESPONSE TO A RESERVE-ADDING INTERVENTION BY THE FEDERAL RESERVE, SOURCES SAID.

THE FED ENTERED THE MARKET AT 1153 EDT FOR A THREE-DAY SYSTEM-ACCOUNT REPURCHASE AGREEMENT AS FEDERAL FUNDS WERE TRADING AT 14 5/8 PCT.

ANALYSTS INTERPRETED THE MOVE, WHICH PUT DOWNWARD PRESSURE ON THE FUNDS RATE, AS A CLEAR SIGN THE CENTRAL BANK IS BACKING OFF FROM ITS TIGHT-MONEY STANCE.

SOME SOURCES BELIEVE THE SIGNIFICANT INCREASE IN UNEMPLOYMENT, REPORTED EARLIER TODAY, PROMPTED THE FED TO EASE. THE JOBLESS RATE ROSE TO 7 PCT IN APRIL FROM 6.2 PCT IN MARCH, THE HIGHEST IT HAS BEEN SINCE AUGUST 1977.

FED FUNDS WERE QUOTED AT 13 3/4 PCT AT 1500 EDT. TREASURY BILL RATES SETTLED BELOW 10 PCT ACROSS THE BOARD. THE DISCOUNT ON THREE-MONTH BILLS SETTLED OFF 43 BASIS POINTS AT 9.95-90 PCT. THE SIX- MONTH AND ONE-YEAR BILL DISCOUNTS WERE 65 BASIS POINTS LOWER AT 9.75-70 PCT AND 9.45-40 PCT, RESPECTIVELY.

NOTE AND BOND PRICES SETTLED 1 TO 2 POINTS HIGHER ON THE DAY. TWO-YEAR NOTES ENDED THE DAY UP 1 4/32 POINTS, FOUR-YEAR NOTES WERE UP 1 20/32 POINTS, 10-YEAR NOTES WERE UP 1 16/32 POINTS AND 30-YEAR BONDS SETTLED 1 30/32 POINTS HIGHER.   END
1447 CDT#

1246 CDT FUTURES PRICES

	HIGH	LOW	LAST	CHANGE	
CORN					
MAY	269	266	268 1/4	UP	2
JLY	279 3/4	277 1/2	279	UP	1 1/4
SEP	290 1/4	287 1/2	289 1/2	UP	1 1/2
DEC	298	294 1/2	296 3/4	UP	1 3/4
MAR	310	306 3/4	308 1/2	UP	1 3/4
CBT OATS					
MAY	155	149 1/2	155B		
JLY	159 1/4	154	159 1/4B		
SEP	162	157	161 3/4A		
SOYBEANS					
MAY	595 1/2	589 1/2	594 1/2	UP	4 1/4
JLY	615 3/4	609	614 1/4	UP	4 3/4
AUG	625	617 1/2	624	UP	4 3/4
SEP	634 1/2	627	633 1/2	UP	4 1/4
NOV	650	644	648	UP	3 1/2

Source: Commodity News Service.

kets are not your competition either. By law a speculator can hold a position in wheat no larger than 3 million bushels. Quite frankly, "the General" couldn't care less what you do with so little wheat. General Mills, Hershey, Cargil, and Continental Grain all use the markets to help secure the goods they will need in the future at a known price, and within reason they will use the markets regardless of price levels. Competition between the public speculator and the large grain com-

panies is nil. The hedger is playing the exact opposite game from the speculator.

Holders of the physical commodity (farmers, warehousemen, and so on) have more need of the guaranteed price for their goods than do processors (who can pass any price rise on along with the processed goods) and therefore hedgers are normally net short on the futures markets, sometimes overwhelmingly so. And yet with the major industries often taking the bear side of the market, commodity prices

FIGURE 3–5

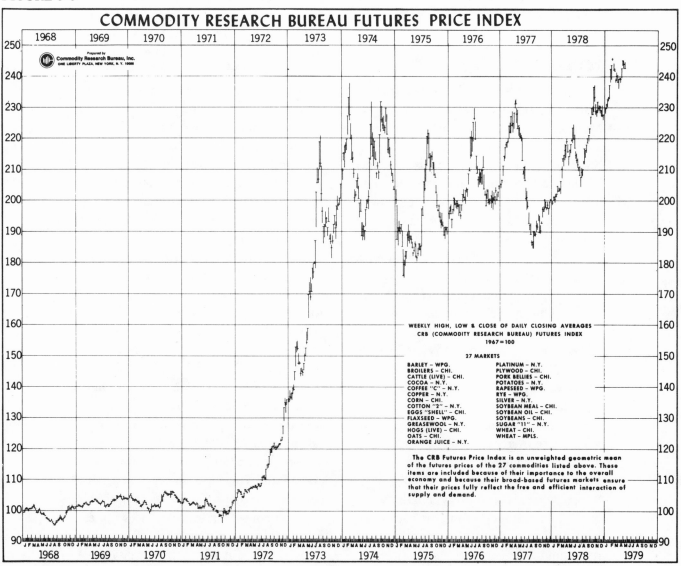

have shown a steady upward bias in recent years. This reflects the effects on commodity pricing of general economic trends, as the inflation of the 1970s carried most commodity prices on a volatile but unmistakable upward climb. (See Figure 3–5.)

As a final check, once a month the Department of Agriculture publishes *Commitments of Traders in Commodity Futures,* outlining the exact positions of all large traders in each commodity futures market. In commodities, the speculator knows exactly where he stands in relation to the large institutions. This he cannot know in the stock markets.

MYTH NUMBER 8

If I can only find the perfect trading system, I'll easily make a million. There are good ways to trade and bad ways to trade. The worst way to trade is to put all your faith in someone else's magic method, as if commodities were a religion. There's always someone selling miracle cures, perpetual motion machines, and sure-fire commodity trading methods. The gimmicks are as various and endless as their purveyors, and the suckers apparently equally innumerable. The eternal human hope of no-risk wealth is particularly ludicrous in commodities, where risk is the name of the game. Yet thousands continue to seek out that one certain and effortless key to riches. Commodities are a superior way of accumulating money, but you can lose—and lose big—especially when greed overcomes sober thought. The annals of commodity trading are littered with the sorry stories of such dreamers. Still, a sucker is born every minute (more often, it sometimes seems, in commodities), and get-rich-quick schemes continue to abound. The beginner should be wary

of all such promises and look closely for the price tag.

If one studies the best known, most well respected writings on commodities, talks to the leaders in the field, and trades for many years, there does emerge into light a consensus about the nature of commodity trading and about the best ways to profitably do it. Most of that consensus is reflected in this book's contents and will provide the reader with the kind of knowledge upon which a rewarding career in commodities trading can be based. The trader will have to work, to think about trading, and learn to employ the information and advice he has gathered. The first lesson is self-reliance. The successful trader builds his own program, for his own needs, to suit his own personality and economic goals. A good trade for speculator A may not be a good trade for speculator B. The trader will find that techniques that work for some won't work for others. Ideally, the speculator will start investing real capital only after carefully studying this text and others, evaluating them with suspicion, and learning to make sound judgments based on realistic analyses. No computer, no formula, no bag of tricks can replace common sense when it comes to commodity trading.

MYTH NUMBER 9

The public speculator is normally "long" in the market because he is more accustomed to buying something than to selling "short." This false argument has shown up in print in a number of books about futures markets. It is true that many beginning traders feel more comfortable buying than selling, but this does not explain the net long position of seasoned traders. While it is exactly as easy for a trader to go short as it is to go long, the speculator serves a vital function by being net long. The net long position of speculators helps right the imbalanced market caused by the long *cash* position of industry hedgers who *must* therefore sell *futures* short. The speculator is not trying to be nice, not to exhibit ignorance or innocence. He is buoying up a market that would sag from excess selling pressure, picking up a profit along the way for doing so.

The distribution of longs and shorts among hedgers and speculators changes, as hedgers may see a need to buy and speculators a profit in selling short. Though historically the speculator ends up long, from day to day trading decisions still must be based on actual price movement and market conditions, including the present distribution of open interest. No sane trader goes long merely to be in conformity with the statistics. The point is that the relative positions of hedgers and speculators in a market's open interest may be an important factor in evaluating the next profitable move, though such a policy of follow-the-leader trading has its drawbacks.

MYTH NUMBER 10

With everyone on low margin, it is only a matter of time before the crash. In 1929, when stocks were bought and sold on margins of 10 percent and less, everyone could wield huge fortunes with small amounts of cash. When prices dipped, margined account owners were called to put up more cash to cover their positions. If they couldn't their stock was sold, sending the price spiraling downward. Due to the fundamental differences between the stock and commodity markets, no col-

lapse of comparable magnitude is possible. (On these differences, see Chapter Four.)

Current commodity market margins serve the same function as the predepression stock market margins (although they are technically different, being surety bonds rather than down payments). Their function is to cover fluctuation in prices. When price moves against a commodity position, the trader will be asked to put up more cash (a "margin call"), but unlike in stocks (where value is tied only to demand for the certificates) futures prices are tied directly to the physical product which is traded in substantial quantities on many cash markets around the country. The futures price cannot vary much from the price of the actual goods. If it did, shorts who must deliver by contract would simply buy the actual commodity and deliver. If the price rose too far above the price of the actual goods in cash markets, longs would simply take delivery against their open positions and sell the goods on the cash market.

The stability of the commodity markets is also bolstered by the large investments of industry hedgers. Their capital resources can withstand sizeable adverse moves and their hedged situations allow them to counteract most such adversity, thus limiting price spiraling before it ruins everyone. Great declines and high peaks do occur regularly, but they always hit a limit by virtue of their connection to the cash commodity and their importance to processors and consumers. In a depression consumers can very well do without ABC Sewing Machines and ABC Sewing Machine stock. They are not going to do without wheat. Corn, oats, silver, and eggs are not suddenly going to find themselves without value. The close monitoring of financial markets, money supplies, and credit levels by the federal government helps give financial futures a stability denied other monetary speculations.

A major difference that should comfort the prospective trader concerns the guaranteed solvency of futures trading. Futures is a "zero sum game": at all times exactly 50 percent of the market is long and 50 percent is short. At the end of every trading day all trades are turned into the exchange's "clearinghouse." If you bought wheat that day the clearinghouse assumes the other end of the deal, and its members guarantee performance on the contract. If the contract crashes, half the players lose. If the stock market crashes, everybody loses.

MYTH NUMBER 11

Commodity speculation is little more than gambling. This last myth is quite joyously true. The speculator who plays the best game will make the most money and have a good time doing it. The best odds in Las Vegas are on the blackjack tables, where a good player can find a house rake-off of only 2 percent. The odds are much worse in roulette or craps. The race track normally rakes off between 15 and 20 percent. In commodities, not only is the game open and going all the time, but the odds can actually be slightly in favor of the speculator.

It is possible to sit at a poker table and play one hand and receive four aces—*once;* or place your money on red on the roulette wheel and win—*once;* or buy corn and watch it go up—*once;* but it is a one-shot proposition. If the speculator is to make any money over any period of time, it requires a program that puts the odds

of a risk situation in the trader's favor. It is not the high roller who takes money out of the commodity markets but the actuary, the person who sticks with the figures and the real moves of the market.

Although for the person playing, games of chance and the commodities game are both gambles, the nature of the two games and their relation to society as a whole are distinct. This doesn't affect trading strategy, which remains essentially risky, but it is an important aspect of the overall picture of the markets' economic function. One can argue that the horse race, the poker game, and the roulette wheel create the risks that players speculate on, that gambling is the means and end of such activities. (Never mind, for the purposes of theory, the economic benefit in jobs, construction, taxes, etc. that gambling brings.) Commodity speculation or futures gambling deals in risks already existent in a capitalist economy. Price changes are an inevitable phenomenon in the modern production, processing, and marketing of goods and services. Risks are present with or without the speculators. It is normal business and consumer activity, not speculators, that causes significant price movements. Foes of the futures markets who accuse speculative traders of driving prices up and down artificially fail to understand the economic context of futures trading, and the real role the speculator has in it: risks are generally shifted away from those in the industry who don't want them and onto the willing shoulders of the speculators. The degree of volatility injected into commodity pricing by speculation is far less than that which would take place in an unregulated, unhedgeable, totally risky market free-for-all.

Chapter 4

STOCKS AND COMMODITIES

AN OLD CONFUSION

Many people believe that commodities trading is like stock trading, only faster. This fallacy has probably cost speculators more money than all other errors put together. The mistaken notion that commodity futures can be bought and sold in much the same manner as stock certificates has persisted despite the facts and is perpetuated as more and more stock traders turn to the rewarding arena of commodities in search of the wealth and financial security that has so far eluded them. Historically, investors began switching from stocks to commodities in record numbers during the late 1960s and throughout the 1970s, fueling the explosive growth in commodity futures trading that has established it as a dominant component of the nation's economic life. It was inevitable that old ideas about stock trading would be carried over into the commodities field. Experience and a history of gigantic losses enforces the lesson that the trader of commodities had best forget his stock trading methods when he switches games. Though commodity trading has long since been recognized as a primary and unique speculative field, many people continue in the old confu-

sion. It may be because of the perceived historical and economic priority of the major stock exchanges (though commodities certainly predate stock certificates). It may be because the ownership of stocks more closely resembles the average person's idea of investment—that is, purchase of property that returns earnings. Whatever the reasons, the old conceptual privilege of stocks hangs on in some minds even as the economic standing of the commodities exchanges sweeps past its rival. (See Figure 4–1.) A review of the distinctions between stocks and commodities and of how they are traded is thus a good way to introduce the game and to dispel the myths surrounding it.

LEVERAGE

For the trader, the key difference between stocks and commodities is margin. It is the "thin" margin in commodity trading that gives the quick markets their characteristic speed and the trader his quick profits or losses. Commodities don't fluctuate more than stocks. Studies show, in fact, that some commodities fluctuate less than stocks. It is not fluctuation, but margin, that alters the significance of price

FIGURE 4-1

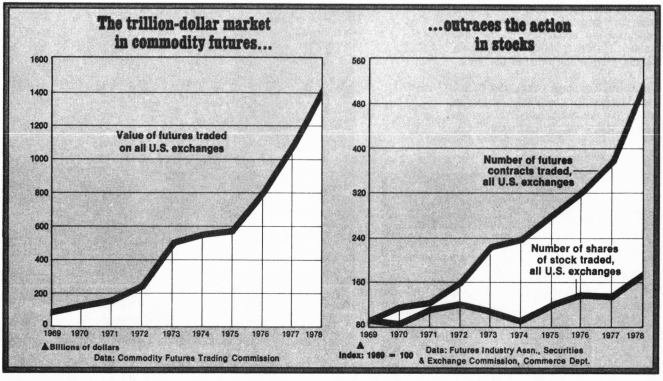

Source: Business Week, June 11, 1979.

changes when you turn from stocks to commodities. Margin determines trading's dangerous opportunities.

Margin itself is simply that amount of capital that the investor or speculator puts down to buy stock shares or control commodity contracts. The fact that the investor owns the stock, while the speculator only controls the contract for a future transaction, transforms the meaning and requirements of margin in each category. The stock buyer's margin is actually a partial payment for ownership, and he must pay interest on the remaining amount. Regulation of security debt is done by the Federal Reserve Board, the stock exchanges, and the brokers. The commodity trader's margin is nothing more than a good-faith deposit, assuring the brokers and the exchanges that the trader will be

good for his positions. The speculator will have to pay for the cash commodity only in the unlikely event that delivery is actually made or taken, in which case the brokerage can readily arrange a compensatory transaction with little loss.

Stock accounts demand margins usually between 50 and 90 percent of purchased stock value. Commodity margins are computed as fixed minimums per bushel or contract. The common margin requirement in commodities normally will be between 5 and 15 percent of the contract value, with less required for low-risk spread positions. The minimum margin for a contract is set by the exchange, but individual brokerage firms may require larger sums for a variety of reasons relating either to the market or to the firm's manner of conducting business. Margins may be raised in the case of a very volatile market or lowered to the minimum when a slump calls for trading incentives. The amount of risk determines the amount of margin, and a firm may raise margin for its own or its client's protection. Exchanges frequently raise and lower margin requirements whenever a market appears to require such regulation. Margin requirements have in the past, and will in the future, double or triple on occasion. Such fluctuation is common and will not affect a trader's program, although it will affect his leverage. Still, it is rare for commodity margin levels to exceed 20 percent.

Capital investment, then, may be greater in stocks, while capital risk (and potential profit) is greater in commodities. A trader buying 100 shares of Acme Dynamic Systems at $25 a share must come up with $2,500 plus commissions when the account is opened. If he is known well enough by the broker to trade stocks on margin, the requirement may be 65 percent of $2,500 or $1,625; if at $30 a share, $3,000 or $1,950; if at $40, $4,000 or $2,600 on margin. A contract of pork bellies at 50 cents per pound is worth $19,000 (38,000 lbs. per contract) and may be bought or sold with a margin perhaps as low as $1,200. Margin for a contract of wheat might be priced at $1,500 whether the wheat is priced at $4.00 a bushel or $5.00 a bushel, even though the total value of the contract varies by $5,000 (5,000 bushels per contract).

The amount of money typically invested in stock and commodity accounts thus differs enormously. Stocks are often added to over a period of years and the average size of the portfolios handled by the brokerage is considerably larger than the average commodity account. It is not unusual for a brokerage to have many accounts containing in excess of $100,000 worth of stocks with a correspondingly large margin account. A trader walking into a commodity brokerage who deposits $50,000 could well have one of the largest accounts on hand. A $5,000 or $10,000 deposit can be sufficient, or enough to trade three or four contracts comfortably. An account with $50,000 worth of stocks must have on deposit no less than $35,000, while an account with $50,000 worth of commodities requires no more, perhaps, than $4,000. The commodities trader wields relatively more economic leverage and has more financial clout than someone with more capital tied up in the stock market.

TIMING

The consequence of this thin margin is that, in commodities trading strategy, timing is everything. The stock holder who buys John Doe, Inc. at $50 can safely watch it fall to $40 or $20 while waiting for prices to rise. He has virtually unlimited "downside flexibility" because of his large margin. The stock trader is playing price appreciation over a relatively long haul. A 10 percent rise or decline can be taken fairly well in stride with the sure expectation that a present recession is beginning to give way to prosperity and that higher personal incomes will find their way into the stock market. A bull market will pull nearly every issue along with it, and sooner or later the stock of any healthy company will hit new levels. Given enough time, a program of buy and hold may well succeed.

The commodity speculator cannot wait out a setback with the expectation that sooner or later everything rises in price. A futures contract for July soybeans is going to become real soybeans in July. By then the trader must have taken his profit or losses or find himself with the cash goods. Once the contract expires in July, traders with open positions must make and receive delivery. That particular July soybeans futures contract is dead. These short lives, as compared to stocks, dictate strategic time frames of very short duration. The seasoned commodities

FIGURE 4–2

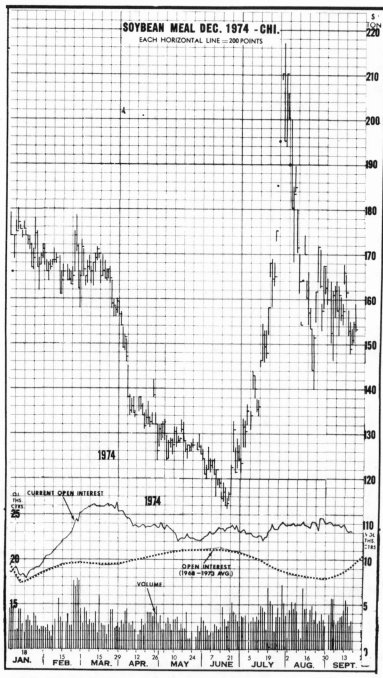

Source: Commodity Research Bureau, Inc.

trader won't sit out a 10 percent move against the value of a contract. Since a 5 or 10 percent leverage is being used to control tens of thousands of dollars worth of commodities, the trader who holds on to a losing price move will end up losing huge sums as his initial deposit is quickly wiped out and the losses mount.

The analytical methods then, successful in stocks, will fail in commodity trading. If I trade stocks I want to know certain hard facts about earnings, future growth, the industry's profile, what other stocks are selling for, etc. I want to know everything about this stock so I can project its price in the future. All this data may be hard to come by and analyze because stock markets are secondary markets while commodities markets are primary. The stock investor needs to know the markets of the company in whose stock he is investing as well as the market for the stock itself. The commodity speculator's concern is the primary market of commodity supply and demand, whose necessary statistics are public and easily available. Even so, if I do trade commodities as if they were stocks, the results will be instructive, and probably ruinous. If I try to trade soybean meal this way, I will join other earnest traders in hours of research and computation. I will want to know how many soybeans are around, what the "crush" or processing figures are, how the hogs are eating, what the price of other feed grains is, and how the export situation stands. Now say that my figures tell me, and the seasonal odds confirm, that soybean meal will rise from a present $176 a ton to $200 a ton in six months time.

Examine the chart for soybean meal. (See Figure 4–2.) Could you have afforded to jump on board and wait for six or seven months for your profits as you might do in stocks? If you bought 3 contracts in January at $176, on a margin of $1,000 per contract, your losses by June 19 (when prices hit the $105 low) would be $21,300 or 710 percent of initial margin. If you had met all your margin calls and bought even more contracts, still hoping for that price rise, your losses would be astronomical. In any case they would probably take you out of trading for a good while, and long before meal hit its promised high you'd be back to blue chip issues and savings accounts (if, that is, you had any capital left). The commodity trader cannot afford to play a long term game. His game is price movement, not eventual earnings, and he must be prepared to play markets where price changes that are inconsequential in stocks can make or break fortunes in commodities. Unlike in stocks, price forecasting takes a back seat in commodities to timing. Learning to survive is the trader's first task. He must begin by thinking about how *not* to lose his money, *not* about how much money he can make. The beginning speculator is not out to build a portfolio but to learn how to stay alive in the market no matter what happens.

HONESTY

The true stories of fortunes won and lost in commodities have generated in turn a wealth of notorious legends about price fixing, cornered markets, and wholesale corruption. Commodity markets have been portrayed as a wild school of anything-goes money sharks, while stocks are represented as the clean and sane repository of hard-earned dollars. The truth is that fraud and dishonesty are a miniscule problem in the commodities game. (Commodity *options* are another case and are treated elsewhere.) This inherent fairness of the system constitutes one of its advantages over other kinds of investment or speculation. And no matter what the reason may be for a price change, legal or illegal, the trader's problem remains exactly the same: How do I profit from the movement of prices? The temptation to blame others for our own mistakes, or naïveté, lies behind many of the accusations against commodity trading. Human history and human frailty tells us that a degree of dishonesty will creep into every enterprise. One should protest abuses wherever they are found, but they are hardly an excuse for one's own shortcomings or a license to escape from the world and its sins. In commodities, as in other things, one proceeds by taking such shortcomings of people and institutions into account when formulating a strategy for success.

The opportunities for fraud in stock dealings easily outnumber those in commodities, for the pricing mechanisms of the former are far more susceptible to manipulation than those of the latter. All stocks are valued on a price-to-earnings ratio. The fundamental figure for computing stock values, and thus for determining the fate of investors and markets, is the earnings statement. This opens monumental doors for fraud, as earnings statements are prepared and released by the interested companies themselves. Fundamental figures in commodities, on crops and herds and interest rates, are produced and published by public agencies and disseminated to all simultaneously through newswires, bulletins, free pamphlets, etc. No such open window will be found in corporate stocks. Thus, current earnings and projected earnings may be nothing but the product of accounting gimmicks. Within limits, many company books could be made to show either a large or small profit or a large or small loss by an unscrupulous accounting executive. Earnings numbers and statements are subject to board room decisions, as they may have political or financial consequences the company wishes to control. A corporation may manipulate or even wholly fabricate its earnings statements, and swindles resulting from this kind of fraud are unfortunately common.

In contrast, the futures price of a contract in corn or eggs or plywood cannot be raised or lowered substantially at the whim of a single corporation or individual. False news reports or inflated harvest projections are quickly detected and discounted in the markets before major moves can occur. The information basic to commodity trading is of such a nature as to be easily double checked, a situation many holders of now worthless stock might find enviable. A massive position taken by a commodity trader must be registered publicly and is thus soon the object of scrutiny and counterreaction by other players. Though very short term effects are possible through manipulation, the important directions and trends of commodity futures prices resist all coercion. One need only look at the federal government's attempts to control farm prices or interest rates to see how even the most powerful agencies fail at this. Those individuals who have tried recently to corner markets and manipulate prices have paid a high cost, monetary and legal, for their flings.

With farmers, buyers, consumers, and regulatory agents all watching and with weather and international politics intervening, no one has a dominant leverage in commodities. Not even supply and demand figures can be counted on for predictable price moves; history reveals that every variety of supply/demand fluctuation has been known to cause every variety of price movement at every level of intensity. The multiplicity of forces influencing commodity futures prices virtually guarantees the overall honesty of the system. Finally, and perhaps most importantly, it should be remembered that futures prices (the key figure in computing trading profits and losses and market movements) are tied to the price of the actual physical commodity. Futures prices are based on real world values, while stock values are more subject to emotion, misleading information, and subtle corporate accounting practices. Happily, the commodity trader need not be concerned with dividends, interest, rents, royalties, handling certificates, proxies, voting, call dates, conversions, or other complications of the stock investor. His concern is just forecasting and trading that little line on the chart that shows the price going up, down, or sideways. The trader need not keep up with new issues or companies. A new commodity contract can be traded like any other, once the basic channels of fundamental information are opened. There is no researching of the corporation's projected earnings, no worries about cash flow, no anxieties about management personnel, and no wondering about the health of subsidiaries. The profitable attraction of commodity trading is in its relative simplicity.

DOING BUSINESS

Of course, there are similarities between stocks and commodities. In either case the public trader does business through the brokerage houses, from the famous nationwide firms to the countless independent dealers. Often the same broker will handle both stocks and commodities (perhaps thereby giving the erroneous impression of an equal expertise in both). Whether in commodities or stocks, this merchandiser will give out tips, brochures, charts, facts, and a dry shoulder when the results are in. Both brokers will service an established account by phone. Both brokers will take your money. Margin accounts appear to have about the same function in both cases, though in fact they are entirely different. Both markets feature nearly instantaneous ticker reporting, and any good newspaper will give quotations of daily price movements for both in the same manner. Many of the terms used in one mean the same thing in the other.

However, the rules under which the commission houses are licensed give the commodity trader an advantage over the stock trader. A stockbroker can use margin accounts in his normal business. The certificates held in margined accounts are registered in the name of the broker; he may borrow against them or sell them to pay his operating expenses. Periodically, stock commission houses can go bankrupt and for the period of time that its accounts are fouled, before other companies can bail it out, the house is like any other bankrupt organization. Its assets belong to its creditors, who get whatever percentage on the dollar they can. The stock trader in such a case is just another creditor.

Clearing Members which trade commodities for public accounts must strictly separate public money from their own assets. No commodity broker can use your money to pay his light bill and no commodity broker can risk account money for his clients without an express legal permission to do so. Traders must decide to risk their own money. That is their responsibility. (The exceptions, of course, are "managed" or "discretionary" accounts.) No trader has lost money due to a Clearinghouse failure in a century of commodity trading. In the securities markets, commissions may be related to the amount of money involved in the transaction, while commodity commissions are simply computed at a flat rate per "round turn," covering both purchase and sale and charged against the account at the time of liquidation.

As objects, a stock and a commodity futures contract have nothing essential in common. One documents real ownership. The other merely commits the holder to fulfill one end of a contractual agreement. Ninety-nine percent of all speculators in commodities never end up owning any commodities. This is perhaps the hardest thing for the beginning student of commodities to understand, and is worth reviewing. Imagine that you don't own any fuel oil at all. Someone else, however, knows that he will want some in 8 months time. You believe, from studying the markets and supply/demand figures, that the price of fuel oil will be *lower* then on the actual cash market than it is today. So, you strike up a futures contract with the person who wants oil and who will make this contract with you because he doesn't want to risk not knowing what the price of his oil is going to be in February when he must buy it for his business. You still don't own any fuel oil, yet you've sold a contract's worth. The months pass. When the contract closes, you buy the actual fuel oil in the cash market at the cheaper price, deliver it to your contract partner

at the agreed upon higher price, and pocket the difference as profit. During those months, as the price of fuel oil went down, the value of the "short" contract position went up. As the holder of the contract, you could have sold the contract to another trader before actual delivery was required and thus made your profit from the contract's increased value without ever owning any oil at any time. (See Figure 4–3.) You take the risk of price moves and take the profit if the move is in your direction. This would be a case of "shorting" the market, as you were short the actual commodity. Imagine yourself the buyer, and imagine the price rising over time, and you have a model for going "long" the market.

In commodity futures, the rights to these contracts, and to the profits or losses accrued as the value of the contract oscillates with shifting prices, are what is traded. Of course, you can see from the example why few futures contracts are actually delivered upon. Actual sellers and buyers use the futures markets chiefly to "hedge" their real positions, either "long" because they are producers of a commodity or "short" because they are processors in need of a commodity. In planning their eventual sales or purchases, these hedgers can take positions in the futures markets to minimize and offset the effects of price changes and then complete their actual transactions in the spot or "cash" market. The speculator exists to provide hedgers enough partners for their positions and to assume unwanted risks. This system of hedging, speculating, and matching long and short positions forms a market structure totally foreign to that of the stock exchanges. (See Figure 4–4.)

While stock traders are bidding for a share of stock which they can place in

FIGURE 4–3

Source: Commodity Research Bureau, Inc.

their safe deposit boxes, the commodity trader is making and closing trading agreements. A stock is a tangible item. The investor owns it. He may store it, sell it, give it away, or cover the walls of his room with the certificates. He buys it at one price either with the expectation of enjoying dividend payments or in the hope that the price will rise so that he may resell it. One share of Acme Dynamic Systems could represent ownership of 1/ 100,000 of that company. One contract of September cocoa is a written agreement to deliver or accept 30,000 pounds of cocoa in September. The shares of Acme are fixed in number and owned by somebody at all times. The number of contracts for delivery of cocoa in September changes constantly. Open interest, the number of contracts extant, can easily

double in a day without a change in price. The trader can trade either the long or the short side of the market with equal ease, and there are always an equal number of longs and shorts in any commodity market. In stocks, the vast majority of positions are long, and selling short requires borrowing of the securities or other complicating procedures.

STRATEGY

Basically, the stock trader chooses an issue on any number of criteria with the expectation that the price of the stock will rise within the next year or so. Is the industry healthy? Is the company sound and moving in the right direction? How are the earnings in the past compared to the earnings of other companies in the indus-

FIGURE 4-4
Estimated average dollar values of net short hedging and long speculative open
contracts (mostly 1954/55–1958/59) (million dollars)

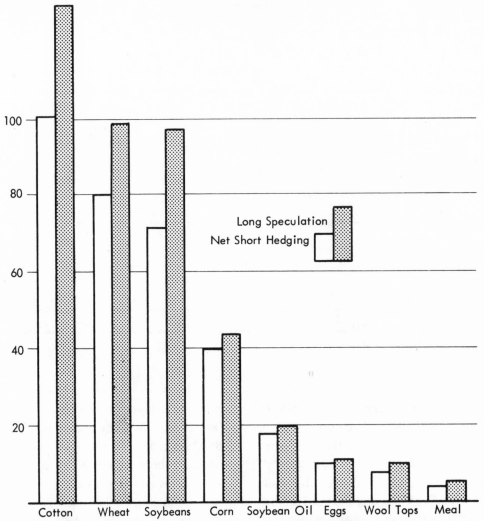

Volume and speculation are greatest on those markets with the greatest hedging interest. Total
long speculation is often greater than net short hedging (short minus long hedging). The difference is
made up by short speculation.

Source: Holbrook Working, "Speculation on Hedging Markets."

try? Who holds the stock? Is it glamorous? Steady? Growing? If I am correct, where will the price per issue be in a year or two? In five years? How is the stock market doing overall? Will the Dow Jones Industrial Average advance to 2,000 or fall to 400? Stock strategy involves know-

ing about the issue, about the market as a whole, and about the character and effect of price moves. Both the stock and commodity trader have fair mobility in trading. The clever trader can work purely technical adjustments to his advantage in the timing of his purchases and sales, while keeping a reasonably interested eye on fundamental aspects of the issues. But the large margin in stocks makes the timing of price moves less important in strategy than other considerations. The major questions during the buildup of a stock portfolio are those of goals and trading mix. Is 10 percent yearly increment good enough? Am I willing to risk more?

The commodity trader does not have this question about trading mix. He knows all of his purchases and sales are going to be speculative before he makes any move. His game is not trading mix, for he will deal in only a few commodities at a time, changing positions often, holding a contract for just days or weeks. He may trade wheat futures for several months, then switch to cattle, copper, or coconut oil as prices fluctuate. He makes his money on the small percentage moves on the very large positions he can control with his margin account. He expects to lose money on more than half his trades, but if he is a successful trader he keeps these losses small and stays in the game, ready for the major price moves. The commodity trader is playing a game of money management rather than trading mix. Which commodity he chooses is less important than how he handles his account.

PRICE MOVES

Commodity prices have no built-in upward bias. Over the contract life span, prices are as likely to be down as up. Bumper crops in corn, wheat, and cotton can drive prices for these commodities down to the government price support level, while potatoes skyrocket because of a blight in Idaho and while cocoa gyrates

madly because of unrest in Nigeria. There are connections between commodities, such as the price of hogs and the price of the corn they eat, and high-priced corn will eventually raise the price of pork, but these are the exceptions rather than the rule, tying together two or three commodities in a very loose relationship. High-priced corn will do little for the price of gold, silver, wool, cotton, plywood, or propane. Charts for May cotton and May potatoes show very dissimilar trends. (See Figure 4–5.) Each commodity, not the overall market, must be judged and played for itself. There is normally no overall bull or bear market in commodities, for commodities is in actuality an aggregate of separate trading markets, each with its own independent fundamental and technical factors. The contract expires close to the cash spot price for that commodity in the current market, regardless of activity in other futures. The commodity trader is seldom caught in the position of having figured a particular commodity price movement correctly, only to have his position ruined by a total market upheaval, as has happened frequently in stocks.

On the other hand, the speculator *is* in the position in commodities of having figured all his factors accurately, forecasting the price move with the best odds, and then watching the individual market he is playing go all to hell anyway. To survive, the trader with a larger size account may manage the risk he assumes in the same manner that an insurance company bears risk. By dividing a determinable risk across a large number of cases, the insurance company can set a program under which it knows it can operate at a profit, even though it does not

FIGURE 4-5

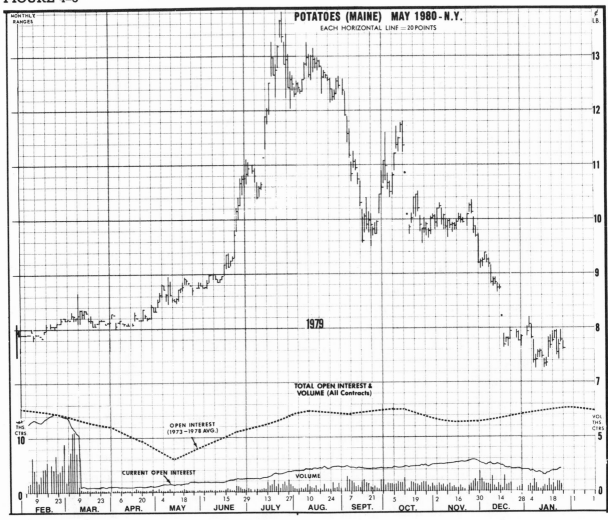

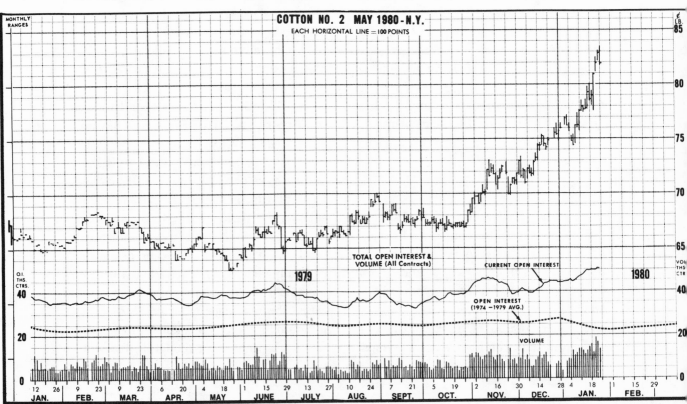

Source: Commodity Research Bureau, Inc.

know what will happen on any particular policy. The insurance company does not know what will happen to any one car, only that out of a hundred thousand cars, 12.7 percent will be involved in accidents in any given year. It knows the cost of the average accident and, by determining the number of accidents and the cost of the average accident, the company knows how much income it must have to run a profit and sets its premiums accordingly. Likewise, the farmer does not worry about any single grain that he sows but merely about the average germination. If his seed germinates at about 60 percent, he knows that he must plant 100 seeds where he wants 60 plants. In the same spirit, the commodity trader should have a trading program consisting of a number of trades, without dependence on any one position, ready to survive a number of different price moves. Numerous losses are balanced against a small number of wins whose profits the trader learns to maximize. It is the profit or loss of the entire program that counts, not any single speculation. The commodity speculator plays positions across the board, testing the water and getting out of adverse price moves. Thus, he is in position when the profit-making moves occur. The speculator who selects just one commodity as though it were a stock, analyzes it thoroughly, and takes a position is playing the wrong game.

The commodity speculator is playing an insurance game, the game of bearing risk. He cannot know whether the price of British Pounds is going up or down (although he may try), but he can figure how far up or down the price can possibly go and the chance of its going there. He knows he is going to lose on at least half of his trades and needs only to see that

his average loss is smaller than his average gain. There are probably as many different methods of speculation as there are speculators, but the trading programs all share two basic functions. The speculator must predict (guess which market to play and which side to take) and manage his position (to that the net profit of his plays).

Commodities trading is what economists term a "zero sum game." Every dollar lost by any trader is made by another trader and the only money that leaves the game is made by the broker through commissions. It is like a poker game with a dime drag out of every pot to pay for rent, cards, and potato chips. While any trader may have a "paper profit," the profit and loss of all traders at all times adds up to zero. This is distinctly different from the stock market, where the total value (and profit) goes up in a bull market and down in a bear market. The total value of all commodity futures contracts changes with price movements, but the total value of winnings will change only as the volume of business changes.

As with stocks, any commodity that becomes too volatile may be suspended from trading until the market has a chance to digest events and to calm nervous traders. Individual exchanges decide on market suspensions or limitations, though they may have to do so in response to requests (as from the federal government). In commodities, however, daily trading limits are specified in advance, at the discretion of the exchange. The limit on wheat, for instance, might be set at 20 cents per session. Unlike in stocks, individual positions in agricultural commodities have preset maximum levels. No comparable regulatory device exists for the stock markets. The commodity trader has to figure his flexibility in responding to price moves by keeping in mind the daily trading limits and the limits on the positions he may take.

THE CAST OF CHARACTERS

Many people do trade both stocks and commodities. But, generally speaking, the types of traders in commodities and the relations between them differ from those in stocks. The talents and financial flexibility demanded by futures trading draw a personality who would probably be restless in the comparatively slow motion world of stocks. This game is not for those looking for an easy, safe investment or for those used to allowing other people to make their investment decisions for them. Commodity speculators, however, make up only a portion of the traders in any market. Not all the traders in commodities have the same profit goals. Much of the volume on any commodity ex-

change represents hedging by industry players. In fact, one study showed that a market serving speculators only simply could not survive. While the speculator is after profits earned on his risk capital, the hedger uses the market to manage and specialize, if not to totally eliminate, his risk. The truly large positions held by grain companies (excused from position limits, as are all hedgers) are not in competition with the speculator for risk profits. This is not true, say, of the Dreyus Fund in stocks. The speculator competes with other speculators, moving among many positions, rather than investing. He profits from his own skills rather than from the earnings of an anonymous conglomerate. One can make money in stocks, to be sure. The action in commodities, however, promises personal and financial returns of an almost unlimited scope for those capable and willing to take the chance.

Chapter 5 ————————————————————

FUTURES TRADING: A BRIEF HISTORY

TRADING THROUGH THE AGES

Commodity trading dates back to the dawn of humanity. The simple barter or exchange of foodstuffs, tools, hides, and fuels stands behind the evolution of today's complex economies. We are still in the business of creating, trading, and consuming material goods. The types of products and the means of exchange have taken on forms our ancient ancestors would hardly recognize, but the fundamentals of need and satisfaction remain the same. There are producers and there are consumers, and society exists in large part to facilitate and organize the transactions of these parties. Commodity futures trading enables the system to control one of its basic problems, that of giving a price to goods when exchange involves long periods of time and great geographical distances.

The first economies, circa 600,000 B.C., were evidently based on bartering. One useful commodity, like a hand axe or flint stone, was traded for another, the equality of their value being a matter of individual traders' judgments. The flaws of the system were fatal, for value became hostage to subjective opinion, shrewd dealers, and variable quality. A standardized mode of exchange—money—arose to replace the old system. (See Figure 5–1.) This made trade physically easier, valuing of goods more uniform, and the spread of trade over regional and global distances a reality. (Of course, the order and degree of this evolution differed from region to region and suffered frequent regression.)

As economic relations became more intricate and the quantity of goods traded became larger and larger, even cash transactions proved of limited usefulness. Merchants, carrying bags of gold to market, were notoriously vulnerable to highway robbery. Samples replaced actual goods as the cost and impracticality of carrying bulky orders from market town to market town grew. In a variety of forms in many nations, arrangements for the future delivery of goods and for future cash payment appeared more and more common. Evidence points to futures agreements in the wheat markets of Abyssinia as early as 1,000 B.C. Wherever and whenever they arise, futures markets bloom when economic conditions and practical realities require sophisticated mechanisms for pricing and distribution.

Scholars generally trace the origins of modern futures trading to the merchant trade fairs of early Renaissance Europe in the eleventh and twelfth centuries. Traders wandered from town to town hawking their wares until volume and the rise of early urban centers prompted the organization of regular trade fairs at key commercial crossroads. Here dealers in cash commodities would meet with interested buyers and sell goods "to be delivered when the next caravan arrives from the east." The use of "forward contracts," a forerunner of today's futures contract, seems to have begun in earnest at the fairs sponsored by the Counts of Champagne in the twelfth century. Gold was left on deposit with houses in major centers of commerce, payable on presentation of credit letters. Thus arose the banking fam-

ilies of the Italian merchant cities, like the Medicis.

Though at first a contract limited to specific buyers and sellers, these "lettres de faire" soon became negotiable documents with characteristics of a bill of exchange and a warehouse receipt. To govern transactions the merchants instituted rules of trade and merchants' courts at the fairs, prefiguring our modern exchanges and regulatory agencies. Soon markets appeared in many cities and a permanent, year-round trading center was established in England. The Royal Exchange of London opened in 1570, its action divided between spot and forward contracts and its players including many speculative dealers. A boom and bust in

FIGURE 5-1

Before Money Was Something You Printed

By Patricia Fanning

Washington

OPEC and others who would like to see the almighty dollar replaced with some other currency for international transactions could get some ideas at the Smithsonian Institution's National Museum of History and Technology these days. They

The Gallery

could forget about their "baskets of currencies" and special drawing rights for a moment and consider clam shells, dogs' teeth, and birds' feathers as alternatives. Those are among the unusual monies of the past now in a special exhibit of currencies presented to the museum by Chase Manhattan Bank.

The most imposing "coin" in the collection is a 90-pound, discus-shaped stone, an example of "fai" money once used in the Yap Islands in the Pacific. The stone has a hole in the middle so that a local plutocrat could lug it about on a long pole. "For sheer bulk," the stone money is "unequaled in the world," says Elvira Clain-Stefanelli, the museum's curator of numismatics and organizer of the exhibit. A smaller, 10-pound version on exhibit had the value of a small pig or 500 coconuts.

Feathers have been floated as the currencies of several societies. Two samples in the exhibit were used mainly for buying

canoes and wives. Natives of New Guinea used tan and reddish-brown feathers from the bird of paradise. Santa Cruz Islanders dealt in "honeybird" feathers plucked from the red breast and head of the tiny "manga" bird. In California, the Darok Indians used woodpecker scalps.

As late as 1900, abalone shells were used in trade by Indians along the West Coast of the U.S. Preferring mixed currencies, the Shasta Indians wrapped their shells with strips of snake skins and strung them on deer sinews. A string of 20 shells bought a beaver pelt.

Among the East Coast Indians, beads made of shells were the coin of the realm. Such wampum "bought everything," says Mrs. Clain-Stefanelli, the curator. Like U.S. foreign aid, it was also used for making peace and sealing alliances. In the 1700s, American settlers even built a factory in New Jersey to make wampum.

In Oceania, porpoise teeth were the island's pennies. About 80 to 100 could be obtained from each porpoise, and they traded at about 1/40th the value of dogs' teeth, which were especially scarce and valuable. Suppliers in San Cristobal raised dogs solely for their high-priced choppers, which were "extracted with great cruelty," the exhibit catalog notes. Big spenders, usually chiefs, dealt in teeth from the sperm whales (one tooth bought a large canoe).

Cocoa beans, still a valued commodity today, sweetened the pot for the Aztecs of

pre-Columbian Mexico, and bricks of tea were legal tender up to the 20th Century in Tibet, Mongolia and southern Siberia. The bricks in turn could easily be broken into small change.

Grain was the ticket in ancient Egypt, though the crop itself was a bit bulky for transacting business. The exhibit has a special ring that was used to represent a certain amount of grain. Hair from elephant tails was braided into currency that was valuable in West Africa. Two or three slaves went for 50 hairs. Rabbit tails were used as money in Olney, Texas, during the Depression. The exhibit has a couple of furry, gray specimens from the great auction of May 13, 1933, when 1,726 tails were bequeathed by the local Chamber of Commerce. They were exchanged for gift certificates.

A druggist in Pismo Beach, Calif., used clam shells to shore up his currency shortage, which was a nationwide problem after President Franklin D. Roosevelt closed the banks in March 1933. A shell could be redeemed at Leiter's Pharmacy for either 50 cents or $1 (the amount was written inside). Money was indeed dear back then, for whenever the large white shells changed hands, the druggist's customers signed their names inside.

Ms. Fanning is a member of the Journal's Washington bureau.

Source: *The Wall Street Journal.*

tulip bulbs sent Holland reeling early in the seventeenth century. A significant futures trading market evolved in Japanese "rice tickets" from 1600–1900, containing most of the provisions of today's futures game, though actual delivery was forbidden. The Dojima rice market pioneered such rules as: contract term duration limits, standardized contracts and grades, independent clearing houses, and certification of trader credit. However, the failure to firmly tie futures prices to actuals caused repeated problems and a closure from 1869–1871, after which it reopened with futures and cash related much as they were in the American markets. Fascinating in itself, the Japanese system had little direct impact on the origin of the American futures business which has its roots in the unique problems and potentials faced by American agriculture in the middle of the nineteenth century.

CHICAGO

The real history of modern futures trading starts in Chicago, where the largest exchanges still flourish today. Early in the nineteenth century the opening of the frontier beyond the Mississippi brought thousands of settlers to till the fertile plains. Farms and ranches prospered and soon a steady stream of corn and wheat was seeking markets to the east. Corn was the leader in the early stages of the Chicago grain trade as the shipment records of corn from 1847–1851 show:

1847	67,315	bushels
1848	550,460	"
1849	644,848	"
1850	1,262,013	"
1851	3,221,317	"

Wheat stockpiles during this period were less burdensome. The amount of wheat shipped from Chicago actually declined from the 1848–1849 levels and did not rise again until 1854. Corn shipments in the period 1850–1856 exceeded those of wheat. Because of these circumstances, historian Harold S. Irwin concluded that Chicago "time" and "to arrive" contracts were pioneered in corn and spread quickly in the 1850s and 1860s to traffic in other grains. (For a complete account, see Irwin's work cited in the Appendix.)

Chicago's strategic location in the evolving pattern of agricultural marketing made it the natural headquarters for the trade. The grains, hides, and meat of the western territories were funneled through Chicago for transhipment east and south or held and processed by the city's rapidly growing industrial sector. An unmatched transportation network was carved out of roads, rivers, canals, lakes, and later was the major factor in the founding of the railroads. Rail service was inaugurated in 1850 but played little part in the early history of the grain trade and futures markets. It was the massive stockpiling of ever larger inventories on the banks of frozen waterways that created the demand for "time" or "forward" commodity contracts.

Farmers, corn crib operators, merchants, millers, and exporters felt the need to better organize this large, new enterprise which by the 1840s had already made Chicago a preëminent international grain center. The Board of Trade of the City of Chicago was founded in 1848 with a membership of eighty-two. The state of Illinois authorized it to train personnel in the inspection and measurement of grain, initiating the quality control essential to mass marketing and futures contracts. Advances in weight measurement, handling, and the standardization of grades set the stage for negotiable warehouse receipts, forward contracts, and eventually futures themselves.

First, however, came the "to arrive" contracts. Farmers would come to Chicago ahead of their product and congregate at stores, street corners, and saloons and make their deals with the merchants. Price fluctuations, even during the short periods covered by these time contracts, could be costly. By the time the wagons or barges had arrived changes in the spot cash price could cause many to default on their contracts as they sought a better deal. "Margin" was one result, being a good faith promise to execute the trade as agreed. But soon speculators saw the opportunity to aid farmers and merchants desiring to quit their contracts and to make a profit along the way. Time contracts would change hands twenty or thirty times until the sheer volume of such transactions made the establishment of permanent futures exchanges the only sane solution.

The Chicago Board of Trade, which had at first discouraged the traffic in negotiable contracts, reversed its early opposition and took steps to regulate the trade. On October 13, 1865 the General Rules of the Board of Trade were adopted, including the margin requirement. Contracts and delivery arrangements were made standard and guidelines for grading, government inspection, open and accessible pricing, financial responsibility, and volume liquidity were set down. Chaos shifted its headquarters from the streets to the pits, where some degree of restraint could be imposed and a limit placed on the more flagrant abuses. Many date the

beginning of modern futures trading from this time, though the organization of trade in commodities other than corn and wheat lagged behind at other exchanges. The rules of the New York Cotton Exchange were promulgated in 1872, formalizing the trade between southern producers, New York exporters, and English importers who had featured time contracts since 1851. Buyers and sellers discovered the hedging value of futures, which spread rapidly after 1870.

Periodic scandals rocked the markets afterwards as colorful speculators made bold moves in the robber-baron spirit of the age. The market corners and price manipulations of those legendary years gave futures trading an unsavory reputation it took a century to shake off. Two presidents of the Chicago Board were suspended for insufficient funds. Speculation increasingly became a war of wits between a few famous traders—market superstars whose spectacular adventures were often more exciting than they were profitable. It was a time when the rugged American individualist moved from the frontier into the market place, bringing with him the same code of fierce independence and shrewd opportunism that had already built the nation's factories and railroads. The morals and genius of these futures pioneers were no better or worse than could be found elsewhere in a society rushing toward unprecedented wealth. (See Figure 5–2.)

The wild days of trading's first half-century passed away under pressure from ever stronger exchanges, angry farmers, and a suspicious federal government. Several times attempts were made to outlaw futures altogether. Federal intervention became serious as commercial farming burgeoned in the twentieth century. Stan-

FIGURE 5-2
20
THE SOUTHWESTERN MILLER

June 29, 1971

—HERMAN STEEN—
Colorful Participants in Futures Speculation Range From "Bet-a-Million" Gates to Patton, Cutten and Livermore — Few Retain Wealth

FAMOUS GRAIN SPECULATORS

THE Board of Trade of the City of Chicago—the rarely used official name of the exchange—was chartered in 1848. Not many persons today are aware that the objective of its founders was to provide a meeting place for buyers and sellers of such diverse commodities as hides, wool, brick, lumber, fish, salt and beef, in addition to corn, oats and wheat.

After quite a controversy, "time contracts" not exceeding 30 days were authorized in 1850 in the case of the three grains. Deals of this kind were dissimilar to the impersonal futures of later years, as they related only to specific lots of commodities. The volume of such trading expanded considerably, especially in the early 1860's, and in October, 1865, rules governing the purchase and sale of grain futures were adopted. Futures trading apparently began at about that time, although quotations were not published regularly until 1870 or 1871, which has caused some writers to state that the futures business began at the later time. This is incorrect, as an examination of contemporary publications quickly reveals; for instance, a history of the Board of Trade itself refers to 1868 as the "year of corners" in grain trading.

FIRST TRADER ALSO IN ELEVATORS

In the course of the past century, trading in grain futures in Chicago has been marked by many dramatic events, a few of which will be summarized here. The earliest of these were the operations of Ira Y. Munn, who may have been the first to undertake large-scale trading. He was the largest grain speculator of the late 1860's and early 1870's, when he also owned or controlled most of the elevators in Chicago as well as a newspaper and several banks. He was so powerful that he was able to compel the railroads bringing grain to Chicago to deliver it to his houses regardless of who might be the consignee. It was later established that he employed a systematic plan of short weights and false grades at his elevators.

The Board of Trade attempted in vain to correct these evils, which ended only after a new Illinois law provided for state warehouse inspection. Munn fought the law in the courts, went bankrupt masterminding a corn market corner that failed, was expelled by the Board of Trade of which he had been president not many years earlier, and he received a knockout blow when the Supreme Court of the United States sustained the Illinois law in a notable decision in 1876.

CORNER TRY BY CINCINNATI BANKER

Beginning in or about 1880, a number of wealthy persons started to trade heavily in grain futures, some as individuals and others in concert. A high point in these activities was reached in 1887, when a Cincinnati banker undertook to corner wheat. The scheme failed, and so did the banker, his bank and a large broker. The banker received a penitentiary sentence for illegal use of the funds of his depositors.

"OLD HUTCH" A CONSISTENT BEAR

One of the by-products of these ventures was the career of Benjamin P. Hutchinson, widely known as "Old Hutch." He observed that most large-scale traders, especially those not thoroughly versed in the business, were usually market bulls, and it was the practice of Old Hutch to watch quietly until their operations moved the market level above what he thought conditions justified and then he would sell short, often in millions of bus. He had been a department store manager, and he often said that the grain pit was the only place where a person could sell goods without limit and without advertising. Old Hutch was a consistent bear, but tradition has it that in 1888 he crossed up his followers by bulling the wheat market and collecting a huge gain in the process. His trading covered many years, and although on various occasions he made large profits he had little left when he retired.

BREAK ICE FOR LAKE DELIVERY

Joseph Leiter, the idle and bored son of the wealthy partner of the first Marshall Field, staged what is perhaps the most spectacular event in Chicago market history through his market operations in 1897-98. He knew little or nothing about grain, but he acquired a huge line of wheat, much of it below 70c per bu, and was on the way to obtaining a large profit as prices marched toward a dollar. Armour Grain Co. broke the incipient corner by dynamiting the ice out of the Soo in December and bringing great shipments from Duluth to Chicago when the lakes were not supposed to be navigable. Young Leiter's paper profit at one stage was above $1,000,000, but when his father settled up with Armour the loss proved to be about two and a half times that amount.

In spite of Armour's vast winnings at the expense of Leiter, the company was liquidated in the middle 1920's to escape being declared insolvent, and George E. Marcy, who was its head for many years when it often engaged in extensive speculations, retired from the pit in almost the same condition.

"BET-A-MILLION" GATES FAILURE

The barbed wire king, John W. Gates, called "Bet-a-Million" Gates because he was said to have once made such a wager, impressed his Wall Street associates with his supposed knowledge of grain trading. Under his leadership they undertook to corner the wheat market in 1905. It is reported that they lost around $2,000,000 to shorts headed by Old Hutch.

PATTEN IN TWO BULL EXPLOITS

A colorful figure was James A. Patten, one of very few big traders whose fortune was intact when he quit. He is perhaps best known for his many bull market exploits, especially in 1909 and 1923, the first aided by a telegraph strike that largely prevented the shorts from ordering corn in from country points to deliver on contract. Although Patten was credited at the time with near-omnipotence in matters having to do with grain, he depended heavily upon his brother George, and after George's death James traded only in small amounts. Several million dollars of Patten money greatly enhanced the facilities of Northwestern University.

HUGE VOLUME OF TRADE BY CUTTEN

Canadian-born Arthur W. Cutten was a famous grain speculator through most of the first third of this century. A chronic bull, he is believed never to have made a short sale, and his trading was so extensive that on occasion he is thought to have been long as much as 60,000,000 bus. His net worth exceeded $200,000,000 in the late 1920's, but he is said to have dropped $50,000,000 in the 1929 stock market crash. There are a legion of stories about Cutten and his generosity to friends; once he put his dentist into the market without the latter's knowledge until he received a check for $400,000. Cutten was suspended from trading in the 1930's for a time by the Grain Futures Administration for exceeding the daily trading limits. His great riches were almost gone when he died.

Almost contemporary with Cutten was Jesse Livermore, a big speculator in stocks who also took giant plunges in grains. His biographer stated that he lost $3,000,000 in 1925 in stocks, made $4,000,000 in the same area in 1927 and then lost $9,000,000 in a Florida land deal. He was accused of having set off the stock market panic in 1929, but that charge is of doubtful validity. A more or less chronic bear in grain, he tangled several times with Cutten, with the honors less than even. He went through bankruptcy several times and was bankrupt when he died by his own hand.

Thomas Howell was one of the last of the big pit operators. Like Livermore, he was usually a bear, believing that bulls nearly always overstay the market. It was common practice with him to move in with short trades in huge volumes when he felt sure that the market was unduly high. He was credited with very large gains at times, but a predominant part melted away in bank stock losses.

Those named here are among the all-time most famous grain speculators. A few others may rank with them, but not many. There have been, of course, hundreds and possibly thousands of other important pit figures over the years, along with an infinite number of other participants in the speculative grain market—all the way from one-shot performers to those who traded more or less regularly for years. How many have won and how many have lost is something that nobody knows, but it seems significant that a great majority of the mammoth traders who reaped fortunes finally "gave it back" before they were through.

dards for quality and trading needed legal sanctions. The Grain Standards Act was passed in 1916. Grain speculation caused by the widespread depression following World War I led to the Futures Trading Act of 1921, declared unconstitutional almost immediately. A better version, the Grain Futures Act, became law in 1922. It empowered the government to deal with the industry through the exchanges rather than through the myriad of traders. The regulatory powers it invested in the U.S. Department of Agriculture, however, proved inadequate.

The Commodity Exchange Act of 1936 strengthened the regulator's hand and spelled out the laws that governed trade until 1975. Regulatory coverage was extended to cotton and other commodities as well as to grains. Stronger authority was granted to combat abuses of the market by traders and brokerage firms. Significant amendments in 1968 established minimum financial standards for all futures commission merchants (FCM), which includes any and all individuals or groups buying or selling contracts for commission. When the dollar value of traded commodities rose to $500 billion in 1973 and new rumors of scandal spread through the industry, it was clear that a regulatory house cleaning was in order. The result was the Commodity Futures Trading Commission Act of 1974 which created the Commodity Futures Trading Commission as market watch dog, replacing the Agriculture Department's old Commodity Exchange Authority.

THE NEW AGE

Since the late 1960s commodity futures trading has entered a revolutionary new age. The changes that shook the industry in the 1970s promise to continue their exciting pace into the 1980s and beyond. Historians will look back at these years and find a turning point in the history of futures, one that signalled profound realignments in the economic life of the nation and of the world. Just as futures trading went into its second century, far-reaching transformations made the recent past seem light years away. Between 1900 and 1965 the nature of the markets held steady, dominated by grains and participated in by a small group of traders and speculators. Today millions are playing the game and there seems no end to the variety of players or of commodities in the new futures era.

The upturn in commodity trading in the mid 1960s owed much to the introduction of successful new contracts, especially those in live hogs, cattle, and frozen pork bellies. The rivalry between the large Chicago exchanges spurred these experiments, helped along by advances in storage and transportation technology. Yet, new contracts had been tried before and withered on the floor. Through trial and error the exchanges had come up with some exceptionally well written and tradeable contracts, but their success has to be seen in the context of other economic forces that were working to push futures into the forefront. Inflation, global economic interdependence, the rising price of oil, changes at the stock exchanges, and increased public sophistication contributed to the futures boom. In a decade of double digit inflation and extreme price volatility, a totally new arena of futures trading opened with the smash debut of interest rate and other financial futures. Trade in gold and silver was begun and in a few short years the historically attractive precious metals were starring on the network news and making headlines around the world. Trading volume set brand new records every single year in the 1970s. Volume in 1979, for instance, was about *eight times that of 1969*. (See Figure 5–3.)

Into these new conditions came a new generation of investors. In the years following World War II stocks and securities had become the favored financial tool as the memory of the 1929 crash and subsequent depression faded into the textbooks. Consumption and capital appreciation headed steadily upwards and the public

became more familiar with the trading techniques of the market. From stocks investors found their way into the techniques of short selling, hedging, arbitrage, convertible bonds, warrants, new issues, and others. An expertise in financial affairs developed, encompassing an ever wider spectrum of the public. This new sophistication, limited though it was, paved the way for the "discovery" of commodity futures.

Meanwhile, reforms (mainly unwanted) at the nation's stock brokerages were assisting the bright career of futures.

FIGURE 5–3

'80s Outlook
Further Gains Seen In Futures Trading

By AL CONLAN
Journal of Commerce Staff

The 1970s were marked by an uninterrupted and dramatic increase in the volume of trading on the nation's futures exchanges and all indications that the decade getting under way' will witness continued impressive growth.

Trading in 1979 approximated 76 million contracts — one side only — an all-time high and the 11th successive year that a record had been established.

During this span volume rose from 9.3 million contracts, an increase of more than 800 percent, and the rate of climb accelerated over recent years with a gain of more than 15 million contracts in 1978 and of over 17 million in 1979.

Established Markets Play Leading Role

Long established markets, such as the soybean complex (soybeans, oil and meal), corn, wheat, live cattle and silver continued to play a leading role.

However, relative newcomers accounted for a significant and increasing volume. These included such items as Ginnie Maes and Treasury bonds on the Chicago Board of Trade, and gold on the Commodity Exchange and International Monetary Market.

The performance of gold futures has been extraordinary, reflecting worldwide trading interest generated by inflation.

Many new markets made their appearance in the '70s. On the Chicago Board of Trade markets initiated during this period included gold, Ginnie Maes, Treasury bonds, commercial paper, and Treasury notes.

On the Chicago Mercantile Exchange trading in feeder cattle and stud lumber had its start. Also, the CME opened the International Monetary Market in May 1972 and that division with trading in gold, Treasury bills and notes; silver coins, and foreign exchanges has recorded rapid growth since its inception with 7.7 million trades in 1979, almost 10 percent of total U.S. trading in futures. The Chicago Board of Trade easily retained

(Continued from Page 1)
its position as the world's largest futures exchange with approximately 33.9 contracts, 23.7 percent above its previous trading peak reached in 1978, and the Chicago Mercantile Exchange — excluding the IMM — posted a record 12.2 million trades, up about 22 percent from its previous peak.

CBT Director C.C. Odom recently attributed the growth in trading on that exchange to a number of factors, including political and economic uncertainties and, of course, inflation which, he noted, makes the futures markets an even more valuable vehicle for users and producers to hedge against price risk.

He also observed that interest rate futures have proven to be ideal hedging vehicles for financial and money market users.

"Growing awareness of commodities as an investment also contributed to the record volume," Mr. Odom said.

Most Active Contract

The most active contract in 1979 was soybeans with 9.1 million trades with corn holding the second spot with 8.7 million trades. Live cattle accounted for 7.2 million transactions. Gold on the

Commodity Exchange and the IMM had a combined total of 10.1 million and silver on the ComEx and CBT 6.8 million trades.

New markets have not been uniformly successful with occasional casualties during the decade but these were greatly outnumbered by those which have taken hold.

A large number of new contracts are in various stages of planning and development. These include such articles as energy futures (fuel oil, gasoline); sunflower; Eurodollar time deposits; more financial instruments, and a contract based on Standard and Poor's index of 500 U.S. stocks.

Long-Range Outlook

Enhancing the longer range trading outlook are the continuing inflation; the projected further expansion in number of markets, and the growing acceptance by various segments of industry and agriculture that futures offer hedging facilities not available elsewhere.

Knowledge of the role of futures markets has been growing but much still remains to be accomplished in this area with industry seminars, university courses, etc., making a significant contribution.

Source: *New York Journal of Commerce.*

When I began trading in 1967 brokers had set aside the smallest, dimly-lit corners of their offices for the "low class" business of commodity trading. Two or three of a firm's thirty or so brokers might handle futures at that time and they were generally ostracized as odd balls playing a hopeless, losing game. Commodities remained a minor item for brokers until the Russian wheat deal of 1972, which dramatically displayed the profit potential and economic validity of futures trading to the general financial community. Brokers might still have ignored the facts and the interest of their aroused clients had not their hand been forced by an attack from another source.

On May 1, 1975 the Securities and Exchange Commission shocked the brokers by deregulating commission rates heretofore fixed throughout the industry. The securities business was thrown into a turmoil. Visions of vulgar discount houses and cut-rate operators disturbed the sleep of those who had controlled business-as-usual. To survive, the brokers (whose earnings depend on commission income) would have to learn to sell other things if rates for stock sales should fall sharply or competition turn too keen. The once forlorn commodity department suddenly commanded attention, for its revenue-generating possibilities were an untapped resource. Whereas an active stock account of $10,000 might generate $1,000 or $2,000 in commissions yearly, a $10,000 commodity account that stays afloat or profits in active trading will return 100 percent, or $10,000, to the brokerage in the course of a year. The attraction was irresistible, and today most of Wall Street's old, prestigious firms are players in the once frowned upon futures markets. Brokerage house personnel have flocked

to seminars, studied trading systems, read crop reports, and pondered pig slaughters in order to cash in on the bonanza. Now clients are encouraged to put some of their capital into futures, and some firms themselves publish market newsletters and organize commodity trading pools and funds. Today almost any brokerage will handle your commodity account—and happily.

In an example of how events may bump into each other in the course of history's random walk, this broker interest coincided with a surge of curiosity on the part of investors. Whether through education, experience, or just plain greed, they learned what futures had to offer. Many others came in search of relief from the economic uncertainty that replaced the optimism of the postwar years. Inflation sent investors searching for ways to store or increase wealth despite an atmosphere hostile to capital survival. A stock portfolio or other formerly "safe" investment returning 12 percent annually turned into a net loser when inflation ran to 13 percent and 14 percent. The profits of 100 percent, 200 percent, or 2,000 percent in futures look, by contrast, like heaven on earth when seen in the context of the last decade's events. (See Figure 5–4.)

Many investors had first grown accustomed to the world of commodity speculation when they dealth in rare stamps, antiques, works of art, and other scarcity items popular as hedges against inflation. The principles took hold and the switch from Picassos and Chippendales to pork bellies and T-Bonds proved less difficult than most had imagined. The argument that futures were unduly risky lost its force as risk became standard even in the most conventional of investments. Speculators, often inspired by the glowing pre-

FIGURE 5–4

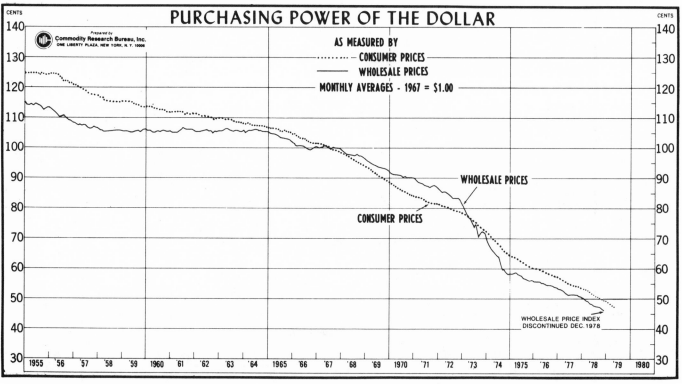

Source: Commodity Research Bureau, Inc.

dictions of brokers eager for commissions, found commodity trading less mysterious than once believed, though the promised grand profits were hard to come by. Enthusiasm and interest were not always matched by knowledge and skill, leaving many newcomers with bitter lessons after their first few trades. This was to be expected in any such circumstance where players are learning a game, and the steady increase in volume indicates that the lessons may be paying off.

Inflation also afflicted the large financial institutions of the nation and gave pain to all whose business costs were directly tied to interest rates and money supplies. The huge quantities of dollars entering the economy as a result of oil price rises and general inflation played havoc with the fiscal operations of the na-

tion. Erratic quantum leaps in interest rates could be devastating to banks, to corporations floating bonds, and to borrowers and lenders of all kinds. (See Figure 5–5.) Commodity futures trading had originated as a way to manage price volatility and control risk and the principle could work for financial commodities in much the way it worked for grains and meats. Necessity is the mother of invention, and as the need for tools to hedge against interest rate and monetary fluctuation increased, the imagination of the exchanges rose to the occasion.

Currency futures took hold in 1972 and have become integral to national and world monetary dealings. Interest rate futures began trading in 1975 when the Chicago Board of Trade introduced its first contracts in Government National Mort-

FIGURE 5-5

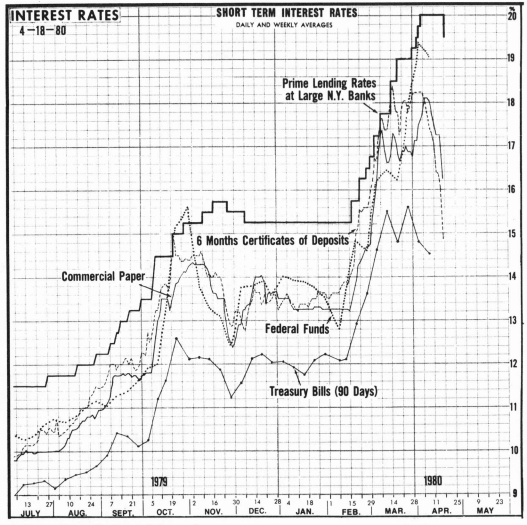

Source: Commodity Research Bureau, Inc.

gage Association (GNMA or Ginnie Mae) futures. The Chicago Mercantile Exchange soon offered Treasury bill futures, which were instant successes. Since then many new financial contracts have appeared wherever the need and profit potential were strong. The usefulness and popularity of interest rate futures brought futures trading to an entire sector of the economic populace that had never considered commodity trading before. Banks, corporations, pension funds, insurance companies, and savings and loan institutions put hundreds of millions of dollars into futures, making them quickly a standard component in the normal operation of their business affairs. These contracts did not compete for trader interest in already established commodities, but rather brought trading to a different dimension of the economic community and trading volume to unheard of levels. (See Figure 5-6.)

New arrivals in the business of futures

FIGURE 5-6

GROWTH OF TREASURY SECURITIES TRADING EXPLOSIVE, OFFICIAL SAYS

WASHINGTON--FEB 12--CNS--A TREASURY DEPARTMENT OFFICIAL TOLD A HOUSE AGRICULTURAL OVERSIGHT SUBCOMMITTEE TODAY THAT SINCE TRADING BEGAN IN TREASURY SECURITY FUTURES IN JANUARY 1976, THE GROWTH RATE OF THOSE CONTRACTS HAS EXPLODED.

ROBERT CARSWELL, DEPUTY SECRETARY OF THE TREASURY, SAID THE ANNUAL TRADING VOLUME IN TREASURY BILL FUTURES CONTRACTS ALONE WAS APPROXIMATELY 2 TRILLION DLRS IN 1979, COMPARED WITH 769 BILLION DLRS IN 1978 AND 322 BILLION DLRS IN 1977.

"CURRENTLY, THE DOLLAR AMOUNT OF TRADING IN THE TREASURY BILL FUTURES MARKET ACTUALLY EXCEEDS THE TOTAL VOLUME OF DEALER TRADING IN THE CASH MARKET FOR TREASURY BILLS," CARSWELL SAID. "IN VIEW OF THE PIVOTAL ROLE OF THE TREASURY BILL MARKET AS A BENCHMARK FOR OTHER MONEY MARKET RATES, THIS GROWTH HAS MAJOR IMPLICATIONS FOR THE EFFICIENT FINANCING OF OUR ECONOMY."

Source: Commodity News Service.

saw a system of economic relationships emerging in the 1960s and 1970s that was unlike any situation former traders had faced. International events had influenced commodity prices as early as the Crimean War (1853–1856), but the interdependency of nations in the world's economy has increased exponentially since World War II. The story of this basic change in global history has been told in commodities—most pointedly in oil. The OPEC oil embargo and subsequent price hikes illustrated how modern nations depended on each other for vital necessities. The message in oil pertains to wheat, corn, cocoa, coffee, gold, currencies—to every commodity. Day by day the world becomes, economically, a global village. The one-nation economies of the past have passed into history and the days when a nation could plan its resources without considering events in far off parts of the planet are gone forever. The commodity trader is caught up in the significance and excitement of this world-historical change, and he plays a game of international scope. The speculator must keep tabs on politics in Africa, religions in the Middle East, troop movements in the Soviet Union, and freezes in Brazil. Price, the ultimate decision-maker in futures, is subject to incalculable influences and unpredictable jolts from anywhere at anytime. Modern futures trading has developed into a key index to global life and every sign indicates it will hold and strengthen this dominant position in the decades ahead.

Chapter 6

EXCHANGES AND TRADERS

THE EXCHANGE

The purpose of the exchange is to provide an organized facility for conducting the business of commodities. The exchange will, depending on its scope and purpose, perform many of the vital functions of commodity commerce—from grading and handling through contract development to cash sales and futures trading. A few exchanges (like the Minneapolis Grain Exchange) concentrate on nonfutures activities related to the handling and sale of actual goods. The primary activity of the major exchanges is futures trading. It was the need to regulate this complex business that first gave rise to the exchanges and which is the source of their continuing importance today (hence the very uneasy relationship between the exchanges and the Commodities Futures Trading Commission).

The exchange, through its governance system, formulates and supervises trading in the contracts offered on its floors. It must oversee the behavior of members, originate profitable and useful contracts, monitor trading activity, set trading hours and limits, arbitrate disputes among members, disseminate market information quickly and accurately without favoritism, provide the means for liquidation or settlement, and be the trader's negotiator with the regulators in Washington. Obviously, the pressures on the exchange can be overwhelming, especially in light of the fact that its decisions may make or break the fortunes of traders when the market goes haywire. Market suspensions and alterations in trading rules have caused uproars in the past as speculators saw golden opportunities or precision strategies foiled by closures or limits. Some have taken their gripes to court and in certain cases have raised the question of a conflict of interest on the part of the exchange's interest in the way the market moves. These have been chronic problems and are sure to be the subject of future debates and developments as the exchanges meet the challenges of modern trade.

In its technical legal form, the exchange is a private, nonprofit, and voluntary association of individuals who gather for the purpose of commodity transactions. Only members of the exchange may trade in its contracts. Thus, investors and speculators may work through member brokers or with firms with ties to exchange members. Membership in most exchanges is limited in number and seats are sold on an availability basis. Large brokerage firms will underwrite membership for its employees to make its trades, and such firms may have many members on the major exchanges. The number of memberships will change over the years with the popularity and health of the exchange, as will the price a seat can command. (See Figure 6–1.) Members include representatives from every corner of the economy concerned: producers, exporters, merchants, warehousemen, brokers, farmers, shippers, bankers, and professional traders. Members may be on the floor and trade in the pits. They also are entitled to reduced commission rates, often about one-half of nonmember rates. Each exchange has its own requirements for membership which may take into consideration the applicant's character, financial background, and company affiliation. Some exchanges have experimented with the rental or leasing of seats and with the sale of "floor permits" for trading in specified commodities. Large exchanges may have two or three divisions where different types of commodities are traded and one

may be a member of a single division or of all simultaneously, depending on the exchange's membership conditions and the amount the trader is willing to pay.

The exchanges establish the rules for trade. They do not set prices, which are determined solely by the movement of the market itself. The exchange trades no contracts for its own corporate benefit. It looks to dues, fees, investments, real estate, rentals, and the sales of information for its income. Of course, the profits of the exchange's individual members are linked to the prosperity of the exchange as a whole. The success of the exchange's operations is translatable into higher incomes for its traders, executives, and employees. The exchange does not exist merely to serve the common economic good. Volume means profit for the members and competition for that business is keen. The boom in commodity trading has meant a sharpening of the contest between the various exchanges, who now scramble to provide high technology services and alluring new contracts.

Traders and investors will go where the profitable contracts are and where they

FIGURE 6–1
Highest price paid for exchange memberships 1968 and 1978

EXCHANGE	1968	1978
Chicago Bd. of Trade	$ 19,800	$215,000
Chicago Merc. Exchange	38,000	255,000
MidAmerica Exchange	2,100	21,400
Commodity Exchange, Inc.	15,000	95,000
KC Board of Trade	12,000	60,000
Minneapolis Grain Exch.	700	14,000
NY Cocoa Exchange	23,500	20,000
NY Coffee & Sugar Exch.	12,000	32,000
NY Cotton Exchange	9,500	30,000
* NY Mercantile Exchange	40,000	47,000

(1968 figure also included right to apply for membership in now-defunct National Stock Exchange.)

Source: Futures Industry Association.

can most easily be traded. Simply explained, the exchange is like a retail store putting new items on the shelf to see what people will buy. It will introduce new products that can bring in new dollars and new customers, not products that compete with established items for money already spent there. It will duplicate products sold by competitors in hopes of draining off some of their revenues, or it will hope to create a similar demand among a different group of customers. A successful commodity will be duplicated by other exchanges, until conditions settle and a clear winner emerges. This has happened in the past with grains, meats, and interest rate futures and certainly will happen with proposed new contracts like stock indexes and energy futures. The revolutionary impact of financial futures came precisely from the recruitment of a large sector of the financial public that had never before traded in futures. T-Bills and Ginnie Maes didn't much attract the old trader whose long success had been in bellies and beans. New traders, with new dollars for the markets, entered the scene and were competed for fiercely by the established exchanges, while new exchanges concentrating in financial instruments were readied for action.

(As a side note, it may be observed that the obstacles thrown in the path of stock index futures and expanded interest rate futures by the SEC and others could be interpreted as a power play by the stock traders and exchanges. Futures hedging of portfolio holdings could decrease volume on the stock exchanges, endangering their profitability and liquidity. In this light it is significant that the first large scale effort to open a new exchange dealing primarily in financials was set up as a subsidiary of the New York Stock Exchange.)

Exchanges have come and gone with the fortunes of their contracts. A core group of ten or eleven exchanges has been around for many years, in and through which mergers and fall-offs have occurred. The fluidity of contracts offered, and to a lesser degree of the exchanges themselves, will make any listing and description obsolete almost as it is written. The persistence, however, of the major exchanges and of the basic commodities they rely upon justifies a quick accounting.

THE CHICAGO BOARD OF TRADE

Founded in 1848, the Chicago Board of Trade is the nation's oldest active commodity futures exchange (the St. Louis Merchants Exchange began in 1836, but no longer trades futures). The Board is the largest agricultural market place in the world, coordinating the sale of billions of dollars of foodstuffs destined for every portion of the globe (See Figure 6–2.) The Board's early preeminence and steady staying power were closely linked to Chicago's dominant place in world grain trading. Thus, it was that for almost a century the history of futures trading and the history of the Board ran hand in hand.

When the Illinois legislature outlawed futures trading in 1867, it was seven members of the Board who found themselves at Cook County Jail. The evolution of hedging at the CBT in the 1870s did much to institutionalize grain futures trading. The Board pioneered in establishing trading procedures, quality control, and accurate weighing. The art of speculation found a home at the Board, where trading volume far outpaced cash grain receipts as early as 1864. The next forty years exhibit a history of great market excitement, as cornering and manipulation flourished.

FIGURE 6–2

CHICAGO BOARD OF TRADE
Monthly Volume of Sales by Contract for 1977 and 1978

1978	Wheat M. Bu.	Corn M. Bu.	Oats M. Bu.	Soybeans M. Bu.	Total All Grains M. Bu.	Soybean Oil Contracts	Soybean Meal Contracts	Iced Broiler Contracts	Plywood Contracts	Silver Contracts	Gold Contracts	GNMA CDR Contracts	GNMA CD Contracts	Treasury Bonds Contracts	Commercial Paper Contracts
January	694,190	1,755,290	31,356	2,978,200	5,459,036	209,509	173,142	3,341	29,066	283,560	2,984	48,423	—	11,486	1,004
February	713,250	1,598,770	37,670	2,223,525	4,573,215	183,384	123,614	5,098	30,771	159,384	5,879	46,723	—	10,241	789
March	1,129,539	3,405,375	59,680	5,057,235	9,651,829	312,735	275,525	8,002	25,071	305,319	3,613	57,065	—	14,179	1,018
April	1,183,810	3,255,390	80,185	4,121,115	8,640,500	266,788	213,593	8,063	24,144	180,273	3,274	57,241	—	19,145	821
May	1,062,815	3,159,135	68,775	3,819,565	8,110,290	258,121	190,169	9,600	21,797	141,659	2,759	60,141	—	25,386	1,148
June	1,121,840	3,147,120	98,530	3,741,875	8,109,365	278,618	224,531	10,619	19,237	134,557	3,921	75,180	—	33,065	979
July	1,133,240	2,495,050	103,785	2,661,615	6,393,690	215,172	191,250	8,427	18,913	143,338	5,604	73,578	—	37,822	909
August	1,311,540	2,662,680	121,290	2,964,765	7,060,275	236,321	207,309	5,088	18,056	206,771	5,834	109,207	—	62,179	1,903
September	1,021,135	1,988,580	119,980	2,561,485	5,691,180	204,271	162,185	3,864	16,346	166,875	5,198	96,119	807	60,314	1,234
October	1,260,055	2,729,205	148,985	4,754,460	8,892,705	285,409	257,331	5,329	24,834	280,918	6,904	110,932	973	87,678	1,958
November	1,271,560	2,723,390	140,975	3,991,825	8,127,750	257,259	260,221	4,009	17,202	342,405	5,236	108,950	1,505	95,246	3,540
December	877,705	1,715,510	67,665	3,510,720	6,171,600	201,697	214,216	3,244	15,046	312,774	5,264	109,602	3,242	98,609	3,464
TOTAL	12,780,679	30,635,495	1,078,876	42,386,385	86,881,435	2,909,284	2,493,086	74,684	261,483	2,657,833	56,470	953,161	6,527	555,350	18,767

1977	Wheat M. Bu.	Corn M. Bu.	Oats M. Bu.	Soybeans M. Bu.	Total All Grains M. Bu.	Soybean Oil Contracts	Soybean Meal Contracts	Iced Broiler Contracts	Plywood Contracts	Silver Contracts	Gold Contracts	GNMA Contracts	Treasury Bonds Contracts	Commercial Paper Contracts
January	576,690	1,746,760	39,290	3,483,480	5,846,480	188,156	172,111	7,209	26,143	206,446	249	23,982	—	—
February	809,650	1,587,375	39,470	2,564,085	5,000,580	144,980	143,082	7,137	28,303	91,127	419	21,745	—	—
March	888,160	1,674,545	41,645	5,061,980	7,666,330	276,391	221,799	6,473	35,929	212,622	321	25,944	—	—
April	693,375	2,093,385	44,885	4,707,420	7,485,065	306,049	272,204	7,190	32,537	154,888	1,762	20,026	—	—
May	597,380	1,803,620	41,785	3,550,120	5,992,905	239,271	194,029	5,226	18,456	136,702	2,359	29,626	—	—
June	846,125	2,437,175	54,200	4,011,990	7,349,490	274,484	231,075	6,219	25,855	158,699	754	32,226	—	—
July	823,740	2,261,105	53,815	2,467,685	5,606,345	193,401	192,068	7,052	21,531	109,748	655	34,642	—	—
August	623,190	1,945,635	55,260	2,311,565	4,935,560	154,282	170,469	4,963	52,121	134,438	911	61,807	3,274	—
September	777,095	2,021,130	44,645	2,377,815	5,220,685	146,212	183,274	4,272	31,976	166,184	540	36,875	7,236	420
October	739,525	2,280,580	34,985	2,733,680	5,788,770	160,122	165,410	3,479	32,840	240,000	1,285	45,363	5,255	969
November	981,600	3,386,590	66,110	3,897,290	8,331,590	240,893	249,153	3,093	29,452	255,098	1,915	43,398	8,957	1,388
December	747,420	1,925,235	33,760	2,813,325	5,519,740	210,805	178,797	2,625	33,627	390,107	2,588	41,787	7,379	776
TOTAL	9,103,950	25,109,135	549,850	39,980,695	74,743,630	2,535,046	2,373,453	64,938	368,770	2,257,059	13,758	422,421	32,101	3,553

CHICAGO BOARD OF TRADE
Annual Volume of Sales by Contract

	Wheat M. Bu.	Corn M. Bu.	Oats M. Bu.	Soybeans M. Bu.	Total All Grains M. Bu.	Soybean Oil Contracts	Soybean Meal Contracts	Iced Broiler Contracts	Plywood Contracts	Silver Contracts	Gold Contracts	GNMA CDR Contracts	GNMA CD Contracts	Treasury Bonds Contracts	Commercial Paper Contracts
1978	12,780,679	30,635,495	1,078,876	42,386,385	86,881,435	2,909,284	2,493,086	74,684	261,483	2,657,833	56,470	953,161	6,527	555,350	18,767
1977	9,103,950	25,109,135	549,850	39,980,695	74,743,630	2,535,046	2,373,453	64,938	368,770	2,257,059	13,758	422,421	—	32,101	3,553
1976	14,869,140	23,046,296	634,425	27,370,894	65,920,755	1,685,312	1,524,312	117,639	233,374	2,011,043	10,940	128,537	—	—	—
1975	11,314,205	24,195,239	772,580	19,566,950	55,848,974	1,489,736	761,056	179,483	285,784	1,952,693	55,304	20,125	—	—	—
1974	11,890,330	23,395,210	997,430	13,656,485	49,939,455	1,620,316	878,182	221,128	339,718	1,505,789	1,143	—	—	—	—
1973	7,837,285	20,374,173	973,766	13,711,529	42,896,753	1,762,747	660,732	331,881	277,121	1,642,272	—	—	—	—	—
1972	4,275,315	9,712,610	208,735	20,218,625	34,415,285	1,110,485	629,697	23,199	216,877	754,045	—	—	—	—	—
1971	2,793,640	10,414,400	226,240	15,619,355	29,053,635	1,537,194	478,327	54,891	218,856	511,391	—	—	—	—	—
1970	2,797,570	10,700,220	459,080	10,156,345	24,133,000	1,907,436	868,413	93,229	47,229	362,624	—	—	—	—	—
1969	3,780,285	8,145,470	668,645	5,004,000	17,696,930	778,824	415,216	92,553	393	47,103	—	—	—	—	—

Note: 1974 total Wheat includes Gulf Wheat Volume.
1976, 1975, 1972, 1971 total Soybean Meal volume includes Soybean Meal 'B' volume.
1967 through 1970 inclusive, entries in Total All Grains column includes Rye volume for those years.
See 1974 Statistical Annual for Choice Steer volume of trading for years 1967 through 1971 inclusive.
See 1976 Statistical Annual for Stud Lumber volume of trading for years 1972 through 1976 inclusive.

Source: Chicago Board of Trade.

C. H. Taylor's three-volume chronicle of the Board's history details countless episodes of speculative adventuring no longer possible in today's regulated markets. There were monthly corners in wheat, corn, oats, rye, and pork products during 1868. Squeezes and defaults resulted in the Board's extension of margin requirements and trading supervision. Yet, human ingenuity persisted and a great era of speculative activity at the Board lasted until the century's close. Speculative trade in wheat in 1900 was said to be 50 to 100 million bushels per day.

In this century the CBT has worked closely with the U.S. Department of Agriculture in devising commodity trading standards, at least up until the advent of the independent Commodity Futures Trading Commission. The Board has also

FIGURE 6–3
Exchange volume 1978 and 1979

	1978	1979	
Chicago Board of Trade	27,362,929	33,870,680	(+ 23.7%)
Chicago Mercantile Exchange	15,153,957	19,930,798	(+ 31.5%)
Commodity Exchange, Inc.	8,973,828	12,952,353	(+ 44.3%)
MidAmerica Commodities Exch.	2,121,189	2,568,950	(+ 21.1%)
Coffee, Sugar & Cocoa Exch.	1,425,339	2,510,179	(+ 76.1%)
NY Cotton Exchange	1,441,209	1,875,126	(+ 30.1%)
Kansas City Board of Trade	755,949	1,037,018	(+ 37.2%)
NY Mercantile Exchange	926,793	828,249	(− 10.6%)
Minneapolis Grain Exchange	284,313	328,799	(+ 15.6%)
Amex Commodities Exchange	16,671	64,319	(+285.8%)
	58,462,172	75,966,471	(+ 29.9%)

Source: Futures Industry Association.

been a leading creator of new contracts: soybeans, 1936; soybean oil, 1950; iced broilers, 1968; silver, 1969; Ginnie Mae, 1975; and Treasury bonds, 1977. Though increasingly threatened by its rivals, the Board remained the dominant exchange in trade volume in 1979, trading some 33.9 million contracts. Its share of the market, though, slipped from 48.2 percent in 1978 to 45.7 percent in 1979, reflecting the success of precious metals, interest rate futures, and currencies on rival exchanges. (See Figure 6–3.) The relative status of the Board in the 1980s and beyond will be decided by its ability to maintain its traditional strength in the agriculturals while meeting the challenge in these new contracts.

THE CHICAGO MERCANTILE EXCHANGE

Organized in 1919, the Chicago Mercantile Exchange grew out of the old Chicago Butter and Egg Board. Its purpose was to formalize the increasing trade in butter and egg futures, with an eye kept open for new contract possibilities. In its first decades the career of the CME was an undistinguished one. Technological

and marketing improvements eroded the futures market in eggs and butter. Contracts in scrap iron, frozen shrimp, hides, and apples sparked little interest (a still controversial law prohibited the contract in onion futures in 1958). After this spotty start, the CME launched a series of successful contracts in the 1960s and 1970s that quickly made it the exchange to be reckoned with. Frozen pork bellies, (uncured slabs of bacon), live cattle, and live hogs became staple items in the trader's deck. Now the nation's second largest exchange, the CME actually surpassed the Chicago Board of Trade in the value of contracts traded, thanks to its precious metals and currencies.

A key ingredient in the CME's formula was the formation, in 1972, of the International Monetary Market. At first a sister exchange, the IMM was incorporated as a division of the CME in 1976. It initiated contracts in foreign currencies and later in U.S. silver coins, copper, gold bullion, U.S. treasury bills and notes. (See Figure 6–4.) Full CME members may trade all contracts on the regular exchange as well as those of the divisions. Division members may only trade on their respective floors. In addition to the IMM, the Asso-

FIGURE 6–4

IMM Foreign Exchange Futures Volume By Contract

Represents trading in British Pounds (introduced in 1972), Canadian Dollars (1972), Deutsche Marks (1972), Dutch Guilders (1973), French Francs (1974), Italian Lira (1972 & 1973 only), Japanese Yen (1972), Mexican Pesos (1972) and Swiss Francs (1972).

Type of Contract	1972	1973	1974	1975	1976	1977	1978	1979*
British Pounds	14,787	31,412	14,033	15,015	33,465	78,701	240,099	404,503
Canadian Dollars	38,804	29,161	3,699	2,677	17,068	161,139	207,654	340,105
Deutsche Marks	19,318	77,264	49,447	54,793	44,887	134,368	400,569	359,369
Dutch Guilders		11,327	1,527	927	392	2,812	3,585	22
French Francs			11,359	6,238	5,968	3,150	4,449	388
Italian Lira	592	143						
Japanese Yen	43,989	125,653	7,239	1,790	1,449	82,261	361,731	290,246
Mexican Pesos	9,717	120,337	90,941	48,547	51,439	17,029	17,844	27,110
Swiss Francs	17,721	22,013	42,505	69,933	37,246	106,968	321,451	406,775
Total Volume	**144,928**	**417,310**	**220,750**	**199,920**	**191,914**	**586,428**	**1,557,382**	**1,828,518**

*1979 figures are based on 10 months' trading only.

Source: International Monetary Market.

ciated Mercantile Market (AMM) of the CME handles contracts in lightly traded items such as eggs, lumber, potatoes, milo, and butter. The CME has representatives in every state of the union and many abroad. Its rules and operations are under the control of the Exchange's Board of Governors, now consisting of twenty-one members. The latest record price for a seat on the CME is $285,000. Volume at the beginning of the 1980s was nearing two million contracts per month, with live cattle futures leading the way.

OTHER EXCHANGES

Eight other major exchanges currently trade in commodity futures in the United States, though rumors of mergers, spinoffs, and closings circulate regularly. Four exchanges (Comex, N.Y. Coffee, Sugar and Cocoa, N.Y. Cotton, and N.Y. Mercantile) share a common trading facility at New York's World Trade Center. Known as the Commodity Exchange Center (CEC), it houses the kind of expensive, high-technology equipment and modern conveniences utilized by the giant exchanges. The competitive pressures of today's markets make this pooling by smaller exchanges an attractive alternative to actual mergers. Three 84-foot long and 11-foot high computer-controlled price display boards instantly report transactions for all active contracts on all four exchanges. The single massive trading floor allows observers to watch the action in each market and enables traders to circulate from pit to pit.

Slated to open in late 1980 is the New York Futures Exchange, the expensive brainchild of the New York Stock Exchange. The NYFE organizers stress their streamlined floor design, electronic price and order reporting systems, and computerized ability to monitor and police trade. As planned, small orders will be directly transmitted through a computerized routing network to printers in the center of each trading ring. Large, influential orders will still be hand carried. These and other state-of-the-art innovations (costing over $6 million) are expected to reduce the number of floor personnel, cut the cost of daily business, and improve the efficiency of trades. Contracts being considered involve U.S. treasury bills, bonds, and five foreign currencies.

Still struggling to be born is the revived and renamed New Orleans Commodities Exchange. It hopes to build on a contract in Texas/Oklahoma short staple cotton instead of the long staple grade currently traded in New York.

Other exchanges and their principal commodities today are as follows:

1. Commodity Exchange, Inc. (Comex): Copper, Gold, Silver, Ginnie Mae, T-bills (world's largest metals market).
2. MidAmerica Commodity Exchange: Silver, Gold, Wheat, Corn, Hogs, Cattle, Soybeans (features MiniContracts).
3. New York Coffee, Sugar, and Cocoa Exchange: Coffee, Sugar, Cocoa.
4. New York Cotton Exchange: Cotton, Frozen Orange Juice, Liquified Propane.
5. Kansas City Board of Trade: Wheat, Milo.
6. New York Mercantile Exchange: Gold, Swiss Franc, No. 2 Heating Oil, Imported Beef, Palladium, Potatoes, Silver Coins.
7. Minneapolis Grain Exchange: Wheat, Oats, Sunflower Seed.
8. Amex Commodities Exchange: Ginnie Mae, T-bills, T-bonds.

The foreign exchange historically of most interest to U.S. traders is the Winnipeg Commodity Exchange where barley, flaxseed, gold, oats, rapeseed, rye, and wheat trade actively. Winnipeg recently increased its membership limit for the first time since the 1920s. Important exchanges in London trade coffee, grain, bullion, cocoa, rubber, wool, oil, metals, and sugar. A complete list of the many exchanges scattered around the globe should be available from your broker.

THE TRADERS

Who are the traders doing business on the exchanges? Individually, they come from all walks of life. In the past, commodities traders represented relatively few social and economic categories, mostly concerned with agricultural products. Today everyone is getting in on the act. As a commodity advisor I have corresponded with doctors, lawyers, housewives, retired persons, penitentiary inmates, dentists, bankers, and white- and blue-collar workers. Large corporations, industrial firms, and investment institutions have joined trading's ranks with increasing frequency. The more variety of contracts the more possibilities for hedging and profit-taking by a wider range of players.

This variety of participants does not change the fundamental number of functional categories into which they fall in the workings of the game. All traders in commodity futures fall into one of two categories: hedgers or speculators. The

Department of Agriculture and the CFTC add a third category called "small traders." This is strictly a procedural classification containing traders of whom the government doesn't gather the information required of large speculators and hedgers. The majority of players, regardless of classification, trade through brokerage house accounts. Their trades are on the floor or in the pits. Some pit traders trade their own accounts on the floor. A scalper is a pit trader who deals for profit in hectic trades of as little as a quarter of a cent. His trades help to keep the flow of offers orderly, matching buy and sell orders. He is constantly taking positions but usually ends the day without a contract commitment.

THE HEDGER

Any person who holds a position on the futures exchange approximately equal to, but opposite to, a position held in the physical commodity (or certain to be held in the future) is said to be *hedged*. Someone who holds or will harvest 1 million bushels of soybeans is *long* soybeans in the cash position. By opening a *short* position on the Chicago Board of Trade for 1 million bushels, the holder of beans reduces or eliminates the risk of price deterioration. If the price drops 10 cents on the cash market where the soybeans will be sold, the loss will be $100,000 (5,000 bushels per contract × 200 contracts × ten cents). But another offsetting $100,000 will have been made as the value of the winning short futures position goes up. When the futures price drops from $8.00 a bushel to $7.90, the short who sold on the futures exchange for $8.00 has now "locked-in" a 10 cent profit. He may liquidate the short position by buying it back

for the now cheaper price of $7.90, realizing the profit needed to offset the decline in the market value of goods held. The actual beans can then be delivered on the cash market at $7.90 without damaging the holder's price and profit projections, upon which a business must be able to depend.

The soybean crusher or merchant who must buy soybeans is *short* the cash product. By assuming an equal *long* position in Chicago the risk of a price rise can be offset. Money lost on the cash market, where he must pay more for the soybeans needed to do business, will be made back on a winning long position on a rising futures market. This is often termed a "buying hedge," as opposed to the producer's or holder's "selling hedge." In a "forward hedge" an exporter may in January go "short" by selling wheat to an Italian firm for March delivery. He simultaneously goes long on the futures exchange for an equivalent March contract. In March he sells off the futures position and buys the commodity at the port, saving transportation costs from the Midwest and hedging his price position.

The price relationship between futures contracts and cash goods in wholesale markets is called "basis." "Basis" is an important term which states the difference between any two commodity prices that are connected but not the same. "Country basis" refers to the price differential between Chicago, where the futures hedge is made, and the countryside point where the cash transactions take place. (Such factors as transportation, storage, handling, and market pressure will determine how much more or less a commodity will cost in Des Moines than it does in Chicago or Seattle.) As long as the country basis remains constant, neither the short nor the long hedger stands to lose money in cash dealings due to price deterioration or rise after hedges have been placed.

If the price on the spot market varies 10 cents from the time the hedger opens his futures position, the Chicago price should also move 10 cents in the same direction. The country basis changes and moves in cycles, depending on the supply/demand factors at play in any given year and locale. The spot cash markets, through the actions of producers, merchants, and buyers will establish the current country basis. Hedgers hope that this basis figure will hold steady for the time they hold their contracts, for hedgers stand to lose money only if the basis spreads or narrows appreciably before hedges are lifted and closed. The hedger may lose money with the hedge if the basis changes, as his separate cash and futures deals will no longer equally offset each other. But unhedged he could suffer far greater losses if the market moves against his cash position. Because basis is not perfect, a hedge does not totally eliminate risk. It keeps risk in intolerable limits. Except in theory, there is no "perfect hedge."

The feedlot operator in Des Moines who expects to have 1,000 head of choice steers ready for market in July can sell 30 contracts of live beef cattle on the Chicago Mercantile Exchange (30 contracts will approximately equal the herd he will be bringing to the cash markets). The operator has no intention of shipping cattle to an exchange-approved delivery point; he probably has a local buyer with whom he does business. But if the price of choice steers drops by July, and the feedlot operator is forced to accept a lower price than he had expected from the local buyer, the price of live cattle futures in Chicago will also drop. The loss or reduced profit that is taken on the cash steers will be closely balanced by the money made on short contracts in the futures market. Risk is thereby lessened in the year's income forecasts. Any windfall profit made in the form of higher prices on the local cash market will be eaten up by losses on the hedge. The feedlot operator stands neither to lose nor to gain, and theoretically has very little interest in price fluctuation once the hedge is placed.

Hedgers entering the futures markets should remember that the hedge is meant to reduce *overall cash risk*. It does not mean that you simply and mechanically adopt a futures position opposite to whatever your cash position may be. To *sell* into a bull market is speculation, not hedging. A bull market is not adding to the cattle breeder's cash risk, and he ought to stay out of it altogether unless he's prepared to speculate dangerously. Futures selling for hedging purposes by producers or those holding inventories should be done in *declining markets*.

The steer breeder has no intention of delivering against his short futures position. As the herd is sold off in the local cash market, futures contracts are bought until the short positions have all been closed out. It makes little difference to the feeder if the futures contract specifications as to grade, weight, point of delivery, delivery date, and so forth do not exactly describe the cattle being actually sold, so long as the value of the beef described in the futures contract fluctuates at a constant premium or discount to the grade he has to sell. The price may be $1.00 per pound in Des Moines and $1.05 in Chicago, but if the price drops to 95 cents in Des Moines it will probably drop to $1.00 in Chicago. The prices may never be the same but direction of price change should be the same in both the local cash position and the futures position. Though there are no perfect hedges, a careful hedging policy aware of basis, market conditions, and futures movements can considerably relieve the uncertainties built into the commodities business.

The hedger, like the speculator, has no intention of actually using the futures contract for acquisition or delivery, though the futures contract is perfectly suitable if fulfillment becomes necessary or desirable. The possibility exists and serves to keep the futures price and the cash price in line so that hedges will work effectively. If cash and futures prices do get out of line, people legally could and would deliver cash goods on the futures markets. In fact, very few contracts are ever filled— probably less than 2 percent. The rest are closed by speculators who don't want the goods and hedgers who do their business on cash markets and lift their hedges as they do so.

Like most things in economics, hedging in practice is not quite as straightforward as in theory. Few topics in the literature on commodities futures occasion such acrimonious disagreement as does hedging. Some find it the ultimate origin and justification of the futures exchanges, while others see it as a minor activity argumentatively exploited by speculators to justify their profits. The truth, as usual, falls somewhere in the middle, as hedging is an essential but imperfect component of the commodities game. Cash prices in a particular wholesale market at the time the hedger wishes to buy or sell the actual goods will be determined to some extent by purely local conditions which will not affect Chicago prices. Hedging in Chicago will not necessarily cover this local fluctuation. It is largely for this reason that sev-

eral futures markets often exist for the same commodity in different parts of the country. Futures markets and cash markets will both reflect national conditions and the overall market situation, but country basis will vary according to local price fluctuations which do not extend to the urbal exchanges. Hedgers, like others in business, will study local conditions in judging their hedges and then act accordingly. While hedgers theoretically will hedge at any price which allows them a profit in their cash operations, the fact is that hedgers rapidly lose interest if they believe the possibility of windfall profit is greater than actual loss on the cash markets. In other words, hedgers speculate on their cash positions by leaving them unhedged if they think this is their most profitable alternative. Guessing correctly when to hedge is of great importance, as is the accurate and timely execution of the order. These complications are of little interest to the speculator who does all his business in one market and has no need of following the country basis.

The trader using the markets for hedging purposes is usually an employee of an enterprise that depends on the predictability of prices for materials sold or bought in order to do business. Grain companies, foresters, banks, and other large hedgers employ trading analysts whose job it is to hedge the company's risks and meet preset price and cost goals. The hedging operations of Cargill or Continental Grain are intricate maneuverings designed to attain average cost goals over time so that profits on actual sales may be healthy ones. Once the desired cost per bushel of wheat for the coming fiscal year has been put into the company's budget, it is up to the trader and purchasing department to see to it that the average price paid does not exceed the limit. Futures trading is absolutely basic to the success of such strategies.

If hedging can be so beneficial, why do not more farmers make use of it? Going into the 1980s, surveys showed only 10 percent of farmers questioned regularly used the markets for hedging. Historically, there has been a gap between farmers and the exchanges that has led to recurrent angry confrontations. Hedging was traditionally the business of warehousemen, elevator operators, grain companies, and others whose business needs and conditions were unlike those of the farmer. The small farmer had little time or know-how to follow the futures markets regularly enough to hedge well. He carried an almost genetic suspicion of those who did trade in futures, for they were the very city dwellers who bought the corn or wheat and who were thus his natural adversaries in the war for a good price. The advent of agribusiness and of national campaigns by brokerage firms luring farmers into futures may alter the old pattern.

Another reason many farmers don't use futures more is margin. Unlike speculators, they are virtually locked into their hedges: liquidate the hedge on an adverse move and the whole hedging scheme collapses. But holding on can mean big margin calls, bigger than the usually capital-short farmer can afford. The average farm runs on bank loans against future crops. Farm bankers have been reluctant to further extend credit for hedging costs many thought of as gambling losses. Brokers argue that since hedging loans are also secured by crops, banks ought to extend credit to cover margin calls. Banks back off from what appears to be great risk and farmers dislike the required monitor-

ing of their books such loans would call for. Arrangements linking farmers, bankers, and brokers in hedging plans have yet to have all their bugs worked out. Brokers complain that they cannot trade speedily and efficiently if every trade must be cleared first through a banking executive. Another option is the "foward contract," with the broker agreeing to buy the crop at a fixed price, enabling him to do the hedging.

Hedging has been a key factor in the tremendous growth of the financial futures markets. For the banks, pension funds, corporations, and investment houses hedging in financial instruments, the same basic principles apply that hold for agricultural hedging. In these cases the commodity is money, the price of which fluctuates with interest rate changes. Sound money management necessitates that risks incurred in the borrowing or lending of funds be reduced by strategic futures trading in interest rate futures.

PIT TRADERS AND SCALPERS

A pit trader may trade his own account or he may take orders from a brokerage house or hedger not large enough to have his own staff. The pit trader is the one who stands physically in the pit and trades contracts by a system of shouting and hand signals. It is through his work in the pit that trading orders are actually executed. Some pit traders hold fairly large positions for weeks at a time, but most who trade for their own accounts hold their positions for very short periods of time. A scalper might hold a position for ten to sixty seconds. In an active pit, ten or twenty seconds may mean two or three fluctuations in price. The scalper cannot and will not hold a losing position through a long adverse price move. The special advantage of being in the pit (for any trader who is handling his account) is largely made up of very quick price trades. For normal speculation, holding a position for several days, weeks, or even months, being physically in the pit offers no particular advantage.

The majority of pit traders take advantage of small price fluctuations that occur in every market. The constant input of buy and sell orders kicks the price slightly up and down as deals are struck. The trader in the pit may buy a temporarily depressed price and sell back a few seconds or minutes later when a large buy order comes in, raising the price in the pit. Such traders in small tics are called "scalpers" and serve the same function as the specialist in a stock market. Scalpers trade for their own accounts, though they are not regulated, as are stock specialists.

Any trader in the pit can quickly "scalp" a price which has dipped and sell the contracts when the price has returned. With such competition for fraction-of-a-cent profits, regulation is simply not required. Any trader attempting to distort a price by holding back on trading would soon find himself undercut by the trader standing behind him. Scalpers rarely profit by more than a few minimum fluctuations of price, except in extremely volatile markets. They can afford to do this because they pay no commissions, unlike the speculator who must figure commission costs into his profit projections.

Like the stock specialist, the scalper's function is to provide liquidity to the market by balancing the number of sell and buy offers in the pit. A rush of buy orders will cause the price to rise. Before it goes

too far, scalpers will start selling, picking up a quick fraction and keeping the buy orders filled. The scalper then swiftly closes out as an excess of selling pressure hits the floor from the ticker rooms of the brokerage firms. Scalpers rarely hold positions overnight and they seldom alter price trends. They function to smooth prices out and to assure incoming orders of a representative price. They also balance the pit itself, trading from side to side or corner to corner, keeping prices fairly uniform.

Pit traders and scalpers often start as runners, phone clerks, or floor employees, working their way up to membership in the exchange and the low cost trading privileges that go with it. They pay scant attention to supply and demand fundamentals, though they may keep charts and are adequately informed on general market conditions. Their profits, however, depend on technical market moves of price in the pit, moves that cannot be played by reference to the fundamentals. They will usually work a single pit, making 300 or 400 trades in a day sometimes. Winners take home anywhere from $50 to $1,000 a day, with stories about legendary $50,000 days. Like other speculators, their fortunes go up and down frequently and dramatically. Contrary to popular assumption, only a very small number of floor traders are consistently successful in the pits. The turnover rate is high. Almost all pit traders and scalpers are young. The work is very demanding—physically and financially. Older traders will be wiped out, emotionally or monetarily, or if successful have moved up to less hectic positions in the futures trade. The same rules applying to other speculators are endorsed by pit traders: have the discipline to follow and respect what the market really does, cut losses short, and trade the price move—not the product. In addition, scalpers may have to estimate who is buying and who is selling in order to surmise how strong or weak the price tic is. Are the sell orders coming from commission house speculators or hedgers? Public or commercial investors? Each trader in the pit must decide quickly which side to take, and each has his own theory about what groups to "fade" (take opposite position from) and which to follow.

THE PUBLIC SPECULATOR

The rapid development and diversification of futures trading has made it impossible to draw a steady portrait of the "average" public speculator. The nature of speculation and the financial requirements imposed by most brokerage firms, however, assure some common characteristics. The speculator will probably be a bit younger on the average than the stock investor, for risk rather than security is his game. His income will be healthy enough to make trading possible ($20,-000–$50,000) but perhaps not so high that tax considerations dampen enthusiasm for speculative profits taxed at a rate of 70 percent or more. Considering this economic bracket, the trader is likely to have a college education and there's a good chance he holds a graduate or professional degree as well. Many will be new to the game (many novice traders only last a year or two), though experienced in other investment areas. The ascending popularity of commodity futures pools and funds will mean a further broadening of the kind of people trading, and a possible categorical distinction between individual and group speculators.

It might be possible for a futures market to exist serving only speculators, but in fact volume of business done on any of the futures markets directly follows the amount of interest in hedging on the part of industry. Industries with the greatest amount of hedging have the greatest volume of speculation on their futures markets. The speculator is after profit and typically couldn't care less if the contract called for delivery of cotton, Mexican Pesos, or box top coupons. The speculator's business is to be long when the price rises and short when the price falls. But the speculator must follow the action and the action follows the needs of the industry. Contracts whose open interest is 35 percent to 60 percent held by hedgers are usually high volume commodities— wheat, corn, soybeans, Ginnie Maes, T-Bonds—and they will most regularly provide the profit opportunities the speculator is looking for. Gold and silver, where international politics and global speculation often dominate the market, are unique kinds of cases where a commodity futures market comes close to being a purely speculative venture, with weak ties to real world fundamentals. They are belief, rather than tangible value, markets.

Like the scalper, the speculator serves a function in the futures markets. By looking out for his own profits, he assumes unwanted risk and helps balance the markets. The speculator makes his profit by buying prices which have fallen below a fair and reasonable estimate of the cash price to come in the future, whether because of a large hedging sale or because of improperly discounted information about coming market prices. (Information is said to be "discounted" when traders estimate its significance and adjust prices before the news "officially" comes out.)

The speculator profits from selling

prices which have risen too far, thereby keeping futures contract prices in line with coming cash prices which are at the price contracts must expire. The question that has never been fully resolved is whether the speculator, in fact, succeeds in performing his function. If he does sell too high prices and buy prices that are too low, he makes a profit and helps level out unwanted price movement, giving a fair price to any who wish to use the markets. The speculator's presence in the market also provides crucial liquidity.

It is still questioned whether the speculator does make profits overall, thereby leveling prices or whether he loses, causing unnecessary price aberrations in the process. Studies of the now prohibited onion markets, with and without speculation, indicate that the speculator performs his function very well and provides a better market while taking his profits. In other markets, speculator stop-loss orders may cause irritating price spurts when they are tripped. (Intentional tripping of clustered stop-orders by pit traders for their own purposes does happen occasionally.)

If the speculator is doing well the markets are improved, but it is difficult to determine over a market just how well the speculators are doing. Position figures are released by the government just once a month and do not indicate intermonth changes in position which would determine profit and loss on the part of the various traders. Hedgers often depress the market or give it a purely technical boost, but there is again no way of determining if the market is stabilized by speculation and who takes the profit for the stabilization of prices. Ticker or newswire readouts will often describe market action in terms of commercial or commission house or floor pressure, and all seem integral to the market's activity. (See Figure 6–5.)

There are large speculators and small speculators trading on the exchange floors. Large speculators hold positions above the "reporting level" and stay with them for a while. A large speculator might

FIGURE 6–5

```
CME LIVE CATTLE SPECIAL: FALLS SHARPLY, THEN REBOUNDS--5/2--CNS

    CATTLE PRICES FELL SHARPLY, HITTING SELL-STOPS ON THE WAY DOWN,
AS LOCALS AND SOME COMMISSION HOUSES WERE ACTIVE SELLERS, SOURCES
SAID. PRICES QUICKLY DROPPED AS MUCH AS 132 POINTS, BASIS JUN.
    HOWEVER, FUTURES THEN RALLIED SHARPLY, WITH JUN REGAINING AS MUCH
AS 60 POINTS AS LOCALS COVERED SHORT POSITIONS AND ON COMMISSION
HOUSE SUPPORT AT THE LOWS.
    SOURCES SAID THE MARKET CONTINUES TO HAVE A WEAK UNDERTONE AND
THIS COULD HAVE TRIGGERED A PORTION OF THE SELLING. HOWEVER, THE
MAJORITY OF THE SELLING APPEARS TO STEM FROM LOWER DRESSED BEEF
PRICES, THEY SAID.
    AT 1155 CDT, PRICES WERE STILL DOWN 97 TO 25 POINTS BUT HAD
GAINED 55 TO 15 POINTS FROM THE SESSION'S LOWS. NEARBY JUN WAS OFF 97
POINTS AT 63.25 DLRS PER CWT.   END
1215 CDT#
```

Source: Commodity News Service.

buy 200 contracts of May pork bellies (7.6 million lbs.) with a margin payment of $240,000 or sell 300 contracts of live beef-cattle (12 million lbs.) with a payment of $450,000. Such positions must be reported to the CFTC. The small speculator will limit his position in a single contract to one or ten or maybe twenty futures contracts and will exit from positions more quickly than the large speculator. Small traders are not required to file position reports with the CFTC. Their positions are derived by subtracting the large traders' commitments from the total number of contracts open at the end of the month. For this reason, no breakdown is possible of the small traders into hedging and speculative categories.

COMMITMENT OF TRADERS

Each month the CFTC publishes a bulletin, *Commitments of Traders in Commodity Futures.* This bulletin usually comes out before the fifteenth of the month after the reporting period and lists the total position of six categories of traders. The breakdown is as follows: Large Speculators, long, short, and spreading; Large Hedgers, long and short; and a final category of Small Traders, which includes both hedgers and speculators whose positions are below the reporting level. The large trader, as discussed above, is one who holds a position in any one market and contract month equaling or exceeding the quantities specified as "Reporting Level" by the CFTC. Large hedgers may be grain companies, shippers, banks, or any institution taking large positions to reduce risk.

The *Commitments of Traders* bulletin gives a pretty fair view of the general tenor of a market. How much of the open inter-

est is hedging? How does my position compare with that of the "smart money" large traders? What are the small traders up to? I may want to remember, in judging the movement of traders in and out of the market, that speculators are much more likely to close their positions if the price moves against them than are hedgers. The hedgers, after all, are making money on their cash positions when the price moves against their futures position.

The bulletin's breakdown on commitments may help to answer some of these questions, but it cannot be used as a predictive device for trading. Staking positions in imitation of large speculators or in reaction to hedgers, in the belief that they know more of the inside story, can be courting disaster. A price move easily sat out by the big holders will wipe out the small speculator. The large hedger is not using the markets for the same purpose as the speculator, so the hedger's position is no forecast by which to make profits. Comparisons of commitments of traders charts with price charts show that small traders are often making money rapidly as large speculators lag behind and hedgers count their losses. (See Figure 6–6.)

In the accompanying figure, the commitments chart has been compiled in the CFTC's *Annual Report* from the individual monthly bulletins. It gives a breakdown of traders in soybean meal in a typical year. From it one can read the number of positions held by each category of trader in each month, the percent of long or short positions held by each category of traders, and the number of traders in each group. Notice that "Open Interest" figures are the same as the combined total of longs (large and small) and as the combined total of shorts (large and

FIGURE 6–6

SOYBEAN MEAL – CHICAGO BOARD OF TRADE
MONTHEND COMMITMENTS OF TRADERS IN ALL FUTURES COMBINED AND THE ANNUAL
AVERAGES FOR OCTOBER 1976 THROUGH SEPTEMBER 1977 (FISCAL YEAR 1977)

MONTH	TOTAL OPEN INTEREST	REPORTING (LARGE) TRADERS								NONREPORTING (SMALL) TRADERS SPECULATIVE AND HEDGING	
		SPECULATIVE				HEDGING		TOTAL			
		LONG OR SHORT ONLY		LONG AND SHORT (SPREADING)							
		LONG	SHORT	LONG	SHORT	LONG	SHORT	LONG	SHORT	LONG	SHORT
					(HUNDRED TONS)						
OCTOBER	31,088	3,836	2,367	5,771	5,771	13,746	18,514	23,353	26,652	7,735	4,436
NOVEMBER	37,843	4,941	3,377	8,732	8,732	15,423	20,424	29,096	32,533	8,747	5,310
DECEMBER	34,379	5,638	3,142	7,338	7,338	13,585	19,587	26,561	30,067	7,818	4,312
JANUARY	31,607	4,392	4,386	4,138	4,138	14,748	17,640	23,278	26,164	8,329	5,443
FEBRUARY	37,441	6,246	4,629	6,897	6,897	14,387	21,330	27,530	32,856	9,911	4,585
MARCH	45,963	9,884	4,424	7,059	7,059	16,696	29,671	33,639	41,154	12,324	4,809
APRIL	53,064	7,396	6,427	10,342	10,342	25,285	30,703	43,023	47,472	10,041	5,592
MAY	50,916	6,066	5,353	9,740	9,762	25,100	29,162	40,906	44,277	10,010	6,639
JUNE	47,020	3,432	4,267	12,214	12,214	25,587	24,653	41,233	41,134	5,787	5,886
JULY	43,936	808	5,725	11,505	11,505	24,936	19,848	37,249	37,078	6,687	6,858
AUGUST	44,916	1,628	5,773	10,049	10,049	25,690	19,770	37,367	35,592	7,549	9,324
SEPTEMBER	43,322	2,038	4,317	12,859	12,859	20,888	16,282	35,785	33,458	7,537	9,864
ANNUAL AVG.	41,791	4,692	4,516	8,887	8,889	19,673	22,299	33,252	35,703	8,540	6,088
			PERCENT OF OPEN INTEREST HELD BY EACH GROUP OF TRADERS								
OCTOBER	100.0%	12.3	7.6	18.6	18.6	44.2	59.6	75.1	85.7	24.9	14.3
NOVEMBER	100.0%	13.1	8.9	23.1	23.1	40.8	54.0	76.9	86.0	23.1	14.0
DECEMBER	100.0%	16.4	9.1	21.3	21.3	39.5	57.0	77.3	87.5	22.7	12.5
JANUARY	100.0%	13.9	13.9	13.1	13.1	46.7	55.8	73.6	82.8	26.4	17.2
FEBRUARY	100.0%	16.7	12.4	18.4	18.4	38.4	57.0	73.5	87.8	26.5	12.2
MARCH	100.0%	21.5	9.6	15.4	15.4	36.3	64.6	73.2	89.5	26.8	10.5
APRIL	100.0%	13.9	12.1	19.5	19.5	47.7	57.9	81.1	89.5	18.9	10.5
MAY	100.0%	11.9	10.5	19.1	19.2	49.3	57.3	80.3	87.0	19.7	13.0
JUNE	100.0%	7.3	9.1	26.0	26.0	54.4	52.4	87.7	87.5	12.3	12.5
JULY	100.0%	1.8	13.0	26.2	26.2	56.8	45.2	84.8	84.4	15.2	15.6
AUGUST	100.0%	3.6	12.9	22.4	22.4	57.2	44.0	83.2	79.2	16.8	20.8
SEPTEMBER	100.0%	4.7	10.0	29.7	29.7	48.2	37.6	82.6	77.2	17.4	22.8
ANNUAL AVG.	100.0%	11.2	10.8	21.3	21.3	47.1	53.4	79.6	85.4	20.4	14.6
				NUMBER OF TRADERS IN EACH GROUP							
OCTOBER	139	42	30	55	55	45	37	114	98		
NOVEMBER	157	50	34	71	71	51	41	136	118		
DECEMBER	156	55	27	70	70	45	41	137	118		
JANUARY	137	34	34	47	47	50	43	111	104		
FEBRUARY	168	61	36	58	58	52	54	138	119		
MARCH	179	71	33	65	65	56	55	155	122		
APRIL	183	53	42	67	67	64	58	151	136		
MAY	141	37	37	60	60	57	44	123	109		
JUNE	131	23	30	59	59	52	46	114	108		
JULY	123	12	41	58	58	42	41	99	109		
AUGUST	131	16	47	61	61	42	46	105	117		
SEPTEMBER	128	21	37	62	62	39	45	106	113		
ANNUAL AVG.	148	40	36	61	61	50	46	124	114		

* LESS THAN .05 PERCENT.

Source: Commodity Futures Trading Commission.

small). This is somewhat confusing at first, but all numbers given *except* for "Open Interest" refer to *positions,* not to *contracts.* It takes two positions for every contract. One long and one short make a contract, someone to deliver and someone to accept delivery, and it is the number of contracts that "open interest" denotes. Thus, if you wanted to know how much of the open interest was held by hedgers, you would add together long and short hedgers and divide by two, giving the number of hedged contracts. The percent of open interest held by hedgers could similarly be found by combining the "percent of open interest" figures for long and shorts and dividing the result by two. For October hedged positions were 13,746 long plus 18,514 short, equalling 32,260 positions or 16,130 contracts which, if you want further mathematics, is 51.9 percent of the 31,088 open interest. The percent of open interest held by hedgers may also be arrived at by adding the 40.2 percent long with the 59.6 percent short and dividing by two, giving 51.9 again. The same procedures can be used to figure totals and percents for each category of the breakdown.

Would you have profited more trading meal if you had followed the large specula-tors, the large hedgers, or the small traders? Take a look at the soybean meal price chart for the period covered by the commitments bulletin and start figuring. (See Figure 6–7). At the end of February large speculators had 6,246 positions long and 4,629 short. Hedgers were 14,387 long and

FIGURE 6–7

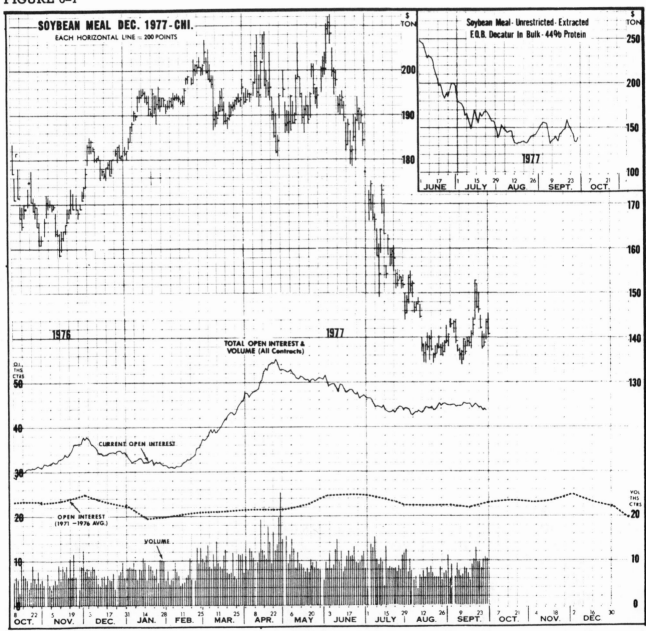

Source: Commodity Research Bureau, Inc.

21,330 short. Small speculators were 9,911 long and 4,585 short. In other words, though both the large and the small speculators went long in meal anticipating a price rise, small speculators were twice as long as short, whereas the large speculators were only one-third as long as short. In fact, figures for the preceding months show small speculators catching the rise of meal from October into June faster and more numerously than did the large speculators. Cross-examining the price and commitments charts, one can watch the changing nature of open interest as prices move up and down and see which traders capitalized the most. The biggest winner in this market was the small trader, followed by the large speculator. Hedgers lost during this action. It is well to know who else is in the market, and where, but the decision on individual positions must be made with primary reference to the individual trader's situation and trading program.

WOMEN IN COMMODITIES

The entrance of woman into the futures game promises to transform the complexion of traders and exchanges, and it deserves to be noted in any account of the industry's evolving character. Like most of economic society, commodity futures trading was a male business until quite recently. With the growing acceptance of women in the business and professional communities, they have begun to make their mark throughout the commodities field. The many new opportunities that have come with the commodities boom have opened new doors to many once excluded from money management, investment, and speculation. Good old capitalism is at work here too, for women—

comprising half the population—represent the single largest untapped pool of potential traders. Volume is volume and dollars are dollars, no matter the spender's gender.

Historically, a major roadblock used to keep a tight control on who traded was financial credibility. An account for commodity trading cannot be opened unless the potential trader can demonstrate sufficient economic credibility. Law, precedent, economic practice, and just plain prejudice all combined to make most woman financial nonentities until the 1970s, when reforms and heightened public awareness began the movement toward more equitable economic identities for the sexes. As working women accumulate more capital, grow eager to put this capital to work, and look for profitable ventures, their positions in futures will inevitably increase.

Progress has been slow but steady. The first woman admitted to membership in the New York Mercantile Exchange, Muriel Edelstein, took her seat in 1964. She went on to become the very successful president of the family's brokerage firm. It was not until some five years later that the Chicago Board of Trade elected its first woman member, and the ranks of the Coffee and Sugar (and now Cocoa) Exchange were not broken until 1978. (See Figure 6–8.) Aside from financial restraints, women traders had to overcome the myth that women were "too emotional" or "too unstable" to handle the wild futures business. Today women are actively trading in a number of pits, screaming and pushing and closing deals with their male colleagues. The very physical nature of pit work puts women, on the average, at a disadvantage (as it does slight or short men). In practice, though,

FIGURE 6–8

The New York Cotton Exchange reports with some dismay that not only does it not have a woman member currently, but also that it has never had any women members, nor has it ever had a woman apply for membership. On the other hand, approximately 14 of that exchange's 200 Citrus Associates are women, though none of them trade on the floor.

The installation of a women's rest room on the Minneapolis Grain Exchange trading floor a few years ago was a sign of changing times in the industry. When the exchange was built in the early 1900s, women were not allowed on the floor.

Source: Commodities Magazine.

Exchange	Recent seat price	Total members	Women members	Percent women
Chicago Board of Trade	$259,500	1,402	22	1.6%
Financial Instrument Memberships (FIM)	130,000	100	8	8 %
Floor Activity Permit	quarterly fees of $250 to $2,500	250	28	11.2%
Chicago Mercantile Exchange	30,000	500	11	2.2%
International Monetary Market (IMM)	155,000	650	60	9.2%
Associate Mercantile Exchange (AMM)	50,000	150	45	30%
MidAmerica Commodity Exchange	17,300	1,205	105	8.7%
Kansas City Board of Trade	60,000	212	1	.47%
Minneapolis Grain Exchange	15,000	420	6	1.4%
Commodity Exchange, Inc.	180,000	350	1	.29%
New York Coffee and Sugar Exchange	33,500	344	1	.29%
New York Cocoa Exchange	26,000	170	3	1.8%
New York Mercantile Exchange	31,000	408	6-8	1.7%
American Commodity Exchange	15,000	500	3	.6%
New York Cotton Exchange	38,000	450	0	0%
Citrus Associates	700	200	14	7%

women have found that high pitched voices and distinctly different appearances can be real advantages in the pit, where recognition is essential for successful trading.

Women now serve in most of the industry's jobs—as traders, floor runners, phone clerks, account executives, researchers, market analysts, managers of commodity departments, and officers of brokerage firms (where women once had to have letters from their husbands in order to open an account). They tend to rise up along the same paths as their male competitors and succeed (or fail) for the same reasons. In interviews they give the rational answer that what makes a good trader (or broker or analysts) are skills, intelligence, and technique. Sound trading methods have nothing to do with anatomy. The fact that brokerage firms are under equal opportunity guidelines means more women in every facet of the business, and by 1980 at least one leading firm had a female vice-president. For women in commodities, the trend is bullish.

Chapter 7

COMMODITY CONTRACTS

MAKING A CONTRACT

The futures trader deals in contracts, not in real goods. As was apparent in comparing stocks and commodities, futures contracts do not exist in the same way as stock certificates. Contracts come into being or are dissolved with every trade. Normally, there is no limit to the number of contracts for a particular commodity or month. In commodities, volume translates directly into contracts (though at any given time daily volume and total open interest may be far apart). The aggregate of futures contracts may very well exceed total real world supplies—not a worrisome condition when we remember that very few contracts result in delivery. (See Figure 7–1.) Delivered soybean contracts totaling 27,287 may sound like a substantial number but is small compared to an open interest of 102,044 and volume of 7,909,135 contracts. The futures trader, however, should never forget that the futures contract is bound by the market for cash goods and is ultimately deliverable. The success of the entire futures system hinges on the contract's utility and thus on the skill with which it is written. Contracts once were scribbled quickly on the backs of saloon napkins. Today, an exchange may spend years of time and many thousands of dollars devising a new trading contract.

The negotiability and quick transfer of the contract are rooted in the standardization of goods and their reception stipulated by the contract. If the commodity can be uniformly graded, easily stored, and conviently delivered, a contract could be written for it. For the contract to succeed, market price conditions and distribution systems must be such as to encourage futures trading. The contract itself must pass the inspection of producers, buyers, and speculators. If any part of it fails to satisfy their requirements (and many have), the contract will go untraded until it is rewritten or dropped. (See Figures 7–2 and 7–3.)

A legally binding publically offered commodity futures contract may only be made on an authorized and regulated exchange by two members of the exchange, one taking the long and one the short position. In its essence the contract calls for the delivery and acceptance of the named commodity at a certain time and place, in grades or with qualities set down by the contract. One contract of March

FIGURE 7-1

CONTRACT MARKET REVIEW

Estimated Average Monthend Open Interest, 12 Month Total Volume of Trading and Deliveries by Exchange, by Commodity, for Fiscal Years Ending September 30, 1977 and September 30, 1978

Exchange/Commodity	Contract Units	Open Interest (Contracts)		Volume of Trading (in Contracts)		Total Contracts Settled by Delivery	
		1977-78	1976-77	1977-78	1976-77	1977-78	1976-77
Chicago Board of Trade (CBOT)							
Wheat	5,000 bu.	42,482	44,341	2,367,980	1,884,344	19,678	26,659
Corn	5,000 bu.	132,131	98,346	6,211,959	4,661,104	25,272	23,750
Oats	5,000 bu.	4,801	2,964	171,220	107,152	5,172	2,201
Soybeans	5,000 bu.	102,044	97,181	7,909,135	7,826,267	27,287	20,264
Soybean Oil	60,000 lbs.	49,329	51,644	2,775,659	2,373,177	8,366	44,159
Soybean Meal	100 tons	44,636	41,791	2,354,960	2,193,064	16,318	25,407
Iced Broilers	30,000 lbs.	2,144	1,993	71,299	59,850	2,153	2,058
Silver	5,000 tr. oz.	237,569	171,557	2,606,950	1,941,843	25,688	28,315
Gold	3 kgs.	2,392	1,260	44,854	9,173	1,993	338
Plywood	76,032 sq. ft.	6,714	6,907	300,302	337,371	5,976	8,885
GNMA's	$100,000 prin. bal.	27,338	10,608	754,225	333,427	956	1,606
GNMA-CD's	$100,000 prin. bal.	577[1]	—	807	—	—	—
Commercial Paper	$1,000,000	683	90	12,938	420	29	—
T-Bonds	$100,000 prin. bal.	7,182	1,405	291,555	10,510	3,313	—
Total CBOT		660,022	530,087	25,873,843	21,737,702	142,201	183,642
MidAmerica Commodity Exchange (MACE)							
Wheat	1,000 bu.	1,999	2,799	191,247	198,739	330	1,676
Corn	1,000 bu.	3,694	4,034	264,887	313,025	400	410
Oats	5,000 bu.	24	149	1,122	7,075	6	30
Soybeans	1,000 bu.	7,343	5,897	997,357	1,082,397	248	2,815
Silver	1,000 tr. oz.	13,231	13,364	425,202	354,527	3,297	1,195
Gold	1 kg.	390	96	20,483	2,602	34	86
Live Hogs	15,000 lbs.	1,222	853	185,593	159,297	46	16
Live Cattle	20,000 lbs.	451[2]	—	2,172[3]	—	—	—
Total MACE		28,354	27,192	2,088,063	2,117,662	4,361	6,228
Chicago Mercantile Exchange (CME)							
Fresh Eggs	22,500 doz.	1,678	2,110	98,506	147,197	458	733
Idaho Potatoes	80,000 lbs.	42	136	234	4,585	11	12
Turkeys	36,000 lbs.	—	26[4]	—	264	25	39
Live Cattle	40,000 lbs.	73,158	45,633	4,659,726	2,804,570	1,113	1,430
Livefeeder Cattle	42,000 lbs.	14,274	4,211	444,248	119,474	662	322
Live Hogs	30,000 lbs.	19,650	13,678	1,694,365	1,203,282	259	271
Lumber	100,000 bd.ft.	7,858	6,573	530,541	436,826	251	309
Stud Lumber		274	—	7,454	—	91	—
Frozen boneless beef	36,000 lbs.	-0-	8[5]	4	33	—	—
Frozen Pork Bellies	36,000 lbs.	9,965	9,431	1,439,987	1,283,297	1,216	1,725
British Pound	50,000	4,962	1,844	230,461	44,869	1,576	507
Canadian Dollar	200,000	2,511	2,214	141,055	129,931	622	735
Deutschemark	500,000	4,006	1,942	328,810	102,627	1,942	955
Dutch Guilder	125,000	395	20	6,248	282	575	12
U.S. Silver Coins	$5,000	40	32	401	272	66	53
Japanese Yen	25,000,000	4,276	1,068	330,055	27,689	1,565	402
Mexican Peso	1,000,000	2,322	1,592	18,659	18,062	243	397
Swiss Franc	500,000	3,887	1,329	285,980	65,505	1,977	869
French Franc	250,000	219	195	4,253	4,269	330	183
Gold	100 tr. oz.	50,204	14,196	2,355,929	570,482	20,828	4,973
Treasury Bills-90 day	$1,000,000	20,404	5,806	531,679	260,265	986	661
Treasury Bills-1 year	$1,000,000	736[6]	—	2,211	—	—	—
Total CME		220,861	112,044	13,110,812	7,223,781	34,796	14,588

Source: Commodity Futures Trading Commission.

FIGURE 7-2

FROZEN PORK BELLIES FUTURES SPECIFICATIONS
Applicable Against February 1979 and Subsequent Contracts Through August 1979

SCOPE OF CHAPTER — This chapter is limited in application to futures trading of frozen pork bellies. The procedures for trading, clearing, inspection, delivery, settlement and any other matters not specifically covered herein shall be governed by the rules of the Exchange.

COMMODITY SPECIFICATIONS — The commodity traded pursuant to this chapter shall consist of Green Square-Cut Clear Seedless Bellies from a federally inspected packing plant. Each belly must bear a United States Department of Agriculture (USDA) Meat Inspection Division inspection legend.

FUTURES CALL

TRADING MONTHS AND HOURS — Futures contracts shall be scheduled for trading and delivery during such hours and in such months as may be determined by the Board.

TRADING UNIT — The unit of trading shall be 38,000 pounds.

PRICE INCREMENTS — Minimum price fluctuations shall be by multiples of $.00025 per pound.

DAILY PRICE LIMITS — There shall be no trading at a price more than $.02 per pound above or below the previous day's settling price.

POSITION LIMITS — A person shall not own or control more than 150 contracts in February; 150 contracts in March; 200 contracts in May; 150 contracts in July or 150 contracts in August, but in no event shall such person's total position exceed 250 contracts net long or short.

INTERPRETATION – Any person making a bid or an offer which would, if accepted, put such person over the position or daily trading limits, shall be deemed in violation of Exchange Rules.

TRADING LIMITS — While restricted to the foregoing position limits, a person shall not trade during one day more than 225 February contracts, 225 March contracts, 300 May contracts, 225 July contracts or 225 August contracts, but in no event shall he trade in excess of 375 contracts.

ACCUMULATION OF POSITIONS — The positions of all accounts owned or controlled by a person or persons acting in concert or in which such person or persons have a proprietary or beneficial interest shall be cumulated.

BONA FIDE HEDGES — The foregoing position limits shall not apply to bona fide hedging transactions meeting the requirements of the Commodity Exchange Act and the rules of the Exchange.

TERMINATION OF FUTURES TRADING — Futures trading shall terminate on the business day immediately preceding the last five business days of the contract month.

CONTRACT MODIFICATIONS — Specifications shall be fixed as of the first day of trading of a contract, except that all deliveries must conform to Government Regulations in force at time of delivery. If any federal governmental agency issues an order, ruling, directive or law that conflicts with the requirements of these rules, such order, ruling, directive or law shall be construed to take precedence and become part of these rules and all open and new contracts shall be subject to such government orders.

DELIVERY PROCEDURES — In addition to the procedures and requirements of inspections and deliveries, the following shall specifically apply to the delivery of frozen pork bellies:

1. *Delivery Days*

   Delivery may be made on any business day of the contract month.

2. *Sellers Duties*

   At time of delivery, seller must furnish a producer certification of other written evidence satisfactory to the Clearing House manager that the bellies were fresh or fresh freezer accumulated (FFA) and not over 15 days old at the time of shipment from plant to approved warehouse. Such evidence or other certification plus a bill of lading, or photo copy thereof, must accompany regular delivery documents.

   Received weights are to be recorded by the receiving warehouse on the itemization of weight sheets which shall show total net weight, lot number, name of warehouse, location and date stored. A copy thereof, certified by the warehouse shall be furnished by seller on delivery in lieu of official weight certificate.

   At time of delivery of inplant inspected pork bellies, the seller shall furnish a producer certificate or other written evidence satisfactory to the Clearing House manager that the bellies were fresh cut not over 48 hours at the time specified in the original order for inplant inspection.

PAR DELIVERY AND SUBSTITUTIONS

PAR DELIVERY UNIT — A par delivery unit is 38,000 pounds of 12/14 pound frozen pork bellies shipped from one federally inspected packing plant in the United States (which upon inspection show 31 or less minor defects.) The unit may contain bellies from hogs which have been slaughtered at one or more USDA federally inspected slaughtering plants, provided that all bellies in the unit have been uniformly cut and trimmed from whole dressed hogs at one federally inspected establishment. All bellies shall bare the identification number of the federally inspected establishment.

QUALITY SPECIFICATIONS IN GENERAL — The bellies shall be typical of those produced from barrows, gilts and smooth sows (no stags or boars permitted).

The bellies shall be boneless and the major cartilages of the sternum and the ribs shall be closely and smoothly removed, leaving a reasonably good lean covering on the face of the belly. Any remaining embedded tips of the cartilages shall be approximately level with, or slightly lower than, the surface lean. The bellies shall be practically free from bruises, skin scalps, skin cuts and objectionable discoloration.

Bellies shall not be excessively oily or soft and the flesh shall not be extremely dark or coarse.

The bellies showing poor workmanship or any condition adversely affecting the end product shall not be acceptable.

Practically all leaf fat and other abdominal surface fat of similar character shall be removed.

The bellies shall be frozen and shall not show evidence of defrosting and refreezing except where sampling or examination has made this necessary to the bellies involved.

The bellies shall be in good condition and show no indication of mishandling or rancidity.

The conditions stated herein are general. For more specific requirements on conformation, quality, workmanship, etc., see the schedule of defects.

PACKAGING — Bellies shall be adequately protected according to trade custom by any one of the following methods: however, each unit must be uniform: (a) Suitably glazed by double dipping: (b) Wrapped in wax paper or in long sheets of polyethylene or other durable plastic film. Not more than four bellies may be included in each wrapping; (c) By enclosing in polyethylene or other plastic film bags. Not more than four bellies may be included in each wrapping unless the entire pallet load of bellies is enclosed in a single polyethylene bag; (d) By encasing the entire pallet load of bellies in a single polyethylene bag to be put on from the bottom up. The bellies must be frozen prior to closing the bag. The bag must be of sufficient weight to give adequate protection to the bellies and must be maintained in good condition.

STORAGE — To be eligible for delivery during the months of February, March, May, July and August, frozen pork bellies shall not have been produced or stored prior to November 1 of the previous year.

Each delivery unit shall be stored and completed within a 15-day period under one lot number and must be stored continuously in only one approved cold storage warehouse.

DELIVERY POINTS — Par delivery of frozen pork bellies shall be made from approved warehouses in Chicago. Deliveries made from approved warehouses outside of Chicago may be substituted with an allowance as set by the Chicago Mercantile Exchange.

INTERPRETATION.– The formula for determining the dollar amount to be deducted for outside Chicago delivery is: Negotiable warehouse receipt weight times the published allowance from the warehouse from which the bellies are delivered.

QUALITY DEVIATIONS AND ALLOWANCES — If the bellies in the sample have no more than a total of 31 minor defect equivalents, the entire lot will be deliverable at par. Bellies with 32-60 minor defect equivalents may be delivered at ½¢ discount. Bellies with 61-75 minor defect equivalents may be delivered at 1¢ discount. Bellies with 76-91 minor defect equivalents may be delivered at 1½¢ discount. Bellies with 92-106 minor defect equivalents may be delivered at 2¢ discount. Bellies with more than 106 minor defect equivalents are nondeliverable.

WEIGHT DEVIATIONS AND ALLOWANCES — Delivery units complying with all other rules of the futures contract but in the following weight ranges are deliverable with the specified allowances.

14/16 pound units — 1¢ allowance

16/18 pound units — 3½¢ allowance

A weight tolerance of ¾ pound on individual bellies is permitted but the number of bellies more than ¾ pound over or under the weight range may not exceed 7 per sample lot.

Variations in quantity of a delivery unit not in excess of 5% of 38,000 pounds shall be permitted at time of delivery. An allowance for shrinkage of ¼ of 1% of the certified received weights must be deducted on the tender notice but this allowance shall not disqualify a unit for delivery because of minimum weight requirements. Payments shall be made on the basis of the certified weights as indicated on the warehouse receipt less the allowance for shrinkage.

Source: Chicago Mercantile Exchange.

FIGURE 7-2 (continued)

PRODUCT SAMPLING, EXAMINATION AND CHECKING FOR CONFORMANCE — The examination shall be performed by the USDA Meat Grading Division. The bellies may be examined fresh in-plant, fresh or fresh freezer accumulation when stored, or at any time in storage. Fresh freezer accumulation (FFA); Shall mean bellies which may be fresh, partly frozen, or solidly frozen, which have been accumulating for a period not exceeding 15 days, and shall be bright in appearance, reasonably free from dehydration causing woody texture and show no indication of spoilage, discoloration or rancidity. The delivery unit must be suitably identified by lot number in a manner satisfactory to the USDA Meat Graders.

If at any time in the examination of the lot (fresh or frozen) there is any indication of contamination caused by harmful materials (including ammonia, brine, dirt, chemicals, filth, rodents, etc.), or if the bellies show evidence of being rancid, slimy, sour or off-condition, the entire lot will be considered ineligible for delivery on the contract and will be rejected without further examination.

If on preliminary examination the entire lot appears to be in good condition, the USDA Meat Grader will select a random sample of 50 bellies which will be examined. If frozen, the bellies must be defrosted. The defrosting must be done in a room having a temperature that does not exceed 60 degrees F. and the bellies must be defrosted to the extent that the specification requirements are visually determinable. The bellies must not be defrosted by submerging in hot water or brine.

An examination of the sample (fresh or defrosted) will be made to determine the number of major or minor defects present. These are listed in the Schedule of Defects and defined as follows:

a. Major Defect — A major defect is a condition of the belly which makes its use for good quality slab or sliced bacon possible only after excessive trim.

b. Minor Defect — A minor defect is a condition of the belly which makes its use for good quality slab or sliced bacon possible only after slight trimming.

Acceptance or rejection of the lot will be based on the number of minor defect equivalents in the bellies in the sample. For the purposes of determining the number of minor defect equivalents, each major defect will be considered to be the equivalent of four minor defects. No more than four minor defects shall be counted against any one belly of the sample.

If upon two consecutive inspections the bellies fail to meet exchange requirements for delivery, the lot shall not be eligible for delivery on exchange contracts at any time thereafter. No more than one reinspection of any lot shall be permitted. Bellies submitted for inspection failing to make weight range specified because of being too light or too heavy do not automatically become eligible for delivery in another category without a reinspection.

PRODUCT SAMPLING, EXAMINATION AND CHECKING FOR CONFORMANCE FOR INPLANT INSPECTION OF PORK BELLIES — In addition to the procedures and requirements of basic rules and regulations pertaining to delivery, inspections, etc., the following shall specifically apply to inplant inspections of pork bellies:

a. Each day's cut shall be kept separate and dated.

b. Contract units shall be presented in combo bins with polyliner such that the integrity of the unit can be maintained. Following examination each combo unit shall be stamped by the grader with the USDA shield identification stamp. The USDA Meat Grader will supervise the sealing of each combo unit and record seal numbers on the USDA certificate. *INTERPRETATION - Only those combo bins in the contract units which have passed examination by the USDA Meat Grader will be stamped with the USDA shield and sealed.*

c. The approved plant shall be responsible for the refrigerated transportation of the product, to and acceptance by an Exchange approved warehouse within a 24 hour period following inspection.

d. The warehouse shall be responsible for checking to see that the seal numbers on the combo units correspond with those on the graders report. Following acceptance of the contract unit by the C.M.E. warehouse, and following weighing of the unit by the warehouse weighmaster, seal the warehouse shall immediately notify the C.M.E. Inspection Department as to weight, seal number, U.S.D.A. certificate number, and warehouse lot number.

e. For inplant inspections, U.S.D.A. Meat Graders shall record seal numbers of the combo units on the inspection certificate and forward them to the warehouse with the truck. The U.S.D.A. Meat Graders shall telephone their results to the C.M.E. on the day the inspection is completed if during business hours, if not, results shall be telephoned to the Exchange by 10:00 A.M. the following morning.

EXCHANGE CERTIFICATE — An Official Exchange Certificate for frozen pork bellies based on an examination made on or after November 1 of any year shall remain in force until 5:00 o'clock p.m. on the first business day of the following September, provided the bellies have remained in the same warehouse and have been kept under proper refrigeration. Exchange Certificates must be in good standing up to 5:00 o'clock p.m. on the business day following the day of delivery.

COSTS OF INSPECTION, WEIGHING, STORAGE, ETC. — On all deliveries made on the futures call, the seller must assume storage charges up to 5:00 o'clock p.m. on the second business day after the date of delivery. The proration shall be on the basis of 1/30th of the prevailing monthly storage rate at the particular warehouse raised to the nearest five cents and multiplied by the number of days remaining to the next expiration date (all months figured on the basis of 30 days). In no case shall handling charges be included in such proration. The storage charges shall be paid in advance by the person holding the product on storage expiration date and pro rata charges prepaid by such holder shall be added to and shown on the tender notice.

The costs of USDA Meat Grading Service and all other charges throughout all phases of the sampling procedure and examination must be paid by the seller; these costs shall include Exchange documentation and related services such as defrosting (if frozen), examination, refreezing and reglazing or rewrapping promptly after examination.

TRADING HOURS: 9:10 a.m. to 1:00 p.m.

CLOSING RANGE: 30 SECONDS — The closing range for all Commodities shall be confined to the final 30 seconds of trading.

Exception: On the last day of an expiring contract the closing range shall be confined to the final 90 seconds of trading.

GENERAL INTERPRETATION - Wherever the words Stock yard(s), Mill(s), Store(s), Warehouse(s), or Plant(s) appear within these Rules regarding the delivery of Exchange contracts, they are understood to be approved.

SCHEDULE OF DEFECTS

Examination for	Major Defects	Minor Defects
1. Conformation	Belly more than 14 inches wide at widest point in a 12/14 pound delivery unit measured on the skin side.	Belly more than 13 inches but not more than 14 inches wide at widest point in a 12/14 pound delivery unit, measured on skin side.
	Belly more than 15 inches wide at widest point in a 14/16 pound delivery unit measured on the skin side.	Belly more than 14 inches but not more than 15 inches wide at widest point in a 14/16 pound delivery unit, measured on skin side.
	Belly more than 16 inches wide at widest point in a 16/18 pound delivery unit measured on the skin side.	Belly more than 15 inches but not more than 16 inches wide at widest point in a 16/18 pound delivery unit, measured on skin side.
	Skippy belly.	Cut from fat back more than 2 inches beyond outermost point of scribe line measured on the face side within 2 inches on either side of exact center (determined on skin side) of the belly.
		Belly less than 6/10 inch thick at thinnest point except for a 3 inch square on the fat back side at the ham end.
		Belly less than 8 inches wide at narrowest point measured on the skin side.
		Belly more than 2-4/10 inches thick at thickest point in a 12/14 pound delivery unit.
		Belly more than 2-7/10 inches thick at thickest point in a 14/16 or 16/18 pound delivery unit.
2. Quality	Oily or extremely soft fat. Dark. coarse lean.	Rough, thick, or coarse skin.

wheat traded on the Chicago Board of Trade is a binding contract committing the seller to deliver 5,000 bushels of No. 2 soft red wheat at certain designated warehouses during the specified month, in this case March. No. 2 northern spring wheat, on the other hand, is traded at the Minneapolis exchange with delivery

FIGURE 7–3

MiniContracts open new trading opportunities in popular commodities.

If you're interested in trading commodities, chances are there's a MiniContract that fits your needs. There are MiniContracts available in commonly traded grains, metals, and livestock.

Building on a base of successful grain contracts, in 1968 MidAmerica became the first midwestern exchange to trade silver; in 1972, the first to trade U.S. silver coins. In 1974, the Exchange became the first in the country to offer gold futures. The same year, a 15,000 pound live hog contract was introduced. And more MiniContracts are under study.

Similar to other contracts, only one-fifth to one-half the size.

In grains, MidAmerica offers convenient 1,000 bushel contracts in corn, soybeans, and wheat. There's also a 5,000 bushel contract in oats.

In livestock there's a 15,000 lb. live hog contract (about 70 head), and a 20,000 lb. cattle contract (about 20 head). These are one-half the size of similar contracts traded elsewhere.

In metals, MidAmerica offers a 33.2 troy ounce gold contract; a 1,000 troy ounce silver contract; and a $5,000 face-value silver coin contract.

MiniContracts have the same delivery months and similar specifications as large-size contracts traded on other exchanges. For example, the corn contract calls for no. 2 yellow corn with the delivery months of December, March, May, July, and September. The maximum daily advance or decline in price is 10 cents. These similarities mean that MiniContracts trade at prices in line with those of large-size contracts at other exchanges.

Compare MiniContracts to the large-size   contracts traded on other exchanges.

1,000 bu. soybean contract instead of 5,000 bu.

1,000 bu. corn contract instead of 5,000 bu.

15,000 lb. live hog contract instead of 30,000 lb.

20,000 lb. live cattle contract instead of 40,000 lb.

1,000 bu. wheat contract instead of 5,000 bu.

5,000 bu. oats contract (same as other exchanges)

1,000 troy oz. silver contract instead of 5,000 troy oz.

33.2 troy oz. gold contract instead of 100 troy oz.

Source: MidAmerica Commodity Exchange.

FIGURE 7-4

CONTRACT DESCRIPTION

ELEMENTS OF THE CONTRACT

Class of Wheat

Northern Spring Wheat of United States origin

Contract Grade

No. 2 Northern Spring Wheat as described by the Official Grain Standards of the United States and with a protein content of 13.5% or higher

Trading Unit

Futures Contracts are traded in "round" lots of 5,000 bushel multiples or "job" lots of 1,000 bushel multiples.

Contract Months

Spring Wheat Futures are traded throughout the year. The five contracts currently used provide for delivery in September, December, March, May, and July.

Final Day of Trading

Maturing Futures Contracts may not be traded during the last seven business days of the delivery month.

Delivery Points

The delivery points for Minneapolis Wheat Futures are elevators located in Minneapolis/St. Paul, and Duluth/Superior. Elevators that meet the necessary qualifications are designated as Delivery Elevators by the Minneapolis Grain Exchange.

Price Quotations and Fluctuations

Prices are quoted in dollars and cents, with fractions of eighths of a cent per bushel. A price change of 1/8¢ is $6.25 for a round lot of 5,000 bushels.

Prices in a single day's trading are prohibited from advancing or declining more than 20 cents from the previous day's close, so a 40-cent trading range is the maximum permitted on any given day.

SETTLEMENT OF CONTRACTS

Off-setting Contracts

Most Futures Contracts are settled by offsetting purchases or sales of the same futures.

The trader who **buys** wheat futures (assuming a long position) may settle his contract by selling an equal amount before the maturing contract month.

The trader who **sells** (assuming a short position) may liquidate his contract with a purchase of an equal number of bushels any time before the contract matures.

Delivery

Futures Contracts may be settled by delivery. During a trading session in the maturing month the seller may serve notice to the Minneapolis Grain Clearing Corporation of intention to deliver. The Clearing Corporation notifies the buyer (long) holding the longest standing contract in the maturing month that a delivery has been tendered. The long must take the delivery intentions to the office of the seller (short) by 1:00 p.m. the next day. Here payment is made with a certified check and the buyer (long) receives warehouse receipts. Delivery may be made, at the option of the seller, any business day in the maturing month.

The buyer may retender the delivery notice. If the buyer receives a notice during a session, on or before the final day of trading of the contract, he may sell the future and retender the same notice to the Clearing House before 12:00 noon the same business day. In other instances the notice is not retenderable. A buyer who holds a warehouse receipt assumes the responsibility of ownership and attendant charges for storage and insurance.

While No. 2NS is the contract grade, No. 1 is deliverable. Also, wheat with 13% protein is deliverable (at a discount).

Source: Minneapolis Grain Exchange.

points in Minnesota. (See Figure 7–4.) February pork bellies is another way of saying 38,000 pounds of uncured bacon of deliverable grade delivered in Chicago in February. June Ginnie Maes are Government National Mortgage certificates with a principal balance of $100,000 and a stated interest rate of 8 percent, deliverable in June. For delivery purposes, certificates for other interest rates may be substituted in an amount equivalent to

$100,000 of Ginnie Mae 8's when calculated at par and under the assumptions of a 30-year certificate prepaid in the twelfth year. (See Figure 7–5.)

The contract life will usually be between twelve and eighteen months. If a contract is held into the terminal month, it may be fulfilled by acceptance of delivery at the seller's discretion or by a cash settlement. Notices of delivery by sellers are required ahead of time, with notice

FIGURE 7–5

Summaries of the Contracts in Table Form

Long-Term U. S. Treasury Bond Futures Summarized

Grades deliverable
Long-term U.S. Treasury bonds not callable for at least 15 years if callable, or, if not callable, with a maturity of at least 15 years. All bonds delivered against a contract must be of the same issue. Deliverers at their option may deliver U.S. Treasury bonds with a face value of $100,000 and stated interest rates of other than 8%, provided that, on settlement, a discount is deducted from the face value of bonds with lower than 8% interest rates and a premium is paid to the bearer of bonds with higher than 8% interest rates.

Trading unit
U.S. Treasury bonds with a stated face value at maturity of $100,000 and an interest rate of 8%.

Price quotations
Price shall be basis delivered Chicago, Illinois, by book-entry system, payment in Federal Funds.

Minimum fluctuations
Minimum price fluctuations shall be 1/32 point per 100 points ($31.25 per contract).

Normal daily limits on price movement
24/32 of a point ($750 per contract) above and below the previous day's settlement price.

Delivery system
Further information available on request.

Commissions
Consult your broker.

Margins
Consult your broker.

Ticker symbol
US

Source: Chicago Board of Trade.

GNMA Mortgage Interest Rate Futures Summarized

Grades deliverable
Mortgage-backed certificates guaranteed for the timely payment of principal and interest by the Government National Mortgage Association (Ginnie Maes) as described in the standard prospectus form HUD 1717, commonly known as modified pass-through certificates and bearing a stated interest rate of 8%. Deliverers at their option may deliver Ginnie Maes with stated interest rates other than 8%, provided that the Ginnie Maes delivered bear the same yield as the 8% Ginnie Mae when calculated at par and under the assumptions of a 30-year mortgage prepaid in the 12th year.

Trading unit
Ginnie Mae with $100,000 principal balance and stated interest rate of 8%.

Price quotations
Price shall be basis delivered Chicago, Illinois.

Minimum fluctuations
Minimum price fluctuations shall be 1/32 point per 100 points ($31.25 per contract).

Normal daily limits on price movement
25/100 of 1% of $1,000,000 on a 90-day basis ($625 per contract) above and below the previous day's settlement price.

Delivery system
Further information available on request.

Commissions
Consult your broker.

Margins
Consult your broker.

Ticker symbol
M

days varying from contract to contract. Alternatives for the seller provided in the contract allow for delivery of the commodity with specified deviations from the par specifications. A scale of premiums and discounts regulates the value of contracts delivered above or below standard. Variations can include weight, grade, and location. Although the contract may be effectively bought and controlled by a nonmember trader, it is the member broker who is responsible for the execution of the contract as written, and whose name appears upon it. If not a member of the exchange's clearinghouse, the broker must have a clearing member finalize the trade.

By limiting the delivery points to one area and the delivery months to less than twelve per year, the volume of business (hence liquidity) increases and a more efficient market is formed. If all wheat buyers and sellers are willing to choose from the limited months offered on the futures market and are willing to trade a single grade of cash and single delivery area, the market serves each of them more reliably and effectively. In a large volume market made possible by a well-written and attractive contract, market orders to buy or sell of nearly any size can be filled with little or no price concession. A farmer may find it difficult to sell one million pounds of potatoes for delivery in October in New Jersey without offering a price considerably below the market, but he can fairly easily sell twenty contracts (at 50,000 pounds per contract) of Maine potatoes on the New York Mercantile Exchange for November delivery.

The farmer may have no intention of holding his potatoes until November nor of delivering them in New York. The potatoes sold on the futures exchange may not even be the same grade that he will harvest in the fall. But as the price of potatoes on the futures exchange goes up or down, the price of potatoes at the farmer's local spot market should follow. As the price of potatoes goes up, the price of all potatoes at all delivery positions should follow fairly closely. The hedging functions of the futures market require this commensurability of contracts and this close linkage of cash and futures prices. If the specifications of an offered contract do not allow for good hedging opportunities, the contract will likely fail. It may become necessary to revise contracts periodically to meet unforeseen changes in market conditions or to improve a contracts' hedging or speculative viability. Once trading has begun, however, a contract may not be altered during its lifetime.

PRICING

The value of a futures contract falls and rises according to supply, demand, and market pressures. The value of the contract changes with the spot price of the actual commodity and with the traders' anticipations of what future cash prices will be. The complexity of futures price influences and cash/futures relations have their own chapters further on. Here it is enough to note that an orderly price structure, entailing sales of cash and futures by traders in many locations, is an absolute necessity. The prevailing futures price on the exchange serves as a touchstone or guideline price for contracts made elsewhere. Although the vast majority of agricultural sales are made by way of cash forward contracts rather than futures contracts, evidence is that futures prices serve as the reference point for these transactions. Though farmers may not be hedging in large numbers (yet), 30 percent of those surveyed by the CFTC kept track of futures prices, 37 percent were familiar with "local" or "country" basis, and 42 percent of those with sales over $100,000 followed futures trends.

Country basis acts, then, as a principal agent in relating cash and futures prices to assure all a fair price. For each major producing locality a country basis will exist, giving the price differential between that location and the futures exchange, reflecting handling, shipping, storage, and other costs. The futures price acts as a universal price, and local prices are established as premiums or discounts from the futures price according to the amount of the basis. Cash wheat may be selling for $4.50 in Chicago and $4.10 in Iowa City. The Iowa City figure is not readily available, but the Chicago cash price is quoted daily in many newspapers. The cash buyer in Iowa City needs only to know that wheat on his cash market brings 40 cents less than it does in Chicago. The farmer twenty miles outside of Iowa City needs only to know that wheat on his farm is worth 3 cents less than wheat in Iowa City. By finding the cash Chicago quotation in the newspaper he can subtract 43 cents and have a pretty close estimate of the price he can expect to receive for his crop.

Commodity merchants keep a book of "country basis" charts from which to figure the offering price to make for commodities in each place in the country where they do business. Often a purchase agreement will simply specify so many bushels or pounds of goods at "Chicago less 43 cents." The farmer and the merchandiser understand that the contract calls for the farmer to receive that day's closing cash quote from Chicago less the country basis. It is quite possible that neither will know the exact price until the next day.

Country basis is of little direct importance to the speculator but is of great importance to the farmer. Government price support programs state a support price for a commodity at a specific locality. Country basis is then subtracted from the support price, reflecting the lower value of the goods in different parts of the country. Were this not the case, a support price of, say, $4.00 per bushel for wheat might find no takers in Illinois and buy literally all the wheat produced in Whatcom County, North Dakota. Through the use of country basis, support prices and selling prices are applied evenly across the nation. Country basis remains relatively constant. For this reason the farmer or processor can hedge on the Chicago futures market even though he has no intention of delivering or accepting delivery from Chicago as specified in the contract he has entered on the futures market. As the price at the futures exchange varies, so will the country basis. Although industry hedgers often make up as much as 80 percent of trading volume on the futures exchanges, fewer than 2 percent of the contracts made for future delivery are filled by actual produce. The rest are closed out (by opposite order) as the actual goods are sold on the country markets at country prices. Delivery remains a possibility, however, as country basis is equal to the cost of getting goods to the market. Any cash dealer could buy the goods in the country and deliver them in Chicago

FIGURE 7–6

READING A BASIS CHART
If the basis chart in an area looks like this—what does it mean?

Soybean Basis { Chicago Nov., Mar., Jly. Future
               { Iowa Track Price

Oct. 1960 — July 1961

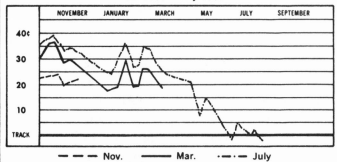

— — — Nov.   ——— Mar.   ·—·— July

For a Farmer it means:
1. Beginning in December, he can look at the November future 11 months ahead, subtract an approximate 20 to 25¢ November basis, and have an estimate of the harvest value of soybeans. He can then:

   a. Decide how many acres to plant

   b. Sell them now — or any time up to harvest — if the futures price looks good to him. If basis holds true, his local price equivalent, figured with the result of the futures transaction, should return about the target price.
   In March, the November future is 276. Basis is 20 to 25¢. He likes the price and sells the future, planning to net 251 to 256 on the beans in November.
   In November, the future is selling at 268. He buys it back 8¢ cheaper than he sold it for, and gains a gross of 8¢. The cash price in his area is 22¢ under the future, or 246, and he sells the grain for 246, adds the 8¢ to make 254. It is in the target price range.

2. All through the growing season a farmer can use basis to check cash price offers—or he can actually sell the crop. Or he might determine that it would pay to carry the crop into the new year.

Supposing he had already sold the November future to lock in an attractive harvest price, but sometime before harvest had a chance to move the hedge to July, eliminating the wide harvest basis and adding about a 13 cent carrying charge. Using the figures of the previous example where he sold the November for 276, aiming for a target price in the 251 to 256 area—he would be looking for about 289 in June (The 276 futures price plus 13 cents carrying charge.) His arithmetic would look like this:

March 15, 1968—Sell November future @ 276 } +6¢
September 25, 1968 { Buy back November contract—270
                   { Sell July at 13¢ over Nov.—283 } +6¢
June 13, 1969—Buy in July future—277
June 13, 1969—Sell cash, same price as July—277

He was aiming at a target price of about 289. Results showed:

Cash price	277
Futures gain	6
Futures gain	6
Gross receipts	289

The example showed this man to be the victim of falling prices if he had not hedged. As it is, he bought the November futures in at lower than the sale price, and the same happened with the July. The gain here, plus his cash price, helped him realize his target price.

He would have achieved the same results had prices gone up, realizing more for his cash sale, but having to subtract losses in the futures market from that. It generally is not good practice to place a hedge, lift it, place it again, lift it, and so on to try to adjust to changing price levels. However, in the event of a genuinely bull market for the cash commodity, a futures position can be readily liquidated.

In short, it is recommended that those who would use the market in their business become thoroughly acquainted with it, then use it as a part of the business when it will help to make or save money.

It's possible to swap a cash speculation for futures speculation by selling cash grain at harvest and buying a futures contract, hoping the price will go up.

Grain has storage charges—live animals do not, otherwise the basis principles and market use are the same for commodities other than grain.

Source: Chicago Board of Trade.

for a price high enough to cover his costs. This, is fact, enforces the country basis. (See Figure 7–6.)

PREMIUMS AND DISCOUNTS

The number of people who can efficiently use the futures market for hedging is increased (again increasing liquidity) by the specifications in the contract. Through specifying in the contract the various grades (other than the standard) that are deliverable, and by establishing for them set premiums and set discounts, producers and buyers have considerable flexibility in their use of futures trading. One need not be a farmer of No. 2 yellow corn (or an exporter of it) to find the Chicago Board of Trade's contract in No. 2 a good hedge or even a good deliverable contract.

Per contract specifications, No. 1 yellow may be delivered at a 3 cent premium to the price quoted for the contract grade. The contract similarly makes provision for the delivery of No. 3 yellow at a set discount. The Chicago Mercantile Exchange's live hog contract calls for par delivery at Peoria, Illinois. Deliveries from approved livestock yards at Omaha, Nebraska, East St. Louis, Sioux City, and St. Paul are deliverable at an allowance of 25 cents per hundred weight. (See Figure 7–2.)

It might be possible to have separate markets for each of the various grades of a commodity, such as corn, or for each of the delivery locations, such as for live hogs. As long as the value of the different grades or different deliveries remains in a fixed relationship, one central market will do, saving everyone a lot of time and trouble. By trading only one grade and allowing delivery of other grades at set premiums and discounts, one market gives a quotation that can be used by all the farmers and processors of that commodity. The central organization of trade in the exchange also makes it easier for speculators, the necessary partners to the hedger's game, to find large and profitable markets.

If the contract is to serve the largest possible audience, it must be set up so that the country basis and the various grade premiums and discounts remain constant. A farmer who will bring in a crop of No. 1 red wheat cannot hedge his crop by selling contracts of No. 2 red wheat in Chicago unless he is confident that the price differential between the two grades and localities will probably remain the same. As long as the contract works properly and the relations between the grades hold steady, he can hedge in Chi-

cago and remove or reduce the risk of a price drop when harvest comes.

CONTRACTS CURRENTLY TRADED

Commodities currently traded on futures exchanges fall into six major categories according to physical type. Classification by substance, always a bit arbitrary, may reveal relations masked by classification according to exchange, volume, or trading characteristics. The purpose of such classifications, in addition to their educational value, lies in the intercommodity relations and trading patterns these groupings can afford. Many traders prefer to deal only in one type of commodity or even in a single subgroup consisting of three or four related contracts. It is important to recognize that certain groups of contracts move together, or in ways tied to one another, and that these movements have their explanation in the physical origins of the commodities. When the price of a particular feed grain passes that of others, buyers will switch, setting off a new market trend. When the price of gold starts to skyrocket or tumble, the best bet is that silver and platinum are not far behind.

Grains. Included here are barley, corn, sorghum, flaxseed, rapeseed, oats, rye, wheat, and soybeans (soybeans are technically a legume, but can be considered a grain for trading purposes). Soybean meal and soybean oil each have their own contract but are often listed and discussed as members of the "soybean complex." Meal and oil, by the way, are among the few semiprocessed products for which futures markets exist. The "grains" category includes the most important commodities in our agricultural industry at the earliest point in their production. They were the first to be widely traded and continue to be volume leaders. Most of these commodities can be used as animal feed. Price changes for these basics will thus be reflected up the agricultural and livestock line all the way to the supermarket shelf.

Animal products. Successful animal product contracts really began with the live hog and cattle contracts at the end of the 1960s. These, together with pork bellies, are by far the most popular contracts in this category. Iced broilers have commanded modest interest, with trade shifting from the initially unsatisfying CBT contract to the more acceptable CME contract. Historically important, contracts in egg futures continued to decline toward extinction during the 1970s. Others in this group are hams, hides, butter, cheese, frozen turkeys, and wool. None of these has traded substantially in recent years.

Metals. The opening of trade in silver and gold helped revolutionize the futures business. They have since become international political barometers, creating unique and treacherous trading opportunities. The popularity of these two traditionally glamorous precious metals as vehicles for speculation and wealth storage has spilled over into the markets for other metals, notably copper and platinum. Defunct or nearly dormant, however, are futures contracts in lead, mercury, palladium, nickel, aluminum, tin, and zinc, trading only a handful to a few hundred contracts a year. Such very thin markets are of little value to the hedger who cannot find the buyer or seller he needs and have little attraction to the speculator who must be able to control his position with a phone call. Volume

is the Catch-22 of commodities trading. Those markets which have a lot of volume serve their customers well and get a lot of volume. (A lively trade in many metals is conducted at the London Metals Exchange.)

Plant products. Grouped here are such items as cocoa, coffee, cotton, orange juice concentrate, Maine potatoes, Russet Burbank potatoes, sugar, plywood, and lumber. Some of these markets have been quite lively in the past (coffee and sugar) while others promise to play increasingly interesting roles in the years to come (plywood and lumber). Inactive or tepidly traded are rubber, apples, and tomato paste.

Financials. This newest category of futures contracts can itself be subdivided. One group is comprised by the interest rate futures contracts for delivery of set amounts of interest bearing items like Treasury Bills, Notes, and Bonds, commercial paper, and Ginnie Maes. A second group is made up by the foreign currencies: British pounds, Canadian dollars, Mexican pesos, German marks, French francs, Japanese yens, and Swiss francs.

Energy futures. A possible candidate for great expansion, energy futures today are represented in the market places by just three modest pioneers: No. 6 industrial fuel oil, propane, and No. 2 heating oil. Only the latter had significant open interest going into the 1980s.

NEW CONTRACTS

New contracts will come into existence as the needs of industry change, as the business community becomes more sophisticated in its marketing practices, and as the advantages of present futures markets become more widely known. Some offerings will fail to attract enough interest to get off the ground. Open interest is self-feeding, high volume makes the market function well, and a well-functioning market attracts heavy use. If the need is great enough and if price fluctuation and delivery conditions are right, a new contract just may flourish. Still, many fall flat. Frozen shrimp, short ribs, and lard were all traded at one time in Chicago, but now only lard barely remains, as refrigeration has allowed shrimp and ribs to be kept long enough to vary supply into varying demand. With the ability to hold stocks, the need to hedge died out and the markets collapsed. New York and St. Louis had important wheat futures markets at one time, but their business declined as changes in the wheat trade and improved communications reduced the special advantages of hedging those markets rather than Chicago's, where the great volume lowers the hedging cost. Even among the much celebrated financial futures, a number of offerings stubbornly refused to gather much open interest or volume.

The introduction of new contracts is vital to the continuing success and effectiveness of the futures trade. It is now familiar history how contracts in live animals, soybeans, gold, and T-Bills captured the imagination (and financial backing) of industry leaders and professional speculators during the commodities boom. Dozens of contracts were developed, proposed, or opened during the renaissance years after 1967. Of the top ten volume leaders in 1978, five (silver, gold, live cattle, live hogs, and pork bellies) had been trading for only a decade or less. In 1979 gold leaped past soybeans to become the commodity volume champion with 10.3 million contracts (all exchanges). Copper, at 2.3 million, and U.S. Treasury Bonds,

at 2.1 million, displaced live hogs and pork bellies from the top ten listing. (See Figure 7–7.) Ranked in terms of the dollar value of contracts traded, Treasury Bills were at the top. The estimated value of T-Bills traded in 1979 was 2.2 trillion dollars or about four times the United States federal budget.

The astounding pace at which new contracts have entered the markets slowed as government regulators began to flex their muscles. The CFTC must approve

FIGURE 7–7

Still growing

The nation's futures industry projects 1980 contract volume will surpass 1979's record-breaking price, despite problems in the silver markets and the embargo on U.S. grain exports to the Soviet Union.

Sources at the exchanges and brokerage houses note that in each year since the growth trend began in 1970, the markets experienced situations which threatened contract volume. Still, the industry grew by leaps and bounds.

Most industry leaders point to financial futures as leading the market this year and in the 1980s. Financial futures volume in 1979 scored the largest percentage gain among commodity groups, 101% over 1978. Metals followed with a 33% gain, livestock and meat 22.5%, and grains and feeds 20.3%.

These commodity groups collectively boosted total industry volume to 74.1 million contracts in 1979 from 56.8 million a year earlier, or a 30% gain. The ten most active contracts last year were: Gold, 10.3 million contracts; soybeans, 9.3 million; corn, 8.7 million; live cattle, 7.3 million; silver, 6.9 million; wheat, 5.0 million; soybean oil, 3.2 million; soybean meal, 2.6 million; copper, 2.3 million, and U.S. Treasury bonds, 2.1 million.

Active commodities posting the largest declines from 1978 included plywood, down from 261,000 contracts to 147,000 contracts, and iced broilers, from 75,000 contracts to 33,000.

Source: Commodities Magazine.

all new contracts for future trading in a process called "contract market designation." Hearings must be held on the effects of the contract, the sectors it will serve, the nature of the commodity itself, etc. Decisions concerning proposed rival contracts are understandably controversial. Charged with the mission of protecting the public at the same time as it encourages the growth of the futures industry, the Commission may designate a board of trade a "contract market" for a new commodity only when certain conditions and requirements are met. It rests with the exchange making the proposal to demonstrate "that transactions for future delivery in the commodity for which designation as a contract market is sought will not be contrary to the public interest." The economics of developing a sound new contract and the politics of securing its approval will undoubtedly remain instrumental factors in the efforts of the futures industry to maintain its momentum and prosperity.

There is theoretically no limit to the number or kind of commodity contracts that may evolve in the decades ahead. Currently being hotly debated are a number of proposed futures contracts based on stock price indexes. Such contracts are aimed at equity portfolio managers and other possible new constituencies. Stock index proposals have run into a storm of criticism and a maze of government officials. Some question whether the contract is, in fact, based on a commodity in the traditional sense. To many it appears mere gambling on stock prices, while to others it represents a bold, creative step into new dimensions. These and other financial futures have caused jurisdictional squabbles between the CFTC, the SEC, and the Federal Reserve Board, all of whom find grounds for claiming regulatory authority over a contract concerning securities. Other contracts imagined or contemplated include shipping rates, freight rates, warehouse rental rates, coal gas, boxed beef, and securities portfolios.

Chapter 8 ⎯⎯⎯⎯⎯⎯⎯⎯⎯⎯⎯⎯⎯⎯⎯⎯⎯⎯⎯⎯⎯⎯⎯

BROKERS AND ACCOUNTS

SELECTING A BROKER

Choose your broker carefully. In an ideal world, all traders would have the knowledge and time to make their own buy and sell decisions and the facilities to send them directly to the pit. In practice, a host of intermediaries stands between the trader and the trade, ready to furnish data, give advice, process and execute trades, and keep account records accurately up to date. The great majority of brokers do their work honestly and sincerely, working hard in the genuine interest of the client's welfare. Unfortunately, the nature of the brokerage business encourages the unscrupulous few. Almost all brokerage houses are run on a commission basis. For every trade made, a fee is paid, regardless of the trade's financial profit or loss. This drives a wedge between the interest of the broker and that of the client. The broker's profit is in the quantity of trades; the client's profit is in the quality of trades.

The most common exploitation of this system is "churning," the purpose and systematic overtrading of an account by a broker purely for the accumulation of fees. Churning accusations may be hard to substantiate, for the record of a churned account can look exactly like that of an account traded with the best interests of the client in mind, or according to a speculator's own instructions. Nowhere does a trading order reveal intention. The preponderance of scandals and abuses reported in the commodities world involve the hoodwinking of naïve clients by fast talking brokers. It is wise to recall that the individual handling your account, except in those few circumstances when you might deal with a firm's top officers, is in reality a salesperson. He or she might know a great deal, or absolutely nothing, about the product being promoted. Proposals to put account executives on a salary basis have as yet gone nowhere. Brokerage firm officers, however, are salaried—and handsomely so. By 1980 65 percent of brokerage industry presidents were earning six figure incomes, no matter company size. Executive vice-presidents were in the $70,000 plus bracket, with most other officers making $40,000 or more.

These cautionary remarks are not meant as a broad indictment of the whole brokerage industry but as a warning to the prospective trader whose innocent attitudes are what make most brokerage

97

abuses possible. If your broker is to do anything more than execute your orders, then you had better get to know this new business partner well. There's no excuse for hiring an incompetent or dishonest person to perform the services so absolutely basic to the successful outcome of an investment.

There are thousands of brokerage offices and branches around the country hoping to cash in on the commodities boom. The number of account executives doubled from 1976 to 1977. Behind this explosive growth was the deregulation of futures trading commissions which took effect in 1978. Previously, commissions had been set by the exchanges, who granted discounts to their members. Brokers had an incentive to join, which kept them under the regulatory eye of the exchanges, surveillance units. Deregulation, while it opened up the business and lessened the cost for the speculator, also meant a leap in the number of nonmember brokers (they must still process trades through a member firm, but the relationship usually stops there). Since that time broker regulation has become more and more a CFTC headache, and the agency encounters a disproportionately large number of complaints about nonmembers. Stricter enforcement of broker transaction requirements and procedural safeguards could counter this trend in the future. The CFTC now licenses brokers and registers all those who act as Futures Commission Merchants. Never do business with unlicensed or unregistered agents. (See Figure 8–1.)

Most of the largest stock brokerage firms handle commodities, so the transition for the stock trader will be a simple one. Many big names in stock brokerage have become big names in commodities

FIGURE 8–1

Required To Register With CFTC*

Basically, anyone dealing in or advising about commodity futures or commodity options is required to register with the Commodity Futures Trading Commission. Registration categories reflect different functions of individuals who provide professional services at different levels in the futures industry, including:

• Futures Commission Merchants—Firms or individuals engaged in soliciting or accepting orders for the purchase or sale of any commodity for future delivery on commodity exchanges.

• Associated Persons—Generally speaking, persons working as account executives for futures commission merchants. Those who deal with customers on their orders in the offices of futures commission merchants, including registered representatives.

• Floor Brokers—Any person who may or may not be associated with a futures commission merchant, but does execute orders for others, himself, or the futures commission merchant's house account.

• Commodity Pool Operators—Individuals or companies who invest, on behalf of a group of people, a pool of money in commodities.

• Commodity Trading Advisors—Individuals who offer advice about the purchase or sale of commodities, but do not actually trade accounts.

*The above general descriptions of types of activities are not statutory definitions. The statutory definition as well as the registration requirements pertaining thereto are found in the Commodity Exchange Act and the rules and regulations thereunder.

Source: Commodity Futures Trading Commission.

brokerage. A large office will employ agents specializing in commodities, some who may only handle soybeans, or gold, or interest rate futures. Trained account executives servicing large hedgers in commodities are featured by many of these firms. Many employ renowned commodities experts to advise account executives and client traders. Most publish market newsletters and a variety of detailed reports on individual commodities. Each branch office is tied into a national information and ordering network designed to provide minute-by-minute monitoring of pit transactions and news events. If convenience is a factor, the trader may be attracted to these firms, which have departments handling the full range of investment opportunities and financial merchandise.

A second option is the speciality firm that deals only in commodities. Often lesser known than the above mixed "wire houses," commodity brokerages can offer less hectic atmospheres and an enterprise undistracted by other markets and investments. Whether to choose a brokerage which handles only commodities or one which handles both commodities and stocks depends on the needs and desires of the trader. A big firm will have established machinery to deal with complaints, should any arise, and the financial security to guarantee its transactions. The money in public accounts cannot be mixed with company funds in commodities, but should a brokerage firm go under your margin account could be tied up for some time.

If you like personal service, and the opportunity to develop your own relationship with your broker, a smaller firm will often be more congenial and less set in its ways. The speed at which your order

is processed, often a key factor in profits, may be greater at a small office doing less business. If a wire operator, the unseen person who sends out the order, has several orders ahead of yours, costly delays can ensue. In a fast moving game like commodities, a few minutes toward the end of a contract life can be significant. If your brokerage handles both stocks and commodities, ask which receives priority when going out over the wire.

A third option is the discount broker. These firms meet the needs of sophisticated traders or speculators with independent advisors who do not want advice from their brokers. The bare bones discount house will simply take your order and fill it as fast as possible, often at a commission rate apporaching only 50 percent of that charged by standard houses. To those trading frequently, the savings are substantial. Discount house agents work on salary, so their goals are accurate fills and fast confirmation. The trader will still require some basic account services and should be sure that discount brokers don't mean discount services. Check to see if the discount applies regardless of volume. Are there hidden costs? Compare minimum starting deposit requirements. Make sure everything is in writing and in compliance with CFTC standards. Ask for public financial statements, audits, and bank references. Know what your recourse is if a trade is improperly executed. The firm should alert you to fundamental trade rule changes promptly, including delivery month notices, margin requirements, contract specifications, and limits on fluctuations. Whether dealing with a discount house, a commodities brokerage, or a full service investment firm, know precisely the kinds of services and information you want and make sure you are getting them. And as your order is what makes the trade, have a long talk with your firm to establish the nature and exact wording of orders that can be placed.

On request, exchanges will provide lists of member and nonmember firms through whom you may trade their commodities. (See also the annual "Reference Guide" issue of *Commodities Magazine*.) Visit several brokers before making a choice, and consider the recommendation of experienced traders whose judgment you trust. When you first enter a new brokerage, either in stocks or commodities, the receptionist will often direct you to the "man of the day" whose turn it is to get all new customers for that day. This is probably as good a system as any for matching brokers and traders, but don't feel obliged to accept him as your broker. If you are not impressed, come again another day or politely ask to see someone else. Expect the broker to question you fully about your financial condition, your personality, and your ability to act responsibly in a risk situation. You are entering into a business relationship with the broker and the firm, and each person in this relationship has a right and an obligation to closely examine the prospective partner. You may be handed a form asking for information about where you work, your income-debt profile, liquid and capital assets, and so on. The brokerage is being honest and straightforward. No one without the means to pay their losses should be trading, so the broker is out to protect you as well as the firm. Counter with specific requests to see financial statements, trading track records (real, not hypothetical ones), research facilities, and other services. A businesslike relationship, set up at the beginning, will pay dividends later.

When comparing brokers, note the differences in opening financial requirements. Some firms may allow you to open with as little as $5,000 in the account; others may require $50,000. Some large firms might not wish to bother with the small trader. When you open the account, read the fine print and make sure the conditions are those you verbally agreed to. You will be asked to sign a basic customer's margin agreement wherein the client accepts responsibility for trading losses and agrees to pay them. The agreement must specify whether the client is to be a single individual, wife and husband, or business partners, who the broker will accept instructions from and what occurs in the event of death. If anyone other than the client, such as a trading advisor or the broker himself, is to manage and trade the account, a limited power of attorney so stipulating must also be signed. A general power of attorney, authorizing the withdrawal of funds by someone other than the client, is rare. Traders should take care when agreeing to any power of attorney arrangements.

TYPES OF ACCOUNTS

The trader may choose from a diverse assortment of different types of commodity accounts. A hard look reveals that, for the individual speculator, there are really only two basic alternatives. One is the account controlled by the client, who studies the market, organizes the trading plan, and gives the position orders. The other is an account managed by someone else, be it a broker, advisor, or a trader, employed by a commodities pool or fund. Many of these latter accounts, designed to meet and exploit the surging popularity of commodities as investments, allow speculators to "play" the market without spending any time researching trends or planning strategies.

In a strictly individual commodity account, the decisions are your own. You may consult the broker, an advisor, a horoscope, or tea leaves, but you are the one who gives the "go" signal on a trade and the one who decides when to close out a winning or losing position. The trader's instruction to the broker is simple: Don't call us; we'll call you. This is the ideal way to trade and eventually the most profitable. Letting someone else trade your commodity account is risky business. You won't have any fun, and trading commodities is a great deal of fun after you get the feel of it. The unique advantages of commodity trading—its freedom, challenge, and excitement—exist only for the trader who depends upon his own individual judgment, on his own skill, intelligence, fast wits, and trading savvy. If at all feasible, reject a broker's suggestion that anyone but yourself trade the account. Trading your own account will be more difficult and time-consuming, but the rewards will be your own. Why share that $50,000 profit in pork bellies with an advisor or fund manager when, with some extra effort, it could all be yours?

Great profits with no effort on your part will not occur in commodity speculation or in any other financial endeavor. Once again, those who are out to make quick risk free bucks are only pouring quick risk free bucks into the pockets of others. In the long run, if you are to make substantial money in commodities, you are going to have to do it yourself. And to the person who can afford to risk $5,000 or $10,000, the self-knowledge and feeling of accomplishment that comes with win-

ning in a difficult game surpasses the purely financial rewards.

There are degrees of independence for individual accounts. You may wish to begin with a "guided account." You and the broker sit down together to establish objectives, trading strategies, buy and sell signals, etc. The broker watches the markets and alerts you for opportunities in keeping with your joint understanding. The final decision remains yours, but you have the benefit of someone who is presumably more knowledgeable and well-informed to assist you in getting off the ground. In a more radical departure from the independent account, a "discretionary" account authorizes your broker, as well as yourself, to make trading decisions and initiate positions. Such a system may be tailored to your own objectives and follow your own program. Its advantage to some is the shifting of responsibility for watching the markets from the client to the broker and the feeling of security that comes with thinking that an "expert" is at your side.

The danger of discretionary accounts comes with this confusion of responsibility and decision making. The client may be happy when a discretionary trade brings in profits and furious when the broker decides to make a trade that ends up costing thousands. This can be hazardous for the broker-client relation. The disadvantage of such accounts is the diversion of responsibility from you to your broker. This dependence will lessen your involvement in the market, sharply curtailing your education in trading.

Your goal for the first year ought to be to learn as much as possible without having to add money to your margin account. Look at your first trades with an eye to being able to play again if you lose and look for a broker who can conservatively guide you, answer your questions, help you hold onto your playing capital, and be as patient and calm as you yourself must be. Once you are ready to play your own game, you will have little use for your broker other than as an executor of your trades. It is possible to become an expert in two or three commodities fairly rapidly, and over time you will do so. Then when your broker calls you with advice or a tip, thank him and evaluate the information for yourself. There's no reason to be jumping into the market all the time, and your broker's word forms only a part of the total supply of information you gather from newspapers, wire services, government agencies, exchanges, and trading associates.

MANAGED ACCOUNTS, POOLS, AND FUNDS

The managed account is still an individual one, though all trading decisions are made by the broker or advisor or computer. Clients are ordinarily not notified before a position is taken, a considerable logistical relief for the brokerage house. The account trades according to the advertised system or manager's program, often computer assisted. More than a few of these, on inspection, boil down to instructing the computer to play diverse markets, place stops, cut losses short, and let the profits run. Most claim to consider both technical and fundamental factors. Each features some "unique" method promising (never guaranteeing) fabulous profits. Although the manager trades the account, the client is responsible for all losses and margin calls. Hence, the initial deposit to open a managed account regularly runs to $25,000 or $50,000 or more,

along with a statement of sufficient net worth. Brokers justify these hefty deposits as necessary for the avoidance of "under capitalization," that time when too little in resources limits the trader's ability to ride out a bad market while waiting for the big move. It should be noted that this may create a situation in which the manager, given great flexibility and relieved of worrying about "small" losses, can end up letting those losses run until the account is wiped out. The surplus funds in such accounts normally pay interest to the brokerage, not to the client.

Managed accounts run by established brokerage firms normally charge only commissions for the service. These, however, can run 50 percent to 150 percent over commissions for nonmanaged accounts. Managed accounts offered by trading advisors or other independent investment agents not receiving commissions do entail fees, often 6 percent of equity per year plus 10–15 percent of profits, and there may be an up-front service charge at the start. If you have money, and are tempted to open a managed account, find a sound and legitimate manager with an approach to the markets that suits your understanding of commodity trading and that matches your financial goals. Demand and scrutinize the manager's and the system's track record, making sure it isn't hypothetical or projected. (See Figure 8–2.) Ask for references. If no references are forthcoming and he waxes vague about his record of trades, the broker is either as inexperienced as you are or the record is a sorry one.

Many of the pros and cons of commodity pools or funds parallel those of managed accounts. The fund is a managed group account into which a typical investor might put $5,000 or $10,000. The big

FIGURE 8-2

The Dunn & Hargitt Trading System
$500,000 Commodity Portfolio

YEARLY PROFIT RECORD

10 Commodities	Trades Per Year	1970	1971	1972	1973	1974	1975	1976(6 mos)	Total
Sugar	16.8	-110,789	-73,014	+268,941	+ 4,728	+205,843	+308,303	-14,485	+589,527
Hogs	26.5	+ 13,390	+17,007	+ 5,775	+172,879	+270,477	+ 91,820	+ 5,287	+576,635
Soybean Oil	30.0	+ 72,174	+50,544	- 60,076	+152,860	+196,960	+157,300	- 2,378	+567,384
Cattle	23.8	- 19,580	+42,802	+ 40,192	+137,260	+175,876	+115,950	+29,024	+521,524
Cocoa	17.5	+115,135	+91,791	- 26,167	+183,075	+ 61,132	+ 22,764	+47,621	+495,351
Copper	14.6	+ 81,746	+32,189	- 9,812	+107,174	+230,178	+ 10,755	+17,876	+470,106
Soybeans	19.5	- 2,110	+14,617	+ 43,035	+221,913	+ 58,805	+ 88,667	+20,845	+445,772
Wheat	16.3	+ 14,525	-34,585	+ 42,791	+ 73,237	+185,985	+134,875	-11,162	+405,666
Pork Bellies	18.5	- 14,584	+99,654	+ 6,315	+ 69,629	+169,138	+ 84,913	-48,696	+366,369
Cotton	14.8	- 27,575	-37,447	+ 82,892	+193,350	+ 38,810	+ 38,767	+26,598	+315,395
Total		+122,331	+203,559	+393,888	+1,316,105	+1,593,203	+1,054,115	+70,529	+4,753,730
% Profit		+24.5%	+40.7%	+78.8%	+263.2%	+318.6%	+210.8%	+14.1%	+950.7%
25% Performance Fee		30,582	50,889	98,472	329,026	398,300	263,528	17,632	1,188,429
Net After Performance Fee		91,749	152,670	295,416	987,079	1,194,903	790,587	52,897	3,565,301
% Profit After Perform. Fee		+18.3%	+30.5%	+59.1%	+197.4%	+239.0%	+158.1%	+10.6%	+713.1%

All results shown in these tables are based on a <u>simulation</u> model using the Dunn & Hargitt Commodity Data Bank.

Average Percent Profit Per Year = +109.7% per year (after commissions and performance fees)

Dunn & Hargitt © 1976 C1

difference here is that this money is not really margin. Fund investors are buying shares of the fund's hoped-for profits and are not subject to losses in excess of the initial outlay. The investor is one of many "limited partners," the managing "general partner" being either an investment house or the subsidiary of a brokerage firm that in turn handles trades and receives commissions. All pool or fund operators must be licensed as such by the CFTC. The third agent involved is the trading advisor, who makes the actual decisions on the fund's positions. As in stocks, the advantages of a fund include professional research and judgment, large capital resources, and diversity of holdings.

Hundreds of pool operators have come upon the scene to capitalize on the lure of commodities profits. They have tempo-

FIGURE 8-3

PERFORMANCE OF PUBLICLY OFFERED COMMODITY FUNDS

Compilation is done for MAR by Jay Klopfenstein of Norwood Securities, 6134 N. Milwaukee Ave., Chicago, IL 60646. Information is taken from public records and reports and is believed to be reliable. However, neither Norwood nor MAR guarantees the accuracy of the data. If you have any questions, contact Mr. Klopfenstein at 312/763-1540

FUND NAME	Date Started	*Offering Value Per Share	Unit Value 10/31/79	Unit Value 11/30/79	Record for Month	Cash Distributions
Ann Arbor Commodity Fund I	8/79	$1,000	$ 810	$ 597	-26.3%	
Antares Futures Fund (Paine Webber, Inc.)	1/78	1,000	922	740	-19.7%	$300
The Dunn Corporation (Limited Partnership)	10/74	1,000	3,687	3,672	- 0.4%	
Galileo Futures Fund (Clayton, A.G. Edwards, & Blunt, Ellis & Loewi)	3/79	1,000	1,016	862	-15.1%	
The Future Fund (Heinold, Blyth Eastman Dillon)	7/79	1,000	1,147	1,213	+ 5.7%	
Harvest Futures Fund (Heinold Commodities, Inc.)	6/78	1,000	3,477	4,549	+30.8%	
Heinold III. Comm. Fund (Heinold Commodities, Inc.)	1/78	1,000	1,163	1,201	+ 3.2%	
Heinold Recovery Fund I (Heinold Commodities, Inc.)	3/78	465	575	578	+ 0.5%	
Heinold Recovery Fund II (Heinold Commodities, Inc.)	3/78	189	213	220	+ 3.2%	
McLean Futures Fund (ContiCommodity Services)	12/78	1,000	1,229	1,347	+ 9.6%	400
McLean Futures Fund II (ContiCommodity Services)	8/79	1,000	716	753	+ 5.1%	
Mountain View Futures Fund (ContiCommodity Services)	9/76	1,000	651	653	+ 0.3%	213.37
The Resources Fund (Heinold/Blyth Eastman Dillion)	8/78	1,000	1,257	1,337	+ 6.3%	
Thomson McKinnon Futures Fund Thomson McKinnon Securities)	11/78	1,000	975	968	- 0.7%	
NORWOOD INDEX (Average performance for the month)					+ 0.2	

* Offering Value Per Share does not reflect deductions for sales or management fees taken prior to the start of trading or during the annual trading period. (i.e. Thomson McKinnon Fund starting value was $942 after deduction of fees; Ann Arbor Fund starting value was $849).

rarily replaced commodity options as the most scandal-prone element in the futures business. Some of the operators of boiler room type telephone solicitations in phony options simply switched over to selling shares in quickly patched together funds, once again inviting unwary investors to make flat payments in hopes of effortless wealth. Many legitimate fund operators do exist and some have scored impressively in the markets, though their results so far tend to correlate with the general swings of the market, suggesting that computer systems and capital depth have made little difference in the long run. (See Figure 8–3.) No authoritative judgment can be pronounced on the pools and funds as yet because of their relatively short history. Few pools have been around for more than a few years. Turnover of executives is high, making past records a dubious measure of future promise. Not very many trading advisors have greater than five years experience handling large sums. A fund is only as good as its advisor, and the advisor only as good as the market allows.

The exact structure of the fund, its service fees, and the relations of its partners should be precisely ascertained before any investment is made. The differences between various funds can be enormous. Some will charge a management fee of a percentage of equity on a regular basis regardless of the fund's profits or losses. Others will not extract a cent unless there has been an absolute profit from all preceding months. The deductions from funds for management fees, commissions, and other "services" have in some cases reached outrageous proportions.

In evaluating a fund, look for certain structural safeguards. The general partner, the brokerage receiving commission,

and the trading advisor should be entirely separate legal entities without financial interdependence. The point is to prevent conflict of interest, such as the churning of the account by a trading advisor who receives compensation in a ratio to volume or commission or who has other ties to the commission house. The prospectus for a fund run by a subsidiary of a large brokerage firm should thus be looked over carefully. (See Figure 8–4). The investor should have the right to withdraw from the fund at least on a quarterly basis. The fund should have a 50 percent dissolution clause, being subject to a dissolution vote of the limited partners if equity should fall below 50 percent of the original assets. No more than 20 percent of total assets should be put into any one commodity. Regular reports of income, losses, and fees charged should be sent to all partners. Check the credentials of the management and trust only those with genuine long-term experience and expertise in commodities trading. When going over a track record, pay particular attention to "downside risk." Has the advisor or the system ever suffered a loss large enough to cause dissolution? Is there a money management program for the investment of some funds in Treasury Bills, and is the surveillance system of the firm an adequate one for monitoring the fund's health?

MARGIN

In all cases other than pools and funds, commodity accounts are margin accounts. Margin is conceptually different in stock and commodity trading, and this difference echoes throughout a trader's relationship with the broker. While stock account margins are in effect down pay-

FIGURE 8–4

CONFLICTS OF INTEREST

The following inherent or potential conflicts of interest should be considered by prospective investors before subscribing for Units:

1. *Relationship among the General Partner, the Advisors and the commodity broker.* The General Partner is a wholly-owned subsidiary of SHS, which will act as the commodity broker for the Partnership. As a result, the General Partner will have a conflict of interest between its responsibility to the limited partners to obtain the most favorable brokerage commission rates and its interest in generating brokerage commissions for the benefit of SHS. Further, the Advisors are also employees of SHS and may have a conflict between their obligation to trade only in the best interests of the Partnership and any interest they may have in generating brokerage commissions for their employer. In addition, the General Partner may have a conflict between its obligation to prevent the Advisors from engaging in excessive trading and its interest in the brokerage commission income going to SHS. Furthermore, R. Parker Crowell, Jr., who is a Vice President and a Director of the General Partner, is the Manager of the Greenwich, Connecticut branch office of SHS and part of the compensation paid to Mr. Crowell by SHS is based on the profitability of that office. For internal accounting purposes in computing such profitability, Mr. Crowell's office will receive credit for a portion of the commissions generated by the Partnership. In order to decrease the likelihood that trades for the Partnership may be made only to increase the income flowing to SHS, or to increase the compensation paid to Mr. Crowell by SHS, SHS has agreed that it will reimburse the Partnership for any commissions received by it in any year which exceed 25% of the average of the month-end Net Assets of the Partnership during such year. See "The Commodity Broker—Brokerage Commissions".

2. *Commission rates to be charged by the commodity broker.* Pursuant to the Customer Agreement between the Partnership and SHS, SHS will act as the commodity broker for the Partnership. Because the General Partner is a subsidiary of SHS, the General Partner may have a conflict of interest between its responsibility to manage the Partnership for the benefit of the limited partners and its interest in obtaining commission rates which are favorable to SHS. However, SHS will charge the Partnership brokerage commissions at 80% of its standard public customer rates. In addition, the General Partner will bear such general and administrative expenses of the Partnership as may be incurred except the fees of the Advisors and legal, accounting, reporting and filing fees and extraordinary expenses, and will receive no compensation for its services to the Partnership. Although the Customer Agreement is non-exclusive, so that the Partnership will have the right to seek lower commission rates from other brokers at any time, the General Partner believes that the arrangements between the Partnership and SHS are consistent with arrangements other comparable commodity pools have entered into with other futures commission merchants and are fair to the Partnership and does not intend to negotiate with SHS to obtain lower commission rates or to refer brokerage transactions to other firms. However, the General Partner will review, at least annually, the commission rates charged to other comparable commodity pools to determine that the commission rates being paid by the Partnership are competitive with such other rates. Each limited partner, by execution of the Subscription Agreement, consents to the execution and delivery of the Customer Agreement by the Partnership and authorizes the payment to SHS by the Partnership of brokerage commissions at the rates set forth in the Customer Agreement.

3. *Distribution of profits.* The General Partner has discretion as to the distribution of profits, if any, to the limited partners. To the extent that profits are retained by the Partnership rather than being distributed, the Net Assets of the Partnership, which determines the maximum commissions payable in any year, will be increased, thereby increasing both the maximum amount of commissions which can be earned by SHS and the amount of funds deposited in segregated accounts at banks which extend overdraft privileges to SHS. See "The Commodity Broker-Customer Agreements". The General Partner intends to distribute a portion of the

FIGURE 8–4 (*continued*)

Partnership's profits at least once per year. However, no distribution will be made if it would reduce the Net Asset Value of a Unit below $1,000 or if the amount of profits realized would result in a distribution which would be too small to warrant the administrative expense which would be involved in making the distribution. In addition, the General Partner does not intend to make a distribution if, in its opinion, the reduction in the amount of assets under management which would result from the distribution would not be in the best interests of the Partnership or the limited partners.

   4. *Accounts of SHS, the General Partner, and their affiliates.* The officers, directors and employees of SHS and the General Partner, as well as SHS itself, may trade in commodity futures contracts for their own accounts. The records of any such trading will not be available for inspection by limited partners. In addition, SHS is a futures commission merchant and effects transactions in commodity futures contracts for its customers. Thus, it is possible that SHS could effect transactions for the Partnership in which the other parties to the transactions are its officers, directors or employees or its customers. Such persons might also compete with the Partnership in making purchases or sales of contracts without knowing that the Partnership is also bidding on such contracts. Transactions for any of such persons might be effected when similar trades for the Partnership are not executed or are executed at less favorable prices.

   5. *Management of other accounts by the Advisors.* The Advisors intend to manage the accounts of clients other than the Partnership. In addition, they intend to trade commodity futures contracts for their own accounts. The records of any such trading will not be available for inspection by limited partners. All of the positions held by all such accounts will be aggregated for purposes of determining compliance with position limits and daily trading limits. See "Commodity Futures Markets—Regulation". As a result, the Partnership might not be able to enter into or maintain certain positions if such positions, when added to the positions held by such other accounts, would exceed the applicable limits.

   6. *Other activities of SHS.* SHS maintains a commodity research department which makes trading recommendations on a daily basis. In addition, SHS has commodity trading programs in which certain customers participate. The records of trading of such programs will not be made available to limited partners. In such programs and in its trading recommendations SHS may take or recommend transactions which are similar or opposed to transactions being made for the Partnership. SHS will not provide advisory services to the Partnership.

   7. *Other commodity pools.* The General Partner or SHS may sponsor or establish other commodity pools which may compete with the Partnership.

   Source: Shearson, Shearson Loeb Rhodes, Inc.

ments, supplemented by broker loans on which interest is due, commodity margin takes the form of a surety bond guaranteeing performance of the contract. When the trader puts up a margin of $800 for five thousand bushels of corn (one contract), he is merely assuring the broker that he can stand an $800 loss in the value of the contract. If the price per bushel were $3.50, the market value of the contract would be $17,500, but the trader would never owe this amount except in the rare event that the contract were held into delivery. In this event the trader would tender a check for the full amount plus handling charges, the margin being applied to the purchase.

If the market moves adversely, the trader could lose the entire margin deposit of $800. That would leave the brokerage with an open position for which it held no deposit protection. An $800 deposit equals 16 cents per bushel, so the initial margin deposit would cover an adverse move of 16 cents above or below the price at which the futures contract was taken.

To protect the firm, the broker will call for more deposit before the price ever reaches such extremes. The trader is generally allowed to lose 25 percent of the original margin deposit. The 75 percent equity required to maintain the account is known as "maintenance margin," and serves to protect the brokerage house extending credit to the trader. Margin calls will be made on the trader whenever losses threaten to endanger the maintenance level. Generally speaking, meeting a margin call violates the rule that losses ought to be cut short, and they should only be met after careful deliberation justifies the risk.

Margin rates for spread positions are set much lower than for single "naked" positions. In a spread, simply defined, the trader takes two different positions—in different months of the same commodity, in different exchanges for the same commodity, and in different but interrelated commodities—and speculates on the changing of the price differential between the opposing positions. This lower margin allows a trader to handle a much larger position with the same initial cash outlay, one of the main attractions of spreads. A trader might have one "leg" in July soybeans and another in August soybeans. While the margin for the single naked position in July could run about $3,000, the margin for the spread between the two months could run as low as $600 for both legs. An investment of $6,000 would thus control a position of 10 contracts long and 10 contracts short in a spread or 2 contracts held naked long or short.

Risk normally is relatively small in spread positions, because as the market moves in price both legs of the spread will move with it. The trader stands to win small percentages of money (but often huge profits or huge losses) as the legs come closer together or widen (depending on which way the spread was taken). In general, risk is reduced by a spread (although the actual risk may still be very great), so less protection and cheaper margin rates follow. Specific margin requirements for spreads, as well as for single positions, vary according to the commodity, the season, and the current condition in the market place. Brokers should supply traders with complete margin schedules and update them continually. (See Figure 8–5). Brokerages on their own volition will sometimes raise margin requirements above the amount stipulated by the exchanges if they consider the price of a commodity to be extremely volatile. Brokers may not lower margin below exchange prescribed minumums.

There is no grace period in commodities between the time the order is placed and the payment for the position. The trader must tender a check on the day of the short sale or long purchase and make additional deposits immediately any time the margin account falls below the amount specified for the contracts held open in the account. When a commodity position is offset (closed) the broker must immediately return a check or deposit the money in the client's account. Margin accounts, by law, are not available for the discretionary purposes of the brokerage. The amount of margin capital required in commodity trading does not normally vary with the value of the commodity. If the margin for pork bellies is set at $1,500, that will be the margin payment recorded in the trader's account whether the price of bellies be 40 cents per pound or 80 cents per pound. However, when markets go wild, margins go with them. During the silver boom of 1979–1980, ini-

FIGURE 8-5
Commodity Futures   Margin Requirements

Shearson Loeb Rhoades Inc

For internal use only

Commodity	O/M	Spread	London	O/M	Spread
Broilers	$ 900	$ 500	Silver (10M oz)	$50,000*	$2,500*
Coca NY (SPOT 3,600 Extra)	2,000	600	Tin (5 Tons)	6,800	1,500
Coffee (Spot month 11,500)*	7,500	500	Copper (25 Tons)	8,000*	1,000
Copper	4,000*	500	Aluminum (25 Tons)	3,500	800
Cotton	1,000	500	Nickel (6 Tons)	3,500	750
Corn (1M BU 125 MidAm)	600	300 (Crop 500)	Lead (25 Tons)	4,000	325
Eggs Chic Merc (Except SPOT)	700	600	Zinc (25 Tons)	3,000	750
Gold (400 oz) NY Merc or WPG	50,000*	3,000*	Coffee (5 Tons)	2,500	500
Gold (100 oz) Comex Chi WPG	12,500*	750*	Rubber (15 Tons)	1,500	400
Gold (32.15 oz) NY Merc or MidAm	4,500*	250*	Cocoa (10 Tons)	2,000	600
Hogs Chi 30M lbs. (15M 450 Mid Am)	900	500	Sugar (50 Tons)	2,300	375
Live Cattle 40M (20M 750 MidAm)	1,500	600	Wheat (100 Tons)	1,000	250
Feeder Cattle	1,800	600	Barley (100 Tons)	1,500	400
Lumber Chi Merc (Stud 1,000)	1,200	600	Sydney Wool (1500 Kilos)	600	150
Oats CBOT or MidAm	400	150			
Orange Juice (1,000 extra SPOT month)	2,000	400	**Foreign Currencies**	**IMM**	
Palladium	2,000	400	Deutschemarks	$ 2,500	$ 500
Platinum	5,000*	400	Swiss Francs	3,000	500
Plywood	700	250	British Pounds	2,500	625
Pork Bellies Chi Merc	1,200	700 (Crop 1,200)	Canadian Dollar	2,000	500
Potatoes Maine	300	200	Mexican Peso	6,000	2,000
Potatoes Russet	500	300	Japanese Yen	3,000	750
Comex Silver 5M (Spot 50M)	25,000*	1,200	French Francs	3,000	750
CBOT Silver 5M (1M 5,000)	25,000*	1,200	Dutch Guilder	2,500	625
Silver Coins NY ($10M)	25,000*	5,000			
Silver Coins Chi ($5M)	12,500*	2,500	WPG Barley or Rye	800	200 (100 Tons)
Soybeans (1M 600)	2,500	600 (Crop 1,000)	WPG Flax or Rapeseed	2,000	500 (100 Tons)
S/B Meal CBOT	1,200	300 (Crop 750)			
S/B Oil CBOT	1,250	300 (Crop 750)	**Inter-Commodity Spreads**		
Sugar NY World No. 11	2,300	475	Chicago Wheat Vs. KC Wheat	$ 750	
Sugar NY DOM No. 12	2,600	475	Wheat Vs. Corn	$ 750	
Wheat (1M BU $300 MidAm)	1,500	400	10M Oats Vs. 5M Corn	$ 600	
Treasury Bonds (CBOT)	3,000	700	1 Cattle Vs. 1 Hogs	$ 1,500	
Treasury Notes	3,000	700	1 Bellies Vs. 1 Hogs	$ 1,200	
GNMA Mortgages	3,000	700			
Treasury Bill Futures	3,000	1,200			
Commercial Paper	3,000	700			
Heating Oil No. 2 (SPOT 5M)	3,500	750			

Eggs will require 25% delivery value *four* days before notice day. Live Cattle and Hogs increase near delivery date. SPOT month generally requires higher margins. # NY Gold & Silver Permit slightly lower, but individual cases require advance approval by Office Manager and NY Commodity Department. Requirements for substantial positions may well be higher. Above relates to established account, and to limited number contracts.

Changes from last week.

FIGURE 8-6

How the market has changed . . .

	"Normal"	Recent Extreme	Feb. 1
Gold			
Initial speculative margin per contract			
CBT	$1,200	$ 6,000	$4,500
Comex	1,000	15,000	5,000
IMM	900	9,000	9,000
MidAm	280	3,000	3,000
Daily limit on price fluctuations per ounce (deferred months)			
CBT	$10	$60	$40
Comex	10	50	50
IMM	10	75	50
MidAm	10	75	50
Silver			
Initial speculative margin per contract			
CBT spot month	$1,500	$30,000	$30,000
CBT deferred months	1,500	16,000	12,000
Comex spot month	1,000	75,000	75,000
Comex deferred months	1,000	1-100 contracts — $40,000	
		101-250 contracts — $50,000	
		251 contracts or more — $60,000	
MidAm	280	2,800	2,800
Daily limit on price fluctuations per ounce (deferred months)			
CBT	$.20	$1.20	$.80
Comex	.20	1.00	.75
MidAm	.20	1.20	.80
Position limit (maximum number of contracts a speculator can hold)			
CBT	No limit	600	500
Comex	No limit	2,000	2,000
MidAm	No limit	10 for Feb. '80 contract	No limit

Source: Commodities Magazine.

tial speculative margin for silver contracts rocketed from averages of $1,000–$1,500 upwards towards $40,000 or more. (See Figure 8–6.)

COMMISSION

After years of discussion, commodity futures commission rates became fully negotiable in 1978. As the major source of revenue for the brokerage house, the commission represents, in fact, a payment for aggregate services, though nominally it only covers the trade performed. Commission rates, then, should reasonably represent the degree of effort made on the

client's behalf by the broker and the firm. Multinational mixed wire houses featuring daily reports, newsletters, hot lines to the exchange floor, and other specialities will naturally charge more in commission than discount brokers who do nothing but phone in your order and keep the records straight. (See Figure 8–7.) Commission rates should be an important consideration in the comparison of brokerages. Their absolute comparison, however, is unjust without the context of the difference in services. (See Figure 8–8.)

Commission is paid only once in commodities—at the time the position is closed (called a "round term" commis-

FIGURE 8–7

Commodity Research

Weekly Report

Commentary on the Chicago Markets

FOOD AND FEED GRAINS

WHEAT

The Iranian crisis continued to unsettle the grain markets and unnerve the shorts. As previously discussed here, the situation is mostly price-bolstering, due to higher production costs, possibly reduced fuel supplies, inflation, pressure on the dollar abroad and the usual short covering touched off by international confrontations. But concern seemed to lessen somewhat this week as world opinion - at least on the hostage issue - mov-

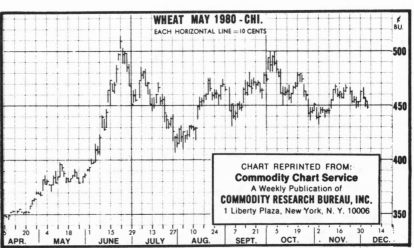

ed solidly behind the U.S. This left wheat and other commodities more responsive to their individual supply-demand profiles. It should be noted that, concurrent with the start of the Iranian crisis, the Soviet Union began a round of fill-in buying of grains, generally thought to include about 2 million tonnes of wheat and 4 million corn. While it is impossible to separate the impact of Soviet buying from the Iranian situation, it is now felt that the bulk of the Soviet fill-in buying is over and no further large purchases are expected until spring.

Consequently, the wheat price advance has lost its zip. U.S. producers, who had been holding off sales for the same reason speculators covered shorts, are now offering wheat more freely. Farmer holding had helped prices get to within about 10¢ of the $4.11 reserve "call" price, but we don't think this level will be sustained. Despite the well-advertised U.S. wheat stock drawdown this season, to 851 million bushels from 925 million on June 1, 1979, there is no shortage of free wheat. Only about 236 million bushels remain in the reserve, out of the original 413 million bushels. Wheat has been trading roughly 65¢ over the reserve release minimum, and reserve wheat therefore remains in release status.

FIGURE 8-7 (*continued*)

WHEAT (Continued)   -2-   December 7, 1979

Heavy rains over the southeastern half of India's winter grain belt helped the crop immensely, but the combined effects of earlier drought (continuing in some areas) and shortages of farm inputs and energy still seem likely to reduce India's winter grain crop by 10%. While China's 1979 grain crop is estimated at a record 311 million tonnes, dry conditions are starting to be noted throughout that country's winter wheat belt. The Soviet Union's expanded winter grain plantings headed into dormancy in satisfactory condition. As in the U.S., where winter wheat seedings are believed to be up 7-10%, increases generally are expected around the Northern Hemisphere. While overall yields in the U.S. are likely to hold 1980 output to about the 1979 level of 2.1 billion bushels, our wheat exports in 1980-81 could be lower than this season's estimated 1.4 billion bushels, resulting in a carryover buildup. We are bearish on the wheat market.

CORN

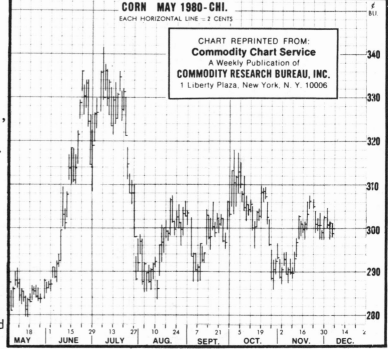

Here also, the past month's price strength reflected a combination of the Iranian situation and coincidental fill-in buying by the Soviet Union, which may have included up to 4 million tonnes of corn. Producers, who are generally bullish, withheld corn from the market and this reinforced the November advance. But this week they became somewhat freer sellers.

The corn market logged some fairly bearish fundamentals in recent weeks, which were never fully digested in the rush to cover shorts over the past month. These include the record November corn crop estimate of 7.59 billion bushels and the consequent carryover buildup expected in 1979-80. That's not encouraging in view of the USDA's decision to drop the acreage set-aside option in the 1980 feed grain program.

As expected, the USDA on November 30 withdrew the reserve release authorization for corn, as the price fell below the release minimum. Only about 530 million bushels of corn remained in the reserve at that time, out of a total supply of 8.872 billion bushels. Withdrawal of the release minimum meant producers would continue to get Government storage payments of 25¢ per bushel per year. Meanwhile, the onus remains on our internal transportation system to move the 2.5 billion bushel exports forecast for this season, and feeding margins remain narrow. A few other negative factors are likely to come into play during the balance of 1979. Many farmers ended up with 10-15 more bushels per acre than expected, and these "bonus" bushels could come on the market soon. More locomotives appear to be available for use in the Western Corn Belt; this could reduce the inordinately large price differential between corn prices in that area and the Eastern Belt, or conversely, it could reduce the demand for Eastern supplies. Additionally, the high cost of storing versus selling and placing the proceeds in short term interest-bearing instruments should stimulate marketings.

These factors leave us somewhat bearish on the corn price outlook.

FIGURE 8-8

COMPARATIVE OVERNIGHT COMMISSION RATES

	Merrill Lynch Rates	Eastern Savings $$	Eastern Savings %	Shearson, Hayden Stone Rates	Eastern Savings $$	Eastern Savings %	Heinold Commod. Rates	Eastern Savings $$	Eastern Savings %	EASTERN CAPITAL CORP. Rates
SOYBEANS	$55.50	$30.50	55%	$50	$25	50%	$50	$25	50%	$25
CORN	$55.50	$30.50	55%	$50	$25	50%	$45	$20	44%	$25
LIVE CATTLE	$55	$30	54%	$50	$25	50%	$50	$25	50%	$25
SUGAR #11	$72	$47	65%	$75	$50	67%	$75	$50	67%	$25
CURRENCIES	$55	$30	54%	$70	$45	64%	$57.50	$32.50	56%	$25
T-BILLS	$62	$37	60%	$70	$45	64%	$60	$35	58%	$25
GOLD (N.Y.)	$56.50	$31.50	56%	$50	$25	50%	$50.50	$25.50	51%	$25
COCOA	$57	$32	56%	$100	$75	75%	$75	$50	67%	$25
LUMBER	$55	$30	54%	$55	$30	54%	$50	$25	50%	$25
PORK BELLIES	$55	$30	54%	$60	$35	58%	$55	$30	54%	$25

COMMISSION SAVINGS

No. of Contracts Traded Per Month	Approx. Monthly Savings At Eastern	Approx. Yearly Savings At Eastern
10	$ 300	$ 3,600
25	$ 750	$ 9,000
50	$1,500	$18,000
100	$3,000	$36,000

Dollar savings on spread trades are even more substantial than those shown for overnight trades.

Source: Eastern Capital Corp.

sion). No commission is paid at the opening of the position. Each commodity commands its own rate of commission, with day trades usually costing less than positions held overnight. Commissions are flat rates per contract, regardless of changes in the value of the commodity or of the size of the order. Though wide ranging, commissions usually run in the range of 0.2 percent to 0.6 percent of the total value of the contract. This results in costs per trade that appear, at first, attractively cheap in comparison with stocks and in light of the value of the contract handled. A commission of $50 on a soybean contract worth over $40,000 sounds like a bargain, and it can be. But the trader must remember that leverage affects commission costs as well as margins. If the commission rate is 0.4 percent of contract value, and the margin is 10 percent of the contract value, the commission becomes 4 percent of the margin

amount, a sizeable chunk in a business where positions may be held for only hours, days, or a few weeks. Even in properly traded accounts, commission charges eat upon a great portion of the original capital, sometimes in excess of 100 percent. Ideally, profits will provide the capital to continue trading.

Most brokerages provide for lower commissions on trades which are opened and closed on the same day ("day trade"). This gives a fair chance to the speculator who competes for profits on minor price dislocations such as might occur during execution of large orders. Day trade commission schedules also apply in the event that a trade is closed and opened again in one day, and it is here that the practical importance of day trades exists for the public speculator. The speculator can keep the position closely covered by a stop-loss order, and in the event that the stop order is tripped and the trader taken out of the market, a new position can be economically put in place if the speculator so desires. The broker, however, must be notified if the trader wishes the closing and subsequent reopening considered a day trade, as normal accounting procedure may not connect the two, resulting in full commission charges being levied on both transactions.

When a commodity position is closed, the trader receives in the mail a transaction slip which lists the commodity purchased, the price at which the position was opened, price closed, gross profit or loss, total commission, and net profit or loss. Combined with the slip received in the mail when the position was first opened, this transaction slip constitutes the trader's official record of business done. A monthly statement from the brokerage lists open positions and total equity in the margin account, including any free margin which has been deposited and is not currently being used, along with the total value of current open positions. This is the minimal amount of information you should expect from your broker, and its accuracy should be checked against your own trading records. Timely, accurate bookkeeping and notification are essential components of brokerage service to be demanded by every trader. The amount of unused equity sitting in your margin account each month as surety for your trades can itself be a drain on finances during times of high interest rates and inflation. If so, some brokers will take a substantial portion of account equity and purchase Treasury Bills on the client's behalf. These same bills can then be used to margin commodity transactions, putting the money to work for you in two ways simultaneously.

MECHANICS

TRADING FLOOR AND PIT

What happens after the customer places an order with the broker? (See Figure 9–1.) Depending on the brokerage firm's facilities, it is sent by teletype or direct phone line either to the firm's branch office in the city where the respective exchange is located or to the firm's station on the floor of the exchange itself. If transmitted, say, to the Chicago branch, the order is recorded on another form marked private wire and given an identification number and time-stamp, recording the date, hour, and fraction of a minute. The written order, usually translated into abbreviations or symbols, goes to a telephone operator connected to the phone clerk at the exchange floor. These thousands of calls, originating with commercial traders, brokerage firms, and speculators, flow into batteries of telephone stations strategically located near the pits and operated by member companies. (See Figure 9–2.) Time stamped again by the clerk, the order goes by runner to the floor broker in the pit who executes the actual trade. The system succeeds remarkably well, and customers may receive confirmation of their trade in two or three minutes or even less.

The pit is the natural outgrowth of the time when commodities were traded in the open air. Choosing a natural hollow in which to do business allowed earlier commodity traders to actively participate in transactions while keeping an eye on all the other traders in the market. The round hollow also made it possible for short traders to step up or down as they tried to monitor the action. These first pits traded without referees: buyers and sellers simply kept finding one another as rapidly as possible while keeping a sharp ear on the trades just consummated by other traders. In this way everyone could keep track of the "going price" and have a starting point from which to haggle. They could just as well make their trade in the nearest tavern (and many did), but pit trading assured each of a trade at a price close to what other people were getting and giving. At some exchanges trading may be done around a large ring, with traders leaning against the rail and making their deals across the ring's hollow. (See Figures 9–3 and 9–4.)

Modern commodity trading is only slightly more formal, as anyone who has witnessed the pushing and shrieking bedlam of the exchange pit can testify. Trading still takes place directly between buyer and seller as rapidly as each can find the other and agree upon a price. Competition is intense and very physical. Floor traders in the pit come out sometimes as bruised and weary as any contact sport combatant. Flying arms and elbows have blackened eyes and broken noses. The Chicago Board of Trade keeps a paramedic on duty to assist infrequent victims of heart at-

FIGURE 9–1
Order Execution Process

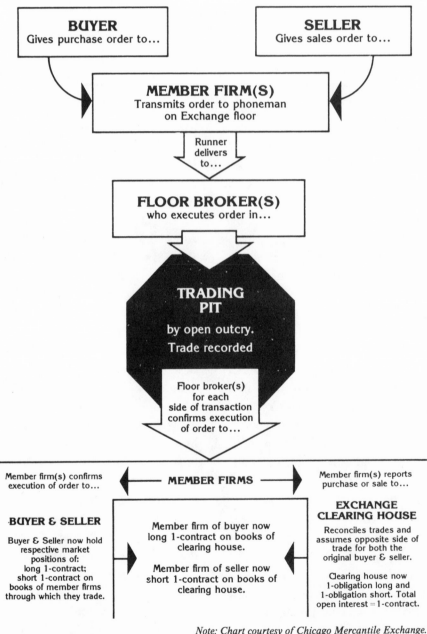

Note: Chart courtesy of Chicago Mercantile Exchange.

FIGURE 9-2

Source: Chicago Mercantile Exchange.

tacks, but usual tasks involve squashed toes, sprained ankles, and traders who faint from overexertion. There can be 300 traders crowding around the 30-foot soybean pit frantically in search of deals worth millions of dollars, so that finding and cornering a broker to trade with before prices tick again inspires brokers to heroic efforts. Getting someone else's attention may mean anything from reaching across and grabbing their shoulder to elaborate theatrics of clowning and demonstration.

Beneath this apparent insanity is a surprisingly organized and efficient structure. The old trading hollow is duplicated on the exchange floor by a set of steps rising from the center, so that the maximum number of traders can see the entire market. The center of the pit is at exterior floor level. A number of tiers or levels will rise above, in an octagonal shape. This eight-sided figure eliminates sharp corners where the view would be congested. Normally, each tier represents a single contract month, with the topmost tier reserved for the current delivery month, providing it with the necessary speedy access to phones and messengers. Where volume is light or commodities related, more than one commodity's futures contract may trade in a single pit. Traders switch from contract month to contract month by stepping up or down in the pit, or wander from one commodity pit to another in search of profitable action. (See Figure 9–5.)

All the screaming and shouting so infamously associated with commodities by an understandably amused public is in re-

FIGURE 9–3
New York Coffee and Sugar Exchange Trading Floor, 1896

Source: New York Coffee, Sugar, and Cocoa Exchange

FIGURE 9–4
Commodities Exchange Center

Source: New York Mercantile Exchange.

ality a safeguard for fairness and equity. All trading must be done by open outcry auction, publicly, and no quiet side deals among friends are legally allowed. (See Figure 9–6.) The trader cries out the number of contracts (or in the case of grains, bushels) he wishes to buy or sell and the price. This makes the voice one of the pit broker's principal financial assets and weapons. But the trader backs up his shouts with hand signals, for nothing specific can be heard in all that din. Upthrust fingers indicate the number of contracts or bushels. If the palm of the hand is held outward, the trader wishes to sell. If the palm is held inward, the trader wishes to buy. Fingers are then turned horizontally to indicate price (usually as a penny or fraction of a cent variation from the going price). (See Figure 9–7.)

When two traders find each other and agree on a price, each will note the number worn by the other, the price, and the number of contracts traded and use this information to "clear up" at the end of the day. How, one may ask, can the pit

FIGURE 9–5

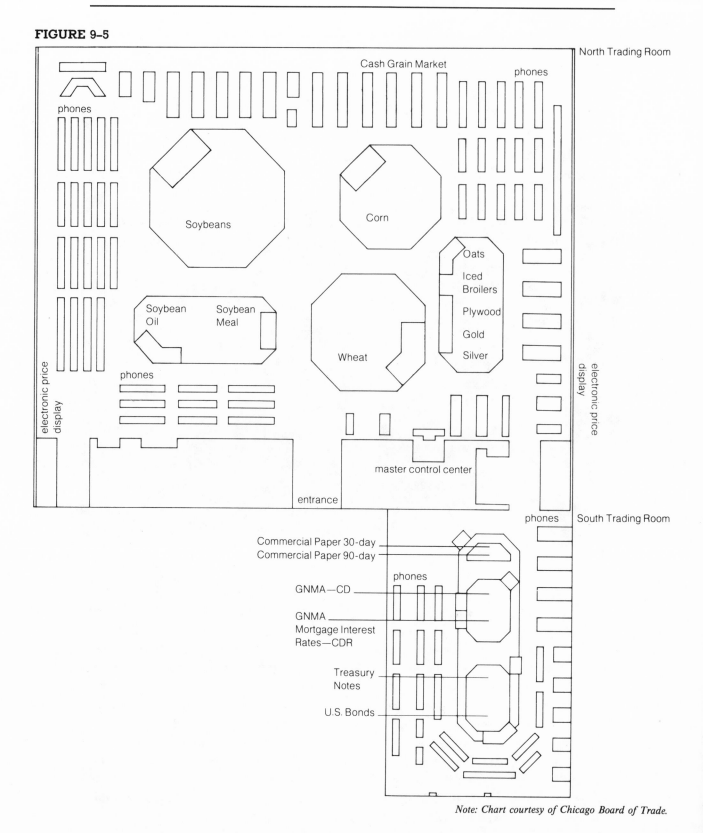

Note: Chart courtesy of Chicago Board of Trade.

FIGURE 9–6

Copyright 1979 by the New York Mercantile Exchange

trader keep it all straight? He or she uses what's called a trader's "deck," a sheaf of papers held like playing cards, containing orders received arranged in an order that tells the broker when and if to execute them. If a brokerage firm order comes up in the trader's deck and is successfully completed, confirmation is sent back by runner to the phone station and on its way to the customer.

An observer, employed by the exchange, takes note of all pit actions and price changes. Trades and prices are time-stamped and immediately entered into the network of commodities communication. Quotes go out on ticker tapes world-wide, and to visual quotation display screens owned or leased by brokers and traders. The exchange's own price display boards, on high walls above the floor, show the price action at every turn. A central computer keeps a record of trading data for recall and analysis. Time is of the essence, and transaction efficiency literally measured in milliseconds. Every exchange experiments regularly with sophisticated new technology designed to quicken, streamline, and increase the accuracy of

FIGURE 9–7

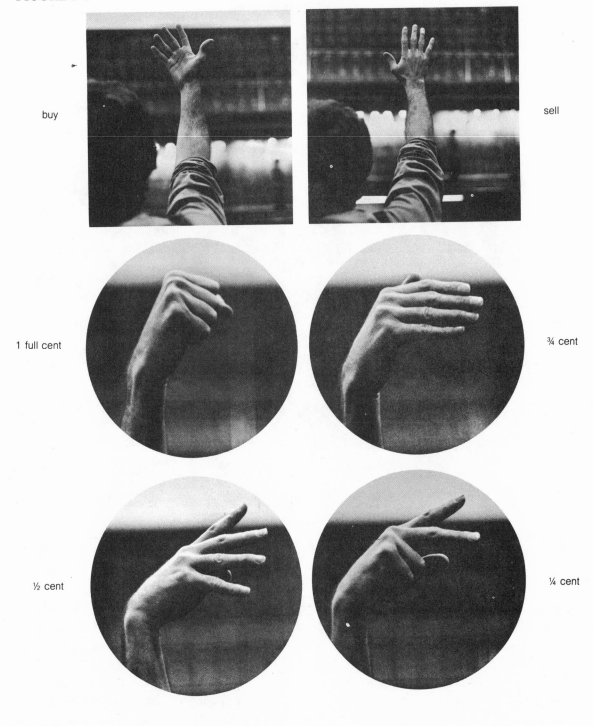

buy

sell

1 full cent

¾ cent

½ cent

¼ cent

floor trading and order processing. Old-fashioned blackboards still have their uses, though, in slow markets. Buy and sell orders are chalked up and stay posted until a matching offer comes along.

THE PIT'S LIMITATIONS

No one has yet devised a system for automating or computerizing the actual futures trade, and pit brokers naturally argue (as do many others) that elimination of the traditional human method would ruin the business. Whatever happens on the technological side, it is unlikely that the pit will be replaced as the center of futures trading anytime in the near future despite its limitations. Direct auction between buyer and seller assures everybody an equal chance at the best possible price, but the physical setup of such a system limits the efficiency of trading, especially in times when the pit is swamped. The big grain pits measure 30 to 40 feet across and average 150 to 200 traders, all yelling and waving their arms at any given time. Sometimes, as at the opening after price-making news the night before, at the close before a holiday, or at the end of the contract, trading becomes so hectic that communications become imperfect and snarled. Confirmation, which is normally immediate, can be held up an hour or more or even until after the close of the trading. This is especially true of larger brokerage houses whose wire facilities may not be able to keep up with the large volume of trade. The pit trader will at all times get the best price he can find for the trades he is given, but this may not be the best price to come across the teletype. In the uproar of the pit, a better bid or offer will have been made which simply was not heard or seen by even an expert pit broker. Possibly, prices will vary from one part of the pit to another in rapid trading, through the discrepancy will not usually exceed a small fraction. If it did, scalpers fast enough to catch the variation could make a lot of money in a few seconds at no risk, while their trades would help pressure prices back into conformity.

If the confusion becomes too great, trading will be suspended, just as in stock trading, to allow the traders time to order their decks and prepare for a more rational go at it. But during the flurry of volatile price moves before a close or suspension, even the ticker may not reflect every price hit with complete accuracy. If prices are moving rapidly, the ticker operator will attempt to report every price hit and will do so to the best of his ability. But even the official tape and quotation board may not show all the activity. Thus, a trade order could be returned to the broker and customer marked "unable," even though similar prices did actually trade. Exchange rules reflect this reality and specifically restrict the public trader's recourse in the event of mistakes or missed executions which cannot be attributed to any person but are rather inherent in the nature of pit trading. Under exchange rules no trader has recourse if the trade was not made at the best price to come across the ticker so long as it was made in the range of prices reflecting the best price the pit representative could find. No trader has recourse in the event that a limit order (to be filled at a specified price or better) was not filled, even though this price was, in fact, hit by the market if such occurred at a time when rapidity of trading made it impossible for the representative to consummate the trade before another buyer or seller stole the deal.

Errors are made from time to time and for these arbitration procedures are set out by the exchanges. Should the trader find an error in the handling of his account and not find satisfaction from the broker, he has recourse directly through the exchange on which the trade was made. Should a brokerage or its representative at the exchange neglect either to fill an order or to close a position, the brokerage must pay the trader a sum equal to the amount lost on the mistake. (Mistakes resulting in profits for the customer remain the customer's.) Further bylaws can be obtained from the various exchanges and should be thoroughly reviewed with the broker who will handle your orders.

HOURS, UNITS, TICKER SYMBOLS

Each exchange sets the hours during which a given commodity may be traded. In most cases, commodities trade for about 5 hours from morning to early afternoon. Trading may begin in all months simultaneously or by call. In a call market, each delivery month is called in sequence until all openings are recorded and continuous auction is in progress. Bells ring to alert traders of the opening and to warn of the close before the final gong sounds. No trades outside set hours are allowed, which makes for frantic trading in the waning minutes of a contract. For many contracts, trading hours are shortened on the final day. (See Figure 9–8.)

In order to simplify trading, commodities contracts are written in standard units. Grains trade in contracts of 5,000 bushels and other physical commodities in units according to weight or volume. One contract of cotton equals 100 bales, a total weight of 50,000 pounds. Soybean

oil trades in 60,000 pound contracts, about the size of one tank car. Units for interest rate futures are in dollar amounts of the respective financial instrument: $100,000 for Ginnie Maes and T-Bonds and $1,000,000 for T-Bills. A contract of lumber equals 100,000 board feet. Odd-lot or "mini-contracts" are traded on the MidAmerica Commodity Exchange. These contracts run one-fifth to one-half the size of regular contracts, with margins proportionately reduced. Mini-contracts cannot be used to cover standard contracts nor vice-versa. Mini-contracts can be a useful, less expensive way to break into commodity trading, though the cost of commissions as compared to profit potential is more than for regular contracts. When trading grains, remember that orders are placed so as not to confuse the number of bushels with the number of contracts. Grains are ordered by the bushel, so that "10 May corn" means 10,000 bushels, or two contracts (*not* ten contracts).

As a matter of policy, most brokerages send their order written out in full or in easily read abbreviations to avoid mistakes. A simple typing error could change the important details of such an order. To save time and tape, however, tape readings are usually sent in ticker symbols. Grains are each noted by their first letter: W for wheat, S for soybeans, C for corn, and so on. All other commodities are denoted by abbreviations which can be read, with some imagination, as the proper name. (See Figure 9–9.)

MINIMUM FLUCTUATION AND DAILY TRADING LIMITS

Commodity exchanges establish minimum fluctuations in price for every com-

FIGURE 9-8

FUTURES TRADING FACTS

COMMODITY	NAME OF EXCHANGE	TRADING HOURS N.Y. Time Mon. thru Fri.	CONTRACT	MINIMUM FLUCTUATION		DAILY TRADING LIMITS (From Previous Close)
				Per Lb., etc.	Per Contract	
BROILERS, ICED	Chicago Board of Trade	10:15 A.M. - 2:20 P.M.	30,000 Lbs.	2½/100¢	$7.50	2¢*
CATTLE (FEEDER)	Chicago Mercantile Exchange	10:05 A.M. - 1:45 P.M.	42,000 Lbs.	2½/100¢	$10.50	1½¢
CATTLE (LIVE BEEF)	Chicago Mercantile Exchange	10:05 A.M. - 1:45 P.M.	40,000 Lbs.	2½/100¢	$10.00	1½¢
COCOA (OLD)	N.Y. Coffee,Sugar&Cocoa Ex.	9:30 A.M.-3:00 P.M.	30,000 Lbs.	1/100¢	$3.00	4¢*
COFFEE "C"	N.Y. Coffee,Sugar&Cocoa Ex.	9:45 A.M. - 2:28 P.M.	37,500 Lbs.	1/100¢	$3.75	4¢*
COMMERCIAL PAPER	Chicago Board of Trade	9:30 A.M. - 3:00 P.M.	$1,000,000 (Face)	1/100 of 1% 90-day basis	$25.00	50/100 of 1%*
COPPER	Commodity Exch., Inc., N.Y.	9:50 A.M. - 2:00 P.M.	25,000 Lbs.	5/100¢	$12.50	5¢
COTTON #2	New York Cotton Exchange	10:30 A.M. - 3:00 P.M.	50,000 Lbs.	1/100¢	$5.00	2¢*
Currencies						
BRITISH POUND	International Monetary Market of Chic. Merc. Exch.	9:15 A.M. - 2:24 P.M.	25,000 BP	$.0005	$12.50	$.0500*
CANADIAN DOLLAR		9:15 A.M. - 2:22 P.M.	100,000 CD	$.0001	$10.00	$.0075*
DEUTSCHE MARK		9:15 A.M. - 2:20 P.M.	125,000 DM	$.0001	$12.50	$.0100*
JAPANESE YEN		9:15 A.M. - 2:26 P.M.	12.5 Mil. JY	$.000001	$12.50	$.0100*
SWISS FRANC		9:15 A.M. - 2:16 P.M.	125,000 SF	$.0001	$12.50	$.0150*
EGGS, SHELL (FRESH)	Chicago Mercantile Exchange	10:20 A.M. - 2:00 P.M.	22,500 Dz.	5/100¢	$11.25	2¢
GINNIE MAE MTGES.	Chicago Board of Trade	9:00 A.M. - 3:00 P.M.	$100,000 @ 8%	1/32	$31.25	64/32*
GOLD	Chicago Board of Trade	9:30 A.M. - 2:35 P.M.	96.45 Troy oz.	$.10/Oz.	$9.60	$40.00
	IMM—Chicago Merc. Exch.	9:25 A.M. - 2:30 P.M.	100 Troy oz.	$.10/Oz.	$10.00	$50.00
	Commodity Exch. Inc., N.Y.	9:25 A.M. - 2:30 P.M.	100 Troy oz.	$.10/Oz.	$10.00	$25.00*
	N.Y. Mercantile Exchange	9:25 A.M. - 2:30 P.M.	32.15 Troy oz.	$.20/Oz.	$6.40	$24.00*
	Winnipeg Commodity Exch.	9:15 A.M. - 2:30 P.M.	400 Troy oz.	$.05/Oz.	$20.00	$10.00
			100 Troy oz.	$.05/Oz.	$5.00	$10.00
Grains-Chicago WHEAT, SOYBEANS, CORN, OATS	Chicago Board of Trade	10:30 A.M. - 2:15 P.M.	5,000 Bus.	1/4¢	$12.50	Wheat 20¢, Soybeans 30¢ Corn 10¢ Oats 6¢ *
Grains-Minneapolis WHEAT	Minneapolis Grain Exchange	10:30 A.M. - 2:15 P.M.	5,000 Bus.	1/8¢	$6.25	20¢*
Grains-Kansas City WHEAT, SORGHUM	Kansas City Board of Trade	10:30 A.M. 2:15 P.M.	5,000 Bus.	1/4¢	$12.50	Wheat—25¢ Sorghum—10¢
Grains-Winnipeg BARLEY, OATS, RYE, RAPESEED, FLAXSEED	Winnipeg Commodity Ex.	10:30 A.M. 2:15 P.M.	20 Metric Tons	10¢/Ton	$2.00	Barley, Oats, Rye $5.00/Ton Rapeseed & Flaxseed $10.00/Ton
HOGS, (LIVE)	Chicago Mercantile Exchange	10:15 A.M. - 1:55 P.M.	30,000 Lbs.	2½/100¢	$7.50	1½¢
LUMBER (OLD)	Chicago Mercantile Exchange	10:00 A.M. - 2:05 P.M.	100,000 Bd. Ft.	10¢/1000 Board Ft.	$10.00	$5.00
ORANGE JUICE (Frozen Concentrate)	New York Cotton Exchange	10:15 A.M. - 2:45 P.M.	15,000 Lbs.	5/100¢	$7.50	5¢**
PLATINUM	N.Y. Mercantile Exchange	9:30 A.M.-2:30 P.M.	50 Troy oz.	10¢	$5.00	$20.00*
PLYWOOD	Chicago Board of Trade	10:00 A.M. - 2:00 P.M.	76,032 Sq. Ft.	10¢/1000 Sq Ft.	$7.60	$7.00*
PORK BELLIES	Chicago Mercantile Exchange	10:10 A.M. - 2:00 P.M.	38,000 Lbs.	2½/100¢	$9.50	2¢
POTATOES	Maine-N.Y. Merc. Exch.	9:50 A.M. - 2:00 P.M.	50,000 Lbs.	1¢	$5.00	50¢*
	Idaho Russ.Chi.Merc.Exch.	10:10 A.M. - 2:00 P.M.	80,000 Lbs.	1¢	$8.00	50¢
SILVER	Commodity Exch., Inc., N.Y.	9:40 A.M. - 2:15 P.M.	5,000 Troy oz.	10/100¢	$5.00	40¢*
	Chicago Board of Trade	9:40 A.M. - 2:25 P.M.	5,000 Troy oz.	10/100¢	$5.00	60¢*
SOYBEAN MEAL	Chicago Board of Trade	10:30 A.M. - 2:15 P.M.	100 Tons	10¢	$10.00	$10.00*
SOYBEAN OIL	Chicago Board of Trade	10:30 A.M. - 2:15 P.M.	60,000 Lbs.	1/100¢	$6.00	1¢*
SUGAR world #11 domestic #12	N.Y. Coffee,Sugar&Cocoa Ex.	10:00 A.M. - 2:43 P.M.	112,000 Lbs.	1/100¢	$11.20	½¢*
Treasuries						
T - BILLS (13-week)	IMM-Chicago Merc. Exch.	9:10 A.M. - 2:40 P.M.	$1,000,000 (Face)	.01 of IMM Index	$25.00	.50*
T - BONDS (Long Term)	Chicago Board of Trade	9:00 A.M. - 3:00 P.M.	$100,000/8%	1/32 Pt.	$31.25	64/32*

*Variable limits go into effect under certain conditions.   **Limit is also maximum range.

Commissions and Margins: CONTACT YOUR BROKER FOR ALL INFORMATION.

All statements made herein, while not guaranteed, are based on information considered reliable and are believed by us to be accurate.

Source: Shearson Loeb Rhodes Inc.

FIGURE 9–9

C.M.E. Symbols

LC Live Cattle	PB Pork Bellies
FC Feeder Cattle	BB Boneless Beef
LH Live Hogs	HM Frozen Hams

A.M.M. Symbols

LB Lumber	B Butter
ST Stud Lumber	P Russet Burbank Potatoes
E Shell Eggs	TK Frozen Turkeys
FE Frozen Eggs	MI Yellow Sorghum (Milo)
NE Nest-Run Eggs	

I.M.M. Symbols

BP British Pound	MP Mexican Peso
CD Canadian Dollar	SF Swiss Franc
DM Deutsche Mark	UC U.S. Coins
DG Dutch Guilder	CR Copper
JY Japanese Yen	GD Gold
FR French Franc	TB U.S. Treasury Bills

Month Symbols

January	F	July	N
February	G	August	Q
March	H	September	U
April	J	October	V
May	K	November	X
June	M	December	Z

Note: When a transaction is made for a delivery month more than a year away, the symbol "NXT" will appear on the ticker. For example, it is March and pork bellies are being traded for delivery in July of both the current year and the following year. A trade for the following year might appear on the ticker as PBN NXT 72.20.

Using these tables, here is an explanation of the following prices:

PBH 67.30	LCZ 40.22	DMM .43150
Pork Bellies	Live Cattle	Deutsche Mark
March	December	June
67.30¢	$40.22	43.150¢
a lb.	a 100 lbs.	a Deutsche Mark

Note: Data courtesy of Chicago Mecantile Exchange.

modity, and prices may move up or down only in multiples of these basic pricing units. This provides for uniformity in the pricing of contracts, ease of trade, and a universal standard by which the value of price moves can be computed. Corn, oats, and soybeans all have minimum fluctuations of ¼ cent per bushel, which for the 5,000 bushel contract means $12.50. (Every one cent price move is worth $50.) Most other contracts trade in "points," each point being equal to 1/100th of a cent (or dollar), and the minimum fluctuation is set at some number of points. Broilers, cattle, and hogs and bellies, for example, vary in price by a minimum of 2½ points, or 2½/100ths of a cent per pound. Foreign currency futures are quoted in dollars or cents per one unit of the foreign denomination with fluctuations in basis points accordingly.

The exchange also establishes a daily trading limit for the price fluctuation of each commodity. These floors and ceilings are set in relation to the previous closing price and protect everyone involved from catastrophic losses possible because of margin leverage. The price of soybeans can only fluctuate in a 60 cent range, 30 cents either way from the preceding day's close. If the price does go "limit up" or "limit down," it is usually in reaction to political news, the release of a crop report, an action by the Federal Reserve Board, or some other equally significant occurrence. In such cases the pit will remain open for anybody who wishes to trade at a price within the permissible range, but no trades will be allowed at prices beyond the published limits. For each commodity, the exchange has contingency rules to deal with markets so volatile that limit moves become common. Each successive day that limit moves occur puts greater and greater pressure on the market. In the event of really drastic news, trading may not take place for several days. Each day the range moves the limit until prices catch up with the public estimation of fair price. In this event, and only in this rare event, it is possible for a trader to lose his entire margin capital supply and more. If trading effectively ceases as a string of limit move days push prices radically up or down, brokerages will be unable to close out the customer's position. Losses of two or three times the original margin outlay can then occur, and the trader is helpless to stop them.

Daily trading limits may be suspended

or adjusted during times of volatility or in the final days of trading. The trader must keep abreast of such adjustments in order to prevent huge losses or to protect sizeable profits. Unless you are already in and the market is going your way, it is best to sit on the sidelines and just observe when a commodity takes to making successive limit moves.

THE CLEARINGHOUSE

After the gong sounds and trading ends, the work of the clearinghouse begins. Each exchange has its own clearinghouse, which is a distinct legal entity charged with "clearing" all the day's transactions and handling all the transfers of funds generated by the execution of trades. The membership of the clearinghouse usually includes a select number of the larger or more prestigious exchange member firms. (See Figure 9–10.) Nobody would have reason to be a member of a clearinghouse who was not also a seat holder on the exchange serviced, but not all seat holders are clearinghouse members. Those who are not must pay an extra fee for the services provided by the clearinghouse members for them in addition to the normal service fees. Members are chosen by the exchange according to specific standards regarding the firm's commitment to the exchange: its financial conditions, business integrity, and ability to perform the services of a clearing member.

Without exception, all transactions on the exchange are made in the names of the clearing members. It is this name, rather than the customer's, that appears on the official record and which determines ultimate financial responsibility. It is the clearing member that must guaran-

FIGURE 9–10

Clearing members

ACLI INTERNATIONAL COMMODITY SERVICES, INC. • 141 W. Jackson Blvd., Chicago, IL 60604 • 987-4400
AGRA TRADING, INC. • 141 W. Jackson Blvd., Chicago, IL 60604 • 435-2900
*AMERICAN TRANSEURO CORP. • 175 W. Jackson Blvd., Chicago, IL 60604 • 427-0890
ANSPACHER & ASSOC., INC. • 222 S. Riverside Pl., Chicago, IL 60606 • 648-1152
*ARON, J. & CO., INC. • 327 S. LaSalle St., Chicago, IL 60604 • 922-8787

BACHE HALSEY STUART SHIELDS INC. • 141 W. Jackson Blvd., Chicago, IL 60604 • 630-7000
BARNES BROKERAGE CO., INC. • 222 S. Riverside Pl., Chicago, IL 60606 • 648-1404
BEAR, STEARNS & CO. • 230 W. Monroe St., Chicago, IL 60606 • 630-4801
BECKER, A. G.—H. S. KIPNIS & CO. • 209 S. LaSalle St., Chicago, IL 60604 • 372-1410
*BRODY, WHITE & CO., INC. • Four World Trade Ctr., New York, NY 10048 • 212/938-9600 • 312/427-4013

CARGILL INVESTOR SERVICES, INC. • 141 W. Jackson Blvd., Chicago, IL 60604 • 435-8300
CARL, JACK, ASSOCIATES • 222 S. Riverside Pl., Chicago, IL 60606 • 648-1938
CLAYTON BROKERAGE CO. OF ST. LOUIS, INC. • 222 S. Riverside Pl., Chicago, IL 60606 • 322-4150
COLLINS COMMODITIES, INC. • 141 W. Jackson Blvd., Chicago, IL 60604 • 922-8282
CONTI-COMMODITY SERVICES, INC. • 141 W. Jackson Blvd., Chicago, IL 60604 • 786-0800
CSA, INC. • 222 S. Riverside Pl., Chicago, IL 60606 • 930-1800

DELLSHER INVESTMENT CO., INC. • 222 S. Riverside Pl., Chicago, IL 60606 • 648-1040
*DISCOUNT CORPORATION OF NEW YORK FUTURES • 120 S. Riverside Pl., Chicago, IL 60606 • 648-1757
*DONALDSON, LUFKIN & JENRETTE SECURITIES, CORP. • 140 Broadway, New York, NY 10005 • 212/943-0300 • 312/332-7660
DREXEL BURNHAM LAMBERT INC. • 230 W. Monroe St., Chicago, IL 60606 • 977-3000
*DUNAVANT FINANCIAL, INC. • 7455 Sears Tower, Chicago, IL 60606 • 876-0360

*EASTON & COMPANY • 1 State Street Plaza, New York, NY 10004 • 212/425-4580 • 312/648-0603
EDWARDS, A. G. & SONS, INC. • 141 W. Jackson Blvd., Chicago, IL 60604 • 648-5259

*FIRST CHICAGO INT'L FINANCE CORP. • One First Nat'l Pl., Chicago, IL 60603 • 732-4000
FIRST MID AMERICA, INC. • 175 W. Jackson Blvd., Chicago, IL 60604 • 427-0690
FIRST WALL STREET SETTLEMENT CORP. • 72 W. Adams St., Chicago, IL 60603 • 781-6500
FREEHLING & CO. • 120 S. LaSalle St., Chicago, IL 60603 • 346-2680
FRIEDMAN, RAY E. & CO. • 222 S. Riverside Pl., Chicago, IL 60606 • 454-4900

GNP COMMODITIES, INC. • 222 S. Riverside Pl., Chicago, IL 60606 • 648-2800
GARVEY COMMODITY CORP. • 141 W. Jackson Blvd., Chicago, IL 60604 • 427-5285
GELDERMANN & CO., INC. • 141 W. Jackson Blvd., Chicago, IL 60604 • 322-6700
*GLASS, GINSBURG, LTD. • 120 S. Riverside Pl., Chicago, IL 60606 • 648-0535
GOLDMAN, SACHS & CO. • 6000 Sears Tower, Chicago, IL 60606 • 876-3930

HEINOLD COMMODITIES, INC. • 222 S. Riverside Pl., Chicago, IL 60606 • 648-8000
HENNESSY & ASSOCIATES • 141 W. Jackson Blvd., Chicago, IL 60604 • 341-0444
HUTTON, E. F. & COMPANY, INC. • 141 W. Jackson Blvd., Chicago, IL 60604 • 435-3333

K & S COMMODITIES, INC. • 222 S. Riverside Pl., Chicago, IL 60606 • 930-1600
KEYSTONE TRADING CORP. • 222 S. Riverside Pl., Chicago, IL 60606 • 648-0347
KING & KING, INC. • 222 S. Riverside Pl., Chicago, IL 60606 • 648-1325
KOHN & COMPANY • 222 S. Riverside Pl., Chicago, IL 60606 • 648-0234

LEVY COMMODITIES • 222 S. Riverside Pl., Chicago, IL 60606 • 663-3910
LINCOLN-STALEY COMMODITIES, INC. • 141 W. Jackson Blvd., Chicago, IL 60604 • 341-9480
LINCOLNWOOD, INC. • 141 W. Jackson Blvd., Chicago, IL 60604 • 427-5853
LIND-WALDOCK & CO. • 222 S. Riverside Pl., Chicago, IL 60606 • 648-1400

MADDA TRADING CO. • 309 W. Jackson Blvd., Chicago, IL 60606 • 786-1500
MADUFF & SONS, INC. • 222 S. Riverside Pl., Chicago, IL 60606 • 648-1234
MERRILL LYNCH, PIERCE, FENNER & SMITH, INC. • 141 W. Jackson Blvd., Chicago, IL 60604 • 786-3636
MILLER, G. H. & CO. • 222 S. Riverside Pl., Chicago, IL 60606 • 648-0400
MILLER-JESSER, INC. • 209 W. Jackson Blvd., Chicago, IL 60606 • 322-1750

O'BRIEN, R. J. & ASSOC., INC. • 550 W. Jackson Blvd., Chicago, IL 60606 • 648-7300
O'CONNOR GRAIN CO. • 141 W. Jackson Blvd., Chicago, IL 60604 • 435-0808

PACIFIC COMMODITIES • 141 W. Jackson Blvd., Chicago, IL 60604 • 922-0357
PACKERS TRADING CO., INC. • 222 S. Riverside Pl., Chicago, IL 60606 • 648-5750
PAINE, WEBBER, JACKSON & CURTIS INCORPORATED • 208 S. LaSalle St., Chicago, IL 60604 • 781-9200
PEAVEY COMPANY • 141 W. Jackson Blvd., Chicago, IL 60604 • 939-0600
PETERS & CO. • 141 W. Jackson Blvd., Chicago, IL 60604 • 939-5955
*PHILIPP BROS. COMMODITY CORP. • 1221 Ave. of the Americas, New York, NY 10020 • 212/575-5900
*PLAZA CLEARING CORP. • One New York Plaza, New York, NY 10004 • 212/747-7000 • 312/876-8700

*REPUBLIC CLEARING CORPORATION • 222 S. Riverside Pl., Chicago, IL 60606 • 648-0400
RICH, SOL & CO., INC. • 222 S. Riverside Pl., Chicago, IL 60606 • 648-1188
RICHARDSON SECURITIES, INC. • 141 W. Jackson Blvd., Chicago, IL 60604 • 435-4600
RITTEN, LOUIS N. & CO., INC. • 141 W. Jackson Blvd., Chicago, IL 60604 • 922-6682
ROSENTHAL & COMPANY • 141 W. Jackson Blvd., Chicago, IL 60604 • 786-0900
RUFENACHT, BROMAGEN & HERTZ, INC. • 222 S. Riverside Pl., Chicago, IL 60606 • 930-1252

SHEARSON LOEB RHOADES, INC. • 233 S. Wacker Dr., Chicago, IL 60606 • 855-6000
SIEGEL TRADING CO., INC.,THE • 100 N. LaSalle St., Chicago, IL 60602 • 236-6789
SMITH BARNEY, HARRIS UPHAM & CO. INC. • 175 W. Jackson Blvd., Chicago, IL 60604 • 621-3600
STERN, LEE B. & COMPANY, LTD. • 141 W. Jackson Blvd., Chicago, IL 60604 • 786-0750
STONE, SAUL & COMPANY • 222 S. Riverside Pl., Chicago, IL 60606 • 648-1200
STOTLER & COMPANY • 141 W. Jackson Blvd., Chicago, IL 60604 • 987-2700

TABOR GRAIN CO. • 141 W. Jackson Blvd., Chicago, IL 60604 • 663-1530
THOMSON McKINNON SECURITIES INC. • 134 S. LaSalle St., Chicago, IL 60603 • 630-5800

WEINBERG BROS. & CO. • 222 S. Riverside Pl., Chicago, IL 60606 • 648-4400
DEAN WITTER REYNOLDS, INC. • 141 W. Jackson Blvd., Chicago, IL 60604 • 726-7200
WOODSTOCK, INC. • 222 S. Riverside Pl., Chicago, IL 60606 • 454-8500

*IMM Clearing Members only.

Source: International Monetary Market, Chicago Mercantile Exchange.

tee the performance of all trades it submits to the clearinghouse. After the close of trading, each clearing member will tally up the slips made out by the pit traders during the actual trading and submit them to the clearinghouse. Every clearing member submits a trade confirmation record on a computer card or magnetic tape for every trade executed on behalf of the firm or its customers, detailing the identity of the traders, the number of contracts, and the price. This information is tallied by the clearinghouse to see that an equal number of purchases and sales are listed for the day and that opposite sides agree. When this balance has been established, the clearinghouse accepts the slips and cards and assumes all contract obligations. It literally becomes the opposite party to every transaction.

The clearinghouse guarantees performance by each long and each short clearing member. All traders then hold positions with the clearinghouse rather than with other traders. In this unique way the financial integrity of each transaction is confirmed and the subsequent liquidation of the individual positions made much easier. A trade may have been undertaken during the day involving the sale of five contracts of cotton on the order of a trader in San Francisco to a trader in Des Moines who had placed a buy order with his local brokerage. After the clearinghouse assumes all the day's obligations, the trader in San Francisco holds a contract with the clearinghouse to deliver cotton, and the trader in Des Moines must accept delivery from the clearinghouse unless the position is closed before the delivery date. Because the clearinghouse holds an equal number of short and long positions, it is in no danger of loss due to price changes and does not itself do any speculating on the markets.

The substitution process enables the clearinghouse to act as the enforcer of all payments and collections. This is done on a daily basis so that all outstanding debts are cleared before the start of the next day's trading. (Sudden huge increases in volume have been known to shut down or curtail trading until the clearinghouse could finish its business.) Once the settlement price for each commodity is set, the clearing firms pay their debts and collect their profits for all outstanding contracts, in cash by electronic transfer. No firm is allowed credit or delay, so that everyone starts with a clear slate every day.

The actual contracts are one step further removed from the speculator by the fact that the clearinghouse deals only with members of the exchange. The brokerage that took the order from the trader in Des Moines owes the clearinghouse for five contracts of cotton. The clearinghouse knows nothing of the speculator. Clearing members owe the clearinghouse, non-clearing brokers owe the clearing members, and individual traders owe the brokers. No one can "pass the buck" up or down the line. Margin is required of the brokerage and deposited with the clearinghouse to assure performance on the part of the broker. This is the main reason that the commission houses are so discreet in their choice of customers and so demanding about their financial situation. Should a customer declare bankruptcy or simply drop out of sight, the brokerage that handled the order is still responsible for the contracts it holds with the clearinghouse. The brokerage will be required to meet any loss that might occur in the customer's account. Otherwise, every time a trade was made the participants would have to investigate the solvency of their opposite, an obviously impossible task in the hectic world of commodity trading. In the event that the brokerage also cannot pay the loss, it will automatically be covered by the clearinghouse itself out of special funds and operating profits. Clearing members must deposit certain funds in anticipation of this possibility. This guarantee, and the role of the clearing members in assuring the performance of all trades, accounts for the fact that exchanges seek well-known and respected brokerages and corporations to serve as clearing members. If somehow the loss on runaway contracts exceeds the resources of the established clearing fund, the clearing firms are obliged to cover the contracts. In over 130 years of trading, no clearing member has left any clearinghouse in a position where it could not cover the commitments of its members out of its own funds, and no trader ever lost money due to the bankruptcy or failure to perform of the individuals and firms on the other side of the trade.

On a modern exchange, the clearinghouse is, in fact, nothing more or less than a computer system operated by employees and clerks of the house. If they are unable to match submitted cards, confirmations are returned to the respective clearing members for reconciliation and corrections. Once the daily clearing process has been completed, the computer compiles a trade register for every clearing member, itemizing commodities held, positions long or short, prices, and transactions. The firm's profits or losses for the day, what it is due or owes as a result of open positions, and how much margin money the firm must forward to secure its positions are also compiled by the clearinghouse and the information sent to members.

The existence of the clearinghouse mechanism vastly reduces the difficulty of trading commodities because all positions are held by one trader and the clearinghouse rather than between individual traders. A speculator in Seattle who bought soybeans in April in a deal whose opposite was a commercial hedger working out of New York can sell them back and close the position any time without the need of finding the original contractee. The other party to the trade may have left the market long before or may hold the short position for several months more.

At delivery the clearinghouse matches warehouse receipts tendered by the "shorts" to the "longs" that are still in the spot trading month, normally giving the first receipt to the oldest standing long. Other systems of ownership dispersal exist, but the warehouse receipts are always tendered to the clearinghouse and then handed to the longs who have agreed to accept delivery and who have stayed around long enough for delivery to become a fact.

ORDER VARIATIONS

The fundamental business of the exchanges and clearinghouses is the accurate execution of very specific buy and sell orders. The customer does not just wander into the broker's office and say "sell wheat." Commodities is a game of control. Over the years a number of order variations and restrictions have evolved to allow the public speculator the greatest possible amount of control over his position without the necessity of continual tape reading and order placement. The speculator wants to sell wheat at a particular price, perhaps at a particular time, in relationship to other prices, and with a specified degree of price variability. Generally speaking, a broker can execute any order that is understandable and that can be transmitted in succinct language. (Some types of orders, such as stop-limits, may not be allowed in certain commodities.) The design of orders that can best accomplish the trader's goals is an essential aspect of any successful trading program. It can make all the difference between catching a price swing at the exact right time and missing it completely.

The various orders discussed below are used by traders to exploit the market if, and only if, it reacts in the manner they wish to exploit. This is not an exhaustive list of all order variants ever used, but it does cover all the kinds most often employed. The order's function, whatever its type, is to see that trades are opened and closed when the trader wants them opened and closed. Any order can be replaced or canceled by a phone call. (See Appendix III.)

At market (MKT). This is the unconditional order for the purchase or sale of a contract at the best possible price the pit trader can get. The broker may bid up or offer down in order to fill the order. In active, high volume markets these orders can usually be filled without substantial price concessions. They are more risky in thin markets where a lack of liquidity reduces the prospects for a quick deal at a favorable price.

At opening (OPG). Order is to be filled as specified at the opening or not at all. If only part can be executed (that is, 7 contracts out of an order of 11), the remainder will be left unfilled. Such an order would be used to exploit any price aberrations expected in the opening minutes of trading.

At close (CLO). Similar to the above. In contrast to securities trading, both OPG and CLO orders in commodities can contain other restrictions and will simply not be filled if these cannot be satisfied.

Good through (GT). Order to rest in the trader's deck until proper conditions are met, with a stated time limit. If it has not been filled by then it will be canceled. *Good this week (GTW)* and *Good this month (GTM)* are orders which will be canceled if they have not been executed by the end of the week or month. Orders may be placed specifying a time limit during the trading day, as in "Good through 11:15." Time orders must conform to the policy of the brokerage as to whether it is stated in local, New York, or Chicago time. *Good till canceled (GTC)* is a common, open-ended time order.

Fill or kill (FOK). This order must be filled as specified immediately upon receipt or canceled. If part of the order can be filled, that part will be executed and the remainder canceled.

Stop order (STP). A stop order rests with the pit broker until other conditions prevail, usually the movement of prices to the level specified by the order. Once that level is reached, the stop is "tripped" and the other executed at the best possible price, as if it were a market order. Stop orders are frequently used to buy or sell contracts only in accordance with the speculator's predetermined game plan and view of price trends. This way the trader only gets into the market when prices are at a level he has determined as promising a profitable trend. The most important stop order is the "stop-loss" order. This order takes the trader out of the market if prices go against the position to a degree sufficient to warrant full retreat. Setting stop orders requires that the speculator plan ahead, judging all the possibilities and protecting himself whatever may occur. Many traders set stops, whether to get in or out, according to their readings of the contract's price charts (showing the range of fluctuation of prices for the contract), or where computer analyses dictate. Thus, oftentimes one can read in reviews of pit action that a flurry of buying or selling was caused by a price move tripping a widely held stop.

Limit order. The word "limit" accompanies orders when the customer only wants to buy or sell at a specified price or better. The advantage of the limit order is in the strict control it gives the trader over prices paid for contracts. Its disadvantage is that it can prevent the successful execution of a purchase or sale when the precise price cannot immediately be found. A trader may see the ticker price go through the limit level and yet not complete his trade if the pit broker does not happen to be in the right place at the right time. This is almost always a matter of chance, not negligence.

Stop-limit. This order combines the "stop" and "limit" options so that the trader controls entrance or exit from the position and sets a limit to the price paid. The limit gives the maximum or minimum acceptable price after the stop has been tripped. Thus, the speculator might set the stop at $5.30 and the limit at $5.35 when buying wheat.

Market if touched (MIT). The MIT order is activated whenever prices hit the stipulated level and executed as a market order that can be filled at, above, or below that price. Chartists may use MIT's to guarantee entrance into a market when prices reach a predetermined extreme range.

Basis orders (BAS). This order is oriented to changes in the basis, or price differential, between two commodity prices.

For example, "Buy five March bellies when May bellies rise to 60.25." In this transaction only the March pork bellies are bought, although the May pork bellies are used to trip the stop. Limits and stop orders may be appended to the basis order, specifying the price range for the month to be purchased.

Spread order. Spread orders are speculations on the basis between two contract prices, only in this case the trader establishes two positions—one in each. In instituting a spread position, the trader is primarily interested in the amount of the basis, not in the absolute price levels of the contracts. The spread order buys one month and sells an equal number of another. The spread may be in two months of the same commodity, in two different but related commodities, or in the same commodity but in two different markets (March over May wheat; Chicago over New York gold, etc.). In spreads the basis will be the condition for the sale and when the set spread has occurred both the purchase and sale will be made. In intermarket spreads it is customary to send the order to the smaller market where the trade is most difficult.

One cancels other (OCO). This is an "alternative" order consisting of two orders, one entered above the last market price and one entered below the last market price. This is done either to liquidate open positions or initiate new positions when the trader is not exactly sure which way prices will move. For instance, a speculator who has bought a contract at $6.63 may place an OCO establishing a sell limit order at $6.93 and a sell stop at $6.33, the fulfillment of either automatically canceling the other.

Scale order. A scale order can be used to scale in contract positions at set intervals as prices move in a certain direction. "Buy 5 March wheat at MKT and 5 each 1¢ down total 25 day" would put the trader in at market price and add to his position one contract (5,000 bushels) at time for each one penny move until five contracts were held. The positions would be established only if the market moved in the direction stated in the order.

Market if tendered. Orders the broker to close a position if notice of delivery is received in the delivery month.

Cancellation orders. It may seem an obvious point, but in the rush of trading some speculators forget to cancel old or suddenly outdated orders. It is well to make certain that unless otherwise noted, all of your orders are "day" orders to be canceled at the close of the day's trading. A "straight cancel order" simply wipes out a previous directive. Cancel orders should contain all the specifics and details of the original order, so that no foul-ups take place at the brokerage office or in the pit. Cancellation orders may also be designed to replace former orders, often by adjusting the directed price level.

As the trader must transmit orders through a broker, wire or phone clerk, and pit broker, such variations should be worked out between the speculator and the broker with a clear understanding of each order's meaning. Usually, a form can be found which will economically fill any need the trader may come up with and any trading combination imaginable. Such orders, while convenient, may cause problems in some commodity pits if a great many traders use similar trading methods and systems, causing spurts and other dislocations when the price hits a level considered significant by many traders. It is for this reason that some of the pits disallow certain orders, and the speculator should determine in advance what kinds of orders are accepted at the markets he intends to play.

STOP LOSS EXECUTION

Imagine that you have been following the corn market and have good reasons to believe that the present downturn will continue for some time. You will give your broker an order to sell 10,000 bushels of March corn short at $3.50 or better, stop loss $3.55, "good till canceled." An order will be sent to Chicago reading "Sell 10m March Corn $3.50." A second order will say "Buy 10 m March corn $3.55 STP GTC." Relayed almost instantly by clerks, phones, and messengers, the order goes to the pit trader who executes it immediately, if possible. If he cannot, a slip of paper containing the order gets put into his deck along with others waiting to be filled. This handful of papers is arranged in his grasp so that all slips read in order according to price. By keeping the deck open to the going price, the orders held can be easily read and filled. Some of these orders may have been in the deck for a month or more, others for only a few minutes. Some will never leave the deck until the end of trading in that particular commodity or month because the price never reaches the level stipulated for execution.

When a buyer has been found and the trade completed, confirmation goes back to the brokerage house and is mailed out to the customer. This confirmation slip is the only official record of holding that the speculator will receive in the course of maintaining the position. The broker will take the requisite margin from the trader's account to secure the position. As long as the market price for corn remains steady, nothing further happens. If the price drops, profits will pile up and the trader may take funds in excess of the margin requirement out of the margin account. If the price rises and the trader holds onto his position, a margin call may be issued, instructing the trader to restore margin to a specified level.

The original order to the broker was actually two orders, both of which were passed along in code to the pit trader. The first was to sell March corn at $3.50 or better. If the prevailing price was lower than $3.50 and he could find no takers at the ordered price, the order went into the deck. The second order was to buy (effectively to liquidate) March corn when and if the price rises to $3.55 (a market order once $3.55 is hit) and will not be executed unless the first order has been filled, at which time the second order— the stop-loss order—enters the deck as a regular stop order.

The result of such paired orders is to ensure that the trader makes the sale at no worse price than he indicates, in this case $3.50. If he can sell at a higher price, he has done better than planned. The second order is designed to take the speculator out of the market should prices rise, causing a loss on the original short sale. The speculator here has indicated he is willing to sit through a rise of less than 5 cents, but at 5 cents he is willing to admit his mistake and have his loss stopped. Buying 10,000 bushels at $3.55 will effectively cover the original short position and take him out of the market. If the market shoots past $3.55 before the stop-loss can be executed, the trader still wants out at the best price available. Thus, in fact, he has entered one limit order, good until canceled, and one stop-loss order which is not to be executed unless the market moves above $3.55.

A buy order would have been handled in exactly the same manner. The original purchase might have been "at the market" and fillable at the prevailing price or a limit order to be filled at a given price or less, good until canceled. The stop loss would have entered the deck when the first order was filled or close to it, ready to close the position at the market once the stop point had been hit.

THE COMMODITY FUTURES TRADING COMMISSION

Government regulation of the commodity futures industry was minimal until 1974, when the Commodity Futures Trading Commission (CFTC) was established to replace the old Commodity Exchange Authority (CEA). The CEA had been an office within the Department of Agriculture, with its roots in the days when almost all commodity futures were in agricultural products. The CEA kept a low profile and interfered only rarely with the cherished independence of traders and exchanges. The phenomenal growth of the industry, the trade in nonagricultural contracts, a series of widely publicized scandals, and the turmoil associated with the Russian Wheat Deal prompted Congress to create the CFTC as a separate regulatory agency analogous to the Securities and Exchange Commission. Since that time the CFTC and the futures industry have been in an awkward period of transition, marked by the persistent antagonisms characteristic of many regulator/ industry relationships and increased in this case by the inexperience of the agency and the resentment of an historically freewheeling business. The outcome of this constantly evolving contest for authority and power will be a major factor in shaping the form of the futures trade in the next decades. (See Figure 9–11.)

The CFTC has a chairman and four other commissioners, appointed by the president subject to Senate ratification. Their terms are for five years, and the CFTC has been reviewed by Congress every four years. The work of the Commis-sion employs hundreds of analysts, lawyers, and surveillance personnel in offices across the nation. (See Figure 9–12.) The CFTC exercises both rule making and enforcement powers over all futures exchanges, commodity futures contracts, commodity options, and persons engaged in the trade and brokerage of futures. The

FIGURE 9–11

INCREASED REGULATION OF FUTURES INDUSTRY INEVITABLE, STONE SAYS

WASHINGTON--MAR 5--CNS--JAMES STONE, CHAIRMAN OF THE COMMODITY FUTURES TRADING COMMISSION, TODAY SAID IT WAS INEVITABLE THAT THE U.S. FUTURES INDUSTRY WILL BE REGULATED MORE, RATHER THAN LESS, IN THE YEAR TO COME.

HOWEVER, HE CALLED ON EXCHANGES TO SHARE THIS REGULATORY BURDEN AND NOT LET THE JOB FALL TO THE CFTC ALONE.

IN REMARKS PREPARED FOR DELIVERY TO THE FUTURES INDUSTRY ASSOCIATION CONFERENCE IN MIAMI, FLA., STONE SAID HE WAS NOT SATISFIED WITH THE CURRENT STATE OF COMMODITY REGULATION.

"NOWHERE NEAR ENOUGH IS DONE TO PROTECT CUSTOMERS FROM ABUSES AT THE RETAIL LEVEL," HE SAID.

HE ALSO SAID NOT ENOUGH WAS BEING DONE TO PROTECT PRODUCERS AGAINST MARKET MANIPULATION, OR TO ASSURE THE "PURITY AND INTEGRITY OF FLOOR PRACTICES ON THE EXCHANGES."

"I WOULD FAVOR REGULATORY ACTION IN EACH OF THESE AREAS," HE TOLD THE CONFERENCE.

TO HELP SOLVE THESE PROBLEMS, STONE ADVOCATED THE ADOPTION OF EFFECTIVE RULES FOR FRONT OFFICE PRACTICE BY COMMISSION MERCHANTS AND THE CREATION OF A MECHANISM TO ENFORCE RETAILING STANDARDS; SUITABILITY RULES TO MAKE SURE THAT CUSTOMERS HAVE THE FINANCIAL RESOURCES AND KNOWLEDGE APPROPRIATE TO THE POSITIONS THEY ARE ENCOURAGED TO TAKE; BETTER MARKET SURVEILLANCE TOOLS FOR THE COMMISSION AND EXCHANGES; AND IF NECESSARY, SAFETY VALVES OR POSITION LIMITS IN TIGHT MARKETS.

STONE SAID THE GOVERNMENT SHOULD INVOLVE ITSELF IN SETTING PUBLIC POLICY AND LEAVE THE MARKET ECONOMIC SYSTEM TO THE PRIVATE SECTOR.

"THE CFTC AND INDUSTRY SHOULD WORK TOGETHER TOWARD A BETTER ALLOCATION OF THE TASK AT HAND," STONE SAID. "THE ENHANCEMENT OF SELF-REGULATION IS AS WORTHY OF YOUR (THE INDUSTRY'S) ATTENTION AS (SELF-REGULATION) IS OF OURS," HE SAID.   END
1508 CST#

FIGURE 9–12
Annual report 1978

PROGRAMS/SUBPROGRAMS

Market Surveillance
- Daily Market Surveillance
- Market Analysis

Research and Education
- Research
- Education

Registration, Audits and Contract Markets
- Audits and Financial Review
- Contract Markets
- Registration

Enforcement
- Reparations
- Customer Inquiries/Complaints
- Investigations
- Litigation

Executive Direction and Centralized Support
- Hearings and Appeals
- Legal Counsel
- Agency Director
- Centralized Administration (Headquarters and Regions)

Registration, Audits & Contract Markets

Audit and Financial Review

Segregation Audits of FCM's	92
General Audits of FCM's	98
Preregistration Audits	71
Clearing Association Audits	8
Customer Accounts Examined (thousands)	82
Customer Equities Represented ($ millions)	511
Audits of Exchange Financial Rule Enforcement	1
Financial Statements Reviewed	1,413

Contract Markets

Contract Markets Designated	9
Contract Rules Approved	174
Rule Enforcement Reviews	4
Trade Practice Investigations	6

Registration

Futures Commission Merchants	372
Associated Persons	12,266
Floor Brokers	2,901
Commodity Pool Operators	670
Commodity Trading Advisors	971
Total Registrations	17,180
Fitness Name Checks Completed	10,099
Fitness Investigations Completed	266
Denial or Revocation Actions	40
Reparations — Reviewed	1,132
Referred for Hearing	336
Customer Inquiries/Complaints Customer Complaints Received	686
Processed	317
Investigations — Open	199
Closed	156

Litigation

Administrative Proceedings	Open	67
	Closed	14
Injunctions	Open	18
	Closed	4

CFTC Program Performance

	FY 1978 Actual
Daily Market Surveillance	
Trader and Broker Reports Processed (thousands)	991
Permanent Record Tables Prepared	7,959
Reports Checked (thousands)	691
Reports Published	725
Compliance and Warning Letters Issued	524
Reporting Requirements — Speculative Limits	125
Market Analysis	
Economic Review of Rule Changes	11
Economic Review of Existing Contract Markets	3
Economic Review of New Contract Market Designations	10

Source: Commodity Futures Trading Commission.

Commission's goals are to prevent deliberate manipulation or distortion of the markets, enforce fair trade processes, certify the financial integrity of the market place and broker community, protect the rights of customers, and provide a forum for legitimate grievances and reparations.

To meet these objectives the CFTC is charged with performing a long list of specific functions and, in turn, oversees the compliance of the industry with federal regulations. Its actions can have a decisive impact on the nature of the futures trade. The CFTC has sole power to designate and authorize futures exchanges and boards of trade as legal contract markets. All proposals for new contracts must be approved by the Commission. It registers all Futures Commission Merchants, floor brokers, Associated Persons, commodity pools, and trading advisors. It lays down the procedures for the protection of customer funds, for establishment of brokerage integrity, and periodically audits the records of FCMs. The CFTC's surveillance division monitors every contract every day, watching for potential abuses such as price fixing, cornering, or extreme volatility so dangerous as to threaten the legitimate functions of the market. Its enforcement division investigates questionable practices and takes legal measures when justified. In its efforts to encourage industry self-regulation, the CFTC has conducted extensive reviews of each exchange's ability and actual record in enforcing its own rules. The Commission may also recognize a national association of the futures industry for the purposes of self-regulation if such an association appears and so qualifies. The Commission's offices regularly gather and publish data on its activities and on the markets, including the much cited *Commitments of Traders* reports.

Futures Commission Merchants are defined by the CFTC as any individual, association, partnership, or corporation that buys or sells futures contracts on commission. FCMs must meet certain financial requirements and submit regular independently audited statements. Associated Persons (APs) are defined as anyone associated with an FCM and who solicits or accepts customers' orders (other than clerks) or who supervises persons so engaged. They, too, must register with the Commission. CFTC regulations also define and require the registration of all Commodity Trading Advisors and Commodity Pool Operators and stipulate fair procedures for their enterprises.

The Commission must review and approve the bylaws, rules, and contract terms for each futures exchange. Extensive hearings on new exchanges and new contracts are commonplace, with revision after revision passing back and forth from the proponents to the regulators. Exchanges must demonstrate that the contract is in the public interest and serves a real economic need. The jurisdiction of the CFTC over all commodities contracts means that it handles a wide diversity of items that may fall under the regulatory umbrella of other agencies, such as the Treasury Department or the Securities and Exchange Commission, in which case interagency squabbles may further delay action. Litigation between the CFTC and the exchanges has upheld the Commission's power to declare a trading emergency and to take corrective measures, including the suspension of trade. Limits on positions, both daily and overnight, are set by the CFTC, and FCMs are required to report the customer's account whenever such limits are reached.

Much of the agency's effort is spent on customer protection, especially in regard

FIGURE 9-13

RISK DISCLOSURE STATEMENT

This statement is furnished to you because rule 1.55 of the Commodity Futures Trading Commission requires it.

The risk of loss in trading commodity futures contracts can be substantial. You should therefore carefully consider whether such trading is suitable for you in light of your financial condition. In considering whether to trade, you should be aware of the following:

(1) You may sustain a total loss of the initial margin funds and any additional funds that you deposit with your broker to establish or maintain a position in the commodity futures market. If the market moves against your position, you may be called upon by your broker to deposit a substantial amount of additional margin funds, on short notice, in order to maintain your position. If you do not provide the required funds within the prescribed time, your position may be liquidated at a loss, and you will be liable for any resulting deficit in your account.

(2) Under certain market conditions, you may find it difficult or impossible to liquidate a position. This can occur, for example, when the market makes a "limit move."

(3) Placing contigent orders, such as "stop-loss" or "stop-limit" order, will not necessarily limit your losses to the intended amounts, since market conditions may make it impossible to execute such orders.

(4) A "spread" position may not be less risky than a simple "long" or "short" position.

(5) The high degree of leverage that is often obtainable in futures trading because of the small margin requirements can work against you as well as for you. The use of leverage can lead to large losses as well as gains.

This brief statement cannot, of course, disclose all the risks and other significant aspects of the commodity markets. You should therefore, carefully study futures trading before you trade.

The undersigned hereby acknowledges that he has read this Risk Disclosure Statement and that he understands its' contents.

_____

Customer Signature

to proper exchange operation and brokerage proceedings. FCMs who trade their own accounts must give priority to customer orders and may not circumvent this priority through any tactic deliberately resulting in a conflict of interest. Supervision of FCMs is mandated, to include frequent reviews of employees and accounts by firm management. FCMs are forbidden to execute a trade for the customer without specific prior approval and must have a written power of attorney to trade on a discretionary basis. Truth-in-advertising statutes of the CFTC pertain to all brokerage, pool, and advisory advertisements; hypothetical or stimulated track records must be labeled as such and a risk disclosure must accompany the promotion. (See Figure 9–13.) Customer suitability standards exist to protect both the FCM and the prospective trader. The CFTC ensures that all the exchanges have fair and equitable procedures for customer grievances and claims. Customers may also take administrative reparations proceedings before the Commission itself. The CFTC may suspend anyone from activity in the futures industry after requisite hearings and may assess fines as penalties for rule violations.

Chapter 10

COMMODITY OPTIONS

FOOLS RUSH IN

In 1971 a cocky young college dropout from Louisiana named Harold Goldstein set up shop in Los Angeles, dealing in commodity options. Options give the holder the right (but not the obligation) to assume a commodity position at a fixed price sometime in the future in return for a set fee. If prices fail to advance (or decline) sufficiently, the fee is lost. Potential profits, on the other hand, are theoretically limitless. So are the profits of the dealer who can talk people into purchasing options without any guarantee that the commodities can be delivered. Goldstein saw his pot of gold.

Commodity options were not a new invention. From 1926 until 1933 they were actively traded at the Chicago Board of Trade in wheat, rye, corn, oats, and other contracts. A boom in options on futures led to a crash, however, when rising prices drove crowds of dealers into the pits in efforts to hedge the options they had sold and which were now sure to be exercised. Prices were forced up by a demand disconnected from fundamentals until the scramble ended and prices plummeted, rendering the options worthless and upset-ting the normal functions of the market. The U.S. government banned the sale of options on all *regulated* commodities. But at the beginning of the 1970s a number of unregulated items (coffee, sugar, cocoa, and metals) came to the attention of a public aware of the fabulous profits many were now making in these goods. They were eager for a piece of the action. Waiting to take their money was Harold Goldstein. (See Figure 10–1.)

Goldstein knew that options had been trading in London since the nineteenth century with considerable success and integrity. He also knew that although the average investor stood in awe of the legendary profits to be made in commodity futures trading, most dared not risk a speculation so potentially ruinous. Most importantly, Goldstein saw that dealing in options on unregulated commodities escaped the jurisdiction of both the Securities and Exchange Commission and the old Commodity Exchange Authority. An options dealer needed no license, did not have to report to an exchange, and did not have to register with any government agency. He could literally just set up shop and start selling, whether or not he really had anything to sell at all.

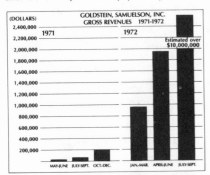

Goldstein's scheme was a classic "Ponzi" scam, named after an early innovator in the mass marketing of nonexistent securities. (See Figure 10–2.) In a Ponzi, investors buy shares, coupons, options, or whatever with the promise of later profits, only to find out in the end that no investment was ever actually made or contemplated. Revenue from new sales is used to pay off a portion of standing investors or, in Goldstein's case, those whose options showed a profit when prices moved. As 80 percent of the speculators should by all probability be losers in commodity speculation, the organizer of the Ponzi stands to pocket a sizeable sum with no risk or effort at all. Unfortunately for Goldstein, things didn't go that way in 1972 or 1973. Unprecedented advances in the markets made many of his options holders big winners, and the claims far outpaced even the new sales ace-showman Goldstein could drum up at his well publicized "investment seminars." Goldstein had never purchased any of the contracts he had promised as hedges against the options. Meanwhile, a long list of financial chicanery on Goldstein's part began to be compiled by state and federal investigators and Goldstein had to fire his own top executives when they tried to stop him from sending over a half-million dollars out of the country.

Legend has it that Goldstein began his adventure with $800 in his pocket. Others contend that his financial backing came from the notorious wizard of international investment fraud, Bernie Cornfeld. No one disputes that by the end of 1972 Goldstein, Samuelson, Inc. was grossing $45 million in premiums for worthless options. By the end of February 1973 the "world's largest commodity options underwriter" was in receivership—bankrupt. Its outstanding debts ran into the tens of millions of dollars, earning a place as one of the largest investment frauds in United States history. Along the way Goldstein had stolen stocks, had forged a letter asserting that his corporation was fully insured, had embezzled untold thousands, had been expelled from the West Coast Commodity Exchange, and in the end had tried to buy himself out of his own company through a dummy foreign corporation in a deal that would have absolved him of any responsibility for past actions. As Goldstein himself put it, "There were really some dirty things going on at Goldstein, Samuelson." (See Figure 10–3.)

Government investigators, lawyers, and officials tracked Goldstein with all the precision of the Keystone Cops. Goldstein had spotted the legal hole and ducked through it. These options were anomalous. They were not on CEA regulated commodities, but as risk speculations of a specific sort they were not securities either. Finally, an angry and frustrated state official in California, Brian Van Camp, turned the tables on Goldstein. Since, in fact, Goldstein was not hedging his options—not actually buying any of the contracts on the futures markets his customers were taking out their options on—then Goldstein was peddling "naked" options. Monies paid out to customers were *not* the results of speculations but returns on investments in the money schemes of Goldstein, Samuelson. As such, Van Camp ruled, these were indeed securities. The trap closed. Van Camp's Commission on Corporations demanded that Goldstein and all options dealers register as securities dealers with the state of California and abide by all pertinent regulations.

FIGURE 10–2

Charles Ponzi's legacy

The investment swindle that immortalized Charles Ponzi is the oldest, and the simplest, in the world. Yet there never seems to be a shortage of credulous victims. Two fascinating versions broke into the open this past week—one a wine fraud in Virginia, the other an oil drilling swindle based in Tulsa, Okla. Both show that sophisticated financiers and businessmen are as likely to take the bait as schoolteachers or widows.

At least $26-million was lost in wine that wasn't there. But perhaps four times as much money vanished in phony oil shelters that trapped big names in U. S. business.

In a classic Ponzi game, the investors' money is never invested in anything. Early investors are paid "gains" out of money that later investors put up. The purest operations are chain letters and pyramid sales schemes. But almost any investment vehicle can be, or can turn into, a Ponzi swindle, so long as new money keeps coming in. Versions in recent years have included offshore mutual funds, commodity options, and cattle investment clubs. Some of the commodity, silver, and coin investment groups being hawked to the public today may eventually prove to be Ponzi frauds.

Johnson's wine. But the old master, Charles Ponzi himself, would have envied the two latest variations. The wine scheme was set up by a Chesapeake & Potomac Telephone Co. employee in McLean, Va., named Robert D. Johnson. The notion was to buy low-grade "industrial" wine in Europe, ship it to the U. S., and sell it to food processors such as Heinz for salad dressings and the like. Johnson offered investors promissory notes to be repaid in nine months at guaranteed returns of 30% to 100%. But as the SEC describes it, there was never any wine or any ships. In fact, wine experts say there's no such thing as "industrial" wine.

Nonetheless, Johnson kept the game going for 10 years—always paying off the notes as old investors kept reinvesting and new investors were attracted by word of mouth. Then, in 1972, Johnson left the phone company and teamed up with John D. Schrott, Jr., who won notoriety 12 years ago by compiling a $10,000 stock portfolio at age 15.

Through Schrott's Vortex Corp., investors were put into limited partnerships managed by Johnson's Ridge Associates. Top executives of Virginia banks,

themselves heavily invested in the partnerships, provided Johnson and Schrott with references. The scheme might have continued if a stockbroker who was losing clients to Johnson hadn't looked into the operation and alerted the SEC.

Several of United Virginia Bankshares' banks were stuck with bad loans, and the holding company says it may lose $3.8-million, not to mention some executives. Some 400 people put more than $26-million in the scheme just since October.

Trippet's oil. Even bigger, the oil drilling fraud was allegedly perpetrated through a series of tax shelter partnerships by Tulsa's Home-Stake Production Co., run by Robert S. Trippet. The SEC declared the company insolvent last September, and Trippet is now being sued by the trustee in bankruptcy as well as by four groups of investors.

The list of Home-Stake's investors, published by the *Wall Street Journal* on Wednesday, reads like a Who's Who of U. S. business and entertainment. The show biz crowd includes Andy Williams, Liza Minnelli, Jack Benny, and Walter Matthau.

The business crowd is astonishing. Among corporate chairmen are Hoyt Ammidon of U. S. Trust, Donald Kendall of PepsiCo, David Mahoney of Norton Simon, Richard Oelman of NCR, J. Stanford Smith of International Paper, Thomas Staley of Reynolds Securities, and Walter Wriston of First National City Bank. Presidents include Time Inc.'s James Shepley, Henry Roberts of Connecticut General Life Insurance, William Morton of American Express, and First Boston's Paul Miller.

As in the wine fraud, the extent and complexities of the scandal are not yet known. But investors may lose as much as $100-million. That could make it the biggest Ponzi scheme ever.

Ponzi's stamps. Certainly, the scheme dwarfs Charles Ponzi's own maneuver in Boston in 1920. His gimmick was postal reply coupons that could be bought in Spain for 1¢ and redeemed in the U. S. for 10¢ worth of postage stamps.

Ponzi promised at least "50% profit in 45 days" and lured 40,000 people to give him $15-million in a mere eight months. It never occurred to anyone that there was no way for Ponzi to redeem the postage stamps for cash. The swindle began to crack when a Boston newspaper learned that less than $1-million in postal reply coupons had actually been issued during the period that Ponzi presumably was investing $15-million. Later, the state froze his accounts. Ponzi protested that if he were allowed to go public, he could use the stock proceeds to pay off all his investors. (Ironically, his company was Securities Exchange Co.—or SEC for short.) Instead, Ponzi went to jail for 10 years and died a pauper in Brazil in 1949.

FIGURE 10–3

Goldstein Admits Options Were Misrepresented, Not Backed

BY JOHN A. JONES
Times Staff Writer

Harold Goldstein, chairman and president of the bankrupt Goldstein, Samuelson Inc. commodity options firm, signed a legal document filed with the federal court in Los Angeles Thursday confirming regulators' allegations that the options his firm sold were not backed by trading on commodity exchanges and that the firm misrepresented the nature of the options.

The document, also signed by Charles T. Rose, a lawyer in the Los Angeles office of the Securities & Exchange Commission, is an outline of the facts agreed to by both sides in the complex civil lawsuit filed by the SEC against Goldstein, Samuelson Inc. of Beverly Hills last February.

The stipulation of facts was submitted to U.S. Dist. Judge Robert J. Kelleher, who will consider them instead of going on with the trial of the case, which has been held over since last summer.

It will take at least a month before the case is finally settled by the court, however.

Goldstein still claims that the options his firm sold were not securities and were not subject to the federal securities laws administered by the SEC. The SEC has maintained that the firm was selling unregistered securities in violation of federal law. The key to the case is whether such options were securities.

The SEC claims that investors who bought options from Goldstein, Samuelson Inc. were, in effect, investing in GSI as a company, as if they were buying securities in the firm.

Judge Kelleher is expected to decide that issue and then rule on the SEC's application for an injunction barring Goldstein and his firm from selling options without SEC registration.

A commodity option entitles the buyer to take a contract on the futures market at a specified price during the life of the option, no matter how high or low the market price may be. The difference between the fixed option price and the fluctuating futures market price offers the buyer the chance to profit—but the fee for the option must be paid whether he wins or loses.

Goldstein's firm has been out of business since it was adjudicated bankrupt last April. Goldstein himself has pleaded guilty to three counts of mail fraud and is due to be sentenced by another federal judge Oct. 29.

The SEC's civil case against Goldstein was the first of its kind in federal court to tackle the key issue of whether options, are securities.

Since the issue was raised by both federal and state regulators early this year, when the commodity options boom was at its peak, new state legislation has given the California Department of Corporations authority to regulate trading in commodities which are not federally controlled. All Goldstein's options were written on such unregulated commodities.

The stipulation filed with the federal court Thursday stated that although the company told its customers and employes that it was "hedging" its options, it stopped hedging within six months of starting business in 1971.

"GSI had covered the options issued from its beginning of business in April, 1971, to September, 1971, in an account with Fenton-Lavine, a member of the West Coast Commodity Exchange, but ceased that practice to generate additional operating capital and to avoid subjecting GSI to the risk inherent in speculating in the futures market," said the documen signed by Goldstein.

In February, 1972, the document said, GSI opened an account at Hentz & Co., a member of the New York Stock Exchange and various commodity exchanges, because there were many inquiries about GSI's hedging methods.

The account was opened "for the sole purpose of making assurances" about hedging and "to reassure accountants and regulatory authorities," the document said. "In reality the Hentz account and subsequent accounts at various brokerage companies were merely a facade."

Among other misrepresentations listed in the document signed by Goldstein was his claim that GSI had a $1 million bond to guarantee customers would be paid if the firm should become insolvent—"when in fact the letter claiming such coverage was from an insurance agency controlled by Harold Goldstein, the insurance agent's signature was forged on a letter dictated by Harold Goldstein and no such bond ever existed."

GSI wrote its options "naked" — without any commodity futures contracts to back them up, the document said.

"GSI paid off old customers' profits with new customers' money, the success of which depended on an ever-expanding inflow of cash from new customers rather than profits generated from commodity or futures trading," it said.

The lawyers agreed that they will submit written legal arguments to the court by Nov. 12. The judge is expected to decide the case some time after that has been done.

Source: *Los Angeles Times.*

Goldstein copped a plea. He was sentenced for three of sixteen counts of mail fraud and spent eight months in a minimum security facility at Long Beach, California. The options scandal briefly awoke a slumbering federal government which enacted the legislation creating the Commodity Futures Trading Commission with jurisdiction over all commodities and options thereon. The ban on options sales in previously regulated commodities remained in effect and rules were laid down on the brokering of the new commodities and of those traded in the London options markets. Meanwhile, Harold Goldstein

persevered. He went back to prison in 1976 after pleading guilty to securities and mail fraud in a gold-ore investment scheme. A few months after his release, Goldstein was back in business, having spotted another hole to run through. His "forward delivery contract" options in gasoline capitalized on the energy price crunch. (See Figure 10–4.) They were big sellers at the beginning of 1980 until grand jury investigations resulted in the "voluntary" suspension of most sales. Critics of government regulation might note how Goldstein and his new partner, Michael Krivacek, spotted this golden opportu-

FIGURE 10–4

Improbable Pitch
An Ex-Convict Flaunts Prison Record to Sell Gasoline-Futures Deals

Harold Goldstein Says That He Can't Risk Mistakes, So Investors Will Benefit

But a Bartender Is Skeptical

By G. CHRISTIAN HILL
Staff Reporter of THE WALL STREET JOURNAL

LOS ANGELES—The woods are full of gasoline-marketing get-rich-quick schemes, but even the Securities and Exchange Commission concedes that Harold Goldstein has added a unique extra touch to his.

"The ultimate in chutzpah," one SEC attorney calls it.

The portly young Goldstein, 34, is chairman of a company called Co Petro Marketing Group Inc. His sales pitch, as presented recently at an "investment seminar" attended by 350 people at the Century Plaza Hotel here, is that small investors can make buckets of money by buying tanker-truck loads of gasoline from Co Petro at today's prices for delivery in the future when prices will be higher.

Goldstein assures his audiences that their money will be in safe hands with him because he has been in jail twice, once for mail fraud and again for mail and securities fraud and currently is being investigated by three federal agencies, including the Federal Bureau of Investigation.

"I'm not going back to prison for anything," Goldstein declares. So, he asserts, "Co Petro has to be 150% legal." In invitations to the Century Plaza seminar, Co Petro actually boasted that Goldstein "knows what he is talking about" because he has been in prison and "he is not about to make those mistakes again."

Taking in Millions

Goldstein's brazen brandishing of his criminal record has nonplused federal regulatory authorities. And the major refiners with whom Co Petro claims to have long-term, fixed-price supply contracts deny such agreements exist—raising questions about whether the company will be able to deliver the promised gasoline on schedule. Nonetheless, Co Petro appears to be taking in millions of dollars from a public fascinated by the possibility of making a killing in gasoline in an era of energy shortages.

While precise sales figures can't be obtained, Co Petro's sales literature shows total income of nearly $5 million in January, much of it from gasoline sales. One federal investigator says Co Petro's growth has begun to explode with the opening of sales offices in different parts of the country. A salesman at the company's Newport Beach, Calif., branch office reports excitedly, "It's just crazy here. We have three WATS lines here, for our national advertising campaign, and they are ringing off the hook."

Source: *Los Angeles Times.*

nity: "This is one of the few businesses left," said Krivacek, "that is completely unregulated."

CARR'S CAPERS

Though Goldstein may have been the most brazen and obnoxious of the options con men, his scheme was nothing new or special. He wasn't the first, or the last. The freshly organized CFTC ran into new options swindles almost everywhere it looked. After the crackdown on American dealer options, London options quickly surfaced as the newest lure in the confidence man's game. Established brokerage firms had handled London options for years without incident, but the imagination (and money) of speculators was captured by a regiment of fly-by-night profiteers who consistently misrepresented the facts and charged outrageous sums for the privilege. They made a science of the "boiler room" telephone solicitation scam, rarely bothering to make the deals they were being paid for. The premiums they charged were often two or three or four times that of the reputable dealers, making even a paper profit on price moves for the speculator virtually impossible. The game hit big in 1977–1978, until James A. Carr did for London options what Goldstein had done for the domestic variety.

Carr appeared in Boston early in 1976. His three piece suits were impeccably tasteful, his conversational manner low key and smooth. He was the very image of financial integrity. He opened his offices on State Street, in the heart of one of the nation's oldest and classiest districts of high finance. With an artist's sense of detail, he added "Lloyd" to the corporation's title, so that Lloyd, Carr, and Co.'s

dealings in London options would trigger subconscious associations with the prestigious Lloyd's of London. The firm eventually filed a belated application for registration as a Futures Commission Merchant, required of all options dealers. Lacking a financial statement, the request was denied by the CFTC in October 1976. A new application was filed on the last day of a three month extension, but CFTC auditors found the company's books "ridiculous." Again the license was denied and again Carr went right on doing business. For another full year Carr tied up the inept and understaffed CFTC in endless courtroom battles and legal disputes, successfully defeating every attempt to close it down by injunction. The federal agency's statutory preëmption of all individual state actions in regulatory matters, except in the event of criminal wrongdoing, effectively froze local authorities and gave Carr his hole in the fence. He was finally chased down by the zealous investigative reporting of a national T.V. news show, which prompted a fraud suit by the state of Michigan in October 1977. Twelve other states joined in, along with the CFTC, but Carr kept selling his options even after a December order to cease and desist. He was arrested early in January 1978.

Then the fun really started. Carr's fingerprints were routinely run through the FBI's computer bank. Government officials and industry advocates were shocked and embarrassed to find out that James A. Carr was not James A. Carr. He was Alan Abrahams, alias Alan Abrams, alias Alan Layne, alias James A. Carr. Abrahams had escaped from federal prison in New Jersey in 1974, where he was serving 4–6 years for other commodities frauds. His criminal record stretched back some twenty-two years and included numerous confidence games, forgeries, and thefts.

Ex-con Abrahams had had the audacity to create a public empire in fraud which at its height employed 1,000 people in eleven offices from coast to coast and which did an estimated $50 million in business in 1977. Carr and his family took up residence in an exclusive waterfront suburb in north Boston, owned three cars (including a Rolls-Royce), and hired a butler and a chaffeur. Even Harold Goldstein must have been impressed.

The Lloyd, Carr, and Co. operation was typical of dozens that flourished at the time. The volatile price swings of commodities had come to the public's attention and whetted its appetite. Like all options schemes, these featured the limited risk nature of options, where the premium is all the customer can lose, though profits are theoretically endless. Much of the business was done by unsolicited phone calls from "boiler room" setups by sales personnel recruited through ads promising exorbitant incomes from commissions. They knew no more than did the customers about commodities, but this mattered little since Lloyd, Carr had no intention of actually purchasing any London options for its clients. Supervisors in gorilla and Superman suits roamed the sales floors, exciting employees to push or coerce prospective investors into parting with thousands of dollars on the flimsiest of promises. When a sale was made, bells rang and staffers stood cheering. One Detroit sales office made more than 50,000 long distance calls in a single month. In one instance a blind customer was told he had lost his initial $9,000 investment, but that an option worth $42,000 had been taken out in his name which he should mortgage his home and business to pay

for. State investigators listened in when the salesman called back and threatened the client with bodily harm. Unlike most, this investor had actually checked out Lloyd, Carr with Dun & Bradstreet and the Better Business Bureau; both gave it a clean bill of health.

Freed on $100,000 bail, Abrahams promptly skipped town. He bungled his great escape, however, when he used a former employee's name in renting a car upon arrival in Florida. A hotel worker spotted Abraham's wife and the two were taken into custody at a resort late in January. Their apparent destiny was the Bermudas, where it was rumored Abrahams had secreted almost $2 million in embezzled funds. Back in Massachusetts, officials estimated that state's investors had poured about $12 million into the coffers of Lloyd, Carr, and Co. As the court cases against Abrahams mounted and the publicity intensified, a humiliated CFTC ordered its staff to draw up a regulation suspending all trading in London options. It had failed for more than a year to stop Lloyd, Carr and some twenty other firms suspected of running similar games. Sixty of the agency's 100 investigators were involved in the cases, making effective surveillance of the $1 trillion business in legitimate commodity futures impossible.

Scheduled to face Congressional hearings on the renewal of its charter in the fall, the CFTC had to act. On June 1 the ban on sales of London options went into effect (See Figure 10–5.) Respectable options brokers protested that the baby was being thrown out with the bath water and that an industry ought not to be prohibited simply because a regulatory agency couldn't do its job. An exception was made to allow dealers in precious and base metals to continue writing options on

FIGURE 10-5

Boiler room sales practices, outright fraud and widespread violations of Commission regulations in the sale of London options to the public during 1978 compelled the Commission to suspend most sales of commodity options in the United States and focused Congressional attention on the regulation of options and other commodity investment vehicles such as leverage contracts.

The Commission suspended option sales on June 1, with the exception of the acquisition by commercial interests of trade options in connection with their businesses and a limited number of strictly controlled dealer options—transactions in commodity options granted or issued on a physical commodity by persons in the business of buying, selling, producing or otherwise using that commodity.

The Futures Trading Act of 1978 subsequently banned commodity option transactions except for trade options and, under conditions set down in the law and to be implemented and supplemented by CFTC, dealer options on physical commodities. At the same time Congress encouraged the Commission to proceed expeditiously with plans to implement options trading through commodity exchanges, one of the cornerstones of the Commission's original plan for the orderly regulation of options trading, and the Commission is proceeding to develop such a program.

In contrast to a commodity futures contract, a commodity option represents the right but not an obligation to buy or sell a commodity at an agreed upon price within a specified time. In the case of "previously regulated" agricultural products, trading of options on domestic exchanges was banned by the Commodity Exchange Act of 1936 and that ban continues. The current legislation permits the Commission to either ban or allow, under regulation, options trading in all other commodities.

Leverage transactions, on the other hand, involve standardized agreements with payments over a period of time for the purchase of a specific commodity for delivery or offset at a later date. Purchases are margined or "leveraged" by a present down-payment with interest and other carrying charges payable over the life of the contract. Section 217 of the Commodity Futures Trading Commission Act of 1974 gave the Commission jurisdiction over leverage transactions in silver or gold bullion or bulk silver or gold coins. The Futures Trading Act of 1978, while requiring continued regulation of gold and silver bullion and coin contracts, extended the Commission's jurisdiction to all leverage contracts, and permitted the Commission to either regulate or ban such transactions.

Relatively few London options—those involving futures contracts traded on London exchanges—were being sold when the Commission first took up options regulation in 1975, and the Commission had no factual evidence or experience on which to ban options outright at that time. Because it felt that commodity options might prove useful in risk-transfer strategies, it developed options regulations designed to protect the public while allowing for continued sale of options. Regulation foundered, however, on the shoals of repeated court challenges and delays, widespread violations, skyrocketing sales and the sometimes downright bizarre excesses of the high pressure sellers who quickly moved into the business. The complexity and size of the enforcement task overwhelmed the Commission's limited resources.

Although some options dealers attacked the suspension as "arbitrary and capricious," courts found that the rulemaking record constructed through the expenditure of an inordinate amount of staff time during fiscal 1977 and fiscal 1978, detailed for all to see the fraud and widespread illegal practices that pervaded the sale of London options. The Commission had already instituted 13 formal administrative actions and 15 injunctive actions and had obtained injunctions against 60 firms and individuals when it suspended options sales. The bulk of the injunctive actions and administrative proceedings involved allegations of the use of boiler room sales techniques, deceptive promotional materials, misleading "canned" telephone sales pitches and misleading disclosure statements. Audits of commodity options firms revealed that the majority of them were ignoring Commission regulations requiring the segregation of funds received in payment for commodity options purchases, putting at risk some $27 million, representing 90 percent of the purchase price of open options positions.

In addition, the majority of options firms failed to meet minimum capitalization requirements. At least six options firms filed for bankruptcy, one of them, having failed to segregate customer funds, listing liabilities of $689,000 to 118 customers who had exercised their profitable options but could not be paid, with another 217 customers holding unexpired options.

Recordkeeping was a shambles and Commission investigators and auditors had difficulty verifying the details of options transactions purportedly effected for Americans on foreign exchanges—details essential to determine whether or not orders for options had been executed or the premiums simply pocketed by the dealers.

Source: Commodity Futures Trading Commission.

FIGURE 10–6

600% profit

It was too good to be true

by Patrick Oster
Chicago Sun-Times

SPRINGFIELD, Va. — A few days ago, a man offered me a 600 per cent profit if I invested $7,500 in crude oil. It seemed almost too good to be true — and, as it turned out, it was. The offer came in a call from Dirk Spencer, a "senior consultant" with R.L. Harrison Petroleum Corp. He said he was British and had once worked for the United Nations helping underdeveloped countries.

Spencer had a smooth sales pitch: My $7,500 would be a nonrefundable fee that would give me temporary control over the price of 1,000 barrels of crude oil. The fee guaranteed that, in July, I could buy the oil at $26 a barrel, no matter what happened to the price in the meantime. I could resell the oil then, and if the price of oil went up, I would make money. If it went down, I would lose.

For me to make a net profit, however, the price had to go up enough to compensate for my $7,500 fee, which, in effect, added a cost of $7.50 a barrel to the $26 fixed price.

I asked Spencer what my chances were of making a profit. He said the best oil was selling on the spot market for about $42 a barrel. And while he expected some softening of price in a few weeks, he believed that after that the price "is going to harden and go through $50."

Spencer warned me that there was a "downside risk" to my investment because oil could drop below my break-even point. But he quickly added: "Now I do not believe for a minute that oil is going to come down." If it did, he said, "we'd be back in the land of the Tooth Fairy and Santa Claus.

"We believe (a $50-plus price) is possible," he said, "very probable, in fact. I have to be very careful about what I say. Privately, I think it's more or less damn sure, but let's talk 'brokerese'."

Spencer wasn't talking "brokerese." In effect, he was talking fraud, said Jack Field, chief of the en-

forcement division of the Commodities Futures Trading Commission.

When I asked for a brochure and other information about the deal or the company, he indicated there was none, that the situation changed too quickly to put it all in writing.

I asked about R.L. Harrison, which Spencer said was "quite an old company."

As it turned out, Harrison had been incorporated in New York October 24, 1979, just four months before.

The company's background, however, was really "irrelevant" to the deal, Spencer assured me. He told me not to worry about detail. "That's the way the oil business works," he said.

"Your transaction is not with us," he said. "The whole transactions are dealt with by banks," he said.

That's not what the banks said. As far as they were concerned, they were just holding or transferring the money Harrison collected from customers.

Spencer said the Amford Bank & Trust Co., for example, would issue me a bill of sale for my 1,000 barrels as soon as I wired my money to Amford, a Nassau-based bank.

Abe Lieber, president of the bank's parent company, said: "We don't know anything about oil contracts." He insisted no officer had proper authorization to involve his bank in the deal.

Derek Anderson, the "chief office executive" of Harrison's Springfield, Va., office, said Spencer hadn't had much experience in the oil business.

"Neither have I, for that matter," he said.

That, however, did not stop Anderson, Spencer or their boss, Joseph Glantzman, from using high-pressure telephone-sales techniques to peddle expensive oil contracts to the public.

After hearing details of Spencer's pitch to me, Glantzman said Spencer, must be "one of the top morons of the telephone-sales business," especially for virtually guaranteeing me a profit, a patent misrepresentation.

"My people are supposed to be knowledgeable about the oil business," said Glantzman, who said he himself had no experience selling oil by phone to customers before he set Harrison up.

Although Spencer had told me there were no brochures, Glantzman, in fact, had some brochures printed up. The initial batch had to be reworked, however, when the listed oil supplier was linked to an oil scam in New York.

The brochure also listed as a reference a purported embezzler of the Amford Bank's funds.

One thing the brochure did not mention was what kind of oil I was buying. Spencer said it was "low sulfur light sweet crude," a highly prized variety because it is cheap to refine.

Anderson told me that the oil had an American Petroleum Institute rating of 27 (a measure of how thin or thick it is). That made it a heavy crude, not a light one.

He said it had a sulfur content of 2.04, which is high, making it costly to refine, and a specific gravity of 16.5, which is heavier than any liquid known to man. It is roughly that of lead.

Glantzman, however, said the oil had a rating of 16.8, a crude so heavy it would have to be used as asphalt. He refused to name the company supplying it.

He acknowledged he should have supervised his Virginia operation more closely.

The C.F.T.C. has been investigating Harrison as part of a review of a suspected network of fraudulent and illegal commodities dealers.

When Spencer approached me, I had decided I would play along, posing as an interested investor.

By the end of my "involvement," the Federal Bureau of Investigation, in search of evidence of fraud, had seized the records of Harrison's Springfield, Va., office, and the New York attorney general had told the firm to shut down or risk indictment. The C.F.T.C. also had told the company it was selling oil in violation of commodities laws.

Glantzman argues with federal authorities who have told him he is dealing in oil without being properly registered as a broker.

He insists he is exempt from federal commodities laws because they cover future-price contracts, not the fixed-price contracts he said he is selling.

Glantzman said he won't do any more business unless he can get the go-ahead from the New York attorney general's office, which has jurisdiction over Harrison's home office which uses a Fifth Avenue address as a front.

Anderson, like Glantzman, was unable to explain the inconsistencies of his company's oil deal. He is busy now with a secret deal of his own, using International Market Consultants, which he set up.

Spencer, though he found the FBI raid "a shattering experience," said he's trying to interest insurance companies in a plan to get the elderly to sell their homes in exchange for a lifetime annuity. "And I'm looking very seriously at the Mexican peso," he said. "It's selling at half price, you know."

Source: Seattle Times.

their inventories if they met strict requirements. One qualified. Talk of a pilot program legalizing options through exchange regulated trade has persisted since and has been a bone of contention between an eager brokerage industry and a very reluctant CFTC.

Meanwhile, the same old con games go on. Only the names and the commodities change. For every Goldstein or Abrahams there are a hundred unscrupulous hucksters waiting to take the public's money. "Deferred delivery contracts" in gasoline quickly replaced London options, sold through the same intense phone campaigns and with the same fraudulent intent. Most try to duck the law by defining the objects sold so as to fall outside the regulatory powers of established agencies. In 1980 there were an estimated 150 commodities con artist firms peddling gold, silver, platinum, diamonds, Mexican pesos, and crude oil—piling up sales totals in the hundreds of millions of dollars. The technique remains the same. Buy a phone list from a brokerage or business. Make repeated and direct phone appeals—oozing in sincerity, expertise, and personal concern. Warn the investor that the train is leaving the station and that he'd better hop on board fast. Tell the customer how to wire his money straight to the firm's bank (the Bermudas are still popular). And watch the dollars pour in. Although common sense should prevent anyone from making investments based on such phone solicitations, the supply of suckers seems infinite. (See Figure 10–6.)

How could it all happen? How could so many people, some with many years experience in the financial world, get taken by the oldest trick in town? The wily Goldstein himself put it bluntly: "Look, I provided a service to greedy peo-

ple . . . who have money falling out of their pockets. They begged me to let them invest in commodity options. Sure, a lot of them lost money. But that's their fault for making a bad investment choice. The magazine and newspaper stories about us were full of warnings. But people still kept investing." Of course, this cheap and ugly "justification" for out and out theft pinpoints only the faults of the investor. Few could make a sound investment choice based on the lies they were told by companies like Goldstein, Samuelson or Lloyd, Carr. And the incompetence of both industry and government in protecting investors from such abuses deserves loud and round condemnation. Finally, it is the peculiar and complicated nature of options themselves that is partly to be blamed, vulnerable as it is to "Ponzi" games. Options themselves do need to be understood. They have been in some cases and places a responsible component of market and financial management.

DEFINITIONS AND MECHANICS

An option is a special kind of deal in the future purchase or sale of something, be it stocks or real estate or commodities. It is not a futures contract, but the right to take a position in such a contract at a stipulated price within a certain length of time. For instance, A thinks that a supermarket chain may be interested in a parcel of land owned by B. A goes to B and makes a deal. A pays B a relatively small sum and thus acquires the option to buy B's property at an agreed upon price on or before some time in the future. The price of the land, say $400,000, is called the "striking" price. The amount A pays to B for the option is called the "premium." The time limit on the option agreement is set by an "expiration date." If A decides to use the option, he will "exercise" it. Now A closes a deal with the supermarket chain, which agrees to buy the land for $500,000. A exercises the option, picks up the land for $400,000, and makes a hefty profit. If the premium paid had been $10,000, the profit would have been 1,000 percent. If the deal had fallen through and the option run out, A would have lost the whole $10,000.

The process is roughly the same in commodities. The speculator pays a premium, usually from 5 to 15 percent, for an option to buy or sell during the life of the contract but only for as long as the option states (1 or 3 or 6 months). The price (per ton, per pound, etc.) is set at the time of the sale, either by the exchange in open trading or by the dealer underwriting the option. That price is good for whenever the option is exercised. Although this may resemble the margin paid in commodity futures, the difference is absolutely crucial. The options trader holds only an option, not a contract. He cannot suffer a real loss as long as the option goes unexercised. If the price fails to move in his favor, he may simply allow the option to run out and forfeit the premium. *The options speculator cannot lose more than his original premium.* There are no margin calls, no unlimited downside risk, and no constant monitoring of price fluctuations. This brought the crowds to Goldstein and Lloyd, Carr.

There are three standard types of options. A "call" option gives the speculator the right to buy the commodity in the future (literally to call the commodity from the hands of the grantor). A "put" option gives the purchaser the right to sell the commodity sometime in the future (literally to put it in a buyer's hands). A "double" option conveys the right to either buy or sell and thus carries a higher premium. If you expect prices to rise, purchase a call option. If you expect them to fall, take a put option. If prices are trading in a narrow range, a double option might be the best bet.

Options are also classified by who underwrites them—that is, by who guarantees the future performance of the option if the purchaser chooses to exercise it. An "exchange" option, such as many of the London options, is offered by an exchange. Its trading floor is the pricing mechanism and its clearinghouse the guarantor of performance. Such exchanges have analogous functions to those of the futures exchanges. If sound, the exchange can solve the major problems with options, reliable public pricing, and responsible performance. (The role of the now defunct West Coast Commodity Exchange in the options fiasco of 1972–1973 demonstrates the limits of such a program.)

A "dealer" option, on the other hand, originates with and depends upon an options dealer. The dealer grants the option and the entire transaction takes place solely between the dealer and the purchaser. A dealer in precious metals might sell options to jewelry manufacturers desiring to hedge their costs. The dealer's inventory stands behind the option as a promise of ability to perform. Dealer options written by brokerage firms or anyone else must be underwritten by actual goods or contract positions; otherwise they are worthless (or "naked"). Options provide another way to hedge against price volatility, gauge pricing trends, and organize commodity marketing.

How would a typical trade work? The

speculator notes in January that silver is selling at $40 an ounce and that analysts predict a short-term price surge in the wake of a miners' strike in South America. The trader buys a one-month call option on a London Metals Exchange 10,000 troy ounce contract. The premium might be $20,000. (Of course, this and other money figures would be in pounds sterling and conversion rates would effect all results.) At such a premium the price will have to rise at least $2 per ounce just to recover the initial outlay. If within the month prices hit $44 and the option is exercised, the profit (minus the premium) would be $20,000 or 100 percent. If prices linger at $40 for 32 days and then hit the highs, the speculator is out of luck and out of his original $20,000. If prices had declined to $35, the loss would still remain only the amount of the premium. Premiums will vary with many factors, including current volatility, striking price, duration of the option, and value of the commodity.

Now, let's complicate the matter with a procedure termed "trading against the call." The silver call option was bought at a striking price of $40. In a week prices hit $44. The owner of the option in this case does not exercise it. Instead, he sells silver in the futures market at $44. Prices soon decline to $42 and the speculator buys out his short for a $20,000 profit (minus commissions). He still owns the option and can trade against it again. After its dip, silver moves up again in a few days, hitting $44. Once more the speculator sells short, only this time prices continue their advance and hit $46. Rather than buy this position out at the market price, incurring a loss, the owner of the option exercises it (at the striking price of $40) and realizes a $40,000 return

(minus the premium). There are risks, however. After their spurt to $44, prices might have continued their decline past $42, limiting or eliminating the speculator's profit.

THE LONDON MARKETS

Options continue to be sold in London where a century of experience and a set of unique institutions and circumstances enable a relatively small and judicious trade to flourish. Options are written against actual cash commodities, thus limiting their speculative availability and strengthening their guarantee of performance. Individual exchanges for coffee, sugar, cocoa, and rubber do both cash and futures business, handle options, and are members of the International Commodities Clearing House. The London Metals Exchange has no clearinghouse and trades take place only between principals. Thus, settlement does not take place before the contract falls due. Even if the contract or option shows a profit early on, it can't be collected until the end of the contract.

The London markets are world commodities markets and their operations differ somewhat from those of their American counterparts. There are usually two sessions in the day, interrupted by a recess. For some commodities, off-hours trading takes place in what is called a "kerb" market, allowing for arbitrage between London, New York, Chicago, and other exchanges. Generally, there are no daily price limits (except sugar). Cocoa and rubber recess when they hit the limit and resume trading without a limit. Daily quotations on the London markets go out over the major wire services around the world.

PART TWO

PRICING

Chapter 11

THE RANDOM NATURE OF MARKET PRICE

RANDOM WALK THEORY

The commodity trader's world pivots on price. After all the reports, bulletins, charts, graphs, rumors, and intuitions, it is the movement of prices that decides the player's fate. Thus, it is useful at some point to talk about the nature of price itself, divorced from the fundamental and technical factors that go into it. Are futures prices the results of processes that can be scientifically analyzed and hence predicted? An entire school of traders and academic researchers believes so and has produced advanced mathematical and statistical evidence to prove it. An equally distinguished group firmly asserts the opposite: that prices change randomly and allow of no patterning or forecasting. They, too, have published intricate studies to support their position. The individual trader need not worry about choosing sides in this arcane controversy, but some general lessons emerge from it that will be useful in playing the futures game.

The economists speak of price changes in terms of negative and positive serial correlation—that is, whether or not one price in a series is correlated to other prices in the series. If prices are related

in the series, technical study of past market prices can give valid forecasts of prices to come. If they are not related, no technical study of the market has any value whatsoever. A market without any serial correlations would be a purely random one. Rather than choose between these alternatives and their rival schools as if they were mutually exclusive, the trader should adopt the random walk theory of market prices as a theoretical Ideal Market. With this hypothesis of randomness, one can study the commodity markets and the nature of supply and demand pricing, measuring actual markets by the theory and the theory by the markets. The theory serves about the same function in economic studies that a 1,000 batting average serves for baseball fans or that a 300 game serves for bowlers. With an ideal game in mind, something exists by which to measure the real.

Put simply, the theory of random walk suggests that short-run price changes in speculative markets cannot be predicted solely on the basis of past prices. The price of a commodity walks randomly about its "intrinsic" value. According to the model, each price change is independent of every other price change, reflecting the

155

FIGURE 11–1

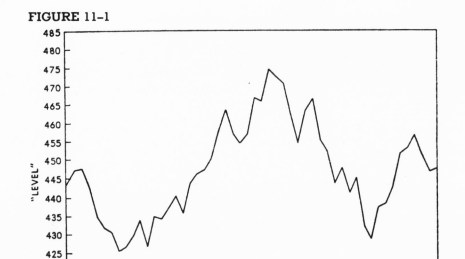

—Simulated market levels for 52 weeks

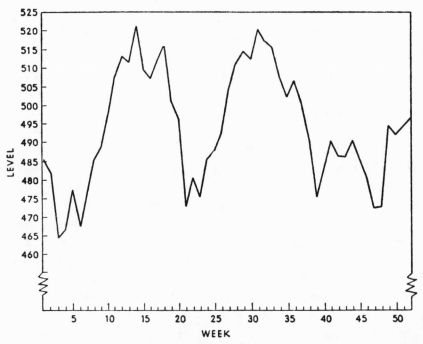

—Friday closing levels, December 30, 1955—December 28, 1956. Dow Jones Industrial Index.

Source: Harry Roberts, "Stock Market 'Patterns' and Financial Analysis," *Journal of Finance,* March 1959.

new information and situation of the moment. The patterns apparent in price charts could be generated just as easily, say the theorists, by flipping coins or by throwing darts. (See Figure 11–1.) At any given time, prices would have a 50–50 chance of going up or a 50–50 chance of going down no matter where they had been before. In theory.

In practice, the conditions of actual markets violate the premises and assumptions of random walk theory in a number of key ways, though it remains the standard by which these variations can be judged. The application of probability statistics and models to life can be tricky. In physics, scientists found that although some radioactive materials break down in random fashion, when the total series is taken a strictly predictable pattern emerges, yet one that cannot predict the movement of a particle at any given moment. This confusing contradiction between a local and a general focus carries over into other analyses. If you flip a coin five times and it comes up heads each time, the chances that it will be heads again on the sixth toss are still 50–50. That's the local view. But if you were to place your bet before any coins were tossed, and looked at the general chances for landing heads six times in a row, the odds would be considerably less than 50–50. Likewise in commodities, the trader speculates in extensive series, not in binary oppositions. The question is really not whether the price will go up or down. The question is how fast, how far, when, and how long? Each random move of the price has weighing upon it numerous pressures trying to influence its direction, pressures the trader has the job of evaluating and responding to.

Although prices may have no memory of their past actions, traders do. The emerging shape of a price move is not simply the product of numbers mechanically selected or spewed out of a programmed computer. Prices in the futures market are really ever-evolving stories that traders tell about the commodities in question, interpretations that may speak of a rosy future or a bleak tragedy. The life of a contract becomes something like the life of a legendary hero: sometimes strong, sometimes weak, faced with adversity, challenged by assaults, entangled in politics, vulnerable to corruption, and persevering to the end. Commodity prices are collectively authored by traders, market forces, and the elements of chance—all working at random yet all contributing to the creation of an eventually coherent, meaningful, and perhaps even profitable pattern. Human ideas and emotions have subtle, often dramatic, influences upon the directions, limits, and shapes of prices. The trader should begin by conceiving of the market as a random walk of prices. This properly chastises him and sets the stage for the uphill fight for profits. Yet, as experience and analysis yield sophistication and savvy, randomness may give way in particular circumstances to trends, motions, and patterns that can be identified and traded if the speculator works simultaneously on the fundamentals, the technicals, and the psychologies of futures trading.

DISCOUNTING

The random walk theory includes the notion of an "efficient" market wherein all new information is speedily and rationally absorbed or "discounted." An efficient market would be composed of a great many equally knowledgeable and informed competitors all seeking the best possible speculative return. The market is imagined to be in a steady state as long as no new information (crop reports, a hike in interest rates, war in the Middle East) disturbs it. If all new information is taken into account fully by these hypothetical geniuses, complete discounting results in a price that reflects the news precisely, as well as events expected to occur. Price becomes an interpretation of the news, a process that can get out of hand when speculators turn a commodity (like gold) into an outlet for their anxieties and hopes. In theory, rational discounting means that actual prices approximate intrinsic value.

But random differences of opinion will make for random discrepancies between actual price and intrinsic value. When highly efficient, the market keeps such motion in a random walk about the intrinsic value. Intrinsic values will change as fundamentals change, but well-informed competitors will soon translate this into a fair new price. The translation, however, may be garbled or inaccurate, as human communication and judgment are flawed. New information will enter the market and affect price at different speeds and with different messages, resulting in the random quality of subsequent price fluctuations. It is this random input and imperfect discounting, rather than fundamentals, that is said to explain the irregular character of short-term futures prices. Price adjustments will have variable directions and impacts, causing prices to overreact, underreact, anticipate, or lag behind the news. Thus, each change in price happens independently of others, though in the end all may eventually conform to the dictates of a new intrinsic value.

The complexities of discounting take the trader into the psychology of the market place. Price moves depend on the attitudes of traders; more concretely, they depend on how each sector of the trade reacts—how strongly, for how long, and in that way. The corporate hedger in T-Bills may have a very different attitude toward a fall in the Federal Funds rate than a trading advisor or a public speculator. The profile of a market, how many kinds of traders, and in what proportion shape the discounting of news and the moves of prices. Responses to market news happen in interreacting stages, from the floor trader to the brokers to the commercial hedgers to the pools and funds to the individual trader. Each discounts news with his or her own interests and trading plan in mind. A good price for one may be a disaster for another. And discounting takes time. The first reaction to an event might be uniformly bearish among a small group of traders receiving the news first. Remember, however, that this reflects an unstable mixture of opinions concerning the commodity's new intrinsic value and the reactions others in the market will have to the news. A bearish response might be solely based on predicting that other traders will have a bearish response. As the word of a bear slide spreads, other groups have a chance to respond. Enthusiastic sell orders will further drive the price down. A number of sell orders merely equal to readily available longs will keep prices steady. A hesitant trickle of sells, or a scattering of sceptical buys, can reverse the original move. Traders make their move in part by anticipating how others will discount the news (as these first traders bet on a bearish response) or by in turn discounting the discounting of others (as these

FIGURE 11-2

TUESDAY.

TRADERS WHO WERE CLEARLY ON THE BEARISH SIDE WERE LAMENTING THAT BULLISH CONSENSUS LAST WEEK IN SOYBEANS HAD DROPPED TO 18 PCT. THEY SEE VERY LITTLE ROOM FOR FURTHER CONVERTS TO BEARISHNESS. BEARS AND BULLS ALIKE WERE INTENSIFYING THEIR "BOTTOM-PICKING" AND NERVOUSLY JOCKEYING POSITIONS SHOULD MAJOR NEWS BREAK.

THERE WERE ONLY A FEW DEVELOPMENTS OF MAJOR SIGNIFICANCE THIS WEEK, AND THE MARKETS REFLECTED THAT. VOLUME CONTINUED TO SLIDE ALONG WITH PRICES.

THE PRIME LENDING RATE HIKE TO AN UNPRECEDENTED 19 PCT RECEIVED WIDE ATTENTION. THE RATE INCREASE BY MAJOR BANKS DID NOT CATCH COMMODITY TRADERS BY SURPRISE, BUT DID TEND TO BLUNT THE RALLY EFFORTS HERE TUESDAY, SOME ANALYSTS SAID.

NORMALLY, INTEREST RATES ARE A MAJOR CONCERN FOR SPREAD TRADERS. WITH THE RATE AT 19 PCT, HOWEVER, BROKERS EXPECT SOME IMPACT ON FLAT PRICES AS WELL AS SPREADS.

BROKERS SAY THE IMPACT ON SPREADS HAS BEEN HEAVILY DISCOUNTED. ALTHOUGH MOST SPREADS HAVE NOT TOTALLY REFLECTED THE INTEREST RATES, TRADERS ARE LOOKING FOR METHODICAL WIDENING IF SUPPLIES CONTINUE TO BE BURDENSOME, PARTICULARLY IN OILSEEDS. THE JLY/NOV SOYBEAN SPREAD IS A GOOD EXAMPLE, THEY SAY, OF A SPREAD THAT HAS NOT COMPLETELY INCORPORATED THE RISING COSTS OF MONEY. HOWEVER, TRADERS ALSO SAY THE INDUSTRY NOW ANTICIPATES EVEN HIGHER RATES AND TAKES THEM AS A GIVEN ELEMENT. CARRYING CHARGES, HENCEFORTH, PROBABLY WILL TRADE MORE ON OTHER VARIABLES, SUCH AS FREE GRAIN STOCKS.

THE INTEREST RATE CHARGED TO FARMERS ON PRICE SUPPORT LOANS FOR 1979 CROPS IS ONLY 9 PCT, LESS THAN HALF THE CURRENT PRIME. PROSPECTS ARE IT WILL BE INCREASED TO BETWEEN 12 AND 13 PCT LATER IN 1980, STILL A RELATIVE BARGAIN.

SOME TRADERS THEORIZE THAT FARMERS WILL BE DRAWN INTO THE LOAN AND RESERVE PROGRAMS IN GROWING NUMBERS, INSULATING MORE OF CARRYOVER SUPPLIES FROM THE MARKET AND TIGHTENING SPREADS TO COMPENSATE.

BUT ANOTHER ARGUMENT MAY HAVE MORE ADHERENTS. THESE TRADERS SAY HIGH INTEREST RATES WILL PUT PRESSURE ON FLAT PRICES BECAUSE FARMERS WILL BE FORCED TO SELL MORE GRAIN QUICKLY THIS YEAR. THIS ARGUMENT STATES THAT FARMERS SIMPLY CANNOT AFFORD TO FINANCE THE HOLDING OF GRAIN OR CANNOT OBTAIN THE FINANCING. DUMPING OF GRAIN WAS NOT APPARENT HERE, BUT MANY TRADERS EXPECT IT AND MAY HAVE BEEN SELLING THIS WEEK TO DISCOUNT THAT FACTOR.

THERE IS PROBABLY LITTLE CHANCE THAT THE NEW STORAGE BINS ON MIDWEST FARMS WILL SIT IDLE IN 1980. TRADERS WILL BE WATCHING FARMER SELLING PATTERNS CLOSELY IN AN EFFORT TO RECONCILE CONFLICTING INTERPRETATIONS OF EXPENSIVE MONEY.   END

0802 CST#

Source: Commodity News Service.

later traders did in going long). The unpredictable balance of responses further encourages prices to take a random walk.

Any trader who stays with the commodity markets for a while will undoubtedly have the experience of seeing a normally bullish change in fundamental supply and demand cause prices to drop. Consider the following case. A trader has lunch with a friend who has just returned from researching an academic study of the Soviet economy. Among many details of his visit, the friend mentions in passing that the Soviet Union has decided to put emphasis on self-sufficiency in feed grains this year and was planting rye and corn in fields normally given to sunflowers. Russia was scheduled to export no edible fats for the year. The trader checks Russian exports of edible fats in the past and finds them to be a significant factor in international trade, especially in the Asian and African markets. Safflower oil is in direct competition with the high-priced, high-quality soybean oil exported from the United States.

The trader buys soybean oil and waits for the world to start buying tons of the stuff as competing products run out. Sure enough, in December alone 30 million additional pounds of soybean oil are sold for export, the news coming across the wire Friday afternoon after the close of trading in soybean oil futures. Monday morning the price *falls* in active trading and never rallies back up to its Friday close. Why? Informed soybean oil traders had been anticipating *50* million pounds and were discouraged by such a small sale announcement. In the process of discounting, the price had already been bid up to reflect the traders' expectations, and when these were not fulfilled, prices dropped sharply.

No matter the commodity or the upcoming news events, prices will probably already be reflecting the traders' interpretations and anticipations. (See Figure 11–2.) The actual move on a day when droughts are announced, interest rates are raised, or housing starts are detailed will be up or down in relation to previous expectations. A bullish factor can mean short-term bear markets and vice-versa. Market prices may also, through discounting, average price increases or decreases into futures estimates based on the probability of foreseeable events like freezes. If a major event like a freeze hits every other year, then 50 percent of the price increase a real freeze would incite would find its way into futures prices as the market plays the odds. In the case of light and scattered freeze damage, the trader might watch the prize *go down* on news of a partially damaged crop.

PROFITS, PRICES, AND DISCOUNTING

In an undiscounted coffee market, futures contracts might sell for $2.10 per pound. Any trader who recognized the possibility of another Brazilian freeze could take a long position. If the freeze did not occur, prices ought to stay about where they were, leaving the trader with a zero loss, zero profit position. If a freeze did hit and prices soar to $2.50, profits per contract would be $15,000, a 200 percent return on a margin of $7,500 (minus commissions). The trader stands to win a little or lose a little in the absence of a freeze, with the added bonus of a large win on the long side if the climate goes his way. Such an undiscounted market would heavily favor the speculator on the long side. Placing the order, such a speculator would help firm the price for coffee futures. Other speculators doing the same would help push the price up even more, until the price finally rests at the point at which speculators are no longer offered lopsided odds. This would be a price which simply no longer tempted speculators into taking long positions without extremely strong and solid evidence for doing so. At this level the price has an exactly equal chance of dropping or rising and the market is said to be "fully discounted."

Should the price rise above the point at which it has a 50–50 chance of advancing or falling the same amount, some speculators will find that they are risking 30 cents in the event there is no freeze (if the price is at $2.40) and standing to gain only 10 cents if there is (if the average freeze brings the price to $2.50). With an equal chance of a freeze or no freeze, speculators who are risking 30 cents against 10 cents will prudently leave the market, weakening the price until it drops back to the point that no further speculators wish to exit.

Any time any trader can find an advantage on one side of the market or the other, either because price is more likely to move in one direction than the other or because it is likely to move *farther* in one direction than the other, he is in effect being offered a premium for instituting a position. In so doing he firms up a too low estimate or weakens one that is too high, speeding the market price closer to a better guess of the price that is going to occur on the cash market at contract expiration. Prices will adjust up or down as speculator demand takes advantage of a too low or too high price, shrinking the premium until it no longer tempts traders into exploiting it. It is by this process of offering profits,

either at the opening of a position or at its close, that the market discounts itself. Any time the price does not include all known factors and known odds of change in fundamentals, a profit is held out, which will be exploited until it disappears. A buy or sell order has the same effect of pressure on the market whether it is used to close an open position or initiate a new position. However, some traders will begin to analyze the market by taking account of the nature of the orders, using open interest as a gauge of market strength or weakness. If massive buying is covering existing shorts, rather than initiating new positions, the market will discount this information difference in its eventual price move.

The net effect of market discounting is that price in a totally efficient, discounted market has at all times an exactly equal chance of going the same distance in either direction. If the market has a 25 percent chance of going up (such as a history of drought every four years), this fact will be reflected in the price. The resting price in all events will be the price at which no speculative advantage is held out to any trader. Of course, new information comes in so often and trader judgments occur so continuously that the resting price or rationally discounted level is rarely found or held for long and the market remains constantly in fluctuation about the hypothetical intrinsic value.

Holbrook Working, in his academic study of the profits accruing to different players in commodity futures markets, concluded that speculators exist essentially on the crumbs of the markets as speculative advantage is exploited by a field of eager watchers before it has time to hold out a substantial meal to anyone. This is an adequate metaphor for a fully discounted market as long as it is remembered that *nobody* is getting the whole meal. If the marketing is working efficiently, crumbs are all that are allowed to exist. The metaphor ought not to be taken too literally, however. Even in the most efficient market the leverage given traders by low margin can return 100 to 1,000 percent in a matter of weeks.

THIN MARKETS

The best discounted markets are those that see the greatest volume of trading. The more traders doing business on a market and seeking advantage by different methods, the less likely is the market to hold out any sizeable speculative advantage to any of them. Such markets will hand out profits, in a random manner. Thin markets can be expected to react to news in a more jerky way and show a generally more volatile price pattern. Thin markets often hold out greater advantages to the speculator because of reduced competition for profits, but they also hold out greater risk. Lack of trading volume can make execution of plays at planned levels of price difficult or impossible, and once a poorly discounted market takes off, its price moves tend to be greater than in better discounted markets. The trader must balance the promise of greater profits against the risk of substantial losses, recognizing the danger of not being able to control a position if liquidity falls so low that the order cannot be executed. Extremely thin markets should be avoided most of the time (check daily volume and open interest figures). (See Figure 11–3.)

THE MODEL

No such thing as a random walk market exists, but by studying this "perfect game" an understanding of the real markets can be had. Where the real-world markets deviate from the ideal, a speculative advantage appears. Where real-world price movement is not random, the chart trader can make money by reading past price behavior. Theory has been largely avoided throughout this book for the simple reason that the vast majority of it has absolutely no pragmatic value to the speculator. Random walk is an exception and is being given, in some brief detail, in the hope of providing a basis for comprehending exactly what a forecasting system attempts to manage and measure.

Some very efficient commodity markets, such as those for wheat, corn, soybeans, and cotton have been shown to closely approximate the ideal over comparatively long periods in the past. Price movement is random and the market is considered fully discounted, free of trends. In shorter terms, inefficiency creeps in— price dips to accept large seasonal hedging sales, new information is not immediately or fully understood, traders do not all receive the same information from the same sources at the same time or come to the same conclusions. Because of short-term inefficiences, trends do exist and it is these that allow a trader to develop better than 50–50 odds in the game. Technical chart rules attempt to mechanically exploit these inefficiences, and it is for this reason that theoretical economists have given study to the rules of chart traders. The effect of chart rules is a direct measure of nonrandomness. (See Figure 11–4.)

In a random walk market the price will fluctuate daily in a narrow range for as long as no new information or expectation of new information applies to the judgment of traders. This random price movement could be accurately duplicated by

FIGURE 11–3

REPEATING VOLUME AND OPEN INTEREST TOTALS--3/25--
--FIGURES OF 3/24--

	VOLUME	OPEN INTEREST
CBT WHEAT	112,925	232,775
CBT CORN	180,680	787,100
CBT OATS	4,150	18,170
CBT SOYBEANS	135,300	497,975
CBT SOYMEAL	7,396	52,184
CBT SOYOIL	6,847	58,770
CBT BROILERS	18	289
CBT KILO GOLD	0	14
CBT 100 OZ GOLD	837	3,233
CBT SILVER	1,285	24,747
CBT PLYWOOD	650	3,283
CBT CD GNMA	13	2,099
CBT GNMA	7,954	46,747
CBT T-BONDS	9,770	58,982
CBT T-NOTES	0	282
CBT 90 DAY COMMERCIAL PAPER	57	391
CBT 30 DAY COMMERCIAL PAPER	6	2
CME BURBANK POTATOES	2	20
CME LIVE CATTLE	25,013	53,849
CME FEEDER CATTLE	2,711	14,191
CME LIVE HOGS	6,346	24,122
CME PORK BELLIES	1,869	21,970
CME FRESH BROILERS	33	793
CME NEW SHELL EGGS	1	49
CME OLD SHELL EGGS	16	43
CME LUMBER	808	10,030
CME STUD LUMBER	10	423
KCBT WHEAT	14,520	101,925
MPLS WHEAT	2,790	34,309
NY SUGAR 11	17,724	73,715
NY COFFEE C	3,148	13,072
NY COCOA	1,695	7,163
NY SUGAR 12	17	4,144
COMEX SILVER	4,286	54,901
COMEX COPPER	7,557	44,550
COMEX GOLD	28,792	143,384
COMEX ZINC	0	10
COMEX T-BILLS	222	529
COMEX GNMA	0	222
NY COTTON	16,153	46,459
NY FCOJ	1,542	6,457
NY LPG	0	1
ACE GNMA	46	1,869
ACE T-BILLS	0	0
ACE T-BONDS	9	79
NY MERC PLATINUM	2,035	7,225
NY MERC PALLADIUM	295	1,875
NY MERC ME POTS	393	3,640
NY MERC IMP BEEF	21	790
NY MERC SILVER COINS	63	326
NY MERC HEATING OIL	31	2,177
IMM B POUND	5,245	14,322
IMM C DOLLAR	1,663	9,126
IMM D MARK	2,883	10,251
IMM F FRANC	0	20
IMM J YEN	1,214	4,621
IMM M PESO	50	2,582
IMM D. GUILDER	0	2
IMM S FRANC	1,613	8,171
IMM SILVER COINS	0	6
IMM GOLD	6,255	27,173
IMM 13 WK T-BILLS	9,641	25,215
IMM 1 YR T-BILLS	0	179
IMM 4 YR T-NOTES	0	74

FIGURE 11-4

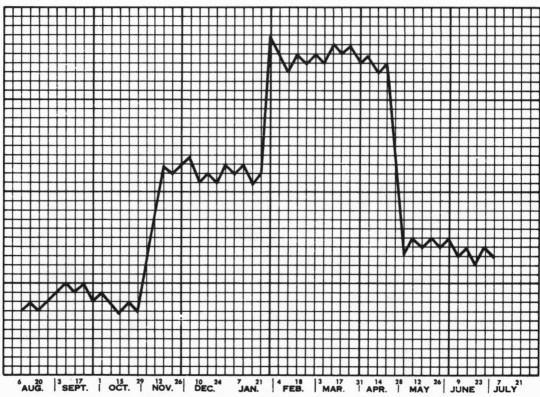

| 6 20 | 3 17 | 1 15 29 | 12 26 | 10 24 | 7 21 | 4 18 | 3 17 | 31 14 28 | 12 26 | 9 23 | 7 21 |
| AUG. | SEPT. | OCT. | NOV. | DEC. | JAN. | FEB. | MAR. | APR. | MAY | JUNE | JULY |

In a random walk market, price change will occur without pattern in the manner of a coin flip. Jogs in the chart occur when new, unpredictable information reaches the market and leave price at a new level of random fluctuation.

the simple flip of a coin and is insignificant to any trader who must pay full commission because movements are too small to cover the cost of exploiting them. These small random fluctuations are called "noise" and any series of upticks would give the trader no more information about his next position than would a series of heads to the bettor on a coin flip. In large, efficient markets such noise has been found to account for 75 percent of all new prices coming across the ticker. About 75 percent of all new prices are in the direction opposite the preceding one, with the result that the price ends in almost exactly the same place that it started from during the time a market is fully discounted. The market may, in fact, move in one direction or the other, rewarding long or short trad-

ers, but no such movement would give information about future movement or help a trader in instituting a position.

According to the model, all information pertaining to price that can be applied has been applied, and no trader who has the money to open a new position has the desire. No trader with the desire has the money. Such fluctuation as occurs is caused by traders closing their positions to go on vacation or opening new positions simply because they have the money and come in a completely unpredictable, erratic fashion.

When new information is released and becomes generally known, the price will jump or drop to a new level and begin the meaningless fluctuation that characterizes a market at rest. In the theoreti-

165

cally perfect market, all traders receive the information at the same time and are equally talented in interpretation. Thus, the price moves quickly and smoothly to its new level. Some traders will think the new information justifies a 4 cent upward adjustment, some might consider 5 cents closer to reality, but agreement will soon solidify and a consensus price will be established. If the new information was expected and the market already discounted in anticipation, the price may rise or drop with the news according to whether it was better or worse than expected. A further refinement would take into account the relative reactions of "insiders," "outsiders," and other sectors of the trading public as each responds in turn.

As news is by definition "new," its effect on the market is random. It can be bullish, bearish, or neutral with equal probability. The Department of Agriculture and other government agencies take great precautions to avoid leaks of infor-

mation and to see that all traders have equal access to governmental reports and releases. This is done to see that all traders have a fair chance at profits in the commodity markets and serves to bring the real markets closer to the theoretically perfect market.

The random walk market is random in the short term as price reacts up and down to essentially nonfundamental purchases and sales, characterized by small sales just sufficient to set a new price. It is also random in the medium term as incoming news is random and the new price level is quickly fitted to the new information. Only in the long run is any bias expected, as commodity prices in general inflate (or increasingly rarely, deflate) in value along with other prices in the economy. Seasonal trends will be efficiently discounted, and long-term bias spreads across a period longer than the life span of any contract, leaving intact the random nature of the market. If corn

FIGURE 11-5

DISTRIBUTION OF LENGTHS OF RUN OF WEEKLY CASH WHEAT PRICES AT CHICAGO

(1883-1934, Excluding 1915-1920)

Length of Run (Weeks)	Observed		Expected Up or Down
	Up	Down	
1	280	295	297
2	147	132	149
3	86	77	74
4	38	42	37
5	15	18	19
6	13	12	9
7 or longer	7	8	9
TOTAL	586	584	595

Source: Holbrook Working, "Prices of Cash Wheat and Futures at Chicago Since 1883," Wheat Studies Vol. II, No. 3, November 1934, pp. 75-124.

prices are to rise, the contract for corn delivery will start at a higher price in a perfect market.

The model fits the short- and long-term reality of actual markets fairly well, sometimes extremely so. (See Figure 11–5.) In the medium term of several weeks or months, when speculators normally make their moves, statisticians have found distinct trends. Were the actual markets perfect, there would be no possibility of improving profit from technical study of past price performance. The next price would bear absolutely no relation to the last price or any number of past prices. The trader would do as well to buy and sell at random as he would following the most sophisticated computer program. Because the markets are not perfect, trends do exist, probabilities and odds surface, and the speculator takes some of his profit by identifying these in time to go along with them. If the analysis is right, the order will help push a trending price to its final goal, or even a little past it, before the correction sets in. This trading has the effect of eliminating the trend by simply ending it—the price more rapidly reaches its destination and the market more fully approximates the random walk. The more trading done on a market, and the more bidding into price changes, the more the market will approach the theoretically perfect market.

IMPLICATIONS OF THE THEORY

If market price did not walk randomly, there would be no need of futures markets and the unique process of discounting they provide. If agricultural, mineral, or financial instrument prices could be absolutely controlled, or precisely forecast by any single system, producers and processors would do so and be able to adequately control their yearly budgeting with cash forward contracts and other commercial devices. Because commodity markets *do* walk randomly, no computer has yet been programmed that can take over the function of an open auction by a large number of traders.

Random walk helps us see that prediction techniques are exceptions to the rule, not magic wands. Because markets are inefficient, trends and patterns do take shape, even if at random. The trader following the market closely can then take advantage of this aberration from the random norm. Viewing technical study as the measurement of flaws in the perfect market gives the trader some method of evaluating the worth of his prediction methods. Such an approach is admittedly negative, but perhaps it is better to be a flaw in a theory than to be in no theory at all, especially if money is being bet on it. Random walk cautions against naïve faith in highly sophisticated "fool proof" trading systems: If there is no hidden pattern in the total market (just randomness), then no advisor or computer can claim to have found the key that unlocks the market's mystery. The market *is* a mystery. This is its essential character. Hence, the importance in trading of psychology, intuition, and the "feel" of the market as complements to technical and fundamental analysis. Since deviations from the random are the product of human acts upsetting the market's random nature, a sensitivity to the moods and minds of a market's traders can be vitally important.

The theory of random walk allows improvement on random buying and selling only if one of the following conditions is met. Under these conditions the market is still considered to walk randomly, although with flaws which hold out a speculative advantage to one side of the market or the other. Such a view seems to most accurately describe actual markets.

1. A bias in the entire supply and demand balance forming the current market. This may happen due to conditions in the cash market such as the glut immediately at harvest or because of marketing peculiarities such as the seasonal lifting of hedges. Flaws in market discounting could be discovered in a study of seasonal behavior for the commodity and each of its contracts. This is one of the most promising predictive avenues.

2. A time lag in the discounting of information. Experienced traders are normally quite humble about their own opinions. A trader who has learned of bullish news will often buy a few contracts and wait for market price to confirm his opinion before buying more. Or a trader might keep his opinions private for selfish reasons, quietly scaling in orders to avoid notice rather than rushing all at once into a huge position and spoiling the market thereby. Instead of jogging neatly to the next resting area, price may trend toward it or even intermittently regress as other traders continue to take positions based on old premises. Several technical devices attempt to define and exploit such trends while profit possibilities still exist. Obviously, the first trader to find the trend will make the most money.

3. Distortion by nonrandom price factor. The market price may react randomly to a price set by supply and demand, fully discounted, but be under the influence of a closely placed factor such as the government loan rate that provides a floor under the price or the CCC offering price that provides a ceiling over the price. In such

a case the price has an equal chance of going up or down, but can go further in one direction than the other.

4. Fundamental price factors may be uncovered which have not been fully discounted because of their obscurity. In this case, the trader has an "angle" to follow until it becomes common knowledge. This was the case of the trader who bought soybean oil on the basis of a tip from a friend back from Russia. Such "scoops" in commodity trading are extremely risky.

5. Markets can be self-fulfilling prophecies. The markets have a long history of forming artificial trends whose sole foundation is the belief or expectation of the traders themselves. Temporary price movements do occur that are simply the product of speculation that affirms its own predictions. This commonly happens in the pit when prices hit a cluster of stop orders and then spurt. More recently, the volume of orders being placed by pools, funds, managed account programs, and commission houses based on computer selection has caused problems when all the analysts are in agreement and the floor is flooded with identical orders.

6. The trader can manage positions so that more is won on correct guesses than is lost on wrong ones. Of the six, this possibility presents the most theoretically sound procedure and the only one which is not subject to discounting. Cut your losses short and let your profits run. There's not a prominent reputable broker, advisor, or observer in the field who doesn't list this as rule number one. All agree that speculators who do come out ahead profit on only a small minority of their trades. A lot of little losses can be more than offset by a few gigantic wins. The trader may (a) win more on winning positions than he loses on losing positions;

(b) win on more contracts when he wins then he loses on when he loses; or (c) choose risks through some combination of the previous five conditions.

Part Three of this text will explore each of these six possibilities as an aid toward the development of a trading program which can coexist with the random walk. Before constructing such a program, however, the trader will need to take a closer look at the details of cash and futures pricing.

Chapter 12

CASH COMMODITY PRICING

CASH PRICE

At first, cash prices don't appear to be a very complicated matter. We see hundreds of them everyday, printed in clearly understandable figures. We pay for things daily without questioning the concept of price though we may protest loudly about the level of price and its speed of ascent. The recessions and inflations of recent decades have taught that prices are not the set and reasonable statement of a thing's worth. They are but momentary stopovers in the wayward journey that is commodity pricing. The simple numbers that tell us, however painfully, an object's price are the end result of a lengthy process of calculations that began long before the thing was produced and which end only when the customer makes the decision to buy at the offered price. In the intricate interim, the price will undergo dozens of adjustments by participants at each stage of production and marketing. Each sets a price, or bids one, which is in reality a kind of speculative guess involving all the myriad factors of cost and profit that determine the life of a business enterprise.

The price of a car, a cup of coffee, a mortgage, or a bushel of wheat should not be thought of as a measure of absolute value. Prices are, rather, ever shifting evaluations of a product's production costs, its current and future supplies, its current and future demand, its projected relations to other commodities and markets, its cost to distribute and sell, etc. The price will also be shaped by the economic climate as a whole and by the success or failure of other business ventures involving the buyers or sellers of the product. The market value of the raw materials contained in the average automobile play a small and highly variable role in the price that appears on the car dealer's sticker. Likewise, the price the auto manufacturer paid for aluminum, copper, rubber, and nylon will only partially depend upon mine output, the rubber tree crop, or the supply of textile fabrics. More important may be the cost of energy, the price of substitutable materials, or the recent wage hikes which were themselves predicated on the price of food and housing. Taking the broadest view, all commodity prices affect all other commodity prices as well as the price of doing business itself. Decisions on the price of a particular object give small attention to the thing itself. The price determination emerges from a total view of the particular business enterprise and its market place. Participants in the market, including the futures trader, have the difficult task of sifting a potentially infinite flow of price factors in search of the few that matter most. The process and function of pricing largely supersede the simple denomination of intrinsic worth or value.

SUPPLY AND DEMAND

The model commonly used to describe price functions in economic activities is that of the free competitive market where producers and prices are ultimately governed by the choices of the sovereign consumer. Unfortunately or not, such markets in their pure form are rarely to be found. At the retail level, the model hardly fits an age of multinational corporations larger in organization and capital than many states and nations. Most major markets are dominated by a small group of companies who minimize price competition in favor of creating a stable market that assures continuous revenues to all. Markets are managed by mutually cooperative producers, and in the age of mass media advertising consumers themselves are managed and often have only a choice among indistinguishable varieties at similar prices. Companies undertaking the production of high technology or capital intensive products involving years of investment and research cannot afford the uncertainties of the free market. Price levels must bring in, on a regular and predictable basis, the revenue necessary to underwrite modern industrial enterprise. To that extent prices and revenues cannot be left to the consumer. Demand and price are managed as much as possible by pro-

ducer influence in the market and sophisticated media management of the consumer.

The problems of the free market can be entirely circumvented by the popular path of government contracting. Demand is further locked in, and prices set high, if the consumer be the Pentagon or other government agency. The risks of market competition can be replaced by years of assured profits, interrupted by only periodic campaigns to sell the "need" for new projects or weapons (whose research and development the government pays for—read "taxpayer"—whether or not the product eventually sells). The size and economic importance of modern producers makes them at times immune to the decisions of the free market—witness the government "bail-outs" of Lockheed and Chrysler. As the free market disappears and price risks for producers diminish, inflation inevitably increases and the modern economic cycle spins.

Thus, classic supply and demand economics no longer accurately describes pricing in the United States other than in small business markets and in agriculture. Today's farms have grown to become multimillion dollar agribusinesses, yet no farmer produces a significant enough proportion of the total production to have any personal control of supply or of the price he will receive for his produce. There is no farm comparable to General Motors, U.S. Steel, I.T.T., or Exxon. The farmer or cattle rancher must be content with the best price that can be gotten from a market over which he has no control. Buyers of farm produce do rival the multinationals in other industries in size relative to market but have not been able to effectively set prices in so volatile a supply and demand market. The final price for farm goods is still largely set by how much stock is to be had and how many people want to have it. This is not true of any other large significant sector of the economy.

With restrictions, the cash price of a commodity will be as high as suppliers can set it and still account for all their produce, and as low as buyers can force it while still getting all the commodity they need to run their operations. In the course of the year, price should adjust to assure that all of the commodity finds a home somewhere. Restrictions of pure demand and supply pricing are regulated by the Department of Agriculture, largely in the form of price floors designed to protect the farmer against too low a price for farm products. These floors (and sometimes ceilings) are administered in a number of ways—through planting restrictions on supply, loan levels, and outright purchases. These programs are made necessary by the difference between the agricultural free market and the controlled markets in energy and other goods the farmer and his family must buy. Unable to dominate the market with three or four fellow producers, the farmer cannot set prices to guarantee a reasonable return and to pay for the ever escalating prices of other goods. Thus, price support programs are meant to give the individual farmer a relative guarantee of return roughly analogous to that which a huge corporation can assure itself. The examples of Lockheed and Chrysler were the exceptions that proved the rule. From 1954 through 1976 there were only 2 years in which as many as five of the 100 largest industrial corporations in the United States lost money.

If free market competition suffers most where individual participants can domi-

nate the field, the futures exchanges appear to be some of the last bastions of free competitive pricing. The structure of the futures markets has preserved competitive characteristics in most cases. The (so far) small role of large corporations in the production end of agriculture has kept that economic sector closer in its operation to the model, while the futures markets have been somewhat of a check on the few multinationals who control the merchandising and export of grain. And the relatively small role now played by raw materials in the eventual computation of product prices (as compared to wages, energy, and regulation) has allowed the commodity markets to continue functioning with supply and demand in their traditional predominant places. The explosive growth of financial futures may in part be explained as a result of inflation. Continuous corporate profits were no protection against the inflation and high interest rates they helped to fuel. Unpredictability once again disturbed stable planning, and financial futures offered a way to battle this new cost of doing business without the danger of production cutbacks, bankruptcies, and lower prices.

The individual consumer or speculator may have as much trouble estimating price movements as has the federal government, considering the vast complexity and variety of the forces at work. Commodity pricing, however, still differs from pricing at the retail level, though many commodity markets without correspondent futures have ceased to resemble the competitive model. In commodities prices go on fluctuating down as well as up, registering from moment to moment and from day to day the ceaseless process of pricing. These fluctuations occur in the main as the results of traditional market actions and reactions, not as edicts promulgated by single individuals or groups. As long as the market actually remains in control, more powerful than any of its participants, then price analysis can proceed in the traditional method of supply and demand estimation.

FUNCTIONS AND FUNDAMENTALS

When the market itself governs prices, prices are allowed to perform their basic allocating functions without prejudicial intervention. As they operate, prices will have a number of significant effects the commodity watcher will note carefully. Price levels will spur, stifle, or halt production plans in enterprises that are susceptible, or "elastic," to price changes. The terms "elastic" and "inelastic" are used by economists and commodity analysts when describing the reactions of prices to demand or supply or of demand or supply to prices. If a product like soybean oil has an "inelastic" demand, fairly wide swings in price will not produce much change in demand. For every commodity there are different degrees, and speeds, of elasticity—perhaps at different times of the year or different locations—that will alter the tendencies of prices. Producers and buyers plan their strategies, and react to the markets, knowing the behavior patterns of price levels and commodities.

Inventory accumulation and liquidation will closely reflect the relative strength of the market price and vice versa. One of the classic functions of price in economic theory is the distribution of goods between storehouse and market, and these will be statistics the trader will study with care. In the case of stored seasonal commodities like the grains or some meats, prices have the special function of rationing supply over time. During the short harvest season, supplies pour in that must be made to last through the crop year, meet reserve and export requirements, and achieve the desired level of carryover. (See Figure 12–1.) Ideally, high prices will ration short supplies and low prices will encourage new demand. At all times there are two kinds of demand. One is for current use and the other for inventory for future use. Thus, prices play a key role in the movement of goods in and out of inventory, from the farmer's bin to the grain elevator, from the grain elevator to the shipping terminal, and from terminal to export. Prices and the movement of goods respond almost immediately to each other, causing many of the price ticks in the cash and futures markets. Special problems can arise at the end of a crop year, or production cycle, as the rationing of the old and the introduction of the new must be timed right or severe price dislocations may ensue.

Inventory holders and suppliers constantly scrutinize the market, looking for a signal that says "sell," "hold," or "buy." These cash players in effect speculate and forecast when taking action in the market. Timing can be just as essential to the cash player as to the futures trader, for both move in and out of the market on the uncertain basis of price judgments. The producer who sells too soon and the merchant who runs out of inventory suffer what can be classified as speculative losses. Everyone in commodities, inside and outside of the futures exchanges, speculates on price changes. The difference is only one of degree, not of kind. Similarly,

FIGURE 12–1

Chicago total stocks of grain on or about the first of the month
(Reported in 1,000 Bu.)

WHEAT

	1978	1977	1976	1975	1974	1973	1972	1971	1970	1969	1968	1967	1966	1965
January . . .	20,722	16,796	18,535	7,914	4,686	6,446	2,785	4,676	6,987	10,406	15,052	9,694	7,944	8,770
February . .	20,238	16,660	16,698	5,147	4,936	5,116	2,654	3,643	6,561	8,412	13,514	9,380	7,822	8,355
March . . .	18,995	16,424	14,744	3,283	3,975	4,115	2,705	3,119	6,060	7,250	11,712	8,893	7,978	8,108
April . . .	18,247	16,163	13,310	1,749	3,738	3,738	2,505	2,697	5,541	6,179	10,180	8,044	7,234	7,502
May	16,077	15,078	12,368	799	2,261	3,309	1,344	2,314	4,120	5,267	10,112	7,926	6,339	5,824
June	12,512	14,530	10,745	382	554	3,204	723	1,782	2,101	5,203	9,241	7,487	5,657	2,895
July	9,306	14,773	10,755	522	216	2,953	479	1,126	1,434	4,239	9,618	8,189	5,054	2,152
August . . .	9,749	19,470	15,188	9,680	4,908	4,027	6,030	6,097	6,942	8,947	15,078	18,091	12,874	9,849
September . .	7,664	21,136	16,221	18,492	7,681	4,716	8,834	5,321	7,752	11,254	16,708	19,999	13,921	10,576
October . .	5,993	21,866	16,805	21,580	8,367	4,565	9,192	5,600	7,984	11,997	16,082	20,586	13,636	11,067
November . .	4,150	20,948	17,630	21,266	9,241	4,013	8,386	3,509	6,069	10,355	15,054	18,493	12,675	10,500
December . .	3,706	20,846	17,222	19,696	9,318	3,636	7,076	2,661	5,318	8,262	12,613	16,801	11,230	9,802

CORN

	1978	1977	1976	1975	1974	1973	1972	1971	1970	1969	1968	1967	1966	1965
January . . .	11,838	16,490	10,602	12,695	16,710	13,958	15,646	17,008	13,296	17,923	15,313	19,540	19,706	26,244
February . .	12,541	16,362	12,589	14,466	17,562	14,781	16,221	16,029	12,749	18,699	19,626	20,454	18,951	24,087
March . . .	13,718	16,151	14,744	16,993	19,537	15,781	17,489	14,947	13,162	19,827	21,904	21,699	21,322	22,899
April . . .	13,235	14,803	13,310	12,950	19,286	16,723	19,085	12,882	12,886	20,380	23,150	25,389	19,879	22,810
May	11,937	9,176	12,368	9,160	13,632	16,735	18,550	10,785	12,704	21,340	21,832	21,832	12,257	19,833
June	8,341	3,986	10,745	5,150	14,855	14,855	14,235	9,589	10,228	8,217	15,575	15,235	11,507	15,389
July	8,786	4,344	9,184	2,367	3,386	13,632	15,208	10,795	10,125	7,731	13,594	10,436	11,758	9,394
August . . .	10,090	4,209	6,148	4,759	5,147	13,124	14,813	10,389	8,982	10,508	12,525	11,893	11,893	7,818
September . .	8,058	7,571	1,424	1,984	5,512	13,982	11,593	8,410	13,251	8,370	9,124	5,609	12,995	8,442
October . .	7,569	10,165	2,875	5,199	7,034	14,396	13,556	6,643	14,175	9,537	9,770	6,534	9,738	10,769
November . .	13,711	12,021	7,906	7,158	6,240	18,127	12,256	10,273	16,739	10,022	9,228	5,172	13,346	10,514
December . .	17,635	12,738	14,878	9,324	10,508	19,259	11,876	14,912	17,604	8,532	14,091	8,004	18,210	16,927

OATS

	1978	1977	1976	1975	1974	1973	1972	1971	1970	1969	1968	1967	1966	1965
January . . .	82	61	245	127	7	238	403	2,532	3,654	1,141	950	2,630	2,379	1,771
February . .	71	43	83	101	26	250	363	2,082	3,200	1,074	505	2,439	2,264	1,548
March . . .	64	40	78	77	61	44	254	1,564	2,463	1,099	400	2,324	2,042	1,512
April	58	43	11	24	17	18	301	1,505	1,314	1,690	274	1,714	1,724	1,129
May	51	41	10	17	9	16	1,058	1,309	1,013	1,359	140	1,480	1,393	1,059
June	46	9	14	8	10	6	823	563	772	1,566	122	1,171	988	1,515
July	45	—	14	—	4	1	696	429	772	1,248	55	655	730	1,101
August . . .	50	—	139	7	48	66	868	691	1,350	1,638	1,048	311	1,967	945
September . .	87	—	240	191	137	257	921	761	1,707	3,473	2,106	1,531	4,212	1,367
October . .	149	82	252	376	156	223	780	575	1,869	4,343	1,576	1,579	4,407	2,448
November . .	177	82	246	362	157	171	747	562	1,991	4,595	1,586	1,467	3,819	2,721
December . .	176	82	165	351	144	61	415	509	2,068	4,549	1,420	1,355	3,280	2,696

SOYBEANS

	1978	1977	1976	1975	1974	1973	1972	1971	1970	1969	1968	1967	1966	1965
January . . .	8,763	7,968	13,429	14,814	6,425	10,888	15,448	17,389	16,833	10,586	7,705	2,304	8,841	8,503
February . .	8,847	8,429	13,814	14,281	7,688	14,965	15,434	17,726	9,539	9,539	6,923	2,498	8,546	9,962
March . . .	8,343	8,919	13,927	12,793	9,395	16,605	16,055	18,263	20,012	10,859	6,892	2,963	9,403	11,538
April	8,341	10,032	13,165	7,576	8,627	17,235	16,287	18,966	20,808	11,556	7,097	4,293	9,877	11,560
May	8,153	11,520	11,936	3,391	8,248	15,034	15,782	15,002	17,689	9,270	5,741	3,861	10,152	10,252
June	8,151	16,700	10,032	1,511	6,350	8,236	12,420	11,798	14,550	5,488	4,545	2,543	8,870	7,475
July	5,373	14,802	8,351	1,419	5,166	5,342	10,367	12,143	9,920	4,086	4,304	797	7,766	4,027
August . . .	4,085	9,671	8,684	1,504	4,132	5,673	7,916	11,987	9,038	3,043	3,704	2,051	4,983	2,082
September . .	1,464	4,621	7,197	1,342	5,054	3,612	8,036	5,636	7,672	2,101	1,154	1,248	2,320	1,531
October . .	2,270	3,904	5,896	2,410	5,013	3,508	3,715	5,019	5,270	3,471	1,068	958	1,331	696
November . .	8,384	7,187	11,193	11,652	12,225	6,194	2,845	15,545	7,993	12,838	11,073	5,574	4,219	8,453
December . .	9,182	8,855	8,922	13,236	15,052	6,475	6,281	15,318	14,000	18,027	13,014	7,495	2,242	11,643

Includes Wheat Afloat and one non-regular elevator

Source: Chicago Board of Trade.

the person who buys a foreign car to take advantage of a temporarily favorable exchange rate is speculating, as is the futures trader who sells a contract of a foreign currency. The next move in the price of that currency will tell which, if either, player made the best deal.

Cash price, then, may be thought of as simply the first price in the general list that includes the prices quoted for each month of the commodity's future contracts. Every trade of a futures contract throughout its trading life is made at a price which is simply the best current guess of the cash market price to come in the future. Cash and futures prices are

tied to each other by their method of estimate and by the terms of the commodity
futures contract. In the delivery month
the contract will "go off" the board at a
price level very close to those found in
the cash markets at the same time. Were
the futures price to inordinately exceed

cash, traders would buy cash and sell futures until prices came back into line. If
futures were well below cash, the same
process in reverse would soon restore
equilibrium. Disequilibriums will persist
from time to time as distortions in some
price factor relationships temporarily pre-

FIGURE 12–2

Source: Commodity Research Bureau, Inc.

vail, but the cash-futures pricing mechanism always pressures prices eventually toward harmony (See Figure 12–2.) Cash prices will often command a small premium over futures in the deliver month due to considerations concerning ease and timing of delivery, location, quality of goods, and handling expenses. In general, cash traders liquidate their futures contracts and make their deals in the most convenient suitable cash market rather than take delivery, though exceptions regularly make some acceptances and deliveries attractive.

The imperfect but strong continuity of cash and futures prices means that the trading in commodity futures entails a good grasp of price mechanisms and factors. The basic forces influencing prices in the cash markets are usually grouped under the heading "fundamentals." Traders spend hours pouring over figures of farmers' planting intentions, spring calf crop, chicks hatched, rainfall in Bolivia, snow cover in Iowa, gross national product in Japan, labor negotiations in Chile, housing starts at home, etc. Any factor directly affecting the cash market price of a commodity can be classified a fundamental, and the fundamentals constitute a helpful but by no means certain index to the movement of futures prices. Fortunately for the trader, a wealth of fundamental information is made available by the government, the exchanges, and the large brokerage houses as well as by the major commodity news services and business periodicals. The U.S. Department of Agriculture publishes the most important reports for the trader in agricultural products; the Federal Reserve Board is the key source for traders in financials, along with the Commerce and Treasury Departments. In fact, one of the arguments that

has always defended futures markets to their opponents has been this organization of price information.

SUPPLY DETERMINANTS

The commodity fundamentalist divides the total supply of any given commodity into specific categories of major determinants, keeping a record of each section and its relative level over time. (See Figure 12–3.) The flow from principal sources of supply will be constantly checked, totaled, and analyzed. In the grains, total supply breaks down into three sections which, when added together, will give the total amount of the commodity to be disposed of over the year. This figure can be compared to years past and, when contrasted to projected demand, provides a basis for estimating cash prices in the near future. The three sources of supply are (1) carryover from previous years; (2) current farmer planting intentions and harvests; and (3) government offerings. Government offerings are set in price by a formula based on the market price and significantly alter supply only if the market price rises sufficiently to make the government goods attractive to buyers. Such sales must be carefully timed so as not to unduly upset the market. For commodities grown in the United States, U.S.D.A. "situation reports" sum up all of the above information in a manner readily understood by the student of fundamentals.

Supply statistics for other commodities can be similarly organized. Supply analysis for international plant products (cocoa, sugar, cotton, and coffee) considers production, carryover, import and export figures, and processing levels (grinding, roasting, ginning, and refining). For the metals, supplies include new production

FIGURE 12–3
Acreage and Supply of Corn in the United States   In Millions of Bushels

Year Beginning October	All Purposes Planted	All Purposes Harv.	Harvested For Grain	Harvested For Silage	Harvested For Forage	Yield, Per Harv. Acre-Bus.	Carry-over, October 1 Farm	Carry-over Term. Mkt.	Carry-over CCC Bins	Carry-over Others[3]	Carry-over Total	Production For Grain	Production For All	Imports[2]	Total (All Supply Grain)
			In Millions of Acres												
1966–7	66.3	5	57.0	7.9	.9	73.1	530	5	134	176	840	4,168	5	1.0	5,011
1967–8	71.2	5	60.7	8.4	1.0	80.1	569.2	5	97.6	156.5	823	4,860	5	1.0	5,687
1968–9	65.1	5	56.0	7.9	.8	79.5	781.8	5	103.3	277.2	1,162	4,450	5	1.0	5,620
1969–0	64.3	5	54.6	7.9	.6	85.9	728.2	5	143.3	241.9	1,113	4,687	5	1.0	5,806
1970–1	66.8	5	57.4	8.1	.7	72.4	575.6	5	111.3	318.3	1,005	4,152	5	4.0	5,161
1971–2	74.1	5	64.1	8.8	.7	88.1	426.7	5	24.5	215.5	667	5,646	5	1.0	6,309
1972–3	67.0	5	57.5	8.4	.5	97.0	751.3	5	26.3	348.7	1,126	5,580	5	1.0	6,700
1973–4	71.9	5	62.1	9.0	.6	91.3	404.6	5	20.3	283.7	709	5,671	5	1.0	6,380
1974–5	77.8	5	65.4	10.8	.6	71.9	287.6	5	——195.1——		483	4,701	5	1.8	5,187
1975–6	78.6	5	67.5	9.8	.6	86.3	191.3	5	——168.2——		359	5,829	5	1.8	6,192
1976–7	84.4	5	71.3	11.3	.9	89.7	229.8	5	——169.4——		399	6,266	5	2.5	6,668
1977–8[1]	83.6	5	70.9	9.3	.6	90.7	446.1	5	——438.0——		884	6,425	5	2.6	7,312
1978–9[4]	79.7	5	70.0	8.6	.5	101.2	659.3	5	——444.7——		1,104	7,082	5	1.0	8,187
1979–80[4]	79.2														

[1] Preliminary.   [2] Includes grain equivalent of cornmeal & flour.   [3] Interior mills & elevators and terminal mkts.   [4] Estimate.   [5] Discontinued, no longer reported.   *Source: Commodity Economics Division, U.S.D.A.*

Salient Statistics of Oats in the United States & Canada

Year Begin. July	Acreage Planted[3]	Acreage Harvested[3]	Yield Per Harv. Acre Bushels	Farm Value of Product Mill. $	Farm Disposition Feed & Seed	Farm Disposition Sold	Owned By CCC July 1	Under Price Support Loans	Under Price Support Purch. Agree.	Under Price Support Total	Deliveries To CCC	Nat. Avg. Support Rate $ Bu.	Average Prices No. 2 White, Portland	Average Prices No. 2 Heavy Chicago
	1,000 Acres				Mil. Bu.			1,000 Bushels					Dollars per Bushel	
1966–7	23,343	17,877	44.9	540	527	277	50,573	22,700	—	22,695	6,500	.60		
1967–8	20,719	16,110	49.3	528	525	268	47,796	37,200	400	36,740	19,500	.63		
1968–9	23,342	17,708	53.7	576	592	359	45,206	89,200	5,700	89,135	35,600	.63		
1969–0	23,561	17,971	53.7	572	586	380	61,088	152,500	10,100	162,600	62,000	.63	.74	.64
1970–1	24,469	18,594	49.2	584	563	355	104,254	108,900	4,800	113,700	26,600	.54	.80	.77
1971–2	21,956	15,705	55.9	546	539	339	168,910			81,900	700	.54	.83	.74
1972–3	20,178	13,410	51.5	509	428	262	178,128			31,800	—	.54	1.02	.88
1973–4	19,147	13,770	47.9	785	404	256	104,942			10,392	—	.54	1.57	1.40
1974–5	17,967	12,608	47.6	933	389	212	24,000			3,900	—	.54	1.96	1.75
1975–6	16,486	13,092	49.0	928	397	245	5,800			3,900	—	.54	1.86	1.54
1976–7	16,734	11,946	45.7	845	353	193	—			5,000	—	.72	1.80	1.71
1977–8[1]	17,733	13,452	55.8	853	459	288	—			83,000	2,000	1.03	1.44	1.36
1978–9[1]	16,385	11,531	52.2							24,000		1.03	1.76	1.34
1979–80[1]	15,038													

[1] Preliminary.   [2] For all purposes.   [3] For grain.   *Source: Statistical Reporting Service, U.S.D.A.*

Supply and Distribution of Soybeans in the United States   In Millions of Bushels

Crop Year Begin. Sept. 1	Supply Stocks, Sept. 1 Farms	Supply CCC	Supply Mills, Elevators[2]	Supply Total	Production	Total Supply	Distribution Crushings	Distribution Exports	Distribution Seed	Distribution Feed	Distribution Residual	Total Distribution
1966–7	4.4	0	31.2	35.6	928.5	964.1	559.4	261.6	47.1	.9	4.9	874.0
1967–8	41.6	0	48.5	90.1	976.4	1,066.5	576.4	266.6	48.6	.9	7.8	900.2
1968–9	60.7	—	105.6	166.3	1,107.0	1,273.3	605.9	286.8	47.3	.9	5.4	946.4
1969–0	70.6	5.3	247.3	326.8	1,133.1	1,459.9	737.3	432.6	48.5	.9	10.8	1,230.1
1970–1	40.6	8.7	180.5	229.8	1,127.1	1,356.9	760.1	433.8	48.1	1.1	15.1	1,258.2
1971–2	20.6	—	78.2	98.8	1,176.1	1,274.9	720.5	416.8	51.0	1.1	13.5	1,202.9
1972–3	11.8	0	60.2	72.0	1,270.6	1,342.6	721.8	479.4	60.8	1.1	19.8	1,282.9
1973–4	9.4	0	50.2	59.6	1,547.5	1,607.1	821.3	539.1	56.1	1.2	18.7	1,436.4
1974–5	64.5	0	106.3	170.9	1,216.3	1,387.2	701.3	420.7	57.2	1.0	21.7	1,201.9
1975–6	75.1	0	109.9	188.2	1,547.4	1,735.5	865.1	555.1	53.5	1.2	15.7	1,490.6
1976–7	86.2	0	158.8	244.9	1,287.6	1,532.5	790.2	564.1	61.0	1.0	13.3	1,429.6
1977–8[1]	32.7	0	70.2	102.9	1,761.8	1,864.7	926.7	700.5	68.0	1.0	7.5	1,703.7
1978–9[3]	59.0	0	102.0	161.0	1,842.6	2,003.6	1,000	760	70	1	13	1,844
1979–80												

[1] Preliminary.   [2] Also warehouses.   [3] Estimates.   *Source: Economic Research Service, U.S.D.A.*

Source: Commodity Research Bureau, Inc.

from ores domestic and foreign, secondary recovery, and government and private holdings. Livestock supplies follow production cycles based on the average life of the animal and time needed to reach market weights. Supplies are analyzed in terms of farrowing and calving intentions, diversion for dairy or breeding purposes, and final slaughter figures. For financial and currency markets, supply analysis is a bit trickier. Variations in absolute supply of mortgages, Treasury Bills, or Deutchesmarks will affect prices, but prices and traders are also sensitive to a set of fundamental financial indicators which direct prices for money instruments. These include total monetary supply in various categories, interest rates of several kinds, price indexes, production and trade statistics, quantity and character of government spending, and other economic news that influences the flow of investment funds in and out of particular financial instruments. (See Figure 12–4.)

Changes in real and projected supply occur throughout the year, altering cash prices and futures speculations on upcoming levels. "Farmers' planting intentions" will later be released as "total estimated acreage" with adjustments for producers who changed their minds. Four times a year this figure will be encompassed in "stocks in all positions" to give a yet more accurate picture of total current supply. U.S.D.A. and other reports continually publish revisions that are anxiously watched by cash and futures traders. For each kind of commodity there are similar predictable reports on changes in the supply picture. To these the trader adds the effect on supply of haphazard events including weather, disease, and politics. Prices will also reflect the difference between absolute and actually available supplies. Goods that can't come to market because of transport problems, labor stoppages, supplier reticence, or government policy must be temporarily discounted.

Ideal weather conditions exist for each agricultural commodity. Any trader quickly learns what to look for in the evening national weather report. Soybeans flower in summer, and if temperatures are too high or humidity too low through the Midwest, fewer blooms will develop and the crop size will be lowered. Ample rainfall will persuade the farmers to wait while the plants pick up the added moisture, making the harvest later and determining whether the September soybean contracts will reflect new crop or old crop prices. Winter wheat is planted and sprouts in the fall and lays dormant under the snow to be harvested in the spring and early summer. An inadequate snow cover will damage the crop. The best yields are produced when soil moisture level is 15–18 percent throughout germination, and this figure may drop to no less than 9 percent after germination without harming the crop. After full structural growth, temperatures in the 80–100 degree range help to firm the kernels and mature the crop.

FIGURE 12–4

Effects of various forces on financial instrument prices

Development	Effect on short term instrument (e.g. T-Bill Futures)	Effect on long term instrument (e.g. T-Bond Futures)
Inflation Accelerates	−	−
Real Growth Accelerates	−	−
Unemployment Rate Rises	+	+
Dollar Depreciates	−	−
Government Deficit Increases	−	−
Larger Than Expected T-Bond Issue Offered	0	−
Larger Than Expected T-Bill Issue Offered	−	0
Coupon Pass (purchase) by Fed	0	+
Fed Raises Target Funds Rate	−	−,+

Source: Commodity Research Bureau, Inc.

Relative humidity below 50 percent will raise the quality of the crop by lowering the risk of rot in storage.

Such parameters, of course, exist for weather conditions relating to each plant and agricultural commodity. The trader becomes familiar with the conditions which will lead to bonus crops and low prices and with those which will damage the crop and raise the price. As a practical matter, no trader need hang on the news each day to see that supplies of the commodity traded are not damaged. Droughts and freezes take time to do their damage, and their lasting effect on prices may not correspond to the first wave of trader response. Commodity newsletters or reports received by the trader or the broker will provide an adequate appraisal of weather conditions and their significance.

DEMAND DETERMINANTS

Factors of demand for each commodity are bunched together in situation reports

under the classification "disappearance." (See Figure 12–5.) "Disappearance" refers to all the individual sales made on cash markets, regardless of the disposition of the commodity. It may be eaten, processed, dumped, lost to disease, given away under a government program, or exported. "Disappearance" may be easily compared to total supply and to disappearance in previous years to judge the demand and supply conditions to come. Will there be a great excess in the future? Is the nation using up its supplies too quickly? Are world production and consumption patterns changing? Will new technology increase or diminish a particular supply or demand figure? Is the demand for one commodity transferable to another? If so, how much and at what price? Demand equations are often more difficult than estimates of supply, given the unorganized nature of the ultimate buyers as compared to the small organized group of producers. While supply changes with farmers' opinions before planting and

FIGURE 12–5

Potato stocks, disappearance and crop production estimates in the U.S.

	Millions of CWT.					Disappearance of Previous Fall Crop Until					Crop Production Estimates—In Thousands of Cwt.			
Year	Jan. 1	Feb. 1	Mar. 1	Apr. 1	Dec. 1	Dec. 1	Jan. 1	Feb. 1	Mar. 1	Apr. 1	Oct. 1	Nov. 1	Dec.	Final
1966	124.2	98.7	74.9		153.6	69.7	93.3	N.A.	N.A.		296,308	299,989	300,940	307,242
1967	128.1	103.6	79.6		161.5	75.1	100.4	N.A.	138.5		301,520	303,160	305,906	305,766
1968	139.2	112.6	86.5		152.8	69.5	91.9	118.5	144.8		289,620	292,962	293,438	295,401
1969	130.4	105.0	81.9		162.8	68.0	90.4	115.9	138.9		305,449	305,141	307,229	312,578
1970	138.1	111.5	87.6		175.1	76.0	100.5	127.3	151.1		320,153	323,485	324,861	325,716
1971	150.0	122.2	96.8		176.4	78.4	103.1	131.3	156.7		316,972	318,462	316,083	319,329
1972	151.4	124.4	98.5		158.6	77.5	102.4	129.4	168.2		295,976	294,498	294,490	296,359
1973	134.4	107.3	83.4	58.3	157.8	90.4	114.5	141.7	165.5	198.0	297,506	298,611	297,352	300,013
1974	133.7	106.6	81.2	55.9	187.9	96.1	120.3	147.3	172.7	209.6	337,767	338,997	340,116	342,395
1975	163.1	133.4	104.1	75.9	186.0	97.8	122.6	152.2	181.4	200.6	307,644	310,250	315,647	322,254
1976	159.1	131.7	104.1	71.6	202.0	88.6	114.9	142.9	169.4	201.4	349,943	349,275	353,386	357,674
1977	174.8	143.9	114.1	81.9	207.0	99.1	128.3	157.8	188.0	218.4	350,588	350,414	352,010	354,570
1978[1]	178.2	149.7	121.0	89.2	218.7	93.8	122.8	149.9	177.9	210.2	353,680	357,670	360,467	
1979[1]	190.5	159.1	128.5	95.3		94.6	123.0	154.0	115.0	218.0				
1980														

[1] Preliminary.   [2] Held by growers & local dealers in the fall producing areas.   *Source: Crop Reporting Board, U.S.D.A.*

Source: Commodity Research Bureau, Inc.

then a few times more with crop conditions, demand factors change daily with all kinds of conditions.

The categories constituting total demand or disappearance for any given commodity are as various as those for supply. In the case of grains, demand analysis concentrates on national and world food situations, especially trends in feed grain composition and usage. Metals demand depends on the health of client industries, developments in production technology, and the variable desire for metals as wealth storage vehicles. Cotton demand is tied to textile enterprises in the United States and Asia. Coffee, cocoa, and sugar are predominantly consumer preference items whose demand is inelastic within fairly large price swings, new demand being generated by marketing and by changes in world income and life style. Meats, too, are an individual consumer item, their individual popularity hinging on income, season, relative price, and shifting preference. The demand for financial instruments comes and goes with changes in interest rates and inflation, which affect the returns offered by other investment vehicles. Consumer sophistication and psychology can play a key part in financials (and some other commodities) when economic conditions are highly unstable.

In general, then, principal demand factors are (1) life style and consumer preference; (2) level of disposable income; (3) population; (4) price of substitute goods; (5) seasonal influences; and (6) conditions of user industries. Running through all these factors, however, is price itself. Changes in price often dramatically raise or lower demand. The elasticity of demand due to price may have historical patterns the trader can consult, charting

how much more will sell at each lower price level and how much less will sell at each higher price level (all other things being equal). Elasticity (or inelasticity), however, is relative over time and space. Auto manufacturers may continue buying copper at steep prices for a while but will in the long run be pushed to find a substitute if prices stay high. Lower prices for some goods might prompt less demand at first, while buyers hold on to adequate supplies and wait for the market to hit bottom. And in the other direction, demand will not necessarily bring lower prices and greater supplies if supply cannot react quickly.

INTERCOMMODITY RELATIONSHIPS

The analytical trader discovers that intercommodity relationships are the most fascinating, and frustrating, computations in the explanation of cash price. Just as the trader must isolate the few relevant factors of an individual commodity's supply and demand, so must he sift out the few decisive facts among the hundreds of relationships a commodity has to other commodities. The price of one commodity reflects the prices of all commodities involved in its own production and marketing; it runs up against the price of the goods and services prospective buyers are paying; and it is challenged by the prices of competitors and potential substitutes. Cash prices are the well trampled crossroads of intercommodity transactions, acting as fluctuating indices to a network of connected commodities, markets, and prices.

Some commodities are part of larger markets, so that an increase in the supply of a competing product is essentially, for pricing purposes, an increase in the supply of the commodity itself. Soybean oil is in direct competition with other digestible high protein fats. Increases in olive production in the Mediterranean or sunflower seed production in the Midwest will tend to lower the price of soybean oil as though more beans had been grown. Beef, chicken, and pork all compete for the consumer's meat dollar, so that changes in the demand, supply, or price of any occasion reciprocal changes in the demand, supply, and price of the others. (See Figure 12–6.) In livestock, demand may act as a function of disposable income. As individual incomes go up, the market may demand more high priced beef in place of relatively cheaper pork, chicken, or fish. The result of lowered disposable income will be greater demand for pork. As the cost of petroleum products soars, it takes with it the cost of synthetic fabrics, eventually boosting the demand for cotton.

Other groups are formed by relationships of raw material to byproducts, such as hogs and the pork bellies cut from them. The supply of hogs will be determined by the demand for pork, hams, etc. and by the cost of feed. Pork bellies, which eventually become bacon, come two from each hog and the supply of hogs will directly determine the supply of pork bellies. The trader studying the price and supply of pork bellies looks immediately to the hogs' situation, then to the price of feed. Much of today's new silver comes as a byproduct of ores mined chiefly for copper, lead, zinc, and tin, so that silver may pull these others up (or down) with it.

Some commodity relationships are ones of overwhelming dependency. The feed-grain complex is one example. The hog-corn price ratio reflects the relationship between the animal and the feed he eats.

Any commodity which comes from an animal will be affected by changes in the feed complex that supports the animal before slaughter. High priced corn will eventually result in high priced hogs and a lowering in the number of pigs farrowed. Fewer hogs brought to market will result in a lowered supply of pork bellies, which are traded in their own cash and futures markets. In the case of soybeans, there is very little market for the unprocessed bean itself. The price of a bushel of soybeans is figured by adding the prices of its two products, soymeal and oil. In turn, planters' intentions as they choose from soybeans, corn, and cotton will depend on the comparative prices of all, the price of fertilizer, the interest cost on farmer loans, etc.

The supplies of money and oil help form the price curves that are interest rates and energy costs. If government price supports remain relatively low, these cause farmers to sell off quickly, depressing prices in the short term. As today's agribusiness is more dependent than ever on bank financing, it is more sensitive to events in other economic sectors and in the money markets. The same holds true for cattle feeders who must borrow to buy replacement stock. A report that housing starts are up, despite attempts to slow them, can send Treasury Bill prices down (along with copper and lumber), as it indicates a failure to curb inflationary growth and thus signals a continuation of rising interest rates. Those same rates and T-Bills would attract investors to the dollar, strengthening it on the currency markets and sending foreign denominations down. At that point gold could lose some of its attraction as a hedge, depressing metals across the board. Or a large move in gold might not be reflected in the dollar market

FIGURE 12-6

HOG SUPPLY WILL LIMIT FED CATTLE PRICE GAINS THIS YEAR, PURCELL SAYS

--BY DIRCK STEIMEL, CNS STAFF REPORTER--

MONTEREY, CALIF.--MAR 25--CNS--CASH CATTLE PRICES WILL NOT RISE
MUCH ABOVE 70 DLRS PER CWT THIS YEAR UNTIL THE HOG SUPPLY IS REDUCED,
WAYNE PURCELL, AGRICULTURAL ECONOMIST FROM VIRGINIA POLYTECHNICAL
INSTITUTE SAID HERE TODAY.

PURCELL TOLD THE CALIFORNIA CATTLE FEEDERS ASSOCIATION MEETING
HERE THAT IN ORDER TO HAVE 70-DLR-PER-CWT CATTLE, 40-DLR-PER-CWT HOGS
ARE NECESSARY, OR A 1.75-TO-1 PRICE RATIO. HOWEVER, HE SAID, THAT
DOES NOT APPEAR LIKELY FOR ANY EXTENDED PERIOD THIS YEAR.

IT IS VERY UNLIKELY THAT CATTLE PRICES WILL BE ABLE TO HOLD MORE
THAN A 1.75-TO-1 RATIO OVER HOG PRICES IN THE NEXT YEAR BECAUSE OF
REDUCED CONSUMER DEMAND FOR BEEF, PURCELL SAID.

THE CURRENT 2-TO-1 RATIO BETWEEN CATTLE AND HOG PRICES (32-DLR
HOGS AND 65-DLR CATTLE), IS THE RESULT OF HOG PRICES OVERREACTING
DOWNWARD BECAUSE OF LAST WEEK'S BEARISH U.S. HOGS AND PIGS REPORT, HE
SAID. BASED ON 65-DLR CATTLE, HOGS WOULD BE ABOUT 37 DLRS PER CWT IF
THE RATIO WERE 1.75 TO 1.

CATTLE PRICES MAY PEAK AT 75 DLRS PER CWT DURING THE MAY-JUNE
PERIOD AS HOG PRICES RECOVER SEASONALLY, PURCELL SAID. HOWEVER, HE
SAID, PRICES ARE NOT LIKELY TO MOVE ABOVE THAT MARK THROUGH THE
REMAINDER OF THIS YEAR.

TO GET ANY SORT OF SUSTAINED PRICE RALLY IN THE FED CATTLE
MARKET, CATTLE FEEDERS NEED A FAVORABLE HOGS AND PIGS REPORT, PURCELL
SAID. HOWEVER, LAST WEEK'S REPORT WAS A "SHOCKER" AND DEFINITELY WILL
HURT THE FED CATTLE MARKET, HE SAID. THE MOST BEARISH PART OF THAT
REPORT WAS THE SOWS FARROWING IN DEC-FEB PERIOD AT 107 PCT OF LAST
YEAR, GUARANTEEING NEAR-RECORD HOG SUPPLIES THROUGH THIS YEAR, HE
SAID.

DEMAND FOR BEEF IS DIRECTLY LINKED TO PRICE AND THE CONSUMER
WILL READILY OPT FOR CHEAPER PORK OR POULTRY WHEN THE PRICE
DIFFERENCES ARE AS GREAT AS THEY ARE NOW, HE SAID.

HOWEVER, PURCELL SAID, WHEN HOG PRODUCERS DO CUT BACK, AS THEY
ARE LIKELY TO DO IN 1981, "WE ARE IN FOR A HECK OF A BULL RED MEAT
MARKET BECAUSE OF THE SUPPLIES." HE PREDICTED A GENERAL UPTREND IN
CASH CATTLE PRICES THROUGH AT LEAST 1983, MAINLY ON THE BASIS OF
TIGHT SUPPLIES.   END
1332 CST#

if gold prices were being driven by international political crises that threatened many nations and their currencies, thus giving no real edge to any one. Gold and silver often have a "rubber band" effect on each other and on other metals, pulling the group in staggered moves in parallel directions—a phenomenon common also in the grain, livestock, financial, and currency groups.

As intercommodity relationships constantly evolve, new factors alter old patterns. The high cost of gas is encouraging plans for the use of agricultural land and crops for energy production. If successful (as it has been in Brazil's use of sugar cane for fuel), this will radically change commodity distributions and prices. Competition of food and fuel affects exports (supply), encourages self-sufficiency abroad (demand), and could transform the general economic picture entirely, depending on political conditions as well. Gasohol production in large amounts would alter price determinants, prompting farmers to switch back from soybeans to corn as new kinds of ratios (corn-alcohol-protein byproduct) influence planting intentions. On the other hand, a massive investment in and subsequent failure of the experiment could wreak havoc on the markets for years to come. In either case, it is highly likely that the increasing intertwining of food and fuel will have a major impact on commodity pricing in the future.

Demand and supply pricing is extremely complex, then, made up a minutiae from all parts of the world's many economies. A trader can easily be buried under an avalanche of tables and logarithms and curves and equations before he realizes that of all the factors only a

few fundamentals are changing significantly at any given time. The trader need not know all the elements that go into a price move—indeed, not even a computer could do it— but only those that are unusual or likely to change. To compare this year's crop size to last year's or this year's money supply and interest rates to last year's, he need really only know the significant unusual factors as understood and explained in newsletters describing the general makeup of a market. A handful of principal components shape the tone of the current market at any one time. Picking these out, and interpreting them correctly, is the fundamentalist's art.

GOVERNMENT POLICIES AND PROGRAMS

Tampering with supply and demand has become a widely accepted tool in the governmental regulation of the modern economic state. Policy and budget decisions regularly influence every sector, making government actions a powerful ingredient in any cash price calculation. Debates go on as to whether this helps or hurts a nation's general well being, but the trend is unmistakable. The most direct pressures are on natural resources, financial transactions, and agricultural production. In each of these three key areas, government programs and regulations have enormous sway over the availability of commodities, their distribution, and their ultimate cost. The lumber and mining industries, for instance, cannot readily increase supplies through more cutting and digging without undergoing lengthy and costly environmental impact hearings. The cost of preserving natural resources must inevitably become a part of the price of using natural resources. In the same way, mineral and timber holdings on federally owned lands have uncertain relations to total supplies while politics and economics do battle.

The growth of financial futures and the recurrent economic crises of the 1970s illuminated, and enlarged, the role of government fiscal managers in monetary affairs. The federal government both supplies Treasury Bills and Bonds through its frequent sales and sets prevailing interest rates through the independent agency of the Federal Reserve Board. Manipulation of the money supply emerged in the last two decades as a favorite "quick fix" for recessions and inflations. (See Figure 12–7.) The price of money will respond actively in the short term to Treasury and Federal Reserve Board decisions on how much money to put into circulation and at what cost. The Treasury, in addition to raising government revenues through such sales, may also sell gold or the Federal Reserve may intervene in the international currency markets on behalf of the dollar. The Ginnie Mae is itself a Government National Mortgage Association certificate, another government creation sold in cash and futures markets and guaranteed by that agency.

But the oldest and most pervasive government management of supply and demand has involved agricultural production. The results have been mixed, as the markets are notoriously tricky ones, and government programs are in flux just about as rapidly as other conditions constituting the agricultural complex. The fact remains that the health of the grain and livestock industries, like that of the banking and financial community, depends on a foundation of government ac-

tions and programs which themselves constantly adjust to the workings of the market place. When the Department of Agriculture attempted to limit surplus production by restricting acreage planted, farmers gave more care to the acres they did plant, bringing supply back up to old levels. Changes in government policy can be expected literally with every session of Congress. The chief intended effect of government policy is to prevent large surpluses while keeping farmer income at some percentage of parity with a previous base period. If surpluses grow, or farmer income either jumps or radically falls, changes in programs and their administration can be expected. A new development has been the use of government restrictions of sales to certain nations the government hopes to punish.

Changes in programs are usually the result of pressure on Congress when someone is either making too much or too little money. In the past, the majority of changes have been tinkering with the current system, with a total revamping about every ten years. The framework of the present system is given below, although shifts in loan rates, parity, and surplus disposal can be expected from time to time.

Parity is a theoretical formula that attempts to keep current farm prices "on par" with nonagricultural prices as they were in some base period. Such prices are samples of those the farmer incurs running his operation and household—labor, taxes, real estate, machinery, and clothing. If, in the base period 1910–1919, a farmer could buy a suit of clothes with the return from 30 bushels of wheat, and if he can still do so, farm prices are said to be at full parity. In fact, farm efficiency

FIGURE 12-7

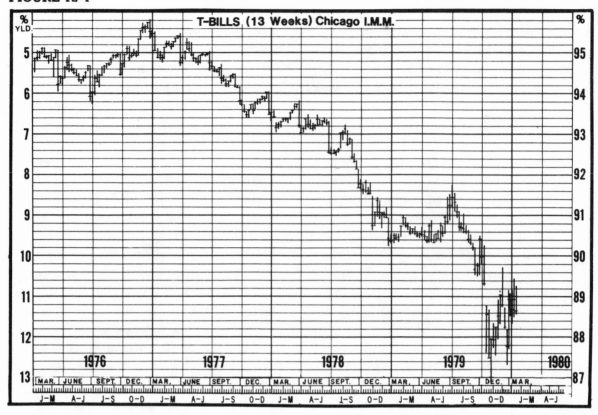

U.S. Money Supply M1 (Demand Deposits Plus Currency) in 1972 $ In Billions of Dollars

Year	Jan.	Feb.	Mar.	Apr.	May	June	July	Aug.	Sept.	Oct.	Nov.	Dec.	Average
1974	243.6	241.8	240.6	239.4	237.4	236.9	235.8	233.5	231.3	230.1	229.6	228.1	235.7
1975	226.6	225.4	226.1	224.6	225.7	227.3	225.5	225.8	225.5	223.7	224.1	222.3	225.2
1976	222.5	223.9	224.1	224.5	225.0	224.1	223.8	223.9	223.7	224.9	225.0	225.3	224.2
1977	225.4	224.5	224.4	224.7	224.5	224.5	226.0	226.4	227.2	227.9	227.4	227.8	225.9
1978[1]	228.4	227.2	226.0	227.2	227.1	226.3	226.3	226.5	227.1	225.6	223.9	222.8	226.2
1979[1]	219.9	216.7											
1980													

[1] Preliminary.   *Source: Federal Reserve System*

U.S. Money Supply M2 (Demand Deposits Plus Time Deposits at Commercial Banks Other Than Large Co's) in 1972 $ In Billions of Dollars

Year	Jan.	Feb.	Mar.	Apr.	May	June	July	Aug.	Sept.	Oct.	Nov.	Dec.	Average
1974	516.1	514.0	512.2	511.7	507.9	507.2	506.1	502.4	498.4	497.4	495.9	493.0	505.2
1975	493.1	493.0	495.2	494.6	497.8	501.6	500.0	501.2	501.0	500.0	501.3	500.3	498.3
1976	503.9	509.3	511.3	513.9	515.5	515.7	517.0	519.0	521.5	525.7	528.7	531.8	517.8
1977	533.1	532.1	532.9	533.5	534.2	535.1	539.1	540.6	542.6	544.4	544.2	544.4	538.0
1978[1]	545.0	543.8	541.6	542.1	541.8	540.9	541.7	543.6	544.8	543.4	542.3	540.1	542.6
1979[1]	534.8	529.6											
1980													

[1] Preliminary.   *Source: Federal Reserve System*

Source: Commodity Research Bureau, Inc.

has increased more rapidly than efficiency in other parts of the economy, so that parity has slipped somewhat. Parity may be maintained at 75–90 percent for basic crops and 60–90 percent for other harvested goods. As farmer income falls or grows relative to nonagricultural prices, a new parity formula will be issued. This will be affected by changes in other U.S.D.A. programs.

Government price support programs fall into two categories: (1) direct purchase of the farmer's crop, or a subsidy payment making up the difference between market and parity price; and (2) payments to farmers for reducing production. Payments to farmers for reducing production are of little importance to the speculator (although they are, of course, important to the farmer). This and the effect of land diversion payments can be read in the reports on farmers' planting intentions and crop estimates. Outright purchase and loan rates, however, simply change the ownership of the product, which finds its way off the cash markets and back on again, influencing prices. (See Figure 12–8.)

The loan program is the most effective government policy for supporting farm prices and has the most profound effect on the cash and futures markets. Before planting begins, the U.S.D.A. will announce its "loan rate" for each commodity under the program. Farmers know this to be the minimum price they will have to accept for their produce and can plan accordingly. If the loan rate were set at $3.50 and the cash market price near or below this amount, the farmer could "borrow" at this rate against his crops from the Commodity Credit Corporation, the Agriculture Department's administrative wing. In order to qualify for the loan, the

crops must be in elevators which have been approved by the CCC. Loan monies received are secured by the stored goods, and the farmer can use them to pay machinery rental costs, labor, and bank loans.

The farmer has until January 31, following harvest, to place most grains under loan (may 31 for corn, April 30 for cotton). This effectively sets a bottom price for the crop. Two months after the cutoff date for making loans, the CCC owns the commodity and the farmer keeps the loaned money, without further obligation to the CCC. At any time before that two months runs out, the farmer may repay the loan and take possession for sale on the cash market. The farmer is then liable for elevator storage costs unless approved on-farm elevators were used. The loan rate thus forms a floor under the price of commodities. If the cash price does not rise above the loan rate by enough to cover storage and red tape costs, the farmer will simply default on the loan and let the CCC have the goods, keeping them off the market.

The actual amount the farmer will receive depends on the local country basis. The loan value often sets the price floor for cash and futures markets since a farmer who qualifies for the loan program will simply sell crops to the government at the loan rate whenever the free market is paying less. Not all farmers will qualify for government loans, however, since these require compliance with acreage limits and other program restrictions. When this nonloan supply is sold on the open market it can (and has) forced both futures and cash prices below the equivalent Chicago government loan rate. Thus, the floor is not perfect and the market price can drop below the loan floor by

FIGURE 12–8

U.S. grain price support operations

Crop Year	Production 000 Bu.	Quantity Put Under Support 000 Bu.	Percent of Crop Percent	Carry Over Stocks at End of Crop Marketing Year Total 000 Bu.	Owned by CCC 000 Bu.	Average Support Rate Dollars Per Bu.	U.S. Farm Price Dollars Per Bu.
WHEAT 1/							
1977-78	1,798,712	223,005	12.0	1,176,700	–	2.25	2.33
1976-77	2,025,793	468,276	23.1	1,112,248	–	2.25	2.73
1975-76	2,142,362	42,744	2.0	665,253	–	1.37	3.56
1974-75	2,122,459	36,500	1.7	434,975	–	1.37	4.09
1973-74	1,705,167	59,600	3.5	340,060	–	1.25	3.95
1972-73	1,544,939	167,100	10.8	438,454	139,100	1.25	1.76
1971-72	1,617,789	460,000	28.5	863,072	367,400	1.25	1.34
1970-71	1,351,558	254,200	18.8	731,478	369,885	1.25	1.33
1969-70	1,442,679	407,600	28.3	884,873	301,200	1.25	1.25
1968-69	1,556,635	453,200	28.9	816,660	162,700	1.25	1.24
CORN							
1977-78	7,081,849	206,253	3.0	1,104,000	–	2.00	2.02
1976-77	6,357,424	274,541	4.3	884,135	–	1.50	2.15
1975-76	6,266,359	145,944	2.3	397,542	–	1.10	2.54
1974-75	5,828,961	85,278	1.5	359,448	–	1.10	3.03
1973-74	5,646,806	260,513	4.6	482,732	414	1.05	2.55
1972-73	5,573,320	395,000	7.1	708,559	689,000	1.05	1.57
1971-72	5,641,112	952,000	16.9	1,126,000	718,000	1.03	1.08
1970-71	4,151,938	324,000	7.8	667,000	330,000	1.05	1.33
1969-70	4,687,057	398,145	8.5	1,005,000	543,000	1.05	1.15
1968-69	4,449,542	404,000	9.1	1,118,000	736,000	1.05	1.08
OATS 1/							
1977-78	601,477	3,769	.7	310,600	–	1.03	1.14
1976-77	747,914	4,371	.6	164,931	–	.72	1.56
1975-76	546,315	3,920	.7	208,104	–	.54	1.46
1974-75	642,042	3,860	.6	224,000	–	.54	1.53
1973-74	666,867	10,397	1.6	255,074	721	.54	1.18
1972-73	691,973	31,400	4.5	409,948	221,000	.54	.73
1971-72	881,227	82,000	9.3	541,000	372,000	.54	.61
1970-71	917,159	113,700	12.4	517,000	359,000	.63	.62
1969-70	965,863	163,000	16.9	499,000	296,000	.63	.58
1968-69	950,689	95,000	10.0	397,000	165,000	.63	.60
RYE 1/							
1977-78	26,160	102	.4	4,100	–	1.20	1.20
1976-77	16,998	144	.8	4,418	–	1.20	2.47
1975-76	14,951	87	.6	4,404	–	1.00	2.36
1974-75	15,958	197	1.2	6,622	N/A	.89	2.51
1973-74	26,263	442	1.7	14,175	N/A	.89	1.91
1972-73	29,183	6,893	23.6	33,270	17,482	.89	.96
1971-72	49,288	20,196	41.0	45,634	33,156	.89	.90
1970-71	36,840	12,168	33.0	27,876	24,549	1.02	.99
1969-70	30,204	6,909	22.9	21,130	16,761	1.02	1.01
1968-69	22,971	4,584	20.0	15,957	11,533	1.02	1.02
SOYBEANS							
1977-78	1,842,647	12,921	.8	161,000	–	2.50	6.42
1976-77	1,716,334	2,249	.1	102,916	–	2.50	6.81
1975-76	1,287,560	2	2	244,636	–	2.00	4.92
1974-75	1,547,383	34,554	2.2	185,036	–	2.25	6.64
1973-74	1,547,165	122,752	7.9	170,882	–	2.25	5.68
1972-73	1,270,630	90,555	7.0	59,637	–	2.25	4.37
1971-72	1,175,989	168,204	14.3	72,000	1	2.25	3.03
1970-71	1,127,100	146,420	13.0	98,800	2,491	2.25	2.85
1969-68	1,133,120	179,499	15.8	229,800	150,190	2.25	2.35
1968-69	1,106,958	340,271	30.7	326,800	171,423	2.50	2.43
BARLEY							
1977-78	447,008	12,408	.8	172,100	–	1.63	1.80
1976-77	415,803	18,019	4.3	125,700	–	1.22	2.25
1975-76	372,461	9,153	2.5	128,713	–	.90	2.42
1974-75	374,386	6,869	1.8	92,000	–	.90	2.80
1973-74	421,527	15,373	3.7	119,003	–	.86	–
1974-75	383,920	6,869	1.8	92,000	–	.90	2.80
1973-74	421,527	15,373	3.7	119,003	–	–	–
1972-73	423,464	41,700	9.8	162,544	50	.86	1.21
1971-72	463,601	89,000	19.2	175,000	79	.86	.99
1970-71	416,139	27,600	6.6	155,000	90	.83	.97
1969-70	427,055	52,000	12.2	236,000	166	.83	.89
1968-69	426,151	123,800	29.1	201,000	125	.90	.92

1/Beginning with the 1974-75 season, the crop year for wheat, oats, rye and barley is June 1-May 31. Prior to the 1974-75 seasons, the crop year for these grains was July 1-June 30.

2/No support programs was implemented for the 1975 soybean crop.

Source: Feed Situation, Wheat Situation, Crop Production, Fats and Oils Situation.

Source: Chicago Board of Trade.

small amounts. After harvest there may not be enough storage elevators to go around, which will force some grain onto the market at any price it can obtain, for the CCC will not loan money on grain that is not properly stored in inspected elevators. Many farmers may not be enticed to go through the trouble of the loan unless cash falls below the loan rate. Also, some misjudgment of market price can occur after the final day for taking the CCC loan, which means some unprotected grain may make it to market even at rates below the loan rate. Finally, some hedging activity will take place on the futures markets regardless of price level; if this hedging is net short in the normal pattern, it can force futures prices below the loan rate on near months immediately after harvest.

Outright government purchases are similar in effect and execution to the loan program. The farmer may contract to sell certain quantities of produce to the CCC at a pegged price, which is usually the same as the loan rate, and deliver or not deliver according to whether a better price is available elsewhere. Under the purchase program, the farmer receives no money until goods are relinquished irrevocably, and storage becomes the responsibility of the CCC. On rare occasions the Department of Agriculture will announce direct purchases on the cash market of commodities whose prices have fallen too low. Such purchases help buoy up the market and are well publicized in advance. These are looked at simply as new demand purchases taking place in a low priced market. The CCC was also the agency responsible for managing government acquisition and market redistribution of grains in the wake of the Soviet embargo of 1980.

Other price support programs are designed to help the movement of United States surpluses to overseas markets. The U.S.D.A. makes direct subsidies to exporters when domestic prices rise above world prices—a frequent situation. Rather than let huge surpluses build up, overwhelming the cash markets and storage facilities, the Department will pay the difference between the domestic and world prices, allowing exporters, to do business abroad. Under Public Law 480, the CCC can give its stocks of commodities to needy nations, use them for barter at less than their total worth, or sell them on long term loans. When the goods exported come directly from CCC stocks, no effect is felt on the cash or futures markets, as these stocks were not competing with "free" stocks and had no price effect. Public Law 480 does allow the CCC, however, to make loans in dollars to foreign nations with the stipulation that the money be spent on specific commodities which are then purchased on cash markets in this country. Such purchase arrangements have in the past accounted for over half our exports of edible oils, though in recent years foreign aid has been a low government priority.

The Reserve is another government program influencing prices. Extra grain is stored in the Reserve in years of plenty to assure food supplies in case of crop failures or other future crises. A payment of 25 cents per bushel currently goes to farmers to hold this grain for the government. If the "release price" is hit in the markets (125 percent of the loan rate), farmers may sell. The farmer is not obligated to release but must settle up with the government if prices reach 140 percent of the loan rate. Penalties are assessed for selling Reserve grain before the release price has been hit. Heavy movement of grain into the Reserve can be a bearish sign for prices.

GOVERNMENT DISPOSAL

While government purchase and loan rates form a rough floor under commodity prices, government disposal forms a much simpler and more effective ceiling to how high prices can climb. CCC stocks are no longer as consistently large as they once were, owing to the success of its other programs and farmer resistance to lower prices, but CCC offerings on the cash market can still be an important factor in pricing when price levels rise sufficiently to make them attractive. Whenever cash prices rise to within grasp of support resale prices, government offerings must be watched closely.

The Department of Agriculture regularly publishes a CCC sales list indicating what stocks of commodities it holds and their offering prices. The price formula is figured independently of cash demand and supply factors to eliminate the absurdity of purchasing grains at a support price while dumping the same grains on a market that cannot sustain the supply at reasonable price levels. CCC grain can be sold if national average cash prices reach 150 percent of the loan rate. If corn were supported at a net loan rate of $2.00 a bushel, the total cost of the grain to the CCC, including interest, storage, handling, and so on (the gross loan rate) could be $2.30. The resale offering in Chicago will be 150 percent of this gross loan rate of $2.30 plus transportation to Chicago of, say, 18 cents per bushel, for a total of $3.63. If the market price rises above this amount, the CCC will sell the grain at market but it will not sell it for less

than $3.63. No trader need figure CCC held stocks into supply unless the market price rises close to this amount.

An exception to the resale formula exists only in the case that the stocks of grains are endangered. Any time the CCC fears that the commodity is likely to spoil, due to too much moisture in the kernels or some other threat, it may sell the endangered goods at the best market price it can fetch. Such sales can be important to corn holdings which do not store well when the corn is full of moisture. Drying processes are available but expensive, and wet corn held by the CCC often makes it to market at prices below the formula. Offering price formulas and amounts of CCC stocks vary from year to year and crop to crop. As the cash market price for soybeans is normally well above the loan rate, very few farmers default on their loans and CCC stockpiles of soybeans are very small. On the other hand, CCC corn deliveries have at times constituted half of Chicago transactions, making resale prices thus a very significant market factor for corn. Massive government stockpiles set a very effective ceiling to cash and futures prices that rarely gives way until stocks are depleted.

PRICING INFORMATION

Quotations of cash prices for most commodities appear daily in *The Wall Street Journal* and the *New York Journal of Commerce.* (See Figure 12–9.) The latter devotes half a page to cash commodity prices and three or four pages to discussion of commodity statistics and news items. Subscriptions to these or comparable publications will give the trader most requisite cash price information. Prices

FIGURE 12–9

Money Rates

Wednesday, April 2, 1980

The key U.S. and foreign annual interest rates below are a guide to general levels but don't always represent actual transactions.

PRIME RATE: 19½% to 20%. The charge by large U.S. money center commercial banks to their best business borrowers.

FEDERAL FUNDS: 19½% high, 5% low. 12% closing bid, 14% offered. Reserves traded among commercial banks for overnight use in amounts of $1 million or more.

DISCOUNT RATE: 13%. The charge on loans to member commercial banks by the New York Federal Reserve Bank. Surcharge to certain large banks: 3 percentage points.

CALL MONEY: 19¼% to 20¼%. The charge on loans to brokers on stock exchange collateral.

COMMERCIAL PAPER: placed directly by General Motors Acceptance Corp.: 17¼%, 30 to 59 days; 16⅝%, 60 to 89 days; 15%, 90 to 179 days; 13½%, 180 to 270 days.

COMMERCIAL PAPER: high-grade unsecured notes sold through dealers by major corporations in multiples of $1,000: 17½%, 30 days; 17⅝%, 60 days; 17¾%, 90 days.

CERTIFICATES OF DEPOSIT: 16¼%, one month; 16⅞%, two months; 18%, three months; 18¼%, six months; 17⅜%, one year. Typical rates paid by major banks on new issues of negotiable C.D.'s, usually on amounts of $1 million and more. The minimum unit is $100,000.

BANKERS ACCEPTANCES: 17.05%, 30 days; 17.20%, 60 days; 17.30%, 90 days; 17.30%, 120 days; 17.05%, 150 days; 16.80%, 180 days. Negotiable, bank-backed business credit instruments typically financing an import order.

EURODOLLARS: 19¼% to 19⅛%, one month; 19 7/16% to 19 5/16%, two months; 19⅝% to 19½%, three months; 19¾% to 19⅝%, four months; 19 7/16% to 19 5/16%, five months; 19 5/16% to 19 3/16% six months. The rates paid on U.S. dollar deposits in banks in London, usually on amounts of $100,000 or more.

FOREIGN PRIME RATES: Canada 16½%; Germany 10½%; Japan 7%; Switzerland 5%; Britain 19%. These rate indications aren't directly comparable; lending practices vary widely by location. Source: Morgan Guaranty Trust Co.

TREASURY BILLS: Results of the Monday, March 31, 1980, auction of short-term U.S. government bills, sold at a discount from face value in units of $10,000 to $1 million: 15.037%, 13 weeks; 14.804%, 26 weeks.

SAVINGS RATES: on instruments offered to individuals; minimum amounts vary. Money market fund-a, 14.68%; six month money market certificate, 14.804%; 30-month savings institution certificate-b, 12%; savings institution passbook deposit-b, 5.5%; U.S. savings bond, 6.5%.

a-Annualized average rate of return after expenses for past 30 days on Merrill Lynch Ready Assets Trust, the largest of such funds; this isn't a forecast of future returns. b-Commercial banks are limited to paying one-quarter percentage point less than savings and loan associations and savings banks.

Cash Prices

Wednesday, April 2, 1980
(Quotations as of 4 p.m. Eastern time)

	Wed.	Tues.	Yr. Ago
FOODS			
Flour, hard winter KC cwt	$9.30	$9.10	$8.25
Coffee, Brazilian, NY lb	n1.80	1.80	1.35
Cocoa, Accra NY lb	z	z	z
Potatoes, rnd wht, 50 lb, NY del	y2.75	2.75	3.35
Sugar, cane, raw NY lb del	.1971	.1901	z
Sugar, cane, ref NY lb fob	.2810	.2910	.2245
Sugar, beet, ref Chgo-W lb fob	.2740	.2840	.1915
Orange Juice, frz con, NY lb	b z	z	1.0110
Butter, AA, Chgo., lb.	1.33½	1.33½	1.18
Eggs, Lge white, Chgo doz.	.60¾	.60¾	.70
Broilers, Dressed "A" NY lb	x.3924	.3939	.4889
Beef, 700-900 lbs, Midw lb fob	.96	.98	1.06½
Pork Loins, 14 down Mdw lb fob	.70	.72¼	.90
Hams, 14-17 lbs, Midw lb fob	.55	.56	.79½
Pork Bellies, 12-14lbMdw lb fob	.27	.27	.48
Hogs, Sioux City avg cwt	e29.70	29.95	44.90
Hogs, Omaha avg cwt	e29.45	29.75	44.15
Steers, Omaha choice avg cwt	60.00	62.00	72.90
Steers, Sioux City ch avg cwt	59.40	60.65	73.25
Feeder Cattle, Okl Cty, av cwt	e70.00	69.00	93.00
Pepper, black NY lb	a.92	.92	.87
GRAINS AND FEEDS			
Wheat, No. 2 ord hard KC bu	3.82¾	3.74¾	3.47
Wht,No.1 dk Nthn 14%-pro Mpls	3.76½	3.73¾	3.44½
Wheat, No. 2 soft red Chgo bu	n3.97½	3.87	3.56½
Sorghum, (Milo), No. 2 Gulf cwt	5.08	5.00	4.04
Corn, No. 2 yellow Chgo. bu	h-n2.57¼	2.55	2.52¾
Oats, No. 2 milling, Mpls bu	1.48	1.48	1.47
Rye, No. 2 Mpls bu	2.15	2.15	2.37
Barley, top-qlty. Mpls bu	2.60-2.80	2.50-2.80	2.65
Soybeans, No. 1 yellow Chgo bu	n5.68¾	5.63¼	7.43
Flaxseed, Mpls bu	6.00	6.10	7.45
Bran, KC ton	88.00	90.00	70.00
Linseed Meal, Mpls ton	145.00	145.00	140.00
Cottonseed Meal, Memphis ton	110.00	110.00	145.00
Soybean Meal, Decatur, Ill. ton	150.50	152.00	193.50
Corn Gluten Feed, Chgo ton	106.00	106.00	120.00
Hominy Feed, Ill. ton	77.00	77.00	69.00
Meat-Bonemeal 50%-pro, Ill.ton	212.50	217.50	256.25
Brewer's Grains, Milw ton	87.00	87.00	79.00
Alfalfa Pellets, dehy, Neb., ton	89.00	88.00	90.00
FATS AND OILS			
Coconut Oil, crd, N. Orleans lb	.36	.36¾	.46⅝
Corn Oil, crd wet mill, Chgo. lb	r.22	.22	.33½
Corn Oil, crd dry mill, Chgo. lb	r.22½	.22½	.34¼
Cottonseed Oil, crd Miss Vly lb	n.20½	.20½	.34
Grease, choice white, Chgo lb	.18½	.18⅝	.27
Lard, Chgo lb	.19¼	.19½	.29¾
Linseed Oil, raw Mpls lb	.28	.28	.28
Palm Oil, Neutral, N.Y. lb	n.30½	.30½	.31¾
Peanut Oil, crd, Southeast lb	a.20½	.20½	.39
Soybean Oil, crd Decatur, lb	n.2007	.2027	.2751
Tallow, bleachable, Chgo lb	.19¼	.19¼	.27½
Tallow, edible, Chgo lb	.21¼	.21¼	.30
FIBERS AND TEXTILES			
Burlap, 10 oz. 40-in. NY yd	n.3815	.3805	.2835
Cotton, 1 1-16 in lw-md Memph. lb	.8012	.8212	.5768
Print Cloth, cotton, 48-in. N.Y. yd	s.68-.70	.68-.70	.61
Print Cloth, poly/cot 48-in NY yd	t.50-.50½	.50-.50½	.48½
Satin Acetate, NY yd	.68	.68	.70
Sheetings, 60x60 48-in. NY yd	.73-.74	.73-.74	.69
Wool, fine staple terr. Boston lb	2.60	2.60	2.10
METALS			
Aluminum ingot lb	p.66-.72	.66-.72	.55½-.60
Copper cathodes lb	p.90½-.95	.87⅝-.96	.95-1.05
Copper Scp, No. 2 wire NY lb.	k.66	.64	.78
Lead, lb.	d.48	.48	.48
Mercury 76 lb. flask NY	405.00	405.00	240.00
Nickel plating grade lb	p3.50	3.50	z
Steel Scrap 1 hvy mlt Chgo ton	96.00	96.00	120.00
Tin Metals Week composite lb.	8.6122	8.6089	7.2627
Zinc Prime Western lb	p.37½-.39½	.37½-.39½	.37½-.39½
MISCELLANEOUS			
Hides, lt native cows Chgo lb	n.51	.51	1.12
Newspapers, old No.1 Chgo ton	65.00-70.00	65.00-70.00	30.00
Rubber, smoked sheets, lb	n.70¼	.70¼	.65¾
PETROLEUM			
Crude, Saudi Arabia light, brl	26.00	.2600	14.55
Fuel Oil, No. 2 NY, gal	g.7500	.7500	.5775
Gasoline, Reg NY, gal	g.9700	.9700	.7300
Gasoline, Unld NY, gal	g.9700	.9700	.7300
PRECIOUS METALS			
Gold, troy oz			
Engelhard indust bullion	501.75	510.80	240.05
Engelhard fabric prods	519.31	528.68	246.26
Handy & Harman base price	500.50	509.50	240.00
London fixing AM 498.00 PM	500.50	509.50	239.75
Krugerrand, whol	a516.00	525.00	250.50
Platinum, troy ounce	p420.00	420.00	325.00
Silver, troy ounce			
Engelhard indust bullion	14.220	13.825	7.309
Engelhard fabric prods	15.264	c14.840	7.492
Handy & Harman base price	14.400	14.000	7.309
London (in pounds)			
spot (U.S. equiv $15.000)	6.950	7.750	3.5325
3 months	7.1995	7.850	3.6235
6 months	7.490	8.210	3.7095
1 year	7.990	8.610	3.836
Coins, whol $1,000 face val	a13,060	12,200	5,300

a-Asked. b-Bid. c-Corrected. d-Dealer market. e-Estimated. g-f.o.b. harbor barge. Source: Oil Buyers' Guide. h-In hopper railroad cars. k-Dealer selling price in lots of 40,000 pounds or more, f.o.b. buyer's works. n-Nominal. p-Producer price. r-Day's trading range. s-Thread count 78x76. t-Thread count 78x54. x-Less than truckloads. y-Maine origin; varies seasonally. z-Not quoted.

Source: *The Wall Street Journal.*

FIGURE 12-10

GRAIN STOCKS

Released: January 25
3:00 P.M. ET

Crop Reporting Board

Economics, Statistics, & Cooperatives Service

U.S. Department of Agriculture

Washington, D.C. 20250

SOYBEAN AND FEED GRAIN STOCKS RECORD HIGH--WHEAT STOCKS UP

January 1, 1980 soybean stocks at 48.2 million metric tons were up 27 percent from a year ago and at a record high level, according to the Crop Reporting Board. Stocks of the four feed grains (corn, sorghum, barley and oats) also were a record high at 203 million metric tons, 7 percent more than January 1, 1979. Changes from last year for individual feed grains were: corn, up 9 percent; sorghum, up 1 percent; barley, down 7 percent; and oats, down 14 percent. Wheat stocks, at 46.6 million metric tons, were up 5 percent from a year earlier.

CORN in all storage positions on January 1, 1980 totaled a record high 6.77 billion bushels (172 million metric tons), up 9 percent from a year earlier and 23 percent more than January 1, 1978. Farm stocks at a record 4.93 billion bushels (125 million metric tons) were up 9 percent from last year. Off-farm stocks, also a record high at 1.84 billion bushels (46.8 million metric tons), were up 10 percent from last year. Indicated disappearance during October-December 1979 totaled 2.28 billion bushels (57.9 million metric tons), up 15 percent from the comparable quarter a year ago.

SORGHUM GRAIN in all storage positions on January 1, 1980 amounted to 646 million bushels (16.4 million metric tons), 1 percent more than a year earlier and 4 percent above the same date in 1978. Farm stocks totaled 234 million bushels (5.94 million metric tons), 2 percent less than last year while off-farm holdings at 412 million bushels (10.5 million metric tons) were up 3 percent. Disappearance during the October-December 1979 quarter was 328 million bushels (8.33 million metric tons), compared with 298 million bushels (7.56 million metric tons) in the same period a year earlier.

OATS in all storage positions on January 1, 1980 amounted to 482 million bushels (7.00 million metric tons), 14 percent less than a year earlier and 15 percent below the same date in 1978. Farm stocks totaled 406 million bushels (5.90 million metric tons), down 15 percent from a year ago. Off-farm stocks amounted to 75.6 million bushels (1.10 million metric tons), down 6 percent from last year. January 1 stocks indicate October-December 1979 disappearance at 92.4 million bushels (1.34 million metric tons), compared with 102 million bushels (1.48 million metric tons) in the same period last year.

Gr 11-1 (1-80)   For Information Call: (202) 447-3843

Source: U.S. Department of Agriculture.

FIGURE 12-11

GNMA 8%
Daily Cash, Bid, Ask, Yield
Pts. & 32nds at Par
1978

JANUARY

	Bid	Ask	Yield[1]
2	HOLIDAY		
3	99.13	96.17	8.43
4	96.10	96.14	8.45
5	96.15	96.19	8.42
6	96.09	96.13	8.45
9	95.16	95.20	8.56
10	95.09	95.13	8.59
11	95.11	95.15	8.58
12	95.05	95.09	8.62
13	95.15	95.19	8.57
16	95.06	95.10	8.61
17	95.11	95.15	8.59
18	95.10	95.14	8.59
19	95.10	95.14	8.59
20	95.10	95.14	8.59
23	95.08	95.12	8.60
24	95.05	95.09	8.62
25	95.01	95.05	8.63
26	95.07	95.11	8.61
27	95.08	95.12	8.60
30	95.08	95.12	8.61
31	95.14	95.18	8.56

FEBRUARY

	Bid	Ask	Yield[1]
1	95.11	95.15	8.59
2	95.09	95.13	8.57
3	95.09	95.13	8.57
6	95.09	95.13	8.57
7	95.09	95.13	8.57
8	95.06	95.10	8.60
9	95.07	95.11	8.59
10	95.05	N/A	8.62
13			
14	95.00	95.04	8.64
15	95.00	95.04	8.64
16	94.22	94.26	8.69
17	94.26	94.30	8.67
20	HOLIDAY		
21	94.21	94.25	8.69
22	94.18	94.22	8.70
23	94.21	94.25	8.69
24	94.31	95.03	8.64
27	95.05	95.09	8.62
28	95.03	95.07	8.63

MARCH

	Bid	Ask	Yield[1]
1	94.29	95.10	8.65
2	95.02	95.06	8.63
3	95.03	95.07	8.62
6	95.04	95.08	8.62
7	95.07	95.11	8.61
8	95.09	95.13	8.60
9	95.09	95.13	8.61
10	95.18	95.22	8.56
13	95.20	95.24	8.55
14	95.18	95.22	8.56
15	95.17	95.21	8.56
16	95.18	95.22	8.56
17	95.19	95.23	8.55
20	95.21	95.25	8.55
21	95.22	95.26	8.54
22	95.16	95.20	8.57
23	95.08	95.12	8.60
24	HOLIDAY		
27	94.25	94.29	8.67
28	94.26	94.30	8.67
29	94.21	94.25	8.69
30	94.21	94.25	8.69
31	94.21	94.25	8.69

APRIL

	Bid	Ask	Yield[1]
3	94.20	94.24	8.70
4	94.22	94.26	8.69
5	94.19	94.23	8.70
6	94.16	94.20	8.71
7	94.19	94.23	8.70
10	94.18	94.22	8.70
11	94.15	94.19	8.72
12	94.15	94.19	8.72
13	94.18	94.22	8.70
14	94.24	94.28	8.68
17	94.28	95.00	8.66
18	94.24	94.28	8.68
19	N/A	N/A	
20	94.09	94.13	8.75
21	94.08	94.12	8.75
24	94.02	94.06	8.78
25	94.08	94.12	8.75
26	94.04	94.08	8.77
27	93.31	94.03	8.79
28	94.01	94.05	8.78

MAY

	Bid	Ask	Yield[1]
1	94.03	94.07	8.77
2	94.02	94.06	8.78
3	94.02	94.06	8.78
4	94.05	94.09	8.76
5	93.28	94.00	8.81
8	93.20	93.24	8.84
9	93.21	93.25	8.84
10	93.20	93.25	8.84
11	93.19	93.23	8.85
12	93.12	93.16	8.80
15	93.17	93.21	8.86
16	93.19	93.23	8.85
17	93.21	93.25	8.84
18	93.13	93.17	8.87
19	93.03	93.07	8.92
22	93.03	93.07	8.92
23	93.01	93.05	8.93
24	92.31	93.03	8.94
25	92.26	92.30	8.96
26	92.16	92.20	9.01
29	HOLIDAY		
30	92.16	92.20	9.01
31	94.21	94.25	8.69

JUNE

	Bid	Ask	Yield[1]
1	92.16	92.24	8.99
2	92.18	92.26	8.93
5	92.16	92.24	8.99
6	92.26	93.02	8.90
7	92.28	93.00	8.95
8	92.24	92.28	8.97
9	92.24	92.28	8.97
12	92.13	92.17	9.02
13	92.19	92.23	9.00
14	92.14	92.18	9.02
15	92.17	92.21	9.01
16	92.17	92.22	9.02
19	92.12	92.16	9.03
20	92.12	92.16	9.03
21	92.06	92.10	9.06
22	92.00	92.04	9.09
23	91.26	92.30	9.11
26	91.21	91.25	9.14
27	91.21	91.26	9.09
28	91.22	91.26	9.08
29	91.20	91.24	9.14
30	91.16	91.20	9.16

JULY

	Bid	Ask	Yield[1]
3	91.18	91.22	9.15
4	HOLIDAY		
5	91.12	91.16	9.18
6	91.12	91.16	9.18
7	91.10	91.14	9.19
10	91.10	91.14	9.19
11	91.12	91.16	9.18
12	91.10	91.14	9.19
13	91.10	91.14	9.19
14	91.12	91.16	9.18
17	91.20	91.24	9.14
18	91.14	91.18	9.17
19	91.16	91.20	9.16
20	91.16	91.20	9.16
21	19.10	91.14	9.19
24	91.08	91.12	9.20
25	91.06	91.10	9.21
26	91.17	91.21	9.16
27	91.30	92.02	9.10
28	92.14	92.18	9.02
31	92.09	92.13	9.04

AUGUST

	Bid	Ask	Yield[1]
1	92.10	92.14	9.04
2	92.25	92.29	8.92
3	93.18	93.22	8.81
4	93.22	93.26	8.79
7	93.24	93.28	8.78
8	93.23	93.27	8.79
9	93.25	93.29	8.78
10	93.03	93.07	8.92
11	93.05	93.09	8.91
14	92.28	93.00	8.95
15	92.25	92.29	8.97
16	92.15	92.19	9.02
17	92.24	92.28	8.97
18	92.25	92.29	8.97
21	93.04	93.08	8.92
22	93.04	93.08	8.92
23	93.13	93.17	8.87
24	93.03	93.07	8.92
25	93.14	93.18	8.87
28	93.12	93.16	8.88
29	93.11	93.15	8.88
30	93.05	93.09	8.91
31	93.09	93.13	8.89

SEPTEMBER

	Bid	Ask	Yield[1]
1	93.09	93.13	8.89
4	HOLIDAY		
5	93.17	93.21	8.86
6	93.16	93.20	8.86
7	93.17	93.21	8.86
8	93.20	93.24	8.79
11	93.31	94.03	8.77
12	94.03	94.07	8.78
13	94.01	94.05	8.78
14	94.01	94.05	8.78
15	94.05	94.09	8.76
18	93.29	94.01	8.80
19	93.15	93.19	8.87
20	92.22	92.26	8.94
21	92.17	92.21	9.01
22	92.08	92.12	9.05
25	92.04	92.08	9.07
26	92.09	92.13	9.03
27	92.09	92.13	9.04
28	92.11	92.15	9.03
29	92.11	92.15	9.03

OCTOBER

	Bid	Ask	Yield[1]
2	92.07	92.11	9.05
3	92.13	92.17	9.02
4	92.09	92.13	9.04
5	92.07	92.11	9.05
6	92.09	92.13	9.04
9	92.09	92.13	9.04
10	92.13	92.17	9.02
11	92.11	92.15	9.03
12	92.16	92.20	9.01
13	92.19	92.23	9.00
16	92.12	92.16	9.03
17	92.12	92.16	9.03
18	92.02	92.06	9.08
19	91.26	91.30	9.11
20	91.20	91.24	9.14
21	91.22	91.26	9.13
23	91.24	91.28	9.12
24	91.20	91.24	9.16
25	91.20	91.24	9.16
26	91.20	91.24	9.16
27	91.02	91.06	9.23
30	90.17	90.21	9.25
31	90.16	90.20	9.25

NOVEMBER

	Bid	Ask	Yield[1]
1	91.16	91.20	9.11
2	91.20	91.24	9.09
3	91.04	91.08	9.16
6	91.08	91.24	9.09
7	HOLIDAY		
8	90.30	91.14	9.13
9	91.00	91.16	9.13
10	91.04	91.20	9.11
13	91.08	91.24	9.09
14	91.04	91.20	9.11
15	91.20	92.04	9.04
16	91.24	92.08	9.02
17	91.28	92.12	9.00
20	92.02	92.18	8.97
21	92.17	92.21	9.01
22	91.24	92.08	9.02
23	HOLIDAY		
24	91.16	92.00	9.05
27	91.20	92.04	9.04
28	91.16	92.00	9.05
29	91.12	91.28	9.07
30	91.12	91.28	9.07

DECEMBER

	Bid	Ask	Yield[1]
1	91.20	92.04	9.04
4	91.23	92.06	9.03
5	91.14	91.30	9.06
6	91.14	91.30	9.06
7	91.10	91.26	9.08
8	91.10	91.26	9.08
11	91.10	91.26	9.09
12	91.08	91.24	9.10
13	91.02	91.18	9.12
14	90.30	91.14	9.14
15	90.28	91.04	9.19
18	90.16	90.16	9.28
19	90.02	90.10	9.31
20	89.27	90.03	9.34
21	89.27	90.03	9.34
22	90.06	90.14	9.29
25	HOLIDAY		
26	90.10	90.18	9.27
27	90.10	90.18	9.27
28	89.24	90.00	9.36
29	89.24	90.00	9.36

[1] Yield computed on ask quote.
Source: Wall Street Journal.

Source: *Statistical Annual*, Chicago Board of Trade.

are also available from brokers and commodity news services.

The majority of price-making data appears in government releases and reports; subscriptions can be had by writing the agency involved (see Appendix). This data reappears quickly in summary by brokerage and advisory service newsletters. Government reports contain just about all the information that is to be had about the commodity markets and most other sources of information are derived from them. They are mostly free and released to everyone at the same time. This considerably reduces the problem of "inside information." The Department of Agriculture publishes "situation reports" on a wide variety of commodities. The Departments of Treasury and Commerce, the Bureaus of Census and of Mines, and the Commodity Futures Trading Commission publish numerous reports valuable to the trader. (The principal reports for the major commodities are discussed in the appropriate sections of Chapter 13.) (See Figure 12–10.)

Most commodity exchanges publish yearbooks containing information about futures contracts traded in their various pits and on the cash markets with which they are associated. Historical price data, tables of monthly highs and lows, and other details are found in these yearbooks, along with a great deal of source material about the commodities and contracts themselves. (See Figure 12–11.) Each exchange also authors a series of pamphlets and books on aspects of commodity trading. Many produce daily or weekly newspapers containing information pertinent to the commodities traded at the exchange. A simple letter of inquiry to the exchange will bring a packet of booklets and a list of further publications, many of them free.

Since a great deal of fundamental information comes from just a few sources, the blizzard of industry publications tends to be very repetitive. Subscription to a newspaper, a couple of periodicals, principal government publications, and a brokerage or advisory newsletter will give the average trader all the information about the fundamentals he would care to know. Daily reading is much more important to developing a feel for the market than are all the correlations and paper work that a man can do with the information constantly pouring in. Keeping abreast of the market is mostly a matter of scanning a manageable and well chosen flow of facts, sifting out significant data, and gauging the tone of individual markets.

Chapter 13

FUTURES CONTRACT PRICING

FUTURES PRICES

The reader will already have noticed that cash prices cannot be discussed without reference to futures prices, and vice versa. The factual connection is simple. Cash price is the single most influential factor in futures price. Whatever goes into the formation of a cash price goes, in turn, into the formation of the futures price. But futures contract pricing entails other elements, including the shifting nature of the cash-futures relationship itself. The study of futures prices often hinges on this relationship. Hedging and speculative trading both place their bets on fluctuations in the correlation between cash and futures prices. This requires an understanding of the difference between cash and futures and of the differing characteristics among futures prices in themselves, even for the same commodity.

In the simplest definition, a futures price represents the best educated guess of a commodity's worth at some distant date. A September contract of wheat bought in April for $4.75 presumably indicates a belief that cash wheat in September will sell for about $4.75. Of course, the model has obvious flaws and no such neat

correspondence can be counted on in fact. The rationing function of prices influences the futures price so that the purpose of a futures price may be more to regulate price and distribution in the short run than to predict prices accurately in the long run. Futures prices are used by various sectors for contrary or divergent reasons: some hope for speculative gain, some hope to set a price for actual delivery, and some are hedging other related commodities. For only a few does the futures price quotation represent an anticipated real cash price.

The futures price is quite literally that: the price that a future quantity of a commodity can command *now*, given all information. *It is the present price of a future commodity, not the future price of a present commodity.* As a price barometer, the futures price serves to inform everyone in the industry of what everyone else is thinking. Futures prices can be "messages" sent back and forth from hedgers and speculators, farmers and grain exporters, and bankers and pit brokers—all using futures prices to carry on a dialogue about the economics of a commodity and their interest in it for the short, medium, and long run. Futures prices act to spell

FIGURE 13–1

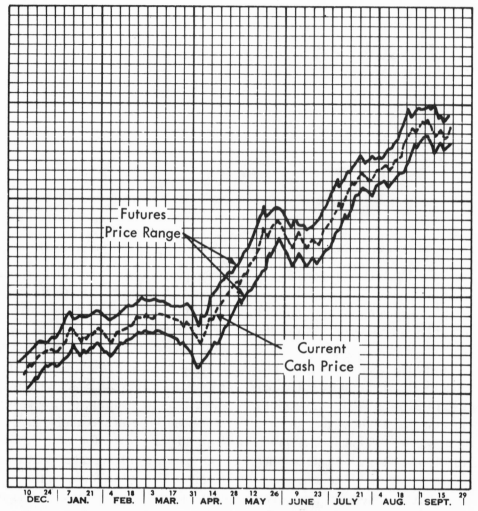

Future prices cannot range far above or below cash prices. A futures price which is too high guarantees a profit to short traders who can buy cash and deliver to fill their high priced futures contracts. Too low a price will prompt longs to buy futures, take delivery, and redeliver on the cash market.

out faith in the market, anxiety over the weather, concern about government policy, satisfaction with recent profits, or impressions of general economic trends. Only as the delivery month nears or begins does the futures price become predominantly predicative in nature. Throughout its life its limits are set by cash price, but its fluctuations are less projected prices than reflections of a temporary pricing and distribution mechanism serving a

complex of economic functions. (See Figure 13–1.)

FUTURES QUOTATIONS

Most large newspapers publish some daily futures price quotations. Comprehensive tables like those of the *Wall Street Journal* (Figure 13–2) cover thirty-five or more major commodities. The capital letters in parentheses following the name

FIGURE 13-2

Futures Prices

Thursday, April 10, 1990

Open Interest Reflects Previous Trading Day.

-GRAINS AND OILSEEDS-

-LIVESTOCK & MEAT-

-FOOD & FIBER-

-METALS-

-FINANCIAL-

Source: *The Wall Street Journal.*

of the commodity denote the exchange: (CBT) for the Chicago Board of Trade, (CMX) for New York's Commodity Exchange, Inc., etc. Next to this are the size and pricing units of the contract. Price quotes are always for the previous day's trading. Down the left hand column are the abbreviations for each contract month of the commodity currently being traded. For each month the columns on the right give the price when trading opened, the highest price of the day, the lowest price of the day, the settlement or closing price, and the net change from the settlement price of the day before. On more detailed tickers the settlement price may actually be two prices—that is, 43.00—42.65. This means that in the last hectic minutes of trading a range of prices bounded by these two was hit. "Nominal" would refer to a price which is a good representation of the prices current in the market when the final bell sounds. "Lifetime High/Low" cites the highest and the lowest prices reached by that particular contract month since it began trading. Open interest tells how many contracts were outstanding at the opening of the day's session. Volume gives how many positions long and short were opened or closed during the session.

BASIS

In an ideal hypothetical market, prices will rise gradually in regular steps from cash through each futures contract: $2.00 cash, $2.10 for the "nearby" contract month, $2.20 for the next contract month, and so on (sometimes called a "contango" market). "Backwardation" or inversion, on the other hand, denotes a market situation in which prices step lower in the future delivery months. The difference between the cash and the futures price

(or between any two commodity prices) is known as "basis." (See Figure 13–3.) Few statistics command the respect and attention of commodity traders as generally as does basis, for reasons that will soon be clear. Before any trade is executed, the trader must have a sense of the strength of weakness of a given futures price. A scrutiny of the basis, its history and direction, aids enormously in completing a comprehensive view of the character of a particular futures price.

With grains or other stored commodities, basis may largely be set by "carrying charge," the standard estimated cost of holding goods from month to month in a grain elevator, bank vault, or bullion depository. This includes fees for storage, inspection, interest, and insurance. Such charges will vary considerably with the cost of money, the availability of storage space, and the demand for the cash product. Basis will be more or less than the carrying charge at times, depending on the season and supplies. The costs and market desirability of storage move the basis: commodities move into storage when the price of storage is favorable and move out of storage when the price is unfavorable. For stored nonagricultural commodities whose supply and demand fundamentals do not change so rapidly, market cycles begin with the model progressive structure of basis increments, factoring in storage, interest, and insurance. The effect is to inspire rising prices, despite a lack of fundamentals, until longs cannot so easily move positions higher and the market collapses. This pattern recurs frequently in silver.

Producers, merchants, and buyers must know, to a fraction of a cent, the prevailing carrying charge and current basis. Without such a system, price differentials

FIGURE 13–3

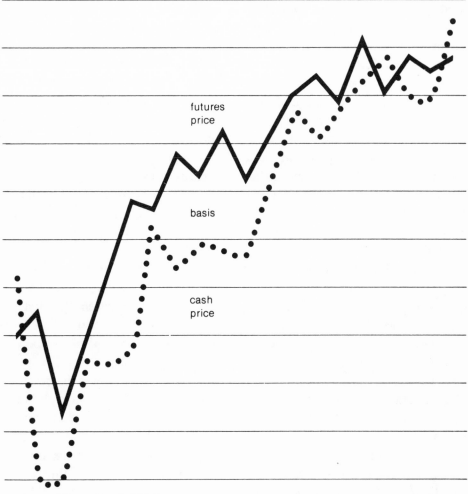

futures
price

basis

cash
price

Source: Chicago Board of Trade.

over time and in disparate locations would fall into chaos. Futures pricing organizes quotes throughout an industry to ensure uniformity and equivalence. The nearby (closest to delivery) contract works as the common price guideline. The actual cash buying of grains takes place according to basis, not flat price. Bids for cash corn to elevators or farmers are quoted as the basis to the nearby futures contract. The bid price might be "10 cents under," "at the board," "5 cents over," etc. The purchaser figures bids by comparing the nearby futures price to the average target price the company has targeted for the year. If prices are favorable and supplies ample, bids will be "under"; as prices rise and if supplies are low, company bids go "over" in a scramble to buy before losses mount too high.

It follows, then, that the cash-futures basis can be an index to supply and demand. If futures prices are abnormally high in relation to cash, the futures trader who buys is paying a premium for a commodity that the cash dealers evidently don't want or need—the forecast should probably have been bearish. If cash is selling at a stiff premium to futures, it means that cash people are willing to pay a high price for goods, a sign of a possible bull market or of an abnormal short-term demand situation which may be overcome before the delivery month arrives.

Basis, and the historical pattern of basis change for the commodity, can be a valuable tool for the trader, as it places an isolate futures price quotation in a meaningful context of cash trends. One futures contract may have a more favorable basis for trading than another month in the same commodity, depending on the pattern and on how each month has been discounted in prior trading. The trader who expects a cash move of 60 cents had better choose his futures contract months carefully if the basis for the nearby month is 20 cents cash-below-futures and the basis for another is 70 cents cash-below-futures. The latter price may already include, through accurate discounting, the anticipated price jump and thus offer little profit (if any). In monitoring market indicators, the experienced trader often finds that a sharp change in the basis signals a dramatic trend in upcoming futures prices.

PRICE FLOOR

As the futures contract approaches and enters delivery month, its price will move ever closer to the cash price. Distant price prediction gives way to near-term real pricing and purchase. Naturally, the trader can guess in August what the September price will be more accurately than he could in December or June. Futures prices will adjust as the months wane, facts become clearer, and estimates more on target. The second reason cash and futures prices coincide is the cash price

forms a floor under the futures contract price and a ceiling above the futures price.

People in the cash commodity business—be they in silver, copper, hogs, T-Bills, lumber, grain sorghum, propane, oats, coffee, or cocoa—watch closely the movement of futures prices. On 1 April a dealer in immediate need of wheat has only one option: to buy in the cash market no matter the price. Buying the next nearby futures contract, May, would do no good, for delivery would still be at least a month away. But as the weeks pass and May approaches, a second option becomes feasible. The dealer can buy cash wheat as usual, or buy the May futures contract as a source of actual goods. Contracts normally expire between the first and the twentieth of the month; if the buyer can wait into or through this period for delivery, acquisition via futures is possible. Since the user of the cash commodity can buy the futures and take delivery, cash price sets the floor for nearby futures. Carefully written contract specifications support this price floor mechanism by assuring the procurement utility of the futures contract.

For example, assume that the price of an August futures contract for some commodity fell to $3.10, while the cash commodity was bringing $3.50. If the industry user can wait a few weeks for delivery, then purchase of the August contract represents a hefty savings of 40 cents per unit over the price of cash goods. A buyer would simply hold the long futures position (with no carrying costs) into delivery and take possession of the actuals at the bargain price. Such a profit would probably be substantially more than that realized in the ordinary handling, processing, or merchandising enterprise the buyer normally depends upon for profits. The shorts who deliver either held commodities which they could have sold much more profitably on the cash market, or must buy in order to fulfill their contract obligations. Either way they stand to lose the 40 cents the buyer rakes in. Dealers who are not able to secure sufficient cash commodities on the cash market may also do their buying on the futures market. This buying may or may not have an impact on the cash market, depending upon the then prevailing activity in both cash and futures markets.

In reality, futures contract prices will rarely, if ever, fall far enough below the cash price to make it profitable for the merchant or processor to buy futures contracts and wait the time required until delivery. Dealers seeking such "guaranteed" profits in a dislocated market would, through their buy orders, drive the futures price up. When the time came to accept delivery, the dealer who bought at the futures price would probably find that the two had come into line. He then covers his futures position and buys from his cash dealer in the normal fashion. There is still a 40 cent profit in the deal, but the result is a satisfactory price correction that brings cash and futures into harmony. In fact, any time that the futures price is too low a guess of the cash price in the expiration month, dealers will move in and establish long positions, driving the futures price up and guaranteeing that it will be a reasonable industry reflection of cash price directions. These continual price corrections will prevent most large dislocations as described above. If cash does sell for considerable premiums over futures, and no quick correction occurs, supply and demand are dictating the undesirability or impossibility of buying futures and holding into delivery.

PRICE CEILING

In a similar way, cash price also sets a ceiling on how high futures prices can climb. The futures contract price will not usually exceed the commodity cash price plus what it costs to store the goods until the delivery month. If it did, people would do just that: buy cash goods, store them, and redeliver against their short futures positions. Assume the carrying costs of a commodity were 5 cents per month. Should the current cash price be $6.10 and the futures price for delivery four months hence be $6.60, any dealer could simply buy cash goods and sell futures contracts. The known costs of storage would be a cumulative 20 cents, leaving a guaranteed profit of 30 cents per unit. The warehouse holding a commodity will normally check futures prices before selling. If the nearby contract offers a profit after carrying charges are added, the commodity will be held off the market, more purchased at cash, and the deal fixed by appropriate short positions in futures. Again, this selling pressure will tend to correct price dislocations.

In summary, a futures contract price that is either too high or too low will grant somebody a guaranteed profit. Taking that profit, the trader will beat the price back into line. The futures markets do not grant guaranteed profits for long, so this process assures that the futures price is the best possible guess of the commodity's future worth. It is by finding prices that are too high or too low that the speculator makes profits. For this reason, speculators keep a sharp eye on the cash markets, basis, and the fundamental factors affecting them.

Like most price factors in commodities, the floors and ceilings provided for the futures contract work only imperfectly. The expiring contract can vary a small amount from the cash price. This variance will be large or small or common or unusual depending in part on the historical frequency of delivery against futures in the particular contract. Silver and Treasury Bills may experience high proportions of delivery, while cattle delivery against futures fluctuates sharply with market conditions, and deliveries of other commodities occur in mere handfuls. Users of the cash commodity have grade requirements, or are in locations, which are not necessarily the same as those specified in the futures contracts. This disjunction allows the two possible sources of supply to be priced separately to some extent. Contract requirements are not absolute in practice, however, and if the two prices vary by too much, a user of one grade will quickly find that he can make do with the bargain grade offered. Or a delivered contract can be traded or resold to a holder of a different grade or one in a different location who is in the same predicament. Insufficient volume can also cause price disparity in the delivery month. As hedgers close their positions and speculators leave the market, price distortions occur caused strictly by the technical functions of traders exiting. Should these swings grow large, traders will again seek profits until the market corrects itself.

INTERMONTH BASIS

The rule that basis is tied to carrying charges applies to intermonth relationships between futures contracts as well as to the cash-futures price structure. Each month that goods are held adds a regular carrying charge increment to the schedule of futures prices. But this progressive upward pricing of contract months is subject to many modifications, the most important of which are seasonal trends and supply/demand distortions. Each unprocessed commodity that has ever been alive has a seasonal curve (historically probable but not exactly predictable), starting with prices fairly low during and immediately after harvest when the market is glutted with cash goods. All futures contract prices for a commodity will thus generally move in a parallel direction while the form of intermonth relationships holds pretty firm. New factors will tend to push all the contract prices up or down together, preserving intact the monthly basis between commodity contracts. This is especially true of distant contract months which are less susceptible to short-term cash market conditions.

What occurs in each year is an adjustment of the carrying charge structure to the specifics of seasonal market conditions. In theory, if the carrying costs are 10 cents, the intermonth basis will consistently hover around 10 cents throughout the year. But the influence of seasonal trends, livestock cycles, or interest rate curves creates a pattern of unequal intermonth differentials. Some months will be priced at more than 10 cents apart, others at less, and these distortions will often persist from year to year in roughly similar arrangements. For instance, cattle prices tend to dip in the late summer and fall in compliance with usual breeding and weaning patterns. Prices of the April, June, and August contracts will each be ahead of their predecessors, but October will often fall below August. (See Figure 13–4.) Likewise, a downturn (or upturn) in later months of an interest rate futures contract would reflect trader judgment of

FIGURE 13–4

DAILY SETTLING PRICES OF THE AUGUST AND OCTOBER 1978
LIVE CATTLE FUTURES ON THE CHICAGO MERCANTILE EXCHANGE

AUGUST 1978
LIVE CATTLE FUTURES
HIGH $61.25
LOW $38.15

OCTOBER 1978
LIVE CATTLE FUTURES
HIGH $59.30
LOW $38.15

Source: Chicago Mercantile Exchange.

when current inflationary (or recessionary) rates would firmly reverse.

The assumption behind intermonth basis in seasonal commodities is that a higher price for the later months following harvest will ration supplies, thus avoiding a complete market glut by farmers and warehouses dumping produce immediately after harvest. The market must pay them to hold the commodity for a while before selling. In fact, overselling after harvest does happen and quickly sets up a premium for the distant contract months as cash prices are depressed. The premium for distant months is enforced by traders in a manner similar to that by which fu-

tures are kept in line with cash prices. When a dislocation occurs, someone is offered a guaranteed profit.

Soybeans provide a good example of normal intermonth basis and seasonal adjustment. The soybean year usually begins in October with harvest. Thus, the first new crop contracts will ordinarily be for delivery in November, followed at two-month intervals by January, March, May, July, and a "clean-up" month in August. September (and sometimes August) can be either a new crop month or a finishing off of the last of the old crop. This depends on when the new crop comes in, making September a very volatile contract in soybeans. It jumps up in price if the new crop appears to be late or drops in price if the new crop abundance hits the market in September.

Disregarding September, the price of soybeans is usually set with the November contract when the size of the United States soybean crop is first known. (This and all other United States seasonal factors, however, must be weighed against exports of South American producers who are on a different seasonal schedule. The same caution holds for any United States seasonal commodity and its foreign competitors.) Prices for the ensuing months will tend to rise on an even scale, representing the cost of storing the soybeans through the year. A typical quote of closing prices might read:

September	$7.39
November	$7.25
January	$7.48
March	$7.66
May	$7.80
July	$7.94
August	$7.91

Here September would be an old crop month, with beans selling at a 14 cent premium over the price expected to come in November when huge supplies of the new crop will inundate the market. Demand must be strong for immediate purchase or the November contract would be bid further up by buyers willing to wait. November sets the new crop price around $7.25. January goes up 23 cents, reflecting carrying charges and a confidence in continued demand. March stands at 18 cents over January, with May and July up 14 cents each. These smaller premiums over the nearer months show some uncertainty among traders, who are hesitant to extend their guesses so far into the coming year. August actually sells at a discount to July,

reflecting the possibility that some beans from the following new crop might make it to market in August, depressing prices. If the new crop does enter the August market, prices will fall even lower in relation to July, expanding the negative intermonth basis. If the new crop doesn't appear until September, August will rise above July in a more normal relation. Discounting goes to work. The 3 cent discount on August now results from a calculation that prices will either fall 20 cents from July or rise 14 cents in line with the average premium. Traders split the difference and bid $7.91.

In January the Department of Agriculture will release a "stocks in all positions" report on soybeans, probably making some adjustment in the reported size of the crop over the current estimates. When this happens the price of all soybean months may rise or fall according to whether the crop is found to be larger or smaller than anticipated, but intermonth basis will remain about the same. If the basis between months is not sufficient to cover the cost of storing the beans (or wheat, corn, etc.) farmers will sell their produce right away, depressing current prices and leaving later prices relatively untouched. This action will restore the normal basis (though it won't raise an unprofitable absolute price level). Speculators can also act to keep basis in line by exploiting any imbalance in prices that may occur by taking a spread position.

SPREAD POSITIONS

Spread positions are instituted to exploit an abnormal price difference between two fundamentally related futures contracts. The contracts may be in two months of the same commodity, two exchanges trading the same commodity, or two entirely different commodities. The trader spreads his positions by simultaneously going long in one contract and short in the other. He speculates on a change in the price spread between the two contracts. A legitimate spread involves *futures* contracts whose price movements have widely recognized and demonstrable connections to each other. (A hedge, on the other hand, denotes a trade that speculates on the price difference between a *cash* and a futures position.) The spread trader cares little about absolute price levels. His concern is whether one contract is overpriced or underpriced in relation to the other. By establishing positions in both, the trader may profit when prices move back into their normal spread as he buys the underpriced contract and sells the overpriced contract.

Each contract position forms one "leg" of the spread. The trader hopes that one leg will travel farther relative to the other in a favorable direction. The immediate advantages of spreads are lower risks and smaller costs. Since the trader holds both short and long positions, he stands to profit on one leg no matter which way prices go. This "limited risk" quality of spreads in a single commodity weakens when the spread is between two different commodities. The potential loss is theoretically smaller than it could have been had the trader held only regular naked positions. Because of this diminished risk, brokers charge less margin deposit for some price-related spreads. Spread margins may be as little as 15 or 20 percent of the cost of a naked position in just one contract. Thus, unwary novices are attracted to overtrade cheap spreads in the mistaken belief that they can't lose. In

practice, spreads are neither risk free nor immune from huge losses. Cheap margins make spreads extremely useful to large industrial users of the markets seeking to set or adjust prices and very attractive to professional traders capable of spreading hundreds of contracts to profit from very small aberrations in normal price relations.

Spreads in two contract months of the same commodity are called "intermonth," "intracommodity," or "interdelivery" spreads. These spreads proceed from the conclusions sketched above about intermonth basis and price floors and ceilings. In theory, the speculator should be able to estimate, by reference to carrying costs and basis, just how far the nearby contract can rise or fall in relation to the distant contract. With this knowledge he can set up the legs of the spread to exploit fluctuations in the basis. Should the price difference between the contract months be greater than the carrying costs, or far less, the speculator may profit from the dislocation with a well chosen spread.

For example, in December the January soybean contract may be selling for 18 cents under the March contract, although the normal carrying charge basis might be 12 cents. The spread should narrow, presenting a trading opportunity. If good reason exists to believe the value of soybeans will go up by March, farmers and warehouses will withhold beans from the cash market and keep them until March to pick up the 6 cent bonus. But this will tend to raise January's price, while the increased supplies for March depress that contract's price. The spread heads for the old average. The speculator profits by buying contracts of the underpriced January and selling overpriced March short. The market pressure of the spread itself helps speed futures prices back to normalcy.

For the 12 cent basis to return, either the March price must fall relative to January or the January price must rise relative to March. The carrying charge floor ordinarily keeps January from falling much more and the ceiling keeps March from rising much more. Both prices can go up or down, but March should go up less or fall more than January. The trader in a spread position between two contracts may lose a good deal on one leg of the spread but he will make more on the other. A trader in such a spread can lose money only if the basis becomes greater and make money only as the two come closer together. The trade order would go in stipulating the desired basis, not the flat prices: "Buy 25 January soybeans, sell 25 March soybeans, spread limit 18 cents." ("25" signifies thousands of bushels, here equaling 5 contracts per leg.) This allows the pit broker flexibility in purchasing the legs while guaranteeing the trader his desired spread. The trade result might look like this:

25 percent or less of regular margins, the normal trade offers more. Yet, what if unexpected Brazilian soybeans hit the global market, driving January down to $6.90 and March to $7.08? The loss to the spread trader would be $0. The loss to the trader holding 2 January contracts long would be $1,000. Limited profits in spreads mean also limited losses. Some traders prefer "contingency spreads," switching in this case from naked long to spread only after an adverse price move actually begins. This would cost the same in commissions as simply liquidating the January loss and selling March or liquidating and rebuying after the price turns up, both of which might be smarter than holding onto a losing spread. And such a spread will only work if the basis narrows, an unlikely possibility here when the nearby contract is pressured by cash events.

The July–November straddle is one of the most popular of the many common intracommodity spreads. (See Figure 13–5.) Soybeans are harvested in September

Buy 25 January @ $7.00	Sell 25 March @ $7.18
Sell 25 January @ $7.22	Buy 25 March @ $7.34
Profit = 22 cents	Loss = 16 cents

Total Trade Profit: $6 \times 5 \times \$50 = \$1,500$ (less commissions).

The margin for one spread position (long and short) might be $600. The speculator here would realize a precommission profit of 50 percent of required margin, a respectable profit with only $3,000 in risk capital. But what if the trader had simply gone long January soybeans? At $1,500 per single long position, only two contracts could be margined with the same risk capital. Precommission profit would be $2,200 or 73 percent of required margin. Unless spread margins are about

and October. During the summer months it may become obvious that there is a great shortage of soybeans for near term demand. There is historical precedence for the United States to almost run out of old crop beans while the impending new crop harvest is excessively large. The incoming crop can't help the summer shortage but promises to be bountiful, dampening later prices substantially but leaving the near summer contracts buoyant. The trader takes a "bull market"

FIGURE 13–5
Spread chart

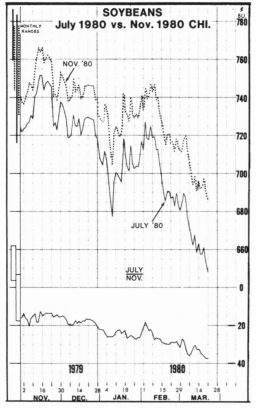

Source: Commodity Research Bureau, Inc.

spread in beans, buying July (or August or September) with the idea that prices will not drop far in a tight market. He balances the purchase with an equal sale of November futures. He has gone long old crop beans and short new crop beans. Tight old crop contracts will generally not fall by much, while a glutted market in November prevents the short side of the spread from climbing.

A "bull spread" is so named because it is expected to work in a bull market. A trader who sold November against January beans would be taking a "bear market spread," with both legs in the same crop year. Such a spread, placed a month or two before harvest, can exploit a widen-

ing of the basis between the two contract months if the near month falls more than the far. This often happens when the market glut comes to pass, depressing spot prices beyond the normal basis pattern. If insufficient elevator storage space is available, cash prices can be depressed severely.

Intermonth spreads are possible in many commodities, including cattle, gold, T-Bills, sugar, and wheat. (See Figure 13–6.) The principle remains the same no matter the substance: anticipate or discover an abnormal price difference and exploit it. Remember, however, that spreads are still speculative. There is no law absolutely forbidding a dislocated basis from growing still more eccentric, overthrowing the "rules" and wiping out the "safe" spread trader.

INTERCOMMODITY AND INTERMARKET SPREADS

Spreads between two different commodities are also common. Substitutability lies behind many intercommodity spreads, such as hogs vs. cattle or oats vs. corn. Hog and cattle prices often fluctuate in close relation to one another as price levels and consumer preference interact. Traders on the floor at the Chicago Mercantile Exchange will watch each pit for signs or travel between them to quickly capitalize on a basis aberration. Other popular spreads include T-Bonds vs. Ginnie Maes, lumber vs. plywood, and platinum vs. gold. (See Figure 13–7.) Again, there must be a reasonable cash connection between the commodities being spread.

Carrying charge floors and ceilings (themselves never completely secure) don't hold for intercommodity spreads.

FIGURE 13-6

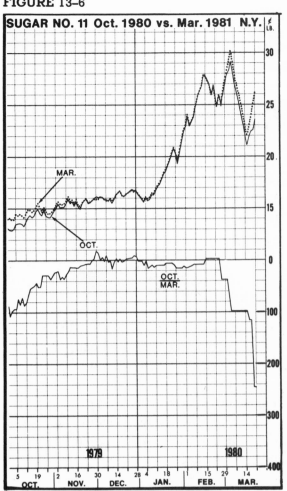

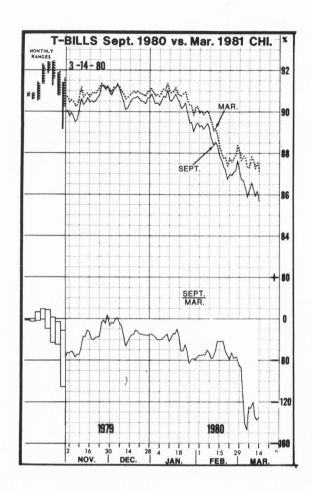

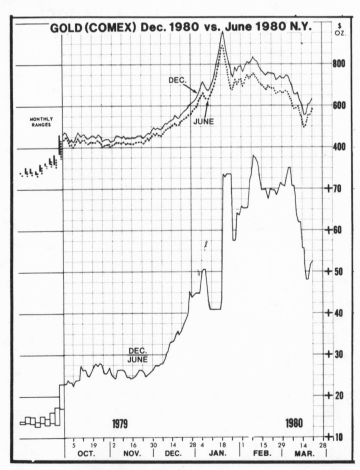

Source: Commodity Research Bureau, Inc.

FIGURE 13–7

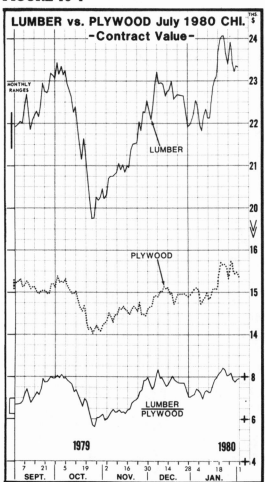

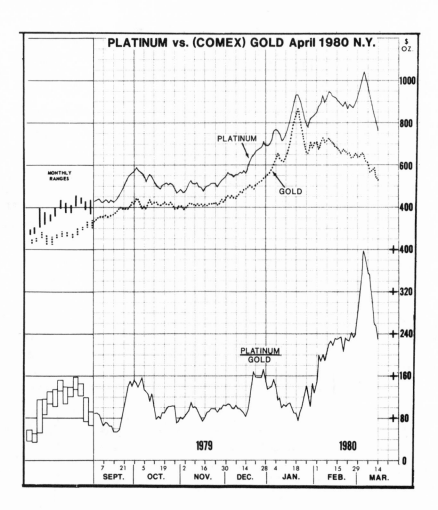

Substitutability, however, and watchfulness among traders set working limits on how far certain commodities can range away from (or toward) each other before corrective trading action is taken. Changes in the yield curve will set off spreading of interest rate futures with different maturities; instruments with similar maturities (T-Bonds and Ginnie Maes) may be spread if one appears overpriced (without good monetary reason).

Some spreads rely upon differences in the seasonal timetables of commodities. Since prices may predictably decline and rise with the unfolding of the crop year, grains harvested at different times can be spread against one another to take advantage of probable strengths and weaknesses, as one price can reasonably be expected to rise more than another depending on the crop year timetables. Spreads of this nature include soybeans vs. corn and wheat vs. corn. Also widely practiced is the spread between the price of soybeans and the combined price of soybean meal and soybean oil. (See Figure 13–8.) If either the beans or the end products (or one of the end products) are overpriced or underpriced relative to the other, a spread can be profitable. If the trader goes long in meal and oil and short in beans, the judgment is that the value

FIGURE 13-8

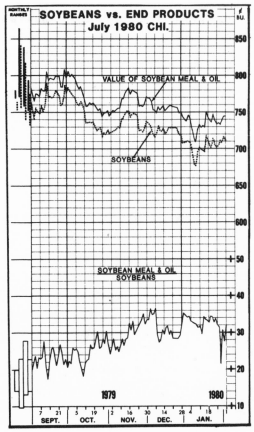

Source: Commodity Research Bureau, Inc.

City. When wheat prices move, they normally do so nationwide. A set of premiums and discounts exists for delivery of different grades and types of wheat at various locations, making calculation of a reasonable intermarket basis feasible. If one of the prices moves out of line, the spread trader can take a profit and help restore the balance.

The spread between May contracts in wheat at Kansas and Chicago is an old standard. The hard red wheat of the Kansas contract is grown further south and west than the soft red wheat of the Chicago contract, so that Kansas goes out to Gulf Coast ports while Chicago goes through the Great Lakes. Hard red may be delivered against the Chicago contract, however, and will be if the price at Chi-

FIGURE 13-9

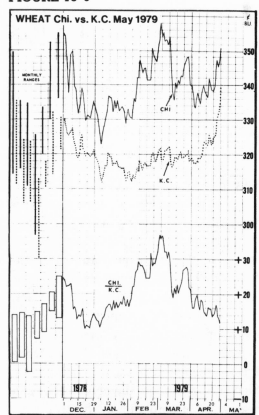

Source: Commodity Research Bureau, Inc.

of the products will increase relative to the price of the beans. This spread is called a "reverse crush spread" because it is the reverse of the usual spread of the soybean crusher. Crushers normally are long the beans (needed for processing) and short the meal and oil (the available product of the crushing operation).

Spreads between the prices of the same commodity as traded on different exchanges exploit aberrations in normal intermarket basis. Very alert traders can scalp a temporary dislocation in a commodity's New York, Chicago, or London prices. The most common form of intermarket spread is in wheat which is traded at Chicago, Minneapolis, and Kansas

cago rises beyond the cost of shipping the wheat to the Chicago ports. Such a high price would offer a guaranteed profit, and thus an effective ceiling is set on Chicago prices relative to Kansas. There is no limit, on the other hand, to the premium Kansas can command over Chicago. In midwinter the trader thus spreads the July contracts, going long Kansas and short Chicago. This is because Kansas tends to lag behind Chicago in winter, as speculators (usually net long) prefer trading at Chicago. As millers and buyers enter the Kansas market in the spring, Kansas gains on Chicago and the spread narrows. Historical studies show this trend in about two-thirds of the years studied. (See Figure 13–9.)

CASH PRICE EFFECTS OF FUTURES TRADING

It has been said repeatedly in this book that futures contracts expire near the cash price in the delivery month and that it is the cash market which determines expiration price. This is indeed usually the case. But futures trading is no different from any other human enterprise. Exceptions to the ideal occur regularly and the system isn't perfect. Futures prices do have an influence on cash markets. That is, in fact, one of their valuable functions, as everyone has an opportunity to effectively "consult" thousands of market watchers before making new decisions about cash positions. Producers, merchants, and buyers will act in response to the collective opinion of the futures market, and a bad guess there can send cash market prices decidedly awry. Before the student of commodities trading joins the chorus that recurrently damns the evil effects of futures on cash business, how-

ever, a longer view of the problem is in order.

The futures market does not and cannot set prices for any substantial length of time, especially if such prices turn out to be out of harmony with the cash world reality. Futures, rather, provide a forum wherein the values of commodities are constantly reestimated. These evaluations remain opinions, always subject to eventual corrections by cash fundamentals and by the opinions of other traders. As they fluctuate, futures prices serve very well the special functions the futures market makes possible: consultative pricing, supply rationing, long range planning, risk reduction, market organization, information dissemination, and new profit opportunity. As long as futures contracts are deliverable, cash prices limit the speculative range of futures prices.

Futures prices, as guesses, can be wrong. They may thus have short term detrimental effects on cash users or producers. In the case of commodities that unduly become the barometers of extraneous emotions about distantly related political problems, harmful effects on industry users are sometimes considerable and costly. But prices fluctuate whether or not there are futures markets. The question becomes: Do futures markets cause a greater degree of harmful price instability than would exist in their absence? Beyond that: Do futures markets make it possible for outsiders to callously use an industry for their own speculative profits? And further: Is the net effect of the futures industry as a whole, in all of its many functions, worth the trouble its imperfections cause? No one has yet shown by historical study that futures markets consistently increase the fluctuations of commodity prices. Some government and private studies, on

FIGURE 13–10

Monthly High and Low Prices of Onions to Michigan Growers, and
Monthly National Average Prices to Growers, September–March

(Dollars per 50-pound sack at 1947–49 price level)

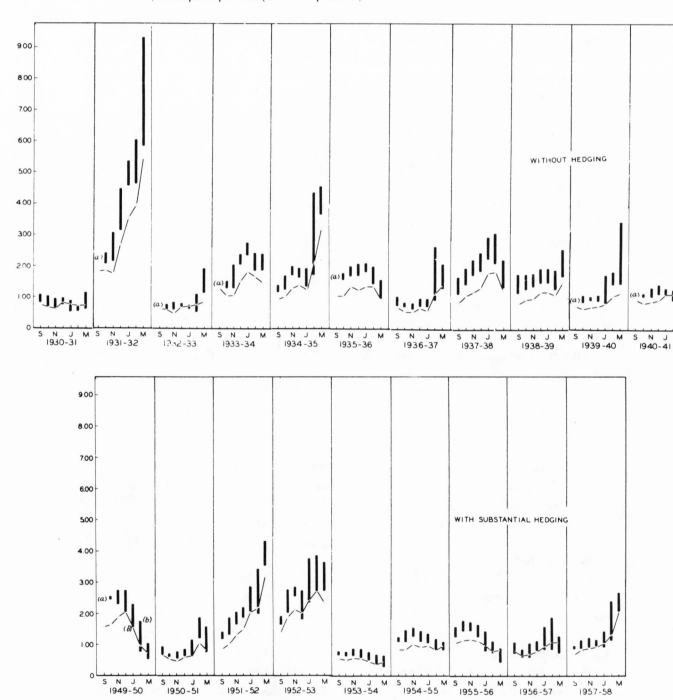

• Michigan price range shown by vertical bars.
ᵃ Quotations lacking or insufficient to establish price range for the month.
ᵇ Missing high or low Michigan price quotation estimated on the basis of Chicago spot quotations.

Source: Holbrook Working, "Price Effects of Futures Trading."

the contrary, suggest that precisely the opposite is the case. After futures trading in onions was prohibited in 1958, studies of the data on prices with and without a futures market show that futures worked to smooth out the otherwise extreme and erratic seasonal motions of price swings. (See Figure 13–10.)

Producers of commodities are naturally reluctant at first to allow speculative traders in distant cities to play important roles in the pricing of goods that constitute their livelihood, especially if agricultural or livestock prices bring little or no profit to the producers. In such instances, futures traders and speculators have made an easy scapegoat. But since, statistically, speculators are normally net *long*, it is hard to imagine how they are responsible for too low prices. Manipulation of prices would, in fact, be far easier without futures markets, for these offer alternative sources of supply and demand (and of pricing) to producers and buyers who would otherwise be at the mercy of whoever controlled the local cash market. It

is much more difficult to control a futures market than one in cash, for there is no physical limit to the number of players who can enter and drive prices up or down. If agricultural prices, more closely determined by free market forces because of the existence of futures, decline relative to the costs of other goods, the problem is a political and structural one within the economy itself—a problem futures can actually help to offset.

The few instances in modern trading history of gross futures distortion by headstrong, irresponsible traders are the exceptions that highlight the otherwise successful operation of this multibillion dollar enterprise. Proper industry self-regulation and government monitoring can prevent most serious abuses. And when the dust does settle after a scandal, one normally finds that the market has righted itself competently; cash dealers have paid a small price for benefits the futures system normally brings them; and the manipulators end up back where they started—or worse.

Chapter 14 ⎯⎯⎯⎯⎯⎯⎯⎯⎯⎯⎯⎯⎯⎯⎯⎯⎯⎯⎯⎯⎯⎯⎯⎯⎯

THE MAJOR COMMODITIES: A FEW FUNDAMENTALS

HOW MUCH ABOUT WHAT SHOULD I KNOW?

The trader in commodities will ask this question often and wonder how to possibly master all the facts available from a thousand authoritative sources. The average speculator faces a list of about forty principal commodity futures actively traded on United States exchanges. Statistics, however, show that only ten commodities in a given year account for about 80 percent of all contracts traded; 90 percent of trading volume involves just 20 different futures. In 1979 gold, soybeans, corn, and cattle together amounted to nearly half the total number of contracts traded. So, the real number of substances and contracts a trader will probably study in depth range from two or three to twenty or so. The professional trader may want to keep charts on all forty markets, but no one can reasonably hope to be an expert in all the fundamental forces and technical factors associated with each.

Fortunately, and this is one of futures trading's blessings, an encyclopedic knowledge of all the details affecting a commodity is not a prerequisite to successful trading. You may know exactly

what the temperature is in the Brazilian coffee regions, how much wheat is stockpiled in Duluth, or what the Chinese demand for cotton will be in the upcoming months, but if you don't know how to follow the price chart and trade it profitably, you might as well spend your research time reading comic books. It's great if you're long in pork bellies and your investigations reveal a 20 percent decline in consumer preference for pork, indicating a switch to a short position might be wise. Yet, actually getting into that position correctly, especially *before* prices really do start down, could well be hazardous, and the placement of stops far more important than current slaughter figures.

Futures trading "experts" like to categorize speculators as either "chartists" or "fundamentalists." Chartists are the ones buried in windowless cells, connected to the outside world only by ticker tapes and subscriptions to chart services. Fundamentalists are those nearly blind, walking computers full of crop statistics, monetary supply figures, interest rate quotations, and supply/demand ratios. The sane trader avoids these extremes, his allegiance ultimately commanded by the real movement of prices. Fundamental analysis helps the trader forecast price changes and assists in evaluating the strength or weakness of a trend. Fundamentals put the trader into place, ready for the trade. Charting forecasts too, but it also guides the trade with advice other than that given by the fundamentals. Following the line that price changes form on the chart, the technical trader plots his entrances and exits, places stops, and takes profits. When placing orders he trades the line, not simply the commodity itself or its statistics. If all the fundamentals look bearish, and the price goes up, don't puzzle. Profit. Never trade against the market, no matter how "illogical" its motion might be if measured by some hypothetical yardstick or sure-fire method. The savvy trader will always tell you straight, "The market is always right."

A balanced approach, then, is the trader's best path. A background knowledge in the commodities you wish to trade essentially complements your technical strategies. Know your commodities, be familiar with the fundamental elements controlling the cash markets, keep an eye on the best sources of information concerning each commodity, and be ready to make your move when the market makes its move. What follows here is a rundown of the major commodities and an introduction to their characteristics.

WHEAT

Grains are the backbone of the world's food supply and also the backbone of the trading system that prices and distributes them. The three major crops of the United States—and thus the principal strengths of our economic place in the world—are wheat, soybeans, and corn. The fundamentals of any single one will bear on the others. Much of what I have to say about wheat applies, with adjustments, to the others. Weather, politics, and global economic currents fundamentally determine the supply and demand, and so the price moves, of these basics. Their importance to humanity's survival increases as population pressures mount. (World population is multiplying at a rate of about 70 million a year.) Wheat and other grains account for about 60 percent of the calories consumed in the developing countries and for about 35 percent in the developed nations. The amount of new acreage, or of acreage that can be taken from other crops or uses, is limited. As income around the world rises, so will the demand for livestock products, and in turn for the grains to feed the cattle and the hogs.

These shifts in the life style of the emerging regions will profoundly affect the direction of world markets in the closing decades of this century. Competition among food, feed, and fuel uses of grain strongly influence grain prices, trade patterns, and production figures. The decisions by the Soviet Union and China to improve nutrition and alter eating habits have had a dramatic impact on the wheat and corn markets. Though the largest producer of wheat, the U.S.S.R. has been a net importer since 1964. Russia's need for wheat helped inspire the age of "détente," which culminated in the Great Russian Wheat Deal of 1972. A different set of political realities turned a similar deal into the Grain Embargo of 1980. Commodities trading became a topic of everyday conversation and food became an instrument of diplomacy. The disturbing question faced by the United States was, "Shall foodstuffs be used as foreign policy weapons?"

Economic, political, and moral dilemmas now entangle the network of the grain trade. The rough parallel between the food producing Western nations and the oil producing Middle Eastern nations was one drawn by many, in and out of government. By assuming the purchase obligation of embargoed grain, the United States Agriculture Department went into the merchandising business in a big way. Politics, in the case of *this* exporter, surpasses weather as the number one determinant of supply and demand. In a world of increasing food and energy shortages, such complications can only intensify as the United States decides to whom it will sell its precious goods. Developing importing nations, on the other hand, may not be able to absorb shipments the United States would like to sell and which those nations would desperately like to buy unless handling, storage, transportation, and distribution facilities are vastly upgraded.

Grain traders must expect constant shifts in import/export balances and alliances. The impact of the 1980 embargo was partly softened by the continuing boom in trade between the United States and the People's Republic of China, which was granted most favored nation trading status. Wheat exports to the PRC advanced sharply, though it by no means could offer a market as immediately large and accessible as Russia's market. The considerable progress of the wheat growing regions of India placed it third among nations in total production, portending long lasting realignments of the trade in that region of the globe. Overall, world wheat production rose—with a few setbacks—from 300 million tons in 1969 to over 400 million tons in 1979. (See Figure 14–1.) World wheat trade passed the 80 million ton level as the 1980s got under-

way. The United States' share of world wheat trade usually exceeds 40 percent. Estimated wheat exports for the first year of the new decade ran to well over 35 million tons.

Wheat futures are traded on the Chicago Board of Trade, the Kansas City Board of Trade, and the Minneapolis Grain Exchange. (Minicontracts of 1,000 bushels are traded at MidAmerica.) The Chicago Board takes by far the lion's share of the futures business in wheat, with about 80 percent of the volume. (See Figure 14–2.) The Chicago contract calls for 5,000 bushels of No. 2 Soft Red Winter Wheat, a type grown in the surrounding area and principally used in processed grain products such as biscuits, cake mixes, and crackers. At Kansas City the contract is for No. 2 Hard Red Winter Wheat. At Minneapolis there are contracts for Hard Northern Spring Wheat and for Hard Amber Durum Wheat. The hard wheats, which make up the majority of the United States crop, are the much sought after bread flour wheats. Durum wheat is used primarily in the manufacture of pasta and macaroni products. (Of course, a variety of grades of wheat may be delivered against a contract according to set premiums and discounts.)

In the United States the winter wheat harvest starts in the South in late May and ends along the Canadian border in late July. (See Figure 14–3.) Sown in September or October, this crop needs moisture in the fall and snow cover for protection during its winter dormancy. Spring wheat is sown as early as practicable and harvested in late summer. The official crop season for wheat runs from 1 July to 30 June of the following year, so that May is generally an old crop contract. July sees the first of the newly har-

FIGURE 14–1

World Production of Wheat   In Thousands of Metric Tons

Crop Year	Argentina	Australia	Canada	China	France	W. Germany	India	Italy	Pakistan	Spain	Turkey	Un. Kingdom	U.S.S.R.	United States	World Total[1]
1968–9	5,740	14,804	17,685	22,000	14,985	6,012	16,540	9,655	6,477	5,477	8,400	3,469	76,500	42,365	307,185
1969–0	7,020	10,546	18,623	23,000	14,459	5,820	18,652	9,585	6,711	4,624	8,300	3,364	62,300	39,263	287,739
1970–1	4,250	7,890	9,023	24,500	12,922	5,492	20,093	9,689	7,399	4,060	8,000	4,236	82,700	36,783	291,108
1971–2	5,680	8,651	14,412	24,000	15,360	7,142	23,832	10,070	6,476	5,457	10,700	4,815	98,760	44,029	322,562
1972–3	6,800	6,510	14,514	26,000	18,123	6,410	26,410	9,423	6,889	4,562	9,500	4,761	85,993	42,046	331,056
1973–4	6,560	12,094	16,459	28,000	17,792	7,134	24,735	8,900	7,800	3,915	8,000	5,003	109,784	46,407	371,600
1974–5	5,970	11,357	13,295	37,000	19,142	7,761	22,072	9,697	7,800	4,534	8,300	6,130	83,849	48,797	356,410
1975–6	8,570	12,024	17,078	40,000	15,013	7,014	24,104	9,610	7,673	4,302	11,500	4,488	66,224	58,078	350,057
1976–7	11,000	11,825	23,587	43,000	16,150	6,702	28,846	9,528	8,691	4,436	13,000	4,740	96,882	58,306	415,100
1977–8[2]	5,300	9,300	19,900	40,000	17,046	7,126	29,082	6,650	8,942	3,988	13,500	5,267	92,200	55,400	381,900
1978–9[1]	7,400	17,600	21,100				31,300						120,800	49,000	435,800

[1] Estimated.   [2] Preliminary.   *Source: Foreign Agricultural Service, U.S.D.A.*

Supply and Distribution of Wheat in the United States   In Millions of Bushels

Crop Yr. Beginning June[5]	Supply — Stocks, June 1[5] — On Farms	Mills, Elevators[3]	C.C.C.	Total Stocks	Production	Imports[4]	Total Supply	Domestic Disappearance — Food	Seed	Industry	Feed — Residual	(On Farms Where Grown)	Total Dom. Disap.	Exports[4]	Total Disappearance
1967–8	144.9	278.5	1.0	424.4	1,507.6	.9	1,933	519.2	71.3	.1	42.6	(42.9)	633.3	761.1	1,394
1968–9	229.5	308.3	.7	538.5	1,556.6	1.0	2,096	519.7	61.3	.1	154.3	(60.8)	735.4	544.2	1,280
1969–0[5]	325.9	490.0	.8	816.7	1,442.7	2.8	2,349	520.1	55.6	.5	188	(61.0)	763.9	603.0	1,367
1970–1	307.1	576.6	1.2	984	1,351.6	1.5	2,236	517.2	62.1	.1	193	(62.0)	772.0	740.8	1,513
1971–2	240.3	489.4	1.8	822	1,618.6	1.1	2,442	523.7	63.2	.1	261	(71.7)	849.3	609.7	1,458
1972–3	355.1	506.3	1.8	985	1,546.2	1.3	2,530	526.9	67.2	.1	203	(47.0)	798.8	1,135.0	1,933
1973–4	133.9	302.8	1.8	599	1,710.8	2.6	2,311	530.3	84.1	—	139	(31.5)	753.5	1,217.0	1,971
1974–5	89.5	157.9	.3	340.1	1,781.9	3.4	2,125	540.8	92	—	—39.1—		671.9	1,018.5	1,690
1975–6	132.7	194.3	—	435.0	2,122.5	2.4	2,560	587.5	99	.1	—35.1—		721.7	1,172.9	1,895
1976–7	235.5	429.8	—	665.3	2,142.4	2.7	2,810	588.0	92	.1	—68.4—		748.6	949.5	1,698
1977–8[1]	426.3	685.9	—	1,112.2	2,036.3	1.9	3,151	586.5	80	.1	—183.3—		849.9	1,123.9	1,974
1978–9[2]	492.9	683.8	—	1,176.7	1,798.7	2	2,978	590	84	—	—150 —		824	1,150	1,974
1979–80															

[1] Preliminary. [2] Estimated. [3] Also warehouses and all off-farm storage not otherwise designated, including flour mills.
[4] Imports & exports are for wheat, including flour & other products in terms of wheat. [5] Prior to 1969–70, data are for crop year beginning July 1. *Source: Economic Research Service, U.S.D.A.*

Source: Commodity Research Bureau, Inc.

vested crop, and lower prices. July, September, December, March, and May are the five contract months traded. The trade unit for wheat and all other grains is 5,000 bushels. Grain trade orders and executions are denominated in bushels, not contracts. "Sell 45 July Wheat" means 45,000 bushels, the equivalent of 9 contracts (not 45). The minimum fluctuation is ¼ cent per bushel, or $12.50 per contract. This is the amount the trader will win or lose each time the wheat price tics. With a maximum daily range of 20 cents from the previous day's close, the speculator stands to win or lose a maximum of $1,000 per contract per day. Margins average $1,500. (This and all other margin figures may vary substantially with the market.) Any trader who holds a position in excess of 500,000 bushels must report his position to the Commodity Futures Trading Commission, and no speculator

FIGURE 14-2

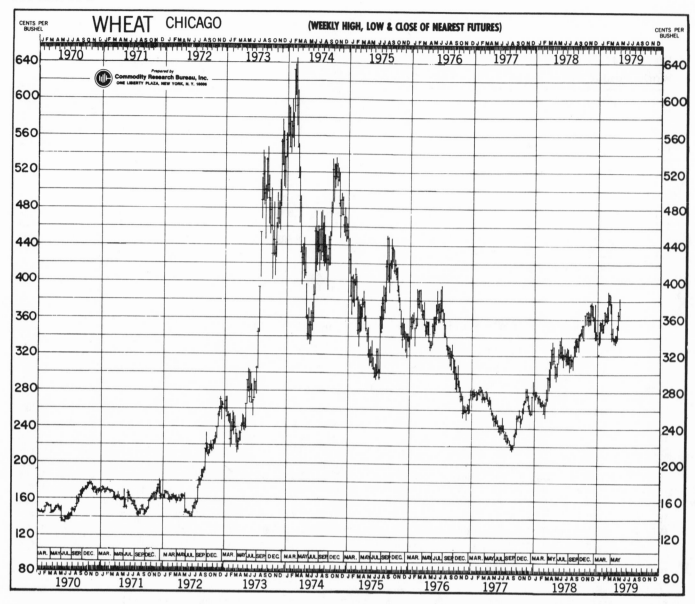

CENTS PER BUSHEL — WHEAT CHICAGO (WEEKLY HIGH, LOW & CLOSE OF NEAREST FUTURES) — CENTS PER BUSHEL

Prepared by
Commodity Research Bureau, Inc.
ONE LIBERTY PLAZA, NEW YORK, N.Y. 10006

Volume of Trading in Wheat Futures at Chicago Board of Trade   In Millions of Bushels

Year	July	Aug.	Sept.	Oct.	Nov.	Dec.	Jan.	Feb.	Mar.	Apr.	May	June	Total
1966–7	806.9	684.1	926.6	719.0	653.3	636.1	648.1	698.3	1,531	1,201	953.7	967.7	10,425.4
1967–8	1,088	1,303	864.9	608.2	832.6	637.8	653.0	522.2	705.2	715.4	587.7	741.2	9,259.5
1968–9	813.3	859.5	742.3	724.0	623.4	500.0	420.6	417.0	464.2	471.4	447.2	447.3	6,930.2
1969–0	571.9	471.1	365.8	282.6	233.2	271.0	200.0	299.1	238.9	256.1	302.9	3,714
1970–1	458.3	534.0	491.1	377.4	343.0	293.3	230.2	247.6	230.7	338.2	267.1	424.1	4,235
1971–2	421.1	371.0	328.9	330.4	322.3	338.7	273.3	244.2	233.0	242.1	197.2	233.1	3,535
1972–3	516.7	1,065	981.7	809.6	774.7	835.4	767.3	810.6	782.5	725.5	927.6	765.1	9,764
1973–4[1]	898.0	758.8	1,018	1,087	1,131	1,130	1,153[1]	970.6	1,137	922.4	864.0	1,026	12,096
1974–5	1,285	1,049	907	1,154	810	653	902	731	768	637	682	858	10,436
1975–6	1,520	1,313	1,062	1,159	960	721	848	1,399	1,472	1,288	1,121	1,758	14,621
1976–7	1,796	1,228	1,876	1,180	1,005	601	577	810	888	693	597	846	12,097
1977–8	824	623	777	740	982	747	694	713	1,130	1,179	1,063	1,122	10,594
1978–9	1,133	1,312	1,034	1,260	1,272	878	889	843	805				
1979–80													

[1] Data prior to Jan. 1973 are for AT ALL "CONTRACT" MARKETS IN THE U.S.
Source: Commodity Futures Trading Commission

Source: Commodity Research Bureau, Inc.

FIGURE 14–3
RECOMMENDED SEED PLANTING DATES U.S.

New England			Middle States			Central and Western States			Southern States		
Crop	Dates to Plant	Weeks to Mature	Crop	Dates to Plant	Weeks to Mature	Crop	Dates to Plant	Weeks to Mature	Crop	Dates to Plant	Weeks to Mature
Corn	May 10 to May 30	14-17	Corn	April 20 to May 30	16-18	Corn	April 1 to June 1	16-20	Cotton	Feb. to May 15	20-30
Wheat (W)	Sept. 1 to Sept. 10	40-42	Wheat (W)	Sept. 1 to Sept. 10	40-42	Wheat (W)	Sept. 1 to Oct. 15	41-43	Corn	Feb. to June	18-20
Oats	April to May	11-15	Wheat (S)	Mar. 20 to Apr. 20	16-18	Wheat (S)	April 1 to April 20	16-20	Wheat (W)	Sept. 20 to Oct. 20	36-40
*Soybeans	May 15 to June 1		Oats	March to May	16-17	Oats	April 1 to May 1	12-14	Oats	Feb., May, Sept.	17
Barley	April to June 20	10-15	*Soybeans	May 15 to June 1		*Soybeans	May 10 to June 5		*Soybeans	May 1 to June 10	
Rye	April to May, Sept.	40	Barley	March to May	13-16	Barley	Fall or Spring	11-13	Barley	April to May	17
Buckwheat	June 1 to June 20	10-15	Rye	Sept. 1 to Oct. 1	40-42	Rye	Sept. 1 to Sept. 30	35-40	Rye	Sept. to Oct.	43
Wh. Beans	May to June	8-14	Buckwheat	June to July	8-10	Buckwheat	June	10-12	Wh. Beans	March to May	7-8
Potatoes	April 15 to May 1	12-20	Wh. Beans	May to June	13-14	Wh. Beans	May 20 to June 10	12	Cabbage	Oct., Mar. to May	14
Turnips	July 1 to Aug. 3	10	Potatoes	March to May	14-22	Potatoes	Mar. 15 to June 1	10-20	Watermelon	Mar. 1 to May 10	16-20
Tomatoes	May 10 to June 1	14-20	S. Potatoes	May to June	10-15	Turnips	July 25 to Aug. 30	10-16	Onions	Feb. 1 to Apr. 10	16-24
Tobacco	Seed bed April	9-12	Cabbage	March to July	8-15	Tomatoes	April 1 to May 25	14-20	Potatoes	Jan., Feb., to Apr.	11-15
Hay	. . . .		Turnips	July	10-12	Flax	May 15 to May 15	15-20	S. Potatoes	May to June	12-15
			Tomatoes	April 20 to May 20	14-20	Tobacco	Seed bed March	15-18	Pumpkins	April to May 1	17-20
			Flax	May	8-10	Hay	April to May		Tomatoes	Jan. to Apr.	14-20
			Tobacco	Seed bed March	15-20				Turnips	Feb., Apr., Aug.	8-12
			Hay, Tim'y	Aug., to Oct.					Tobacco	Seed bar March	18-20
			Hay, Clover	Feb. to April					Cow Peas	May 1 to July 15	6-8

W-Indicates Winter
S-Indicates Spring
*Maturity period for Soybeans is undetermined. Soybeans planted as late as July 1 will mature.

WHEAT HARVEST TIME OF THE WORLD
The following shows the month of the wheat harvest in the wheat growing sections of the world:

January	New Zealand and Chile
February and March	East India, Upper Egypt
April	Algeria, Central Asia, China, Japan, Morocco and Texas
June	Turkey, Greece, Italy, Spain, Portugal, South of France, California, Louisiana, Mississippi, Alabama, Georgia, Carolinas, Tennessee, Virginia, Kentucky, Kansas, Arkansas Utah, Missouri and Oklahoma
July	Roumania, Bulgaria, Austria, Hungary, Czechoslovakia, South of Russia, Germany, Switzerland, France, South of England, Oregon, Nebraska, Minnesota, Wisconsin, Colorado, Washington, Iowa, Illinois, Indiana, Michigan, Ohio, New York, New England, Montana and Ontario, Canada.
August	Belgium, Holland, Great Britain, Denmark, Poland, Quebec, Western Canada, Columbia, North and South Dakota.
September and October . .	Scotland, Sweden, Norway and North of Russia.
November	Peru, South Africa and Australia.
December	Burma and Argentina

CORN HARVEST TIME OF THE WORLD

January	New South Wales			
March and April	Argentina	September and October	. .	Europe
April and May	South Africa	October	.	United States

Source: Chicago Board of Trade.

SOYBEAN HARVEST TIME OF THE WORLD

April and May	Brazil	August thru October . . .	Russia
July thru September . .	Indonesia	October	United States
Sept. and October. . .	China (PRC)	October and November . .	Canada

may hold a position exceeding 3 million bushels. Position limits do not apply to bona fide hedgers as defined by CFTC regulations.

The *Statistical Annual* of the Chicago Board of Trade and the Commodity Research Bureau's *Commodity Yearbook* both give full layouts on the supply and demand of and for wheat throughout the world, along with trading statistics and other vital data. (See Figure 14–4.) (These publications cover all the commodities and are essential reference tools for the trader.) The Department of Agriculture issues its *Crop Production Report* regularly, including a "Prospective Planting Report" and other bulletins which keep the trader up to date with statistics. The U.S.D.A. also periodically issues the *Wheat Situation Report,* probably the most useful publication available to the trader. This and other publications are available free to anyone who enrolls on the automated mailing list. The Agriculture Department's *Grain Market News* comes out weekly, giving the trader a variety of solid facts and reliable estimates concerning every facet of the wheat trade. U.S.D.A. reports and bulletins are instantly disseminated in digest form by the news services subscribed to by most brokers and many traders. Of great interest is the Department's *Quarterly Stocks of Grains in All Positions,* outlining the stocks of wheat and other grains throughout the United States by size, location, and ownership. This is one of the most important reports issued by the govern-

FIGURE 14–4

CHICAGO BOARD OF TRADE
Highest/Lowest Recorded Cash
No. 2 Winter Wheat
$ per Bu.

Year	Highest	Month Occurred	Lowest	Month Occured
1978	$3.86	November	$2.28-1/4	March
1977	2.97-1/4	November	2.01-3/4	August
1976	3.97-3/4	February	2.40-3/4	November
1975	4.52-3/4	January	2.90-1/2	July
1974	9.91-1/2	February	3.30-1/2	May
1973	6.81-1/2	December	2.09-1/4	March
1972	2.70	December	1.40	June
1971	1.82	December	1.40	September
1970	1.83n	November	1.35	May
1969	1.34	September	1.25-1/4	August
1968	1.60-1/2	February	1.13-1/2	September
1967	1.83-1/2	March	1.45-1/4	November
1966	2.03	July	1.61-1/4	April
1965	1.69	November	1.45	July
1964	2.25-1/2	January	1.43-3/4	July
1963	2.33-1/4	November	1.79	July
1962	2.25-1/4	July	2.02-3/4	February
1961	2.15-1/2	January	1.91	July
1960	2.26	March	1.83-3/4	July
1959	2.18-1/2	September	1.77-1/2	June
1958	2.32-1/4	March	1.79-3/4	September
1957	2.46	January	2.06-3/4	June
1956	2.45-3/4	December	1.95	June
1955	2.39-1/2	January	1.83-3/4	August
1954	2.40	March	1.83	June
1953	2.32-1/4	March	1.73	July
1952	2.56-1/4	January	2.06-1/2	July
1951	2.67-1/4	December	2.19-1/4	July
1950	2.44	December	2.06	August
1949	2.42	April	1.79	August
1948	3.18-1/2	January	2.12-3/4	August
1947	3.21-1/2	November	2.13-1/2	January
1946	2.39	December	1.79	January
1945	1.80-1/2	November	1.60-1/2	August
1944	1.73-1/2	January	1.53	July
1943	1.74-3/4	December	1.43-1/2	January
1942	1.42-3/4	December	1.07	February
1941	1.28-1/4	December	.85	February
1940	1.16	April	.69-3/4	August
1939	1.10	September	.59	July
1938	1.16	February	.59-1/2	August
1937	1.51	April	.92	November
1936	1.44-3/4	December	.90-1/2	June
1935	1.31	October	.81	July
1934	1.16-1/4	December	.75-1/2	April
1933	1.17-3/4	July	.45	January
1932	.70-1/2	January	.44-1/2	December
1931	.84-1/2	May	.45	August
1930	1.29	January	.71-3/4	November
1929	1.48	February	.98	May
1928	2.15	April	1.06-1/2	August
1927	1.58	May	1.21-3/4	October
1926	1.94	January	1.30	September
1925	2.20-1/2	January	1.35-1/4	April
1924	1.91	December	1.02	March
1923	1.38	March	.96-1/2	July
1922	1.73	May	1.00	August and September
1921	2.06-3/4	January	1.00-1/2	November
1920	3.50	January	1.58	November
1919	3.50	December	2.21	August
1918	2.42	December	2.17	January, February, March, April, May
1917	3.45	May	1.51-1/2	February
1916	2.02	October	.98-1/4	June
1915	1.68	February	.98	August
1914	1.33	September	.77-3/4	July
1913	1.15-3/8	January	.80-3/4	October
1912	1.22	April and May	.85	November and December
1911	1.17	October	.83-1/4	April
1910	1.29-1/2	July	.89-1/2	November
1909	1.60	June	.99-1/4	August
1908	1.11	May	.84-1/2	July
1907	1.22	October	.71	January
1906	.94-3/4	May	.69-1/8	August and September
1905	1.24	February	.77-7/8	August
1904	1.22	September, October and December	.81-1/4	January
1903	.93	September	.70-1/4	March
1902	.95	September	.67-1/2	October
1901	.79-1/2	December	.63-1/8	July
1900	.87-1/2	June	.61-1/2	January
1899	.79-1/2	May	.64	December
1898	1.85	May	.62	October
1897	1.06	December	.66-1/2	April
1896	.94-3/8	November	.53	August
1895	.81-1/2	May	.48-7/8	January
1894	.63-3/4	April	.50-3/8	July
1893	.85	April	.54-3/4	July
1892	.91-3/4	February	.69-1/4	October

Source: Chicago Board of Trade.

ment and often will set the stage for a rapid price advance or decline. It is issued as of the 1st of January, April, July, and October and is sent out about the 20th–25th of the month.

All of these reports rely almost exclusively on statistical data viewed from different perspectives, although the *Situation* report also includes conclusions and forecasts in paragraph form. The tables can be incomprehensible, or simply a waste of time, unless the trader is looking for specific information. Such reports are best used as reference material after the trader has decided what facts he needs to know. Private newsletters and reports most often merely repeat the U.S.D.A.'s findings, or try to predict them, adding their own advice along the way—which the trader ought to take with great caution.

Supply consists of carry over from year to year and of current production. United States imports of wheat (mainly for seed and special purposes) are minimal. A substantial portion of the carry over is controlled by the government's Commodity Credit Corporation, the agency that administers price support programs through loans and crop purchases. The CCC acts to keep carry over stocks out of the market as part of its price support actions. The price per bushel paid by the CCC in its loan program sets the ordinary price floor and ceiling for the crop (though cash prices have been known to violate these levels). Prices will usually fluctuate in a range around the support price, making it a key reference point for the trader. Knowing where all the supplies that might possibly come into the market are, and how many bushels they add up to, is still only knowing part of the story. The fundamentalist needs to know not only prices and amounts but location and ownership

as well. Where are these bushels? Who owns them? How easily and how fast can they reach which markets? Short-run price changes may depend on the answers to these questions.

Wheat demand is far harder to predict and statistically compute than wheat supply. The government may know fairly accurately how many acres have been planted, what the yield average is, etc., but we can only know vaguely how many bushels of wheat in processed forms the average consumer will buy. Commercial exports, as a form of demand, are on the other hand a central focus for wheat analysts, as are exports under government food programs. As long as the price of wheat exported by other producer nations is lower than the government support price here at home, wheat exports will be very sensitive to crop surpluses abroad.

Wheat normally makes its seasonal price low during the month of June or July, dipping during harvest and rallying over the ensuing months. It is said that a wealthy trader once left his son all he needed to make a fortune: "Buy wheat July 1st and sell wheat December 1st." While this does not work every year, it is in conformity with the general price trend. Speculators will tend to go long after harvest as dealers sell short on hedges, with both gradually reversing and liquidating toward winter. This trading pattern itself can be a counterpressure to the seasonal price trend it is based upon.

A wheat future is characterized by wide swings in the normal range of an active market. A rise of 6 cents followed by a drop of 8 cents and another rise of 5 cents can occur as a regular pattern. Because of this wide swinging pattern, wheat is one of the more difficult of the commodity markets to trade, making harder the handling of a position through the use of stops and requiring substantial backup for the trader who wishes to ride out the storm.

CORN

Corn is the single largest crop harvested in the United States. Successive bumper crops pushed totals from 4.6 billion bushels in 1969 to over 7 billion bushels in 1979. (See Figures 14–5 and 14–6.) The United States grows about 47 percent of the world's corn and maize supplies, or almost as much as all other nations combined. World production has climbed steadily in recent years, with Brazil, China, and the European nations leading the way. United States exports approached the 2 billion bushel level, the U.S.S.R. and Japan being primary customers. Because corn is the major ingredient in the world's evolving livestock feed grain complex, the expanding role of meat in the diets of many developing nations promises to influence the corn trade throughout the foreseeable future.

FIGURE 14–5
World Production of Corn or Maize   In Millions of Metric Tons

Crop Year	United States	Argentina	Brazil	Mexico	South Africa	France	China	India	Italy	Bulgaria	Hungary	Yugoslavia	Romania	Indonesia	U.S.S.R.	World Total
1966–7	105.9	8.0	12.8	8.2	9.6	4.3	21.7	4.9	3.5	2.2	3.9	8.0	8.0	3.7	6.8	239.4
1967–8	123.5	6.6	12.8	8.0	5.2	4.2	25.5	6.3	3.9	2.0	3.5	7.2	6.9	2.4	8.0	253.5
1968–9	113.0	6.9	12.7	8.5	5.0	5.4	23.5	5.7	4.0	1.8	3.8	6.8	7.1	3.1	7.4	243.3
1969–0	119.1	9.4	14.2	6.5	6.2	5.7	24.3	5.7	4.5	2.4	4.8	7.8	7.7	2.3	10.1	260.0
1970–1	105.5	9.9	13.5	8.7	8.6	7.6	26.4	7.5	4.8	2.4	4.0	6.9	6.5	2.9	7.8	255.1
1971–2	143.3	5.9	12.9	9.1	9.4	8.8	25.3	5.1	4.5	2.5	4.7	7.4	7.9	2.6	8.6	292.1
1972–3	141.6	9.0	13.8	8.1	4.2	8.2	22.0	6.2	4.8	2.9	5.5	7.9	9.5	2.0	9.8	286.3
1973–4	143.4	9.9	15.0	9.0	11.1	10.7	28.0	5.8	5.1	2.6	5.9	8.3	7.4	2.9	13.2	314.7
1974–5	118.5	7.7	16.4	7.8	9.1	8.7	30.7	5.6	5.0	1.6	6.2	8.0	7.4	3.0	12.1	286.5
1975–6	147.3	5.9	17.9	9.2	7.3	8.2	32.0	7.0	5.3	3.0	7.1	9.4	9.2	2.6	7.3	321.6
1976–7[1]	157.9	8.8	18.8	9.6	9.6	5.5	31.4	6.3	5.3	3.0	5.2	9.1	11.6	2.6	10.1	336.3
1977–8[2]	161.7	7.8	18.0	9.7	9.5	8.1	31.4	6.0	6.3	3.0	6.3	10.2	9.6	2.3	9.0	341.6
1978–9																

[1] **Preliminary.**   [2] **Estimated.**   *Source: Foreign Agricultural Service, U.S.D.A.*

Distribution of Corn in the United States   In Millions of Bushels

Year Beg. Oct.	Wet Corn Milling (Grind)	Corn Meal[4]	Corn Flour Etc.	Hominy Grits (Food)	Breakfast Foods[3]	Distilled Liquors	Fermented Malt Liquors	Total Shipments	Seed	Livestock Feed[5]	Exports (Incl. Grain Equiv. of Pdt's.)	Total Utilization	Domestic Disappearance
1969–70	216	28	6	19	23	31	43	366	13	3,795	612	4,801	4,189
1970–1	242	24	8	17	23	24	45	383	17	3,581	517	4,494	3,977
1971–2	246	21	10	14	24	25	45	385	15	3,997	796	5,183	4,387
1972–3	284	20	12	13	24	29	45	427	16	4,304	1,258	5,991	4,733
1973–4	295	19	14	13	25	33	47	446	18	4,205	1,243	5,896	4,653
1974–5	315	18	13	10	24	16	49	445	18	3,226	1,149	4,826	3,677
1975–6	343	18	15	11	24	21	50	482	20	3,592	1,711	5,793	4,082
1976–7[1]	362	17	17	10	25	21	53	505	20	3,587	1,684	5,784	4,100
1977–8[1]	380	17	18	10	25	22	57	529	18	3,709	1,948	6,208	4,260
1978–9[2]									18	4,000	1,950	6,525	4,575

[1] Preliminary.   [2] Estimate.   [3] Assumes sizeable quantities of corn flour are purchased by breakfast food mfg. from the dry milling industry.   [4] Regular & degermed.   [5] Feed & waste (residual, mostly feed).   *Source: Commodity Economics Division, U.S.D.A.*

Source: Commodity Research Bureau, Inc.

FIGURE 14–6

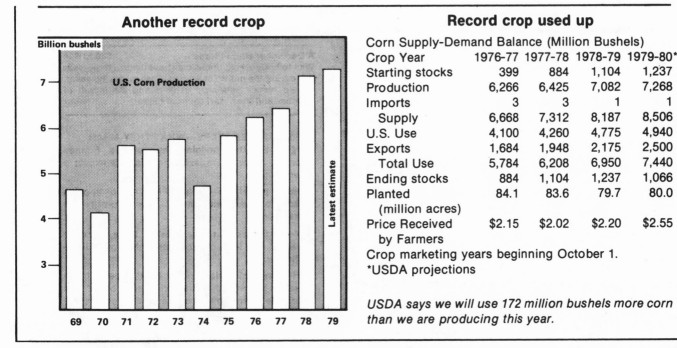

Another record crop

Billion bushels

U.S. Corn Production

Latest estimate

69 70 71 72 73 74 75 76 77 78 79

Record crop used up

Corn Supply-Demand Balance (Million Bushels)

Crop Year	1976-77	1977-78	1978-79	1979-80*
Starting stocks	399	884	1,104	1,237
Production	6,266	6,425	7,082	7,268
Imports	3	3	1	1
Supply	6,668	7,312	8,187	8,506
U.S. Use	4,100	4,260	4,775	4,940
Exports	1,684	1,948	2,175	2,500
Total Use	5,784	6,208	6,950	7,440
Ending stocks	884	1,104	1,237	1,066
Planted (million acres)	84.1	83.6	79.7	80.0
Price Received by Farmers	$2.15	$2.02	$2.20	$2.55

Crop marketing years beginning October 1.
*USDA projections

USDA says we will use 172 million bushels more corn than we are producing this year.

Source: Farm Futures.

Surplus inventories and storage of corn along the waterways around Chicago inspired the first heavy volume in forward contracts and futures at Chicago in the 1840s. Today, 99 percent of all corn futures trade on the floor of the Chicago Board of Trade. Trading volume leaped from 8 million bushels in 1969 to 43 million bushels in 1979, ranking corn third in yearly volume statistics. The huge open interest in corn reflects heavy industry hedging, running about 55 percent or more of positions held. The stability and liquidity of such a market and margins frequently half that required for wheat or soybeans keep speculator interest high. (See Figure 14–7.)

The regulation 5,000 bushel No. 2 yellow corn contract at Chicago has trading months of March, May, July, September, and December. The crop year begins near 1 October. The minimum price fluctuation is ¼ cent per bushel, each tick equaling $12.50 per contract. The trading range from the low to the high is a maximum of 20 cents, with the market allowed to fluctuate from 10 cents higher to 10 cents lower than the previous day's closing price. CFTC reporting levels and position limits for corn are the same as those given for wheat (and for soybeans).

The most significant publication relating to corn is the *Feed Situation* report issued by the Department of Agriculture, published in February, April, August, May, and November. The report publishes authoritative corn statistics for past years and estimates of crops and yields in upcoming seasons. For the farmer and trader are articles on government loan and price support policies. Current and projected supply/demand statistics and foreign trade figures are also featured. The importance of this bulletin is a reminder

FIGURE 14–7

that corn and its trade must be analyzed within the total perspective of the feed grain complex, including statistics for other grains and trends in use and consumption.

Grain Market News, mentioned in connection with the wheat trade, is also valuable for following the corn market. Likewise, the *Crop Production Reports* issued on the tenth of each month are vital

indicators in that they set the existing supply of corn for the current crop year. As in the case of the corn blight of 1970, a production report which first indicated a damaged crop can set the tone of the market of the next two years. This report is followed very closely by the trade when following corn statistics. In a strongly hedged market like corn, traders may be inclined to consult the CFTC's *Commit-*

ment of Traders data in order to size up their own positions as compared to those of the industry and the professionals.

In addition to corn, oats and barley constitute important portions of the feed grain supplies. (See Figure 14–8.) When

FIGURE 14–8

SUPPLY AND DISPOSITION
Feed Grains

Supply					Disposition				
					Domestic Use				
Marketing Year 1/	Beginning Stocks	Production	Imports	Total	Feed	Food, Industry, and Seed	Total Domestic	Exports	Total Use
				Million Bushels					
CORN									
1978-79 2/	1,104	7,081	1	8,187	4,000	575	4,575	1,950	6,525
1977-78 3/	884	6,426	2	7,312	3,709	551	4,260	1,948	6,208
1976-77 3/	399	6,266	2	6,668	3,587	493	4,100	1,684	5,784
1975-76	361	5,829	2	6,192	3,592	490	4,082	1,711	5,793
1974-75	484	4,701	2	5,187	3,226	451	3,677	1,149	4,826
1973-74	708	5,671	1	6,380	4,205	448	4,653	1,243	5,896
1972-73	1,126	5,573	1	6,700	4,310	423	4,733	1,258	5,991
1971-72	667	5,641	1	6,309	3,978	409	4,387	796	5,183
1970-71	1,005	4,152	4	5,161	3,581	396	3,977	517	4,494
1969-70	1,118	4,687	1	5,806	3,796	393	4,189	612	4,801
GRAIN SORGHUM									
1978-79 2/	191	748	—	939	525	7	532	220	752
1977-78 3/	91	793	—	884	473	7	480	214	693
1976-77 3/	51	719	—	771	428	6	434	246	679
1975-76	35	753	—	788	502	6	508	229	737
1974-75	61	623	—	684	431	6	437	212	649
1973-74	73	923	—	996	694	7	701	234	935
1972-73	142	809	—	951	660	6	666	212	878
1971-72	90	876	—	966	692	9	701	123	824
1970-71	244	684	—	928	684	10	694	144	838
1969-70	287	730	—	1,107	638	9	647	126	773
OATS									
1978-79 2/	311	602	1	913	510	85	595	10	605
1977-78 3/	165	751	2	918	511	85	596	11	608
1976-77 3/	205	546	2	753	490	88	579	10	588
1975-76	223	642	1	866	562	85	647	14	661
1974-75	307	601	4/	908	584	82	666	19	685
1973-74	463	659	4/	1,123	674	85	759	57	816
1972-73	597	692	3	1,292	722	90	812	19	831
1971-72	571	881	3	1,455	742	95	837	21	858
1970-71	548	917	1	1,466	779	97	876	19	895
1969-70	424	966	2	1,392	735	104	839	5	844
BARLEY									
1978-79 2/	172	447	10	629	200	162	362	30	392
1977-78 3/	126	420	10	555	158	168	326	57	383
1976-77 3/	128	373	10	511	158	161	319	66	386
1975-76	92	374	16	482	182	148	330	24	354
1974-75	146	299	20	465	180	151	331	42	373
1973-74	192	417	9	618	232	147	379	93	472
1972-73	208	423	17	648	244	142	386	70	456
1971-72	184	464	12	660	270	141	411	41	452
1970-71	269	416	10	695	289	138	427	84	511
1969-70	225	427	13	665	250	136	386	10	396
TOTAL FEED GRAINS									
1978-79 2/	1,778	8,878	12	10,668	5,235	829	6,064	2,210	8,274
1977-78	1,266	8,390	12	9,669	4,851	811	5,662	2,230	7,892
1976-77	783	7,904	14	8,703	4,663	748	5,432	2,006	7,437
1975-76	711	7,598	19	8,328	4,838	729	5,567	1,978	7,545
1974-75	998	6,224	22	7,244	4,421	690	5,111	1,422	6,533
1973-74	1,436	7,670	10	9,117	5,805	687	6,492	1,697	8,119
1972-73	2,073	7,497	21	9,591	5,936	661	6,597	1,559	8,156
1971-72	1,512	7,862	16	9,390	5,682	654	6,336	981	7,317
1970-71	2,066	6,169	15	8,250	5,333	641	5,974	764	6,738
1969-70	2,054	6,810	16	8,880	5,419	642	6,061	753	6,814

1/October-September for corn and grain sorghum; June-May for Oats and Barley.
2/Chances are about 2 out of 3 the final outcome would fall within the ranges.
3/Preliminary.
4/Less than 500,000 bushels.
Source: U.S.D.A. Economic Research Service-Feed Situation.

Source: Chicago Board of Trade.

prices of corn are high, wheat may also become a substitute for feed corn, being a more nutritious though more expensive feed for animals. When the trader studies the supply of corn in the United States, he must also study the supply of barley and oats to enable him to assess the total feed grain situation without depending too heavily on the corn picture. Planting and production estimates must also take account of prices for crops that may compete with the feed grains for certain kinds of acreage. Escalating soybean prices could divert significant acres from corn if the return appears profitable.

Much of the corn grown by farmers throughout the United States never leaves the farm. It goes to the feeding of animals raised on the farm and after harvest it is chopped up and stored away in silos. Proportionately small amounts of processed corn are sold for a variety of food and industrial product uses. Dry processed corn goes into corn meal, grits, and cereals. Wet processed corn is used for corn sugar, corn oil, and corn syrup. Some corn is sold for brewing and some to make starch.

However, about 80 percent of United States corn is fed to hogs, beef and dairy cattle, poultry, sheep, and other livestock. Thus, many of the statistics relating to these markets are also of interest to the corn trader. Available from the Department of Agriculture and from most brokers subscribing to commodity news services are livestock-feed grain price ratios, the hog-corn ratio being most often quoted. This ratio is the number of bushels of corn equivalent in price to the value of a hundred pounds of live hogs. (See Figure 14–9.) At a ratio of 22.5, corn is cheaper at harvest in October than at 14.9

in September. If the price of hogs is relatively high in comparison to corn prices, the farmers will feed more of the cheap corn to their hogs rather than sell the corn on the open market. The price of corn bears directly on the price and supply of pork, beef, and broilers. The hog-feed, cattle-feed, and broiler-feed ratios are closely watched by farmers who must decide whether hog prices are high enough to justify heavy feeding or whether the return does not make the effort worthwhile. Hog ratios are taken as the leading indicator because hog inventories may be raised and lowered more quickly than those for other livestock, thus reflecting feed grain changes faster.

An often decisive factor in analyzing the corn market is government price support and loan activity. By agreeing to loan farmers a certain price for their corn, provided a portion of acreage is diverted, the government places an artificial floor below which the cash and futures market normally will not dip. Since the farmer is able to default on his loans with no penalty, handing over his crop and effectively "selling" it to the government, the Agriculture Department ends up with large supplies of corn. These are owned by the Commodity Credit Corporation which can sell them on the open market when prices reach a certain level. The CCC and affiliated U.S.D.A. programs have been the natural instruments used when the federal government has wished to regulate or suspend grain exports. CCC sales act as a ceiling above which the market normally will not advance. As in most other walks of modern life, government action must be analyzed as a fundamental factor in the corn trade.

About 70 percent of commercial corn

FIGURE 14–9

HOG – CORN PRICE RATIOS [1]
Monthly Average
Omaha

Crop Year	Oct.	Nov.	Dec.	Jan.	Feb.	Mar.	Apr.	May	June	July	Aug.	Sept.	Avg.
1978[2]	25.5	23.6	23.4	—	—	—	—	—	—	—	—	—	—
1977	22.8	20.0	21.4	22.6	24.0	22.1	20.4	20.9	20.6	21.9	24.5	25.1	22.2
1976	13.7	14.4	16.3	16.4	16.8	15.9	16.0	18.8	20.7	23.8	26.4	24.8	18.7
1975	21.2	19.4	18.5	18.6	18.6	17.7	18.3	17.7	17.6	16.8	16.2	15.1	18.0
1974	10.6	11.0	11.8	12.6	14.1	14.3	14.1	16.4	17.9	19.4	18.6	20.7	15.1
1973	17.8	16.9	15.7	14.8	13.4	12.5	12.1	10.2	10.0	11.2	10.5	10.3	13.0
1972	21.8	20.6	20.5	21.5	23.3	25.4	23.4	19.5	17.1	20.0	20.8	18.4	21.0
1971	17.2	16.7	16.6	19.7	20.6	19.0	18.2	19.7	21.5	22.8	23.5	22.6	19.8
1970	13.3	11.7	10.6	11.0	13.2	11.9	11.3	11.8	12.2	13.9	15.1	16.3	12.7
1969	22.5	22.8	23.6	23.1	22.9	22.4	20.0	19.3	18.3	19.6	15.8	14.9	20.4

[1]No. bushels of corn equal in value to 100 lbs. of Hog Liveweight.   [2]Preliminary.
Source: U.S.D.A. Economic Research Service – Feed Situation

STEER – CORN PRICE RATIOS [1]
Monthly Average
Omaha

Crop Year	Oct.	Nov.	Dec.	Jan.	Feb.	Mar.	Apr.	May	June	July	Aug.	Sept.	Avg.
1978[2]	26.8	26.4	26.6	—	—	—	—	—	—	—	—	—	—
1977[2]	23.6	20.7	21.1	21.6	22.2	22.7	23.3	24.5	23.8	25.6	26.5	27.8	23.6
1976	16.1	18.0	17.4	16.1	16.0	15.9	17.5	19.0	19.2	21.5	24.2	24.2	18.8
1975	17.4	17.7	17.6	16.0	14.9	13.8	16.6	14.8	14.2	13.4	13.8	14.3	15.4
1974	10.9	10.9	11.1	11.8	12.5	13.1	15.0	17.6	18.2	17.2	15.0	16.6	14.2
1973	17.9	16.7	15.8	17.4	15.7	15.5	16.7	16.1	14.2	13.7	13.1	12.0	15.4
1972	27.3	25.1	24.7	27.1	28.1	30.6	29.8	24.9	20.8	20.5	19.5	19.0	24.8
1971	28.3	29.0	27.6	28.5	29.5	28.6	27.6	28.1	30.8	31.0	29.5	27.1	28.8
1970	21.2	20.3	18.8	19.9	22.0	22.1	22.7	22.7	21.9	23.0	26.7	28.3	22.5
1969	23.6	23.4	23.9	23.6	24.4	26.0	25.2	23.8	24.1	24.3	22.1	20.9	23.8

[1]Based on price of beef steers 900-1,000 lbs. choice instead of average grade all steers previously published.   [2]Preliminary.
Source: U.S.D.A. Economic Research Service – Feed Situation

BROILER – FEED PRICE RATIOS [1]
Monthly Average
U.S.

Crop Year	Oct.	Nov.	Dec.	Jan.	Feb.	Mar.	Apr.	May	June	July	Aug.	Sept.	Avg.
1978[2]	2.9	2.8	2.9	—	—	—	—	—	—	—	—	—	—
1977[2]	3.0	2.6	2.5	2.8	3.0	3.0	3.3	3.2	3.5	3.9	3.2	3.2	3.1
1976	2.4	2.3	2.2	2.5	2.7	2.7	2.6	2.6	2.7	3.0	2.9	3.1	2.6
1975	3.5	3.4	3.0	3.1	3.2	3.0	3.0	3.1	2.8	2.8	2.7	2.6	3.0
1974	2.5	2.6	2.4	2.7	2.9	2.9	2.8	3.1	3.4	3.7	3.6	3.6	3.0
1973	2.9	2.5	2.3	2.5	2.8	2.7	2.7	2.7	2.5	2.6	2.3	2.6	2.6
1972	2.9	2.7	2.5	2.9	3.0	3.5	3.9	3.3	2.9	3.2	4.0	3.5	3.2
1971	2.8	2.7	2.5	2.8	3.1	3.1	2.7	2.8	3.0	3.3	3.0	3.2	2.9
1970	2.6	2.6	2.4	2.6	2.8	2.7	2.7	2.9	3.0	3.2	2.9	3.0	2.7
1969	3.3	3.2	3.0	3.2	3.0	3.1	2.9	3.0	2.9	2.9	2.8	2.8	3.0

[1]Number of lbs. of broiler grower feed equal in value to one lb. broiler weight.   [2]Preliminary.
Source: U.S.D.A. Economic Research Service – Feed Situation.

Source: Chicago Board of Trade.

is grown in the Corn Belt—Iowa, Illinois, Minnesota, Indiana, Nebraska, Ohio, Missouri, and South Dakota. As the corn is harvested in the Midwest and moves east, early season prices in Chicago will be high and the premium over country will normally decrease as the season wanes. Harvested during the months of September and October, it makes a harvest low about this time. The astute trader is reluctant to take a long position prior to harvest for fear of a price decline as corn supplies increase in the fall. The corn futures market is so large that it often has an open interest two or three times that of the wheat or soybean markets. In an average year corn price swings are normally more moderate than in wheat and thus are easier to trade.

SOYBEANS, SOYBEAN MEAL, AND SOYBEAN OIL

In less than forty years, the once lowly soybean transformed the face of American agriculture. An unimportant, ignored crop before World War II, the soybean and its products were "discovered" in subsequent years and justly celebrated as cheap and easy sources of protein, fats, and oil. Simple to farm, inexpensive to process into basic foodstuffs, in great demand worldwide, the soybean began its meteoric rise in the 1960s. The price of soybeans soon tripled, responding to the Russian wheat sale, the devaluation of the dollar, investment interest from Japan and other importers, and the new recognition of futures trading here at home. (See Figure 14–10.) In many minds, soybeans became the instantly recognized symbol of futures trading.

Soybeans are the number one cash crop grown in the United States. U.S.D.A. crop estimate for 1979–1980 was 2.2 billion bushels, twice the figure for 1967. Soybean

FIGURE 14–10
CHICAGO BOARD OF TRADE
Highest/Lowest Recorded Cash Price
No. 1 Yellow Soybeans
$ per Bu.

Year	Highest	Month Occurred	Lowest	Month Occurred
1978	$7.34-1/2	May	$5.43-1/2	February
1977	10.45	April	4.82-1/2	October
1976	7.27-1/2	July	4.36-3/4	January
1975	7.05-1/2	January	4.04-1/4	December
1974	9.31	October	5.19-1/2	May
1973	12.27	June	4.22	January
1972	4.31-1/2	December	3.01-1/4	January
1971	3.50	July	2.87-1/4	April
1970	3.06-1/4	October	2.48	January
1969	2.73-1/2	August	2.27-1/2	September & December
1968	2.75-1/2	May	2.38-1/4	October
1967	2.99-1/2	January	2.47-3/4	November
1966	3.78	July	2.63-1/2	January
1965	3.10	April	2.37-1/2	October
1964	2.96-1/2	December	2.51	June & July
1963	2.94	November	2.49-3/4	January
1962	2.59	September	2.33-1/4	October
1961	3.09	May	2.32-3/4	October
1960	2.34	December	1.96-1/2	November
1959	2.36	May	2.05	December
1958	2.29-1/2	January	2.02	October
1957	2.51-1/2	January	2.16-1/4	December
1956	3.07	June	2.20-3/4	September
1955	2.87-1/2	January	2.19	October
1954	4.00	July	2.61-1/2	November
1953	3.08-1/4	April	2.47-1/2	October
1952	3.30	July	2.72	October
1951	3.36	February	2.65-1/2	September
1950	3.26-1/2	July	2.15	October
1949	3.20	August	2.12	October & November
1948	4.43	January	2.35-1/4	October
1947	4.07	November	2.92	September
1946	3.51	October	2.22	February

Source: Chicago Board of Trade.

exports bring in more revenue than any other United States crop ($6.9 billion in 1978 compared to $5.9 billion for feed grains and $4.6 billion for wheat). The United States' share of total world soybean production has consistently exceeded 60 percent, although Brazil, Argentina, and China play increasingly important roles in the supply picture. United States exports for 1980 are projected at over 800 million bushels, or more than triple the figure for 1967. About 40 percent to 50 percent of the crop is exported, mostly in the form of meal and oil to Europe, Japan, and other advanced, developed nations. (See Figure 14–11.)

Ninety-nine percent of soybean futures contracts are traded at the Chicago Board

FIGURE 14–11

World Production of Soybeans   In Thousands of Metric Tons

Year of Harvest*	Argentina	Brazil	Canada	China[2]	Colombia	Indonesia	Japan	Korea, South	Mexico	Romania	Taiwan	Thailand	United States	U.S.S.R.	World Total
1967	20	716	220	6,800	80	416	190	201	121	41	75	53	25,269	543	36,543
1968	22	654	246	6,950	87	420	168	245	270	47	73	45	26,575	528	39,740
1969	32	1,057	209	6,480	100	389	136	229	300	51	67	61	30,127	434	40,516
1970	27	1,509	283	6,200	95	498	126	232	240	91	65	70	30,839	603	41,811
1971	59	2,077	280	6,900	106	475	122	222	250	165	61	67	30,675	535	43,556
1972	78	3,666	375	6,500	122	516	127	224	375	186	60	80	34,581	258	47,646
1973	496	7,876	397	10,000	114	541	118	246	510	244	61	115	42,117	424	63,912
1974	485	9,892	301	9,500	114	589	133	319	420	298	67	114	33,102	360	56,513
1975	695	10,810	367	10,000	169	590	126	311	625	213	62	121	42,113	780	67,914
1976	1,400	12,200	250	9,000	75	522	110	295	280	213	53	105	35,042	480	61,171
1977[1]	2,600	9,950	517	9,500	109	480	111	319	470	190	52	135	47,947	545	74,095
1978[3]	3,200	13,500	441	10,000	126	500	140	351	250	200	60	135	49,271	650	80,352
1979															

[1] Preliminary.   [2] Mainland.   [3] Projected.   * Split year includes Northern Hemisphere crops harvested in the late months of the first year shown combined with Southern Hemisphere crops harvested in the early months of the following year.
Source: Foreign Agricultural Service, U.S.D.A.

Salient Statistics of Soybeans in the United States

Crop Year	Planted Alone (In Thousands of Acres)	Acreage Harvested (In Thousands of Acres)	Yield Per Acre (Bushels)	Farm Price ($ Bu.)	Farm Value (Million Dollars)	Pounds Per Bushel Crushed — Yield of Oil	Pounds Per Bushel Crushed — Yield of Meal	U.S. Exports — Grand Total	Bel.-Luxem.	Denmark	Canada	W. Germany	Japan	Netherlands	Taiwan	U.S.S.R.
1966–7	37,294	36,546	25.4	2.75	2,554	10.6	47.7	261.6	8.8	14.8	24.2	32.7	60.7	36.0	11.0	—
1967–8	40,819	39,805	24.5	2.49	2,434	10.6	47.4	266.6	8.7	15.5	21.7	32.0	73.7	36.8	10.6	—
1968–9	42,265	41,391	26.7	2.43	2,689	10.61	47.43	286.8	10.2	11.8	37.9	30.5	69.9	42.7	16.6	—
1969–0	42,534	41,337	27.4	2.35	2,664	10.66	47.36	432.6	16.1	18.4	70.0	41.8	101.4	57.4	21.2	—
1970–1	43,802	42,249	26.7	2.85	3,215	10.83	47.39	433.8	13.2	21.4	42.2	53.0	102.8	57.9	19.6	—
1971–2	43,472	42,705	27.5	3.03	3,560	10.98	47.43	416.8	5.7	16.2	31.3	52.0	107.4	64.1	23.9	0
1972–3	46,885	45,683	27.8	4.37	5,551	10.59	47.04	479.4	8.2	17.4	22.1	54.7	121.0	84.3	19.6	31.5
1973–4	56,675	55,667	27.8	5.68	8,787	10.77	47.17	539.1	13.2	12.5	37.9	72.9	98.8	101.1	20.5	.7
1974–5	53,507	51,341	23.7	6.64	8,070	10.51	47.49	520.7	5.6	5.9	26.9	51.0	96.9	77.7	24.4	0
1975–6	54,550	53,579	28.9	4.92	7,618	10.94	47.27	555.1	17.7	15.1	28.0	45.6	118.1	130.5	32.8	11.4
1976–7	50,226	49,358	26.1	6.81	8,769	11.09	47.81	564.1	15.1	11.3	31.6	55.9	118.3	110.5	25.6	30.3
1977–8[1]	58,760	57,612	30.6	5.88	10,352	10.89	47.37	700.5	17.5	15.6	9.7	56.0	133.6	150.2	31.4	27.3
1978–9[1]	64,044	63,003	29.2	6.42	11,838											
1979–80[1]	68,801															

[1] Preliminary.   *Source: Crop Reporting Board, U.S.D.A.*

Source: Commodity Research Bureau, Inc.

FIGURE 14–12

Volume of Trading in Soybean Futures at the Chicago Board of Trade[1]   In Millions of Bushels

Year	Jan.	Feb.	Mar.	Apr.	May	June	July	Aug.	Sept.	Oct.	Nov.	Dec.	Total
1966	1,791	1,456	1,313	1,300	1,410	1,927	1,291	1,300	1,020	1,067	1,096	790.2	15,761.2
1967	793.1	429.7	478.6	312.6	310.6	462.4	409.1	428.4	449.0	635.6	493.9	322.2	5,525.2
1968	432.1	275.3	283.6	311.0	302.5	408.1	465.6	447.8	400.4	676.0	435.4	280.5	4,718.3
1969	355.5	306.9	320.6	360.1	329.2	286.1	341.0	261.9	482.2	983.0	604.6	373.5	5,004.6
1970	485.9	412.8	394.1	497.7	389.1	1,132	1,485	874.5	722.9	1,470	1,185	1,107	10,156
1971	1,266	837.0	903.2	934.9	1,039	1,440	1,548	1,384	1,384	1,925	1,678	1,226	15,565
1972	1,441	1,371	2,133	2,086	1,732	1,543	1,398	1,665	1,150	1,559	2,039	2,100	20,217
1973	2,152	1,344	1,387	1,241	1,342	875	757	876	577	992	1,176	993	13,712
1974	1,021	1,045	1,224	1,187	1,234	1,194	1,103	1,122	885	1,368	892	1,173	14,816
1975	1,409	1,204	1,473	1,497	1,483	1,400	2,117	1,893	1,621	2,204	1,759	1,508	19,568
1976	1,533	1,298	1,215	1,450	2,410	3,414	2,638	2,333	2,480	3,023	2,893	2,678	27,365
1977	3,484	2,564	5,062	4,707	3,550	4,012	2,468	2,312	2,378	2,374	3,897	2,813	39,621
1978	2,978	2,213	5,057	4,121	3,820	3,742	2,617	2,965	2,561	4,754	3,992	3,511	42,331
1979	3,701	4,901	5,038	4,319									
1980													

[1] Trading on this market represents approximately 98% to 99% of all trading in Soybeans.   *Source: Commodity Futures Trading Commission.*

Highest and Lowest Prices of May Soybean Futures on the Chicago Board of Trade   In Cents per Bushel

Year of Delivery		June	July	Aug.	Sept.	Oct.	Nov.	Dec.	Jan.	Feb.	Mar.	April	May	Range
		Year Prior to Delivery							Delivery Year					
1967	High	323¼	342¼	343¼	342	311¾	304	300	291⅝	289¾	292½	288⅜	284½	343¼
	Low	291⅝	310	320¾	305⅞	299	295⅛	290¼	286	283⅝	285	280⅜	279¾	279¾
1968	High	294	281¼	279¾	278	275½	276⅝	277	279¼	279	278¼	273¼	273½	294
	Low	281½	277⅛	275⅛	270⅝	270⅜	272½	273⅛	274	276	272⅝	269	270⅛	269
1969	High	271¼	268¼	264⅝	264¼	264¼	268⅜	267	268⅝	268⅛	266½	266¾	268	271¼
	Low	264⅛	260⅜	260	257⅝	258	262¼	263	264⅞	265¾	262⅜	261¾	265	257⅝
1970	High	249⅛	252⅝	250⅜	252⅞	260⅞	263¼	258	260⅝	263½	262½	266⅞	270	270
	Low	244⅜	245⅞	246¾	246⅝	250¼	253¼	252¼	254¾	257⅞	258½	259½	262¾	244⅜
1971	High	308	314½	314	305¾	322½	318¾	308¾	317	314	309¼	299⅜	299¾	322½
	Low	298⅛	295½	289¾	288½	298⅜	304½	298¼	301⅜	306	297¾	286½	290½	286½
1972	High	332½	351¼	343	338¾	340	334¾	329⅞	325½	336½	349	361¼	359⅞	361¼
	Low	309½	328	322	315	317⅛	312¼	318¾	310	316¾	333	341¾	342⅞	309½
1973	High	339	343½	352	360¼	364½	390¼	437½	469	635	665	749	1020	1020
	Low	328½	328⅛	328⅞	344½	343	355¾	387¾	413¾	460	530	543	748	328⅛
1974	High	684	794	906	702	676½	639½	648½	665	690	655	617	557½	906
	Low	546	545	670	610	527	521	587	584	623	596	530	521	521
1975	High	603	887	880	857	971	907	816	742	624½	615½	614	544	971
	Low	531	594	726	711½	798	746	707½	575	505	487¼	535½	503	487¼
1976	High	538	661	680	637	604	526	522	505	499	492¾	489½	536½	680
	Low	498	512	592½	571	507½	473½	457½	461	477	464¾	466½	478	457½
1977	High	711	784	709	771	690	691	712	741	793	899	1076½	1030	1076½
	Low	606	638	610	632	619	624	673	694½	718½	776	908	913½	606
1978	High	807½	670	598	589	581½	650	630½	619	596	747½	746	745	807½
	Low	670	580	520	522½	532½	573	591½	565	566	593	647½	693	520
1979	High	691	639	673½	697	753	736	727	733	805½	792	775½		
	Low	620¼	606	606	646½	674	669	681	685	723	747	714		

Source: Chicago Board of Trade.

Source: Commodity Research Bureau, Inc.

of Trade, where contract volume for 1979 numbered 9.3 million contracts. (See Figure 14–12.) Soybean oil and soybean meal also placed in the top ten of the volume leaders, making soybeans and related products the single most traded complex in the world. Contract months for soybeans are January, March, May, July, August, September, and November. (Meal and oil substitute October for November and add a December contract as well.) Beans trade in the standard 5,000 bushel unit, meal contracts are in 100 ton lots, and oil in 60,000 pound loads. Other trading facts for beans, meal, and oil (respectively) are as follows: minimum price fluctuation, ¼¢/bu, 10¢/ton, .01¢/lb.; daily price range limit, 30¢, $10, 1¢; reporting levels, 500,000 bushels, 50 contracts, 50 contracts. Low margins, high liquidity and good spread possibilities have made soybean products very attractive to speculators over the years.

Soybeans are harvested during a short period of time—from September to November in the United States and from March to May in Brazil and the southern growing regions. The impact of South American and other exports on the sensitive world trade in soybeans instructs the trader to watch crops and weather in those areas carefully. Historically, there has been little carryover of crops from year to year in soybeans. Thus, prices will normally rise evenly after harvest to ration out supplies, and exports sell at whatever world price levels dictate.

The *Fats and Oils Situation* report covers soybeans and soybean byproducts and is published five times annually. This report sets forth the current and past supply and demand situation for soybeans and byproducts and makes price forecasts for the upcoming season. These situation re-

ports reflect what the U.S.D.A. actually thinks will happen to the price of a commodity and therefore offer unusually valuable information to the trader. As soybean meals competes with other animal feed, the *Feed Situation* report ought also to be consulted, along with figures regarding livestock supplies. Due to its high protein content, soybean meal is an attractive and special feed component, though again its demand will fluctuate in relation to the prices of other feed grains. The *Livestock and Meat Situation* report, the *Weekly Grain Market News,* and the other grain related publications already mentioned in this chapter contain essential statistics for analysis of the soybean complex.

Soybeans are not in themselves a very popular food item. The demand for beans is a result of the demand for its two products, oil and meal, and this price determining structure must be kept in mind when discussing the soy markets or trading in soy contracts. The complex of fundamentals for meal and for oil together in turn comprise the fundamentals for soybeans when added to other factors such as acreage competition and yield, weather, government programs, and international events. (See Figure 14–13.)

Soybeans are processed into meal and oil by crushing. A key statistic in the soy market is the "crush margin" for the processor, the amount of revenue processed oil and meal will generate versus the cost of the soybeans themselves. Crush margin quotations come across the newswires regularly and indicate supply, demand, and profit trends for each element of the complex. Since a method was developed for improving the flavor of soybean oil, it has become the major vegetable oil in the United States and the principal ingredient in most salad oils and margarines. Oil

FIGURE 14-13

Supply and Distribution of Soybean Meal in the United States   In Thousands of Short Tons

Year Begin. Oct.	For Stocks Oct. 1	Supply—Production		For Edible Protein Pdt's.	Total	Distribution				Price Per Ton Bulk, Decatur	
		Total	For Animal Feed			(Domestic) Feed[2]	Exports	Shipments to U.S. Terr.	Total	44% Protein	49 or 50% Protein
1968–9	145	14,581			14,726	11,469	3,044	56	14,569	74.12	82.46
1969–0	157	17,596			17,753	13,514	4,035	67	17,616	78.45	86.61
1970–1	137	18,035			18,172	13,406	4,559	61	18,126	78.51	84.33
1971–2	146	17,024			17,170	13,110	3,805	63	16,978	90.20	98.20
1972–3	192	16,709			16,900	11,920	4,745	52	16,717	228.99	253.42
1973–4	183	19,674	N.A.	N.A.	19,858	13,766	5,548	36	19,350	146.35	160.57
1974–5	507	16,701	16,437	265	17,209	12,501	4,299	50	16,850	130.86	141.26
1975–6	358	20,754	20,395	359	21,112	15,552	5,145	61	20,758	147.77	157.68
1976–7	355	18,488	18,101	388	18,843	14,001	4,559	55	18,615	199.80	218.73
1977–8[1]	228	22,371	21,961	410	22,599	16,209	6,080	67	22,356	163.56	179.45
1978–9[3]	243	23,750	23,325	425	23,995	17,325	6,250	75	23,650	182.00	

[1] Preliminary.   [2] Includes small quantities used for industrial purposes, estimated at 30,000 tons annually.   [3] Estimate.   *Source: Economic Research Service, U.S.D.A.*

Supply & Distribution of Soybean Oil in the U.S.   In Millions of Pounds

Year Begin. Oct.	Production	Stocks Oct. 1	Exports & Shipments	Domestic Disappearance							Non-Food					
				Total	Food					Paint & Varnish	Resins & Plastics	Other Drying Oil Pdt's	Other Inedible[3]	Foots & Loss	Total Non-Food
					Short-ening	Mar-garine	Cooking & Salad Oils	Other Edible	Total Food						
1966–7	6,076	462	1,105	4,837	1,691	1,273	1,353	58	4,375	96	97	7	61	201	462
1967–8	6,032	596	993	5,096	1,816	1,234	1,494	44	4,588	86	97	7	59	259	508
1968–9	6,531	540	899	5,756	1,978	1,290	1,967	36	5,271	87	94	7	61	236	485
1969–0	7,904	415	1,448	6,328	2,255	1,415	2,150	37	5,857	94	79	7	48	243	471
1970–1	8,265	543	1,782	6,253	2,077	1,381	2,288	34	5,780	82	65	6	52	267	472
1971–2	7,892	773	1,440	6,440	2,089	1,413	2,469	38	6,009	81	55	4	40	251	431
1972–3	7,501	785	1,086	6,685	2,230	1,491	2,469	39	6,229	81	57	4	44	270	456
1973–4	8,995	516	1,461	7,256	2,321	1,513	2,884	30	6,748	91	77	5	55	280	508
1974–5	7,375	794	1,090	6,518	1,882	1,486	2,680	22	6,070	83	58	3	44	260	448
1975–6	9,630	561	1,034	7,906	2,416	1,691	3,274	24	7,405	94	66	3	44	294	501
1976–7[1]	8,578	1,251	1,607	7,454	2,189	1,568	3,165	25	6,947	85	83	4	58	278	508
1977–8[2]	10,288	767	2,115	8,211	2,281	1,584	3,324								
1978–9[2]	10,800	729	1,875	8,625											
1979–80[2]		1,030													

[1] Preliminary.   [2] Forecast.   [3] Includes soap, fatty acids & other miscellaneous.   *Source: Economic Research Service, U.S.D.A.*

Source: Commodity Research Bureau, Inc.

prices, and thus the fate of the soybean complex, will depend in the future on the success of nations now expanding their edible oil exports and on the popularity of competitors here at home—like sunflower seed oil.

Soybean meal feed is used much like feed corn, but with consideration for its high protein value. This makes the supply of other low protein feed grains less important a factor in the demand for soybean meal than the relative price of hogs, cattle, poultry, and other livestock. The volatility of meal, and thus of bean prices, has been explained by some as the result of this lack of competition in high protein feed grains. As rich meal cannot be easily replaced in the feed grain formula, demand remains relatively unaffected by price swings within a fairly large range.

Each month the U.S.D.A. issues a report on the previous month's crush of soybeans and how many tons of meal and oil were produced. This "crush report" is significant since it gives the demand for the current product, as the crushers usually only crush the amount of beans they feel they can sell. If the prices are low for both the byproducts, then the crusher may simply shut down the plant and wait for prices to advance before crushing any more soybeans.

A 60-pound bushel of soybeans, when crushed, yields 11 pounds of soybean oil and 48 pounds of soybean meal, with one pound of waste lost in the process. To determine whether it is worthwhile for the crusher to crush soybeans at the current price, the trader will multiply the current price of soybean oil times 11, multiply the price of meal per pound by 48, and add them together to get the value of the soy byproducts. That value can then be compared to the cost of the bushel of beans to reveal the processor's margin. If soybeans are selling for $7.62 a bushel, oil at 25.9¢ a pound, and meal at $210 a ton, the crushing margin would be 26.4 cents per bushel. With an average favorable margin being 30¢, the trader could estimate a possible slowdown in crushing activity from such figures and a subsequent "bear" in futures prices of beans.

Speculators will often play the spread between the prices of oil, meal, and beans, buying futures contracts of whichever is the cheapest relative to the other and figuring that eventually the processor will come into the market and thereby bring the prices back into line, at which time the speculator will liquidate for a profit. If the speculator feels that bean prices will

continue to deteriorate and the spread widen between the price of beans and meal and oil, he will play a "reverse crush spread" in which he buys soybean oil and soybean meal and sells soybeans in the futures market, figuring that the products will rise in value relative to the price of beans. Spreads are also popular between any two of the three contracts in the complex and between old and new crop months.

COTTON

The United States and the Soviet Union compete for the world cotton production record, together accounting for about 40 percent of the globe's crop. China is the third largest producer, followed by India, Turkey, Brazil, and Pakistan. Both the United States and the U.S.S.R. may consume from 60 percent to 80 percent of their own production in any given year. The world cotton supply and demand scene is complicated by a number of special qualities. United States cotton exported to developing nations may return as cheap textile imports, depressing domestic demand and prospective plantings. The price of oil and petroleum products bears directly on the price of cotton in two ways: through petroleum based competitors in the synthetic fabric complex and through escalating fertilizer and farming costs. The speculator must keep an eye, then, not only on basic supply and demand factors (weather, insects, acres planted, and yields) but also on the trends in world textile production and in crude oil pricing. (See Figure 14–14.)

At one time in American history cotton markets were among the most active in existence, dating back to the middle of the nineteenth century and starring some

FIGURE 14–14

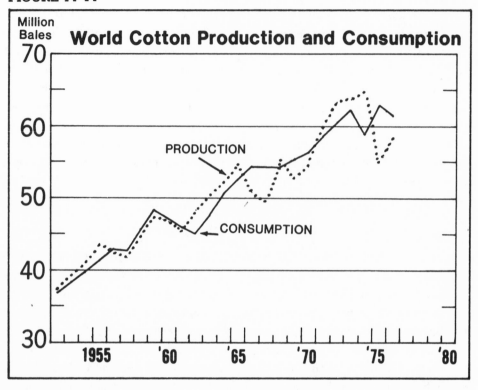

World Production of Cotton   In Thousands of Bales[3]

Year Begin. Aug. 1	Argentina	Brazil	China	Egypt	India	Iran	Mexico	Pakistan	Israel	Sudan	Colombia	Turkey	United States	U.S.S.R.	World Total
1966–7	400	2,050	8,500	2,098	4,600	530	2,240	2,149		890	405	1,760	9,860	9,480	50,921
1967–8	340	2,750	8,900	2,014	5,300	545	2,000	2,400	131	900	465	1,825	7,215	9,370	49,653
1968–9	520	3,320	8,300	2,013	4,900	770	2,450	2,433	154	1,050	640	2,005	11,030	9,200	55,195
1969–0	670	2,675	8,100	2,497	4,850	760	1,750	2,470	183	1,135	590	1,845	9,950	8,850	52,730
1970–1	390	2,740	9,200	2,346	4,400	710	1,440	2,502	163	1,130	540	1,845	10,269	10,800	54,396
1971–2	400	3,135	10,200	2,351	5,800	680	1,715	3,263	169	1,125	590	2,420	10,270	11,000	59,759
1972–3	575	3,000	9,800	2,369	5,370	965	1,780	3,237	186	920	630	2,505	13,890	11,100	63,187
1973–4	585	2,465	11,700	2,258	5,530	920	1,500	3,037	173	1,090	620	2,365	13,300	11,100	63,522
1974–5	790	2,440	11,500	2,018	5,950	1,095	2,230	2,925	230	1,015	700	2,760	11,525	12,250	64,601
1975–6	615	1,825	10,700	1,762	5,350	640	910	2,370	225	500	560	2,215	8,500	11,730	54,339
1976–7	785	2,550	10,000	1,828	4,750	720	1,045	1,930	247	735	685	2,190	10,650	12,050	57,359
1977–8[1]	1,050	2,120	9,200	1,840	5,570	820	1,627	2,550	295	885	645	2,650	14,525	12,750	63,800
1978–9[2]	1,050	2,200	9,600	1,875	5,700	700	1,500	2,300	370	850	375	2,300	10,900	12,500	59,800

[1] Preliminary.   [2] Estimate.   [3] U.S. is in running bales (500 lbs.); all others are 478 pound net weight bales.
Source: International Cotton Advisory Committee

Source: Commodity Research Bureau, Inc.

of the most famous speculative traders of bygone eras. Cotton futures trading peaked in the 1920s. In the late 1940s the dollar volume of trading still surpassed that of all other commodities combined, and of the stocks traded on the New York Stock Exchange. As production and marketing conditions changed, an elaborate structure of government regulations and supports came to govern the cotton industry, and trading activity waned. In 1967 the New York Cotton Exchange introduced the new, No. 2 cotton contract which has been trading successfully ever since, breaking open interest and volume records in 1979–1980.

The contract calls for 50,000 pounds, or 100 bales, of middling grade cotton for delivery at a number of southern and interior ports. With a minimum price fluctuation set at 1/100 cent per pound, each 1 cent move equals $500 per contract. The daily range limit is 4 cents, 2 cents either way from the preceding day's close. (This and other limit rules for trade may often be altered or suspended during the delivery month.) The CFTC reporting level is 5,000 bales, and the speculative position limit on position is 30,000 bales. Contract months are March, May, July, October, and December, along with two more months from the next year's calendar. Harvest is generally completed by October. The reduction in net United States cotton acreage has been accompanied by a steady movement of production into Texas and California, now the leaders in quantity and quality.

Cotton comes in a very large variety of types. Three measurements are used in cotton classification. *Grade* refers to the color purity of the cotton and to its "trash" content (U.S.D.A. standards). *Staple* denotes the length of fiber most characteristic of the bale. These very precise readings fall into five general categories, from "short staple" (under $\frac{13}{16}$ of an inch) to "extra long" ($1\frac{3}{8}$ inch or longer). Each staple has different textile uses and is suitable for different production machinery. "Medium long" ($1\frac{1}{32}$ to $1\frac{3}{32}$) is the dominant American crop. A difference of $\frac{1}{32}$ of an inch may mean $10 a bale or more to the farmer. Finally, "mi-

cronaire" tells the thickness of the fiber, which is actually a hollow tube of cellulose. "Premium mike" is the basic contract measurement for No. 2 New York cotton, with premiums and discounts for variances.

Government farm programs have been among the most important deciding factors in cotton price trends in recent history. The techniques available to the U.S.D.A. have included mandatory acreage diversion, voluntary diversion and set-aside, target price supports, loan programs, and disaster payments. The loan program for a time became the center of the industry, acquiring more than 10 million bales in the early 1960s. Liquidation of much of this stock, and reforms in the loan and pricing systems, have relieved some of the depressive influence on cotton prices and cotton futures markets. Ideally, the loan program offers the farmer a short-term parking facility during the maneuvering for better profits.

The single greatest variation in the supply-demand equation for cotton is the crop size, the occasion for annual market hysteria. Cotton's growth characteristics are "indeterminate," flowering and fruiting over a long period, making yield estimates hazardous. (See Figure 14–15.) Weather affects cotton crops persistently and unpredictably. Disease and insects have been the cotton farmer's enemies, the control of the latter (especially the boll weevil) involving expensive petroleum based insecticides often regulated or banned because of environmental dangers. The control of insects has been a major cost factor in many acreage shifts from cotton to soybeans in the South.

Cotton demand is not easy to compute, involving the trading program in trying to accurately estimate cloth inventories,

FIGURE 14–15

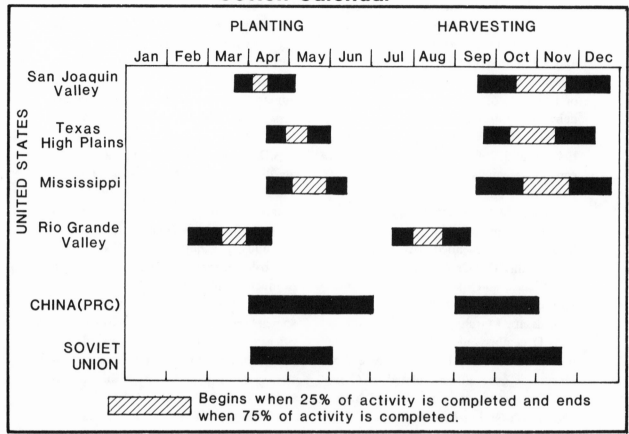

Cotton Calendar

Begins when 25% of activity is completed and ends when 75% of activity is completed.

Supply and Distribution of All Cotton in the United States   In Thousands of (480-Lb. Net Weight) Bales

Crop Year Beginning Aug. 1	At Mills	In Public Storage	Else-where	Total	CCC Held	Total Stocks	Current Crop[2] Less Ginnings	New Crop[3]	Total[4]	Imports	City Crop	Total	Mill Consumption	Exports	Total
		Privately Owned — Carryover, Aug. 1					Ginnings						Distribution		
1969–0	1,638	1,572	400	3,610	2,911	6,521	9,857	6	9,863	52	40	16,534	8,114	2,878	10,992
1970–1	1,423	947	360	2,730	3,030	5,760	10,106	127	10,233	37	77	16,108	8,204	3,897	12,101
1971–2	1,641	1,908	400	3,949	303	4,252	10,107	40	10,147	72	81	14,552	8,259	3,385	11,644
1972–3	1,540	1,357	80	2,977	257	3,234	13,227	3	13,230	34	10	16,504	7,769	5,311	13,080
1973–4	1,500	1,881	350	3,731	198	3,929	12,608	145	12,753	48	20	16,750	7,472	6,123	13,595
1974–5	1,439	1,886	200	3,525	218	3,743	11,189	30	11,214	34	10	15,000	5,860	3,926	9,786
1975–6	1,132	4,074	275	4,511	970	5,481	8,151	47	8,198	92	5	13,776	6,986	3,178	10,179
1976–7	1,210	2,234	150	3,471	123	3,594	10,300	85	10,385	38	54	14,073	6,480	4,673	11,153
1977–8[1]	1,054	1,791	75	2,588	332	2,920	13,933	144	14,077	5	0	17,002	6,236	5,219	11,676
1978–9[1]				4,057	1,269	5,326	10,405	90	10,495	5	14	15,840	6,100	5,700	11,850

[1] Preliminary.   [2] Less ginnings prior to Aug. 1.   [3] Ginnings prior to Aug. 1 end of season.   [4] Includes inseason ginnings.
Source: Economic Research Service, U.S.D.A.

Source: Commodity Research Bureau, Inc.

the quantity and quality of raw cotton inventories held by mills, the competition from other new fibers which come and go over the years, the usage trend in foreign textile industries, and the always crucial and unknown price of oil. Elusive domestic disappearance figures are usually less significant in tracing cotton prices than are export statistics. Cotton has been a notoriously difficult commodity to predict the price for, and should continue to offer traders an exciting and challenging market.

For information, the cotton trader should turn first to the *Cotton Situation* report issued bimonthly by the U.S.D.A. This report sizes up the cotton market as the government sees it and makes forecasts for price shifts in upcoming months. Here can be found historical data, broad overviews, and statistics on domestic mill use and exports. With these in hand, the trader will wish to follow closely the *Cotton Production Reports,* issued monthly during the crop year, to see if production is in fact falling into line with government estimates. Available from the U.S. Census Bureau are a variety of reports on cotton ginnings, domestic consumption, stocks in mills and storage, exports, cotton goods inventories and orders, and cotton quality. As with any commodity, the speculator and the trader should also avail themselves of the information provided by the trading exchange itself. The New York Cotton Exchange publishes an assortment of useful and timely reports on many aspects of the cotton market.

HOGS AND PORK BELLIES

Frozen pork bellies have long been one of the glamour items of the commodity markets. This contract's funny sounding name has earned it a prominent place in most popular discussions of commodities, while its very exciting and profitable trading characteristics bring a different kind of smile to the traders and speculators themselves. Pork bellies are nothing more exotic than uncured bacon, a slab of pork cut from the underside of the hog. Each hog yields two bellies. The bellies make up about 11 percent, or 24–28 pounds, of the average hog. Frozen pork belly contracts began trading at the Chicago Mercantile Exchange in 1961, experiencing a phenomenal popularity in just a few short years. Live hog contracts followed in 1966 at the CME and today both enjoy a roughly equal standing with bellies maintaining an edge in volume and open interest. Hogs and bellies are an exception to the rule that speculative interest follows hedging interest in the development of a market, for both contracts remain predominantly speculative in their trading makeup. Producers and processors have other hedging devices in the way of fairly flexible alterations in farrowings (births), slaughterings, and quantities in storage, leaving the markets to the speculators.

For live hogs, contract months are February, April, June, July, August, October, and December, plus two months from the forthcoming year. The contract unit is 30,000 pounds of U.S.D.A. Grades No. 1–4 Hogs averaging in weight between 200 and 230 pounds. Adjustments are available for deviations in weight, grade, quantity, and delivery location. Minimum price fluctuation is .025 cents per pound with a 1 cent move equaling $300 per contract. Daily limit is 1½ cents per pound above or below the preceding close. Reporting level is 50 contracts. Position limits are 300 contracts for any one delivery month and 750 contracts long or short in all months. (As usual, these limits do not apply to bona fide hedgers.)

Frozen pork belly months are February, March, May, July, and August plus one month from the upcoming year. The size of the contract is 38,000 pounds, about equal to a car lot commonly used in the trade. The deliverable grade is 12–14 pound bellies, federally inspected and containing no more than the stipulated number of defects. (An elaborate schedule of defects is described in the contract specifications.) Minimum price fluctuation for the futures contract is .025 cents, with a daily trading limit of plus or minus 2 cents per pound from the previous close. A 1 cent move equals $380 per contract. Position limits are 250 contracts of all months combined.

Hog and belly fundamentals are almost exclusively set by domestic production, slaughter, and consumption trends. The farrowing of hogs goes on all year long, with traditional periods of increase in the spring and fall. It takes about four months for gestation and about 5–7 months growth to reach market weight. Thus, the hog farmer must make an initial decision on how many pigs to produce some 9–11 months before they will hit the market. The hog cycle emerges from this necessity as farmers increase or decrease farrowing plans in reaction to price and storage data and in reaction to seasonal factors and feed grain costs. Demand for hogs is constituted by demand for bellies and other pork products and by the relative cost of competitors like beef, poultry, lamb, and fish. As farrowings and slaughters in any given year tend to be about equal, the amount of pork and bellies in storage may be a decisive factor in price movements. Pork demand figures are quoted in terms of consumption per person per year. (See Figure 14–16.)

The supply of pork bellies directly follows the quantity of pigs moving through the slaughterhouses. Stocks in storage, bacon slicing trends, and per capita consumption are thus all statistics the trader will watch along with farrowings. As in the case of corn, the pork belly trader keeps a close eye on the hog feed ratio to determine whether feed is cheap relative to the price of hogs and, therefore, whether the farmer will continue to feed the hogs as long as possible or slaughter them the moment they reach the minimum marketable weight. The textbook figure for an average, break even ratio is 15:1 (the price of 15 bushels of corn being equal to the price of 100 pounds of hogs). At ratios dipping toward 12:1, cutbacks in farrowing and accelerated marketing may be expected; at ratios upwards of 20:1, the reverse may occur. (See Figure 14–17.)

Statistics on the movement of pigs into the market, on the rate of slaughter, on storage, and on cash price come regularly across the daily commodity newswires. The major report for the trader is the *Livestock and Meat Situation*, issued bimonthly by the U.S.D.A. It contains commentary on the markets, much information for farmers, and data that can be useful in predicting long term price shifts. Once again, the *Feed Situation Report* should be consulted regularly, with special consideration to interpreting how hog farmers may react to changes in the feed complex situation. *Hogs and Pigs Reports* are issued quarterly in December, March, June, and September. These reports give detailed breakdowns on the farrowings, on the sizes of the litters, and on the pig crop by six month periods. Naturally, the quantity of hogs that will enter the market in the forthcoming six months may be estimated by reference to real far-

FIGURE 14–16

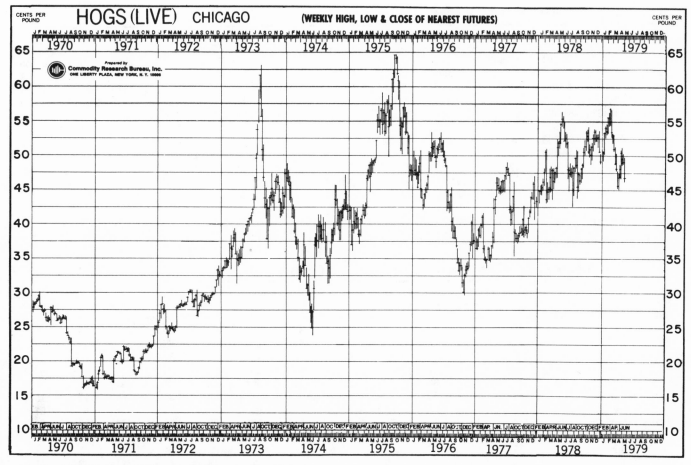

Salient Statistics of Pigs and Hogs in the U.S.

Year	Spring[2] Sows Farrowed (In Thousands of Head)	Spring[2] Pigs Saved	Fall[3] Sows Farrowed	Fall[3] Pigs Saved	Total Pig Crop	Value of Hogs on Farms, Dec. 1 $ Per Head	Value of Hogs on Farms, Dec. 1 Total Million $	Hog Marketings Ths. Head	Quantity Produced (Live Wt.) Mil. Lbs.	Value of Production Mil. $	Hogs Slaughtered in Thousand Head — Commercial Federally Inspected	Other	Total	Farm	Total
1969	6,323	46,521	5,745	42,155	88,676	39.00	2,225	88,074	20,600	4,561	75,682	8,156	83,838	1,134	84,972
1970	7,134	52,126	6,882	49,588	101,921	23.50	1,584	86,919	21,823	4,955	78,187	7,630	85,817	1,235	87,052
1971	7,303	51,918	6,297	46,006	98,512	28.50	1,780	98,644	22,832	3,991	86,667	7,771	94,438	1,210	95,648
1972	6,512	47,523	5,967	43,053	90,828	42.00	2,477	89,555	20,919	5,245	78,759	5,948	84,707	1,158	85,865
1973	6,459	46,125	5,864	41,998	88,199	60.40	3,663	82,419	20,154	7,738	72,264	4,531	76,795	1,095	77,890
1974	6,372	44,792	5,466	38,952	83,954	44.90	2,457	85,504	19,976	6,838	77,071	4,691	81,762	1,321	83,083
1975	4,973	35,530	4,952	35,656	71,186	80.40	3,959	73,595	16,799	7,751	64,926	3,761	68,687	1,193	69,880
1976	5,777	42,177	5,850	42,218	84,395	47.00	2,583	75,744	18,111	7,844	70,454	3,330	73,784	1,175	74,959
1977[1]	6,050	42,960	6,009	43,202	86,162	63.10	3,571	81,962	19,372	7,634	74,018	3,285	77,303	1,139	78,442
1978[4]	6,015	42,341	6,375	45,840	88,181						74,142	3,145	77,287		
1979[4]	6,903	49,356													

[1] Preliminary.   [2] December—May.   [3] June—November.   [4] Breeding intentions.   *Source: Statistical Reporting Service, U.S.D.A.*

Average Live Weight of All Hogs Slaughtered Under Federal Inspection   In Pounds Per Head

Year	Jan.	Feb.	Mar.	Apr.	May	June	July	Aug.	Sept.	Oct.	Nov.	Dec.	Average[1]
1973	238.9	247.0	236.9	238.7	242.5	244.6	245.5	240.3	239.7	242.3	247.0	249.0	241.8
1974	245.8	243.5	244.9	245.5	246.0	248.6	247.2	243.2	243.1	243.1	244.7	245.5	245.1
1975	242	236	236	238	240	244	241	237	238	240	246	246	240.3
1976[2]	243	236	236	236	239	240	238	236	236	238	243	239	238.3
1977[2]	234	233	234	236	239	241	239	237	235	239	243	239	237.4
1978[2]	236	233	234	237	241	244	241	239	239	243	248	247	240.2
1979[2]	241	237											

[1] Average is weighted by Federally inspected slaughter.   [2] Preliminary.   *Source: Department of Agriculture.*

Source: Commodity Research Bureau, Inc.

FIGURE 14–17

U.S. Frozen Pork Belly Storage Stocks (In Thousand Pounds, as of First of the Month)

Year	Jan.	Feb.	Mar.	Apr.	May	June	July	Aug.	Sept.	Oct.	Nov.	Dec.
1967	44,921	50,191	67,803	91,284	108,506	100,453	88,993	60,577	33,275	20,796	32,098	48,756
1968	68,882	66,810	77,182	92,099	115,682	129,377	102,949	59,462	27,393	15,809	20,437	33,774
1969	49,076	46,699	56,173	76,035	96,249	96,670	84,284	46,755	21,719	12,167	19,565	26,074
1970	38,697	37,017	47,094	61,068	74,004	82,061	67,250	39,300	20,393	9,823	21,043	42,054
1971	76,437	81,561	83,004	111,579	131,262	146,093	140,778	105,015	70,504	50,654	53,057	68,004
1972	86,065	84,092	88,090	107,013	131,189	133,069	105,727	69,933	35,792	16,691	22,175	34,167
1973	39,278	32,388	30,764	46,406	50,205	54,980	48,817	26,270	10,186	9,140	15,397	31,580
1974	48,758	48,499	53,083	65,237	78,707	87,290	70,470	39,621	21,762	12,850	22,274	38,441
1975	49,514	40,374	42,846	51,771	65,645	65,470	53,389	22,995	10,057	7,418	17,645	33,532
1976	44,722	37,386	38,526	51,176	60,144	63,799	49,258	25,773	8,689	5,858	9,708	24,946
1977	42,906	38,338	36,364	52,806	69,539	80,658	62,695	29,901	9,640	5,241	4,230	20,642
1978[1]	23,747	19,013	15,738	39,631	70,740	82,336	75,036	44,762	21,006	7,554	19,936	41,112
1979[1]	54,367	39,457	37,209	58,135								

[1] Preliminary. *Source: Crop Reporting Board, U.S.D.A.*

Monthly Cash Pork Belly Prices—Fresh—12–14 Lbs. In Cents Per Lb.

Year		Jan.	Feb.	Mar.	Apr.	May	June	July	Aug.	Sept.	Oct.	Nov.	Dec.	Year
1972	High	39	37	36	35	36½	40	42½	42	49	40¾	44	46	46
	Low	31	30	31	33	34	32	37	37	39	36½	39½	44	30
1973	High	51	54½	55	52½	55	57	84	93	74	63½	65	58½	93
	Low	47	45	47	46½	49	54	57	73	62	57	57½	54	45
1974	High	67	64	50	47½	38½	47½	59	65	65½	62	63	65½	67
	Low	57	51	41	38½	32½	26	49	50½	50	56	53	57	26
1975	High	64	65	70½	72¼	77½	87	103	115½	106	101	86	72	115½
	Low	57	59	57	65	68	76½	84½	94	95½	75	71½	65	57
1976[1]	High	78	73	70½	77	76	82	78½	77	73	59	44½	52½	82
	Low	68	60½	62¾	68	69	75½	68	68	50	40	39	39	39
1977[1]	High	57	55	53	58½	60	61½	72	73½	62½	54	46	61	73½
	Low	48	46	46	52	53	55	57	58	46	41	41½	43	41
1978[1]	High	62½	73	80	76	70	65	62	65	64	65½	61	62	80
	Low	55	64	67¾	63	62	52	54	52	57½	56½	56	50	50
1979[1]	High	66	64¾	60½	56½									
	Low	54	59	50	48									

[1] Preliminary. *Source: National Provisioner.*

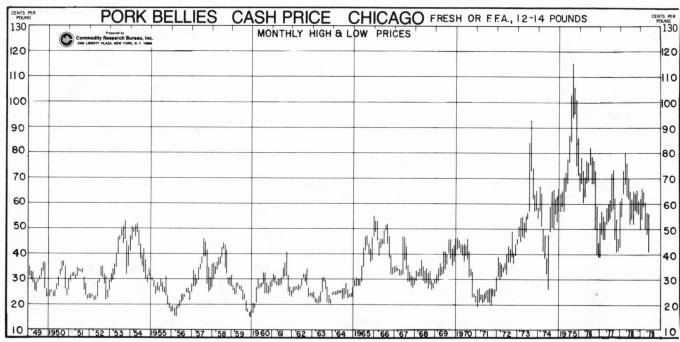

Source: Commodity Research Bureau, Inc.

rowings for the last six months and supplies of live hogs. Farrowing intentions have significance but should be read within the broader context of the hog cycle and of price pressures on the farmer. Pork belly traders pay particular attention to the *Monthly Cold Storage Reports,* which often have a violent effect on the market, causing limit advances or declines on days following the report (usually issued midmonth). The *Yearbook* of the Chicago Mercantile Exchange contains all the salient statistics on hogs and bellies, including volume, cash and futures prices, and supply and demand data—all of which will aid the trader in staking out

FIGURE 14–18

WEEKLY SLICED BACON PRODUCTION
Retail and Commercial Production, Under Federal Inspection
(In Thousand Pounds)

Week Ending	1979			1978			1977		
	Retail	Commercial	Total	Retail	Commercial	Total	Retail	Commercial	Total
Jan. 6	18,269	7,553	25,822	18,432	5,966	24,398	—	—	25,361
13	23,714	9,325	33,039	21,618	7,471	29,089	—	—	26,788
20	23,596	8,147	31,743	19,335	7,225	26,560	—	—	27,660
27	21,546	8,017	29,563	20,548	6,882	27,430	—	—	27,633
Feb. 3	21,486	8,139	29,625	21,477	7,230	28,707	—	—	26,315
10	18,798	7,763	26,561	22,023	6,887	28,910	—	—	26,533
17	19,028	7,518	26,546	21,289	7,142	28,431	—	—	24,199
24	16,958	7,202	24,160	17,832	6,633	24,465	—	—	23,988
Mar. 3	18,856	8,376	27,232	17,981	6,681	24,662	20,778	6,026	26,804
10	19,182	8,206	27,388	16,638	6,621	25,259	23,407	6,722	30,129
17	.....	.....	.....	16,712	6,448	23,160	20,253	6,086	26,339
24	.....	.....	.....	15,018	6,692	21,710	20,021	5,856	25,877
31	.....	.....	.....	15,230	6,649	21,879	19,953	6,066	26,019
Apr. 7	.....	.....	.....	16,433	6,949	23,382	19,617	6,259	25,875
14	.....	.....	.....	17,724	7,432	25,156	19,030	5,700	24,730
21	.....	.....	.....	18,037	7,242	25,279	18,456	5,759	24,215
28	.....	.....	.....	18,762	7,391	26,153	19,574	5,813	25,387
May 5	.....	.....	.....	19,928	7,589	27,517	18,239	5,740	23,979
12	.....	.....	.....	18,616	7,703	26,319	18,765	5,880	24,645
19	.....	.....	.....	18,817	7,550	26,367	18,789	6,310	25,289
26	.....	.....	.....	18,628	7,030	25,658	17,462	5,557	23,019
June 2	.....	.....	.....	15,769	6,317	22,086	18,175	5,478	23,653
9	.....	.....	.....	18,964	7,582	26,546	20,137	6,838	26,975
16	.....	.....	.....	18,900	7,843	26,744	20,996	6,494	27,490
23	.....	.....	.....	20,277	7,803	28,030	21,867	6,289	28,156
30	.....	.....	.....	21,048	8,091	29,139	20,986	6,308	27,294
July 7	.....	.....	.....	23,420	7,222	30,642	19,518	6,534	26,052
14	.....	.....	.....	21,764	8,373	30,137	21,151	6,723	27,784
21	.....	.....	.....	22,547	8,799	31,346	21,131	7,029	28,160
28	.....	.....	.....	22,873	9,203	32,076	21,304	6,888	28,192
Aug. 4	.....	.....	.....	21,743	8,568	30,311	20,562	6,409	26,971
11	.....	.....	.....	21,761	8,385	30,146	22,134	8,221	30,355
18	.....	.....	.....	21,033	8,037	29,070	20,977	6,939	27,916
25	.....	.....	.....	20,700	8,402	29,102	21,275	7,087	28,362
Sept. 1	.....	.....	.....	21,838	8,586	30,424	19,112	6,575	25,687
8	.....	.....	.....	19,280	7,307	26,587	20,533	6,450	26,983
15	.....	.....	.....	21,879	8,552	30,431	21,632	7,031	28,633
22	.....	.....	.....	21,146	8,127	29,273	21,304	7,231	28,535
29	.....	.....	.....	21,563	7,683	29,246	21,114	6,411	27,525
Oct. 6	.....	.....	.....	20,149	7,480	27,629	18,749	6,433	25,182
13	.....	.....	.....	18,908	7,916	26,824	22,578	7,230	29,808
20	.....	.....	.....	19,746	8,351	28,097	21,722	7,736	29,508
27	.....	.....	.....	18,829	8,287	27,116	21,439	6,637	28,076
Nov. 3	.....	.....	.....	18,580	8,649	27,229	22,084	7,220	29,304
10	.....	.....	.....	19,623	8,080	27,703	21,485	7,316	28,801
17	.....	.....	.....	19,105	8,817	27,922	21,385	7,075	28,460
24	.....	.....	.....	16,759	6,460	23,219	16,213	5,971	22,184
Dec. 1	.....	.....	.....	19,507	10,811	30,318	21,269	6,714	27,983
8	.....	.....	.....	21,223	7,933	29,156	20,945	7,174	28,119
15	.....	.....	.....	20,761	8,119	28,880	20,825	7,032	27,857
22	.....	.....	.....	20,710	7,837	28,547	19,212	6,594	75,806
29	.....	.....	.....	16,556	6,616	23,166	18,378	5,329	23,707

Source: Chicago Mercantile Exchange.

a position. The U.S.D.A. also publishes a "Weekly Sliced Bacon Production" report which, though it may be a few weeks behind, gives a good representation of demand. (See Figure 14–18.)

Pork bellies, like other seasonal commodities, have a seasonal price pattern in which prices advance and decline throughout the year in a cyclical pattern. Slaughter surpasses demand from November to April, accumulating storage stocks into a May peak, after which stocks and slaughters decline. Normally, pork belly prices are low in the fall and winter and then advance into the spring with the normal contract highs reached in July and August. However, seasonals are often honored more in the breach than in the observing, and the trader who hopes to buy on seasonal lows in December will as often be wrong as right. The balance of price influencing factors may shift. Intermittent upsurges in demand occur regularly with pork, especially at Easter, Christmas, and during the summer holidays. Bacon demand seems relatively constant despite price unless swings of an extreme nature should occur.

Many traders like to use the pork belly market for "day trading," going in on the opening in the morning and closing out the position at the end of the day. In general, day trading is not a successful technique, and in pork it can often prove disastrous. All too often the trader will take a position for a $100 profit in the morning, get locked into a $200 loss by nightfall, and hold on until he has earned or received a $300 or $400 loss. There's little sense in taking such substantial beatings in the mere hope of a $100 profit. Day trading in bellies should be approached with extreme caution.

Bellies and hogs are also very popular spreading contracts in which the trader buys one month and sells another, hoping that the spread between the two will widen and yield him a safe profit. The February–July and February–August spreads attract many traders, as they are based on the seasonal trends. Again, however, this is not a fail safe operation. Seasonal trends are only a probability, and by now you've learned enough about hogs to guess that the individual contract months are unusually independent of each other. Thus, basis spreads can be dangerous. One cannot be too sure that an intermonth basis will remain stable in the pork belly market with anywhere near the regularity of those in corn, wheat, oats, and other grains and oil seeds.

CATTLE

Initiated by the Chicago Mercantile Exchange in 1964, live cattle futures shattered a 100 year old myth that contended that only inanimate products, easily graded and susceptible to long-term storage, could trade successfully. Cattle went on, despite the early opposition of the livestock industry, to become one of the top ten commodities and a consistently attractive vehicle for producers, buyers, and speculators. Cattle market fundamentals operate, by and large, free from the entangling network of global interdependence, though as demand and price continue to rise, beef imports play a more and more important role in short-term price shifts. (Imports still account for only about 10 percent of consumption). The domestic market is populated by a few large buyers and a great many suppliers. This, coupled with the historically steady increase in per capita consumption, makes supply trends and statistics the favored items in the analyst's workbook. (See Figure 14–19.)

There are two CME contracts in cattle,

FIGURE 14-19
CATTLE AND CALVES

Cattle Supply and Distribution in the United States   In Thousands of Head

Year	Cattle & Calves on Farms Jan. 1	Imports	Calves Born	Total Supply	Federally Inspected	Other[2]	All Commercial	Farm	Total Slaughter	Deaths on Farms	Exports	Total Disappearance
1970	112,369	1,168	45,871	159,408	33,817	5,280	39,097	463	39,559	4,297	88	43,944
1971	114,578	991	46,738	162,307	34,225	5,049	39,274	445	39,730	4,442	93	44,265
1972	117,862	1,186	47,682	166,730	34,688	4,144	38,832	434	39,335	5,126	104	44,565
1973	121,539	1,039	49,194	171,772	32,329	3,607	35,936	477	36,506	6,487	273	43,266
1974	127,778	568	50,873	179,229	35,674	4,125	39,799	722	40,528	6,110	204	46,842
1975	132,028	389	50,183	182,600	40,798	5,322	46,120	750	46,870	6,992	196	54,058
1976	127,980	984	47,440	176,404	43,430	4,574	48,004	722	48,726	5,190	205	54,121
1977[1]	122,810	1,133	46,088	170,031	43,413	3,960	47,373	700	48,073	6,000	107	54,180
1978[1]	116,375	1,253	43,839	161,467	40,570	3,013	43,583	617	44,200	5,700	122	50,022
1979[1]	110,864											

[1] Preliminary. [2] Wholesale and retail. *Source: Economic Research Service, U.S.D.A.*

Number of Cattle & Calves on U.S. Farms & Ranches on Jan. 1, by Classes   In Thousands of Head

Year	Total Cattle & Calves	Beef Cows	Milk Cows	Total	For Beef Cow Replacement	For Milk Cow Replacement	Other Heifers	Total	Steers 500 lbs. & Over	Bulls 500 lbs. & Over	Heifers, Steers & Bulls Under 500 lbs.
1970	112,369	36,689	12,091	48,780	6,431	3,880	6,132	16,443	15,265	2,272	29,609
1971	114,578	37,877	11,909	49,786	6,664	3,843	6,113	16,620	15,610	2,327	30,235
1972	117,862	38,807	11,778	50,585	6,987	3,828	6,399	17,214	15,999	2,376	31,688
1973	121,539	40,918	11,624	52,541	7,436	3,874	6,434	17,743	16,555	2,466	32,229
1974	127,788	43,008	11,286	54,293	8,226	3,942	6,821	18,988	17,802	2,645	33,942
1975	132,028	45,472	11,211	56,682	8,879	4,095	6,509	19,482	16,373	2,987	36,302
1976	127,980	43,888	11,087	54,974	7,196	3,958	7,393	18,546	17,083	2,845	34,531
1977	122,810	41,389	11,035	52,424	6,529	3,888	8,057	18,473	16,885	2,665	32,363
1978[1]	116,375	38,809	10,939	49,748	5,845	3,896	7,970	17,711	16,779	2,544	29,595
1979[1]	110,864	36,989	10,853	47,843	5,519	3,936	7,431	16,886	16,321	2,401	27,413

[1] Preliminary. *Source: Crop Reporting Board, U.S.D.A.*

Farm Value, Income & Wholesale Prices of Cattle & Calves

Year	Per Head $	Total Million $	Gross Income From C. & C.[2] $	Prime	Choice	Good	Choice	Good	Choice Feeder Steers at K.C.	Cows, Utility Omaha	Vealers, Choice- So. St. Paul	Argentina[4]	Over 1,050 Lbs. Choice	Up to 1,050 Lbs. Good	Stockers & Feeders Good
1966	133.0	14,443	10,615	26.31	25.71	24.00	25.76	24.83		17.83	32.41	12.09	24.04	23.34	23.71
1967	149.0	16,212	10,726	26.10	25.29	23.74	25.40	24.62		17.22	31.61	9.59	25.56	24.92	24.54
1968	148.0	16,241	11,447	27.86	26.87	24.79	26.89	25.96		17.94	33.75	9.19	25.66	25.04	24.92
1969	158	17,390	12,781	30.67	29.45	27.14	29.56	28.53		20.29	38.90	9.29	27.86	27.02	29.71
1970	179	20,160	13,935	30.02	29.36	27.04	29.42	28.51		21.32	44.82	12.70	29.75	28.80	31.61
1971	184	21,113	15,247	33.37	32.39	29.38	32.54	31.46		21.62	46.30	18.79	32.68	31.86	37.12
1972	208	24,520	18,579	36.65	35.78	33.43	35.60	34.72		25.21	55.09	27.25	36.19	35.43	42.20
1973	252	30,584	22,814	44.80	44.54	42.01	44.25	43.11	53.17	32.82	64.08	39.88	44.56	43.29	47.38
1974	293	37,477	18,350	43.10	41.89	38.71	42.11	40.97	37.88	25.56	49.63	39.74	49.62	47.88	42.86
1975	159	21,000	17,982	41.39	44.61	39.45		43.12	33.91	21.09	40.44	63.13	41.96	40.43	33.26
1976[1]	190	24,335	19,803		39.11	35.87		37.98	39.40	25.31	45.18				
1977[1]	206	25,252	27,055		40.38	36.70		38.96	40.18	25.32	48.19				
1978[1]	232	27,029	44,661		52.34				58.78	36.79	69.24				
1979[1]	403														

[1] Preliminary. [2] Excludes interfarm sales & Gov't. payments. Cash receipts from farm marketings plus value of farm home consumption. [3] Weighted average prices of beef steers, sold out of first hands for slaughter. [4] Argentine special for chilling, at Liniers market near Buenos Aires. Prices converted to U.S. $ at current rate of exchange. [5] Prices converted to U.S. $ at current rate of exchange. *Source: Economic Research Service, U.S.D.A.*

Source: Commodity Research Bureau, Inc.

"Live" and "Feeder," with the Live Cattle contract pulling in about five times the volume and open interest of Feeder. (Feeder are those animals weighing 500–650 pounds, being sold to feedlots; live cattle are full grown, weighing between 1,050 and 1,200 pounds, being sold for slaughter.) Live and Feeder contracts call for delivery of 40,000 and 42,000 pounds respectively, with scheduled adjustments for deviations in weight, yield, grade, quality, and delivery. Contract months for Live are January, February, April, June, August, October, and December; for Feeder, they are March, April, May, August, September, October, and November. For both contracts, minimum fluctuation is .025 cents per pound, the daily range is 1½ cents above or below the previous close, and the reporting level 50 contracts. The value of a 1 cent move in Live Cattle is $400 per contract; in Feeder Cattle, $420. Position limit is 300 contracts net long or short in any delivery month for both contracts.

To understand cattle markets and cattle cycles, a basic idea of the producing and marketing structure is required. (See Figure 14–20.) In the first stage, the owner of the cow-calf operation makes breeding decisions based on current prices. Gestation takes about nine months, with the majority of calves born within forty-five days of 1 April and weaned within forty-five days of 1 October. After weaning, depending on the farmer's own operation and needs, most of the calves will be sold to a rancher, probably in another region, who specializes in bringing them up to the prefeedlot weight of 500–700 pounds. Transition to the conditions of the feedlots causes substantial shrinkage and death loss. There the animals are custom fed with precise diets of grains, fats, proteins,

and other additives. Slaughter weights are usually reached after about 6–8 months in the lot, after which the cattle are sold to the meat packer for actual killing and dressing. A 1,000 pound steer yields about 600 pounds of wholesale meat and 400 pounds of byproducts. The whole process, from conception to retail pricing and sale, takes from 2½ to 3 years. Cattle fundamentals turn around this long-term process and are interpreted by paying particular attention to the statistics for each stage of the procedure and their relation to supplies, demands, and prices for every other stage and for the market as a whole.

Many factors other than consumer demand influence shifts in cow herd size. Since cattle are the number one source of feed grain demand, changes in the feed price situation should be monitored closely. Crop production reports are likewise of interest, as are land use figures as more and more grazing acreage is lost to industry and housing, driving up real estate and tax costs for the farmer or rancher. Developments in the production and marketing of other meats will affect beef to some extent, with pork traditionally being the major substitute food.

The trader in cattle futures will watch most of the publications mentioned in connection with hogs and pork bellies. Other bulletins of interest include the *Meat Animals Annual Summary,* the *Livestock and Poultry Inventory,* the *Cattle and Calves Report,* the *Special Range Reports, Cattle on Pastures,* and *Shipments of Stocker and Feeder Cattle and Sheep.* Contract specifications, daily and monthly futures prices, and other data appear in the Chicago Mercantile Exchange *Yearbook.*

Cattle prices do not have an annual rise

FIGURE 14–20

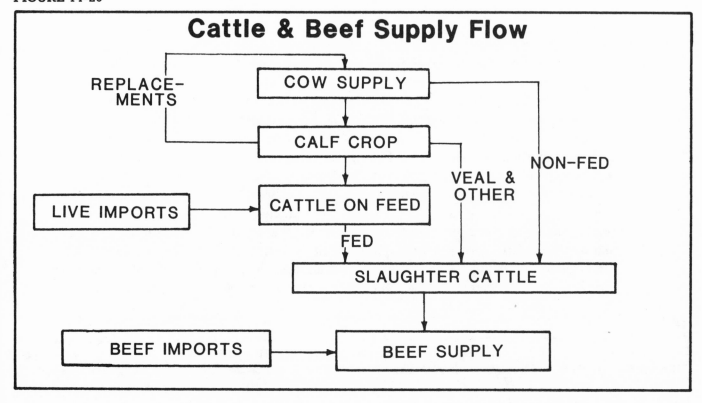

Cattle & Beef Supply Flow

CATTLE CYCLES SINCE 1930:

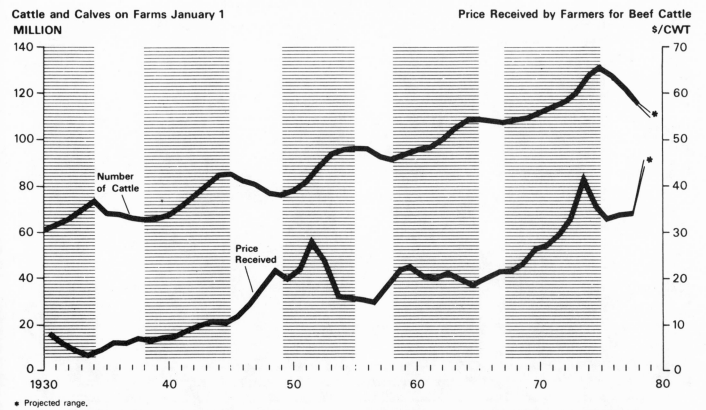

Cattle and Calves on Farms January 1
MILLION

Price Received by Farmers for Beef Cattle
$/CWT

* Projected range.

The shaded sections are periods of herd building. Prices tended to be highest when cattle numbers were low and increasing. Other important price-making factors were consumer buying power and supplies of competing meats.

Source: Commodity Research Bureau, Inc.

and dip similar to those for other agricultural commodities. Rather, cattle prices run in cycles lasting about three to four years. It takes this long for herd size decisions, be they cutbacks or expansions, to have their maximum impact on supplies. A much reported and discussed cycle took place between 1975 and 1979 as producers reacted to low cattle prices, high feed prices, and drought and inflation. Cattle and calves on farms dropped from 132 million head to 110 million head, eventually forcing the upward surge in cattle prices after 1977. (See Figure 14–21.) Initially, the short-term price effect may be opposite the desired long-term effect as a rush of slaughtered animals hits the markets in efforts to thin current supplies, driving prices further down instead of up. Meanwhile, calves and heifers are held back for breeding, not to be full grown and marketed for three to five years, creating the sought after downturn in supplies and the reservoir needed for when prices again reach an acceptable level. Herd expansion, in fact, began to register in 1980,

FIGURE 14–21

Source: Commodity Research Bureau, Inc.

signaling the next step in the cycle. Increased numbers of cattle will find their way to market to take advantage of high beef prices, supplies will eventually grow heavy, prices will fall, and the cycle will begin again.

A great deal of money has been spent by large companies and economists in attempts to scientifically predict prices and cycles, but so far they have failed. When a cycle will begin, how long it will hold, and how well it will hold depends on too many factors outside the strict limit of cattle supplies and prices. The trader need only be aware of the cycles, watching for reversals every two to four years. The cattle markets can be traded with less anxiety than other, more volatile futures contracts because of the dominance of these long-term factors.

METALS: GOLD, SILVER, AND COPPER

One of the most dramatic episodes in modern futures history has been the fabulous career of the precious metals. In the relatively few years since trading began, metals futures have continually commanded the world's attention as volume and price shattered records and over-turned traditional economic relationships. In 1979 newcomer gold actually displaced the agriculturals to rank number one in contracts traded on United States exchanges, the result of an astonishing bull market fueled by the United State's and Iran's war of nerves, the Soviet invasion of Afghanistan, record worldwide inflation, and the abundance of petro-dollars in search of a safe home. A climate of political and economic turbulence created an atmosphere in which it seemed that anything might happen, and probably

would. Though there were some real supply shortages, the fundamentals of metals futures had become predominantly those of international affairs and finance. With the continued decline of the United States dollar, the precious metals suddenly became the preferred value haven, a much sought after storage place for monies threatened by inflation, war, taxes, currency fluctuations, popular unrest, high interest rates, and widespread pessimism about the economic future. (See Figures 14–22 and 14–23.)

Whether the metals markets can sustain the pressure and pace of their first years is anybody's guess. If global politics and international economics do remain the fundamentals in the metals futures markets, more uncertainty and volatility are likely. The same tumultuous kind of developments that inspired the gigantic bull markets of 1979–1980 could well be the undoing of those markets, and not just through the collapses that must inevitably follow all such steep upsurges. Intervention by worried governments or market regulators, scared by these conditions, could strangle the futures trade. Silver went into this kind of crisis at the peak of the boom when fears of a squeeze caused a tight lid to be clamped on new positions. The entanglement of metals markets in the increasingly unstable network of global tensions makes them far more vulnerable to catastrophe (as well as to great profit making swings) than domestically centered and stabilized markets. But whatever forms they take, the metals markets are sure to continue their preëminent role in world affairs into the coming decades.

However, excitement and media coverage surrounding metals price reactions to events in far-off lands should not be al-

FIGURE 14–22

world gold production
thousand fine troy ounces

	1971	1972	1973	1974	1975	1976	1977**
South Africa	31,389	29,285	27,495	24,388	22,938	22,936	22,600
Canada	2,243	2,079	1,954	1,698	1,654	1,686	1,740
U.S.	1,495	1,450	1,176	1,127	1,052	1,048	1,030
other noncommunist	4,398	4,899	5,002	5,341	5,261	6,243	6,460
total noncommunist	39,525	37,713	35,627	32,554	30,905	31,913	31,830
USSR*	6,700	6,900	7,100	7,300	7,500	7,700	7,900
other communist*	270	270	270	270	270	270	270
total communist	6,970	7,170	7,370	7,570	7,770	7,970	8,170
world total	46,495	44,883	42,997	40,124	38,675	39,883	40,000

Source: U.S. Bureau of Mines.
*estimated
**preliminary

central bank gold reserves
million fine troy ounces

	1950	1960	1970	1976
Austria	1.4	8.3	20.2	20.9
Belgium	16.8	33.4	33.4	42.2
Canada	16.6	25.3	22.6	21.6
Denmark	0.9	3.1	1.9	1.8
France	17.8	46.9	100.9	101.0
Germany	0	84.9	113.7	117.6
Italy	7.3	62.9	82.5	82.5
Japan	0.2	7.1	15.2	21.1
Latin America	45.5	38.9	30.9	29.7
Middle East	7.5	15.9	27.9	31.6
Netherlands	8.9	41.5	51.1	54.3
Norway	1.4	0.9	0.7	1.0
Portugal	5.5	15.8	25.8	27.7
South Africa	5.6	5.1	19.0	12.7
Spain	3.2	5.1	14.2	14.3
Sweden	2.6	4.9	5.7	5.8
Switzerland	42.6	62.4	78.0	83.3
U.K.	81.8	80.0	38.5	20.9
U.S.	652.0	508.7	316.3	274.7
other	34.2	32.6	51.1	45.7
world total	951.8	1,083.7	1,049.6	1,010.4

Source: Chicago Board of Trade.

lowed to totally obscure the persistence of fundamentals in the old sense of the word. Metals are still industrial commodities over which supply and demand still exercise an influence. The same general program of analysis concerning production, distribution, consumption, etc. ought to be applied when trading the metals.

Descriptions of the market and predictions of price moves should take place within the context of the general economic picture and with reference to the stage of the business cycle. Commercial inventories will be large at the beginning of an expansion, holding down price rises. In time supplies will be depleted as con-

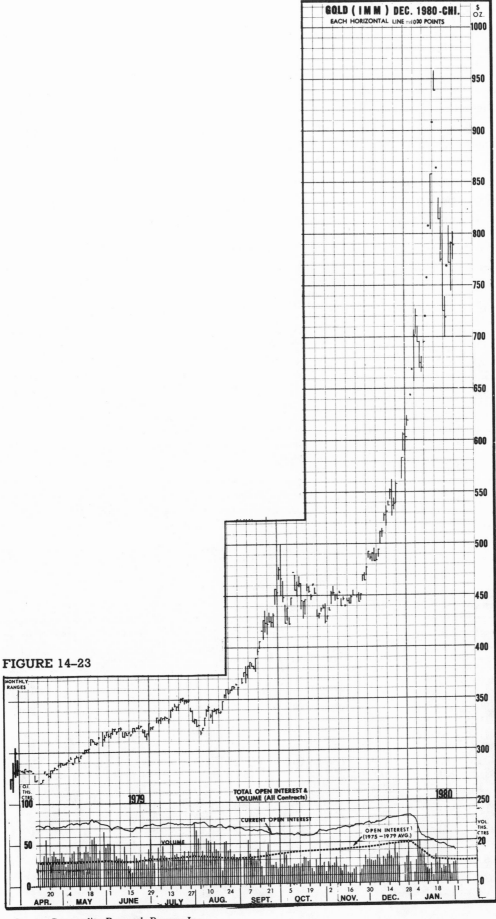

FIGURE 14-23

Source: Commodity Research Bureau, Inc.

sumption takes an upturn and factors other than supply play an increasing part. Rising interest rates at the height of expansion (or inflation) will make the metals more attractive in comparison to bonds and securities. Inflation will aid in driving up the price of metals until a break in one or more fundamentals occurs: interna- tional tension may ease, an induced recession may bring slackening demand, or a drop in interest rates may send investors back to less risky vehicles. The metals trader will have to scrutinize all the major economic indicators—GNP, consumer price index, industrial capacity utilization, money supplies, and productivity—as

FIGURE 14–24

U.S. Consumption of Silver, by End Use   In Thousands of Troy Ounces

Year	Bearings	Brazing Alloys & Solders	Catalysts	Dental & Medical	Electroplated Ware	Batteries	Contacts & Conductors	Jewelry	Mirrors	Photographic Materials	Sterling Ware	Coins, Medallions[2]	Total Net Industrial Consumption	Coinage	Total Consumption
1966	569	18,419	2,683	2,457	21,486	12,517	33,676	6,349	2,946	48,435	30,894	2,564	183,696	53,852	237,548
1967	600	15,391	5,847	2,690	17,897	11,405	26,777	5,751	2,174	50,306	30,269	1,925	171,032	43,851	214,883
1968	451	15,124	2,310	3,094	15,279	5,764	25,805	4,538	1,744	41,607	28,349	1,228	145,293	36,833	182,126
1969	481	16,549	4,081	1,591	12,706	3,799	34,555	3,011	1,510	41,380	20,291	1,592	141,546	19,408	160,594
1970	383	14,035	1,999	1,804	11,437	6,342	25,183	5,119	1,386	38,044	19,115	3,556	128,404	709	129,113
1971	355	12,085	1,730	1,485	10,909	5,631	27,954	3,447	1,112	36,073	22,729	5,636	129,146	2,474	131,620
1972	344	12,214	3,430	1,991	12,716	6,044	36,434	4,870	1,225	38,251	27,163	6,381	151,063	2,284	153,347
1973	375	17,736	5,988	3,022	14,542	4,155	40,209	5,778	2,579	51,979	40,100	9,477	195,941	920	196,861
1974	416	14,514	7,293	2,401	13,179	4,195	31,218	5,235	3,947	49,579	22,147	22,272	177,015	1,017	178,031
1975	458	13,582	8,785	1,503	8,717	4,253	27,211	12,734	3,150	46,074	23,717	7,186	157,650	2,740	160,390
1976	273	11,198	12,267	1,942	9,534	3,490	32,329	10,995	4,622	55,530	19,815	8,240	170,559	1,315	171,874
1977[1]	520	12,586	8,937	2,227	6,834	5,789	31,293	8,056	2,130	53,670	16,690	4,254	153,845	91	153,936
1978[3]	400	11,000	8,800	2,000	7,300	6,200	31,500	7,200	2,000	60,000	19,200	2,900	159,500	100	159,600
1979															

[1] Preliminary.   [2] Includes commemorative objects.   [3] Estimate.   *Source: Bureau of Mines.*

Consumption of Refined Copper[2] in the United States   In Thousands of Short Tons

Year	Cathodes	Wire Bars	Ingot & Ingot Bars	Cakes & Slabs	Billets	Other	Wire Mills	Brass Mills	Chemical Plants	Secondary Smelters	Foundries	Miscellaneous	Total Consumption
1966	196.0	1,396.0	259.0	234.3	264.0	10.6	1,370.8	928.5	2.3	19.7	38.6		2,360.0
1967	166.8	1,254.6	149.1	153.1	202.0	9.8	1,240.2	650.4	2.4	9.0	33.6		1,935.6
1968	164.5	1,191.7	169.6	122.4	221.6	10.5	1,189.3	652.5	1.6	6.4	30.6		1,880.3
1969	241.1	1,270.8	179.8	172.5	258.4	19.6	1,296.3	797.1	3.1	7.0	38.7		2,142.2
1970	247.0	1,275.8	145.7	157.1	202.0	15.7	1,338.7	660.6	2.2	7.0	34.7		2,043.3
1971	309.4	1,236.9	118.3	154.8	182.3	17.7	1,324.9	655.8	1.5	6.9	30.4		2,019.5
1972	425.3	1,331.9	141.4	160.5	161.4	18.2	1,526.3	667.2	.9	10.0	34.5		2,238.9
1973	531.2	1,356.0	147.8	193.4	174.7	33.9	1,672.3	714.4	N.A.	10.6	N.A.		2,437.0
1974	579.7	1,136.7	143.1	178.0	138.6	18.1	1,474.3	670.2	.7	9.2	19.4	20.4	2,194.2
1975	527.9	722.8	72.5	97.7	75.7	4.1	1,061.3	439.0	.5	4.5	14.0	15.3	1,534.5
1976	846.0	768.0	93.5	123.8	84.0	8.6	1,346.0	574.9	.5	3.1	15.4	19.7	1,991.9
1977[1]	965.5	861.3	90.2	115.0	103.3	11.2	1,511.2	628.6	N.A.	6.6	N.A.	N.A.	2,185.0
1978[3]	1,110.6	877.0	105.0	129.8	125.5	8.1	1,669.4	682.6	N.A.	3.9	N.A.	N.A.	2,391.9
1979													

[1] Preliminary.   [2] Primary and secondary.   [3] Estimate of 36,000 tons included in total.   *Source: Bureau of Mines.*
Source: Commodity Research Bureau, Inc.

well as those fundamentals specifically bearing on the supply or use of a particular metal. (Auto sales indicate demand for catalytic converters using platinum, housing starts indicate demand for copper in wiring, etc.) The trader is challenged to evaluate these factors and then to weigh them against the political and international fundamentals. This is a dangerous game, especially in a hot market populated by professionals trading for clients willing to pay any price and to wield huge positions. (See Figure 14–24.)

Metals prices tend to move together as a group, with gold or silver pulling copper, platinum, and others along with it. Speculators satiated with gold and silver, or fleeing an exhausted market, have taken to trading in other metals, much to the consternation of copper hedgers and others who complain loudly of the effects the speculators have on their operations. All traders, speculators, or hedgers must keep a sharp eye on the swings of the other metals markts. (See Figure 14–25.)

Gold: Gold futures prices are tied to the gold markets in New York, London, Paris, Zurich, and Hong Kong. The "fixed" price at London, set twice daily by bullion dealers, acts as an international reference point. The most active futures contracts trade on New York's Commodity Exchange, Inc. (Comex) and the CME's International Monetary Market. These contracts are in 100 troy ounces. Limits, trade rules, and margins may vary wildly with the condition of the market. Taken together, the exchanges offer contracts for every month of the year extending over a 23-month period.

Gold supplies come from new mine output, private holdings, and bank and government stocks. World production declined during the 1970s, though high

prices may cause some reversals in this tendency. South Africa, producer of over half the world's gold, estimates possible output between 1980 and 2030 at 20,000 metric tons. Gold markets react very sensitively to supply fluctuations on a daily and weekly basis occasioned by auctions, sales, and purchases of existing stocks. Traders follow announcements of government sales and plan their moves accordingly. Recent efforts to dampen gold price rises with increased sales have failed to work, as the supply of currency chasing gold was just too overwhelming (this, again, a reflection of oil money and inflation). The large gold deposits held by Western banks have historically been the bedrock of the free world monetary system, a structure undergoing painful adjustments under pressure from floating currencies and the wealth displacements caused by astronomical oil prices. The greater above ground physical liquidity of gold, as compared to silver, most often allows the market to ride out even the most hysterical gyrations, as a small international group of dealers, bankers, and government agents may exercise restraint through their considerable holdings.

Silver: Once upon a time silver was a surplus commodity kept afloat by U.S. Treasury purchases at above market prices. Redemption of monetary certificates for silver ended in 1968 and the precious metals were soon divorced from currencies. The notorious volatility of the silver markets since reflects a thin above ground supply and one that thus is vulnerable to action by a very few large speculators. The 800 percent boom in silver prices from 1979–1980 sent many small investors fleeing, though some took hefty profits with them, while open interest declined and trading became a power play between

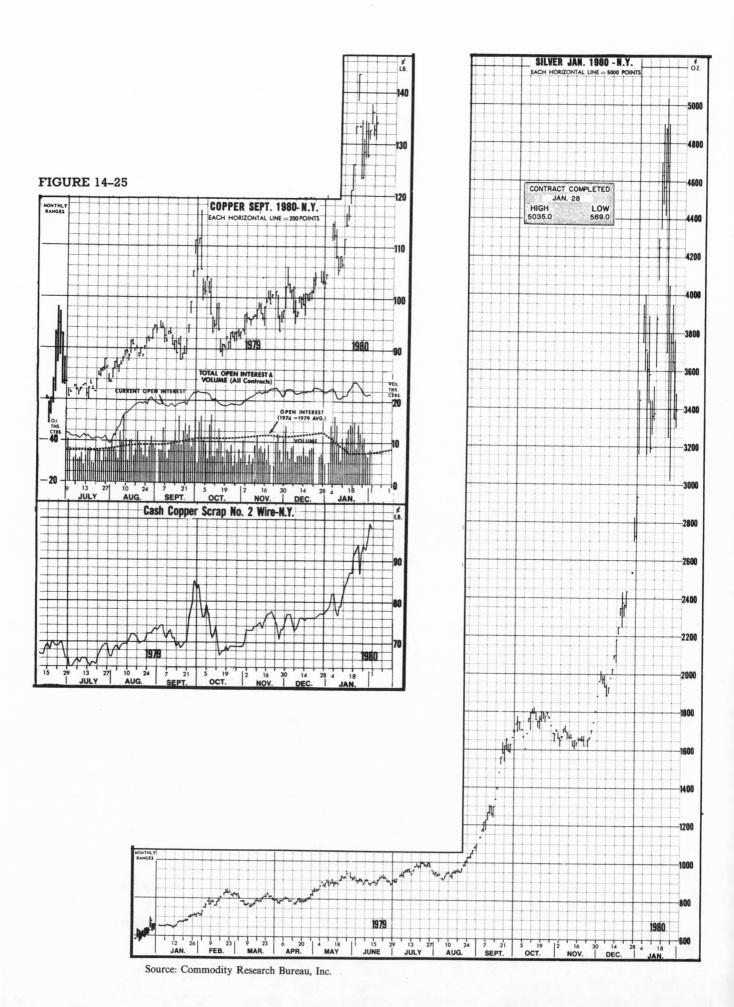

FIGURE 14-25

Source: Commodity Research Bureau, Inc.

the large traders and the exchanges. Contracts for 5,000 troy ounces trade at Comex and at the Chicago Board of Trade in variable months over a 23-month period. Rules, limits, and margins are set by the exchanges in response to market conditions.

Silver supplies flow in from mine output and industrial recovery. About 75 percent of new silver is recovered from lead, zinc, copper, and other ores so that factors for these metals always influence silver and vice versa. Now that minting of negotiable coins has virtually ceased, silver's major use is in photographic materials, electronic hardware, and sterling silverware. The United States is by far the world's leading consumer of silver. In assessing the fundamentals related to supply and demand, the silver trader compares elements of supply (mine production, secondary production from coins and scrap, and government sales) to rates of industrial use in order to estimate to what degree speculative silver holdings may be called on for commercial use (and what reception this demand may receive). Current studies predict a near-term decline in silver stocks with industrial recovery and industrial consumption down, while in the long run mine output should increase in response to record prices. The U.S. Bureau of Mines puts world silver resources at 18 billion ounces.

Copper: Major copper producers around the world include the United States, Chile, U.S.S.R., Canada, and Zambia. As a widespread, world commodity, copper's price is sensitive to production changes and import-export fluctuations. Traders must watch for labor unrest, strikes, transportation breakdowns, accidents, old mine exhaustions, and new explorations. The nationalization of copper

production facilities in a variety of nations means the trader is more than ever tied to government and political activity; a mine may remain in operation despite losses or supply gluts out of a commitment to employment, social progress, or other noneconomic factors. Upheavals in unstable countries may play havoc with prices and supplies. A handful of multinational corporations are involved in the copper trade, and their actions are often an index to future copper trends.

Copper consumption concentrates in durable consumer goods, so that copper tends to follow the general business cycle. Copper joined in the great metals boom of 1979–1980. Its performance, like those of silver and platinum, were helped along by real shortages outpaced by industrial and speculative demand. The heavy spillover of "buy-at-any-price" investors into copper from the gold and silver markets, however, sent prices temporarily far above levels harmonious with supply/demand statistics. Copper entered the 1980s with sudden glamour, much to the dismay of some industrial hedgers and users accustomed to a more predictable and tranquil market. Under pressure from worried investors, copper too became a precious metal and a hedge against economic uncertainties.

The 25,000 pound copper contract trades at the Comex in variable months over a 23-month period. Price changes are registered in multiples of five-hundredths of a cent per pound, equivalent to $12.50 per contract, a one cent move equaling $250. Normal daily price range is 5 cents per pound above or below the previous close.

Information: Statistical data on the metals trade, cash, and futures is available from the respective exchanges. The Federal Bureau of Mines publishes a number of relevant reports, as does the U.S. Census Bureau. World statistics may be had from the American Bureau of Metal Statistics and the British Bureau of Non-Ferrous Metal Statistics. The Bureau of the Mint and the Department of Commerce furnish data on silver use and foreign trade.

FINANCIAL FUTURES

Interest rate futures scored some spectacular successes after their introduction in 1975, setting new trading records and drawing a new sector of the economic community into the futures markets. These contracts were created to meet an unprecedented instability in the price of money itself, a figure which is roughly a direct translation of interest rates. Futures markets have proved themselves to be the best known method for managing the risks of price volatility, so it came as no surprise when exchanges once associated with soybeans or pork bellies began trading in GNMA mortgages and Treasury Bills. These markets arose for the same reasons and follow the same basic principles as their agricultural and livestock forerunners. When the future price of a commodity, in this case the money needed to do business, becomes sufficiently unpredictable and wide swinging, that commodity becomes a candidate for a futures contract that can reduce or eliminate risk. From 1932 to 1964 corporate bond yields varied only slightly, keeping close to the 4–5 percent range from 1957–1966. Short-term rates, though more active, kept to relatively calm cycles. These old patterns were destroyed by the political and economic tumult that characterized the late 1960s and the 1970s. The interest rate on U.S. Treasury Bills stood at 5.1 percent in Sep-

tember 1968. By 1980 rates had hit 20 percent, with an erratic history of ups and downs in between. (See Figure 14–26.) Business as usual in financial circles could not proceed without a new tool for hedging against such potentially calamitous variations.

Many analysts see a continuation of the boom in interest rate futures into the 1980s and beyond. The realization of these hopes for the newcomers will depend on how conditions influencing interest rates change in the coming decades and on how active the government's hand becomes in controlling politically sensitive money market prices. It may be questioned whether or not the interest rates offer the same long term stability as markets as do the agriculturals. After the initial fanfare, a shaking out of contracts is already underway, even as new variants seek approval to trade. The same chaos in economic realities that motivated the creation of interest rate futures could alter or even destroy them in the future. Most likely from current trends, trader interest will join forces with contract efficiency and market conditions to narrow contracts down to a few lasting instruments, as has traditionally occurred in the introduction of other markets and commodities.

This promises to be one of commodity futures trading's fastest changing areas, one not easily described with any hope of eternal accuracy. The details of financial futures can involve economic intricacies requiring volumes to unravel. Elaborate systems of high finance, often accompanied by difficult mathematical calculations, tax the patience and skill of the average trader. Fortunately, little of this complicated inside machinery need concern the speculator, who knows that when all is said and done prices can only go up, down, or sideways. The hedger, a professional investor for institutional money users and dealers, already knows how the system works and need only learn how to trade in the futures market (a comparatively easy assignment). What follows here is a discussion of the bare essentials regarding the fundamentals of interest rate futures. (Those wishing to delve deeper into this fascinating world should consult the growing number of publications specializing in the field; see Appendix I.)

In all interest rate futures trades, the trader buys or sells a contract for delivery of a specified amount of financial instruments. These instruments have, in them-selves, fixed rates of return, set either by an interest rate affixed at sale or by the difference between what the investor paid for the instrument and its value at maturity. For GNMA certificates, for example, the face interest rate is 8 percent. For U.S. Treasury Bills, the government sells the bills at a price depending on the prevailing rate of interest, so that at maturity the difference between price paid and face value approximately equals the rate prevailing at the time of sale.

Now, obviously the price an investor is willing to pay for an interest-governed financial instrument depends on how favorable its rate of return is as compared to the prevailing interest rates and for re-

FIGURE 14–26
INTEREST RATES

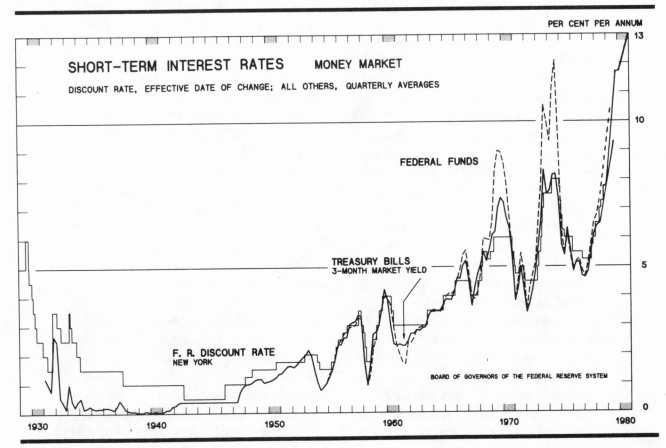

Source: Commodity Research Bureau, Inc.

turns on other instruments. An 8 percent certificate is not very attractive when the prevailing rate is 13 percent and inflation is at 14 percent. On the other hand, an 8 percent certificate might sell at a premium should interest rates ever fall below 8 percent. Financial instruments, then, are priced at sale to give a certain *yield,* and that yield is pegged to current interest rates. An 8 percent certificate may yield the investor 13 percent on his funds if the price he pays for the instrument is well below "par," or face value. Thus, the higher prevailing interest rates go, the higher expected yield rates go, and the lower prices for financial instruments will go. If interest rates and yields decline, prices for interest rate instruments will rise. The trader in these contracts must always remember: Interest rates and prices move *inversely* to each other. (See Figure 14–27.)

It follows that price quotations for financial instruments are given in percentages of par value. Treasury Bill futures are priced at $100 less the yield, as they are sold at a discount rather than with a fixed "coupon" interest rate. (Rates were called coupons because actual coupons were attached, to be clipped and mailed in as claims for interest payments by the bearer.) A quote of 88.04 would mean a discount of 11.96, reflecting short-term interest rates in the 12 percent category, making the 11.96 yield a sufficient one. Ginnie Maes, Bonds, and Notes are quoted as percentages of par with minimum fluctuations of $\frac{1}{32}$. A price of 94–01 translates as 94–$\frac{1}{32}$ percent of par, indicating that for 8 percent Ginnie Maes the surrounding interest rates are in excess of 8 percent, so the certificate sells for less than face value to increase the yield. A price of 101–24 would be 101–$\frac{24}{32}$ per-

cent of par, indicating a prevailing rate below 8 percent, so that the certificate carrying an 8 percent coupon sells for more than par, bringing the yield into line. Commercial paper quotations are given as an annualized discount from 100—that is, a discount of 6.54 would be quoted as 93.46.

Interest rate traders closely follow what is called the "yield curve." (See Figure 14–28.) The yield curve expresses the relation of yields to maturities, and many speculators trade this line as well as the line on the price chart. A "normal" yield curve rises with length of maturity and then levels off, as investors are usually willing to accept lower yields on short-term instruments in return for the greater liquidity and relatively smaller risk of these securities. A fundamental of the yield curve is that short-term financial instrument values are affected less by temporary interest rate fluctuations than are long-term instruments that "lock-in" rates for long periods of time. In times of great fluctuations, the investor wishes to stay out of long-term commitments until prices settle down, keeping his money turning over in early maturing instruments. Variations in the curve, or an inversion putting short-term yields higher than long-term yields, may tell the trader something about expectations for future movements in interest rates and signal trades in only part of the curve or of one maturity group against another.

Yields and prevailing rates, like all other prices, fluctuate daily in the market place where monetary commodities are bought and sold. The supply and demand picture for financial instruments involves a chief supplier, the United States government; other suppliers like corporations issuing commercial papers; a regulatory and

FIGURE 14-27

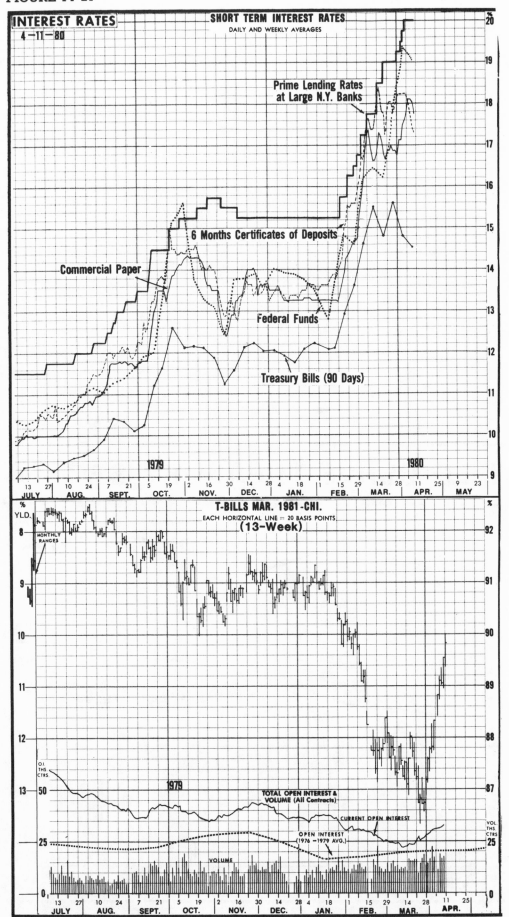

Source: Commodity Research Bureau, Inc.

FIGURE 14–28

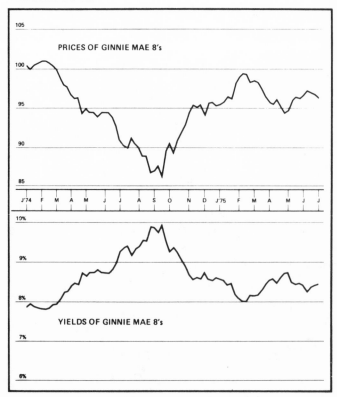

Source: Chicago Board of Trade.

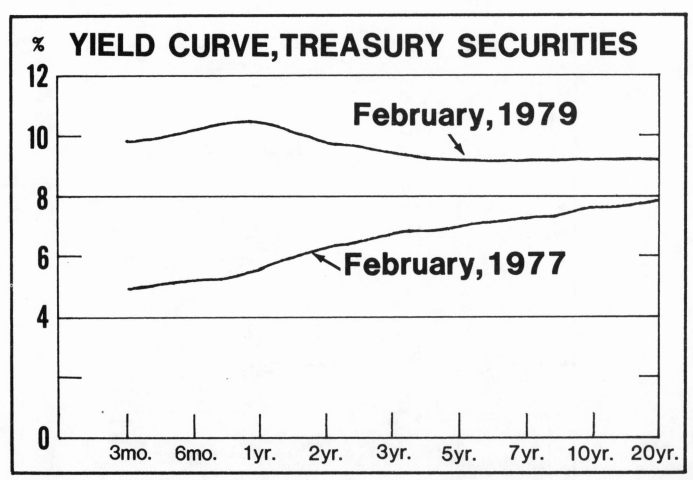

Source: Commodity Research Bureau, Inc.

distribution structure headed by the Federal Reserve Board and populated by dealers and investment institutions; and a demand sector that is in reality the nation's economy as a whole.

The heart of the action is the Federal Reserve System (though even this mighty institution has been threatened by past crises). The System, made up of member banks, organizes the financial transactions of the nation. Banks borrow and lend money back and forth daily to meet obligations. The rate these banks charge each other is the Federal Funds rate, which stays abreast of the Federal "discount rate," the amount charged by the Federal Reserve for monies borrowed from it. The manipulation of this rate by the Board is a major tool in managing the total money supply, availability of credit, interest rates, and economic progress as a whole. About every two days the Treasury or some other government agency will hold an auction, buying or selling securities to raise funds for government expenses or to buy securities to provide infusions of cash into the market place. The yields on these securities bid by dealers are extremely important trendsetters in the financial futures markets, and every trader watches closely as the market responds to the results of the latest government auction.

Federal Reserve actions and policies constitute the single most significant indicator for financials, altering reserve requirements for member banks (thus controlling the amount of cash available in the supply channels) and setting rates and auctions to bolster its policies. Yet, the Fed itself is always reacting to a large number of fundamental economic indicators the trader should be aware of in predicting Fed policies and futures trends. These include the various price indexes,

measures of production and employment, gauges of wholesale and retail demand, data on inventories, housing starts, auto sales, import-export balances, personal income, and government deficits. The price movements of other key financial commodities, such as the United States dollar and gold, can also be influential factors.

Many different interest rate contracts trade at the nation's exchanges. For current details and descriptions the trader should consult a knowledgeable broker and write to the respective exchange. Generally, interest rate contracts have fallen into the following categories:

1. TREASURY BILLS. This is the most widely used money market instrument issued by the Treasury to manage its cash position and to finance short-term requirements. The short-term and liquidity of T-Bills have made them very popular with institutional hedgers holding older long-term bond portfolios.

2. TREASURY NOTES AND BONDS. Notes are intermediate maturity government securities in 2, 4, or 4–6 year denominations. Bonds are long-term obligations of 15 or 20 years. The fortunes of these issues on the market are quite sensitive to steep increases in interest rates which normally will drive investors to short-term instruments, killing the bond markets.

3. GNMA (Ginnie Mae). Ginnie Mae certificates, in contract units of $100,000 at 8 percent, are backed by pools of Government National Mortgage Association guaranteed FHA or VA loans. They have been promoted at particularly attractive hedging vehicles for savings and loan associations, mortgage dealers, and others involved in the financing of real estate transactions.

4. COMMERCIAL PAPER. Recently, large corporations have found that issuing their own promissory notes is

a profitable alternative to bank borrowing. Funds needed for capital investment or other business expenses are financed through the sale of CP issues with maturities of 5 to 270 days. The paper must be rated A-1 and P-1 by Standard and Poor's and Moody's, respectively.

Another group of financial futures actively traded on United States exchanges is that of the foreign currencies. (See Figure 14–29.) Strong markets in the British Pound, the Canadian Dollar, the Japanese Yen, the Swiss Franc, and the German Deutschemark flourish at the IMM and are proposed for the New York Futures Exchange. Their analysis would involve turning the fundamentals for securities upon the United States dollar and studying the economic fundamentals for the particular nation involved. Currencies float up and down against one another with fundamental events around the globe and have been especially influenced by the financial activities of the OPEC oil nations. The eventual approval of contracts in stock-exchange related items seems inevitable and will bring the trader yet another vast new economic field to play in and master.

FIGURE 14–29

THE TRADING PROGRAM

Chapter 15

THE ART OF PRICE FORECASTING

FUNDAMENTAL FORECASTING

Commodity price changes cannot be scientifically predicted. Price forecasting is an art, which means it involves human intuition and flexibility as well as mathematical precision. Every price change situation is slightly different from every other, as the mix of factors has infinite possibilities. Computer analysis can figure an enormous amount of information into a trading prediction, but it can only do so by partially ignoring the uniqueness of each situation. Overelaborate forecasting models average together inherently random incidents and assume more uniformity and consistency in the markets than really exists. They are comforting to traders because they offer the kind of "scientific" and "technological" sophistication that has worked so well in many other fields. But the markets remain human and random. The trader cannot escape from the agony (or joy) of making his own subjective decisions and of taking responsibility for the trade, even if it only means evaluating the computer's choices. The trader has to size up forecasting methods, rely upon those he trusts, and apply those which are relevant to each trading opportunity. If there were a perfect, scientific way to forecast commodity prices, the futures markets would long ago have ceased to function.

It should also be said that price forecasting is often overemphasized in commodity trading books and other futures literature. Detecting a price move is only the bare beginning of the trader's journey toward the hoped for pot of gold. More hard work comes in trading the line that prices form as they actually move across the price chart. Riding a price move profitably demands as much, if not more, art and skill as the forecasting of price. Forecasting the direction of prices won't yield a cent of profit unless the trader learns how to work that move to the best advantage through a carefully planned trading program.

Market forecasting systems are divided into fundamental and technical studies. As we have seen, fundamental forecasting relies on study of the demand and supply factors—"the fundamentals"—that make up market prices. Fundamental forecasting seeks to find changing aspects which have not yet been found and discounted by the market at large. Technical study, on the other hand, attempts to find trends and patterns in the market place itself rather than in the basic demand and supply for the commodity. Technical factors would include price chart formations, volume and open interest statistics, historical price patterns, and other data primarily concerned with trading itself. Some traders claim to rely solely upon fundamental or technical analysis. The consensus is, however, that the best forecasting systems include elements of both. The trader must check many indicators of various kinds, without prejudice, before confirming a price forecast.

Two basic types of information are found in the study of fundamental price factors. Fundamentals may reveal the possible *range* within which the commodity can be expected to trade. In this the study of natural or government imposed price floors and ceilings is crucial. Having staked out the general price range, the trader can also attempt to uncover elements of supply and demand which are likely to change in the near future. The speculator can scoop his competitors by being among the first to discount news that has not yet been widely assimilated. There is real art involved here, for the trader must calculate how important or decisive a certain change in fundamentals will be in itself and in relation to other factors.

How far can price go without running into major flak from competing products? Will government policy intervene to offset the anticipated move? Can other traders be counted on to discount the news in the same direction? How deep and how long will the effects be of a change in the particular fundamental? Will a chain reaction be set off in other factors or commodities that will further change the trends?

What factors have determined prices up to now and how stable are they? If the trader can answer these and like questions, he has a good fundamental basis for "guesstimating" prices in the near future. Although the number of elements which determine the price of any commodity at a given time are nearly infinite, there are usually only a handful that critically affect a price change. Factors which seldom or never change will seldom or never change prices. The number of certified grain storage elevators in the Chicago area will have a direct price effect in the delivery month, but it does not fluctuate from year to year. The relative impact of a fundamental factor has to be decided before its influence on prices can be guessed.

Floors and ceilings for commodity prices have a reciprocal relation to changes in fundamental factors. Floors and ceilings, as discussed above, must be known for each commodity the speculator wishes to trade or the real importance of fundamentals will be impossible to gauge. If corn were priced at $3 a bushel and CCC wheat offered at $4.10, a set of price boundaries exists for wheat. Near-month wheat selling at $4.00 has an exactly equal chance of going up or down in price, but it is going to begin running into heavy flak at $4.10 as large CCC held stockpiles enter the market. If the wheat price exercises its option to fall, it can fall all the way to, say, $3.60 before it triggers heavy demand from cattlemen and hog farmers making purchases of cheap wheat for feed. In the absence of other information, wheat is a better sale than purchase in such a situation. The trader has no idea in which direction the price is going to move, but he knows it cannot rise much more than 10 cents. On the other hand, it can drop

40 cents if the extreme thing happens. In commodities, extreme things happen all the time.

The first rule of fundamental forecasting, then, is *choose your risks* so that the potential profit is at least three or four times potential loss. *Never sell a price that is near its natural or government imposed floor. Never buy a price that is near its ceiling.* In the above case, 10 cents is far too much money to lose with a short position in a climbing market. The trader should limit this loss through the placement of a stop loss order at a price above the sale price, to take him out of the market if the price goes against him. An important part of position management is figuring the ratio of possible gains to possible losses, calculating the rough probability of each and trading accordingly. Fundamental analysis provides some very useful guidelines for estimating such ratios.

FUNDAMENTAL ERRORS

Fundamentals are notoriously easy to misinterpret. The trader, novice, or professional cannot be warned too often about the pitfalls of forecasting on the basis of fundamentals. A fundamental event (drought, interest rate change, housing boom) is never, in and of itself, either bullish or bearish. Its effect may push prices up, down, or sideways depending on the total market complexion. A huge carry over in corn is not necessarily indicative of lower prices if prices are already near their low. It could be bullish news if the surplus has been overzealously discounted, or neutral if the figures are historically about normal. A related point is that new fundamental information is only "new" if the market has not accu-

rately absorbed it. News items are reprinted countless times in the guise of up-to-the-minute bulletins. A story read by a trader about an increase in the money supply may be hours or days behind the Federal Reserve Board's announcement and weeks behind the market's anticipations. Even if newswire reports seem hot, check around before concluding that you've scooped the opposition.

A key lesson is that fundamentals are unreliable when it comes to timing market entrances and exits. Traders who rush off to buy or sell on the basis of news flashes almost inevitably limp home broke. Fundamentals are an excellent source of information for determining market trends and limits, but they are a very dangerous way of picking precise and profitable places to establish futures positions. A common error in such cases is lack of perspective. The trader sees a headline: "60,000 Head of Cattle Contaminated!" Is the news bullish? With a total cattle population of well over 100 million, the news is not likely to have much of a lasting effect.

The speculator should be suspicious of comparisons. "Lumber Milling up 20% over December" could be a bearish signal unless, of course, December's figures were down 40 percent from the previous period. In reading fundamental comparisons, the strength of each of the events must be well inspected before a comparison of the two is meaningful. This especially pertains to popular year-to-year comparisons. The trader should also look cautiously at differences in short- and long-term effects. A sharp rise in grain prices will raise costs for livestock feeders, eventually causing production cutbacks and higher prices. But the short-term effect of herd liquidation will be lower prices as markets are glutted. A depression in housing starts may cause a temporary decline in lumber and plywood prices, but the relative ease of closing mills and reducing supplies can cause higher prices in the long run.

Price ceilings and floors also invite confusion. Time after time the markets reinforce the lesson that prices can and do drop below the cost of production. The cost of production is not an absolute price support factor. Once the product is on the market, supply and demand take over and the market disregards costs whenever it can. Producers may have no choice but to sell at a loss, for the costs of financing inventory and renegotiating outstanding loans will demand that some return is better than none. The old adage of the livestock packer still stands: "Sell or smell."

TECHNICAL FORECASTING

Technical forecasting proceeds by analyzing the price and trading data of the market itself, cash and futures. It is not concerned primarily with the fundamental factors that shape supply and demand. The underlying assumption of the technician is that fundamentals are too numerous and unpredictable to be of much use. Moreover, he argues that fundamentals do not themselves determine prices: Rather, it is the interpretation of the market (including fundamentals) by the traders as a whole that determines prices. Thus, the most direct and relevant approach, say the technicians, is to study the patterns of real market behavior.

The favored method of technical analysis is construction of charts (in dozens of varieties) showing past price behavior. Technical considerations also involve other trading statistics, but the primary tool remains the price chart. The chart tells all the technician needs to know: the

actual direction of prices and their historical tendencies. It makes no difference whether price drops are due to an altered supply and demand curve, the seasonal lifting of long hedges, or because some traders closed positions to use the money for other purposes. The price drops in any event, and it is the drop which is significant to the trader. If, for example, Canadian Dollar prices have had difficulty passing a certain level of the price chart, that is the factor which influences the technical trader in choosing his position. Nobody wants to buy or sell past that level. *Why* doesn't matter.

If price moved in neat jogs as predicted by the random walk model, technical trading would consist of a mere set of mechanical rules. One would buy any price above the resting area represented by random minor fluctuation with the sure knowledge that price is speeding to a new level and hold the position until the price drops, reversing the trend. Or one would sell any price that is hit below the resting area and hold the short position until the price stopped sinking. Such rules would serve to speed the price to its new level, making the unpredictable jobs extremely abrupt and short-lived. The context would be one of getting on the price movement as early as possible through the use of resting stop orders without setting the stop order so close that it is tripped by insignificant shifts in the resting market. Traders who set their stops too far from the resting area would find their orders unfillable or filled at a price far away from their stop, as no trading took place during the rapid spurt to the new level. (See Figure 15–1.)

But as we have seen, random walk is not a perfect description of the reality found in commodity markets. Sometimes there will be such "channel" trading op-

FIGURE 15-1

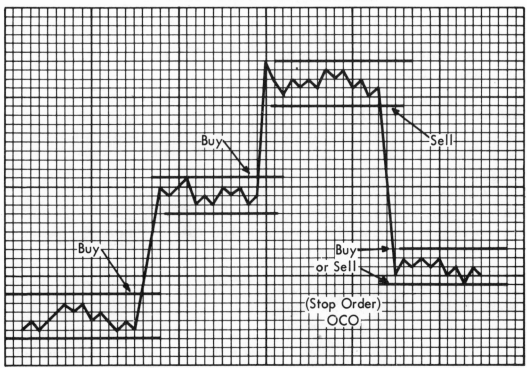

RANDOM WALK WITH BUY-SELL SIGNALS

Were random walk an accurate description of real markets, buying any rise and selling any dip beyond a level of significance would yield effortless profits.

portunities, yet almost always the prediction has to be somewhat more complicated than a simple buy and sell rule. The existence of trends in the real markets requires some technical method of deciding when a trend is about to begin and when it is about to end. Most technical tools attempt to perform these two critical tasks and thus enable the trader to capitalize on price behavior no matter the reason behind it. The goal of chart reading is to discover price trends as soon as possible, forecast their probable range and duration, and pick advantageous positions for getting into and out of the trend.

"A price at rest tends to stay at rest. A price in motion tends to stay in motion." These are tenets of the chart trader, though they also serve to underscore his

chief problem: picking the reversal, catching the moment when a resting price goes into motion or when a moving price comes to rest. A price at rest exhibits an established floor or ceiling for itself which is merely the graphic presentation of demand and supply and market conditions too complex for practical comprehension. When the price breaks through its resting channel, it is said to "signal" a buy or sell move to the trader. A price that is trending establishes a similar floor or ceiling for its trend that can be read in the formation on the chart. When the floor or ceiling is ruptured, the trend can be expected to end. The alert trader will be following a price move with the intention of profiting from both its ups and downs. If holding a long position, the speculator should also be figuring how and when to switch to the short side. Whether it takes a day or a year, every price that goes up must eventually come down—and vice versa—and the trader should be ready to profit when it happens.

CHART CONSTRUCTION

The most commonly used charting method, and the one used generally throughout this book, is the vertical line chart. A single vertical line is drawn for each day's price activity, showing the range from high to low. A small horizontal line crossing the vertical price line indicates the day's closing price. Vertical line charts may be used to illustrate prices on a weekly, monthly, or yearly basis. Their very popularity is another argument for their usefulness, as charts from different sources may be easily compared, giving technicians everywhere a kind of common language for price analysis. Such charts can be constructed and maintained on a daily basis by anyone. Normally, the vertical axis of the chart shows price and the horizontal displays the units of time (days, weeks, months, etc.). (See Figure 15–2.)

FIGURE 15–2

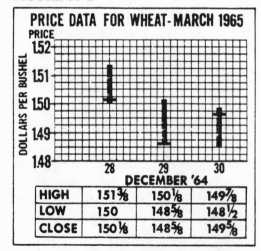

Source: Commodity Research Bureau, Inc.

FIGURE 15–3

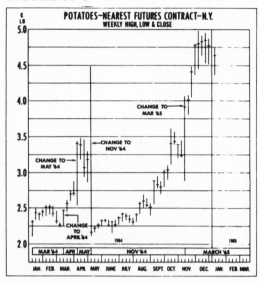

Source: "How Charts Are Used in Commodity Price Forecasting," published by Commodity Research Bureau, Inc.

Charts representing periods longer than a month often trace the movement of a single contract or of cash prices at a certain location. In the case of contracts, the chartist moves over to the next nearby contract when the previous one expires in order to put together a price chart extending beyond the life of any one contract. There is a problem with such transitions, however, as they can cause erratic jumps in the chart so constructed that do not reflect accurately the reality of the market. Such jumps are rather due to crop year changes or varieties of inter-month basis, not to radical moves in the price of one contract. Contracts for later delivery normally sell at higher prices. This upward jog will be picked up by the continuation method, showing an apparently important trading session which did not in fact exist. These jumps can be especially large when the next nearest contract is for delivery of the new crop year, which sells at prices not directly related to the old contract prices. (See Figure 15–3.)

The continuation chart shows the apparently large price jumps which occur as the old contract expires and the new gets picked up. The change to November is a new crop year, which sells at a much lower price than did the expiring old crop contract. At crossover, old contract potatoes sold as high as 4.5 cents per pound in the final days, while the new contract started out just above 2 cents. The apparent leap in prices must be ignored by the astute chart trader.

READING CHART FORMATION

What does the trader do after he has plotted a contract's prices on the chart?

Analyzing the chart begins with a few simple observations. (See Figure 15–4.) First, dominant trends. For July Copper we can see a mid-October to mid-February rise followed by a precipitous decline. In the very short-term, prices seem to be stabilizing into a possible channel. Long- and mid-term periods show great volatility, but over long enough time spans that trend can be isolated and traded. Prices could continue down, but we would expect them to meet a floor near one of the old lows. The contract-high ceiling near $1.50 leaves plenty of room on the upside for long traders, should the other indicators justify it.

How relatively significant is the apparently steep ascent of copper prices? From

FIGURE 15–4

Source: Commodity Research Bureau, Inc.

FIGURE 15-5

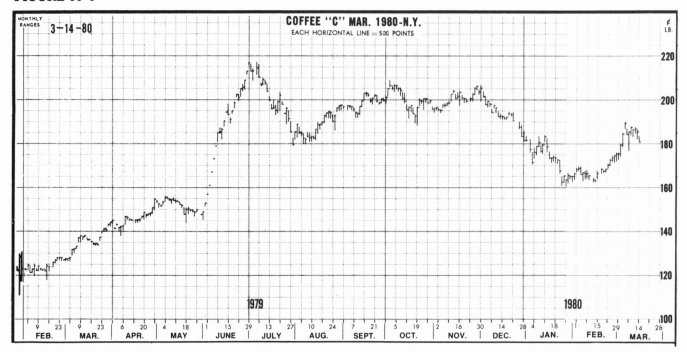

COFFEE "C" MAR. 1980-N.Y.
EACH HORIZONTAL LINE = 500 POINTS

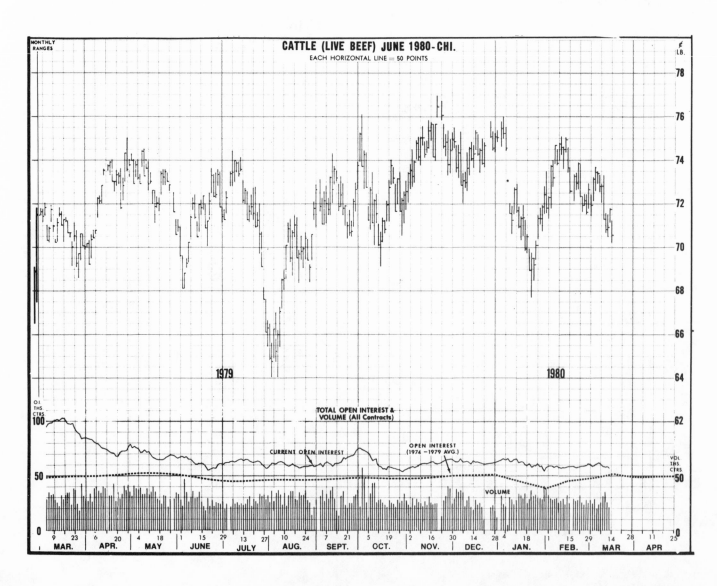

CATTLE (LIVE BEEF) JUNE 1980-CHI.
EACH HORIZONTAL LINE = 50 POINTS

TOTAL OPEN INTEREST &
VOLUME (All Contracts)

CURRENT OPEN INTEREST

OPEN INTEREST
(1974-1979 AVG.)

VOLUME

a low around 80 cents, prices rose almost 90 percent—an extraordinary jump. The bulk of it occurred over a four-month span, plenty of time for the trend to be discovered and capitalized upon. Even if the trader had waited until the price went through the old high at $1.17 to buy in, the move from mid-January to mid-February was worth over $7,000 per contract.

On the other hand, charts can be very deceptive, distorting the significance of a price trend. (See Figure 15–5.) The March coffee charts shows that from mid-June through December, prices hovered in an apparently narrow channel range of $1.80 to $2.20. The range covers only the distance between *two* of the chart's heavy black price demarcation lines. Now compare the chart for June cattle. Here, with one short exception, the price ranges from 68 cents to 76 cents, covering *four* heavy lines. One would assume that the range of cattle prices is greater than the range of coffee prices and thus that cattle is the greater risk. In fact, however, the 40 cent range in coffee represents a risk of $15,000 (1¢ move = $375), while the 8 cent range in cattle represents a $3,200 risk (1¢ move = $400). The superficial implication of a chart depends on the accident of its construction; the real meaning depends on the trader's skill in reading it. The knowledgeable technician would find that the stop-loss positions indicated by the June cattle chart (above or below the range) present an acceptable risk, while those of the March coffee chart do not. When constructing, reading, or comparing charts, pay close attention to relative sensitivity, which is determined by the incremental units chosen for each axis. You may have to smooth out some charts or accentuate others in order to bring their graphic de-

pictions into harmony with trading realities.

Beyond the assessment of general trends and price ranges, charts exhibit certain basic patterns which repeat themselves. Most of these patterns are consistent with an understanding of market discounting, and if a pattern can be shown to occur before a major price move with any reliability, it can be used for prediction. Chart traders contend that such consistency does occur, that identifiable patterns formed by price lines repeat regularly and in ways that signal profitable trades. One advantage of such patterns is that they appear in any commodity (or stock, for that matter) for which a price chart can be constructed. Instead of undertaking the impossible task of knowing all the fundamentals of one commodity or all the fundamentals of every commodity, the technical trader need only master a single system of chart and data analysis which can then be applied to any commodity. Although technical trading methods do vary considerably, most chart readers recognize a number of elemental chart patterns that are now widely used in technical forecasting.

CHANNELS

A market which is trending up or down presents potential profits for any trader who goes with the trend before it comes to its end at the next resting area. Prices will often fluctuate in a perceptible range even as they continue their predominant trend, forming a "channel" on the chart. (See Figure 15–6.) Trend lines are drawn in along the highs and lows of the range to form the graphic channel. The support line for uptrending prices is drawn by con-

FIGURE 15-6

Channels

Resistance and breakout

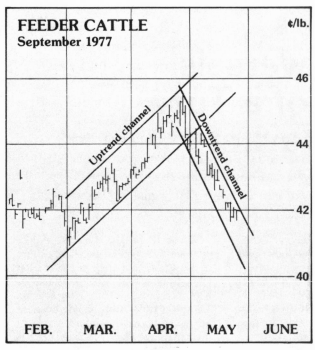

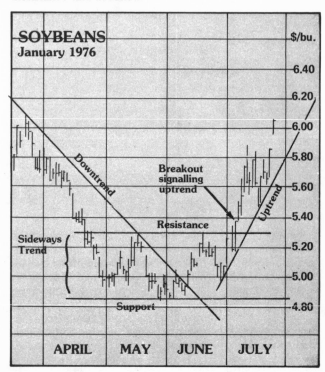

Source: "Charting Farm Markets," by Brock and Marten, Top Farmers, Inc.

necting the lows and the resistance line is drawn by connecting the highs. Prices may fluctuate within the channel for weeks without significance to the chart trader so long as they continue the trend. Once the price breaks out through the support line, prices are considered to be weakening and unable to maintain their momentum. For downward trending prices, the support line is drawn connecting the high points of the market channel and the resistance line is drawn connecting the lows. When the support line above the channel is broken, the price is considered to be firming, unable to drop further. Trend lines may be curved as well as straight. Sideways trends are charted in the same way and interpreted in similar fashions, though in this case the trader

will probably not have a position in the market until the price breaks out of the channel, whereas in uptrend and downtrend channels the breakout signals a change in a position held during the life of the trend.

SUPPORT AND RESISTANCE LEVELS

Most chart formations are, in reality, different shapes that price support and price resistance take. Chart patterns exhibit the different locations, directions, and durations of "pressure" levels for a commodity price. A pressure level is defined as a level which the price has a hard time penetrating. Price may enter a pressure level area several times but fail to penetrate it and move on. Or it may break through, in which case the old resistance level may become the new support level and the old support level become the new resistance level. These pressure levels may be single points on the chart or extended lines covering months of trading. The "strength" of support or resistance will be much discussed by traders and partly estimated by how often prices have traded to or at the pressure level. The more the level has held, the stronger it is considered to be. But frequent attacks on the pressure level may drain off traders until the break-out occurs.

One simple pressure level formation is the *double top* or *double bottom*. (See Figure 15–7.) In the August live hogs chart, prices climbed to 46.50 before running out of steam and descending. When prices reacted at 40.00, they once again headed

for 46.50 but failed to penetrate that former high. The sign was given that long pressure was simply not sufficient to produce higher prices. After that prices could only trend sideways or down. A short sale was thus indicated by the charts. The 46.50 level was found to be a *resistance area* for live hog prices. The same formation can be found at the bottom of price drops, indicating a long position is in order. Double bottoms form at what are generally referred to as *support areas*.

A common variation on price action at a support or resistance level is the *head and shoulders* formation. (See Figure 15–8.) This pattern is usually interpreted as a major reversal indicator. It begins by forming the "left shoulder," a strong upward breakout to new highs on increased volume. A minor downtrend and consolidation follows, after which another up-

FIGURE 15–7

Double top

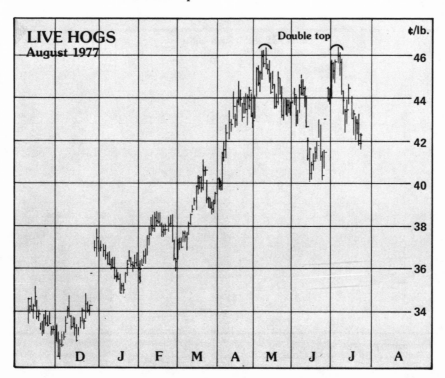

FIGURE 15–8

Head and Shoulders

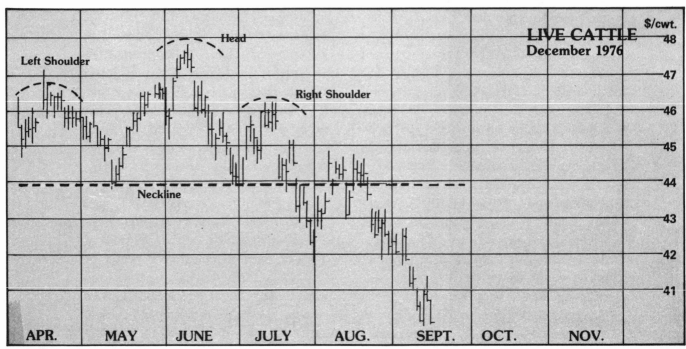

Source: "Charting Farm Markets," by Brock and Marten, Top Farmers, Inc.

FIGURE 15–9

Source: Commodity Research Bureau, Inc.

trend breakout forms the "head" as volume declines. After falling back again, prices make one last attempt to continue the uptrend, but without technical or fundamental support this "right shoulder" is only a prelude to a collapse. The significant chart signal of this pattern is the "neckline," which joins the three lowest points of the formation. When the neckline is broken through, the reversal begins, and is commonly believed to extend at least as long as the distance from the lowest point in the formation to the top of the head. This is the time to sell. An inverse head and shoulders can be formed at the bottom of a downtrend and is read in the same manner.

Another pressure level formation is the "1–2–3." (See Figure 15–9.) First prices rise substantially to a dramatically high level, point #1. Then resistance sets in, people refuse to pay at that price, and prices drop sharply to level #2. Producers and market bulls try to rally prices up again, but continued resistance holds the upswing to level #3. Once prices test this area and succumb, the downward slide sets in, confirmed by breaking past level #2 and continuing the decline for a long while.

RESTING AREAS

A number of patterns are formed by markets that are "resting" before continuing their trends. Major among these are *pennants* and *triangles*. (See Figure 15–10.) When a price slows to a stop, it will often go through a period of discounting represented on a chart by an ever narrower range of price fluctuation. Daily trading ranges from high to low grow smaller and smaller, typically comple-

FIGURE 15–10

TRIANGLES AND PENNANTS FORMATION

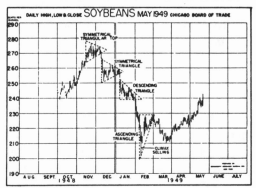

Source: "How Charts Are Used in Commodity Price Forecasting," published by Commodity Research Bureau, Inc.

mented by a steady decline in trading volume. Price is said to be consolidating as the market reaches a consensus. The pictorial result is a triangle with a wider range of prices at the "mast," narrowing off toward the tip of the formation. As with a trend line, a line is drawn connecting the highest prices in the pattern. A second line connects the lowest prices. When either of these lines is broken, new information has entered the market, upsetting the discounting which was taking place.

Purely symmetrical triangles are said to be price neutral, serving as consolidating areas until consensus breaks down and prices head either sharply up or down. Descending triangles indicate a perpetuation of declining prices, while ascending triangles signal an imminent return to rising prices. Breakouts from triangles are typically very steep. False breakouts are common, however, and an embarrassment to chart enthusiasts who counter that such breakouts can be depended upon to return to the trend line before the critical breakout occurs.

CHART EVENTS

The list of possible chart formations is theoretically endless, limited only by the imagination of the chartists. Chart patterns are, like other beauties, in the eye of the beholder. With a little ingenuity, almost any series of price changes can be made into a recognizable shape—spires, diamonds, bells, cornucopias, and wedges have all been traced by different traders. Some technical information taken from chart performance does not signal a pattern, but one particular important event, often taking place in a single trading session. *Gaps, islands,* and *reversals* are figures that fall into this technical category. (See Figure 15–11.)

A session which trades above both the previous trading range and the one to follow is called an *island.* It takes its name from the fact that on a chart such a day's trading appears isolated from other trading. A large gap separates it from other price marks. A *gap* shows up on the chart whenever prices take extreme leaps and no contracts are traded at the intervening

price levels. Such gaps usually indicate a day of market frenzy. Gaps normally fall into one of three groups. The first group is the common gap, which occurs when no trading takes place at a certain price between two days. Chartists will watch in later sessions for prices to return and fill in these gaps. The second group is the breakaway or runaway gap, which is formed as prices move rapidly out of resting or trending areas. The third group is the exhaustion gap, which produces an island and marks the reversal of a trend. In the case of an island, the price jumped so fast as to leave ground uncovered. The resultant price was unsustained by trading subsequently, and prices fell back. The appearance of a stranded island often tips off traders to a major reversal. *Reversals* are commonly characterized by active trading and a wide range for the day's prices. This will show up on the chart as a comparatively long vertical bar. Such lines at the end of a long trend translate into signs of a possible reversal. If they are confirmed by trading in the days to follow, a position ought to be taken in the new trend.

Often more than one formation will be found in a chart at the same time, such as a triangle inside a larger uptrend or a downtrend channel which may occur inside a larger, longer lived uptrend channel. Generally speaking, the trader gives weight to the formation that suits his purposes according to the period of time he prefers to trade. It is crucial, when plotting chart patterns, to keep in mind the duration of a price move and the practicality of staking a position based on the particular chart formation. Short-term trading will be more strongly affected by smaller formations than will long-term trading. For the trader who wishes to hold

FIGURE 15–11

an open position for several months or the life of the contract, smaller formations which occur along the way can be disre-garded so long as they don't indicate a major change in the long-term direction of price. (See Figures 15–12 and 15–13.)

FIGURE 15–12

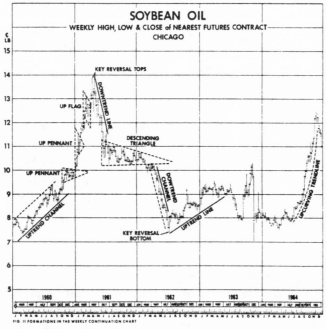

Source: Jiler, "How Charts Are Used in Commodity Price Forecast-ing," Commodity Research Bureau, Inc.

FIGURE 15–13

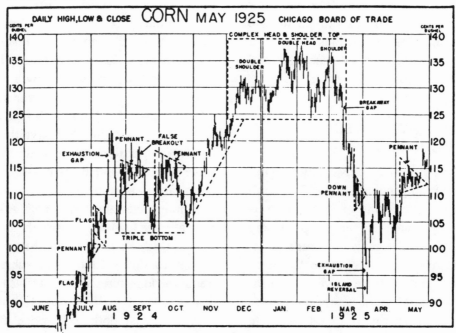

Different commodities have different chart characteristics, and the technical trader can narrow the field of formations according to the commodity he is watching. Heads and shoulders are common and considered important in cotton trading, while the most frequent configurations in wheat are usually trend lines and triangles. Often a technical trader who believes he has discovered a significant formation in a particular contract will check the charts of other months for the same commodity to seek confirmation of his findings. The interrelationship between contract months of a commodity often carries over to the formations which appear in each of their charts, particularly between contracts close to each other on the calendar.

In the reading of any chart formation, it is important that the underlying explanation of what is happening be held in mind. Random walk, trending, discounting, floors and ceilings, and fundamentals all help in the interpretation of charts and help prevent some of the more spurious reasoning that can come from technical study. Finding chart patterns in time to profit from their predictions is easier if the trader knows what to look for and exercises his imagination carefully.

MOVING AVERAGES AND OSCILLATORS

Technical devices universally attempt to measure impending change. The computation and charting of "moving averages" is yet another way of producing "buy" and "sell" signals. The trader monitors the relation between some "average" price and current price moves, establishing a position when the new price diverges far enough from the average to indicate a new trend. A simple moving average is calculated by adding together the daily closing or mid-range prices of a commodity for some number of days and then dividing the sum by the number of days used. This produces the average for the set. Each day the average is refigured by dropping the oldest day in the series and adding the most recent, resulting in a "moving" average with a constant number of days. Common moving averages are 4, 5, 9, 10, 15, 18, and 20 days, but the trader can use any number he deems most reliable for judging trends. The moving average can then be plotted on a chart together with the futures contract price. (See Figure 15–14.) When the daily price crosses through the average, a trend change is underway.

With a simple moving average, each trading day in the set has the same weight in the calculation of the average. The oldest day has as much numerical weight as the newest. Some traders thus use a "front-weighted" average, mathematically computed to give progressively more weight to recent prices. This average still only considers a short span of time, usually less than three weeks. The "exponentially smoothed" moving average takes the entire price history of the contract into account and assigns weight by a mathematical formula. Technical traders disagree about which kind of average to use and about how many days give the most helpful information. Many prefer to chart three simple moving averages—short, medium, and long range—to further refine their interpretations and signals. A short-term average (3–4 days) alerts the speculator to possible changes; a mid-term average (9–10 days) confirms a substantial trend; the long-term average (18–20 days) charts a trend in its broadest contours.

Averages smooth out price fluctuations, sacrificing detail to compose a

FIGURE 15-14

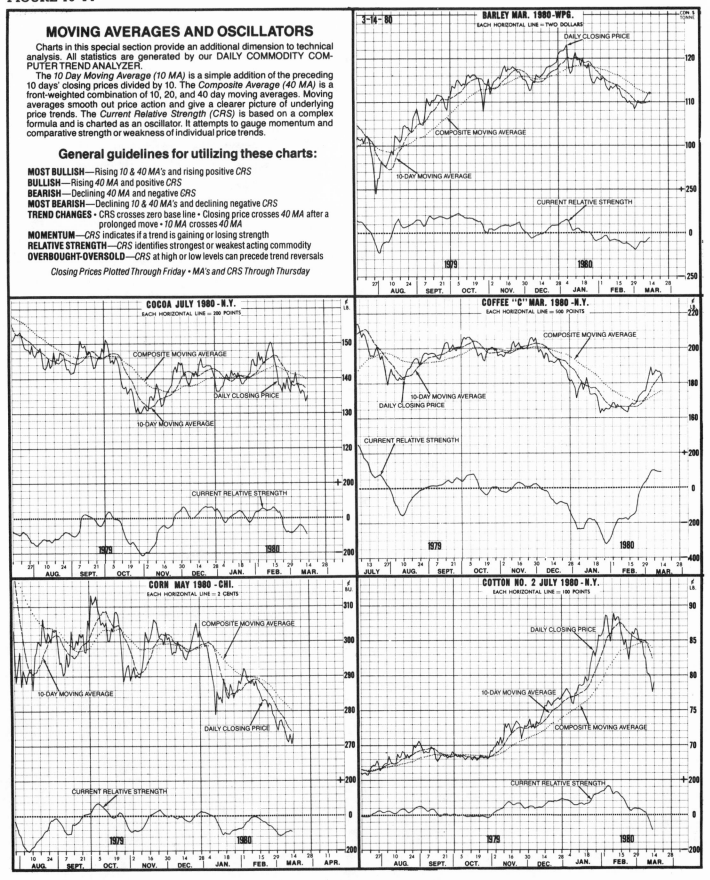

MOVING AVERAGES AND OSCILLATORS

Charts in this special section provide an additional dimension to technical analysis. All statistics are generated by our DAILY COMMODITY COMPUTER TREND ANALYZER.

The *10 Day Moving Average (10 MA)* is a simple addition of the preceding 10 days' closing prices divided by 10. The *Composite Average (40 MA)* is a front-weighted combination of 10, 20, and 40 day moving averages. Moving averages smooth out price action and give a clearer picture of underlying price trends. The *Current Relative Strength (CRS)* is based on a complex formula and is charted as an oscillator. It attempts to gauge momentum and comparative strength or weakness of individual price trends.

General guidelines for utilizing these charts:

MOST BULLISH—Rising *10 & 40 MA's* and rising positive *CRS*
BULLISH—Rising *40 MA* and positive *CRS*
BEARISH—Declining *40 MA* and negative *CRS*
MOST BEARISH—Declining *10 & 40 MA's* and declining negative *CRS*
TREND CHANGES—*CRS* crosses zero base line • Closing price crosses *40 MA* after a prolonged move • *10 MA* crosses *40 MA*
MOMENTUM—*CRS* indicates if a trend is gaining or losing strength
RELATIVE STRENGTH—*CRS* identifies strongest or weakest acting commodity
OVERBOUGHT-OVERSOLD—*CRS* at high or low levels can precede trend reversals

Closing Prices Plotted Through Friday • MA's and CRS Through Thursday

picture of general tendencies. With a short-term moving average, the increased sensitivity of the average will cause more signals on smaller fluctuations, more trades, and more commission payouts. The speculator will get on board of trends fast, but he will also gamble on more losing false trends. A longer range average will reduce the number of trades and whipsaw losses, but it will also put the trader into position much later in the trend. Another strategic problem involves defining the signal itself. How far must price penetrate which average to justify a change of position? Again, there will be a trade-off, as caution reduces both losses and profits. One solution is to use two or three averages, or a composite.

An "oscillator" measures price changes rather than price levels. Its goal is to calculate the momentum of price changes over a given period—to test the strength or weakness of prices at a given moment. For example, a simple 5-day oscillator would be computed as the difference between prices now and 5 days ago. The result would be a positive or negative number and could be translated into a chart showing oscillation above or below a given zero line over time. A declining oscillator that remained above zero would *not* denote a declining price: What it would mean is that prices were no longer going up as fast as they once were. Thus, the trader might begin to look for the end of a trend, based on its current relative strength.

Ocsillators can also be used to assess the "velocity" of a price move. If the price skyrockets quickly, creating a big positive jump in the oscillator, the trader begins to look for exhaustion of buying interest and retracing of the gain. This would be an "overbought" market. An "oversold" market could be monitored as well. Such signals work better in volatile trading markets than in ones dominated by long-term trends. During a strong bull or bear move, the oscillator may repeatedly register an "overextended" market although no reversal of trend subsequently ensues. Oscillators come in all shapes, sizes, and degrees of mathematical complexity.

VOLUME AND OPEN INTEREST

Volume and open interest refer to the trading activity for the day and the number of open contracts which exist. These two figures are reported daily, along with market prices, in most newspapers and wire service reports. They are used by technical traders primarily as a backup to confirm predictions and interpretations of market price behavior. Used alone, they are usually considered to be of little predictive value.

Commodity futures contracts differ from things sold in cash markets and especially from stocks in that the supply of futures for any commodity is in as great a supply as there are people willing to make agreements to trade. The supply of common shares of stock in General Motors, or the supply of bushels of wheat, is fixed and the price will vary according to how many people want to hang onto GM or wheat. The price of a commodity or stock fixed in supply will be set by demand. Interest in that commodity or stock will necessarily show up as a higher price. But commodity futures contracts come into existence any time a buyer and seller conclude a contract. At the beginning of a trading cycle, only a few such people have as yet entered into agreements for those distant contract months. Over the course of the contract, more people usually enter the market, both as sellers and as buyers. The number of agreements extant is called the *open interest,* which is just a name for the number of contracts which are open at any given time.

When a trader takes a position, then, the effect on open interest is determined by the nature of the other trader in the contract arrangement. If I begin trading by buying 5 coffee contracts from a seller who previously had no position, 5 new contracts are created and open interest increases by 5. If the seller is in fact closing out a previous long position of 5 contracts, however, then I am in effect assuming his position and the open interest remains the same. If we both had previous positions and are both liquidating old positions, then the open interest will decrease by 5 contracts. The technical effect of trading activity on prices is a result

of the mix of trades arranged, not of mere quantity.

Open interest normally builds over the life of a contract before tapering off near expiration, and exhibits a seasonal pattern which must be consulted before raw data can be interpreted. (See Figure 15–15.) It is not enough to know the total open interest on a given date; the trader must also know the seasonal pattern and what is normal for that date. He is interested in whether open interest is unusually high or low, not in its absolute level. Most chart subscription services will provide the seasonal open interest pattern along with current open interest and volume, normally in one of the contract charts giving price data. (See Figure 15–16.) Volume also follows a seasonal pattern to a much slighter degree, but is of little consequence.

Technical traders find that volume and open interest behave in predictable ways

FIGURE 15–15

OPEN INTEREST

Start of Trading   Contract Expiration

As the season progresses, more and more people usually enter into agreement. Open interest then peaks and tapers back down to nothing as stocks of cash goods are used up and contracts held as hedges are closed.

FIGURE 15–16

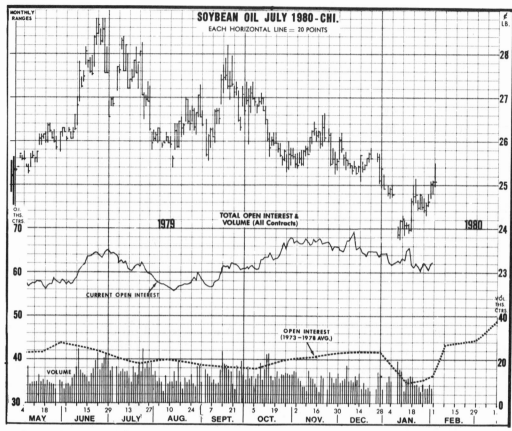

Source: Commodity Research Bureau, Inc.

in conjunction with certain price moves, and vice versa. The norm is then used by chart traders to confirm predictions based on formations made by price alone. At a major top after a long price rise, high volume of trading and a sharp decrease in open interest is interpreted as confirmation of the end of the trend. Positions are being closed in a hurry. At a major bottom, found through chart analysis, a sharp decrease in open interest is considered confirmation of the chart signal. Conversely, a large increase in open interest under heavy trading is considered confirmation of a new move about to get under way. When a chart formation breakout has been found, the trader ex-

pects a new trend and will look at volume and open interest for confirmation.

Traders have established four rules regarding volume and open interest:

1. Price up—Volume and open interest gains indicate that longs are in control, raising prices by intensive bidding for contracts. Price is strong.
2. Price up—Volume and open interest declining indicates that the primary source of buying pressure comes from shorts who are covering their positions with purchases. Price is weak.
3. Price down—Volume and open interest up means shorts are in control of the market, coming into it in increased numbers and forcing prices lower. Market is technically weak.

4. Price down—Volume and open interest down indicates tired longs are liquidating their positions. Market is strong, ready for new buying and price advance.

Seasonally adjusted open interest can be compared with the "positions of large traders" data in order to predict changes in the positions of hedgers and large speculators by those who wish to keep a close watch on market tone. With a large short hedger interest in the latest "commitment of traders" report (which is at least two weeks old) and a decrease in open interest resulting in higher prices, the trader is left with the hypothesis that hedgers are lifting their hedges, leaving the market to speculators. For confirmation of chart formations, seasonal adjustment can be forgotten on a day-to-day basis, as the trader is interested in major changes on a single day. Seasonal adjustment cannot be ignored in the look at market tone.

LIMITS OF TECHNICAL FORECASTING

Even the staunchest random walk theorists acknowledge the existence of trends and patterns in actual commodity markets. Considerable dispute arises, however, on the subject of their readability and predictability. Both agree that technical indicators can be found after the fact (all commodity traders have 20/20 hindsight), but the free walker presents a convincing case against any kind of forecasting. The multiplicity of technical trading systems, some of them beyond the comprehension of all but mathematicians

and computers, argues that the foolproof method is yet to be found. The persistence of the technical devices discussed in this chapter, though also testimony to the old saying that "hope springs eternal," implies some degree of practical utility. The successful trader will probably employ all at some time or another, learning which to consult as market conditions and prices evolve. The best way of looking at technical trading is as a "guesstimating" input to be added to other information on the way to a composite conclusion. Both technicians and random walkers might agree on one thing: The accurate prediction of the future in commodity markets is extremely difficult.

A final cautionary note. Technical trading methods have a habit of becoming "self-fulfilling prophecies" that thus are self-destructing. If any one market device returned profits effortlessly, it would be used constantly until it was discounted away. As a particular trading method becomes widespread, it is common for a flood of orders generated by the system's signals to hit the market at once, causing a "technical" rally or decline. Aware of the origin of the orders, other traders shrewdly leap in to the opposite position and prices retrace their technical gains. Discounting of the trading methods being used in a particular market now occurs regularly as more and more traders grow knowledgeable about their adversaries' methods. Thus, the utility of one technical signal can be diminished or destroyed by its very usefulness and popularity—demonstrating once again that the market will not abide a master.

Chapter 16 ——————————————————

SEASONALS AND ODDS

SEASONAL TRENDS

Should you buy wheat in August? Is an April downturn in cattle prices expected or unusual? What are the chances of making money on a short sale of cocoa in March if prices were lower in February? How often in the last fifty years have corn prices risen from October to November? Questions like these can be answered by reference to the historical data of seasonal price patterns. Study of past price changes will reveal the "odds" for any anticipated move, telling if an offered risk is a long shot or a house favorite. There are no certain bets in futures trading, but the chances of success increase as the trader learns how to estimate the probability of a specific contemplated price swing.

Any unprocessed commodity that has ever been alive has a seasonal price pattern that can be calculated and graphed. Every plant has a time of harvest when the market is well supplied with the produce and a time when the produce is scarce. Every animal eats feed that is expensive at one time of the year and cheap at another time. Most animals have a natural mating season or traditional time of farrowing and an optimum marketing time; to hold

them longer costs space and feed and raises their marketing price. Any trader wishing to trade commodities must know when a commodity is cheap and when it is dear. He must know its seasonal price pattern.

The computation and charting of seasonals and odds combines both fundamental and technical forecasting. The premise of a seasonal trend is obviously grounded in the rules of supply and demand, production, and distribution. The calculation of odds works on the technical assumption that past market behavior forms patterns that are predictable and profitable. In this combination the trader is able to balance market indicators of differing kinds and to check trading decisions against both fundamental and technical signals. This helps explain why the use of seasonals and odds is one of the most respected of trading tools. It greatly assists the speculator in the analysis of a market's character. If the motivating factors for a seasonal trend are known, their dominance or absence in any given year will help predict the price move as it obeys or disregards the norm.

The first guidelines to emerge from contemplating seasonal trends are simple.

Rarely buy a commodity after it has passed its seasonal highs. Rarely sell a commodity after it has passed its seasonal lows. The price of a commodity in a glutted market may well go up, but it may not go up very far. Any commodity at its time of scarcity may drop in value on the cash markets, but it is not likely to drop appreciably. In either case the trader would probably be wasting time and money, for it is the large price moves that bring profit to the futures trader.

It may be argued that any forecasting method so simple and well known as seasonals would be quickly discounted away by the markets, smoothing out the trend and eliminating any advantage for seasonal speculators. It hasn't happened, though the grain seasonals have been recognized for a century. Were seasonal patterns 100 percent repetitive at exactly the same time every year, and were all traders to discount this information in the same way, then seasonals would lose their usefulness. But the functioning of the markets is more complex than that, and seasonals themselves are far from perfect. Because any new season may violate the norm, or fall somewhat above or below it in price, some traders will take positions actively

FIGURE 16–1

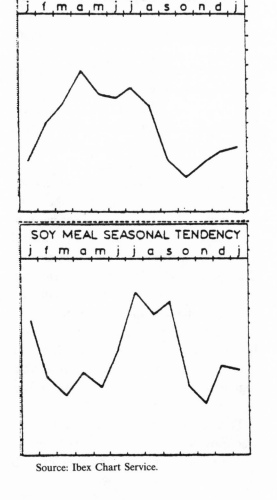

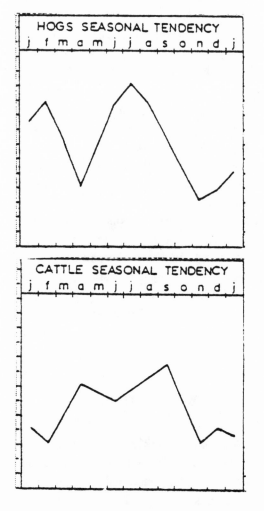

Source: Ibex Chart Service.

against the seasonal trend. This is not done out of ignorance. Consulting seasonal trends does not mean slavishly believing in them. The data of past seasonal price changes may be the key evidence in a decision to trade against the seasonal pattern, if other conditions give weak support to the trend's elemental factors. Two traders are required on opposite sides for every contract: If everyone went long or short in compliance with the seasonal, the market would collapse: Fluctuations up and down within the general movement of a trend are profitable enough for some traders to risk bucking the odds. The paradox is that the very imperfection of seasonal trends operates in the market place to counteract discounting and preserve the curves produced by seasonal factors.

Grain seasonals follow the natural cycles of planting and harvesting. Prices will advance during the spring, decline as harvests begin, and advance again with the rationing of supplies and the onset of winter. The seasonal trend may be displaced a month or two either way with the fortunes of production, weather, and marketing. The surges of spring and winter will be preceded by corresponding dips. Cattle peak around April and September, with lows into June, November, and February. Hogs rise sharply from spring into August, falling off into winter. Soybean meal and oil have distinctive seasonal graphs derived from their relation to soybeans. FIGURE 16–1.)

CASH AND FUTURES SEASONALS

Although roughly accurate, this account of seasonal trends is just a first step. For the person concerned with commodity futures trading, there are numerous

seasonals for each commodity. There are, of course, the *cash seasonals.* These give the pattern of highs and lows for the cash commodity at some specified location over the duration of the year. A common seasonals table will list the average price for each month, arranged in order by crop year. (See Figure 16–2.) These figures tell the trader exactly when the commodity is scarce on the cash markets, when it is abundant, and the rate of price change between these two times. All traders, whether they chart seasonal patterns or not, must have a fair idea of cash seasonal patterns in their heads. Otherwise, they will be vulnerable to buying a contract that has peaked or selling one that has hit bottom.

The agricultural commodities traded on futures exchanges also have a set of *futures seasonals.* This set will be made up of the seasonal price trend charts for each of the available contract months. March, May, July, October, and December are cotton contract months; each exhibits seasonal characteristics of its own. These reflect storage costs from time of harvest to time of expiration, new or old crop, and other factors that distinguish one contract from another in the same commodity. The March contract will follow the trend set by the cash seasonal in a different way than the December or October contracts. When trading the July contract, the speculator interested in confirming a trend with seasonal indicators will want to check the historical data for July cotton contracts, not for March or May, to assure himself of the maximum degree of correlation in conditions affecting price.

To trade in futures, the speculator must first know what time it is in the commodity's seasonal year. That information will

FIGURE 16–2

SOYBEANS – NO. 1 YELLOW
Average Monthly Cash Price – Chicago
per Bushel

Crop Year	Sept.	Oct.	Nov.	Dec.	Jan.	Feb.	Mar.	Apr.	May	June	July	Aug.	Avg.
1978 . . .	$6.47	$6.76	$6.66	$6.79	–	–	–	–	–	–	–	–	–
1977 . . .	5.21	5.05	5.77	5.87	5.65	5.57	6.53	6.81	7.09	6.79	6.54	6.43	6.11
1976 . . .	6.59	6.23	6.58	6.86	7.08	7.25	8.33	9.74	9.50	8.18	6.29	5.66	7.36
1975 . . .	5.55	4.97	4.70	4.59	4.65	4.74	4.66	4.71	5.21	6.25	6.64	6.30	5.25
1974 . . .	7.57	8.33	7.58	7.28	6.33	5.68	5.56	5.76	5.23	5.15	5.58	5.97	6.33
1973 . . .	6.50	5.62	5.65	5.95	6.17	6.39	6.23	5.56	5.42	5.47	6.97	7.55	6.12
1972 . . .	3.48	3.33	3.64	4.13	4.49	5.81	6.24	6.53	8.99	10.87	8.60	9.08	6.27
1971 . . .	3.12	3.12	3.00	3.08	3.09	3.18	3.37	3.49	3.49	3.47	3.51	3.55	3.29
1970 . . .	2.81	2.90	3.00	2.93	3.03	3.06	3.04	2.91	3.03	3.21	3.38	3.29	3.05
1969 . . .	2.61	2.38	2.42	2.47	2.55	2.59	2.58	2.64	2.70	2.71	2.89	2.79	2.61

Source: U.S.D.A. Economic Research Service – Grain Market News

SOYBEAN OIL – CRUDE
Average Monthly Cash Price – Decatur
per 100 Lbs.

Crop Year	Oct.	Nov.	Dec.	Jan.	Feb.	Mar.	Apr.	May	June	July	Aug.	Sept.	Avg.
1978 . . .	$26.70	$24.91	$25.84	–	–	–	–	–	–	–	–	–	–
1977 . . .	18.80	21.00	22.60	20.90	21.60	26.60	26.80	28.80	26.90	25.90	26.30	27.80	24.50
1976 . . .	20.70	21.80	21.00	20.90	22.40	26.50	29.60	31.30	28.30	23.80	21.10	19.20	23.88
1975 . . .	21.40	18.90	16.80	16.20	16.30	16.60	16.30	15.80	17.60	20.90	20.40	22.50	18.31
1974 . . .	42.30	40.40	38.00	33.60	29.40	29.10	28.20	23.60	23.30	27.50	28.50	24.40	30.69
1973 . . .	23.10	20.40	26.00	28.60	36.40	30.20	28.20	29.40	31.60	40.50	43.30	40.70	31.53
1972 . . .	9.60	9.60	9.70	10.10	13.00	13.90	15.00	17.10	19.30	22.40	33.50	24.80	16.50
1971 . . .	13.20	12.50	11.70	10.90	11.00	11.70	11.90	11.40	10.70	10.30	10.10	9.80	11.30
1970 . . .	14.00	13.90	12.40	12.30	12.10	12.20	11.20	11.40	12.80	14.50	14.50	12.80	12.80
1969 . . .	10.60	10.90	9.60	9.60	11.50	12.20	12.20	11.30	11.10	11.50	11.60	12.10	11.18

Source: U.S.D.A. Economic Research Service – Fats and Oil Situation.

Source: Chicago Board of Trade.

only be significant, however, if he is familiar with the normal cash seasonal pattern. To open the actual position on the market, he will have to choose a single contract month to purchase or sell. For this he needs the second, futures seasonal for the particular trading month decided upon. A comparison of that seasonal with cash, and with the current market, will aid in the ultimate determination of the most probable and profitable trading opportunity. A series of simple calculations for both cash and futures will quickly reveal if the contemplated trend has a decent chance of succeeding.

CHARTING SEASONAL PRICES

Cash seasonals can be calculated quite easily by averaging the monthly cash price data. This can be obtained from the Commodity Research Bureau's annual *Commodity Yearbook,* from the annual statistical volumes published by the exchanges, or from USDA situation reports. Constructing a cash seasonal graph consists of simply averaging monthly data for a number of years and plotting the results on graph paper. The cash prices listed for January from several years are added together and divided by the number of years in the sample to produce an average cash price for January for the commodity. This point is plotted on the graph. The same is done for each consecutive month until a pattern is formed indicating the average highs and lows for the commodity over a year. Whether the trader chooses to plot a ten year, twenty year, or hundred year pattern will depend upon his trading methods, the history of the commodity,

FIGURE 16–3
Sample corn cash seasonal

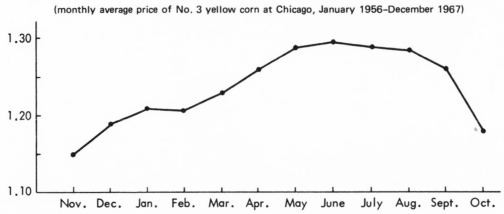
(monthly average price of No. 3 yellow corn at Chicago, January 1956–December 1967)

FIGURE 16–4
Sample soybean meal cash seasonal

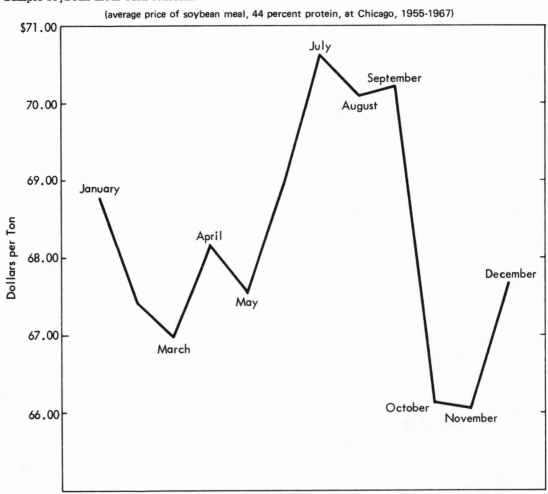
(average price of soybean meal, 44 percent protein, at Chicago, 1955-1967)

and the information being sought. (See Figures 16–3 and 16–4.)

Premade charts are readily available showing visually the *real cash behavior* for various lengths of time: daily for the past year, weekly for the past ten years, or monthly for the whole century. (See Figures 16–5 and 16–6.) These can be of

FIGURE 16–5
Daily cash price chart

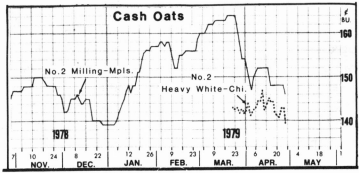

FIGURE 16–6
Monthly cash price chart

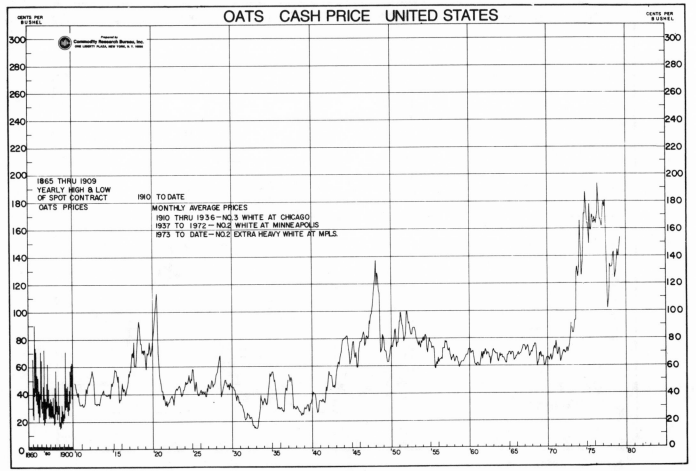

use to the trader interested in how his commodity is shaping up against its normal position on the market. The charts show the actual performance of cash prices in certain time frames. These are *not* cash seasonal charts, though the performance of prices in any given year shown on these charts could be compared to the expected performance as shown on a chart of averaged seasonal prices.

Likewise, *continuation charts* are not graphs of seasonals. (See Figure 16–7.) They instead depict the movement of futures prices during some period of time, and again can be compared to the expecta-

tion represented by the cash seasonal chart—but with caution. Nearest futures graphs are made by charting the price behavior of a contract until it expires, and then continuing the chart by immediately resuming with the next nearest contract until it expires, and so on. These charts can be useful in focusing on the current market and its place in history, but must not be confused with a chart of *average* cash price seasonal patterns. Cash graphs, continuation or nearby futures graphs, and charts of cash seasonals are three different things and contain different kinds of information. A cash seasonal chart pic-

FIGURE 16–7
Nearby futures continuation chart

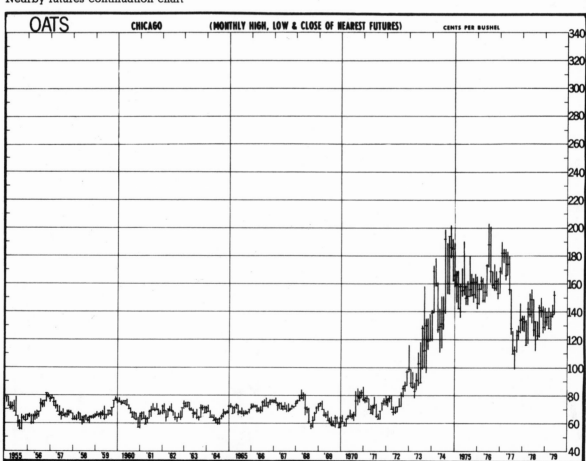

Source: Commodity Research Bureau, Inc.

tures the *average* seasonal pattern rather than the pattern of actual individual years, months, weeks, or days in a string, as do the other two kinds of charts.

Using a large number of years as a base period (ten or more) for the cash seasonal graph helps correct any distortion that might be introduced by an extremely aberrant season. Chartists will often go back in time as far as they have data which comes from a market similar in conditions to the modern market. The employment of computers enables the computation of general seasonal tendencies involving all relevant and available historical price information. Some discrepancy may exist between the general seasonal tendency chart and the chart for cash seasonal

prices in any given base period, of course, depending on the size of the sample and the number of aberrant years within it. This presents no particular problem to the trader constructing an average cash seasonal, but it does remind him to choose the period for the average with deliberation and care. A quick look at the statistics from which the chart will be made quickly reveals how far back to extend the averaging. Soybeans, for instance, now trade in a range which is $4 or $5 above that of ten years ago, due to vastly increased demand for soymeal and oil. Averaging cash prices for the past twenty years would produce a chart lower in price, although roughly the same in shape, despite increased acreage and changes in produc-

FIGURE 16–8

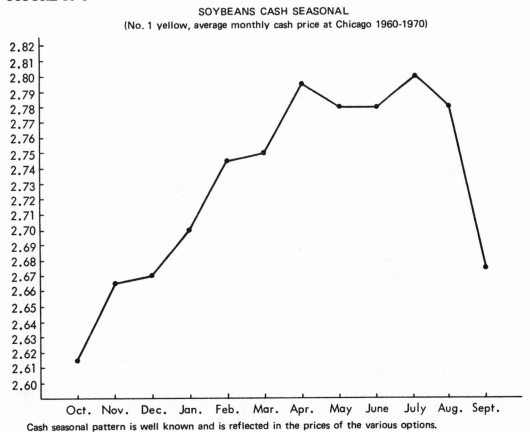

SOYBEANS CASH SEASONAL
(No. 1 yellow, average monthly cash price at Chicago 1960-1970)

Cash seasonal pattern is well known and is reflected in the prices of the various options.

FIGURE 16–9

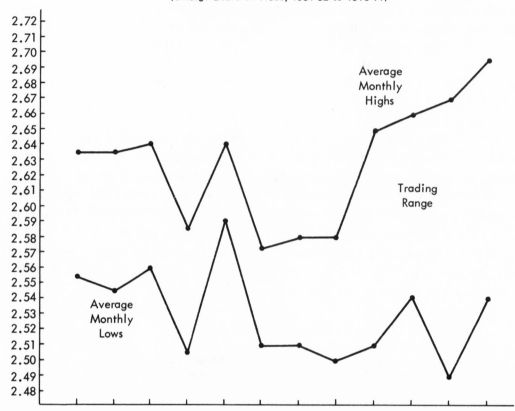

SEPTEMBER SOYBEAN CONTRACT AVERAGE HIGHS AND LOWS
(Chicago Board of Trade, 1961-62 to 1970-71)

The trader, of course, does not trade cash soybeans and must choose a single option which will exhibit a seasonal pattern of highs and lows all its own. The wide divergence between highs and lows in August and September reflects the fact that the September contract can be a new crop or old crop contract.

tion technology. In fact, the cash seasonal chart for soybeans based on the period 1960–1970 (see Figure 16–8) matches almost exactly the general seasonal chart for soybeans published in 1980 (see Figure 16–1) and reportedly based on an extensive computer analysis of recent and distant prices.

The process for producing a *futures seasonal* is identical except that two lines are normally drawn, plotting the average high and average low throughout the life of each contract month. (See Figure 16–9.) Plotting each contract visually is not strictly necessary. Specific information

can be taken for contract months directly from the statistical tables. Plotting all the contracts for a particular commodity will, however, produce a visual impression of what is going on and might well be undertaken for at least one commodity. When done, the trader will have one seasonal graph for cash and four or more futures graphs.

CALCULATING THE ODDS

Charting the information found in cash price lists and futures highs and lows lists gives a nice picture of what is going on.

But once the understanding of the seasonal tendency is had, charting becomes an unnecessary exercise. The trader can, instead, pull his information for trading directly from price lists by calculating the odds for different price moves at different times. Calculating odds rather than drawing charts has the further advantage that it can be refined almost without end to fit precisely the trading situation at hand. The trader can figure the chances of a contract dropping in price compared to the previous contract or he can figure the odds of its dropping from one month to the next. Odds of successfully profiting from the purchase or sale of a futures contract, at least in terms of seasonal tendencies and actual price history, can easily be computed and referred to. What results is a percentage answer, expressing what has been the normal change in the past between any two given dates. This information could be graphed as well. Calculating the odds is merely another route to evaluating a trade's potential based on seasonal price behavior, and one that takes less time than charting.

The prudent trader will simply never take a position when the odds based on past performance are against him. In the absence of other information, *expect the usual,* and you *usually* will be right. To know what is usual, the trader calculates, say, the odds of December wheat trading for more than August wheat based on figures for the last twenty years. The current market is made up of many factors both normal and unique to this particular year, as were the markets of each of the years in the past. While a crude calculation of odds will leave out the 5 percent of market conditions which are unusual this year, it will pick up the 95 percent that occur every year, even though this 95 percent

consists of factors largely unknown. The aberrant factors in this year's price may receive sufficient emphasis in newsletters and other information sources to judge how reliable the seasonal odds may be.

There are all kinds of theoretical and practical limitations to the crude calculation of odds based on past market behavior, but such odds have one distinct advantage. They are based strictly on hard data and mathematical percentages. They are not caught up in the subjective vagaries of market rumors and guesses, pit excitement, and crop report reaction which figure largely enough in the trader's prognosis. "Everybody's excited about cocoa, the market looks good, the price should rise!" All well and good, but what are the cold odds that the price of cash cocoa will rise this month? And what are the odds for a particular futures contract going up? And how far can it be expected to go?

GENERAL CASH ODDS

There are two types of odds and two subdivisions for each type that are important to the commodity speculator. These are:

CASH ODDS	General Cash Odds
	Specific Cash Odds
FUTURES ODDS	General Futures Odds
	Specific Futures Odds

To calculate the two types of cash odds, the speculator needs a list of monthly average cash prices for a substantial time period. This is the same information used to calculate the general cash seasonal graph. Wherever found, in yearbooks or statistical annuals, these figures will ultimately be derived from official USDA reports. Wheat is used here, although the procedure would be identical for other commodities. From the cash lists the trader isolates that portion (if not all) that gives the data relevant to the trade he is contemplating. In this case the trader is trying to decide whether to establish a position in the December wheat contract. The time of year now is August, so the table would be as follows:

Of course, a glance at the chart for the general cash wheat seasonal tendency would disclose a strong upward bias in prices from July to December. (See Figure 16–10.) But the chart tells only of the general tendency. It doesn't reveal particulars or show the years when wheat prices failed to obey the rules. Now our wheat trader wants to know the actual odds for success. From his broker, his newsletter, his study

Wheat (No. 2 Red Winter) monthly average cash price at Chicago

Year	July	Aug.	Sept.	Oct.	Nov.
1960	185	188	193	197	202
1961	194	190	198	201	205
1962	215	211	207	205	210
1963	184	183	197	215	217
1964	143	146	149	152	155
1965	148	155	158	159	166
1966	190	190	186	172	176
1967	150	149	151	152	145
1968	128	122	120	125	132
1969	130	127	131	136	141
1970	145	152	167	174	177
1971	154	145	145	153	160
1972	153	176	202	211	228
1973	308	475	511	475	547
1974	440	434	441	503	486
1975	342	382	406	384	349
1976	337	301	289	272	260
1977	220	208	220	227	259
1978	322	332	342	351	368

FIGURE 16–10

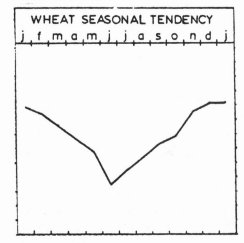

of the fundamentals, his technical signals, or a combination of these, he has concluded that this year wheat prices will once again rise during the late summer months and into winter. He is not satisfied to know that the general historical tendency is in his favor if he goes long December wheat. He wants to know how strong the odds are before deciding how many contracts to buy. And he wants to know when to get out of his positions. Are the odds for an August–November price rise better or worse than for a September–November rise? Once he has his position in mind, the trader has formalized questions that can be answered mathematically with odds from the chart of cash prices:

Question: In the last nineteen years, how many times has Chicago cash wheat averaged a higher price in November than it did in August?

Answer: In fourteen of the nineteen years sampled, November's price was higher than August's.

General Cash Odds: 74 percent chance of a rise in prices from August to November.

Conclusion: General cash odds heavily favor a rise in monthly average cash price for the trading period contemplated.

SPECIFIC CASH ODDS

Specific cash odds refine the data used to calculate the general cash odds. A 74 percent chance for November to rise over August seems great, far better than the speculator could do in Las Vegas or Atlantic City. But the experienced trader still wants to know more. What has happened in the intervening months? Were there signals before August that indicated the direction a specific year's prices would take? Thus a bettor further tests markets by limiting the sample of years to those in the past which exhibited behavior similar to this year's. Displacements in seasonal price curves, or inversions of them, usually create price patterns that repeat and which are thus tradeable. How prices have behaved so far during the present crop year will indicate which past crop years and price patterns are relevant.

The price of wheat historically drops during late spring and early summer. The scarcity of wheat stored over the winter eases with the rationing of supply and the influx of new crop harvestings. Prices come down from winter highs. Each year the trader can expect a seasonal low to be hit sometime in the May–August period. When this low strikes will determine how a trader looking to spot the summer-to-winter price rise will act. If the low falls in July, a long position might profitably be held into November. If the low hits in September (or later), the trader going long in July or August loses his shirt. Seasonal trades are vulnerable to dislocations and brief reversals, which accumulate losses and possibly force the trader out on large margin calls before the expected seasonal move occurs.

So, the speculator wants specific odds for conditions as close to this year's as possible. In the current season, let us say, the average price in August is running well ahead of the average price in July. The hint is that the seasonal low was probably struck early in the summer. Based on this, the trader makes a new series of inquiries:

Question: This year cash wheat prices are averaging higher in August than they did in July. How many years out of the last nineteen in our table has this occurred?

Answer: Eight (1960, 1964, 1965, 1970, 1972, 1973, 1975, 1978).

Question: In these specific eight years, how many times has the average cash price in September been higher than in August?

Answer: Eight. In every single year that prices averaged higher in August than in July, they also averaged higher in September than in August. Odds in such cases for a September price rise, and thus for a profitable long position, are 100 percent.

Question: In these specific eight years, how many times has the average cash price in October been higher than in September?

Answer: Six. In two years, 1973 and 1975 (years we can see from the table were characterized by extraordinary and volatile price swings), the average price stood lower in October. The odds for a price rise are 75 percent in those specific years in which average prices were higher in August and September.

Question: In these specific six years when prices averaged higher in August, September, and October, how many times did November average higher than October?

Answer: In all six years, giving odds of 100 percent for these specific cases. Of those two years, 1973 and 1975, that had broken from the pattern, 1975 turned back upward with the seasonal tendency to close November slightly ahead of July but well below the highs of August and September.

Specific Cash Odds: The specific odds for a price rise from August to September are 100 percent; for September to October, 75 percent. For the six years that rose from July through October, the odds for November are 100 percent; for the eight years that prices rose from July to August, the odds for an October to November price rise are 87 percent.

Conclusion: The specific cash odds look extremely good for the trader who proposes to establish a long position in wheat when August averages higher than July. A decline in the odds for October might suggest closing the position and taking profits early that month except that those

years showing price declines were recognizably extreme aberrations. Unless current year price behavior resembles that of those volatile seasons, holding into November appears a good risk. But, in any case, the trader must remember that the odds are only probabilities; they have no power to force events to comply with expectations. This could always be the year when the 100 percent record is shattered.

If, on the other hand, prices in August had been averaging *lower* than prices in July, a different set of specific odds would be formulated. They would advise more caution to the trader. In ten years out of nineteen, prices did average lower in August than in July. Of these ten, six reached an average September price equal or higher than July's, but by very small amounts. The big seasonal push came in October, when all six of these again averaged higher and eight of the original ten averaged upward relative to September. Of the ten July–August declines, seven averaged higher in November than in July (from 4 to 46 cents). In conclusion, the drop into August signaled uncertainty for upcoming prices, and risks for long traders, though the seasonal tendency was still influential. A speculator could hold a long position in such circumstances, but he would have to be prepared for more reversals, some losses, and a shaky recovery of prices.

These calculations simply tell the trader what has happened to cash prices in past years that were similar to the year he is trading. The why of a past year's performance can be researched and reasonably pinpointed. The why of the current year remains speculative. The trader can only *expect the normal* unless extraordinary and incontrovertible evidence suggests the contrary. Board room rumors, market letters, and technical information might suggest a short position in wheat from August to November, but if prices have risen since July, such a position would be folly. The "shorts" might be correct, but the odds are heavily against them. Long shots and "house bets" pay the same, so there is no reason in such circumstances to wager on the long shot. The successful commodity speculator will not take a futures position unless the general and specific cash odds are substantially and clearly in his favor.

GENERAL FUTURES ODDS

The trader knows that the cash wheat market historically experiences a price rise from August to November and is warned by this normality away from taking a short position. The trader, however, buys and sells futures contracts, not cash wheat. The significance of this difference must be taken into account when figuring the odds for a planned trade. Contract months in wheat for winter delivery will already be priced higher in August to discount the normally expected shortages and higher prices. These contracts have sold at higher prices throughout their trading lives in reflection of this usual cash seasonal pattern. The trader cannot make money by simply purchasing the December wheat contract and watching it go up. The trader has little use for the information that the December future is selling for more than the July. He *knows* this to be the case already.

What the speculator *is* interested to know are the odds of the December futures contract price rising further, or hav-

ing to adjust lower in price, between now and the December expiration. To answer this question, he recalculates his odds for the December contract. The calculation is made in the same way as for cash odds, but now different tables of information are needed. The relevant statistics for futures odds refer to the history of the December contract rather than to the cash market. The trader wants to compute the chances for a contract going up or down in price during a particular segment of the trading year. To do this, he consults the table showing the "Monthly Range of Futures Prices." For each contract month the table lists the highest price and the lowest price that were hit during each calendar month of the trading year. Because contract prices often cover a considerable spread of prices, and because the use of stop orders allows the trader to use that part of the spread that is profitable (highs for selling and lows for buying), an average monthly price would be of little help.

The listed "High" prices will be used for calculating the odds for rising prices; the "Low" for calculating chances for lower prices. Each exchange publishes a yearbook that includes the table of monthly historical highs and lows for each month for each commodity listed on the exchange. Let us assume that the trader wishes to know the chances for the December contract going up in price between 1 August and the end of November. From the Chicago Board of Trade's *Annual* the speculator picks out the table for the December contract. Data is usually given for ten years, so the trader wishing a larger sample might check two yearbooks published ten years apart. The result would be as follows:

December wheat contract: monthly range of futures prices

Year	July High	July Low	Aug. High	Aug. Low	Sept. High	Sept. Low	Oct. High	Oct. Low	Nov. High	Nov. Low
1960	193	189	193	190	195	191	199	195	204	198
1961	205	199	207	203	208	203	205	201	206	202
1962	222	218	219	211	216	198	212	200	210	203
1963	194	182	187	182	207	184	217	204	218	205
1964	151	144	149	144	151	146	151	147	153	149
1965	154	148	162	153	166	160	166	160	166	161
1966	200	188	200	190	200	172	177	166	180	168
1967	164	156	163	149	157	150	156	151	152	143
1968	139	130	131	121	126	118	130	120	134	127
1969	147	125	134	126	136	132	138	134	142	135
1970	155	143	166	149	173	161	177	167	180	166
1971	162	149	152	143	154	142	163	146	168	158
1972	165	151	198	163	232	193	224	207	247	218
1973	350	254	521	350	543	442	502	402	511	418
1974	487	422	486	426	498	408	536	475	525	448
1975	409	312	467	379	447	405	433	377	384	328
1976	420	354	355	318	344	286	310	269	279	249
1977	261	232	240	225	255	229	263	241	283	257
1978	339	307	334	301	345	325	368	334	378	353

With this table the trader can determine how high or how low the December future went in any given month or period. And he can figure the general or specific futures odds for his contemplated trade. Using the table, the trader picks out the period he wishes to trade and calculates the odds as he did for the general cash odds. If he wishes to buy wheat on 1 August and sell at the end of November, he wants to know whether the December wheat future usually goes higher during November than it did in August. This may or may not accord with the movement of cash prices during the same period. The questions posed will be similar to those in the cash odds computations.

Question: During the last nineteen years, how many times has the December wheat futures contract price gone higher in the month of November than it did during August?

Answer: In twelve of the last nineteen years the November high exceeded the August high.

General Futures Odds: The odds are 63 percent in favor of the December wheat contract price hitting a higher price in November than it did in August.

Conclusion: General futures odds favor a rise in the price of the December wheat contract from August through November. A long position would be supported by the odds.

If the trader had been contemplating a short position, the general futures odds for a decline in price during the period could just as easily be computed. In seven of the nineteen years sampled the price of the December contract in November hit a low that was lower than that for August. Odds for the short side would be 37 percent.

SPECIFIC FUTURES ODDS

From the general futures odds the trader knows that the past price performance of the December wheat futures contract favors a rise in price from August to November. For specific odds the calculations can be refined in any number of ways: excluding years without a 10 cent change in price, eliminating those years in which the price was less than $2 a bushel, etc. Again, the most obvious refinements are those that produce a sample similar to the current trading year in known characteristics.

The seasonal trader will be aware of certain pricing habits in the market for the December contract. The December contract will go at a premium in late spring as speculators bet on the higher prices expected for winter. As the size of the new crop becomes apparent, the pre-

FIGURE 16–11

Source: Commodity Research Bureau, Inc.

mium for December usually falls and a correctional low occurs in midsummer. Afterwards, prices resume the seasonal rise toward winter and the expiration of the contract. Indeed, a look at the "Monthly Range of Futures Prices" chart does show that the August "High" was lower than or equal to the July "High" in thirteen of the last nineteen years, or 68 percent of the time. The beginning of August, one might conclude, would be a problematic time to initiate a long position in the December wheat futures contract. By waiting to see if the price in September rises above the August "High," the trader might considerably improve his odds. Let us assume that the trader decides to wait a while, and that the August "High" once again falls below the "High" for July:

Question: In how many of the last nineteen years has the "High" in September been above the "High" in August?

Answer: In thirteen of the last nineteen years the September "High" rose above the August "High" (68 percent of the time).

Question: In those specific thirteen years, how many times did the November "High" rise above the September "High"?

Answer: In ten of those specific thirteen years the November "High" exceeded the September "High." (One year, 1965, showed an unchanged "High" from September through November.)

Specific Futures Odds: In years when the September "High" surpasses the August "High" the odds are 77 percent in favor of the November "High" surpassing the September "High."

Conclusion: Past price behavior counsels that the best odds for a long position in the December wheat contract can be had by waiting until the September price "High" confirms the upward seasonal

tendency by breaking the ceiling of August's "High." A long position might then be reasonably held until the beginning of the delivery month with good expectation of a profit and little statistical risk. (See Figure 16–11.)

PLAYING THE ODDS

Speculators make their money of the futures markets by selling prices which are a little too high and buying prices which are a little too low. It makes no difference if the dislocated price was caused by excess hedging or by a cumulative incorrect guess on the part of all traders. Any system of pointing out incorrect prices for exploitation is simply trying to mechanically determine these incorrect prices so that the speculator may profit from them. In figuring the odds the trader is really researching how many times the futures market has been priced too high or too low and how it has made its corrective adjustments. It is a method of prediction based on the assumption that cumulative mistakes of traders (inaccurate discounting) repeatedly made in the past will repeat themselves in the future. It should not happen, but it does, as there are other forces in the market persuading or tempting the aggregate of traders (each with differing purposes and understandings) in and out of their positions.

If the market is perfectly discounted, the calculation of odds will not return a profit because the market will not make mistakes in judgment over and over again. No technical system, for that matter, will return profit in theory. But in practice, as we have seen constantly, the market is human and imperfect and patterns of mistakes do appear to occur. For every adherent of a trading theory there will be another trader ready to take the opposite position, either on the basis of another theory or in a shrewd practice of scalping profits on price moves largely influenced by the signals of well known trading systems.

All of the factors that encourage hedgers to hedge and speculators to speculate add together to form the complexity of the market and its variety of positions. The number of variables is in fact infinite, and precludes a total or scientific knowledge of any market or any price move. Nonetheless, fairly constant patterns do emerge over time, just as chart patterns emerge from the random walk of prices. Of all these patterns, seasonal price tendencies are the most consistent and reliable. Given these observations on the patterns of price moves and seasonals, the trader does have a rational basis for prediction by figuring the odds. Speculators who calculate that there is a 77 percent possibility of the December wheat futures contract rising in price from September through November have the opportunity to profit from that knowledge. By doing so they help to correct the market by buying the current price and selling it later at a higher price.

In the process of discovering price dislocations and exploiting them, speculators assist the market in functioning more smoothly by eliminating historical mistakes. Yet, the fact that speculators do smooth out market price makes it impossible for a simple odds sheet to be printed up and handed out. So many speculators working the same odds would quickly render the exercise profitless. And the odds will change, slightly or substantially, from year to year with the specific conditions of that year's market. The trader playing the odds will find that, once again, the

responsibility for successful trading is his own. He will have to figure and use his own odds and apply them in concert with the other data and rules that compose his trading program.

A NOTE ON NONAGRICULTURAL SEASONALS

All the seasonal tendencies and odds discussed in this chapter have concerned the "life cycle" commodities. The seasonal price patterns of these commodities are repeatedly reliable because they are ultimately determined by the physical and natural order of planting, harvesting, and distributing. There may be minor changes in the actual production cycle of agricultural commodities, especially as new technology is employed or new growing areas prosper. But nature itself continues to place limits on when wheat can be sown or cocoa harvested.

No such firm and absolute framework exists for the production or demand cycles of nonagricultural commodities. Some traders and market observers like to formulate "seasons" for metals or financial instruments. To some degree there may be perceptible historical patterns in the price changes of these commodities. But two major flaws make me sceptical of the results. First of all, statistical data for these is either skimpy, very recent, or it covers a period of time when changes in the industry and market were so enormous as to make comparisons useless. Progress has indeed occurred in agriculture, but the effect has not been nearly as transformative as in copper or lumber. Secondly, and more importantly, seasonal tendencies for nonagriculturals have no ground in a reliable external framework that would hold steady over time. The effect of the "business cycle" or tax season could be cited, but it hardly compares with the uniformity and strength in the influence of the natural growth cycles of plants and livestock (though technology has perhaps affected the seasonal tendencies of cattle and hogs more markedly in recent years).

Certainly, odds can be computed for any commodity for which historical price data can be found. You can go to the statistical yearbooks and calculate the odds that silver prices will rise from April to May or that T-Bills will fall from December to January. The results might look impressive. But if I flip a coin 100 times and it comes up heads 72 times, the chances for it hitting heads on the 101st try are still 50 percent, not 72 percent. Unless a demonstrable and persuasive set of fundamental facts supports the price pattern of the seasonal, the "odds" so calculated are merely a mathematical game. They cannot be soundly relied upon for price forecasting or trading.

Chapter 17

PICKING THE TURNS

Commodity trading *is* simple, but it *is not* easy. All of us who trade the markets understand this principle well.

Part of the reason it is not easy is that we compound our problems by losing sight of our objective. We tend to be confused by the fluctuating values (after all, does it *really* matter if we buy or sell on the low or high of the day, isn't what really matters whether we bought at a lower price than that for which we sold?) and the minuteness of increments and often lose sight of the goal of picking major turns in prices.

Stop and think. If you had one ability in this game, surely the ability to pick trend changes would be at the top of your request list. To be able to say, "Yes, the price is heading down toward 20 cents, but it will not drop to 19 cents and will, in fact, head back up toward 30 cents," would be a skill which would rank you at the top of your profession.

For, in essence, if you have the skill to pick market turns you have the skill to start yourself on a very successful path toward profits. Picking a turn is not the end in itself, for if the change in direction of price is to be short-lived or if it is to

be of small magnitude, and you are unable to distinguish these features, then you won't know how much capital to commit to the turn in price or whether to buy/ sell at a single level or to scale in additional purchases/sales as the turn rolls on. The ability to pick turns won't make you a total winner in and of itself, but without that skill it will be very difficult to become a winner at all. With that skill, you are at least well on the way to high achievement.

There are various forms you can use to force yourself to watch for market turns. We often have to come up with a method to force ourselves to watch for key events. Otherwise, they pass us by. Though obvious in retrospect, they were never detected at the time they occurred.

So, this chapter will be devoted to working with a form which will allow you to trade the market from one side while always watching for a turn in price and always allowing yourself the option of reversing your position to trade the opposite side. I have found this form very helpful in my own analysis and trading and you should also. (See Figure 17–1 and 17–2.)

Let's use the August Pork Belly con-

FIGURE 17-1

COMMODITY _August Pork Bellies_

DATE	GO LONG AT	STOP	GO SHORT AT	STOP
3/10	42	39.9	STAY SHORT	45.05
11	42	39.9	STAY SHORT	45.05
12	42	39.9	STAY SHORT	45.05
13	42	40.9	STAY SHORT	45.05
14	42	40.9	STAY SHORT	45.05
17	42	40.9	STAY SHORT	45.05
18	42	41.9	"STOPPED OUT"	—
19	42	42.9	—	—
20	STAY LONG	42.9	—	—
21				
24				
25				
26				
27				
28				
31				
4/1				
2				
3				
4				
7				
8				
9				

* For additional copies of this form, write Dr. Bruce Gould, Box 16, Seattle, WA. 98111.

FIGURE 17-2

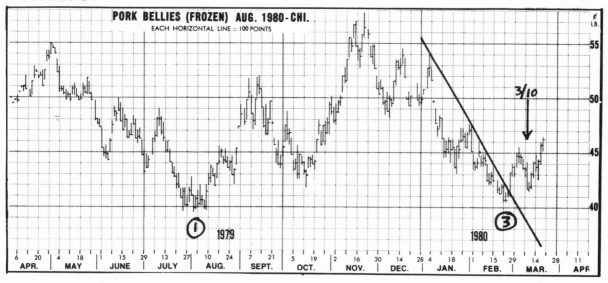

tract as our first example. I have started each of these examples so that you could have a form half completed.

On Monday, March 10, the market dropped substantially. Note the type of pattern we have here. First, the market was in a major bear pattern, but it had broken out of its downtrend. It was headed back toward the February lows. The February lows, at that point, were a number 3 point on a 1–2–3 pattern. If the February lows could hold, there was a good working point from which to work the long side of this market. As I have been watching hogs and bellies both from the short side for some time, I was using the short side of the market here at our starting point. As you will note on the chart, we are "staying short" bellies, but watching for a turn in price. When the stop price of 45.05 was hit, I changed the conclusion that this was a major bear market to one that it was an advancing market and should now be worked from the long side, as the number 3 point should hold for some time.

If you will look at the form, you can

see that what it allows you to do is to maintain your position ("STAY SHORT"), while trading the opposite side of the market at no risk. In a sense you are allowed to "pick the bottom on the long side as many times as you wish without actually investing capital." I use the figure 42 cents here as the point to "go long." If the market had dropped below 42 cents down to 39 cents, on the "paper trading side of the form" we would have brought at 42 cents and been stopped out at 39.9 cents. Then we could decide either to "go short again at 39 cents with a stop perhaps at 36.9 cents" or simply to stand aside on the long side.

The form thus allowed us to maintain our short position until stopped out while at the same time trading the market from the long side at no expense. *WHAT GOOD DOES THIS DO?*

(1) It familiarizes you with a long position. Since you have one at all times, you desire one; (2) it enables you to perfect your skill in picking market turns; (3) it keeps your short position always subject to reversal; (4) it forces you to focus your

attention on the market, always watching for a turn in prices; and (5) it helps you keep price in perspective by allowing you to freely trade either side (or both) and never to forget that commodity prices simply move across the page in an endless cycle.

As the wheat market was turning downward (see Figures 17–3 and 17–4), and by March 10 was already in a major downtrend, one's primary position had to be to work this market from the short side. The form reflects that "stay short," with a trailing stop initially at above 460, later declined to 440 where the stop is eventually hit. As of March 10, you had wheat well within the downtrend and there was no reason to buy wheat.

Does that mean you should ignore the long side? No. Never forget that "all markets turn." It is simply a matter of time. I once read that "everything happens to everyone once, if you live long enough." While that is not exactly true, it does mean that a great many experiences come into the lives of most people. And it is absolutely true that all markets turn. WHY DO WE WATCH A MARKET FROM THE LONG SIDE WHEN YOU HAVE A NICE PROFIT ON THE SHORT SIDE? Because *all markets turn.* We watch the market from the long side while playing the short side because one day the long side *will* be the *best* side of wheat prices. Today the short side is the best, but one day the long side will be the best.

It is a bit like the saying of Willie Sutton, "Why do you rob banks? . . . Because that is where the money is." Why do we watch the long side of the market while trading the short side? Because one day—we absolutely know for certain—the long side will be the better side on which to bet.

Now take wheat, with rapidly declining prices. The only reason to buy is that you have an uptrend line. On March 17 that uptrend line is broken. The other reason to buy is that the January 10 low was a number 3 point, and if that holds then prices will have to stop *before* they get to 425. So, while trading short and having the market go with you, you can pick various areas at which you would buy long and place your stop loss and see how you do. Buying wheat at 440 with a stop at 419 (a) violates buying a market which has broken to the downside of a downtrend line but (b) is well within the principle of buying a market approaching a number 3 point before it hits that number 3 point. The form keeps you on your toes by allowing you to trade both sides of the market at the same time, while risking capital only on one.

The test of your skill as represented in the form should be this:

> *Test:* Which side of the market am I doing the best on:
>   a. The side I am actually trading?
>   b. The side I am trading on paper opposite to the side I am investing in?

Your answer should always be:

(1) The majority of the time, I am doing better in side (a).
(2) But for a brief period of time, I will always do better in side (b) and this is the period when prices change direction.

Take lumber. (See Figures 17–5 and 17–6.) Again, a major bear market. No reason to buy except one: you are looking for a possible number 3 point as price races downward toward contract lows. If a 1–2–3 is formed, the downtrend will have to stop somewhere before it reaches

FIGURE 17–3

COMMODITY ___July Wheat___

DATE	GO LONG AT	STOP	GO SHORT AT	STOP
3/10	440	419	STAY Short	460
11	440	419	STAY Short	460
12	440	419	STAY Short	450
13	440	419	STAY Short	450
14	440	419	STAY Short	445
17	440	419	STAY Short	445
18	440	419	STAY Short	440
19	440	419	"STOPPED OUT"	440
20	440	419	—	—
21	440	419	—	—
24				
25				
26				
27				
28				
1				
4/1				
2				
3				
4				
7				
8				

FIGURE 17–4

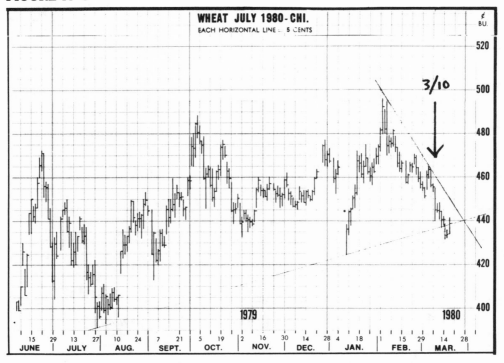

WHEAT JULY 1980 - CHI.
EACH HORIZONTAL LINE = 5 CENTS

below its October lows. By definition, if a 1–2–3 is formed, the downtrend will have stopped sometime before price reached number 1 point. There is no other reason to buy. The economy is shot to hell as far as home building is concerned, interest rates are at levels undreamed of, and the housing industry is laying people off en masse—no reason to buy at all.

So, in actual practice stay short; keep your stop trailing above the current highs. But, for the purpose of the form, always pick the bottom. Force yourself to guess where the decline will end (every decline always ends) and see how skillful you are in doing so.

The form will let you know how correct you are in questions (a) and (b) and how skillful you are in picking the market turns.

There are, in reality, two steps in this process.

(1) Staying with your position which is making you a profit, while trading the other side on paper, and

(2) At one point, getting out of the profit position and making the switch to the other side—sometimes even *before* the stop loss takes you out.

I know this is not what I have written many times—that you should allow the market to take you out with the hitting of your stop loss—but I still remain true to that principle. Over the long run, if your stop takes you out you will be much better off than if you continually "guess" that the market will turn and take yourself out.

But every skill has different levels, and certainly a higher level of achievement in the commodity trading skill is to be able to get out on your own with the profit without waiting for the stop to take you out. By definition, the offsetting of a posi-

FIGURE 17–5

COMMODITY   _JULY LUMBER_

DATE	GO LONG AT	STOP	GO SHORT AT	STOP
3/10	210	196	STAY SHORT	220
11	210	196	STAY SHORT	220
12	210	196	STAY SHORT	220
13	210	196	STAY SHORT	220
14	210	196	STAY SHORT	220
17	210	196	STAY SHORT	212
18	210	196	STAY SHORT	212
19	210	196	STAY SHORT	212
20				
21				
24				
25				
26				
27				
28				
31				
4/1				
2				
3				
4				
7				
8				

FIGURE 17-6

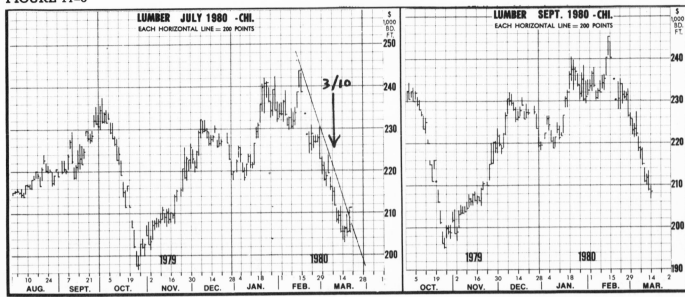

tion through the tripping of the stop loss means you offset at a price worse than you could have received. A stop is not hit until the market has turned, so all stop offsets always are at a price less than the best price possible for your position.

A really skilled trader will (a) give the bias toward letting the stop offset his position but (b) from time to time will offset without waiting for the stop to be hit. The lumber example is a good one. If you truly believe the number 3 point will hold above the number 1 point, then as the price declines closer and closer toward number 1, you may simply wish to offset the short position "at the market" rather than wait for your stop to be hit. You can then decide whether to wait and see if the number 3 holds, or even reverse your position and take a long market position based on your experienced judgment that the number 1 contract low will not be broken.

Now take gold and the form. (See Figures 17–7 and 17–8.) The difference is stark. For lumber there was a number 1

point. For wheat there was a trend line. For bellies there was a clear holding and upthrust. But for gold there wasn't anything to stop the collapse. Here the form is true. Don't pick prices out of thin air and buy at those levels. You have to have something to work from. Five hundred dollars may be a psychological level so you could chose that, but otherwise simply stay short and "pass" on the opportunity to take a long position *until* the market gives you something to work from for that long position. Otherwise, you will see how difficult picking market bottoms can be where there is nothing but space into which price is collapsing.

By March 10, the cocoa market was in a downdraft and prices looked headed lower. (See Figures 17–9 and 17–10.) But it was also in a major sideways trend with the number 1 point still safely and quietly sitting there, unviolated. Now at some point you have to decide whether you will continue to work from the long side of this market, from the short side, or stand

FIGURE 17–7

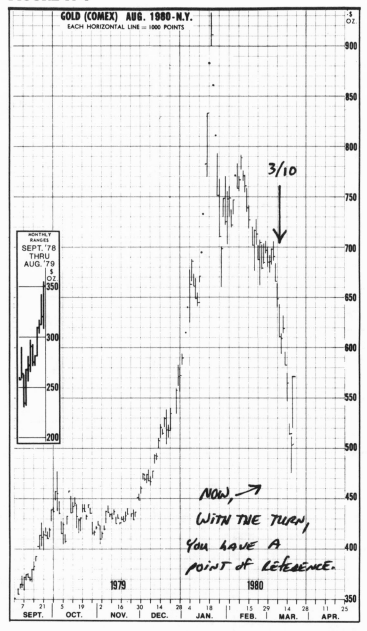

aside. The decision to remain short is based on the collapse which occurred the middle of February. But the desire to go long is based on a chart pattern which clearly has shown no weakness since that mid-February collapse, even though there was plenty of opportunity to do so. If you compare the closing price today (March 19) with the closing price on February 22, the bottom of the collapse, you will see that prices are actually up in the last month. Now, if the market moves up through 140 or perhaps 142, a person may wish to believe the number 3 point has been set and is holding and may wish to return to the long side of this market. That

FIGURE 17–8

COMMODITY _August Gold_

DATE	GO LONG AT	STOP	GO SHORT AT	STOP
3/10	—	—	STAY SHORT	750
11	—	—	STAY SHORT	700
12	—	—	STAY SHORT	700
13	—	—	STAY SHORT	650
14	—	—	STAY SHORT	650
17	500	450	STAY SHORT	600
18	500	450	STAY SHORT	600
19	500	450	"STOPPED OUT"	550
20				
21				
24				
25				
26				
27				
28				
31				
4/1				
2				
3				
4				
7				
8				
9				

FIGURE 17-9

COMMODITY ___MAY COCOA___

DATE	GO LONG AT	STOP	GO SHORT AT	STOP
3/10	140 +	Contract Low	STAY SHORT	140
11	140 +	C.L.	STAY SHORT	140
12	140 +	C.L.	STAY SHORT	140
13	140 +	C.L.	STAY SHORT	140
14	140 +	C.L.	STAY SHORT	140
17	140 +	C.L.	STAY SHORT	140
18	140 +	C.L.	STAY SHORT	140
19	140 +	C.L.	STAY SHORT	140
20				
21				
24				
25				
26				
27				
28				
31				
4/1				
2				
3				
4				
7				
8				

FIGURE 17–10

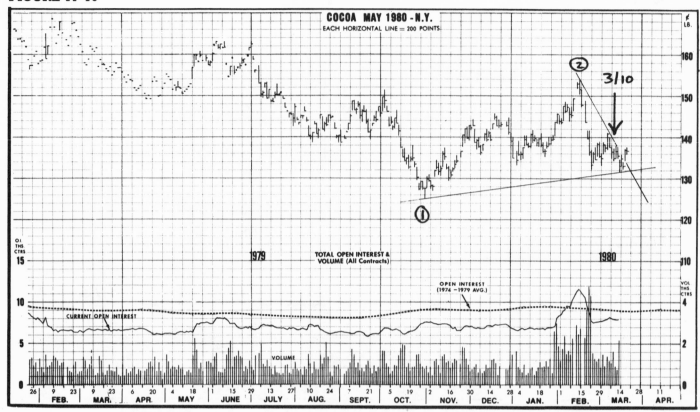

is why you can have, as the form illustrates, the same price level for both, initiating a long position and offsetting a short position. And the price level for initiating the long position need not be "buying on a dip"—it can be buying on strength. The illustrations in this chapter so far have all been about buying the declining market on weakness, but in the case of a market like cocoa you probably would not wish to buy on weakness, since weakness after this prolonged sideways pattern would be a much weaker pattern than buying another market after a long period of collapse when it nears the number 1 point.

So, the form can both keep you in your position and keep you alert to a possible change in direction, and use the same price level for both offsetting the open position and initiating the new position. Cocoa is a good example of how this would work for markets in similar patterns.

Some time ago I mentioned that a leading hard money advocate was recommending the purchase of the German mark and I said that if you thought it would go up, you might wish to consider it for a purchase also. A few weeks back, before the market moved to contract lows and the number 3 point in the making turned out to be false, the mark looked like it might be a possible long position.

The mark illustrates the point that I have made several times and wish to make again, and really can't make too many times. There are *two* skills in successful commodity trading: (a) forecasting price and (b) trading the line. Of the two, (b)

FIGURE 17-11

COMMODITY _Deutsche Mark – June_

DATE	GO LONG AT	STOP	GO SHORT AT	STOP
3/10	—	—	STAY SHORT	58
11	—	—	STAY SHORT	58
12	—	—	STAY SHORT	57
13	—	—	STAY SHORT	57
14	—	—	STAY SHORT	57
17	—	—	STAY SHORT	56
18	—	—	STAY SHORT	56
19	—	—	STAY SHORT	56
20				
21				
24				
25				
26				
27				
28				
31				
4/1				
2				
3				
4				
7				
8				

is far, far more difficult. Price can only stay stable, go up, or go down. Since few prices stay stable, price really can only go up or down. It is a 50/50 proposition and often a fool on the corner has as equal a chance of knowing where price will be in 30–60–90–120 days as does the president's team of economists.

The skill of (b) trading the line is more important and more difficult. The Deutsche mark may well be at a higher level at some time in the future, but riding through the collapse into the void will ruin virtually all but the most highly margined. As you can see from the form (see Figures 17–11 and 17–12), there is no place to go long at, and until the market gives us a point to work from, all you can do is simply trail your stop on the short side and wait the long side out. (But even waiting the long side out is *doing* something. *It is waiting,* an activity requiring much discipline.) (I recall the critic who said, "Young man, sleeping through

FIGURE 17–12

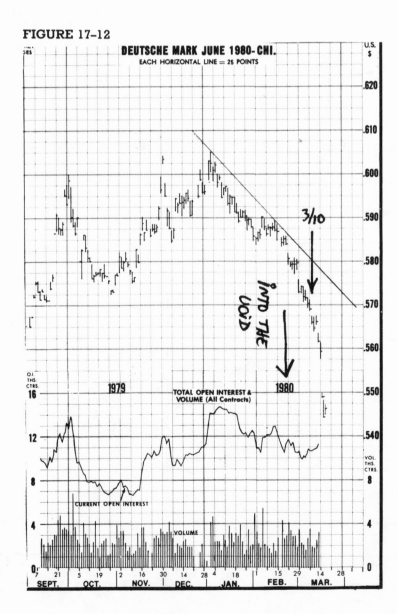

FIGURE 17–13

COMMODITY _DECEMBER T-BILLS_

DATE	GO LONG AT	STOP	GO SHORT AT	STOP
3/10	—	—	STAY SHORT	88
11	—	—	STAY SHORT	88
12	—	—	STAY SHORT	88
13	86	85	STAY SHORT	88
14	86	85	STAY SHORT	88
17	86	85	STAY SHORT	88
18	86	85	STAY SHORT	88
19	86	85	STAY SHORT	88
20				
21				
24				
25				
26				
27				
28				
31				
4/1				
2				
3				
4				
7				
8				

the play *is an opinion* in and of itself.") There is no point at which to buy yet, so the form allows you to stay short while still watching for the turn which will come—while not suffering great financial loss.

Again, you have the problem with the T-bill contract, as of March 10, being in outer space. (See Figures 17–13 and 17–14.) There is no point to work from to mark the bottom of the decline. When a market is making contract lows or contract highs on a regular basis, you have no frame of reference for estimating the point at which the decline will stop.

Now you can simply say, "I know the decline will stop because interest rates for T-bills above 14 percent won't occur." That is a worthwhile opinion, but never bet too much in the commodity markets strictly on the basis of your opinion. Opinion and 40 cents may buy you a cup of coffee, as they used to say, although the way prices are moving opinion and $1.00 may not buy you a cup in some areas. Again, what the form forces you to do is to *see the difficulty* of picking market tops and bottoms without losing so much money in the process that you don't have any left to trade with when you finally

FIGURE 17–14

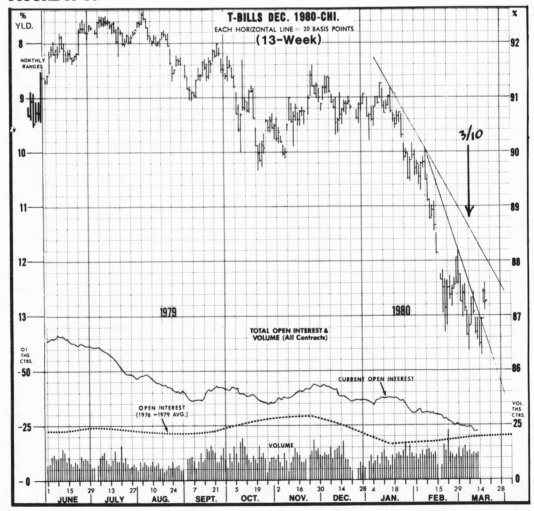

perfect your skill as a successful market top or bottom trader. It allows you to take the gigantic risk (buy gold at $500 with a stop at $450, casually entered, but in true life would you like a $50 stop for gold?) and learn your mistakes without losing your capital.

Now, I truly believe that interest rates will change direction and that prices for T-bill futures will move upward. That will happen. When? Now, that is another question. Timing in commodities isn't something—it is everything—and the "when question" is the dividing question which separates success from failure. T-bills will rise. But will they first make another stab at contract lows? My own view is yes. The bottom has not yet been seen. The skill now comes in trading such a market *or* in having the ability to pass it by and look for another easier to trade.

The illustrations and prices used in this chapter are not meant to be absolute perfection. For example, I may have a price like cocoa at 140+ and another price like the Deutsche mark at 56, but in actual trading I always put stops a small increment on the most distant side of an even number, so the actual figures used in trading would not be something like 40 cents, it would either be 40.02 or 39.97. The purpose of the form, however, is mainly to keep you alert to both sides of price— to allow you to still keep a position when price is moving with you and yet monitor the other side of the position, watching for the turn to come.

The problem with watching only one side of a market is that you tend to think only in terms of that one side. If you are long wheat, you can see *nothing but* the

reasons for wheat to advance. And you tend to become mesmerized by price because of your position. Now, suppose you are long wheat in the form but also trading the short side of wheat in the same form. What soon becomes obvious? The fact that your long side is losing money after money after money, while your short side is making profit after profit after profit. This trading of both sides at the same time quickly allows you to understand why you are losing in your main position and forces you, often much quicker, to reverse your position or to simply offset the losing position, stand aside, and wait for the dust to clear while you analyze the taking of a new position.

In summary then, watching both sides is very valuable. You will not do it without some specially designed program to help you do so. A simple form like this is all you need. This allows you to follow both sides, to learn the skills of trading either side, and to quickly determine whether you are a better paper trader or a better actual trader. If you are better on paper than with actual money, then simply use the form to trade both sides and quit trading with money altogether until you reverse the balance. There is no need to pour money into the markets until you are skilled at doing so. The money goes quickly enough for everyone. (It is just that the skilled know how to get it back.) By using this form, you should be able to further develop all your skills at initial market watching. It should be helpful.

* This chapter is adapted from "Bruce Gould on Commodities"—A biweekly newsletter published at Box 16, Seattle, WA. 98111.

Chapter 18

MANAGING THE COMMODITY ACCOUNT

THOUGHTFUL PLANNING

Nothing is more important in futures trading than thoughtful planning. Behind the exciting spectacle of split second trades, screaming pit brokers, and fortunes won or lost stands the overshadowing necessity of calm deliberation. The hectic public scene represents only the end result of thousands of hours of planning a trading strategy, researching price moves, and calculating every potential response to every potential market swing. The reason why the professionals can move so fast is that they have done their homework. They have a strategy and they follow the rules of the game. They respond quickly to any situation because they have already anticipated its likelihood and prepared a response accordingly. Whether the futures trader is an industry hedger, full-time professional, or novice speculator, he must carefully devise a program that lays out in detail the proposed purposes and methods of his contemplated trades. The impatient trader should remind himself that the majority of losers in the futures markets are the hot-headed people who rush into trades on flimsy evidence and without a thoughtful plan for managing the positions acquired.

The trader begins, before investing any money, with critical self-analysis—personal and financial. Are you (or the company you are trading for) qualified, in personality and portfolio, for futures trading? How will futures trading fit and serve your other economic enterprises? Are you prepared for the hours of work required to formulate a successful trade and monitor its execution? Can you keep cool in a fast-moving crisis? Will your basic financial situation (or that of the company) be damaged if you lose *all* of the money budgeted for the proposed commodity account? If you are not prepared to do the work required to develop a trading program and manage a commodity account, forget futures, or spend substantial time investigating brokers, advisory services, and funds before investing. When you employ any of the latter, you are purchasing a trading program, one that remains your responsibility to thoroughly evaluate.

A lengthy and complete review of your total financial status is a prerequisite to any form of futures trading. It is irresponsible for you to take monies needed for necessities and use them as risk capital (and it is irresponsible for a broker to allow you to do so). The money you put

318

into futures trading is money you should be prepared to lose without fundamental damage to your overall fiscal position. Futures speculation should come only after monies are assured for food, clothing, housing, and insurance and probably only as a complement to other less risky investments that make up the bulk of a well-rounded portfolio. No one should ever lose their house or their children's college fund because of losses in the futures market. Similarly, a hedging program is supposed to aid in corporate money management and planning, not act as a drain on required capital. Every trader should know his net worth, assets, liquid assets, upcoming income and expenses, real and projected liabilities, etc. Budget only a portion of your *extra* cash to futures trading. Once you have determined how much you can afford to lose in futures, you are ready to consider what kind of plan best fits your situation.

Once this is calculated, the next move is to establish the purposes and goals of your life in futures trading. Are you in it just for fun? Is your goal modest profits over a short span of time or a set amount regardless of how long it takes? Do you want to trade a few commodities occasionally or several very frequently? When and how do you plan to get out of the market? The trading program you devise should be consciously tailored to suit your own goals and to reach them successfully. How you combine the elements of futures trading discussed in this book so that they form a unique and profitable individual plan will determine your future in futures. This is how it should be. Pick and choose your methods to meet objectives set out in the cool meditation of thoughtful preparation. If the program fails to deliver profits as planned, don't panic. Don't turn

frantically away from the plan to grab haphazardly at other options. Get out of the market. Take a stroll. Rationally re-ëvaluate the program and what went wrong. Pinpoint mistakes, change the plan, and proceed with care as you experiment with new methods.

Remember, the hard statistics are against you. The majority of traders lose money. The winning minority profits from the skillful execution of a well-researched and tested trading plan. Although this book is *not* a commodity trading manual and does *not* offer detailed trading plans, it is written with the conviction that a study of the contents will give the reader a head start in the race to join the successful few.

POSITION MANAGEMENT

The intention of every trading program is profitable position management. In a perfectly discounted market, the trader's chances of picking profitable positions correctly are 50–50. A program of buying and selling at random will break him at the rate at which he pays commissions. He must improve on this 50–50 proposition by at least the 5 or 10 percent it costs to play the game. This is done by not taking all the risks offered at random. The speculator must *choose his risks* deliberately. He can also improve his odds *by making more on winning positions than is lost on losing positions.* This may or may not mean *winning on more positions than he loses on,* depending on the relative sizes of the wins and losses. Although money management is the key to the financial health of the commodity account, position management is the art that distinguishes the net winners from the net losers.

One reminder is vital to the proper

management of any commodity program. Margin equity is not money. Money can pay the rent, buy a car, or finance a trip to Bermuda. Commodity margin can only buy commodities, unless it be removed from the account. The stock market is often used as a place to store excess money and put it to work until it is needed for other purposes. Money cannot be stored in a commodity contract. Commodities are a speculative venture, not a media for wealth storage. Up until recently, margin deposited with the brokerage firm was used to maintain a speculative position; excess funds sat sterile and dormant. Today most firms offer the trader an interest-bearing account in conjunction with his margin account. The interest-bearing account may involve commercial paper, Treasury Bills, or negotiable CD's. Monies are transferred back and forth from this account to the commodity account as needed. If your broker cannot offer such a program, shop around for one who can. Though such an arrangement does bring added income on the investment, the monies so deposited are still responsible to the futures game you are playing and are thus not as "safe" as accounts held separately from the margin account. Money placed in a commodity account is best viewed as so many game tokens, allowing the trader to hold a position in the game, and whose numbers indicate how he is faring. Only if margin is viewed as a collection of game tokens can the trader achieve that dispassionate objectivity essential to the execution of a skillful game.

The trader's primary goal the entire time he is playing commodities should be to stay in the game. Any position that could knock him out of the game, if the worst possible thing happened, is simply too risky to be taken. Each play is considered like each hand in an all-night poker game: It is a single instance in a series, and is played with the larger view as to what will happen to the entire margin account should the play go wrong. A good commodity program will most often spread across a large number of plays carefully calculated to avoid risking any more tokens than are absolutely necessary to try out the position. Even the best market analyst expects to be wrong about 60 percent of the time. His wins have to cover a large number of losses and provide at least enough surplus to cover commissions. A typical winning commodities program sees something like 40 percent correct guesses result in profits, 40 percent wrong guesses bring a depletion of margin, and 20 percent plays that just meander for no appreciable profit or loss (though costing money in commissions).

RULES TO PLAY BY

The major part of any position program is having one in the first place. A program should cover all possible contingencies that can happen to an open futures position. The trader should know *before* he opens a position on the commodities market exactly how much margin he is prepared to lose, and he should set a stop loss order to make sure that he does not lose more. He should know in advance when he will add to his position to increase his profit, and how. He should know what indicators mean "get out," and let the market signal him when to do so. If each play is looked at as a tentative feeler put out to test the market and to be taken back if conditions are not comfortable, most of the rest of the rules normally applied to commodity programs become unnecessary. Experience and the advice of many experts yield a basic set of rules to play by:

1. *Cut your losses short and let your profits run.* This is the supreme and universal law of futures trading. Almost every rule for successful trading is an attempt to put this law into practice. But human nature exhibits a persistent tendency toward egotism that prevents many traders from admitting their mistakes before it is too late. The more ways you build into the plan to force the closure of losing positions, and the more you design to maximize profits on the winners, the better your chances of ending in the black.

2. *Never answer a margin call.* A call from your broker asking for more money to maintain a position simply means that you have a position which is eating up game tokens. A margin call is a sign you have stayed around too long in a position that is not winning. While this is a good rule of thumb for the novice trader, there are times when you should go by the general concept and not by the letter of the rule. "Never answer a margin call" simply means do not let any position cost you more than you had planned to lose. Stop loss orders at positions you have selected should take you out of the position before it degenerates to this extent. There will be times when the noise in the market will cause swings bigger than what would be required to generate a margin call. In these situations you should select your stop point based on your analysis, not merely on the margin required for the position.

3. *Avoid thin markets.* Markets with comparatively little open interest or volume have less liquidity and are "thin." When a thin market takes off in a trader's

favor, a great deal of money can be made. When major news hits the market, however, it can send price dramatically higher or lower. It will be impossible to close the position quickly. Thin markets are occasionally played by seasoned traders "on a flyer." A trader who fully understands what he is doing and has his trading on a firm footing can afford a flyer, more for the sport than for the winnings. He knows what a flyer is, knows what proper playing is, and will never risk his chances of market survival just for sport. There must be enough money in reserve to cover even the most drastic possible event.

4. *Use stop losses to get out of a losing market at a predetermined price.* Position management requires knowing, *before* you make a trade, precisely when you'll cut your losses short. Every potential trade should be analyzed to reveal the probable extent of both an adverse and a favorable price move. No trade should be entered into unless the potential profit is at least three or four times the potential loss. The price at which the loss stops being acceptable is pinpointed and the stop loss order entered there. Whether a market quickly hits you for a loss, or slowly and gently wanders in the wrong direction, the market is still breaking you. Discipline demands that you set your stops and abide by them—*actually,* not mentally. Never move your stop orders further into adverse territories in hopes of a market turnaround.

5. *Let the market pay.* Profit objectives should not be set as absolutely as stop losses. Letting profits run is the only way to counterbalance the long list of small losses inevitably taken by even the best of traders. There's no harm in watching profits mount. The position ought to be closed out and winnings counted only

when the market actually runs out of steam. A market that has already coursed a long way can look precarious at a glance when, in fact, no significant indicators point to a change in the trend. The trading program should detail in advance, before the heat of a large move, exactly what degree of price event at what point in the move will take the trader out of the market. Let the profits accumulate until the market has broken its trend in fact, according to whatever trend measurement is used. Don't second guess the market. If it has a mind to go your way, don't argue. Listen and profit.

6. *Don't trade against the market.* Trading against the demonstrated market trend is a great way to cut your profits short and let your losses run. All the indicators in the world may be telling you that plywood futures prices can only go up, but if prices have been down for the last five days, don't be a fool. Stay out and wait for the move to begin. If you miss the first few steps, think of the deduction from your earnings as insurance against the losses you would have suffered if you had gone in and prices had collapsed. Anyone who tells you that a price "just has to go up" or "just has to go down" hasn't been around the markets very long. Prices do what they want to do. They obey no one's command.

7. *Never average down.* This is a maneuver of traders who refuse to admit their errors, preferring to buck the trend and increase their losses. Averaging down is a process carried over to commodities from the stock market, where it is also a bad practice. The trader who went long at 2.80 finds himself in a losing position at 2.70. The logic of averaging down is that the trader can buy another contract at the lower price and average the two long positions out at 2.75. The market

thus has only to come back half as far to return the lost money. No sane trading program, set out in advance, would ever call for instituting a long position in a falling market, which is precisely the tactic in averaging down. Increasing a losing position increases the number of contracts that are returning a loss.

In attempting to average down, the trader buys positions when the market is clearly telling him to stay out or go short. The original loss of 10 cents could have been taken with little more than a wince, and without committing more margin capital to a dubious effort at outsmarting the market. Once out of his original long position, the trader has a much better chance of looking at the market objectively, choosing to stay out or go short. He can rationally decide what determines a change in the downtrend and set stop orders that will reinstate his position when the market shows signs of being ready for the upswing. Averaging down doubles the number of the trader's potential losing positions in a usually vain, hope-inspired gamble that the recognizable market trend will suddenly reverse. The same objections hold true for averaging up when holding a short position in a rising market.

Of course, there are circumstances under which experienced traders will average down: when they are looking to put on sizeable positions and the scaling down gives them added flexibility. They, however, have learned to do this from experience, have the capital to finance the operation, AND planned the entire trading operations before they took on the first contract.

8. *Be a movement trader.* This is the lesson distilled from a number of the above rules. The commodity futures trader can easily lose sight of one simple and overriding fact: The futures trader

trades price moves, and nothing else. It is the actual movement of prices, up or down or sideways, that brings the trader his profits. In this fundamental way he is not trading soybeans or gold or Swiss francs. He is profiting from the motion of prices that can be graphically seen on a price chart. The trader who forgets this rule and trades as though soybeans or gold or Swiss francs had a "natural" or "normal" price that could be relied upon as a guide to position management will soon be out of the game.

9. *Spread your money around.* From the fact that the speculator trades price moves and not commodities, it follows that margin money should be diversified among a number of different contracts. The trader who spends years studying only corn (as I did) will find it a useless occupation if corn price moves present no opportunities during those years for sizeable profits. Meanwhile, price moves elsewhere are missed. Speculators should set a limit on the percentage of margin capital invested in any one commodity, with a ceiling of 25 percent. The idea is to try out a number of commodities until one takes off. The losers can be left behind and the winner followed until gains exceed losses.

10. *Beware of overtrading.* There is a vast difference between a healthy diversification of commodity positions and a suicidal program of overtrading. The average trader will find it almost impossible to hold open positions in more than ten commodities at any one time. Sleepless nights and constant calls to the broker will make the financial payoff eventually a bad bargain and the quality of attention given each position correspondingly inadequate. Overtrading can also involve too many positions in a single commodity, to a point where the indicators cannot justify so large a gamble even if the portion of margin capital is still under the self-set limit. Of course, overtrading also moves more of your money out of the market and into the broker's pocket.

11. *Get comfortable on the short side.* More traders should be urged to make no distinction of preference between going long and going short. If you still have trouble selling a commodity you don't own, or taking a position in a declining market, turn the price chart upside down and pretend prices are rising. A trading program will be crippled if denied the resource of the short sale. If you're in a losing long position, and a price decline is signaled, for heaven's sake switch sides and go short.

12. *Take the money and run.* A commodity margin account is properly started with a sum of money that the player can afford to set aside for a game. If the game is played well this sum will grow, and if it grows to the point that it is more money than the trader cares to use for a game, money ought to be taken out. There is no such thing in commodities as a paper profit. Keep the margin account small enough so that it can be considered game tokens. When there is more, take it and run. It is easy in commodities to become hypnotized by large winnings, to grow greedy and obsessive as if the accrued dollars were an end and not a means. Traders unable to leave the markets when they are ahead will only leave the markets when they are broke.

STOP ORDERS

Let us assume now that the trader has a plan. He has analyzed his reasons for speculating in the futures markets, budgeted an affordable sum, investigated brokers, and opened an individual account.

He has spent some months reading books on futures trading and has prepared himself by following the markets daily and trading them on paper. He monitors about a dozen commodities, becoming familiar with their fundamentals, and watches the action of the technicals and the charts. All the preparation now comes down to the moment of action. The skillful execution of the trade itself will be, in fact, the major determinant of success or failure. Price forecasting and market analysis form the foundation, but fortunes are won or lost by the artful exploitation of price moves through position management. The trader must choose when and where to enter, when and where to exit, and how to execute the move his indicators point toward. Knowing the rules, he looks for a way to manage his positions so as to limit losses and encourage profits to accumulate.

The best all-around position management tool is the stop order. For the person directing his own trading program, the vast majority of positions will be entered and closed through the use of stops. As discussed in chapter 8, a stop order is a market or limit order which cannot be filled by the pit trader until the market meets the conditions specified in the order. The only orders which do not go into the pit trader's deck are those that can be filled immediately and those which specify that they are not to be held. "At market," "Fill or Kill," and time orders such as "At Opening" or "At 11:00" which attempt to take advantage of technical market trends like the Friday sell-off are the only frequently used orders which do not await placement. The stop order is used to gain as much precision, in price and timing, as is possible in the establishment or liquidation of the position.

Often the trader will seek to determine in advance what constitutes the end of a resting period of trend and enter a stop order to be filled if and when prices make a substantial breakout. The chart for May sugar shows a classic sideways channel from January through September. (See Figure 18–1.) The trader following the sugar market in this period will not, of course, hold any open positions, as margin capital sunk into such a dormant market is just wasted. What he will do is place a stop order to put him in if the conditions are right. If the fundamental indicators consulted point to an eventual rise in prices, the speculator may place a stop order at an entry point above the channel as suggested by technical and chart analysis: "Buy May 80 sugar at 11.75 Stop: Good 'till Canceled." This order could be placed in February (1979), as soon as the sideways channel establishes itself, and left standing for months until filled.

If the order is filled, the speculator will match this order with a "stop loss" order to sell set below the first, designed to take him out of the market if prices decline sufficiently following his purchase. If the upward move does occur, the trader may decide to "scale in" additional purchases every time the price moves up by, say, 1 cent. Corresponding adjustments in the stop loss orders will simultaneously be made. The new stop orders to buy will put the trader into additional positions only if the market continues to reward his long position. He will also be deciding what price behavior he considers indicative of an end to the trend, trailing his stop orders to take him out of the market. In this manner he may get most of the profit offered without finding himself in the situation of having to decide when the market has paid him enough.

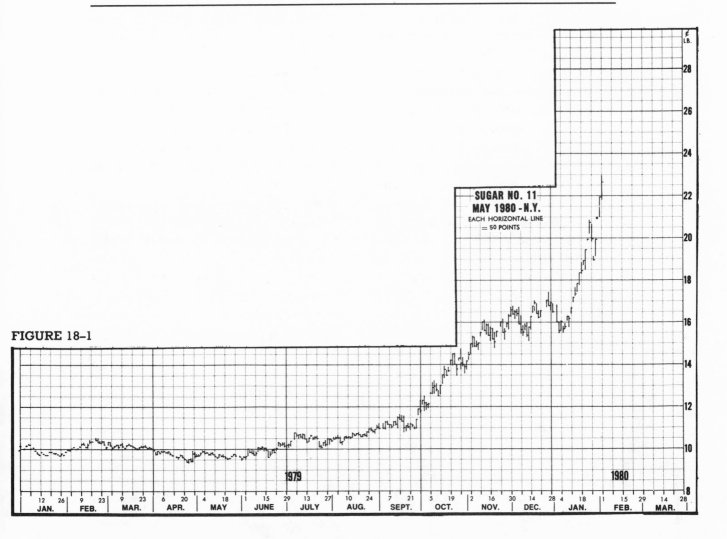

FIGURE 18-1

SUGAR NO. 11
MAY 1980 - N.Y.
EACH HORIZONTAL LINE
= 50 POINTS

In the case of the sugar trader, his first buy stop order would have been tripped at 11.75 on September 25. A conservative trading plan might then have called for placing five new stop orders to buy at 1 cent intervals (12.75, 13.75, etc.), trailing stop loss orders perhaps at 2.10 behind. On February 1, when prices reached 22.75, the six contracts purchased would represent a profit of $57.120 (less commissions).

Stop orders are used to (1) enter positions if market price hits a predetermined level, (2) expand a position if the market continues its positive move, (3) protect profits which have been accumulated or margin which has been committed to new position, and (4) to close out the position when market conditions appear to signal the end of the trend. The process is identical for either uptrending or downtrending markets or for long or short positions.

PLACING STOP ORDERS

In placing stop orders, the trader must determine how large a price fluctuation can simply be classified as noise. Noise is the random fluctuation that occurs within any price formation on the chart. In the May sugar chart, the noise level for the January–September period was about 50 cents. Fifty cent moves were common and indicated nothing about the course of prices to come. This estimate of noise helped the trader choose his entry levels and stop loss points. For the September U.S. treasury bonds chart (See Figure 18–2), noise movements of 20/32 during the February–September period were ordinary and without predictive value. In this particular period of the chart, a movement of less than 20/32 could be ignored; a stop loss order would have best been positioned 20/32 above any sell order or 20/32 below any buy order. In so doing, the trader would be announcing in advance the amount of loss he is

willing to take if he is wrong—in this case, $625.

The speculator knows at the onset of the trade that he stands to win as much as the market will give him (at the rate of $31.25 for each 1/32 tick in price), but he has generally limited his loss to $625. To this he would have to add the commission charge of, say, $75. The results, in practice, will vary, as it is possible for the order to fill at a price above or below the stop price once it is ticked. In that case, losses could exceed $625, but usually not by much unless a rare series of limit moves prohibited liquidation. Placing the stop loss order closer than 20/32 to the

FIGURE 18–2

price at which the position was opened would have limited losses to even less. But this runs the high risk of having the stop tripped by mere noise. At all times the stop loss ought to be as close as possible, limiting losses tightly but not to the extent that the trader risks being knocked out of the market by price swings of a random nature.

Now, some traders will argue that the use of stops needlessly takes the trader out of the market when, if he persisted and stayed in, he could eventually catch the price move forecast in the first place—and without paying two commissions to do it. The trouble with this argument is that (1) it violates the rule against letting losses run and (2) it proceeds on the *hope* of a price move rather than with the real market trend.

For example, let's look at the case of the speculator in September T-bonds. In March the trader forecasts the collapse of the market and enters a stop order to sell at 90–00, with a stop loss at 90–20. His order fills on April 20 and he happily watches prices fall. At the same time he moves his stop loss orders down. On May 4 the market hits its first bottom and begins to rebound. The trader now faces the choice: Does he discipline himself and follow his stop loss program (now set at 89–00) for a small profit or cancel his stop loss and ride out the reversal until the market goes back his way? Many traders, unable to admit error and convinced of the accuracy of their forecasts, would vote to hold on to the position.

What happens in each case? The trader who abandons his stops and rides out the reversal has suffered a loss of over $2,000 per contract by June 29, forcing margin calls and hampering his ability to trade in other commodities. The T-bond market will not finally move conclusively into profitable territory until September, causing this trader to waste his margin and his trading time for more than four months—all to save a commission cost of $75.

The trader who let himself be stopped out at 89–00 makes $1,000 per contract, less commission, and resumes watching the market. In early July he catches the second downward dip at 91–16 and is stopped out again on the second upturn at 90–16 for another $1,000 per contract gain. On August 23 he catches the third downward move at 90–16 and rides it to 88–16 for $2,000. On September 22 he sells at 88–16 and this time rides the collapse as far as he wants, cushioning minor reversals with his sizeable profits or dashing in and out at will. In the four months another trader was holding a margin depleting position, this trader picks up an extra $4,000 per contract, minus $300 in commissions, and still gets on board in time for the big move.

A simple rule can be developed from this comparison: Never set a stop loss so far back it would be cheaper to leave the market and pay a commission to return at a later date and never set a stop loss so close that it closes the position due to meaningless noise. Paying out two or three commissions is a small price for insurance against being stuck for huge losses or for the right to use your capital for other positions until the market resumes its favorable trend.

The amount of noise common to a particular futures contract changes over the life of the contract. Setting stop loss orders requires an inspection of the current chart for the contract being traded. Looking once more at the September T-bonds contract, it is evident that as soon as the collapse was underway in October, price volatility increased dramatically. Moves of 48/32 became common and some such large figure would have to be used for placing stops in the market during these months.

Three things can happen to a protected position in any commodity. The market can go against the trader, taking him out at a roughly predictable loss—depending upon the volatility of the market. The market can trend sideways until the trader sensibly abandons his original forecast and closes for a slight gain or loss. Or the price can go with the open position, rewarding the trader as it goes. In the case that a profit is returned, the distance from the going price to the stop loss becomes larger than considered necessary on the basis of significance (noise level) and the stop loss is continually moved up (or lowered) so that it still provides protection. A stop order can be designed to continually trail the action and protect it as the market makes its swings.

Stop orders are an excellent way for the trader to follow a plan with discipline. The trader may be without a position in several markets. He watches them closely, however, waiting and preparing to go onto either the long or the short side when the market tells him its direction. It is much easier to be calm and rational, taking advantage of every possible angle, before the battle begins and before the excitement drives traders into a frenzy. Quietly anticipating the possibilities, the trader works out his plan ahead of time for each alternative. He figures the respective price moves that will indicate positions on the long and short side, how much loss he is willing to take, how he is going to add contracts to his position if he is right, how his stop losses are going to trail, etc. When

the move begins and other traders scramble, his orders will be in place and his plans will be unfolding logically. Likely, he will be just as frantic as the other speculators in the market, but his market actions will be rational—even if he himself is not.

ADDING TO A WINNING POSITION

Once the speculator has chosen a point at which to enter the market, he must decide then how much to risk: one or two or ten or fifty contracts? And if prices do move in the direction forecast, how does the trader add to his initial positions safely and profitably during the unpredictable period between breakout and reversal? First, the commodity trader should never commit, at initial entry, all the contracts he has contemplated selling or buying for that commodity—even if he can afford it. For the average speculator, one or two contracts will suffice to keep the trader's interest, test the market, and take advantage of correctly estimated market swings. If the price does continue to head in the forecast direction, the trader can then implement a plan for adding to his position according to a set schedule, without depositing more money to the account if he manages his additions conservatively. Such plans will depend on the amount of available trading capital, the trading plan's goals, and the market's character, but one could easily move from one contract to twenty or thirty in a big market move of two or three months duration. In any case, the trader should never commit more than about 25 percent of the account to any single position and never add to it in a way that threatens to wipe out initial profits.

If the market rewards the first contracts taken, the trader can then "scale in" additional contracts at regular intervals, bringing up his stop loss orders at the same time. (See Figure 18–3.) The trader may enter with two contracts, add two more after a reasonable profit, and move the stop loss to protect his gains. He now has four contracts in a winning position, with only two endangered by a price reversal. If the original gain were substantial, it could finance the margin on the two additional contracts. If the move continues, orders are scaled in each time the price makes a specified move (10 cents, $10, 30/32 of a percent, etc.). The trader may stop adding to the position when it reaches a predetermined size (a cautious move

FIGURE 18–3

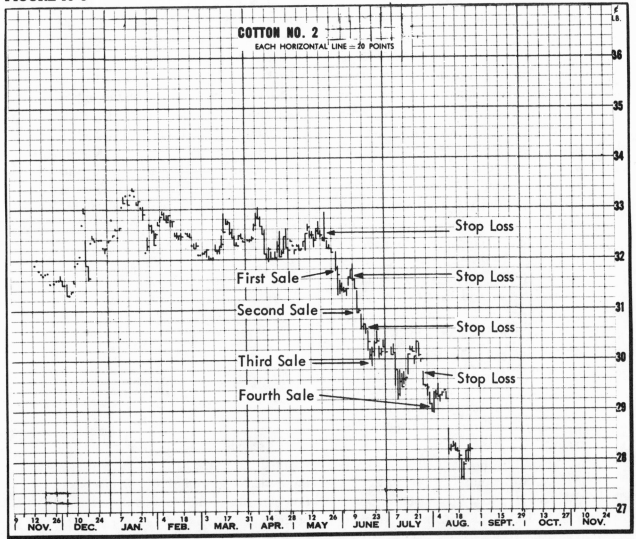

Orders are scaled in, adding to the position so long as the move continues profitable. With each addition, the stop loss is moved down to cover as much of the total position as possible. A single stop-loss level cancels the entire position.

Source: Commodity Research Bureau, Inc., with additions by author.

that limits profits) or continue adding contracts until the market finally turns and forces a loss on the final two contracts (thus paying out a known amount for the opportunity of going all the way with the market move). Orders to scale in will likely be stop orders, each identical except for incrementally higher (or lower) target prices and stop losses.

Eventually, all markets do turn. If at all possible, they will do so at precisely the worst time. Should the trader have a great number of contracts clustered near the turning point, a reversal will sweep them all up and transform an imminent fortune into a ruinous disaster. Initial profits should be guarded by stop losses and additional contracts spaced to enter in an evenly distributed fashion. Never get into a situation where a conceivable market swing could wipe out all your winnings. Keep the majority of contracts in any one commodity below (or above) the stop loss. In this way the trader will always have a protected win at a small cost should the market suddenly turn against him. When the reversal comes the trader may stand to lose on his last two contracts entered, but he will have four or six or eight others on the winning side of his stop loss if it has been kept trailing at roughly the same interval at which new contracts are added. In actual trading conditions price moves and executions will not occur this exactly, but the principle of scaling in will remain the best way to manage positions profitably.

The trader who enters all his contracts at once, at the outset, stands to lose on them all if prices immediately reverse. Yes, he will make less on his contracts if he scales them in as prices move favorably, but he will also greatly reduce his risks. Remember that the successful speculator thinks in terms of a total series of trades and a total trading program. It makes no sense to squeeze every last dime out of a projected trade if it means risking the solvency of the whole commodity account. Only a steady, long-term, disciplined plan of increasing the odds, cutting losses, and letting profits run will return profits consistently over time. Be content to take home 50 or 60 percent of the maximum that *might* have been made, *theoretically,* if you had bet the limit from the first. Keep cool, don't be greedy, follow your plan, and you'll be three steps ahead of most futures speculators.

There will be times when the speculator who has sizeable capital does enter five or ten or more contracts at the outset. Afterwards, new positions are scaled in fewer and fewer at a time until the single last contract is established and the complete position set. This will "pyramid" the trader into the price move, with the base of the pyramid at the starting point and the body tapering off in the direction prices are headed:

```
    X
  X X
  X X X          PRICE
  X X X X        RISING
X X X X X

X X X X X
  X X X X
  X X X          PRICE
  X X           FALLING
  X
```

Such a schedule of scaling has the advantage that, from the earliest time possible, the trader is hopeful of a profitable position by virtue of the fact that the number of his winning contracts always exceeds the number of his losing contracts. Having established five contracts which are showing a profit, he trails the stop loss order to their level and opens four more contracts. He is now safe on five and risking four. If the price move continues his way he risks three more contracts, trailing his stop to the level at which he bought the second batch. He now has a protected profit on five contracts, a break even position on four, and three in the fire. If the move goes on in his favor, he will have twelve contracts on the winning side and the option to pyramid three more. Depending on when the reversal comes, he will lose on considerably less than half his positions; if he completes the pyramid before the reversal, profits will be impressive. The stop loss order, of course, offsets all contracts in the position—those close to the action and those bought or sold long ago—retaining large profits on the early ones to more than cover losses on the few that took a beating.

It is also possible, and perversely popular, to guarantee *losing* by pyramiding in reverse. This clever trader starts with two contracts, adds four more with his winnings on the first, then eight, and so on, guaranteeing that at all times his most recent positions will rack up losses on a price reversal that more than eats up the winnings on the smaller, earlier positions. On occasion you will read of an account manager (usually soliciting clients) who has built an account from $10,000 to $150,000 to $1,500,000 through such a precarious system. In the run after attention getting paper "profits," which are no more than increases in account equity that are not real as long as the dangerous position is held, the account has been made literally to stand on its head. It can only balance like that shortly, and then collapse. An upside down pyramid has no base. It can be expanded indefinitely, at maximum risk to the trader (and maxi-

mum profit to the commission hungry broker), until the reversal takes out the last batch of positions and topples the whole unsound edifice.

Improper scaling can only be profitable if the trader arbitrarily sets a limit on his position and closes it before the reversal comes, a feat requiring extraordinary forecasting abilities and personal self-control. This move keeps profits intact, but in doing so it assures the speculator of missing out on any truly large moves. Once built, a proper pyramid can stand for a major move, and the market will take care of closing it. A reverse pyramid yields no signals as to when to get out and is thus estranged from the market. Any time a trader must choose to let himself out of the market, something is wrong, as he is missing an opportunity to further exploit it. *Let the market decide.* If the player has more than half his position endangered, he is forced to offset it himself, at his own imperfect discretion, rather than letting the market indicate when it is finally through. The temptation to close out a winning position and take small profits is great, but must be overcome. Large price moves always look risky and get riskier looking the further they move from their original plateau. By taking profits out of a risky looking market, the trader assures himself a string of small profits. He is going to lose more often than he wins, and must pay commissions; by keeping his profits small, he will lose overall. Only the market knows how far it can go and it doesn't know until it gets there. The successful futures trader is the one who has a plan that puts him in the market reasonably soon, keeps him riding a price move to its actual end, and takes him out of it with a hefty portion of his profits intact.

ORGANIZATION

Futures speculation is a serious business enterprise (though it is also exciting and fun). As such, it requires proper organization and accurate bookkeeping, without which no amount of position management or price forecasting will be of the slightest value. New positions cannot be opened unless the success (or failure) or previous positions is known. Contracts cannot be chosen and margined unless the present amount of working capital is known. Price forecasts can't be made or stops set unless historical price data is at hand. It will take some time for the novice speculator to gather his materials and put his system into operation. Once intact and functioning smoothly, its day-to-day maintenance will require little time relative to anticipated returns, demanding only a few basic checks of records and information sources before daily position decisions are made. An enormous amount of time and money is saved if the speculator develops a system of logical, easily consulted records that suit his trading program and provide quick, correct answers to his questions.

First, every trader will be equipped with a basic library of price and commodity information. Along with a daily subscription to a newspaper with full futures quotations, this will include recent yearbooks and statistical publications of the major exchanges and the Commodity Research Bureau's *Commodity Yearbook.* For the technical trader, a number of chart services offer subscriptions that will bring any assortment of graphic market data one would care to inspect regularly. For the fundamental trader, the reports and bulletins of the relevant government agencies mentioned in earlier chapters will be a necessity, either directly from the

source or as reprinted by newswires, advisory services, or brokerages. The trader also keeps a sharp eye on the major news magazines and broadcasts, as well as on speciality publications, to monitor current events and developments.

The broker should be another principal source of information and organizational assistance—providing newsletters, reports, and other research services. Check to see how up to date such material is and how it compares in accuracy and timing with government announcements and the publications of other firms and advisors. Almost all large brokerage firms and most advisory services will send free samples of their literature upon request.

The most important papers received from the broker, however, are confirmation slips and monthly statements. The trader should keep his own separate records and check the two against each other regularly. Make sure you protest immediately any trade made inaccurately or without proper authorization. The monthly statement will list a credit or *cash balance.* This signifies money deposited into or withdrawn from the account, plus or minus money realized from positions actually closed out. This balance figure does not include money the trader stands to win or lose from positions that remain open at that date. More important for managing positions is the trader's *equity statement.* (See Figure 18–4.) The closing balance of the equity statement shows how much the account would be worth if all positions were closed at the previous day's closing levels. The figure would be calculated by taking the above mentioned cash balance and then adding and subtracting the amount of unrealized gains and losses. Commission must be included somewhere in the calculation to arrive at an accurate

FIGURE 18-4

SHEARSON, HAMMOL & CO. INCORPORATED FOUNDED IN 1902
OFFICES IN PRINCIPAL CITIES FROM COAST TO COAST
MEMBERS OF THE NEW YORK STOCK EXCHANGE

PA ◯ NO. ◯ ACCOUNT WITH

ALL CHECKS, INSTRUCTIONS, SHOULD BE SENT TO THE OFFICE SERVICING YOUR ACCOUNT.

STATEMENT DATE MO 01 DAY 30 YR 79

ACCOUNT NUMBER 113 1082 00

MR BRUCE G GOULD
P O BOX 15
SEATTLE WA 98111

ENTRY DATE MO DAY YR	BOUGHT OR RECEIVED	SOLD OR DELIVERED	DESCRIPTION	PRICE	UNREALIZED LOSS	UNREALIZED GAIN	TYPE
			COMMODITY POSITION EQUITY				
		1	5 BU MAY FLAX WPG	287 1/2		12.50	8
			NEW BALANCE JAN 31			231.86	8
			NET EQUITY			244.36CR	**
		1	CAK MCH SB OIL CHI	833		408.00	9
		1	CAK MCH SB OIL CHI	891		360.00	9
		1	CAK MCH SB OIL CHI	901		300.00	9
		1	CAK MCH SB OIL CHI	901		300.00	9
		1	CAK MCH SB OIL CHI	891		420.00	9
		1	CAK MCH SB OIL CHI	909		252.00	9
		1	CAK MCH SB OIL CHI	891		360.00	9
		1	CAK MCH SB OIL CHI	923		168.00	9
		1	CAK MAY SB OIL CHI	873		354.00	9
		1	CAK MAY SB OIL CHI	901		186.00	9
		1	CAK MAY SB OIL CHI	891		246.00	9

THIS IS AN EQUITY STATEMENT

This statement which we refer to as an "EQUITY STATEMENT" is not to be confused with "REGULAR MONTH END STATEMENTS".

The closing balance represents the cash balance as shown on your regular month end statement plus or minus the unrealized gains or losses on your open contract positions as of the above date.

SHEARSON, HAMMOL & CO. INCORPORATED FOUNDED IN 1902
OFFICES IN PRINCIPAL CITIES FROM COAST TO COAST
MEMBERS OF THE NEW YORK STOCK EXCHANGE

PA ◯ NO. ◯ ACCOUNT WITH

ALL CHECKS, INSTRUCTIONS, SHOULD BE SENT TO THE OFFICE SERVICING YOUR ACCOUNT.

STATEMENT DATE MO 01 DAY 30 YR 79

ACCOUNT NUMBER 113 1082 00

CONTINUED

ENTRY DATE MO DAY YR	BOUGHT OR RECEIVED	SOLD OR DELIVERED	DESCRIPTION	PRICE	UNREALIZED LOSS	UNREALIZED GAIN	TYPE
		1	CAK MAY SB OIL CHI	879		318.00	9
		1	CAK MAY SB OIL CHI	942	60.00		9
		1	CAK MAY SB OIL CHI	934	12.00		9
		1	CAK MAY SB OIL CHI	930		12.00	9
		5	M BU JUL WHT K C	135 1/8	143.75		9
			NEW BALANCE JAN 31			8,535.02	9
			NET EQUITY			12,003.27CR	**

THIS IS AN EQUITY STATEMENT

This statement which we refer to as an "EQUITY STATEMENT" is not to be confused with "REGULAR MONTH END STATEMENTS".

The closing balance represents the cash balance as shown on your regular month end statement plus or minus the unrealized gains or losses on your open contract positions as of the above date.

statement. The net equity will tell the speculator exactly what he has to work with and how his account has fared. A close inspection will also tell how much of the trader's debits come from commission payouts.

On his own, the trader should draw up a number of record sheets as his semi-official trading data. A personal *account record* will detail the date of each cash transaction and each addition or subtraction of trading results and commissions, with the appropriate figures and their character (withdrawals, profits, etc.). It is imperative that this record be updated daily so that a real picture of results and available capital serves as the backdrop to every new trade. A *monthly statement* will show each and every trade and all its specifics: dates opened and closed, price bought (sold), number of contracts, margin, stop loss points, price at liquidation, profit (loss), commission, etc. The position record is the speculator's personal trading profile. By studying it he can discover the pattern of his errors and the reasons for his mistakes. As in any game, it is easy to forget small losses and to remember large gains. Small profits and losses account for the majority of any trader's moves, and it is important they be remembered, for analyzing these will give the best picture of how a trader is doing and of what he is doing right and wrong. If a number of large losses is showing up

over time, even in an account that is on the whole profitable, the signal is to take a look at stop losses and other management techniques to isolate the flaw.

A set of records should also be kept for each commodity and contract traded. This will include daily entries of prices (open, high, low, close), volume and open interest, and notes on information from fundamentals, charts, newsletters, brokers, and advisors. What emerges, *before* a trade is made, is a current profile and historical background for the commodity and contract. This provides the foundation for decisions to enter, set stops, add positions, and liquidate. A wise trader might follow a commodity this way for months, until he spots the breakout for which he has been waiting. Chances are very high that he will catch it sooner, ride it farther, and exploit it better than the unorganized and unprepared speculator who rushes in to trade in the wake of already demonstrated interest. Such records also enforce the lesson that no speculator need be in all, *or any,* of the commodities at one time. Waiting is just as important, if not more important, than acting. The patient speculator who trades his game with the hunter's careful step knows that success largely depends on skillfully arranging to be at the right place—at the right time—with a clear idea of what to do when the quarry finally springs.

Glossary

Accumulate Adding to a commodity position over a period of time during market fluctuations, rather than all at one time and price.

Acreage allotment That portion of a farmer's acreage which he may plant in crops and still receive the benefits of government price supports and financial assistance.

Acreage reserve A program of the Department of Agriculture wherein the farmer receives payments from the government for not planting basic commodities on part or all of his acreage allotment.

Actuals The physical commodity, such as corn, wheat, silver, or Treasury Bills, as opposed to the futures contract which is merely a slip of paper.

Arbitrage The simultaneous purchase and sale of similar or identical commodities in two different markets, in hope of profiting from the difference in price.

Ask An offer to sell at a designated price.

Backwardation Market situation in which prices are progressively lower in the future delivery months than in the nearest delivery month. Also called an "inverted" market. Back-wardation is the opposite of "contango."

Basis The price difference between two related commodities or contracts. Basis most often denotes (1) the difference in price between the cash commodity and its corresponding futures contract and (2) the difference in price between the various futures contract months of a commodity. "Country basis" refers to the recognized price difference between cash goods in the local country market and the price of the nearby (nearest to delivery) futures contract.

Bear A trader who believes that prices will decline; a bear market is one in which prices are declining. Market indicators are thus often classified as "bearish" or "bullish" (see BULL).

Bid An offer to purchase at a specified price.

Break A rapid decline in prices usually set off by an unexpected news or crop report which caught the commodity traders totally unprepared for such bearish events.

Breakout The sharp surge of a commodity's or contract's price out of a prevailing price level.

Broker   An agent who, on behalf of the customer, is involved in the actual purchase and sale of the commodity future on the appropriate futures exchange.

Brokerage   The fee charged by the firm which handles the customer's order.

Brokerage house or firm   The partnership or corporation which handles, for a fee, various buy and sell orders for commodity clients.

Bucket shop   An illegal practice wherein the supposed broker does not execute ordered trades, rather pocketing the customers' money instead. Ideally, the bucket shop hopes to survive by paying off the claims of a minority of "winners" with the money handed over by the majority of "losers."

Bull   The opposite of a bear. The commodity trader who believes that prices will advance over the near or long term. Such an advancing market is called a "bull market."

Buy-in   To cover or liquidate a short position by buying back a previously sold futures contract.

Call   An exchange-designated period of buying and selling during which an official calls the contract months and a price or range of prices is established.

Carrying charges or costs   The cost of storing and holding a commodity, such as the cost of insurance, storage, inspection, and interest, which is passed on to the commodity futures trader who receives delivery on the cash commodity until he passes such delivery to another party. Carrying charges also can determine the price difference between commodity contract months ("intermonth basis").

Cash Commodity   The actual physical commodity which can be seen, stored, eaten, cashed in, etc. and which is available for immediate delivery.

Cash forward   The process whereby a cash dealer will sell cash commodities for delivery at a specified date in the future.

Cash market   A general national or specific local market in which cash commodities are bought and sold.

Cash price   Current bid or offer for a cash commodity; usually given in terms of a designated location and grade.

Certificated stocks   Stocks of a commodity which have passed the rigorous tests established by the various exchanges and certified as deliverable on the futures exchanges in fulfillment of futures contracts.

CFTC   The Commodity Futures Trading Commission. A federal agency charged with regulating the business of futures trading.

Central bank: A financial instituion that has official or semiofficial status in a federal government. Central banks are the instruments used by governments to expand, contract, or stabilize the supply of money and credit. In the United States, the Federal Reserve Board exercises many of the powers of a central bank.

Charting   The process whereby price or other important data is transferred from mathematical figures to representation on a piece of graph paper for visual analysis. A tool in "technical" trading.

Churning   A method whereby an unscrupulous broker will, over a period of time, make numerous purchase and sale transactions in the account of a customer in an unethical effort to provide a significant financial return for himself and his brokerage house in the form of the excess trading commissions so generated.

CIF   The cost, insurance, and freight required to ship actual commodities to a point of destination.

Clearinghouse   A separate corporation established by the futures exchange to guarantee daily performance on all transactions. The clearinghouse must process all the day's trades and then assume the opposite position to each buy or sell order, thus facilitating initiation and liquidation of contracts and prompt payment of credits and debits to margin accounts.

Clearing member   A member of the clearinghouse. Usually, a well known brokerage or industry firm that has met the high financial standards set by the exchange. Exchange members who are not clearing members must have all trades cleared through a clearinghouse member.

Clearing price   The closing price for the market for the day and the price at which all transactions are cleared at the clearinghouse for the purpose of margin requirements.

Close, the   The end of the trading session during which those traders who wish to liquidate do so and the last price of the commodities traded is known as the closing price.

Commercial stocks   Commodity in-store in public and private warehouses or elevators, at important markets, and afloat in vessels.

Commission   The fee charged by the brokerage house for execution of a commodity futures trade. Commissions are set by the brokerage firm and charged per "round term"—that is,

after the initiated position has been liquidated.

Contango   Market situation in which prices are progressively higher in the future delivery months than in the nearest delivery month. Also termed a normal or a carrying charge market.

Contract   A formal legal document between two parties whereby one party agrees to perform in a certain manner with respect to the other party and vice versa. In futures trading the contract is the unit of trade, being for delivery of 5,000 bushels of wheat or purchase of $1 million in Treasury Bills, etc.

Contract grades   The grade of the actual cash commodity which may be delivered against a futures contract as set forth in the rules and regulations of the futures exchange and futures contract.

Contract market   An organized commodity futures market so designated and authorized by the CFTC.

Contract Month   The month in which futures contracts may be satisfied by making or accepting delivery (see *Delivery month*).

Corner   To purchase such a large position in the commodity markets that, in effect, the trader controls the market and can force prices to respond to his dominant position by moving in a direction which will return a substantial profit to the trader.

Country elevator   A storage facility in the country in which the actual cash commodity is stored during a period when the owner wishes to hold the commodity prior to shipping it to the eventual user.

Country price   The price for the commodity which prevails in the actual country site, usually quoted in terms of a premium or discount to the nearby futures contract.

Cover Liquidation of a short position by the purchase of futures contracts to close out their previous sale.

Crop year The crop year generally begins with the first of the month during which the bulk of the crop is harvested and extends to the previous month in the following year.

Crush The method whereby the raw soybean is taken into a processing plant and crushed to yield the high protein products of soybean meal and soybean oil.

Crush spread A futures position (see *Spread*) wherein the trader simultaneously buys soybean futures contracts and sells soybean oil and soybean meal futures contracts to benefit from an imbalance in their relative prices. A "reverse crush spread" would be the sale of soybean futures and a simultaneous purchase of oil and meal.

Day order Orders that are good for one single day only. If they are not filled during that day they are automatically canceled and must be entered again to be effective on the second day.

Day trader A trader who enters and liquidates a position during a single day, holding no position overnight.

Deferred or distant contracts Those contracts on the futures market which are for delivery months beyond the current closest trading months.

Delivery The tendering of the physical commodity in the form of a warehouse or other receipt to the floor of the exchange during the delivery month in response to a short position held on the futures market. No actual delivery of the commodity is made—merely delivery of a piece of paper evidencing where the cash commodity can be located.

Delivery month The month (January, March, etc.) in the future when the contract may be delivered upon and which thus gives its name to the contract—that is, May cocoa, December copper, etc.

Delivery points The various locations specified in the futures contract where the cash commodity may be stored and delivery made from.

Differentials The price distinctions between various grades and locations of commodities.

Discretionary account A commodity trading account wherein a third party, either the broker or another person, is authorized to make trading decisions and order positions. This arrangement must be made by the explicit written consent of the client.

Discount (1) The amount by which a price is lower than another price (opposite of *Premium*). If cash goods are selling at a discount to the nearest futures contract, cash prices are lower than futures. (2) To take price factors and influences into consideration in the formation of a market price in anticipation of the actual event. Thus, news events may have no impact on prices if they have already been discounted by knowledgeable traders.

Equity The residual value of a trading account if one assumes that all actually open positions where closed at present market prices.

Eurodollars   United States dollar deposits held abroad.

Evening up   Terminating a futures position in advance of a significant news event so as not to be caught in a financially unsecure position should the news be other than anticipated.

Exchange for physical (EFP)   A simultaneous transaction between two traders wherein one trader buys physicals and sells futures contracts while the opposite trader sells physicals and buys futures contracts.

Execution   The actual filling of a customer's order by a floor broker or pit trader at the exchange.

Ex-pit transaction   A procedure which is legal under certain circumstances whereby trades are executed outside of the actual futures pit, usually involving an exchange of cash and futures positions by industry users.

First notice day   The first day of the delivery period when notices may be given by the shorts to the longs of their intention to deliver on the contracts to which they are short and of the precise amount they intend to deliver. First notice day varies with each commodity.

Floor broker   A member of the exchange who stands in the pit and executes orders on behalf of his clients—and sometimes for himself.

Floor trader   An exchange member working the pit principally for his own account (see *Local*).

Fundamentalist   A trader who bases his market decisions upon an analysis of supply and demand statistics and other cash market factors.

Futures   Contracts which relate to a cash commodity to be received and to be delivered at some specified time in the future under terms as set forth in a legally binding contract and subject to the rules and regulations of the futures exchange.

Futures commission merchant   An individual or company who solicits, accepts, or executes order to buy or sell futures contracts for clients in return for payment. FCMs must be licensed by the CFTC.

Hedger   A person in the cash commodity business who, in order to pass the risk along of dealing in cash commodities, engages in transactions on the futures exchanges of an opposite or offsetting character to his transactions in the cash market. The hedger tries to pass his risks along to the futures speculator and to manage his own prices and risks more exactly thereby.

Inverted market   A futures market where the nearby contracts are selling at a price higher than the distant contracts, often due to a heavy near-term demand for the actual cash commodity.

Invisible supply See *Visible supply.*

Key reversal day   A trading day in which the price range for a particular commodity makes a higher high price than it had during the previous trading day, and also makes a lower low price than it had during the previous trading day, and then closes at a price below the close of the previous day. An indication for the "chart trader" that the near-term top of the market has been reached and that prices will decline in the near future.

Leverage   The financial power gained by risking only a small amount of money to control a large position in commodity futures, meaning that a small change in the commodity's value can result in large profits or large losses. (Losses are never "great.")

Life of contract The period of time between the opening of trade on a particular futures contract month and its expiration at the end of the delivery month. Usually less than twelve months but up to twenty three months in some cases.

Limit move The maximum price advance or decline from the previous day's settlement price that is permitted in one day's trading session as set forth by the rules of the exchange.

Liquidity A market is "liquid" when there is a large enough number of traders to make entering or exiting the market easy.

Liquidation The sale of a contract to offset a previously made purchase or the purchase of a contract to offset a previously made short sale. Liquidation is loosely used for any operation which cancels a previously existing position.

Loan price The amount of money per unit which a cash commodity producer may borrow for his crop, provided he has been in compliance with other strictures laid down by the government's loan program. The loan price serves as an influence on cash price.

Local A floor trader working for his own account.

Long A trader who has bought futures contracts hoping for a price advance and who has not liquidated is said to be "long" the market. (Opposite of "short.")

Margin The amount of money put up by a commodity futures trader with his broker as a "good faith deposit"

to assure performance of the contract. Margin is the deposit money that allows the trader to control the futures contract and which gives him the right to profit or lose by its change in price. Margin minimums are set by the futures exchange and may be raised by the brokerage firm.

Margin call A request by the brokerage firm that the customer add capital to his commodity account to cover an unrealized loss which has occurred in his position, resulting in a paper deterioration of his original margin capital by about 85 percent of original margin.

Maturity The period of time during which shorts may deliver on their short positions to settle their commodity commitments. Usually, this is the period between the first notice day and the expiration date of the commodity future.

Maximum price fluctuation The maximum amount the contract price can change—up or down—in a single day, as fixed by the exchange.

Member commission The commission charged to a member of an exchange for the execution of a commodity future order in the pits of that exchange. It is usually considerably less than the commission charged to non-members, which is one reason exchange memberships cost anywhere from $30,000 to $250,000.

Minimum price fluctuation The smallest increment of price movement possible in trading a given contract.

Moving average A mathematical system used by technical commodity traders for averaging near-term prices relative to long-term prices to determine if the trend of prices is up or down, whether a purchase or sale should be made, and at what level.

Nearby The nearby futures contract is the month closest to delivery at any given time. (Opposite of distant and deferred contracts.)

Negotiable A contractual agreement which itself can be bought and sold by any number of parties before eventual conversion into cash is said to be negotiable.

Net position The commodity position held by a trader which is either the greater amount of the long position minus the short position or the short position minus the long position.

New crop The supply of a commodity which will be available after harvest and which will then play a role in the market place.

Nominal price An artificial price set by the reporter at the exchange to give an idea of where commodity futures were traced, even though there may have been no actual transactions at that price. It is usually the difference between the bid and the ask price at the close of the trading day.

Notice A slip of paper by a short in the futures market advising the exchange and the members who are long of his intention to make an actual delivery of the cash commodity in the form of a receipt.

Notice day Any day during the delivery month when notices of intent to deliver may be made by those traders who are short.

Offer Indicates a willingness to sell a futures contract at a given price.

Offset The liquidation of a futures position.

Old crop The crop which has already been harvested and which is pres-

ently in the pipelines of distribution throughout the country.

Omnibus account An account carried by one Futures Commission Merchant with another FCM in which the transactions of two or more persons are comingled and carried in the name of the originating broker, rather than designated separately. A restricted practice.

Open contracts Contracts which have been bought or sold and are still outstanding, not having been liquidated, are said to be open.

Open interest The total of nonliquidated contracts which presently exist for any commodity future or contract month.

Opening, the The period at the beginning of the trading session, officially designated by the exchange, during which all transactions are considered made "at the opening."

Opening range The range of futures prices at which the contract traded during the opening moments of the session.

Original margin The amount of money originally required for each commodity contract which the trader wishes to buy or sell.

Overbought A technical term referring to a market that has had a sharp advance no longer considered supportable.

Oversold A technical term referring to a market that has had a sharp decline in prices no longer considered supportable.

Paper trading A system whereby a commodity trader makes simulated trades on paper rather than by taking actual commodity positions in an effort to practice before trying the real thing.

Parity A government determined price that is supposed to put farm commodity prices on a par with other prices in the economy. This price is usually determined by a formula which takes into account relative prices in a past period considered to have been normal.

Pit The area on the exchange floor where trading of futures contracts takes place.

Point The minimum unit of measure for commodity futures prices.

Position The holdings of a commodity trader, either long or short, is said to be his position in the market.

Position limit The limit, set by federal law, which a commodity trader can hold in futures contracts unless he is a bona fide hedger.

Premium The opposite of discount. The price difference between one commodity futures contract and another or between various grades of cash commodities, the one with the highest price holding the "premium" over the others.

Price averaging The procedure of buying or selling contracts over a period of time to arrive at an average price for the total inventory targeted by a trader or his company.

Primary market Important distribution centers at which spot commodities are originally accumulated for shipment into commercial channels.

Prime rate The interest rate charged by banks to their biggest and most credit worthy customers. Other interest rates normally are scaled up from the prime rate.

Purchase and sales statement (P & S) The statement sent by a broker to a customer when the customer's position has been reduced or closed out, detailing all transactions and results.

Pyramiding Normally considered to be the use of paper profits on established positions to buy or sell further futures contracts. May be done by increasing positions in steady, greater, or lesser numbers.

Rally A sudden upward movement in prices in a market that has been declining.

Range The high and low prices for a specified period of time.

Reaction A market adjustment downward after prices have advanced substantially during any given period.

Realizing profits or losses Liquidating market positions so as to realize actual gains or losses.

Recovery Opposite of a reaction, a market adjustment upward after prices have declined substantially during a given period of time.

Registered representative A person employed by and soliciting business for a Futures Commission Merchant.

Reversal A trading session when the market closes at a lower price than it did during the previous session after making a new high.

Round turn The process of buying and then selling a commodity futures contract is said to be a "round turn" regardless of the order in which the buy or the sell occurred. When you have liquidated a position you have made a round turn and must pay the commission for it.

Scalper A speculator who buys and sells for his account with great rapidity and who is willing to accept small profits on each. Scalpers are normally pit traders, as distance and commissions made scalping virtually impossible for nonfloor traders.

Settlement price   The closing price of the day or an average of the various closing prices of the day. Settlement prices are used to determine margin calls, prices for deliveries, and trading ranges for the next day's trading session.

Short   Opposite of long. A trader who has sold futures contracts is said to be short the market, meaning that he has sold something he does not yet own. He must either buy the cash commodity and deliver it to fulfill his short position or else buy back his futures contract in the market by placing an offsetting buy order.

Short squeeze   A term used to describe a situation in which traders who are short are unable to buy the actual cash commodity to deliver and are, therefore, forced to go into the futures pit and buy futures contracts to liquidate their positions at high prices set by the squeezers.

Speculator   One who attempts to profit by changes in the price of a commodity and who is not using the futures market in connection with industry use of the actual goods.

Spot price   The price of an actual cash commodity "on the spot" at a particular cash market location.

Spread   A trader may spread his position and attempt to reduce his risks by simultaneously (1) buying and selling different contract months of the same commodity, (2) buying and selling the same commodity on two different exchanges, or (3) buying and selling two different but price related commodities. In each case the speculator hopes to profit by a significant change in relative prices.

Switch   A term, also known as "rolling forward," for liquidating a futures position in one contract month and switching it to another month in the same commodity.

Technical rally or decline   A price movement attributed to conditions in the market itself rather than to fundamental cash factors. A big technical move will often reverse itself after a short time to correct for the effects or profit taking.

Technician   The technical trader is the opposite of the fundamentalist. He trades on the basis of market factors alone—that is, past price history, open interest and volume, price charts, market psychology, etc.

Terminal elevator   A major grain storage facility usually at key points in the United States where commodities come from wide points of distribution to be stored until ready for overseas shipment or processing domestically.

Tender   The process whereby a party who is short in the market makes delivery upon his short position by delivering the actual commodity in the form of the receipt.

Tick   A minimal change in price—up or down.

Trading limit   A term used to describe either the limit on the trading range for a session or the limit on the number of contracts which a single commodity trader may hold.

Trading session   That period of time during a single day when commodity futures contracts are traded.

Trend   The general price direction of the prices of a particular commodity or futures contract—either up, down, or sideways.

Variation margin The term used to describe a situation where a paper loss has resulted in an original commodity position to the extent that the brokerage firm no longer feels secure with the original margin and will require that the client put up additional margin to protect the house against the paper loss.

Visible supply The amount of a commodity which can be located throughout the United States at the major known storage points. The actual commodity which can be counted and accurately known. *Invisible supply* refers to uncounted stocks in the hands of wholesalers, manufacturers, and ultimate consumers and sometimes to producers' stocks which cannot be counted accurately.

Volume of trade The number of contracts which are bought and sold during any trading period—day, week, month, year, etc. Counted are only longs or shorts, as it takes two to make a contract.

Appendix I

Sample commodity orders

ORDER PREPARATION MANUAL—COMMODITIES—ILLUSTRATION

USE FOR COMMODITIES ONLY

ADDRESS	C G B OF T KSC GRAINS	C G MERC	WPG	MPLS GRAINS	NY/LDN COMDYS	N Y COF & SUG	N Y CTN EXGE	COMEX N Y	OTHER	ORDER NUMBER	C.F.O. NUMBER
	☒ OBT/CX	☐ OME/CX	☐ OCG/CX	☐ OMP/CX	☐ OCC	☐ OCF/CC	☐ OCO/CC	☐ OCY/CC	☐ _____	CG 15	
										BY ORDER CLERK ONLY	BY ORDER CLERK ONLY

Line 2: ☐ CXL   BASIS ☐ BAS   COMMODITY _____ MONTH   PRICE _____   ☒(hatched)   STOP ☐ STP   ☐ SPREAD   ☐ SWITCH   ☐ SCALE

Line 3: ☐ CXL   ☒ BUY   QUANTITY **10**   COMMODITY **MAY WHT** MONTH   PRICE OR 'MKT' **MKT**   OR BETTER ☐ OB   STOP ☐ STP   STOP LIMIT PRICE ___ LMT   OR   MARKET IF TOUCHED ☐ MIT   LMT   ON CLOSE ☐ CLO   EOS / EDS   ☐ WHEN DONE   OR ☐ AND ☐

Line 4: ☐ CXL   ☐ SL   QUANTITY   COMMODITY MONTH   PRICE OR 'MKT' ☐ PT?   OR BETTER ☐ OB   STOP ☐ STP   STOP LIMIT PRICE ___ LMT   OR   MARKET IF TOUCHED ☐ MIT   LMT   ON CLOSE ☐ CLO   PREM./DISCT. MONTH   ☐ OVER   ☐ UNDER

Line 5: SPECIAL INSTRUCTIONS   NOT HELD ☐ NH   LEAVES ☐ LVS   GOOD 'TIL CANCELLED ☐ GTC   GOOD THIS WEEK ☐ GTW   GOOD THIS MONTH ☐ GTM   GOOD THRU ☐ GT _____ (DATE OR HOUR)   TODAY ONLY ☒ DAY   IMMEDIATE FILL OR KILL ☐ FOK   AT OPENING ONLY ☐ OPG

Line 6: NO FORMER ORDER ☒ NFO   CXL FORMER ORDER ☐ CXL   REPLACEMENT CANCELLATION INSTRUCTIONS

Line 7: ACCOUNT NUMBER **G O — 7 5 4 2 — 6 — 8 9**   NEW ☒ N   LIQUIDATING ☐ L   NEW ACCOUNT ☒ NA   ☒ T 4

Line 8: MISCELLANEOUS INFORMATION (28 CHAR. MAXIMUM)   EXECUTED PRICE

Line 9: GIVE UP ☐ GU   FIRM'S SYMBOL (4 CHAR. MAX)   BY TELETYPE **CFN** (QTY) OPERATOR ONLY

Line 10: CUSTOMER'S NAME   **ROBERT STEINBERG**

Reynolds & Co.
FORM 33-308

MARKET ORDER

```
●

●   OBT/CX CG 15

●   BUY 10 MAY WHT MKT
    DAY
●   NFO

●   60-7542-6-89 N NA T4
    CFN 10

●

●

●
```

TELETYPE IN-PUT

An order to BUY or SELL at the prevailing Bid-Asked price.

When entering orders in grains the quantity shall always be designated in units of 5,000 bushels per contract, written as 5 (one contract); 10 (2 contracts); etc. All other commodities (i.e., wool, cotton, etc.) are designated in contract units as 1, 2, 3, etc.

Note that "MKT" appears in the price field. Do *not* use a dash (—) in the price field when entering a market order. Exchange specifications require the use of "MKT," except in special cases which are described later.

Since this is a market order it has been designated as a **"DAY" order on Line 5 (all market orders are "DAY" orders).**

Also illustrated is the term "NA," on Line 7, which indicates that this is an order for a new account. Such notation is necessary only on the first day of activity of a new account.

Source: The sample orders on pp. 310–40 are from *Order Preparation Manual* of Reynolds Securities Inc. © Reynolds & Co. 1971. Reproduced by permission.

ORDER PREPARATION MANUAL—COMMODITIES—ILLUSTRATION

USE FOR COMMODITIES ONLY

ADDRESS										ORDER NUMBER	C.F.O. NUMBER
	C G B OF T KSC GRAINS ☐ OBT/CX	C G MERC ☒ OME/CX	WPG ☐ OCG/CX	MPLS GRAINS ☐ OMP/CX	NY/LDN COMDYS ☐ OCC	N Y COF & SUG ☐ OCF/CC	N Y CTN EXGE ☐ OCO/CC	COMEX N Y ☐ OCY/CC ___	OTHER ☐	RW 70 BY ORDER CLERK ONLY	BY ORDER CLERK ONLY

Row 2: ☐ CXL | BASIS ☐ BAS | COMMODITY | MONTH | PRICE | STOP ☐ STP | ☐ SPREAD | ☐ SWITCH | ☐ SCALE

Row 3: ☐ CXL | ☒ BUY | QUANTITY **5** | COMMODITY **MAY BLY** MONTH | PRICE OR 'MKT' **3250** | OR BETTER ☐ OB | STOP ☒ STP | STOP LIMIT PRICE ___ LMT | OR | MARKET IF TOUCHED ☐ MIT | ___ LMT | ON CLOSE ☐ CLO | EOS / EDS | ☐ WHEN DONE | ☐ OR ☐ AND

Row 4: ☐ CXL | ☐ SL | QUANTITY | COMMODITY MONTH | PRICE OR 'MKT' ☐ PTS | OR BETTER ☐ OB | STOP ☐ STP | STOP LIMIT PRICE ___ LMT | OR | MARKET IF TOUCHED ☐ MIT | ___ LMT | ON CLOSE ☐ CLO | PREM./DISCT. MONTH | ☐ OVER ☐ UNDER

Row 5: SPECIAL INSTRUCTIONS | NOT HELD ☐ NH | LEAVES ☐ LVS | GOOD 'TIL CANCELLED ☒ GTC | GOOD THIS WEEK ☐ GTW | GOOD THIS MONTH ☐ GTM | GOOD THRU ☐ GT | (DATE OR HOUR) ___ | TODAY ONLY ☐ DAY | IMMEDIATE FILL OR KILL ☐ FOK | AT OPENING ONLY ☐ OPG

Row 6: NO FORMER ORDER ☒ NFO | CXL FORMER ORDER ☐ CXL | REPLACEMENT CANCELLATION INSTRUCTIONS

Row 7: ACCOUNT NUMBER **4 1 — 6 0 3 2 — 6 — 4 8** | ☒ N NEW ☐ L LIQUIDATING | ☐ NA NEW ACCOUNT ☒ T 4

Row 8: MISCELLANEOUS INFORMATION (28 CHAR. MAXIMUM) | EXECUTED PRICE

Row 9: GIVE UP ☐ GU | FIRM'S SYMBOL (4 CHAR. MAX) | BY TELETYPE **CFN** (QTY) OPERATOR ONLY

Row 10: CUSTOMER'S NAME **PAT LOGAN**

Reynolds & Co.

FORM 33-308

STOP ORDER

TELETYPE IN-PUT

OME/CX RW 70

BUY 5 MAY BLY 3250 STP
GTC
NFO

41-6032-6-48 N T4
CFN 5

A stop order to buy (sell) becomes a market order when a transaction occurs at or above (below) the stop price after the order is represented in the "PIT".

ORDER PREPARATION MANUAL—COMMODITIES—ILLUSTRATION

USE FOR COMMODITIES ONLY

C G B OF T KSC GRAINS ☐ OBT/CX	C G MERC ☒ OME/CX	WPG ☐ OCG/CX	MPLS GRAINS ☐ OMP/CX	NY/LDN COMDYS ☐ OCC	N Y COF & SUG ☐ OCF/CC	N Y CTN EXGE ☐ OCO/CC	COMEX N Y ☐ OCY/CC	OTHER ☐

ORDER NUMBER TM 51 / BY ORDER CLERK ONLY

C.F.O. NUMBER BY ORDER CLERK ONLY

2 ☐ CXL | ☐ BAS (BASIS) | COMMODITY / MONTH | PRICE | STOP / STP | ☐ SPREAD | ☐ SWITCH | ☐ SCALE

3 ☐ CXL | ☐ BUY | QUANTITY | COMMODITY / MONTH | PRICE OR 'MKT' | OR BETTER ☐ OB | STOP ☐ STP | STOP LIMIT PRICE ___ LMT | OR | MARKET IF TOUCHED ☐ MIT | LMT | ON CLOSE ☐ CLO | EOS / EDS | ☐ WHEN DONE / ☐ OR ☐ AND

4 ☐ CXL | ☒ SL | QUANTITY **3** | COMMODITY **MAY BLY** / MONTH | PRICE OR 'MKT' **3250** / ☐ P.T.S | OR BETTER ☐ OB | STOP ☒ STP | STOP LIMIT PRICE **3240** LMT | OR | MARKET IF TOUCHED ☐ MIT | LMT | ON CLOSE ☐ CLO | PREM./DISCT. / MONTH | ☐ OVER / ☐ UNDER

5 SPECIAL INSTRUCTIONS | NOT HELD ☐ NH | LEAVES ☐ LVS | GOOD 'TIL CANCELLED ☒ GTC / TODAY ONLY ☐ DAY | GOOD THIS WEEK ☐ GTW / IMMEDIATE FILL OR KILL ☐ FOK | GOOD THIS MONTH ☐ GTM / AT OPENING ONLY ☐ OPG | GOOD THRU ☐ GT | (DATE OR HOUR)

6 NO FORMER ORDER ☒ NFO | CXL FORMER ORDER ☐ CXL | REPLACEMENT CANCELLATION INSTRUCTIONS

7 **8 4 — 6 8 7 0 — 6 — 2 1** ACCOUNT NUMBER | NEW ☐ N / LIQUIDATING ☒ L | NEW ACCOUNT ☐ NA / ☒ T 4

8 **V S   P U R C H   3 3 0 0   9 / 1 5** MISCELLANEOUS INFORMATION (28 CHAR. MAXIMUM) | EXECUTED PRICE

9 GIVE UP ☐ GU | FIRM'S SYMBOL (4 CHAR. MAX) | CFN (QTY) BY TELETYPE OPERATOR ONLY

10 CUSTOMER'S NAME **CARL RICHARDS**

Reynolds & Co.

FORM 33-308

STOP LIMIT ORDER   (At Different Prices)

OME/CX TM 51

SL 3 MAY BLY 3250 STP 3240 LMT
GTC
NFO

84-6870-6-21 L T4
VS PURCH 3300 9/15
CFN 3

TELETYPE IN-PUT

A stop limit order to buy (sell) becomes a limit order executable at the limit price, or at a better price, if obtainable, when a transaction occurs at or above (below) the stop price after the order is represented in the "PIT."

Note that the illustration has a limit price which differs from its stop price. This order will become a limit order of 32.40¢ when the commodity sells at 32.50¢ or less. It will then be executed at not less than 32.40¢, if obtainable in succeeding trades.

ORDER PREPARATION MANUAL—COMMODITIES—ILLUSTRATION

USE FOR COMMODITIES ONLY

ADDRESS	C G B OF T KSC GRAINS	C G MERC	WPG	MPLS GRAINS	NY/LDN COMDYS	N Y COF & SUG	N Y CTN EXGE	COMEX N Y	OTHER	ORDER NUMBER	C.F.O. NUMBER
	☐	☐	☐	☐	☐	☐	☒	☐	☐	BE 74/	
	OBT/CX	OME/CX	OCG/CX	OMP/CX	OCC	OCF/CC	OCO/CC	OCY/CC _____		BY ORDER CLERK ONLY	BY ORDER CLERK ONLY

	BASIS			COMMODITY		PRICE		STOP					
2	☐ CXL	☐ BAS			MONTH			☐ STP	☐ SPREAD				
									☐ SWITCH		☐ SCALE		

		QUANTITY		COMMODITY	PRICE OR 'MKT'	OR BETTER	STOP	STOP LIMIT PRICE		MARKET IF TOUCHED		ON CLOSE	EOS	WHEN DONE
3	☐ CXL	☐ BUY	MONTH			☐ OB	☐ STP	LMT	OR	☐ MIT	LMT	☐ CLO	EDS	☐ OR ☐ AND

		QUANTITY		COMMODITY	PRICE OR 'MKT'	OR BETTER	STOP	STOP LIMIT PRICE		MARKET IF TOUCHED		ON CLOSE	PREM./DISCT.	
4	☐ CXL	☒ SL	3	MAY	OJ	2750 ☐ P.T.S	☐ OB	☒ STP	2750 LMT	OR	☐ MIT	LMT	☐ CLO	MONTH	☐ OVER ☐ UNDER

			NOT HELD	LEAVES	GOOD 'TIL CANCELLED	GOOD THIS WEEK	GOOD THIS MONTH	GOOD THRU	(DATE OR HOUR)
5			☐ NH	☐ LVS	☒ GTC / ☐ DAY TODAY ONLY	☐ GTW / ☐ FOK IMMEDIATE FILL OR KILL	☐ GTM / ☐ OPG AT OPENING ONLY	☐ GT	
	SPECIAL INSTRUCTIONS								

	NO FORMER ORDER	CXL FORMER ORDER		
6	☒ NFO	☐ CXL		REPLACEMENT CANCELLATION INSTRUCTIONS

	ACCOUNT NUMBER		NEW	NEW ACCOUNT
7	1 5 — 1 6 4 2 — 6 — 0 3		☐ N ☒ L LIQUIDATING	☐ NA ☒ T4

	MISCELLANEOUS INFORMATION (28 CHAR. MAXIMUM)	EXECUTED PRICE
8		

	GIVE UP	FIRM'S SYMBOL	BY TELETYPE	
9	☐ GU	(4 CHAR. MAX)	CFN (QTY) OPERATOR ONLY	

	CUSTOMER'S NAME
10	JOE MULLINS

Reynolds & Co.

FORM 33-308

STOP LIMIT ORDER   (At Same Price)

OCO/CC BE 74

SL 3 MAY OJ 2750 STP 2750 LMT
GTC
NFO

15-1642-6-03 L T4
CFN 3

TELETYPE IN-PUT

This type of order is identical with the stop limit order in Illustration No. 3, except that the limit price, in this case, is the *same* as the stop price. Exchange specifications require that both the stop price and the limit price be entered, even though they are the same.

ORDER PREPARATION MANUAL—COMMODITIES—ILLUSTRATION

USE FOR COMMODITIES ONLY

| ADDRESS | C G B OF T KSC GRAINS ☒ OBT/CX | C G MERC ☐ OME/CX | WPG ☐ OCG/CX | MPLS GRAINS ☐ OMP/CX | NY/LDN COMDYS ☐ OCC | N Y COF & SUG ☐ OC.F/CC | N Y CTN EXGE ☐ OCO/CC | COMEX N Y ☐ OCY/CC | OTHER ☐ ____ | ORDER NUMBER **CT 94/21** BY ORDER CLERK ONLY | C.F.O. NUMBER BY ORDER CLERK ONLY |

Line 2: ☐ CXL | BASIS ☐ BAS | COMMODITY ____ MONTH | PRICE | STOP ☐ STP | ☐ SPREAD | ☐ SWITCH | ☐ SCALE

Line 3: ☒ CXL | ☒ BUY | QUANTITY **10** MONTH **MAY** | COMMODITY **WHT** | PRICE OR 'MKT' **138** | OR BETTER ☐ OB | STOP ☐ STP | STOP LIMIT PRICE ___ LMT | OR | MARKET IF TOUCHED ☐ MIT | LMT | ON CLOSE ☐ CLO | EOS / EDS | WHEN DONE ☐ / OR ☐ AND ☐

Line 4: ☐ CXL | ☐ SL | QUANTITY MONTH | COMMODITY | PRICE OR 'MKT' ☐ P.T.S | OR BETTER ☐ OB | STOP ☐ STP | STOP LIMIT PRICE ___ LMT | OR | MARKET IF TOUCHED ☐ MIT | LMT | ON CLOSE ☐ CLO | PREM./DISCT. MONTH | OVER ☐ / UNDER ☐

Line 5: SPECIAL INSTRUCTIONS | NOT HELD ☐ NH | LEAVES **5** ☒ LVS | GOOD 'TIL CANCELLED ☒ GTC | GOOD THIS WEEK ☐ GTW | GOOD THIS MONTH ☐ GTM | GOOD THRU ☐ GT ____ | (DATE OR HOUR) | TODAY ONLY ☐ DAY | IMMEDIATE FILL OR KILL ☐ FOK | AT OPENING ONLY ☐ OPG

Line 6: NO FORMER ORDER ☐ NFO | CXL FORMER ORDER ☐ CXL | REPLACEMENT CANCELLATION INSTRUCTIONS

Line 7: ACCOUNT NUMBER **4 C – 6 3 7 1 – 6 – 1 1** | NEW ☐ N / ☒ L LIQUIDATING | NEW ACCOUNT ☐ NA / ☒ T 4

Line 8: MISCELLANEOUS INFORMATION (28 CHAR. MAXIMUM) | EXECUTED PRICE

Line 9: GIVE UP ☐ GU | FIRM'S SYMBOL (4 CHAR. MAX) | BY TELETYPE CFN (QTY) OPERATOR ONLY

Line 10: CUSTOMER'S NAME **ROGER FARRELL**

Reynolds & Co.

FORM 33-308

CANCELLATIONS

```
●

●   OBT/CX CT 94/21

●

●   CXL BUY 10 MAY WHT 138
    LVS 5 GTC
●

●   4C-6371-6-11 L T4
    CFN 10
●

●

●
```

TELETYPE IN-PUT

There are 3 types of CANCELLATIONS:

(1) Simple Cancellations   (Illustration No. 15).
(2) Change of Price Only   (Illustration No. 16).
(3) Change other than Price   (Illustration No. 17).

The basic rule is to describe the order being canceled *exactly as it was originally entered.* However, when changing only the limit price, you may use an abbreviated format showing (in the gray area) only the price being canceled (see next illustration).

In this illustration of a "simple" cancelation, note that the address (Line 1) is completed in addition to the gray area on Line 3 ("CXL"). The order to be canceled is completely described on Line 3. Notice also, on Line 5, that this cancellation "LVS 5" (of the original 15). This partial cancellation procedure is preferred over complete cancellation and reinstatement.

It is the duty of the Order Clerk to enter the CFO number in the upper right corner. *Failure to enter a CFO number may cause the cancellation to be delayed.*

ORDER PREPARATION MANUAL—COMMODITIES—ILLUSTRATION

USE FOR COMMODITIES ONLY

ADDRESS	C G B OF T KSC GRAINS	C G MERC	WPG	MPLS GRAINS	NY/LDN COMDYS	N Y COF & SUG	N Y CTN EXGE	COMEX N Y	OTHER
	☐	☐	☐	☐	☐	☒	☐	☐	☐
	OBT/CX	OME/CX	OCG/CX	OMP/CX	OCC	OCF/CC	OCO/CC	OCY/CC ___	

ORDER NUMBER CR 82 / (BY ORDER CLERK ONLY)   **C.F.O. NUMBER** (BY ORDER CLERK ONLY)

② CXL / BAS — BASIS ☐   COMMODITY (MONTH)   PRICE   ☐ STOP ☐ STP   ☐ SPREAD   ☐ SWITCH   ☐ SCALE

③ CXL ☐ / BUY ☒ — QUANTITY **2**   COMMODITY **OCT No. 11 SUG** (MONTH)   PRICE OR 'MKT' **328**   OR BETTER ☐ OB   STOP ☐ STP   STOP LIMIT PRICE ___ LMT   OR   MARKET IF TOUCHED ☒ MIT   LMT   ON CLOSE ☐ CLO   EOS / EDS   ☐ WHEN DONE   OR ☐ AND ☐

④ CXL ☐ / SL ☐ — QUANTITY   COMMODITY (MONTH)   PRICE OR 'MKT' ☐ P.TS   OR BETTER ☐ OB   STOP ☐ STP   STOP LIMIT PRICE ___ LMT   OR   MARKET IF TOUCHED ☐ MIT   LMT   ON CLOSE ☐ CLO   PREM./DISCT. (MONTH)   ☐ OVER   ☐ UNDER

⑤ SPECIAL INSTRUCTIONS — NOT HELD ☐ NH   LEAVES ☐ LVS   GOOD 'TIL CANCELLED ☐ GTC   GOOD THIS WEEK ☐ GTW   GOOD THIS MONTH ☐ GTM   GOOD THRU ☐ GT ___ (DATE OR HOUR)   TODAY ONLY ☒ DAY   IMMEDIATE FILL OR KILL ☐ FOK   AT OPENING ONLY ☐ OPG

⑥ NO FORMER ORDER ☒ NFO   CXL FORMER ORDER ☐ CXL   REPLACEMENT CANCELLATION INSTRUCTIONS

⑦ ACCOUNT NUMBER **7 5 – 8 3 1 2 – 7 – 4 6**   NEW ☒ N   LIQUIDATING ☐ L   NEW ACCOUNT ☐ NA   ☒ T 4

⑧ MISCELLANEOUS INFORMATION (28 CHAR. MAXIMUM)   EXECUTED PRICE

⑨ GIVE UP ☐ GU   FIRM'S SYMBOL (4 CHAR. MAX)   BY TELETYPE **CFN** (QTY) OPERATOR ONLY

⑩ CUSTOMER'S NAME **LAWRENCE STANTON**

Reynolds & Co.
FORM 33-308

MARKET IF TOUCHED ORDER ("MIT")

OCF/CC CR 82

BUY 2 OCT NO 11 SUG 328 MIT
DAY
NFO

75-8312-7-46 N T4
CFN 2

An "MIT" order to buy (sell) becomes a market order when a transaction occurs at or below (above) the "MIT" price after the order is represented in the "PIT."

"MIT" orders are entered on the opposite side of the market than are stop orders.

TELETYPE IN-PUT

ORDER PREPARATION MANUAL—COMMODITIES—ILLUSTRATION

FOR COMMODITIES ONLY

	C G B OF T KSC GRAINS	C G MERC	WPG	MPLS GRAINS	NY/LDN COMDYS	N Y COF & SUG	N Y CTN EXGE	COMEX N Y	OTHER	ORDER NUMBER	C.F.O. NUMBER
	☐	☒	☐	☐	☐	☐	☐	☐	☐	**SB 12**	
	OBT/CX	OME/CX	OCG/CX	OMP/CX	OCC	OCF/CC	OCO/CC	OCY/CC _____		BY ORDER CLERK ONLY	BY ORDER CLERK ONLY

Row 2 — CXL ☐ BAS ☐ — COMMODITY — MONTH — PRICE — STOP ☐ STP — ☐ SPREAD — ☐ SWITCH — ☐ SCALE

Row 3 — CXL ☐ BUY ☐ — QUANTITY — MONTH — COMMODITY — PRICE OR 'MKT' — OR BETTER ☐ OB — STOP ☐ STP — STOP LIMIT PRICE ___ LMT — OR — MARKET IF TOUCHED ☐ ___ MIT — LMT — ON CLOSE ☐ CLO — EOS / EDS — ☐ WHEN DONE — OR ☐ AND ☐

Row 4 — CXL ☐ SL ☒ — QUANTITY **2** — MONTH **FEB** — COMMODITY **BLY** — PRICE OR 'MKT' **MKT** ☐ P.T.S — OR BETTER ☐ OB — STOP ☐ STP — STOP LIMIT PRICE ___ LMT — OR — MARKET IF TOUCHED ☐ ___ MIT — LMT — ON CLOSE ☐ CLO — PREM./DISCT. MONTH — ☐ OVER — ☐ UNDER

Row 5 — SPECIAL INSTRUCTIONS — NOT HELD ☐ NH — LEAVES ☐ LVS — GOOD 'TIL CANCELLED ☐ GTC — GOOD THIS WEEK ☐ GTW — GOOD THIS MONTH ☐ GTM — GOOD THRU ☐ GT — (DATE OR HOUR) — TODAY ONLY ☐ DAY — IMMEDIATE FILL OR KILL ☐ FOK — AT OPENING ONLY ☒ OPG

Row 6 — NO FORMER ORDER ☒ NFO — CXL FORMER ORDER ☐ CXL — REPLACEMENT CANCELLATION INSTRUCTIONS

Row 7 — ACCOUNT NUMBER: **1 6 — 3 5 6 0 — 6 — 6 7** — NEW ☐ N LIQUIDATING ☒ L — NEW ACCOUNT ☐ NA ☒ T 4

Row 8 — MISCELLANEOUS INFORMATION (28 CHAR. MAXIMUM) — EXECUTED PRICE

Row 9 — GIVE UP ☐ GU — FIRM'S SYMBOL (4 CHAR. MAX) — BY TELETYPE CFN ___ (QTY) OPERATOR ONLY

Row 10 — CUSTOMER'S NAME **NICHOLAS DALTON**

Reynolds & Co.

FORM 33-308

AT THE OPENING ONLY ORDER ("OPG")

OME/CX SB 12

SL 2 FEB BLY MKT
OPG
NFO

16-3560-6-67 L T4
CFN 2

TELETYPE IN-PUT

"At the Opening Only" ("OPG") is an order to be executed at the opening in the commodity or not at all, and any portion not so executed is to be treated as canceled.

It is Reynolds & Co.'s policy that orders received at the exchange 15 minutes prior to the opening of the market will not be guaranteed to make the opening.

To be sure that you make the opening, enter your order as early as possible in the morning before the opening.

Orders received after the close of the Exchange will not be held over for the following morning unless the New York office, to meet emergency conditions, so specifies.

ORDER PREPARATION MANUAL—COMMODITIES—ILLUSTRATION

FILL OR KILL ORDER ("FOK")

Reynolds & Co.

FORM 33-308

TELETYPE IN-PUT

A "FILL OR KILL" order is a market or limited price order which is to be executed in whole, or in part, as soon as it is represented in the "PIT" and the portion not so executed is to be treated as canceled.

Note that the definition for "FOK" in commodities differs from the definition for stock orders. The definition that is applied here is synonymous with the stock definition for an "Immediate or Cancel" ("OC") order. Nomenclature used in stocks, in many cases, is the same as commodities but their meanings may have significant variations. Careful attention should be given to every illustration and definition appearing in this manual and in the Order Preparation Manual, which deals mainly with listed securities.

ORDER PREPARATION MANUAL—COMMODITIES—ILLUSTRATION

USE FOR COMMODITIES ONLY

ADDRESS	C G B OF T KSC GRAINS	C G MERC	WPG	MPLS GRAINS	NY/LDN COMDYS	N Y COF & SUG	N Y CTN EXGE	COMEX N Y	OTHER	ORDER NUMBER	C.F.O. NUMBER
	☐	☐	☐	☒	☐	☐	☐	☐	☐	WS 49 /	
	OBT/CX	OME/CX	OCG/CX	OMP/CX	OCC	OCF/CC	OCO/CC	OCY/CC _____		BY ORDER CLERK ONLY	BY ORDER CLERK ONLY

Line 2: CXL ☐ | BASIS ☐ BAS | COMMODITY | MONTH | PRICE | (hatched) | STOP ☐ STP | ☒ SPREAD ☐ SWITCH ☐ SCALE

Line 3: CXL ☐ | BUY ☒ | QUANTITY 5 | SEP MONTH | COMMODITY CG WHT | PRICE OR 'MKT' | OR BETTER ☐ OB | STOP ☐ STP | STOP LIMIT PRICE ___ LMT | OR | MARKET IF TOUCHED ☐ MIT | ___ LMT | ON CLOSE ☐ CLO | EOS / EDS | ☐ WHEN DONE ☐ OR ☐ AND

Line 4: CXL ☐ | SL ☒ | QUANTITY 5 | DEC MONTH | COMMODITY MPLS WHT | PRICE OR 'MKT' 2 ☒ PTS | OR BETTER ☐ OB | STOP ☐ STP | STOP LIMIT PRICE ___ LMT | OR | MARKET IF TOUCHED ☐ MIT | ___ LMT | ON CLOSE ☐ CLO | PREM./DISCT. MPLS MONTH | ☒ OVER ☐ UNDER

Line 5: SPECIAL INSTRUCTIONS | NOT HELD ☐ NH | LEAVES ☐ LVS

| GOOD 'TIL CANCELLED ☐ GTC | GOOD THIS WEEK ☐ GTW | GOOD THIS MONTH ☐ GTM | GOOD THRU ☐ GT ___ | (DATE OR HOUR) |
| TODAY ONLY ☒ DAY | IMMEDIATE FILL OR KILL ☐ FOK | AT OPENING ONLY ☐ OPG | | |

Line 6: NO FORMER ORDER ☒ NFO | CXL FORMER ORDER ☐ CXL | REPLACEMENT CANCELLATION INSTRUCTIONS

Line 7: ACCOUNT NUMBER 7 0 – 5 0 4 2 – 6 – 3 6 | ☒ NEW N ☐ LIQUIDATING L | NEW ACCOUNT ☐ NA ☒ T4

Line 8: MISCELLANEOUS INFORMATION (28 CHAR. MAXIMUM) | EXECUTED PRICE

Line 9: GIVE UP ☐ GU | FIRM'S SYMBOL (4 CHAR. MAX) | BY TELETYPE CFN ___ (QTY) OPERATOR ONLY

Line 10: CUSTOMER'S NAME THOMAS LOVELL

Reynolds & Co.

FORM 33-308

SPREAD ORDER

- OMP/CX WS 49

- SPREAD
  BUY 5 SEP CG WHT
- SL 5 DEC MPLS WHT 2 PTS MPLS OVER
- DAY
- NFO

- 70-5042-6-36 N T4
- CFN 5 5

TELETYPE IN-PUT

Although these types of orders have the appearance of a switch order, they are used primarily when a client wants to assume new positions both ways.

A spread order can be traded as: (1) same market, same commodity; (2) same market, related commodity; (3) * different market, same commodity (illustrated above).

The "PREM/DISCT." and the "OVER" or "UNDER" designations are required on all spread orders (unless the price is "MKT") for clarity to the floor broker, *omitting either is likened to omitting the price.*

By making such orders spread, the Account Executive insures that his customer will receive the proper commission rates and margin rates, which are in some cases reduced amounts under regular rates, when applicable.

* In doing orders between different markets, it is customary to send the order to the smaller of the two markets. Such orders are extremely difficult to execute, and may be accepted only without Firm responsibility, as it is physically impossible for our brokers to execute simultaneously in two separate markets.

Appendix II

Information sources

A. Books: an annotated checklist

Hundreds of volumes have been written on the futures markets. A handy, Basic guide for the average speculator is the Chicago Mercantile Exchange's free pamphlet entitled *Bibliography and Information Source List*. For a comprehensive compilation, consult the Chicago Board of Trade's *Commodity Futures Trading: A Bibliography, Cumulative Through 1976* (Chicago, 1978) and subsequent annual supplements.

The few titles listed below represent books widely respected in the futures industry. This subjective selection also includes the books that have been most useful to me in my own trading and writing. I here gratefully acknowledge my debt to their authors as well as to a host of publications and experts too numerous to cite.

Angrist, Stanley W. *Sensible Speculating in Commodities* (New York: Simon and Schuster, 1972). (A basic, lucid introduction with emphasis on technical trading.)

Belveal, L. Dee. *Charting Commodity Market Price Behavior* (Wilmette, Ill.: Commodities Press, 1969). (The technicals explained.)

————*Commodity Speculation with Profits in Mind* (Wilmette, Ill.: Commodities Press, 1967). (A broad overview.)

Cootner, Paul H., ed. *The Random Character of Stock Market Prices* (Cambridge: MIT Press, 1964). (Essays on random walk in theory and practice.)

Gold, Gerald. *Modern Commodity Futures Trading* (New York: Commodity Research Bureau, 1975). (A popular introduction to trading.)

Gould, Bruce G. *Commodity Trading Manual* (1976, Bruce Gould Publications, Box 16, Seattle, WA. 98111—A day by day procedures guide to trading).

Gould, Bruce G. *How to Make Money in Commodities* (1979, Bruce Gould Publications—one simple trading method discussed in considerable detail).

Hieronymus, Thomas A. *Economics of Futures Trading for Commercial and Personal Profit* (New York: Commodity Research Bureau, 1977). (A sophisticated, outstanding exploration of the economic functions of futures, with emphasis on hedgers and industry users.)

Irwin, Harold S. *Evolution of Futures Trading* (Madison: Mimir Publishers, 1954). (An authoritative and fascinating account.)

Jiler, Harry, ed. *Forecasting Commodity Prices: How the Experts Analyze the Markets* (New York: Commodity Research Bureau, 1975). (Each essay demonstrates forecasting methods for a different commodity.)

Kaufman, Perry J. *Commodity Trading Systems and Methods* (New York: John Wiley, 1978). (Contains advanced technical trading methods.)

Loosigian, Allan M. *Interest Rate Futures* (Homewood, Ill.: Dow Jones-Irwin, 1980). (Well written introduction for anyone with little background.)

Powers, Mark J. *Getting Started in Commodity Futures Trading* (Cedar Falls: Investor Publications, 1977). (A short, simple explanation for the beginner.)

Schwarz, Edward W. *How to Use Interest Rate Futures Contracts* (Homewood, Ill.: Dow Jones-Irwin, 1979). (Helpful for speculators and hedgers in financial futures.)

Stigum, Marcia. *The Money Market: Myth, Reality, and Practice* (Homewood, Ill.: Dow Jones-Irwin, 1978). (Essential explications for anyone trading the financial instruments or just trying to understand them.)

Teweles, Richard J.; Harlow, Charles V.; and Stone, Herbert L. *The Commodity Futures Game—Who Wins?—Who Loses?—Why?* (New York: McGraw-Hill, 1974). (One of the very best and most comprehensive books on futures trading, though its chapters on playing the game get lost in overelaborate mathematical considerations.)

B. Addresses of futures exchanges

Each futures exchange publishes an assortment of materials relating to its operations, its contracts, and the markets in general. All will provide a great deal of this information free upon request. A fee is usually charged for statistical yearbooks and book length volumes.

Amex Commodities Exchange, Inc.
86 Trinity Place
New York, NY 10006
(212) 938-6000

The Board of Trade of Kansas City
4800 Main Street, Suite 274

Kansas City, MO 64112
(816) 753-7802

The Chicago Board of Trade
141 W. Jackson Blvd.
Chicago, IL 60604
(312) 435-3500

The Chicago Mercantile Exchange
444 W. Jackson Blvd.
Chicago, IL 60606
(312) 648-1000

Commodity Exchange, Inc. (Comex)
Four World Trade Center
New York, NY 10048
(212) 938-2900

MidAmerica Commodity Exchange
175 W. Jackson Blvd.
Chicago, IL 60604
(312) 435-0606

Minneapolis Grain Exchange
400 South Fourth Street
Minneapolis, MN 55415
(612) 338-6212

New Orleans Commodity Exchange
231 Carondelet St., Suite 403
New Orleans, LA 70130

New York Coffee, Sugar, and Cocoa Exchange, Inc.
Four World Trade Center
New York, NY 10048
(212) 938-2800

New York Cotton Exchange
Four World Trade Center
New York, NY 10048
(212) 938-2650

New York Futures Exchange
20 Broad Street
New York, NY 10005
(212) 623-4949

New York Mercantile Exchange
Four World Trade Center
New York, NY 10048
(212) 966-2600

C. Goverment reports

Many government agencies regularly publish reports containing fundamental data for commodities trading. Subscriptions to most of these are available free upon request. The following are only the major publications often cited by traders; a complete list can be had from the respective agencies.

Crop Reporting Board
U.S. Department of Agriculture
Washington, D.C. 20250

Agricultural Prices (M)
Agricultural Situation (M)
Cattle (Jan., July)
Cattle on Feed (M)
Cold Storage Report (M)
Crop Production (M)
Eggs, Chickens, and Turkeys (M)
Grain Stocks (Q)
Hogs and Pigs (Q)
Livestock Slaughter (M)
Potato Stocks (5 × yr.)
Prospective Plantings (Jan., Apr.)
Weekly Weather and Crop Bulletins (W, fee)

Economic Research Service
U.S. Department of Agriculture
Washington, D.C. 20250

Agricultural Outlook (M)
Agricultural Supply and Demand (9 × yr.)
Cotton and Wool Situation (Q)
Fats and Oils Situation (5 × yr.)
Feed Situation (6 × yr.)
Foreign Agricultural Trade (M)
Livestock and Meat Situation (M)
Poultry and Egg Situation (8 × yr.)
Sugar and Sweetener Report (M)
Wheat Situation
World Agricultural Situation (3 × yr.)

Commodity Futures Trading Commission
233 S. Wacker Dr.
Chicago, IL 60606
(data for Chicago Markets)

61 Broadway
New York, NY 10006
(data for New York Markets)

Commitments of Traders in Commodity Futures (M)

Superintendent of Documents
U.S. Government Printing Office
Washington, D.C. 20402

Business Conditions Digest (M, fee)
Construction Review (M)
Copper, Quarterly Report (Q, fee)
Foreign Agriculture (W, fee)
Housing Starts (M)
Treasury Bulletin (M)
Weekly Business Statistics (W)

Forest Service
U.S. Department of Agriculture
Washington, D.C. 20250

Demand and Price Situation for Forest Products (A)
Forest Survey Reports

Cotton Division
Agricultural Marketing Service
U.S. Department of Agriculture
4841 Sumner Ave
Memphis, TN 38122

Long Staple Cotton Review (M)
Weekly Cotton Market Review (W)
Cotton Price Statistics (M)

Bureau of the Census
Suitland, MD 20233

Business Conditions Digest (M)
Current Business Reports: Green Coffee (Q)
Current Industrial Reports (M) (Q)
  1. Confectionary and Chocolates. 2. Cotton. 3. Fats and Oils, Oilseed Crushings. 4. Fats and Oils, Production, Consumption and Stock. 5. Flour Milling. 6. Inventories of Brass and Copper 7. Copper Products. 8. Cotton Goods.

Bureau of Mines
Mineral Industry Survey
4800 Forbes Ave.
Pittsburgh, PA 15213

Copper Industry (M)
Gold and Silver (M)
Platinum (Q)

INDEX